Spaghetti Westerns

Cowboys and Europeans
from Karl May
to Sergio Leone

CHRISTOPHER FRAYLING

I.B.Tauris *Publishers*

LONDON • NEW YORK

This book is dedicated to Helen and
the wild bunch

Revised paperback edition published in 1998
by I.B. Tauris & Co Ltd
Victoria House, Bloomsbury Square,
London WC1B 4DZ
175 Fifth Avenue, New York NY 10010

Reprinted in 2000

In the United States and Canada distributed by
St. Martin's Press
175 Fifth Avenue, New York NY 10010

ISBN 1 86064 200 4

A full CIP record for this book is available from the
British Library
A full CIP record for this book is available from the
Library of Congress

Library of Congress catalog card: available

Printed and bound in Great Britain by WBC Ltd,
Bridgend

Contents

Illustrations

General Editor's Introduction

Spaghetti Westerns changed the face of the most venerable and characteristic genre of American cinema. They represented an extraordinary and potent cross-fertilization of American and European cultures, creating their own superstar – Clint Eastwood – and revitalizing the careers of a posse of western veterans such as Lee Van Cleef and Guy Madison. Like some of Sergio Leone's best-known films, Christopher Frayling's scholarly study of the Spaghetti Western, first published in 1981, has now achieved classic status. For years it has been cited as a seminal work and second-hand copies have been at a premium. We are delighted to be able to reprint it as part of a policy of making available again important critical texts. Frayling took seriously a genre which many at the time dismissed as at best a bastardization and at worst a perversion of the Hollywood Western. He combines detailed readings of individual films with an analysis of the production context and of the then little-known tradition of European westerns in literature and film. He explores the social and political dimensions of the spaghettis as well as their distinctive cinematicity. He examines the landscape, the costumes, the music, the acting, the violence. He has contributed a new introduction bringing his thinking on the genre up to date, correcting errors and looking back at the intellectual milieu which produced the book in the first place. Beautifully illustrated and stylishly written, this study makes a welcome return to the cinema bookshelves.

Jeffrey Richards

Acknowledgments

I should like to thank Graham Cox, Geof Wood and Robert Reiner; Ernie Hampson; Mike Wallington, Noel Purdon and Eric Mottram; Roger Smither, David Penn and Anne Fleming; Angela Carter, Howard Brenton, Eduardo Paolozzi and Reg Gadney; Bernard Myers (a fund of information on railway lore), and especially Tony Rayns — all of whom discussed with me some of the ideas contained in this book, at various stages in its drafting; Sergio Leone, with whom I had a brief correspondence; the staff of the BFI Information Department; United Artists, Columbia and Rafran Cinematografica, stills from whose films appear in this book, and who kindly supplied most of them; the BFI, Fred Zentner, Tony Williams, and the assistants in the Librairie de la Fontaine (Paris), who helped me track down further stills; and *Cinema* (Cambridge), the journal which published an earlier version of the section on the 'Dollars' trilogy. I would also like to thank the participants in a joint Exeter and Warwick Universities Conference on *Cultural Responses to Mexico*, with whom I had many interesting discussions; the Italian Society at the University of Bath (who listened); and ex-Professor Christopher Cornford of the Department of General Studies at the Royal College of Art (who allowed me to lecture on the subject): all these experiences helped clarify my ideas. I hope they still seem clear. My aim throughout has been, if possible, to enhance the reader's appreciation of these movies, rather than simply to exploit it.

The stills reproduced in this book first appeared in films distributed by the following companies, to whom thanks are due: Avco Embassy, Columbia, Gala, Golden Era, MGM, Miracle, Paramount, Toho, 20th Century-Fox, United Artists, Universal, Warner, and especially Rafran (Rome).

I wish to thank the following for permission to reproduce material: Editions Dargaud for the drawing by Morris from the 'Lucky Luke' comic *Chasseur de Prime* (1972); the Karl May Verlag (Bamberg) for the original 'Winnetou' illustrations by Sacha Schneider; The Johns Hopkins University Press for material from Umberto Eco, 'The Myth of Superman' (*Diacritics*, Spring 1971, pp. 14-22).

Christopher Frayling

1 (*Left*) 'The Bounty Hunter', drawn by Morris for a French 'Lucky Luke' comic of 1972
2 (*Below*) American history, Spaghetti Western-style. In Morris and Goscinny's 'The Bounty Hunter', the story of George Washington and the cherry tree becomes part of a hired gun's biography
3 (*Bottom left*) Three bizarre gunslingers walk down the main street of a Western town. From an early *Mad* magazine feature, entitled 'Hah! Noon!'
4 (*Bottom right*) An Italian Western comic, dating from the end of the Spaghetti boom. Many of the films, and especially those directed by Sergio Corbucci, relied on cutting effects derived from comic-strip graphics

Preface (1998)

At the end of April 1997, I was invited to join a panel of speakers at an international Festival of *Eurowestern* which took place in a cinema next to a railway station in Udine, near Venice. The other panellists at the festival included Horst Wendlandt (who produced the best of the Karl May *Winnetou* films in the mid-1960s), Gojko Mitic (who played a succession of noble Indian chiefs in East German historical epics of the 1970s, and who now plays Winnetou the Warrior at the annual Karl May Festspiele at Bad Segeberg), Tonino Valerii (who was Sergio Leone's assistant before directing *My Name Is Nobody*), Joaquin Romero Marchent (whose career in Spanish Westerns began with *El Coyote* in 1954 and ended with the notoriously bloody *Cut-Throats Nine* in 1973), Luis Enrique Bacalov (the Buenos Aires born composer of soundtracks for *Django, Sugar Colt, Quien Sabe?, The Price of Power* and others), Tinto Brass (director of the over-the-top-gothic *Yankee*), Enzo Castellari (director of the stylish and anti-racist *Keoma*) and Franco Nero (best known in this context for his performance as Django and as Polish/Swedish mercenaries in Sergio Corbucci's political Westerns), plus two young scholars of the Italian Western Luca Beatrice (author of *Al cuore, Ramon, al cuore/Aim for the Heart, Ramon* – an art historical analysis) and Carlos Aguilar (author of a Spanish analysis of the films of *Sergio Leone*). Which just about covered the territory. The climax of the festival was a screening of five Lumière fragments of 1896 and some Joë Hamman French Westerns of 1912, accompanied by Bacalov on the piano. At one point, he played variations on *The Good, the Bad & the Ugly*. There was also an evening of British Westerns pre-1913 (including two produced by Cecil Hepworth), but I had to leave before then.

Discussion wasn't easy: the many languages which were spoken in that railroad cinema resembled the babel of sound on the set of an international Western of thirty years before. But it was certainly animated.

In my panel session (called, alarmingly, *Faccia A Faccia*), the first question from the floor concerned the title of this book. Wasn't the phrase 'Spaghetti Westerns' – which the book had made famous, said the speaker, and launched into the public domain in Europe – an insult to Italian film-makers? A phrase, like 'Pizza Express' and 'Burger King', which implied junk food, mass-production and a total lack of individuality? A phrase which had led to countless jokes about 'heavy on the bolognaise' and thus encouraged a flip attitude to "a significant Euro-contribution to film history". Perhaps I would care to explain what thoughts the phrase conjured up in *my* mind – for the benefit of the assembled film buffs, most of whom were Italian, under thirty-five, and had never seen these films on the big screen before. I replied that Sergio Leone himself had once told me that he, too, had been unsure whether or not the phrase was intended as a put-down: so unsure that he delayed reading this book for a while (or rather, delayed having it read to him by a long-suffering and bilingual assistant in 1981–2) because he feared from the title that it might be patronising and condescending – like the earliest reviews of his films in Europe and America. But Leone had come to realize that the phrase 'Spaghetti Westerns' could, in fact, be a term of endearment. Originally, he said, he had taken its meaning too literally: "I thought it was quite subtle – maybe the spaghetti had replaced the lassoo". Then he realized that the word 'Spaghetti' was simply being used as a synonym for 'Italian':

> "Like today, when we talk of 'Pizza Connection'; today, though, Spaghetti is out of fashion – no? Pizza is in. But there was nothing malicious about the phrase. Just a way of defining national origins, taken up by the Americans. It was some Europeans who took this label in a

critical spirit to stigmatise an entire genre. It's crazy. As if one were to criticise American films set in ancient Rome by calling them 'Hamburger Romans'. I've never heard *Spartacus* or *Ben-Hur* referred to as 'Hamburger Romans'. Have you?"

Actually, the term 'Spaghetti Western' *was* often used as a pejorative in America in the 1960s and 1970s, meaning "not at all like the real thing". But it was this book which persuaded Leone that 'Spaghetti Westerns' need not necessarily be a put-down. True, Leone was still keen to distance *his* work from rotgut Spaghettis – "when they tell me that I am the father of the Spaghetti Western", he once said to me through a haze of cigar smoke, "I have to reply 'how many sons of bitches do you think I have spawned?'" – but he accepted that, until the craze got completely out of hand in the late 1960s, there were interesting things to be said and written about at least some of them; the legitimate ones, rather than the "products of the great gold rush which followed *Fistful of Dollars*".

I then quoted, for the benefit of the audience at *Eurowestern*, from Professor René Konig's sociological study of fashion *The Restless Image* (1973), where he had had this to say about Spaghetti as a type of food:

> "It originated in the East; it is now a food known throughout the world that has spread far beyond the borders of Italy. It even changed its function as it did so: to begin with it was a typical poor man's food; today, particularly outside Italy, it has become a symbol of sophisticated cuisine, and is a popular speciality".

Fistful of Dollars, too, originated in the East – with Kurosawa's *Yojimbo* – and the resulting gold rush of between four hundred and four hundred and fifty films had indeed "spread far beyond the borders of Italy": originally treated as typical poor man's cinema (especially if the poor man happened to come from south of Rome), it had since become a symbol of . . . well, not quite sophistication, but let us say innovative and sometimes fascinating and exciting film-making while remaining a popular speciality. So, 'Spaghetti Westerns' was more apt than it looked. Enough said?

The questioner seemed happier. But there were still a few murmurs of discontent from around the Cinema Ferroviario. There were, incidentally, no Americans present so far as I could tell.

What struck me most forcibly about this exchange and indeed about the whole Festival – apart from the fact that I had never shared a cinema with hundreds of Eurowestern buffs before – was just how much had changed since I wrote *Spaghetti Westerns* way back in the late 1970s. Young scholars all over Europe now write learned monographs about the Italian or Italian-Spanish Western boom of the 1960s, or deconstruct Karl May's novels and the films derived from them (*Old Shatterhand ritt nicht im Auftrag der Arbeiterklasse*, by Christian Heermann, 1995, and *Karl May im Film* by Christian Unucka, 1980), or analyse the East German epics of the 1970s (*Gojko Mitic, mustangs, marterphäle* by Frank-Burkhard Habel, 1997). And they turn to this book – as I learned to my surprise at *Eurowestern* – for intellectual stimulus; it has become the text that launched a thousand theses – the text which 'founded' the serious study of Eurowesterns as Italian or Spanish or German phenomena rather than ersatz American ones. Websites are full of unacknowledged chunks of it. The growth of research in this area has opened up some interesting new questions, to which *Spaghetti Westerns* did not and could not supply the answers. Like, what was the role of Spanish expertise/ directors/precursors in the making of 'Italian Westerns'? Many of these films were in fact Spanish co-productions, most of them had Spanish desert locations, while a significant number were wholly Spanish even though they've been subsumed under the wrong generic title. This book concentrates on the *Italian* production context. And what of the contribution of the pioneering films of Joaquin Romero Marchent? The town of 'San Miguel' in *Fistful of Dollars* was originally built for one of his *Zorro* movies. Carlos Aguilar has begun to research this topic, but there is still much basic fact-finding to be done. Another question: what of the distinction between films pitched at 'third run' cinemas in Italy, and those – such as the bigger budget Leones, Corbuccis, Tessaris and Sollimas – which played at 'first run' cinemas in the big cities? The distinction seems to go well beyond the size of the budget and the eminence of the stars. Christopher Wagstaff (in the essay *A Fistful of Westerns* – a contribution to *Popular European Cinema*, ed. Dyer & Vincendeau, 1992) has mapped out a fascinating study of audiences in 1960s Italy – which partly reinforces my conclusions, partly shows how I tended to approach these different 'levels' of film-making in different ways rather than analysing and revealing how the 'levels' really operated. Your average low-budget Spaghetti played to audiences which went to the pictures several times a week, talked through the boring bits, enjoyed plenty of action and noise, liked heroes who dressed in style and smoked a lot of *toscani* cigars, were accustomed to an arbitrary intermission while the projectionist changed reels, and unless captivated by a surprise ending liked to walk out before the end. This sociology of cinema-going helps to explain at least some of the recurring features of the films themselves. Franco Nero speculated in a 1993 interview that "Spaghetti Westerns were for a certain kind of audience – the workers, I think. Mainly workers, boys . . . yes, all kinds of workers – and the workers they fantasize a lot, and they would like to go to the boss in the office and be the hero and say 'Sir, from today, something's gonna happen'. And then – bam, bam! they want to clean up the whole world". He was probably right. In this sense, the Italian Westerns hark back to the era of silent movies in America, or 'B' movies of the 1930s, when films made direct contact with similar audiences (in the city and the country), and when the horse did as much thinking as the itinerant cowboy.

There have, since the publication of *Spaghetti Westerns*, been further full-length studies of the films of Sergio Leone and especially the Westerns – from Italy (*Sergio Leone* by Oreste de Fornari, 1984; *Sergio Leone* by Francesco Mininni, 1989; *Directed by Sergio Leone* by Gianni di Claudio, 1990; *Sergio Leone* by Roberto Lasagna, 1996); from France (*Sergio Leone* by Gilles Cèbe, 1984; *Leone* by Gilles Gressard, 1989); and from America (*Film Semiotics, Metz and Leone's trilogy* by Lane Roth, 1982; *Once Upon a Time* by Robert C. Cumbrow, 1987). Plus surveys of the entire genre (*Westerns all' italiana* by Massimo Moscati, 1980; *C'era Una Volta Il Western Italiano* by Lorenzo De Luca, 1987; *Seul Au Monde dans le Western Italien* by Gian Lhassa, 3 vols, 1983; *Macaroni Westerns in Japan* by Takuya Nikaido and others, 1995) and even an informative journal devoted to the subject and called *Westerns all'Italiana*, published since 1983 in Anaheim, California, under the editorship of Tom Betts and Tim Ferrante. There have been ten full-length books in the English language alone about Clint Eastwood (including one by me), all of which have at least one chapter on the 'Dollars' films, most of which attribute the innovations in these films to the actor as well as the director. A huge, and sad to report not always accurate, filmography of *Spaghetti Westerns – the Good, the Bad & the Violent*, by Thomas Weisser, was published by McFarland in 1992: given the many different titles of individual Spaghetti Westerns – when they were released in different territories and on video – not to mention the occasional 'American' pseudonyms of cast and crew, anyone who takes on a "complete filmography" is living very dangerously.

Meanwhile, directors and actors now look back on the era of the Spaghetti Western as a golden age of popular Italian film-making. When Rome and Madrid (for interiors) and Almeria (for locations) were bustling with wranglers, technicians, set-builders, actors, translators and all the paraphernalia of international co-productions. When Fellini, Pasolini and Bertolucci were at the height of their very considerable powers – part of a film economy which was booming, sustained by more visits to the cinema per week per adult than any other country in the world (540 million cinema visits per annum to 13,000 cinemas). Today, the surviving directors and actors of that era tend to observe ruefully that most of Cinecittà has gone, all of Italy has television, and the spread of terrestrial and satellite channels plus home video has killed off the popular genres which sustained and dominated the industry of thirty years ago. Many of the key figures have died since I wrote this book: among them, directors Sergio Leone, Sergio Corbucci and Duccio Tessari; actors Lee Van Cleef, Gian Maria Volonté, Klaus Kinski, Fernando Rey, Fernando Sancho and Henry Fonda. The *Karl May Museum* in the Villa Shatterhand, Radebeul, near Dresden – which was turned by the Communist regime in the 1950s and 1960s into a museum of American imperialism: same collection of Native American artefacts, very different captions – has, since the dismantling of the Berlin Wall and the collapse of Communism, turned back unashamedly into the Karl May Museum. Dean Reed – the Woody Guthrie of the DDR, who appeared in five Spaghetti Westerns and several East German ones, having defected from the U.S.A. in the late 1960s – was found face down in a lake on his estate in 1985, after announcing on television that "I fear growing old in a country that's not mine". 'Ringo' is now a brand of Italian chocolate biscuit, and the name 'Django' at last seems to have been copyrighted: in the 1960s, anyone could use it in a film's title; between 1966 and 1973, twenty to thirty Westerns claimed to feature 'Django' somewhere in the story whether or not the scriptwriters originally put him there. The character proved especially popular in West Germany. According to Franco Nero, a film of his called *Mafia* was retitled *Django in Sicily* when released there. At the time *Spaghetti Westerns* was written, *Django* was banned in Britain: now it is available on video and the notorious *Django, Kill* was recently shown (in a fuller version than was released in the 1960s) on BBC television.

Mainstream surveys of Italian cinema, and indeed of the Western, still tend to be dismissive and patronising about Spaghettis – even thirty years on. Exceptions, where the Western is concerned, include Phil Hardy's *Aurum Film Encyclopedia* (1983), Ed Buscombe's *BFI Companion to the Western* (1988) and Kim Newman's *Wild West Movies* (1990): all British. American surveys on the whole agree with Brian Garfield, whose *Western Films* (1982) expresses "a deep disgusted revulsion toward them", refers to Italian Westerns as "childish, contrived, morally offensive but fitfully entertaining" and to this book as "a dense tome which tells us much more than we want to know about the subject". Mr. Garfield, incidentally, is the author of *Death Wish*, so it might be dangerous to disagree. Where Italian cinema is concerned, most serious commentators seem in the end to agree with the critic Lino Miccichè, who wrote – of Leone in particular and Italian Westerns in general – in *Il cinema Italiano degli anni '60* (1975):

"[Leone's] exclusive point of reference turns out to be, not the history of the West, even as filtered through the epic that the American film industry has made of it, but the cinema epic itself – that is to say, not history, nor the myth, but the history of cinema and the representation of the myth. A case of 'cinema about cinema' – a phenomenon which is not infrequent in contemporary films, and which is generally indicative (with rare exceptions) of a notable impotence in the perception and definition of 'what is real', since these films bear witness to a kind of closed (and aesthetically vicious) circle, an inert 'perpetual motion' within the form. Far from being 'critical cinema' (as some critics, with a fetish for such categories, have suggested), this parasitic cinema of the *dilation* of allusion and hyperbole which is always to be compared with 'what has already been said' – risks becoming a showy apology for existing cinema, a passive re-reading of the myth via the 'myth', all leading to the words 'The End', for the end credits and the blank screen can be the only coherent conclusion."

Good Italian films, added Miccichè, are about the real world and lived experience: these Westerns were about the world as refracted by the cinema; about going to the pictures. He wrote this in 1975. A few years later he would surely, like everyone else in town, have applied the term 'postmodernism' to this phenomenon – for the Italian Westerns, whether they were in some cases a form of 'critical cinema' or not (a reference to an article I wrote for the journal *Cinema* in 1970), were certainly a very early example in popular cinema of film explicitly about film: a reworking of a traditional genre, with the addition of a lot of irony, a suspicion of grand narratives and a lexicon of "references" or allusions which would make sense to local Italian audiences and hold their attention while mainstream critics from further North wrung their hands about "perpetual motion". Historical surveys of Italian cinema prefer to concentrate on neo-realism, existential angst and Visconti, rather than on films which are every bit as Italian but which tip their hats to Hollywood. The generation of Hollywood directors known as 'the movie brats', who went to film school in the late 1960s and studied the films of Leone and Corbucci on moviolas in the classroom, picked up on this attempt to make a tired genre feel fresh again and used similar strategies in their own work – especially John Carpenter, George Lucas, John Milius and Steven Spielberg; they were followed in this by 'the video brats' Quentin Tarantino and Robert Rodriguez. And so it came to pass that a hero who had started life in Italy as a mixture of James Bond, Che Guevara, Hercules and Judas, had become by the late 1970s a new kind of Hollywood hero as well: the hero as style statement, rather than as crusader. The superhuman hero whose catch-phrases and clothing tell you all you need to know about him. Part of the hall of mirrors of big budget film-making, in the post-studio era.

Another important change which has happened

since *Spaghetti Westerns* was first published is the spread of videotape and laserdisc, which have made available many of the European Westerns of the 1960s in a bewildering variety of versions: for some reason, Japan is *the* place for laserdiscs of minor Spaghettis. When this book was being researched, I either had to see the films in out-of-the-way cinemas (with a tape recorder secreted on my lap, to capture the dialogue and the music), or if I wanted to freezeframe I had to hire 16 mm versions and thread them up on a Steenbeck. Now, Spaghetti can be studied and tasted in the home. I know collectors with literally hundreds of these Westerns – recorded off-air somewhere in the world, or else prerecorded. Great for research, but one of the joys of the *Eurowestern* Festival was seeing these films on the big screen, in glorious Techniscope, projected as they were originally intended to be projected. This does not happen very often these days. On television, Spaghetti Westerns either look like big faces and empty yellow landscapes – in pan and scan versions – or like letterboxes inside rectangles: either way, much of the impact is lost. And, since Spaghettis were an attempt by Italian film-makers to recapture all the wide-eyed excitement of films they had first seen in their childhood during the 1930s and 1940s – before Freud and alienation rode the range – the *impact* was a very important ingredient.

Although it has had – and maybe will continue to have – quite a shelf-life, *Spaghetti Westerns* is very much of its time where method and argument are concerned. A time when the 'holy trinity' of Linguistics, Marxism and Psychoanalysis tended to dominate film studies, and when many of us hoped these theoretical perspectives would answer all the BIG QUESTIONS about cinema. In fact, they were to turn 'meeja studies' into a discipline which seems terrified of the visual image: we thought then that they might help to explain the image rather than explain it away. When I wrote *Spaghetti Westerns* in the late 1970s, the redhot debates of the moment were:

- could popular cinema (as distinct from the arthouse work of Godard, Godard and Godard) ever be *really* political?
- was the Italian Western just another example of cultural imperialism?
- was Brecht a useful guide to the distancing effects of some of these films, or were they just a form of cinematic showing-off?

- why did the 'moment' of the Italian Westerns appeal so much to children of Marx and Coca Cola in Europe, especially the generation of May 1968?
- was there a general theory of ideology which could usefully explain the repertoire of themes which recurred in these films, or was such a general theory too undialectical?
- was the comic-strip violence of Italian Westerns preferable to the crusading variety of its Hollywood counterpart?

I have to confess that sometimes the prose in which these big questions were discussed was as leaden as the bullets in Django's machine gun – like a wall of words between the readers and the movies: my defence, after some seventeen years, is that the book was written in the firm belief that cinema really *mattered*, and that too much heavy analysis was being devoted to Hollywood in general and John Ford in particular. The answer at the time was *not* to avoid heavy analysis in itself but to apply it to non-Hollywood cinema. The book was also written in defensive mode: I wanted to persuade *someone* out there to take these movies seriously; and I wanted to blaze a trail through the then-new discipline of cultural studies by adopting as wide a variety of critical approaches as possible. If I was completely re-writing the book today, I would try and avoid some of the over-complicated arguments and much of the technical language. I would certainly avoid the lengthy sub-clauses, full of second thoughts, which often break up my sentences. And the over-use of the word "perhaps". One argument I would beef up, though, would be the argument about images of masculinity and the role of female characters in the Italian Western.

At the *Eurowestern* Festival in Udine, I happened to mention to fellow-delegates during the coffee break between two afternoon films that, unlike all the other popular Cinecittà genres of the 1960s – the sentimental weepy, the commedia all'Italiana, the peplum, the horror film, the 'Mondo' film and the spy story – the Spaghetti Western was almost exclusively concerned with a masculine universe in which men strutted their stuff and did nasty things to one another, usually in homo-social spaces such as saloons or gun duels or hideouts in the desert. It was as if the stylish, self-contained hero would be diminished in some way if ever he happened to develop a relationship with a woman. As for gay characters, when they appeared at all they were usually fetishists and/or giggling psychopaths who enjoyed torturing people. The film cycle which preceded the Italian Westerns – the 'sword and sandal' adventure, or 'peplum' – was much more sophisticated in this respect. Why might this be? Where the delegates at Udine were concerned, it was as if I had thrown down a public challenge to Italian manhood. Not only had I been guilty of promoting the phrase 'Spaghetti Westerns', I had also implied that machismo might be out of date. There were plenty of women in Italian Westerns, said one. The West in reality was a mainly masculine place, like the epics of ancient Greece, added another. Granted there was an unusual emphasis on the 'style' of the hero, but what on earth was wrong with that? I replied that one of my female students had likened the experience of watching *The Good, the Bad & the Ugly* to "being at a football match where all the men stare at each other". She had felt excluded from the party. The *Eurowestern* delegates, of both genders, did not see the point of the discussion at all. Time to watch the next film, Franco Giraldi's *Sugar Colt* (1966), where the bespectacled hero begins the story working as a Professor in an academy for the self-defence of young ladies. Several jokes later, he becomes an unbeatable gunslinger.

Spaghetti Westerns were, with one or two exceptions, a celebration of a masculine world where men were men and women – on the rare occasions they appeared – seemed to like it that way: the understated masculinity of the classic Hollywood Western (which belonged to the same world, only less so) had turned into in-your-face closeups of rugged faces, twitching hands and fetishised weaponry, maleness as spectacle and style, and sometimes into extraordinary feats of atheleticism and grace. The audience stared at the protagonists staring at each other. The women were usually, as the cliché goes, madonnas or whores and sometimes both at once. The politics of the Spaghetti Western, which could be quite radical, did not extend very far into sexual politics – and in this they were quintessentially mid-1960s movies.

Surprisingly, the violence – or more accurately the brutality – of Italian Westerns has become less of an issue over the last twenty years. A recent survey of *Screen Violence* (edited by Karl French, 1996) scarcely mentions them, preferring to concentrate on Peckinpah's *The Wild Bunch* as the watershed film. And yet, Peckinpah himself said he would never have made the films he did in the late 1960s if it hadn't been for Leone's example. Maybe the rural quality of much of the violence in Italian Westerns – like a farmer putting an animal out of its misery – plus their emphasis on the elaborate rituals which precede the moment of death, as well as their puppet-show atmosphere, now look quaint beside the more sophisticated urban mayhem of Lynch, Cronenberg, Tarantino and Rodriguez and the post-1960s emphasis on schlock-horror special effects.

Assorted errors of fact in *Spaghetti Westerns* have been pointed out to me – in reviews at the time of first publication, letters from readers since, magazine articles, and as a result of the hard work of filmographer *extraordinaire* John Exshaw. These errors usually arose from the patchiness of my research sources at the time, or from the fact that I was translating titles and lines of dialogue – from Italian or French – of films which had not been released in the U.K. I am delighted to have the opportunity to put them right, in the order they appear (page numbers in brackets). Where the *Prologue* is concerned, the early Italian Western *La vampira indiana* (p. 29) was in fact directed in 1913 by Vincenzo Leone (or 'Roberto Roberti'); I should also have mentioned a 1916 American film called *Argonauts of California* – restored in the late 1970s – which plays like *Birth of a Nation II* and has the San Francisco vigilante committee hanging Spaniards from out of courtroom windows: this would have helped reinforce the chapter's main argument. *Cabiria* was made in 1914, not 1913. In the chapter on *The Studio* (chart pp. 71–2), some filmographic confusions inevitably crept in. Hercules: *The Strength of Hercules* (1960) is not a peplum, but a modern-day comedy; and three extra Italian 'Herculeses' should have been added – *Maciste against Hercules in the Valley of Woe* (1962), *The Conqueror of Atlantis* (1965, with Kirk Morris as 'Eracle'), and *The Avenger of the Mayas / Hercules against the giant Goliath* (1965). Maciste: *The Gladiator of Rome* (1962) was not in fact a Maciste movie; but *The Valley of the Resounding Echo* (1964) is. The *Ursus* list omits *The Invincible Three* (1963). William Price Fox, in his article for *The Saturday Evening Post* (p. 70) referred to "the producer Mr. Mattei": he must have misheard; the associate producer of *The Greatest Robberty in the West* was in fact called Maffei. Illustration 28 (p. 80), which purports to be from *Django*, is in fact from Lucio Fulci's *Colt Concert* aka *The Brute and the Beast* or *Massacre Time* (1966) which was re-titled as a Django movie for German release. The full title of the notorious *Django, Kill* (p. 82) was *Django, Kill! (If You Live Shoot!)* and it is Mexican baddie Zorro, or Sorro – rather than Hagerman or Alderman – who is extremely fond of his pet parrot: the Italian print reveals this not to have been a *Django* film at all; the Tomas Milian character was originally called Barney. My list of seventeen *Django* films released between 1966 and 1974 was based on French sources (so the dates and titles refer to that particular market), and includes other entries which were not strictly-speaking *Djangos*: *Django the Condemned* (1967), a Spanish production, originally featured a hero called 'Reese O'Brien' and was re-titled a year after original release; *Nude Django* (1968) was a German sexploiter rather than an Italian Western; *Django Always Draws Second* (1971) started life, bizarrely, as *His Name was Pot . . . But They Called Him Allegria*. On the other hand, *Kill, Django . . . Kill First* (1970, directed by Sergio Garrone), *Even Django Has His Price* (1971, released on video in Britain with the delirious title *Django's Cut Price Corpses* and directed by Luigi Batzella), and the Spanish *Diango, A Bullet for You* (1966, directed by Leon Klimovsky) should have been included on the list. A Corbucci-approved sequel to the original *Django* – called, inevitably, *Django Strikes Again* – was released in 1987, directed by Nello Rossati with Franco Nero again in the lead role. Sandokan (p. 92) was in fact played by Ray Danton, although Lex Barker did appear in some of the Salgari adaptations. Mario Bava's *Arizona Bill* and *La Strada per Fort Alamo* (also p. 92) were one and the same film released under different titles. Vincenzo Leone's *Fra Diavolo* (p. 96) was made in 1925, and was the first *feature-length* version of this old standby. In the *Karl May and the Noble Savage* chapter, I wrote that "not one" of the Winnetou stories was available in English – unaware that *Winnetou 1 and 2* had just been translated by Michael Shaw for The Seabury Press, New York (I read the books in French translation, as by 'Charles May'); I also somehow confused (p. 113) James Bond villain Adolfo Celi with Mario Adorf, the Swiss actor who later appeared in Peckinpah's *Major Dundee*. The chapter *The 'Dollars' Trilogy – Decors and Details* states that a mortar shell breaks

the beam from which The Good is about to be hanged (p. 171) in *The Good, The Bad & The Ugly* when in fact the shell breaks just about everything *but* the beam; the farmer in the same film is not played by Fernando Rey (p. 173) but by Spanish actor Antonio Casas – who resembles him. Later in *The Good . . .*, the Union captain at Langstone (or Langston) Bridge refers to "the most potent weapon in war": since his preferred drink comes in green glass bottles wrapped in straw, it is more likely to have been wine than whisky. One of the stills from *Once upon a Time in the West* (p. 211, top right) needs reversing.

At the beginning of the critical filmography (p. 256), I should have mentioned *The Monthly Film Bulletin* for November 1971 – making a total of three checklists of pseudonymns. Corbucci's *The Great Silence* (1968) was finally given its British première on BBC television a few years ago under the title *The Big Silence*. In *A Professional Gun* (1968), the Tony Musante character was known as Eufemio in Spain and as Paco Roman everywhere else; in *Companeros* (1970), which was not really "a sequel" (p. 236) the Tomas Milian equivalent was called Vasco or El Vasco rather than Basco; in *A Genius*, aka *Nobody's the Greatest*, Terence Hill played a character called 'Joe Thanks' who was later rechristened 'Nobody', at least in the title, on wider European release. Sergio Leone (p. 258) was born in Rome rather than Naples – although he spent part of his childhood in wartime Naples; *The Colossus of Rhodes* was an Italian-Spanish-French co-production; and actor Gary Raymond wasn't in *Sodom and Gomorrah*. My filmography of Leone's Westerns – through a series of typos – includes German actress Marianne Koch three times: in fact, the part of the Colonel's sister in *For a Few Dollars More* was played by Rosemary Dexter, the part of Maria in *The Good . . .* by Rada Rassimov. The credits for *My Name is Nobody* should have read "Photography: Giuseppe Ruzzolini (Italy/Spain), Armando Nannuzzi (America)". Domenico Paolella was born on 15 October 1915 (rather than 1918). *Winnetou the Warrior* (1963) had an Italian production input. Sergio Sollima was born on 17 April 1921, in Rome; in his film *Run, Man, Run* (1968), John Ireland played 'Santillana' while Donald O'Brien was Cassidy. Composer Luis Enrique Bacalov was born in Argentina rather than Spain.

Still with the critical filmography, Gianni Garko

did not first appear as Sartana in *Guns of Violence* (1967): his first appearance as the character, in the same year, was as a *villain* in *One Thousand Dollars On the Black*, directed by Alberto Cardone. *Guns of Violence* was an alternative title for *10,000 Dollars Blood Money* (1967, directed by Romolo Guerrieri). The Sartana character then came to be associated with director Giuliano Carmineo (or Carnimeo – the sources just cannot agree about this). Klaus Kinski's autobiography has at last been translated – after twenty years – as *Kinski Uncut* (1996). It seems that Riz Ortolani may not, in fact, have written the score for *Apaches' Last Battle* – a German-Yugoslavian-Italian-French co-production: some sources claim that Winnetou regular Martin Bottcher wrote it, while others have stuck with Ortolani. Whoever the composer, the film starred Lex Barker as Old Shatterhand rather than Stewart Granger as Old Surehand. In *Today It's Me, Tomorrow You*, Tatsuya Nakadai plays a mad Mexican rather than "a samurai warrior". Perhaps the most significant error in my filmography is the treatment of the creative relationship between Ennio Morricone and Bruno Nicolai. I tended for some reason to present them as equal partners ('Music: Ennio Morricone and Bruno Nicolai') when I should have written 'Music by Ennio Morricone, conducted (or sometimes directed) by Bruno Nicolai'. Nicolai did write the scores for a couple of Italian Westerns, but they are nowhere near the quality of Morricone's.

Where the 'cut sequences in Leone's Westerns' are concerned, many of these sequences have now been restored in Italian video versions, or in international videos and laserdiscs. So readers can compare my versions – translated from Italian scripts – with the real thing: they are pretty close. Less close are my hastily scribbled lines of dialogue from films I saw in the darkness of the cinema.

I quote Ramon Rojo (in *Fistful of Dollars*) as saying (p. 185):

"When a man with a Winchester meets a man with a pistol, the man with a pistol is a dead man".

In fact, the old Mexican proverb goes "when a man with a .45 meets a man with a rifle, the man with a pistol will be a dead man". I still prefer my version, but it is not quite accurate.

And I quote Calvera (in *The Magnificent Seven*) as saying (p. 219)

"You *stayed* . . . why?"

In fact, the line goes:

"You came back – for a place like this. Why? A man like you – why?"

Finally, some typos: Zinneman should be Zinnemann; Fernando Sancha should be Fernando Sancho – throughout; Carlo Ponto should be Carlo Ponti; Aldo Guiffrè should be Aldo Giuffrè; Bice Valerian should be Bicc Walerian; Dalia (in *The Colossus*) should be Diala; *Helzapoppin'* should be *Hellzapoppin'*; and Gian Maria Volonté "starred in" rather than "appeared in" the two films mentioned (p. 146).

I would like warmly to thank John Exshaw, whose eagle eye spotted a number of these errors, the many readers who have written to me with suggested amendments over the years, and Lorenzo Codelli who invited me to be a panel speaker at *Eurowestern* in Udine. Also Ed Buscombe, who put me in touch with Lorenzo and who sat next to me at the Festival taking notes – for some reason – on cowboys in bathtubs.

When *Spaghetti Westerns* was first published, most of the reviews were generous. "A critical model for future genre studies", wrote Gary Crowdus in *Cinéaste*. "Unquestionably the single best book written about the Western", added Scott Simmon in *The Journal of Popular Film and Television*. Philip French in *The Observer* recalled the gauntlet he had thrown down in 1977 – "A major study remains to be written on the European Western and its relationship to the American version" – and added "He's written it". Robert Reiner, in *New Society*, concluded that "the book is a major contribution to the understanding of film in society, and is as much fun as the movies it discusses". A double-edged comment? I hope not. My favourite line came from Robert Hewison in the *Times Literary Supplement*, when he began his review "The Professor of Cultural History at the Royal College of Art has taken his chair in both hands". Some were bemused by the subject. Others appalled by it. Most were pleased that I had adopted a contextual approach – with plenty of material on the social, economic, historical and political background – and that I had concentrated so heavily (from pp. 141–216) on the films of Sergio Leone. The characteristic *Variety* headline read US WEST, ITALO STYLE IN BRITON'S ANALYSIS. One of the recurring comments was that I had somehow managed, in *Spaghetti Westerns*, to write for "film scholars and the hang 'em high brigade" both at the same time. Which I take to be a great complement.

At the end of the *Preface* to the 1981 edition, I wrote:

"The written sources which I have found most useful are listed in the Select Bibliography. In addition to the books about how best to approach the problems of film and society, these include several interviews with Sergio Leone and other directors of Spaghettis (in French, Belgian, German, Italian, Spanish and American periodicals), surveys of Italian formula cinema, critical writings on aspects of Italian and American Westerns, and articles on the political sociology of Southern Italy. The emphasis I have given to Westerns made in other European countries than Italy and Spain may seem rather surprising. It was not originally intended. But I discovered, during the writing of this book, that an understanding of the Italian Western to some extent depended on an understanding of the European Western in general – and that meant that the German Westerns of the 1930s and 1960s (and, to a lesser extent, some French and Soviet Westerns) had to be taken into account as well. Some books and articles about these are also listed in the Bibliography. The rest of my research took place 'in the field' – the field being cinemas in England, France, Switzerland, West Germany and Italy. This research led me into some bizarre situations. Two stand out in my mind.

One is sitting in a tiny village hall near the shores of Lake Geneva, watching the infamous *Django*. The print of this Italian-Spanish co-production which I saw was dubbed into French (from Italian), and had German subtitles. I was surrounded by Italians who could not understand a word of it. But when Django (Franco Nero) yelled, 'Espèce de salaud', before dispatching a bunch of Mexican bandits, the audience roared its approval. That, apparently, was a language which was internationally recognised. The other is sitting in the dining hall of Trinity College, Cambridge, opposite the guest of a Fellow in Classics (the guest was at that time studying the love poetry of Catullus), who, when the port came round, lowered his voice and admitted me how he had once worked as an extra (a Mexican heavy) in a Spaghetti Western called *Seven Golden Boys* (he thought produced by Cathay Films), which was being shot in North Africa when he happened to be there on his holidays; apparently, his job was to hold the horses. What better symbol of the connections between Cinecittà's 'classical' epics and the Italian Western?"

Well actually, the film had the working title – I have subsequently discovered – of *Tre ragazzi d'oro* or *Three Golden Boys* (1966), but was released as *Tre pistole Contro Cesare* or *Three Guns Against Cesare* and re-released in 1968 as *Tre pistole per un massacro* or *Three Guns for a Massacre*. The co-producers were De Laurentiis (Rome) and Casbah Film (Algeria). It was called in America *Death Walks In Laredo*. So it wasn't in fact Cathay Films. And there were far less than *Seven Golden Boys*. But what the hell? It is still a great anecdote.

Christopher Frayling
February 1998

Preface

First, a word about the title of this book. The term 'Spaghetti Western' was first coined by American critics of the Italian Western, and was intended as a pejorative; back home in Italy, the films came to be known — rather defensively — as 'Macaroni Westerns'. This started a craze among film journalists for applying culinary labels to 'inauthentic' or 'alien' Westerns: 'Sauerkraut Westerns' (produced in West Germany), 'Paella Westerns' (international co-productions shot in Spain), 'Camembert Westerns' (produced at Fontainebleau), 'Chop Suey Westerns' (made in Hong Kong), and, most recently, 'Curry Westerns' (financed and made in India). Hollywood Westerns have traditionally been known as 'oaters'; perhaps a more suitable label, in the light of this craze, would now be 'Hamburger Westerns' (John Wayne representing the pure beef variety). It is doubtful whether the Duke would have found much to say in favour of yet another European brand — the 'Borsch Western': yet, late in 1977, a block-busting Western based on the stories of Bret Harte and called *Armed and Very Dangerous* was packing them in all over Moscow; it was filmed (by the veteran Soviet director Vladimir Vainshtok) in Romania, Czechoslovakia and Southern Russia, and had as its main theme the discovery of oil in the Arizona desert. The oil-barons were the baddies.

I prefer to use 'Spaghetti Western' in a descriptive sense (for movies made in Italy and Spain) — and also as a term of endearment. No 'racist' slur is intended. Professor René Konig, in his sociological analysis of fashion, *The Restless Image*, has this to say about spaghetti:

> It originated in the East; it is now a food known throughout the world that has spread far beyond the borders of Italy. It even changed its function as it did so: to begin with it was a typical poor man's food; today, particularly outside Italy, it has become a symbol of sophisticated cuisine, and is a popular speciality.

A more appropriate label (despite its origins) to apply to the better Westerns made in Italy would be difficult to imagine. So 'Spaghetti Westerns' it is.

Second, in answer to the question 'Where does this book stand?' — a question which reviewers always seem to ask about film books these days — it will become readily apparent that it adopts several different critical perspectives, derived in the main from sociology, history and film theory. Although I firmly believe that the only film criticism that is worthwhile is located within a coherent framework of theory, I also believe that a study of formula cinema (of the type represented by a genre such as the Spaghetti Western) demands a *transdisciplinary* approach to questions about production (the studios) and consumption (the Italian film-going public, in the first instance), thus a variety of critical perspectives which can help inform the reading of a specific body of film texts. These perspectives can then be brought into focus through the actual process of reading. Such a bombardment of formula films from a variety of disciplinary perspectives will not, I hope, be confused with methodological timidity — for timidity of this kind can all too easily fall into the trap of hedging every single statement with a multitude of 'pluralistic' qualifications, and such qualifications, often a hidden defence against accusations of 'Formalism', 'Marxism', 'Structuralism', or, perish the thought, 'Freudianism', can in turn all too easily become simply an excuse for panic-stricken woolly-mindedness. In short, a transdisciplinary approach seems to me to be appropriate for a study of formula films; pluralism for its own sake, or eclecticism, does not. Rather than being a theoretical maverick who wanders, dazed, into every available academic corral, I have attempted to pen my object of study within as many of the contemporary theories about how best to approach the problem of film and society as seemed useful for a full understanding of it: these include narrative analysis (Will Wright's

Sixguns and Society and especially Frederic Jameson's critique of that book), generic criticism (John G. Cawelti's *Six-Gun Mystique*), structuralism (Umberto Eco's 'Myth of Superman'), the sociology of the cinema (Jeremy Tunstall's *The Media Are American*), political sociology (Edward Banfield on 'amoral familism') and a Marxian critique (James Roy MacBean's *Film and Revolution*). There are, of course, other theoretical perspectives which could have contributed to my frame of reference: I could, for example, have referred more explicitly to the current debate about the production and distribution of social knowledge (the 'market place' of ideology) which is so central to fashionably *marxisant* writings on cinematic practice. This mode of inquiry can undeniably help to establish the 'limits of consciousness' (in Lucien Goldmann's phrase), or the repertoire of preferred definitions of reality, out of which the film industry may construct a coherent consensus at a given time (making this consensus seem 'natural', or 'responsible', in the process); it can even provide an explanation, in these terms, as to why a specific film production seems to look like this, rather than like that. To give an example: auteurist critics of the Western (such as Andrew Sarris) are fond of celebrating what is special about an individual director's 'vision of the West' — as if an unlimited number of such 'visions' were available to the director at any one time; by locating, or situating, this director's films within an all-embracing theory of ideology, a critic can reduce this unlimited number of 'visions' to one dominant 'vision' (supported by a socially constructed 'consensus') to which the director may be said to subscribe, of which he may (in rare cases) be attempting a critique, or 'fragments' of which may be identifiable in his work. That is why I have discussed the 'quasi-narrative' function of ideology in my analysis of Will Wright's *Sixguns and Society*. But there must come a point when such an approach can provide no more than *one context* within which to read specific film texts. The Althusserians' emphasis on the 'social knowledge' inscribed within the text as an object — to the exclusion of questions about production ('How did this film come to be made?' 'What process did the film go through, to become the finished product?'), or about reception ('Why did audiences choose *this* film or *this* genre of films as opposed to that one?', 'What was particularly exciting or attractive about this director's work?') — often encourages them to elevate that 'social knowledge' (or ideology) to the status of a simple, exclusive grid through which the director must see and the audience must look. In consequence, to adapt John Berger's comment on this mode of analysing specific artefacts, they cannot incorporate the *act* of film-making, or the *act* of looking at films, into their theoretical model. The experience of the film-maker must be irrelevant, as must the audience's experience of his experience. If one wants to ask the sort of questions about culture and society that a critic like John Berger seeks to ask, then one's conclusion (like his) will surely be that 'ideology partly determines the finished result, but it does not determine the energy flowing through the current. And it is with this energy that the spectator identifies.' In the case of the pure hack (and there are plenty of those working in Italian formula cinema), this 'energy' may be minimal; but that does not, of course, mean that it is thus to be excluded from one's theoretical model.

Further, the concept of the 'Ideological State Apparatus' (much loved by these fashionably *marxisant* critics) has recently been misinterpreted to mean that social knowledge is produced by the ruling class, and transmitted through cultural and educational institutions controlled by the bourgeoisie into the otherwise empty minds of the working class; it thus ignores (in John Mepham's words) that 'it is not the bourgeois *class* that produces ideas, but bourgeois *society*. And the effective dissemination of ideas is only possible because, or to the extent that, the ideas thus disseminated are ideas which for quite different reasons do have a sufficient degree of effectiveness both in rendering social reality intelligible and in guiding practice within it for them to be apparently acceptable.' In other words, the dominant ideology may set the limits of 'popular' forms of knowledge (as we have seen), but it rests for the most part on the voluntary and spontaneous 'consent' of subordinate classes (rather than *directly* on repressive State Apparatuses), and is, in consequence, most significantly manifest in commonsense, everyday 'knowledge'. So the recovery of the 'deep structures' latent in everyday 'knowledge', if it is to avoid the accusation of bland reductionism, can only take the form of 'concrete analysis of concrete situations' (in Paul Hirst's words). From the point of view of this study, I found the self-styled Althusserians' opaque restatement of the old base/superstructure heresy of little use: for the relationship between Italian formula cinema and Italian society is clearly a relationship (in these terms) *within the superstructure*, and thus requires some understanding of the internal dynamics of that superstructure (an understanding which must take into account, specifically, the production methods of the studios, the audiences at which the films are aimed, and the fact that those audiences tend to vote with their feet). Some of these 'Althusserians' have not only succeeded in misrepresenting Althusser (by caricaturing his concept of 'State Apparatuses'), but have also preferred to look out of the library window, rather than at the *screen*.

In short, I chose not to rest my analysis, or to base the questions I sought to ask, on the current debate about the production and distribution of social knowledge, for three main reasons. First, because I believe that there is more to a film, even a formula film, than simply a static text for experts in social theory to decipher. Films may even have a *purpose* beyond the simple propagation of commonplaces: a great deal more than 'raw' ideology seems to me to be running through the gate of the projector. Second, because I do not believe that film audiences are as mindless as these experts have had to presuppose. Indeed, the labels which are currently applied to the general subject-matter of this study *all* seem to presuppose a mindlessness, or supineness, on the part of film audiences — perhaps an index of how prevalent the concept of 'repressive apparatuses' really is, even among non-Marxists. Some call it 'mass culture', others 'popular culture', others 'media culture'; but as Frederic Jameson has pointed out, the term 'masses' is an anachronism probably dating from the 1920s and 1930s, the idea of 'the people' comes to us from nineteenth-century populism, and the concept of a media culture is derived from McLuhan, with his stress on technological determinism. Italian formula films of the 1960s and early 1970s were certainly popular, and were the product of an industry which seems to have been directly in touch with its audience: towards the end of this period, Italy, with help from co-producers, was producing over 200 feature films a year (a total surpassed only by India, especially Bombay, and Japan), could support nearly 13,000 cinemas (a total surpassed only by the USSR and the USA), and registered over 540 million cinema attendances per annum (a total surpassed only by the USSR and India); perhaps

this had something to do with the fact that Italians (mainly Northern and Central Italians) only owned 11 million television sets (a total surpassed by the USA, USSR, Japan, West Germany, the UK and France). So 'popular culture' was certainly a going concern. But the main trouble with these labels ('mass', 'popular' and 'media') is that they all imply that formula films are something to be enjoyed by 'them', not 'us'.

The third reason why I did not wish to become deeply embroiled in the current debate about ideology is that this book is about one specific film genre — the European Western, and, in particular, the Italian Western: I did not intend to end up on the platform of some critical guillotine, muttering, 'It is a far, far meta thing that I do now, than I have ever done before . . .' To have had both feet planted firmly in the air would surely not have helped me come to grips with this particular film genre, one of the most down-to-earth in modern formula cinema. The need for a systematic study of the Italian Western phenomenon has been noted by many critics, both here and in Italy, for some time. In the most recent edition of *Westerns* (1977), Philip French says that he feels that 'a major study remains to be written on the European Western and its relationship to the American version': French now considers that the things he said about Spaghettis in the 1973 edition of his book were 'patronizing and unduly dismissive'. And Lino Miccichè, in *Il cinema Italiano degli anni '60* (1976), reckons that the Italian Westerns are 'a curious and important cultural phenomenon, about which a full, general study would be most welcome, covering not only the common — and variant — archetypes in the films, but also the common (and more rarely different) sociological implications'. The recent full-length studies of the American Western (by Cawelti, Nachbar and Wright) have tended to neglect Italian Westerns -- and, on occasion, have even included actively misleading statements about them. My book is intended to fill what I take to be a significant gap in the literature about this particular type of formula cinema. And, as far as possible, to set the record straight.

Why 'formula cinema'? The term seems to me to sidestep some of the problems associated with the more general labels which academics have applied to *lumpen* culture. It has a strong economic connotation (describing, as it does, films which emerge from an industry substantial enough to produce conveyor-belt products) — as well as a generic one. And *with reservations* one might add that the term implies a judgment about how films are received by the audiences which pay to see them. John G. Cawelti (in *Adventure, Mystery and Romance*, 1976) neatly (perhaps *too* neatly) distinguishes between 'formula' products, and their 'serious' counterparts, precisely in terms of their *reception*: 'serious' works 'tend toward some sort of encounter with our sense of the limitation of reality, while formulas embody moral fantasies of a world more exciting, more fulfilling, or more benevolent than the one we inhabit'. This distinction has been recently made in another way, by Pierre Barberis, as one between 'works which engage in a process of *enhancing* our understanding of reality' (a process which involves both author and audience) and 'ideological productions, which *accept* a given view of the world, and transmit it' (of statistical, or perhaps sociological interest only); and in yet another way by Roland Barthes, as a distinction between 'the text of bliss ... the text that disconnects ... unsettles the reader's historical, cultural, psychological assumptions, brings to a crisis his relation with language' and 'the text of pleasure ... the text that comes from culture and does not break with it, is linked to a *comfortable* practice of reading'. If we accept this distinction completely, we must assume that 'formula cinema' characteristically operates from within the heart of a particular society's ideological consensus. To take the example of the traditional Hollywood Western again: if explicitly political themes happen to be introduced into the formula, the field of ideological battle is a well-prepared one, in which the values of 'individualism' or 'populism' fight it out with each other in a variety of combinations — all keeping well within the broad consensus of opinion. This melting-pot of ideas is labelled 'pluralism', yet the contents somehow never come to the boil — with the ingredients actually *struggling* with each other, or challenging any foreign bodies which might have fallen into the soup. Films which stand *outside* this broad consensus ('oppositional films', 'serious works', 'texts of bliss') may thus be expected to challenge not only prevailing ideas, but also the accepted 'naturalistic' ways in which these ideas tend to be represented: an aesthetic challenge (and, of course, an economic one — since formulas are great box-office) as well as a political challenge. If such films wish to '*enhance* our understanding of

reality', to set up an 'encounter with our sense of the limitation of reality', they must first *unmask* the confidence trick of 'naturalism', and somehow teach the viewer not to accept the reproduction of the world in its immediate appearance as the only 'reality', or as something to do with 'nature'. This is the way, it seems, in which films can 'bring to a crisis' the audience's 'relation with language'. It is, of course, asking a lot of 'serious works' — for the whole of Western cinema (and especially formula cinema) has up until very recently been dominated by a 'naturalistic' aesthetic: to make such an explicit challenge financially viable, with a sizeable public, can only be an uphill task. Nevertheless the challenge must in some way be financially viable, since movies cost so much.

Which brings me to another controversy, very much alive since the release of Bertolucci's *1900* — and that is whether such a challenge can ever emerge, however tentatively, from *within* formula cinema. If we accept the rock-hard distinction between 'formula' works and their 'serious' counterparts, this would seem to be an impossibility. After all, if an industry is large enough to produce films in a conveyor-belt way, and if the products of this process are defined as 'ideological *productions*, which *accept* a given view of the world', then it is pretty unlikely — to say the least — that they will ever overstep the consensus in a significant way. In the case of the Italian Westerns — which were produced (with the aid of American capital) by Cinecittà (a giant studio which is partly owned and controlled by the Italian state and which was opened by Mussolini in April 1937) — it is even more unlikely. Lino Miccichè, writing about the films of Sergio Leone, concludes that they are really 'a showy apology for existing cinema' — and the various stages of his argument locate his conclusion very much within this debate about the consensual role of formula cinema:

> Leone's later films provide abundant evidence of the basically abstract nature of his cinema. In fact, his exclusive point of reference turns out to be, not the history of the West, even as filtered through the epic that the American film industry has made of it, but the cinema epic itself — that is to say, not history, nor the myth, but the history of the cinema and the representation of the myth. A case of 'cinema about cinema' — a phenomenon which is not infrequent in

contemporary films, and which is generally indicative (with rare exceptions) of a notable impotence in the perception and definition of 'what is real', since these films bear witness to a kind of closed (and aesthetically vicious) circle, an inert 'perpetual motion' within the form. Far from being 'critical cinema' (as some critics, with a fetish for such categories, have suggested), this parasitic cinema of the *dilation* of allusion and hyperbole — which is always to be compared with 'what has already been said' — risks becoming a showy apology for existing cinema, a passive re-reading of the myth via the 'myth', all leading to the words 'The End', for the end credits and the blank screen can be the only coherent conclusion.

For Miccichè, Leone's films — the best of the Italian Westerns — not only *accept* the traditional ways in which Hollywood has represented 'the myth of the West', but, by implication, actively *support* them as well. Any suggestion that out of the Italian Western formula may have emerged a form of 'critical cinema' (this is a reference to an article I wrote for *Cinema* in 1970) is reading too much into a genre which continued to operate from well within the consensus.

Yet, it will be one of the contentions of this book that the two main strategies which 'critical cinema' has adopted — to shock the spectator into a questioning of what he or she is seeing, and a recognition of ideas which he or she can think about after the film is over — are discernible in the better Italian Westerns. The first strategy is a Brechtian one — 'laying bare the device', stimulating the audience to question the visual conventions being used, reminding the audience that it is watching a film, and so on: this can take the form of 'a film within a film' (Fellini's *8½*), or using the camera and soundtrack in unexpected ways (Godard's *Wind from the East*). It can also take the form of making accepted visual conventions more *obvious*, more *explicit* than ever before — and a film like Leone's *Once Upon a Time in the West* seems to me to fit into this category: Leone does not exactly 'lay bare the device', but he does draw attention to devices which have characteristically been understated, or unobtrusive. And in this way he keeps the audience at arm's length. The second strategy takes the form of an extreme stylisation which is intended to be at odds with the (accepted) reproduction of

the world in its immediate appearance, or with the everyday experience of the viewer: the melodramatic expressionism of a Chabrol or a Fassbinder is perhaps the most obvious example of this at the moment. Leone's melodramatic expressionism (an *extension* of the formulae of the traditional Western) perhaps qualifies as well. These two strategies — as much as the more explicit criticisms of the 'myth of the West' contained within his films — appear to constitute the bases of Leone's 'critical cinema': he exploits the Hollywood Western, at the same time as 'deconstructing' it — an act of demythologisation, rather than demythicisation, if one may put it that way. Such an exercise, both a celebration and a denunciation, could only have happened from *outside* Hollywood, from *inside* a formula genre, and from an industry which has a lot of confidence in its audience. Perhaps this form of 'critical cinema' was even possible *within* the consensus represented by the Italian film-going public, in which case the definitions of 'the formula' outlined above may perhaps be adapted to accommodate the phenomenon. Of course, the vast majority of Italian Westerns, embodying as they do 'fantasies of a world more exciting ... than the one we inhabit', do not require such an adaptation. So perhaps the Cawelti/Barberis/Barthes concept of 'formula products' remains unscathed. But it seems to me equally possible that a formula system (such as Cinecittà's) *can* produce variations the value of which is more than 'just sociological'. In Panofsky's famous words, 'while it is true that commercial art is always in danger of ending up as a prostitute, it is equally true that non-commercial art is always in danger of ending up as an old maid'. To put it another way, a few of the best Italian Westerns deserve to be taken very seriously indeed.

One final point. If I have pillaged the language of literary criticism to analyse what I consider to be the most significant aspects of these works ('style', 'authorship', and so on), and the terminology of linguistics ('syntax', 'grammar', etc.) to communicate their unusual emphasis on 'critical cinema', this does not necessarily mean that I believe (1) in the direct application of literary critical methods to cinema or (2) in the sign-language (or even cliché-language) of cinema as directly related to linguistics: it simply means that the *analogies* have proved useful to me, given the fact that cinema criticism has yet to evolve a technical language of its own (Saussure reckoned that linguistics would be just one branch

of semiology — but the omniverous conceptual
equipment of linguistics seems to have swallowed
up the whole 'science' of semiology in one gulp).
Indeed, the *transdisciplinary* nature of this book
reflects my belief that recent attempts to make
film criticism into an autonomous discipline have
been far from convincing. They may even have
been misleading.

The written sources which I have found most
useful are listed in the (very) Select Bibliography.
In addition to the books — already mentioned —
about how best to approach the problem of film
and society, these include several interviews with
Sergio Leone and other directors of Spaghettis
(in French, Belgian, German, Italian, Spanish and
American periodicals), surveys of Italian formula
cinema, critical writings on aspects of Italian and
American Westerns, and articles on the political
sociology of Southern Italy. The emphasis I have
given to Westerns made in other European countries
may seem rather surprising. It was not originally
intended. But I discovered, during the writing of
this book, that an understanding of the Italian
Western to some extent depended on an understanding of the European Western in general — and
that meant that the German Westerns of the 1930s
and 1960s (and, to a lesser extent, some French and
Soviet Westerns) had to be taken into account as
well. Some books and articles about these are also
listed in the Bibliography. The rest of my research
took place 'in the field' — the field being cinemas in
England, France, Switzerland, West Germany, and
Italy. This research led me into some bizarre situations. Two stand out in my mind. One is sitting in a
tiny village hall near the shores of Lake Geneva,
watching the infamous *Django*. The print of this
Italian-Spanish co-production which I saw was
dubbed into French (from Italian), and had German
subtitles. I was surrounded by Italians who could
not understand a word of it. But when Django
(Franco Nero) yelled, 'Espèce de salaud,' before
dispatching a bunch of Mexican bandits, the audience
started shouting its approval. That, apparently, was
a language which was internationally recognised.
The other is sitting in the dining hall of Trinity
College, Cambridge, opposite the guest of a Fellow
in Classics (the guest was at that time studying the
love poetry of Catullus), who, when the port came
round, lowered his voice and told me how he had
once worked as an extra (a Mexican heavy) in a
Spaghetti Western called *Seven Golden Boys*
(Cathay Films), which was being shot in North
Africa when he happened to be there on his holi-
days; apparently, his job was to hold the horses.
What better symbol of the connections between
Cinecittà's 'classical' epics and the Italian Western?

End of song, beginning of story . . .

Prologue
The European Western:
Sutter and His Gold

Men murdered themselves into this
democracy . . .

> D.H. Lawrence,
> 'Fenimore Cooper's Leatherstocking Novels',
> a critical essay (1923)

Rancher: They call this country Hell's Gate and
that's what it has been from the earliest people
in here. When my dad came here it was nothin'
but a bunch of savage Indians and Jesuits. Ole
Thomas Jefferson said he was a warrior so his
son could be a farmer so *his* son could be a poet.
And I raise cattle so my son can be a merchant
so *his* son can move to Newport, Rhode Island,
and buy a sailboat and never see one of these
bastard-ass sonofabitchin' mountains again.
Si: Who was Thomas Jefferson?
Rancher: Guy back East.

> Thomas McGuane, *The Missouri Breaks*,
> Scene 267 (1976)

Is Achilles still possible side by side with powder
and lead? Or is the *Iliad* at all compatible with
the printing press or even printing machines?

> Karl Marx, *The Grundrisse* (1857)

In January 1848, James W. Marshall found 'some kind of yellow mettle' near Sutter's Mill, in the Sacramento Valley, California. By 1849, claims had been registered all over the valley, on land which had been granted to Johann August Suter (or Sutter) by the Mexican Governor of California some seven years before. At the close of 1850, there were 50,000 men panning for gold in the area. Up until that time, Sutter's dramatic rise to fame (which made him the first self-made multi-millionaire in American history) had followed the classic pattern. He had emigrated from Europe (dodging a bankruptcy charge and deserting his wife and children in the process) without a thaler in his pocket. On arrival in New York, he had managed to earn enough dollars from odd jobs to join a wagon train to the West. He had reached California (after various adventures *en route*), determined to make the inhospitable virgin land (then a province of the Republic of Mexico, ruled from Monterey) into a profitable garden. By 'fabricating' a colourful European past, he had managed to acquire some letters of recommendation, and, ultimately, a land grant from Governor Alvarado. By 1848, a combination of entrepreneurial initiative, cheap labour (mainly Mormons, Indians, Hawaian Islanders, white half-castes, and out-of-work soldiers), original ideas about irrigation, the first steam-mill ever built in the Far West, the cash to buy out surrounding small farms, and a lot of luck, had made Sutter's New Helvetia project (at the mouth of the Sacramento River, near the site of what is now the city of Sacramento) into a fabulously successful concern. Sutter's empire included distilleries, grist-mills, agricultural land, and stock-raising compounds, and he was in the process of building a saw-mill — to sell timber to the neighbouring settlers. But in 1849, when the Gold Rush began in earnest, this empire abruptly collapsed. The events of 1848-9 shattered Sutter's faith in the rewards which the Lord showered on hard-working entrepreneurs. He spent

the rest of his life trying to persuade the American authorities to grant him some compensation for the land which the forty-niners had stolen from him (apart from anything else, in law he owned most of what had become the great city of San Francisco). But he was unsuccessful, and, although he was solemnly presented with a commission as General during the celebration of California's fourth anniversary as the Golden State, he died disillusioned, broke, and more than a little crazy, at the age of seventy-three.

The standard near-contemporary accounts of Sutter's experiences (which include *The Sunset Land* by the Rev. John Todd (1870), *Hutchings' Illustrated California Magazine* (1857), and Simeon Ide's *Conquest of California*) are unclear about Sutter's response to the discovery of gold on his property. When Marshall (the contractor on his mill) first told him about the yellow nuggets, Sutter 'thought he had gone mad'; but after various on-the-spot experiments, and consultation of an encyclopaedia, he was convinced. Marshall immediately rode back to the mill (over thirty miles away) in the pouring rain, 'with no supper'. The following morning, when they *both* went to look at the 'strike', 'they were equally excited', and were mainly concerned about keeping it a secret. A Mormon soldier (one of Sutter's workers), or the female cook at the mill — the accounts differ — overheard them, however, and the news had spread around the Rio de Los Americanos within a matter of days. 'Sutter's own indiscretion' may have added fuel to the flames; but there was a delay of about a month (probably because the story took a lot of believing), before panning began in earnest.

Todd, in particular, was committed to the notion that the Gold Rush which resulted from Marshall's 'strike' had 'greatly benefitted the great mass of people' and had 'advanced civilisation' by the great migration of miners from all over the world which ensued. He was also impressed by what Captain

Sutter had achieved on his 'grant of land' before 1848. The first part of Sutter's life clearly contained most of the ingredients of a classic 'pioneer' Western (penniless and flamboyant European Protestant makes good, by turning the desert into a garden). But those, like Todd, who sought to mythologise it always had a problem with the events which followed the Gold Rush. If Sutter was in the right, then the forty-niners were all trespassers, claim-jumpers and arsonists: in other words, the popular stereotype of 'Gramps', with his pick-axe and prospector's burro, was the stereotype of a villain. Not a very auspicious start to a series of events which so 'greatly benefitted the great mass of people'. If, on the other hand, Sutter was in the wrong (a land giant from Monterey no longer being valid, perhaps), then his earlier career as an enterprising pioneer must in some way have been tainted. The ambiguity is nicely captured in the portrait of General Sutter done by the Swiss painter Frank Buscher in 1866. In this portrait (painted nearly a quarter of a century after Sutter's 'fall'), the General is shown standing against a background which represents 'the wilderness' (the Great American Desert, and the Rocky Mountains). He is wearing a straw hat, and is dressed in 'urban' clothes (frock-coat, formal shirt and tie); he sports a flamboyant grey cavalry moustache, and sideburns. The relationship between the figure of Sutter and the 'wilderness' is thus a relationship between tamer and tamed. But Buscher's treatment of the General's eyes clearly shows the ambiguity of this relationship: there is a twinkle in them, but also a sadness and a world-weariness. Hugh Honour has interpreted the portrait as 'the very image of the genial adventurer': but Buscher seems to me to have been trying to capture the image of a man who *had been* 'the genial adventurer', and who *had a reputation* as a 'pioneer', but who could only look back on the experience with regret. Whether or not this is so, the dime-novelists and others concerned with popular stereotypes of the West were in no doubt about the symbolic significance of the Gold Rush, and about the need to write Sutter out of history: they opted decisively for 'Gramps'; New Helvetia became the wilderness, and the nuggets became the Holy Grail. There were, of course, mythological precedents for this (did they but know it): the geologists now tell us that the story of Jason and the Golden Fleece was also the story of an arduous 'pioneer' trail, followed by a flagrant example of claim-jumping (Medea being the mine-owner's wife).

The Rev. Todd also had strong views about Sutter's relationship with the Mexicans. He asserted that the owner of New Helvetia was *relying* on the expected takeover of power when California became a State of the Union; the border country which (largely due to Sutter's efforts) was by 1848 a highly productive sector, had become one of the most valuable tracts of land in the West even before the Gold Rush, and according to Todd, Sutter was convinced that California's 'unavoidable' destiny would prove very much to his advantage. (There is some evidence that the Mexican authorities were becoming increasingly alarmed by rumours of Sutter's connivance with American agitators.) The most recent account of the development of the West (Richard A. Bartlett's *The New Country*, Oxford, 1974) in a sense continues this tradition by analysing the Gold Rush in terms of the foundation of frontier democracy, and the inevitable advantages which statehood brought to those who were lucky enough to be participating in that foundation.

> Gold was, of course, the beginning of modern California, and was the principal source of her wealth for at least a generation after 1848. The gold seekers came in just after the treaty of Guadeloupe Hidalgo (the treaty which in effect recognised the inevitability of the sweep across the Continent), and for the first score of months after the great rush of 1849, there was hardly the shadow of government control there. Political scientists and sociologists have always been intrigued at the remarkable way in which mining communities, exploiting streams and digging up lands and constructing jerry-built hovels, liveries, saloons, assay offices, and hotels where they had no legal ownership, ran their affairs by means of buckskin-and-flannel governments that had evolved of themselves. Surely a part of their success lay in the general prosperity of the thousands who flocked in. It was equality to begin with, or very nearly so, and every man for himself; and for a time, almost any hard-working man could make a living. In such a free society the man with ingenuity could greatly enhance his chances by applying his resourcefulness to the conditions at hand.

For Bartlett, the Gold Rush has 'something unreal, storybookish about it', and he demonstrates the significance of the sudden and overwhelming response that the discovery of gold produced, by a suitably 'storybookish' example.

James Marshall, the man credited with the discovery, was not Spanish, nor Mexican, nor a mountain man, nor, as far as we know, had he ever trapped or hunted. Marshall was instead one of those thousands of men, most of them nameless, who drifted west with the times. He and thousands of others were like dust devils, whirling hither and yon in search of a destiny they rarely contemplated and never wholly understood. Probably they sought primarily the One Big Chance, but their restlessness, one suspects, is not wholly explained by the lust for great riches. There must have been present the elements of curiosity and adventure too. Call it some aspect of the human spirit. What else explains Marshall and his kind? . . . Drifting men of Marshall's type, for whom the entire West had become a piece of real estate to hunt over and exploit — these were the kind of people who first felt a faster pulse at the news of gold. By the summer of 1848 settlers, sailors and soldiers, Mexicans — everyone in California it seemed — was after gold. But it was Marshall's kind who constituted the vanguard.

So, the story of the forty-niners tells us much about the origins of 'buckskin-and-flannel governments', and about the spirit which enabled American drifters like Marshall to endure such hardships for a destiny they never wholly understood. The fall of a charlatan like Sutter seems a tiny price to pay.

Between 1925 and 1936, three European artists (of radically different political persuasions) saw in the Sutter story a chance to relate the classic 'Western' to Old World cultural and socio-political concerns of the moment. The clash between the 'storybook' account of the Gold Rush, and the allegory of Sutter's rise to fame, provided them with a perfect opportunity to view the 'Western' from a European perspective. In 1925, the French novelist, poet and intellectual 'Blaise Cendrars' (Frédéric-Louis Sausser) published *L'Or. La Merveilleuse Histoire du General Johann August Suter*. Cendrars' novel was an attempt, in the words of one critic, to 'seize the world of travel and marvellous adventure with the speed, and at the unusual angles, of a cinema camera'. (Cendrars had collaborated with Abel Gance, and was keen to explore the possibilities of what he called 'a *cinematic* use of lan-

guage'.) This was translated into American a year later as *Sutter's Gold*. In 1930, the Soviet film-maker Sergei Eisenstein (who was visiting Hollywood at the time) made Cendrars' novel into a screenplay for Paramount; the film was never shot, but the screenplay (written 'with some help' from Ivor Montagu and Grigori Alexandrov, Eisenstein's co-director on some of his most famous Soviet features of the 1920s), entitled *Sutter's Gold*, together with Eisenstein's sketches for its shooting, have survived. In 1936, the Tyrolean film-maker Luis Trenker (then an ardent supporter of the Nazi regime) made *Der Kaiser von Kalifornien* (*The Emperor of California*), also based on Cendrars' *L'Or*. In the same year, Hollywood's 'reply' came in the form of *Sutter's Gold*, a film made by James Cruze for Universal Studios.

A French novel, a screenplay by the most inventive of Soviet directors, a Nazi propaganda film, and a classic Hollywood Western by one of the founding fathers of the genre, who had already made *The Covered Wagon* and *The Pony Express* — the story of Sutter's gold, in all its various incarnations, is a unique example of what happens to a classic Western in the hands of those who attempt to relate it to 'alien' views about politics and society, and there is even a standard Hollywood account for comparison. It thus provides a useful context for studying the European Western.

The story had obvious appeal for Cendrars, Eisenstein and Trenker: in addition to the 'travelogue' aspects (Sutter's odyssey), it contained the symbolic ingredients for a critique of unrestrained American capitalism, for an analysis of the relationship between European cultural values and the myth of the frontier, and for a close look at the values of popular Hollywood cinema. Hollywood could not cope with the Eisenstein version — but James Cruze (whose career was on the skids) was given the chance to 'reply', by presenting Sutter as the central character in a traditional Western drama.

Of course, these European artists did not decide to adapt *Sutter's Gold in vacuo*: in each case, there was an appropriate cinematic tradition, and a structure within the home film industry which made the productions feasible. These structures — sharply differentiated by the type of relationship which existed between the political regime in power and the established means of film production — did, however, all have one major characteristic in common: they favoured some 'comment' on the value-system of Hollywood, at the same time as favouring competition with Hollywood films (or Hollywood 'imperialism') on terms which the public would accept as at least compatible with the original.

Eisenstein's Sutter project, for example, grew out of a political and cinematic context within which it was crucial for the developing Soviet film industry to compete with (as well as comment on) legendary successes such as D.W. Griffith's *Birth of a Nation* and James Cruze's *The Covered Wagon*. Equipment and film stock were both scarce. Many of the founding fathers of the Russian film industry had emigrated. Features were costly to make and (certainly in the 1921-4 period, but to a lesser extent afterwards as well) a whole series of 'substitutes' were evolved, to encourage experimentation without too much financial risk: theatrical 'events' which were intended to lay bare the principles of cinematic montage; recut 'versions' of Hollywood films which had somehow made their way to Moscow; short features pieced together with spliced extracts from a variety of film sources; newsreels using archive footage, with a minimum of specially shot material; and so on. At the same time, cinema managers (especially in Moscow and Leningrad) could on the whole be trusted to toe the Bolshevik line, provided they were regularly supplied with features to show, and provided audiences could be found for them. But, as Lenin himself was well aware, the Soviet industry could not hope to achieve the output of the Hollywood, Paris or Berlin studios for many years: the most the regime could expect was a certain *proportion* in the programmes shown — double features consisting of 'entertainment pictures specially for advertising and revenue (of course with no indecency or counter-revolution) and pictures prepared under the title of "From the life of peoples in all countries" — pictures with a specifically propagandist content. . . . The cinema owner has the right to add to the programme or change it, but with a certain censorship and on the condition that the proportion is maintained. . . . Within these limits they should be given a broad initiative' (Lenin, memo of January 1922).

Up until 1928, therefore, several Moscow cinemas came to be identified by the public with a certain genre of commercially successful foreign movies — such as French crime serials (preferably by Louis Feuillade), American romances (preferably with Douglas Fairbanks and 'Manushka' Pickford), slapstick comedies (preferably with Keaton or Chaplin) or Italian epics (preferably starring Bartolomeo Pagano as Maciste the muscle-man). When Fairbanks and Pickford visited Moscow in July 1926 (as 'ambassadors'), so much footage was shot while they were there that the Commissariat of Education was able to piece together a full-length comedy entitled *Kiss Me Mary Pickford* (made by one of the Kuleshov collective, Sergei Komarov) after they had gone: this 'eccentric' film was about the adventures of a film-actor who refused to wash 'the kiss of Manushka' off his cheek, and scenes from the actor's life were intercut with documentary footage of the Fairbanks visit. In short, there was some necessity to emulate Hollywood (for commercial reasons) at the same time as to criticise the ideology of some of its most successful products. More avant-garde film-makers (such as Vertov) might try to challenge the hegemony — the dominant 'codes' — of Hollywood, by redefining notions of cinematic *form*, and by adapting techniques to the political needs of the moment (attempting, in essence, to found a Marxist cinematic aesthetic); but there was also a need to keep cinemas full (if for nothing else, so that movies with a 'specifically propagandist content' could be slipped in as 'B' features). Even in the mid-1920s, film-makers (avant-garde *or* mainstream) could not afford to *ignore* Hollywood — whether the artist was in conflict with Hollywood semiologically, or whether he was prepared to accept the dominant 'codes' of Hollywood cinema (whilst challenging its values) to keep urban cinemagoers happy. After all *The Battleship Potemkin* had been replaced at the Second Goskino cinema, in June 1926, by Buster Keaton's *Our Hospitality* (possibly as a result of pressure from Party bureaucrats), despite an article in *Pravda* which had quoted Mary Pickford to the effect that she had found the film 'a very, very moving experience'. And other large studios (from outside America) were also having great successes on Soviet screens: the great hits of 1925 had been Fritz Lang's *Nibelungen* and the Italian *Maciste*. Hence a certain fascination with Hollywood techniques among some avant-garde film-makers in this period, particularly those who belonged to the 'Factory of the Eccentric Actor', which often resulted in an 'eccentric' reappraisal of successful Hollywood genres (with the aim, in Lenin's words, of 'turning the conventional inside out, distorting it slightly in order to reveal the logic of the usual'). During and immediately after the period of the New Economic Policy, the cult of 'Americanism' (as it was later called) was permitted — and cowboys features prominently in at least two Soviet films, *The Extraordinary Adventures of Mr West in the Land of the Bolsheviks*, and *One of Many* (a part-animated short). In *Mr West*, Boris Barnet (later to become a director in the Kuleshov collective) played Jed, a cowboy bodyguard who saves Mr West from the bizarre machinations of a gang of villains, and who in the last reel gets the girl, Elly, as well.

By the time Eisenstein actually went to Hollywood (in the first instance, to study the use of new sound techniques), the situation in the Soviet film industry had changed a lot (the anniversary of 1927-8 had, for example, stimulated an extraordinary number of home-made features), and it was becoming much more difficult to experiment with American films (by recutting and so on). There had been complaints *every year* since 1923 (at the annual Party congress) that imported films, and derivatives, tended to 'propagate bourgeois influence', but in 1928-9, something was at last being done about it. Eisenstein's training, and his most sustained experiments with film language, had, however, all happened between 1923 and Stalin's dramatic volte-face of 1928, at a time when small groups of film-makers could still indulge themselves in ways which were later to be attacked as 'formalist', 'avant-gardist', or 'Americanist'. *Sutter's Gold* needs to be located in this earlier context.

Der Kaiser von Kalifornien was made within a production structure which had certain (very slight) similarities with the Soviet industry in the 1920s. The Nazis had not nationalised the German film industry. The Party had a controlling interest in two of the largest studios, Tobis and Ufa, largely because powerful financiers who were in sympathy with their policies were prepared to let this happen. (In the Soviet Union, of course, there was no well-established film industry to control.) But again, there was a need to compete with Hollywood imperialism, and again, Goebbels evolved a policy which laid stress on newsreels (as 'B' features), as opposed to costly propaganda feature films which the public might not want to see. 'Entertainment' pictures (preferably historical reconstructions, which might epitomise the German spirit by recounting the deeds of great men in great times) were to become the most characteristic product to be sponsored by the Ministry of Popular Enlightenment

and Propaganda at this time. Later, the German film industry was to be nationalised (in time of war), but in the mid-1930s, despite a whole hierarchy of committees (to 'purify' the personnel of the industry, to vet scripts, to vet finished films, to sponsor, to oversee, to oversee the overseers, and to arrange for the Führer's private viewings), the basic need was to encourage people to go out to the cinemas, in the hope that they would arrive early enough to see the newsreels. (Only in wartime was it thought necessary actually to lock the doors after the newsreels had begun.) The SS might complain in the mid-1930s that Hollywood films should be banned as ideologically unsound, but the Ministry of Propaganda could not afford to let this happen. Fewer than 100 features or featurettes with overtly propagandist content were made during the whole period of Nazi ascendancy: such 'flag-waving' (as the Ministry styled it) was to be handled through the media of posters, radio broadcasts, and, of course, mass rallies. Goebbels himself was particularly keen to emulate the 'folkloric' aspects of epic Hollywood Westerns in his 'entertainment' features, and the German public clearly enjoyed seeing them (even if, as Richard Grunberger states, after 1940 German children preferred the game of 'Aryans and Jews' to 'Cowboys and Indians').

The Hollywood Westerns and historical epics which appealed (for very different reasons) to both Sergei Eisenstein and Luis Trenker were never, of course, subject to quite such direct political pressure: nevertheless, directors and scriptwriters associated with 'epic' reconstructions of great moments in American's past were quite capable of manipulating history in ways (whether technical or ideological) which both Stalinist and Nazi propagandists might well admire — sometimes even responding in a direct way to political pressure from outside the industry. Consider, for example, the extreme case of *Old Ironsides* (released in 1926), made by James Cruze shortly after his greatest success, *The Covered Wagon* — and featuring several cowboys from the earlier film, this time playing American sailors. *Old Ironsides* was originally set up by the US Navy as a public relations exercise (to coincide with a 'Save the USS *Constitution*' fund, since *Ironsides* was to chronicle the exploits of that ship in 1804-5). The Secretary of the Navy, Curtis D. Wilbur, had suggested the idea, using a Hollywood newspaperman to 'convey his suggestion' to the Paramount bosses, and navy personnel and equipment were to

5 Douglas Fairbanks and Mary Pickford, Hollywood's ambassadors, pose in front of the latest product of Henry Ford's assembly line, in the mid-1920s

6 *The Extraordinary Adventures of Mr West in the Land of the Bolsheviks*, an 'eccentric' production made by Lev Kuleshov's film workshop in 1924. Mr West, an American tourist, and his cowboy bodyguard, find out what is *really* going on in Moscow

7 A sea-going replica of the USS *Constitution*, which was constructed for the filming of James Cruze's *Old Ironsides* (1926), with assistance from the Navy Department

8 A wagon train is trapped in a box canyon, during James Cruze's *The Covered Wagon* (1923). Some critics asked why the wagon-master had parked over night in such an unlikely place: the answer was, of course, that it made for a very spectacular sequence

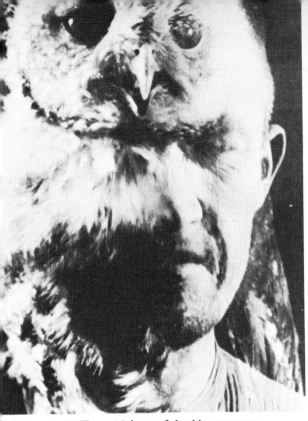

9 (*Above left*) 'Eccentric' use of double-exposure: one of the police spies – 'the owl' – in Eisenstein's *Strike* (1925)

10 (*Above right*) Eisenstein poses for a studio photograph in New York, 1930. This was taken before the Soviet film-makers went to Hollywood

11 Three Eisenstein sketches for *Sutter's Gold* (1930), drawn before the script outline had been completed. They show (1) the opening sequence, in a 'Swiss village', (2) the crossing of the desert, and (3) Sutter's Fort. These sequences were to be filmed in the Paramount Studio, and at Lasky's ranch

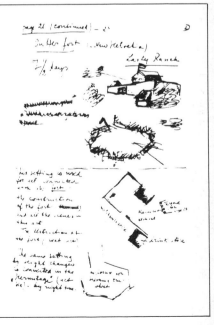

be put at the production company's disposal. Wilbur had been concerned that the US Army was benefiting from Hollywood epics made about World War One (*What Price Glory?*, for example), while the Navy's role in the war had not seemed significant enough to merit such 'epic' treatment; the story of the USS *Constitution*, on the other hand, involving as it did victories against British frigates and French privateers, and 'police action' against Barbary pirates in the Mediterranean, seemed tailor-made for a blockbusting Hollywood epic (with the battles to be filmed in 'Magnoscope'). The Paramount Corporation readily agreed to this 'suggestion', eventually spending $2,500,000 on the film; this sum was, in fact, more than four times as much as was needed to 'Save the USS *Constitution*', but, according to Tom Flinn, 'the Navy, secure in the knowledge that the film would be seen by more people than would visit the ship in a decade, did not seem to care'. The première of *Old Ironsides* was attended by the Secretary of the Navy, 25 admirals, and 300 naval officers. That Cruze's 'historical epic' should be concerned with one of the first examples of the intervention of American armed forces in the affairs of another, less 'enlightened' country (intervention which the film symbolised by the image of the *Constitution* — no less — guns blazing as she blows the Barbary pirates out of the water) may prompt the question why the big studio bosses allowed themselves to be so easily influenced by the suggestions and resources of the Navy Department, in the middle of a decade of 'isolationism'. Whatever the reason (and however characteristic or uncharacteristic *Ironsides* was, as an example of the *engagé* historical reconstructions which Hollywood sponsored), when James Cruze was asked to make *Sutter's Gold* in 1935 (after Paramount had, for a variety of reasons, taken fright over Eisenstein's proposal) he clearly had a good track record for setting the history of nineteenth-century America straight — in other words for sorting out the ideological muddle which the Sutter story seemed to contain. He had even helped to make a modern-day 'Gold Rush' film, *Helldorado*, in 1934. What better choice for the 'reply' to a project which B.P. Schulberg had told Eisenstein was 'not really the type of subject that would interest Americans. Foreigners might come along and think so in their endeavour to find something indigenous, but real natives, no. It was their history, past and dead now.' Perhaps Schulberg was right:

James Cruze's version of *Sutter's Gold* was the biggest money-loser in the history of Universal Studios.

If the structures within the home film industries of Eisenstein, Trenker and Cruze favoured the making of a version of *Sutter's Gold* at this time, in each case there was an appropriate *cinematic* tradition as well. Eisenstein, for example, had a whole series of precedents, all dating from the 1921 to 1928 period in Soviet film history (as we have seen). In 1921, one of Kuleshov's theatrical experiments on what could be done 'without the use of actual film' had been a version of a Jack London story, which he entitled *Gold*: in this experiment, three criminals (one of them played by Pudovkin) had killed each other over a stolen gold ingot. Another film by the Kuleshov collective (*The Death Ray*, 1925) had been an attempt to comment on the values and techniques of popular Hollywood films (still the staple cinematic diet for the vast majority of urban Russians at the time) — and especially Pearl White serials. One of Kuleshov's experiments in 'creative geography' had involved apparently placing Gogol's monument in Moscow next to the White House. By 1926, according to Jay Leyda, 'D.W. Griffith and James Cruze represented the serious American film' for the new generation of young film-makers: *The Covered Wagon*, for example, was used as a 'model' in analysing American cutting methods. The first film by the 'Factory of the Eccentric Actor', entitled *The Adventures of Oktyabrina*, had been about a fantastic, but symbolic, attempt by an Englishman, a Frenchman and an American (called Curzon, Poincaré and Coolidge) to rob the State Bank of gold, with a climax which involved the robbers' frustration by an agile young pioneer. By the late 1920s, Charlie Chaplin's *The Gold Rush* had become another 'model' for Soviet directors, encouraging the poet Mayakovsky to cite it as an example of 'why foreign films beat ours, both generally, and in artistic quality'. This fascination with the best of Hollywood cinema, combined with the recurring interest which film-makers showed in gold robberies as a symbolic theme, go a long way towards explaining why Eisenstein was drawn to the *Sutter's Gold* project. Under the New Economic Policy, a fascination with Hollywood (and an attempt to comment on American film technique) need not *necessarily* entail a challenge to the hegemony of Hollywood film genres, as we have seen. These genres could, for example, be turned 'inside out', and exploited for fresh purposes. Eisenstein's own experiments with the 'circus style' of acting, at the Central Moscow Theatre of the Proletkult (as well as in his first feature, *Strike*, 1925), and his analysis of 'principles of acting' derived from circus and vaudeville, help explain why he adapted Cendrars' novel the way he did. For example, the prominence he was to give to 'Beppo the Circus Dog' in *Sutter's Gold* becomes comprehensible when one recalls the scenes involving the police spy with his performing bear in *Strike*.

Luis Trenker, a Tyrolean with Italian citizenship, had been making 'nationalist' films since 1933, the year Hitler became Chancellor of Germany. Sometimes (as in *Der Rebell*, 1933), these had concerned the destruction of young patriots through contact with the values of an 'alien' power (such as France), and they were characteristically located in romantic mountain settings. According to the *Film-Kurier* of August 1933, 'Hitler said he had seen the film *Der Rebell* four times, and each time with a new enthusiasm.' Goebbels, in his diary for 1933, called *Der Rebell* 'a first-class production of an artistic film'. Stylistically, Trenker's early films resemble the more famous 'mountain films' of G.W. Pabst and Leni Riefenstahl — romantic sagas (such as *The White Hell of Piz Palu*, 1929 and *The Blue Light*, 1932) about the relationship between adventurous German heroes (or heroines) and the mountains they sought to conquer. Arnold Fanck, who was the first to exploit this genre, had 'discovered' Trenker (as well as Riefenstahl, and Harald Reinl — of whom more later), and used him as a stunt man on various occasions: by the time he made *Der Rebell*, Trenker was a great box-office attraction in Germany (according to David Stewart Hull he had 'a screen personality somewhat like that of John Wayne in the United States'). Although he was not a German, Luis Trenker was a firm supporter of the National Socialist Party during the early years of the regime (he was later to fall out with Goebbels, and reject his former association with Nazism). The success of *Der Rebell* in high places gave Trenker the opportunity (and the budget) to make *The Prodigal Son*, a prestigious production of 1934. This film (shot in the Tyrol and New York City) concerns the adventures of a young mountain guide, Tonio, who meets a rich American and his daughter in his local village, and goes to visit them in New York. After working as a steeple-jack (on sky-scrapers), Tonio is sacked (because he is 'a foreigner'). He eventually gets a job as a boxer, and at a spectacular fight in Madison Square Garden he is 'rescued' by the girl and her father. Tonio returns to the Tyrol in time to take part in a folkloric ritual known as *Rauhnacht* (a 'nationalist' version of Hallowe'en), at the end of which he is chosen as king of the festival, and marries the local peasant girl who has been patiently waiting for him throughout the movie. Critics at the time were especially impressed by Trenker's 'newsreel' presentation of New York in the Depression, and by the climactic visual moment when the mountains of the Tyrol blended with the skyscrapers of New York. *The Prodigal Son* won the Grand Prix at the Venice Film Festival of 1935. At a time when Goebbels was concerned about the difficulty of combining 'artistic quality', box-office success, and unimpeachable ideology, Trenker's films impressed him a lot. German audiences apparently did not want to see an endless succession of 'parade' films, and attempts to mythologise the early history of the Nazi party (such as the disastrous *Hans Westmar*, 1933, which started life as *Horst Wessel* but had a last-minute title change since it was thought to give the Party's pet martyr a bad name) had been less than successful. For the time being, at least, Trenker seemed to combine a flair for cinema — a flair which put him in the same league as successful Hollywood directors — with authentic zeal for the Nazi revolution. But he was not a party bureaucrat, and by the time he made *Der Kaiser von Kalifornien* in 1936 Trenker was no longer Goebbels' favourite. The script for the film had, of course, been vetted by the Reichsfilmdramaturg, but location shooting took the unit to the American West, out of the reach of the Ministry of Propaganda, and Goebbels was worried about how the Party's scarce film funds might be spent out there; so Trenker was only granted $30,000 for location work (which effectively meant that the unit would have to use European locations for most of the exteriors). Nevertheless, Trenker's earlier film work helps explain why he felt drawn to the Sutter project. *Der Rebell* had been about the destruction of a student patriot at the hands of 'aliens'; *Der verlorene Sohn* had concerned the corruption of a Tyrolean, through contact with the 'decaying capitalism' of America; in all Trenker's films, considerable emphasis had been given to pioneering odysseys (of the 'mountain' variety), in which *rites de passage* were used to symbolise the hero's strength of purpose. Cendrars' *L'Or* must have seemed an ideal story to adapt as a 'peg' for all these thematic and visual motifs. In Jean-Jacques Rousseau's novel *La Nouvelle Héloïse* (1762), the mountain-men of the Haut Valais know that there is gold beneath their feet, but they refuse to mine it, since that would destroy the purity of their way of life: Trenker had found an ideal vehicle for his Tyrolean brand of Rousseauism in the story of Sutter's gold.

James Cruze was filming his version of *Sutter's Gold* at almost exactly the same time as Trenker. A second-generation immigrant to the United States from Denmark, and later a close friend of another famous immigrant to the Hollywood community, Erich von Stroheim, Cruze (born Jens Cruz Bosen) had started out as an actor in historical stage melodramas produced and written by David Belasco. (Belasco, incidentally, was later to contribute to the first Spaghetti Western worthy of the name by writing the melodrama on which Puccini's opera *The Girl of the Golden West* was based.) After a brief period of acting in film serials such as *The Million Dollar Mystery* (1914), James Cruze had directed his first film in 1918. He achieved international recognition as a film-maker with his 1923 ten-reel epic *The Covered Wagon*, made for Famous Players-Lasky. This film (which had been turned down by three directors before Cruze agreed to take on the daunting task) followed the fortunes of a wagon train from Westport Landing across the desert to Oregon, 2,000 miles away: it was filmed on location, mainly in Utah. *The Covered Wagon*, Cruze's most successful film, and a key to the development of the American Western genre, set the tone for all his subsequent films.

First of all, it was immaculately researched: as Cruze said at the time, 'There wasn't a false whisker in the picture. The dust raised by the wagons was real dust, the Indians were real Indians, the beards of the pioneers were real beards.' (The young Henry Hathaway was in charge of the props.) But the loving recreation of detail, and the spectacle of the action sequences — 100 wagons fording a river, a buffalo hunt, an Indian attack, a prairie fire, the raising of the American flag after a prayer meeting in the wilderness — had to compete with the banality of the central story (as in all Cruze's big-budget films), in this case an interminable romance between virginal heroine (Molly Wingate, played by Lois Wilson), and courageous hero (Will Banion/J.

Warren Kerrigan), with interruptions from the leering villain (Sam Woodhull/Alan Hale). The simplicity of this romance may, as one critic has suggested, 'partly locate the origins of the Western form in popular sentimental literature of the nineteenth century', but certainly, to today's audience, it does detract from the justly famous (if rather static) sections of the film which evoke the epic drive westwards. The Indians may have been 'real Indians', and the location may have been a genuine box canyon in Nevada, but, as was pointed out at the time, the pioneers of the story seem to show a marked disregard for common sense when they park their 100 wagons directly beneath an open ridge, in the heart of Indian territory — simply for a spectacular photographic effect; even Cruze had to admit that this scene made the wagon-master look a 'damn fool'. When *The Covered Wagon* was first released, it was praised by American critics for its authenticity of detail (rather than for any 'realism' of the story), and for being 'the one great American epic that the screen has produced' (it was, in fact, the first Hollywood epic not to be directed by D.W. Griffith). On the strength of its success, Cruze became the highest-paid director in Hollywood and was granted the budget of $2,500,000 by Paramount to make *Old Ironsides*. From the point of view of the Navy Department, he must have seemed the best man for the job: the direction simply required an ability to handle spectacular battle sequences combined with a proven 'ideological soundness'. But apart from these attributes there were also recurring themes in James Cruze's work which made him a safe choice for Universal's version of *Sutter's Gold*, after the Eisenstein/Paramount project had fallen through.

One of the most memorable climaxes in *The Covered Wagon* occurs towards the end, when Joe Dunston, a courier for the US Army, tells the wagon-master about the discovery of gold in California. Some of the pioneers immediately decide to part company with the Oregon train, to throw in their lot with the forty-niners. Jesse Wingate (the wagon-master, and the heroine's father) tries hard (but silently, of course) to dissuade them, by stressing the hardships they have already endured in their search for the promised land of Oregon. But the wagon train splits up, and even Banion (the hero) decides to seek his fortune in California. (He later returns to Oregon and his faithful woman, after conveniently finding enough gold to set them both up, and killing the villain.)

One critic has written about this sequence in *The Covered Wagon*, 'even at this early stage in the development of the genre it was confronting — in the opposition between farming and mining — one of the central debates in American culture'. The split in the trail does symbolise this debate (Oregon versus California), but Cruze characteristically blurs the issue (rather than 'confronting' it) by allowing the resolution of the romantic plot to depend on his sympathetic characters (Will and Molly) getting the best of *both* worlds. Jesse Wingate's strong views on the purpose of the wagon train (to take the pioneers to the lush pastures of Oregon) are undercut by the ease with which Will makes his fortune in California (even if he does return). The last half-hour of *The Covered Wagon* manages to present the issues which the Sutter story epitomised, without actually coming down on one side or the other, or indeed showing the audience that the issues were part of an interesting problem at all.

Despite all this, James Cruze was not the first choice to direct *Sutter's Gold* (which was originally to have starred Francis L. Sullivan in the title role) after Paramount had handed on the rights to film Cendrars' *L'Or*. Howard Hawks was called in during the final stages of preparation, and he probably directed a few sequences before Cruze took over. But Universal's new script for *Sutter's Gold* seems to have been much more in tune with Cruze's proven talents (on *Covered Wagon* or *Old Ironsides* form, at least). In particular, much 'historical' detail on the campaign of John C. Fremont against the Mexicans and Klamath Indians in 1846-7 — a campaign which led to the declaration of the 'Republic of California' — had been added to Cendrars' original story by the time Cruze's services were engaged. Fremont had marched against the Mexicans with sixty men, including Kit Carson (played in the film by Harry Carey, although never once mentioned in the book), and was known to have stayed at Sutter's Fort (with a reluctant Sutter) while waiting for arms and ammunition: in Cruze's version, the 'set-pieces' which show the engagements between Sutter/Fremont/Carson and the Mexicans are among the most 'epic' in scale (and clearly used up much of the budget). Universal's script (in this respect like Cendrars' book) was also very episodic, plotting the story of Sutter's rise and fall chronologically, from his youth in Switzerland to his death in Washington, in a series of rather

static tableaux — so the transitions from scene to scene required written titles (of the narrative 'silent' variety) to paper over the gaps. As the Sutter wagon train battles across the wilderness in the early part of the film, for example, a title reads 'Wagons rolling Westward ... endlessly Westward.' Cruze's career may have been in decline (this was to be his last important film), but the brief to combine historical detail (the Fremont sequences), 'silent' technique (to keep the story moving) and 'ideological soundness' (to relate Sutter's experiences to mainstream Westerns, after the Eisenstein débâcle) must have made him an obvious choice.

The context within which they worked, and the known 'form' of the various artists who tackled the Sutter story between 1925 and 1936, need to be borne in mind as we look in detail at the four versions of *Sutter's Gold*.

Blaise Cendrars' *L'Or* (1925)

1 Suter emigrates

The story of Cendrars' novel opens in May 1834, in the town square of Runenberg, canton of Basle. The peasants are singing as they return home from work. There is a stranger in town — 'a tall, thin man, not old, but with a face already ravaged' — who is first seen leaving the syndic's house, after asking for a certificate of origin and a passport 'to go on a long journey'; this has been refused (since the syndic does not know him) and the man spits into the fountain in disgust as he leaves. It transpires that there is a warrant for the arrest of the stranger — called Johann August Suter — in Basle, but by the time the syndic hears of this, Suter is over the frontier, in France. Inquiries show that Suter is deeply in debt, and that he has deserted his wife and four children. He is a native of Kandern in the Grand Duchy of Baden, and his family has for generations been associated with the paper-making trade there (his uncle Frederick, for example, was a paper-maker and printer who distributed revolutionary pamphlets during the French Revolution, smuggling them from Switzerland to Strasbourg). The current generation of Suters has, however, turned rather 'eccentric', with a particular penchant for strange Protestant religious sects. We next see Suter in Burgundy, robbing a small party of Germans of their clothes, and forging a letter of credit at a local printer's. He eventually reaches Le Havre, where — 'bankrupt, a fugitive, a tramp, a vagabond, a thief and a forger' — he boards the steamship *Esperance* for New York. The scene abruptly changes to New York harbour: 'all the flotsam and jetsam of the Old World is disembarking — shipwrecked men, unhappy men, discontented men, free men and escaped men, men who have staked everything on one card and lost, men whose lives a romantic passion has uprooted'. German socialists, Russian mystics, Fourierists, Carbonari, Calabrian brigands and Greek patriots, most of them 'with the police of Europe at their heels'. Against this backdrop, Suter tries to scrape together a living: he shanghaies Irish immigrants, 'selling' them to a shady employment agency; he is bookkeeper and messenger in a Swedish match firm; he is a draper, a druggist, a delicatessen, a peddler; 'he is ringmaster in a circus, blacksmith, dentist, taxidermist. He sells Jericho roses from a gilded wagon. He boxes a giant Negro, wins a slave and a purse of a hundred guineas. He learns eight languages.' Eventually he opens a saloon (Edgar Allan Poe is a solitary drinker there), and within two years has learned enough about business, and heard enough stories from pioneers, to leave for St Louis, Missouri, with some German merchants, in the hope of making his fortune there. 'He knows the Jews who finance such things, and who outfit enterprises of this nature. He also knows which officials can be 'bought'.' The scene abruptly changes again, this time to the Missouri delta. Suter is a farmer, and is beginning to take an interest in 'the enchanted land' he has heard so often about — the West.

2   Suter crosses the desert

Suter sells up and with the proceeds buys three covered wagons and a double-barrelled shotgun; then he joins thirty-five traders bound for Santa Fe, 800 miles away. Fairly early on in the journey, he becomes separated from the wagon train, and settles (briefly) with the Indians, from whom he learns about the legends of California. After that, he decides to return to Missouri, to prepare for a longer journey: 'he is a haunted man' (this sequence, and the debate which it symbolises, may in fact have been derived from Cruze's *Covered Wagon*, which was released two years before). We next see Suter at Fort Independence, Missouri, about to set out across the Great American Desert with a large wagon train: 'The trail stretches for thousands of miles. Strung along it at intervals of a hundred miles

are wooden forts. . . . Their garrisons are continually on the alert. War with the Redskins is a war of atrocities. No quarter! Woe to the hapless party that falls into an ambuscade of the scalp-hunters. Suter has no hesitation. Mounted on his mustang, Wild Bill, he gallops in the van of his convoy, whistling an air from *The Carnival of Basle* between his teeth. His memory goes back to the little urchin at Runenberg to whom he had given his last thaler. He reins in his horse. "Heads or Tails". The doubloon spins towards heaven like a mounting lark, Heads to win, Tails to lose. It falls flat upon his open palm. Heads! He spurs his horse forwards, full of a new confidence. This was his first hesitation. It will be his last. From now on — forward to the goal.' The other members of the first Independence party begin to leave the wagon train *en route* (all except three women), but Suter presses on; by the end of the trail (the Southern Rockies) two of these women have left and the third has died. Since the trail has become too dangerous by land (it is Apache country), Suter decides to complete his journey to California by sea. Aboard ship, we are introduced to Beppo, or Beppino, a mongrel sheep-dog which had belonged to the girl who died — Maria, from Naples: 'All that Suter has gained in four years of American life is this half-breed circus dog who walks on his hind legs and smokes a pipe with the sailors.' After various changes of ship, Suter arrives in Honolulu, where he gets the idea of employing forced Kanaka labour on his land in California. 'Africa was too far away, and the lookout on slave ships was too close. No profit there! But he liked the idea of giving the laugh to the International Regulations, and avoiding the right of search, by starting a slave trade of his own in these uncharted seas.' So he sets up the Pacific Trade Company, as a means of transporting the Kanakas to the place he has decided to name New Helvetia. After that, he sets sail for California in a Russian trading vessel. The scene changes to the valley of the Sacramento, where Suter has decided to settle. . . .

3   Suter's empire

Within six months, Suter has 'under his orders' a work force of poor white settlers, Mormons, Indians and Kanakas; by his second year, he is able to buy ranches from neighbouring Russian colonists. 'Hard unremitting work and a will of iron seldom fail to impose a new order upon the face of nature', and Suter is aided by his clever decision not to 'take sides' in the growing American-Mexican conflict: while giving covert support to those who want to see California as part of the United States, 'he beats back the Indians to please the Mexicans at the same time'. Somehow, he manages to give the impression that he is on the side of the Mexican government, the American activists *and* the Indians (many of whom are working for him). An armed band made up of ex-soldiers from Honolulu, ships' deserters, and 'down and out Russians and Germans' protects him at all times. Captain Fremont (who appears fleetingly) is amazed by the efficiency of this para-military unit. By this time, Suter has organised an irrigation system, imported a lot of livestock, built 'Kanaka villages' for his workers, and is even considered credit-worthy enough by the banks to raise money for a steam-driven mill to be pulled across the continent by sixty yoke of white oxen; so that by the time California has entered the Union (partly as a result of Suter's 'promises, bribes, drinks . . . and his slaughter of the savage tribes', at a time when the Mexicans are convinced of 'his moral character'), he is 'the largest landowner in the United States'. He pays off his creditors in Europe, and invites his family to join him. But a chance blow by Marshall's pickaxe abruptly brings an end to Suter's empire. . . .

4 Suter's fall

Suter spends more and more time reading the Apocalypse: 'Lord God, if this was in the order of providence, why did I not profit from it? Why did I deserve total ruin?'; 'these towns, these villages, belong to me. And these families, and their workers, their beasts, their happiness — all belong to me. . . . ' Slowly his grip on reality begins to go. He talks a lot now about his 'poor Kanakas', and discusses the moral regeneration of the Indians with Father Gabriel 'their protector'. He feels personally responsible for all the sin and debauchery which has followed in the wake of the Gold Rush: 'The beast of the Apocalypse is now at large . . . and the world is upside down.' But, in more rational moments, he complains that 'the mere thought of the sum of money which all this represents makes me sick'. When he considers fleeing, he questions whether 'I have the right to abandon this country, to which I have given my life, and which (I feel it) will yet have mine'. Eventually, he decides to send one of his sons to law school, in preparation for a mighty legal battle. . . .

5 The myth of Suter

It is a public holiday, celebrating the fourth anniversary of California's entry into the Union. Suter is venerated by the crowds as he rides through the streets on a white horse. In City Hall, the Mayor presents him solemnly with a commission as general, and gives a long speech, which describes how Suter arrived in the village which is now San Francisco, six years ago: 'He traverses arid plains under a burning sky, he scales mountains, penetrates valleys, crosses ranges. . . . In spite of famine, hunger, thirst, and fever, in spite of fierce savages who lay snares for him and lurk in the bush, like the traveller in his own Alpine country, whose eyes, as he travels, never leave the summit, covered with eternal snows, which is his final goal, and who thinks only of the pure and life-giving air he will find upon the peaks and the panoramic view that will lie outspread at his feet, he passes onward and onward, his eyes fixed upon that spot where the sun, night by night, plunges his golden sphere in the fair ocean of the West. Behold him like Moses . . . standing erect upon the crest of the Sierras. His eyes flash. His soul expands. At last he beholds the promised land.' The Mayor's stress on the mythic aspects of Suter's odyssey is obviously intended to be a substitute for any real recompense, for when it looks as though the lawsuit may go Suter's way, shortly after this speech (which is cheered by the audience), 'the public's judgment' (swayed by free drinks from Suter's enemies) reveals itself in the burning down of The Hermitage, his home. Desolated by this act, and by the fate of his children (his daughter a nervous wreck, his eldest son a suicide, one child dead, another in Europe), Suter retreats more and more into the Apocalypse, muttering, 'Thy Will be Done. Amen.' Eventually, he decides to go to Washington, where various swindlers charge him exorbitant legal fees.

In 1870, he joins the 'Herrenbrutter', a German-American Communist sect run by Johannes Christitsch Litiz, and spends his time reading the Book of Revelation: 'The great harlot who has given birth upon the sea is Christopher Columbus, discovering America. Anti-Christ is Gold . . .' In Washington, he meets Marshall again, now a lunatic. A group of street urchins (to him 'the Army of the Just') cruelly tell him that he has at last won his case. Although he has not (Congress is not in fact in session, since it is a Sunday), he has a moment of happiness as he dies of the shock. The novel ends with the words: 'The succession is still open. Those who have the right can still file claims for a few years. Gold! Gold! WHO WANTS GOLD?'

Some of the above quotations will have given an idea of Cendrars' extraordinary futuristic style: both the story and the style of writing have a staccato quality which more than one critic has styled 'cinematic'. Each of the major 'set-pieces' (New York harbour, the trek across the desert, the arrival in California, the development of the farm, the Gold Rush, the lawsuit, the final sequence in Washington) is compounded of a series of 'visual' impressions, arranged in the form of a collage. Cendrars makes no attempt to 'link' the main events in the story (as we have seen, this was to present Universal's scriptwriters with a problem), and he usually symbolises key decisions, or crucial moments, by use of a 'visual' icon (the coin, the dog, the saw-mill, the Book of Revelation, and so on).

Eisenstein's screenplay for *Sutter's Gold* (1930)

It is easy to see what attracted Sergei Eisenstein to Cendrars' book: apart from its thematic content, its use of aural and visual impressions at times resembles his own 'experiments' with cinematic montage. He found Cendrars' *L'Or* in Paris and took it with him to Hollywood, where Paramount had offered him a loose agreement to work on a movie project of his choice, with pocket money, for six months. (Three years before this, Douglas Fairbanks claimed that he had 'signed' Eisenstein to 'fashion any story he likes', for United Artists in Hollywood: but, not surprisingly, nothing came of it.) Ivor Montagu (who was part of the 'team' in 1930) recalls how Cendrars' 'extraordinary tale, full of moral lessons, was turned by Eisenstein — with some help from the rest of us — into what I still regard as a marvellous script. We took it to Paramount, who simply pointed out to us that nobody in America was interested in history, and it was very old fashioned of us to think otherwise.' He believes that the true reason for the rejection of *Sutter's Gold* lay in a 'bitter internal struggle within Paramount ... the really fierce battle between those who supported us and those who tried to defeat them by proving how shameful we really were': the kind of 'in-fighting that constantly occurs in most large organisations', and also 'the general fear that existed in Hollywood in those days ... of anybody with intellectual pretensions;

and the brutal fact is that not only did we have intellectual pretensions, but we had them written all over us'. King Vidor (one of the few film-makers Eisenstein respected in Hollywood) also thinks that the main reason for the rejection of the script was 'a failure of communication' between Eisenstein's views on film-making and the more cautious views of the Paramount bosses. The decision was thus partly political, but not wholly so. The story itself was, in the words of Norman Swallow, 'of a kind to appeal to a convinced socialist'. But its moral and social messages were also 'indirect and oblique'. This 'indirectness' may well have struck the Paramount bosses as smacking of 'intellectual pretensions', quite apart from the 'socialist' aspects of the script. Whatever the reason, Paramount had a fully-fledged script on their hands, and they did not want to film it.

Eisenstein had marked up his copy of *L'Or*, underscoring what he considered to be important passages and writing suggestions for possible visual treatments in the margin. When he actually started work on the script (after a period of inactivity in Hollywood, in the summer of 1930), he first wrote a précis with Ivor Montagu's help, then some notes on incidents and characters. The next step was to visit the Sacramento Valley (and, incidentally, to be photographed standing next to a 'Trails of '49' poster), to 'soak up the scenery' and make sketches, and then to look at the San Francisco waterfront, sketchbook in hand. The script itself was written at great speed, with Eisenstein dictating it verbally, Montagu and Alexandrov correcting it as he went along, and Paramount typists (in relays) preparing the various drafts. Perhaps because of this, there are various inconsistencies, or repetitions, in the finished script: for example, Maria's dog, which dies at the end of Reel 2, reappears at New Helvetia in Reel 3, presumably because Eisenstein, who had decided earlier (despite the novel) to use the dog for symbolic purposes during the trek across the desert, was adapting the New Helvetia section directly from his marked copy of the book. Like all Eisenstein's later scenarios, it reads, in Ivor Montagu's words, like 'a romantic poem, based on historical fact, embodying a social theme'. Although clearly in 'an advanced stage of visualisation' *Sutter's Gold* is far from being a standard shooting-script.

Eisenstein chose to emphasise certain incidents which Cendrars had only mentioned *en passant*, and to give them much more symbolic weight. Examples of this process include Sutter's work with the circus in New York; his prize-fight with the Negro; his relationship with Maria (relocated in New York, at an earlier stage in the story); his acquisition of the bizarre sheep-dog, Beppo (again, placed earlier in the story); his tossing of the coin; his battle with some fearsome coyotes in the desert (coyotes are given the briefest of mentions by Cendrars, simply providing colourful 'context'); his entry into San Francisco; scenes involving Sutter and his family (Cendrars gives them very little emphasis until late in the story); Sutter's death (relocated on the steps of the San Francisco court-house); and a whole series of tussles with officialdom (the police at the prize-fight, immigration officials at San Francisco harbour, the Mexican soldiers, the sinister, black-clad lawyers). Since Eisenstein originally went to Hollywood to find out about American sound systems, it is not surprising that the scenes in Cendrars' novel which make use of aural impressions should be given great emphasis: songs ('a song of California', 'the Eldorado song'); sounds which link scenes (church bells in Switzerland, clocks in New York, the 'symphony' of Sutter's odd jobs, the 'symphony' of devastation the Gold Rush brings); sounds which represent memories (of Maria, of Switzerland); sounds which symbolise various motifs in the story (the court-room as battlefield), sounds which are used to play *against* the image ('satisfied' sounds, as the visuals betray Sutter's inner sadness). An account of Eisenstein's changes to the original story will give a good idea of the kind of scenario he was writing.

1   Sutter arrives in New York

The scene is a fairground: Sutter has become a fortune-teller, and is dressed in Oriental clothes, with a blackened face, as 'the fakir'. In the next scene he is a blacksmith (his face blackened with smoke). Then he is shown pulling out the tooth of a horse, then tearing a tooth out of a man's mouth. After various other occupations, he is seen selling portraits of Washington and medallions, from a tray. 'All these passing episodes are in sound, the tunes of one single melody . . . although they retain their natural and recognisable sound.' This sound eventually becomes circus music. We are introduced to Maria and her dog (the dog 'wears a sailor's cap and smokes a pipe'): Maria is singing about those who have the courage to go out and seek new paths, 'to seek a new Eldorado'. Sutter listens to this,

'rapt', then goes to another booth, where a man is shouting a boxing challenge to the crowd: the challenge is to fight a giant Negro, and the prize is $100 and a young slave. There is a long fight sequence, which is broken up by police officers (for such activities are illegal). Sutter escapes with his prize-money (although not the slave), and sets out on a wagon with the girl and the dog, as the 'Eldorado' song is reprised on the soundtrack.

2   Sutter crosses the desert

Sutter and Maria (accompanied by some missionaries) reach the edge of the desert, and stand looking at three totem poles. 'Sutter takes a coin out of his pocket. He spins it. "Heads or Tails". . . . His eyes follow the coin as he sees it glitter against the deep blue of the sky. "Hey!" — suddenly shouts one of his companions, and Sutter ducks abruptly down on his horse, avoiding an arrow in its flight. The arrow lodges in a totem pole. Mary is the first to fire. A group of Indians is galloping towards them. . . . A scattered volley. Some Indians fall . . . there follows a fearful hand to hand struggle beneath the terrible faces of the totems. . . . The desert is enormous and the struggling group is tiny in comparison with the endless immensity of the desert. The Indians break and run. . . . Two of the missionaries help a wounded colleague to mount, and, without staying for a word, they gallop back down the trail. Mary shouts at them to stop. . . . They do not hear. She bites her lip and tears come into her eyes. And Sutter walks, searching on the ground for the coin on which he has staked his fortune. He recognises the spot on which it fell. Over it lies a dead Indian. He turns him, and kneels down to examine the coin. Mary watches him in horror. "We win!" shouts Sutter. "Heads!" He picks up the coin, rises and shows it to Mary. Mary is content and smiles. Sutter borrows the refrain of her song: "Forward, forward, fortune awaits you". Abandoned by all companions, small and helpless in the immensity of the desert, they leave the silhouettes of the Indian gods and set out towards the setting sun. The West is their goal. . . .'

This sequence is followed by a surprise confrontation between Mary and four trappers in a forest: she is dressed in her circus clothes, they in 'furred leathers'. They gaze at her 'as beasts gaze at a lump of raw meat'. After fighting among themselves, they drag Mary into the bushes. Sutter rescues her, while the circus dog fights with the trappers' 'enormous dogs'. Eisenstein makes the scene seem extremely violent. After this, Sutter, Mary and the dog continue on foot into the desert. As Mary dies, in exhaustion and delirium, and as Sutter prepares a makeshift grave for her, a ring of coyotes, 'howling with sarcastic laughter', begin to close in. 'The dog turns its head back towards the grave. It is anxious and undecided. Sutter departs into the distance. The coyotes close in towards the grave. The dog, in desperation, howls and whimpers. It moves its feet, uncertain where to turn. Sutter is farther, ever farther away. Frantic with despair, the dog runs to the grave, takes up a fighting position, and, with its hair bristling wildly and baring its fangs, it faces the coyotes. The ring of coyotes comes ever nearer to the grave. The cat-like glimmer of their eyes now forms a circle. Ready to die, the circus dog growls. Sutter's figure grows ever distant and more distant, until swallowed by the shadows of the night. . . .'

3   The court scene

As Sutter brings action against 17,221 persons, fog descends on San Francisco, and groups of sinister people ('black figures, in strange black cloaks') start to arrive by ship. 'Dossier after dossier is written by the black-clad figures.' As the sailors watch these people arriving, they mutter, 'This will be no lawsuit — this will be a battle.' In a long court-room scene (added by Eisenstein), the presentation of each document is punctuated by 'the sound of a faraway shell exploding', and by 'the growl of Sutter's hundreds of enemies'; whatever is going on in the court-room, the soundtrack suggests that we are watching a violent military action. Eventually, just as Sutter is beginning to feel that victory is approaching, the enraged mob sets fire to his son's office, where all the documentary evidence is stored. The son rushes over to his office, to 'perish with a shriek amidst the flames'. As the President of the Court adjourns the suit, and as the black-clad lawyers coldly pack their papers by the light of the fire, Sutter collapses. . . .

Eisenstein's script for the abortive *Que Viva Mexico* (which was begun a few months after *Sutter's Gold*) stresses that each of the various 'sections' of the film should be accompanied by a different Mexican folk-song: 'tales from different parts of Mexico brought together in one unified cinematic work'. In a sense, *Sutter's Gold* represents a similar experiment with sound, and, as will be

have been noticed, there is far less dialogue than music and 'natural sounds' (often used expressionistically) on the soundtrack. But *Sutter's Gold*, like *Que Viva Mexico*, is far more than simply a technical experiment. The various themes which recur in the screenplay (attitudes to westward expansion, the moral ambiguities of the Gold Rush, Sutter's own motivations, for example) suggest why Eisenstein wanted to adapt Cendrars' novel (and why Hollywood must have seemed an appropriate place to do it). The 'coin' sequence (where Sutter's choice is explicitly linked with 'manifest destiny' in the form of the destruction of the Indians), the 'coyote' sequence (where the 'circus' trappings of New York confront the horrors of the wilderness), and the 'trappers' sequence (where the traditional terrain of the 'noble savage', at least to European artists, is shown to be inhabited by primitive, mindless representatives of 'civilisation', who look on those women who are unfortunate enough to cross their path as 'beasts gaze at a lump of raw meat' — this over thirty years before John Boorman's *Deliverance*) all make Sutter's 'odyssey' seem like a peg on which to hang a variety of ideas about the myths of westward expansion. Eisenstein may have seen all this in Cendrars' *L'Or*, but, as will be seen from my summary, the equivalent section of the original novel never really stresses the symbolic significance of the 'odyssey' beyond the specific story in hand. The Indians, the coyotes and the trappers were all Eisenstein's invention. In *L'Or*, although Sutter hears a great deal about fearsome savages, the only Indians he actually meets are friendly ones. As for Sutter's response to the Gold Rush, there is less of the hysterial Protestantism which Cendrars emphasises, and more of an aggressive faith in the American legal system. Sutter is less of a rogue in Eisenstein's version (most of his illegal actions can be attributed to the petty-mindedness of officials), and he is never shown supporting the opposing sides in the Mexican War; but he becomes much more dangerous as the lawsuit progresses (shooting trespassers, for example). His maltreatment of the Indians is suggested visually ('the Indian workers are feeding at a long trough, gathering the mush with their hands as it pours out of the rolling barrel'), while the Father Gabriel subplot makes the briefest of appearances. The Indians are Sutter's workers, rather than his slaves. But the central 'message' of *L'Or* — with all its ambiguities — remains intact. Sutter, his family and his dream are all destroyed by the Gold Rush. Before 1849, Sutter builds up an empire by exploiting his workforce and making good entrepreneurial use of his land; after the discovery of gold, his empire collapses as his workers leave him, and as his land is invaded. It is not a case of 'innocence destroyed by corruption': rather, it is a case of one mythology (European Protestant makes good, even if it means exploiting others) confronting another (a 'storybook' Eldorado, hewn out of the wilderness). In Eisenstein's version, Sutter does not seem to think for one moment that the Almighty is judging his previous sins. His last words are 'Thank you' as he dies on the steps of the Court of Justice; he is in a sense *accepting* his destiny, accepting that the myth of the West is destructive of the Old World values he had been taught to believe in, just as his 'odyssey' had demonstrated to him that the quest for the Holy Grail (a European myth) was liable to end in violence and genocide. He thus comes to accept that his type of possessive individualism (involving the cunning exploitation of the fruits of the earth) must give way to another, initially more anarchic, type (ushering in what James Joyce styled 'the era of "the almighty dollar" ').

Luis Trenker's *Der Kaiser von Kalifornien* (1936)

Luis Trenker's *Der Kaiser von Kalifornien*, with Trenker himself playing Johann August Suter, was seen by most critics at the time as embodying (not surprisingly) a very different set of values from those of Cendrars and Eisenstein. The French critic Carl Vincent called it 'a passionate hymn to the superman inspired by the spirit of conquest and struggle'; another critic saw *Der Kaiser* (subtitled 'The Heroic Story of Suter') as 'a denunciation of decaying capitalism as symbolised by gold and by America' (and related this theme to Trenker's earlier films, in particular *The Prodigal Son*). This 'denunciation' is articulated through rhetoric — both verbal and technical — from an ideological base which has few points of contact with Eisenstein's debate in *Sutter's Gold*. In Cendrars' *L'Or* Suter expresses his critique of the American dream in language gleaned from the Book of Revelation; in Eisenstein's version, Sutter might have understood his problem better if he had read *Das Kapital*; in Trenker's *Der Kaiser*, Suter turns to the work of Ernst Moritz Arndt, the Christian nationalist poet of

the early nineteenth century, but it might just as well have been *Mein Kampf*. Trenker makes Suter's odyssey into another version of the 'mountain film'; New Helvetia is transformed into 'a place in the sun'; and the central theme becomes the conflict between a distinctly Teutonic brand of agrarian mysticism and the commercialism or small-mindedness of a less 'spiritual' group of people, the forty-niners. An account of some of the key sequences in *Der Kaiser von Kalifornien* will give a rough idea of the tone of Trenker's film.

1   Suter hounded out of Germany
Der Kaiser opens in a town square in Germany, where a poster (containing slogans by Arndt, including 'Overcome Tyranny and Arrogance') is being read. Suter is a printer of such posters, and we see the police raiding his establishment (just as he is running off some slogans about 'the spirit of Napoleon and Metternich'), and confiscating his equipment. 'What is wrong with the work I am doing?' asks Suter; 'I am just an official, I don't discuss politics', replies the policeman. (Trenker, who also wrote the script, here 'fuses' two characters from *L'Or* — Suter and his uncle Frederick — to make Johann appear as a hounded nationalist agitator.) Suter rushes out into the street (the policeman gives an order not to shoot) and, after wandering for a while, climbs up the steps to the cathedral belfry. As he looks down on the town, he contemplates suicide, but then remembers one of the slogans (by Arndt) he was printing — 'Heaven is too high for a base man.' At this moment, the 'spirit' of Ernst Moritz Arndt appears to him (dressed in a cloak, and a broad-rimmed hat). 'Is the world still beautiful?' asks the spirit. 'There is room for everyone ... conquer yourself if you can.' Suter then has a vision of endless landscapes and rolling seas, which blends into a series of images of stone angels and other Christian symbols, as he rushes down the stairs again, to say farewell to his wife and children. Before saying his tearful goodbyes, he prays with his wife, and blesses his two boys as they sleep. Then he sets out on his journey, across the town bridge, and into the morning mist; a montage of cloudy skies, and rolling seas (through which he walks), fades to a map of the Mississippi basin. . . .

2   Suter crosses the desert
Three 'baddies' are riding through a valley. On a bluff overlooking the valley we see some Indian

warriors. The villains are ambushed, while Suter and his two companions help one of the warriors, whose horse has bolted in the excitement. At an Indian encampment, the three 'baddies' have been tied to poles. Suter and his two German comrades chat amiably with the Indians, and smoke the pipe of peace. For some reason, they talk to the Indians in English ('Thank you so much for your kindness and help'). (This sequence, very loosely derived from the section of Cendrars' novel which deals with Suter's *first* exodus from the Missouri delta, also owes much to the popular novels of Karl May, which I shall discuss in Chapter 3.) Suter releases the 'baddies', whips them hard (with a smile on his face), then sets out again with his two friends. A map plots their progress through the desert, and we are shown a montage of 'desert' effects (sand dunes, sun, the skeleton of a cow). Eventually, the three thirsty travellers have only Suter's horse to carry them. When this horse collapses, Suter cannot bring himself to shoot the beast (an emotional scene, showing the German's love of animals). He leaves his two friends, who can go no further, and searches for help. After shooting in the air to attract attention, he comes across a large wagon train; but although these 'pioneers' are able to look after Suter's friends, they also are in a bad way, so Suter rides off into the mountains, where he hopes to find water. When the trail ends, he leaves his horse (another one), and climbs up the side of a steep rock canyon. As he ascends the rock face, there is a montage of shots of the Grand Canyon, while the soundtrack plays a stirring theme (in fact a mixture of the 'Horst Wessel Lied' and 'The Star-Spangled Banner'). After his epic climb, he struggles to the canyon rim and surveys the scene: it is still fairly arid, but there is some water. He returns to the wagon train, and tells the 'pioneers' of his find. 'But the earth is as dry as a bone,' they say. 'Hold your head up high,' he replies; 'it will soon be fertile.' 'Would it not be better by the ocean?' they suggest. 'No, we will stay here.' . . .

3   The growth of San Francisco
The scene is a music hall in San Francisco. A large girl is singing a German cabaret song. In the audience are various 'decadents': some Chinese, smoking opium, a few black whores, and the villain (the 'baddy' we have met already) with his henchmen. The next time we see San Francisco, the city is celebrating its anniversary. Suter, much aged, rides through the streets on a white horse, in the uniform of a general, and crowds by the roadside cheer him as he enters the City Hall. Inside, the Mayor not only presents him with his commission but tells him that further honours are in store: 'In the name of Washington, I appoint you Senator' (so much for the land of the free). The Mayor then asks him if he will renounce his claims against the State and the citizens of California. In reply, Suter makes a long speech during which he insists on his rights more vehemently than ever. (Although the crowd is by now against him, Suter addresses them as if they were participants in a Party rally.) Shortly after this, the villain whips up feeling against 'the General', and personally supervises the burning of his property. Suter's remaining friends die in the ensuing mayhem, but the chief villain is killed during a shootout – which takes place in the courtyard of Suter's blazing fort. In the final sequence, the elderly Suter is seen laboriously climbing the steps of the Capitol in Washington. At the top of the steps, he again meets the 'spirit' of Arndt, who asks, 'Why fight? You cannot stop progress.' A montage of skyscrapers and heavy machinery illustrates Arndt's sentiments. 'Right or Wrong – who knows?' The legend of Suter will continue to live on, in the forests of California.

The central themes of *Der Kaiser* are expressed in ways which are characteristic of Trenker's earlier work: the visual associations between the belfry, the canyon wall, and the steps of the Capitol are obviously intended to provide outward and visible signs of the aspirations of the central character (and recall technical effects of a similarly rhetorical nature in *The Prodigal Son*); the montages (the land, the sea, the sky, the desert) – answering Arndt's question 'Is the world still beautiful?' – represent the streak of agrarian mysticism which can be found in all Trenker's early films (from the 'mountain' phase onwards); and the combination of epic grandeur with highly sentimental 'domestic' scenes is reminiscent of the scenarios of both *Der Rebell* and *The Prodigal Son*. Whether or not *Der Kaiser* was intended to compete with Hollywood films on their own ground, Trenker's 'vision' of the West (and treatment of the ambiguities in the Sutter story) clearly owes more to developments in the German cinema of the day than to the *Covered Wagon* genre: Suter's odyssey is a personal one (symbolising his own conquest of the elements, and superiority to other 'pioneers'); and like Karl May's Old Shatterhand he likes to think he has more in common with the 'noble savages' than with some of the riff-raff that is going West. Suter is no longer the rogue of Cendrars' original story. In *L'Or*, he is a robber; in *Der Kaiser*, he is robbed (by the 'baddies' in the desert). In *L'Or*, he supports both sides of the American-Mexican conflict; in *Der Kaiser*, no reference is made to this conflict, since the 'enlightened' Mexican Governor approves of Suter's efforts to make 'this land a new home for thousands' (unlike his aide, who would deny them living room in the sun), while the Americans are all associated with the Gold Rush — so there was no way that Suter could come out of the conflict with his land and his honour intact. In *L'Or*, he is involved in the slave trade, and is accused by Father Gabriel of exploiting the Indians; in *Der Kaiser*, he has a 'paternalistic' relationship with his workers (we see him offering them cigars and, later, pleading with them as his 'good friends' -- part of Trenker's rejection of the Marxists' stress on the class struggle, perhaps). Suter is not simply thinking of himself when he tells Marshall that he should keep the discovery of gold a secret: he reckons that the land will shortly be swarming with 'tramps and rogues' if the word gets out, and — in National Socialist terms at least — he is proved right (as the San Francisco music hall sequence was presumably intended to show). When Suter reveals that behind his apparent *bon-homie* there lies an extremely violent temper (while whipping the villains at the Indian encampment, or while making his extraordinary speech to the angry crowds in City Hall), we are clearly intended to continue identifying with him. And, unlike the two other European adaptations of *Sutter's Gold*, personal identification is a key feature of *Der Kaiser*: Trenker's use of the family subplot (and especially his treatment of the younger, more Aryan boy) and his *personalisation* of the main theme (through the invention of the black-bearded villain) ensure that we view those who oppose Suter's lawsuit as all bad. Suter does not leave Europe because he is a criminal in search of a new life: he leaves because the petty officials of his provincial town ('We are just officials, we don't discuss politics') cannot cope with his Nationalist/ Christian ideology and his urge to stand up and be counted. Since all the main issues in the film revolve around such personal relationships (Suter and the

officials, Suter and Arndt, Suter and his family, Suter and the black-bearded villain), the 'indirect and oblique' quality of the original allegory is lost in one big question which expects the answer 'yes'. (Trenker's popular screen persona must have helped in this process.) In short, if Suter does not like something, we are not expected to like it either. He does not like those who fail to appreciate the 'spiritual' qualities of the land (such as the money-grubbing bankers who call in his debts); those who are not prepared to endure some form of 'sacrifice' (such as the workers who prefer gold-panning to harvesting); those who opt to be middle-men (marketing the gold), rather than honest toilers with their hands (such as the black-bearded villain and his henchmen); those who hesitate before obeying a leader of 'vision' (the 'pioneers' who want to continue to the ocean); those 'tramps and rogues' who are parasitic on great cities (the audience in the music hall). The message, like the central character, the music, and the technical effects, is rhetorical: if you accept Suter, you accept everything he stands for, and there are beautiful visuals to carry you over the 'difficult' stages in the argument. Trenker was clearly not very interested in the historical (or even fictional) aspects of the Sutter story ('I appoint you Senator'!), even if some care seems to have been taken over authenticity of detail. But he did make full use of one passage from Cendrars' *L'Or*, and that was the speech by the Mayor of San Francisco. As we have seen, this speech (which provides a self-consciously 'mythic' account of Sutter's odyssey, likening him to the traveller in his own Alpine country whose eyes 'never leave the summit') was undercut in the original novel (where it was supposed to represent the only 'reward' the citizens of San Francisco were prepared to offer him). In *Der Kaiser*, however, sentiments of this kind dominate the entire film. It is rather chilling to discover that one of the cherished myths of the classic Western — turning the desert into a garden -- can so easily be manipulated in this way.

James Cruze's *Sutter's Gold* (1936)

James Cruze's attempt to bring Sutter back to *Covered Wagon* territory, as we have seen, involved a considerable amount of extra historical research, in the form of a long, detailed and expensive sub-

12-15 Four sequences from Luis Trenker's *Der Kaiser von Kalifornien* (1936): Suter (with German friends) crosses the desert; two noble savages appear on the horizon; Suter (played by Trenker himself) oversees his work-force; and the forty-niners arrive

16-19 Four sequences
from James Cruze's
Sutter's Gold (1936):
Sutter (Edward Arnold)
is hounded out of his
local village; the
Mexicans are defeated,
with assistance from
Kit Carson, so Cali-
fornia can now become
a state; winter at
Sutter's Fort; Sutter,
now an eccentric old
man, takes his lawsuit
to Washington

plot about Fremont, Carson and the Mexican War. Predictably enough, this Universal release of 1936 was the only adaptation of *Sutter's Gold* in which the raising of the American flag was intended to be some sort of dramatic climax. Cruze's version was also the most *detailed* account (requiring 'silent' titles, not for expressionist effect as in Eisenstein's adaptation, but simply to keep the lengthy story moving). The film begins in Switzerland, where the young John Sutter (played by Edward Arnold) finds himself wrongly suspected of murder. He flees to America, leaving his wife and children behind. In New York, after a series of odd jobs, he meets Pete Perkin (played by Lee Tracy as a wise-cracking sidekick who never stops talking) and is enthralled by the stories he hears (from returning pioneers) about the opportunities to be had (by those resourceful enough to grasp them) in the fabulous territories of the West. After crossing the desert with Pete Perkin (in true *Covered Wagon* style), he decides to cover the last leg of the journey by ship. Harbouring at the Sandwich Islands, he changes ship, only to discover (to his horror) that the vessel is breaking international regulations by trafficking in slaves. Towards the end of the journey, therefore, he stage-manages a mutiny (cruelty on board helps him drum up support), takes charge of the ship, and, on arrival in Mexican territory, frees the slaves — promising to take them with him as 'colonists'. After he has been granted some land by the Mexican authorities, he begins to convert New Helvetia into the 'colony' he has dreamed about. But, even after clearing the land, he discovers that it may never be economically viable (and he finds it difficult to hold the 'colony' together). New Helvetia is saved in the nick of time, however, when some Russian ranchers (who own the adjoining territory with its precious timber) decide to sell up and return to their homeland. (The role of Russian colonists in California — which gets a cursory mention in Cendrars' *L'Or* — becomes a central theme in Cruze's film. Cendrars refers *en passant* to Russian trading ships in San Francisco harbour, Russians in Suter's para-military unit, and a few Russian colonists whose ranches Suter can afford to buy during his second year in the valley. In Cruze's version, not only do the Russian colonists save New Helvetia when they give up the struggle and return home, but the villainess of the piece, whose bad advice to Sutter neatly sidesteps the moral dilemma of the original allegory, also happens

to be a Russian countess who has stayed behind. The enhanced role that the Russians play must have necessitated some extra historical research: in 1841, a group of Russian ranchers *did* sell up, because of the difficulty of getting permission from the Mexican authorities to extend their holdings, and because the fur trade in sea otters was no longer a going concern. This extra research must have seemed worthwhile. After the trouble Eisenstein had with Paramount, what better 'revenge' than to lay the blame for all Sutter's problems at the Russians' door?) Sutter has fallen in love with one of the Russian colonists — the evil Countess Elizabeth Bartoffski (played by Binnie Barnes) — and she moves to New Helvetia when her compatriots leave. Despite the fact that Sutter has proved himself to be on the side of the angels (in the battles between Fremont/Kit Carson and the marauding Mexicans), he rapidly becomes infatuated with the countess, although even Pete Perkin can see that she is a scheming 'gold-digger'. When gold is discovered by Marshall in 1848, the countess persuades Sutter to prevent his 'colonists' from having any share in the fabulous wealth that lies beneath his land. This so angers his 'colonists' (and the miners from surrounding regions who have heard about the gold strike) that they take great pleasure in deserting their previous employer and riding roughshod over what used to be considered his property. When the American flag was raised, Sutter was at the height of his power and influence; now he is rapidly reduced to near poverty, and the mercenary countess (who sees that there is no more to be gained from their association) does not hesitate to leave him. Before the Gold Rush, Sutter's wife (played by Katherine Alexander) and children had decided to make the long journey to join him. When they arrive (Sutter's selfless wife providing a complete contrast to the evil countess), they persuade him to start a legal fight with the State and citizens of California to recover his rightful property. Although his family is destroyed in the ensuing mayhem, Sutter continues to have hope: at first he pesters local officials, then tries to influence Congress in Washington with writs and petitions, through three successive administrations. Eventually, still with the trusty (and wise-cracking) Pete Perkin by his side, he dies, unsuccessful, in Washington, in 1876. Those he has met in Washington (and especially the children) have come to accept him as an amiable but slightly batty old man. 'Hope was not abandoned, when Death at last claimed him.'

The most striking feature of James Cruze's version of *Sutter's Gold* is its spectacle, and its use of detail. Edward Arnold's make-up, for example (obviously immaculately researched) makes him look more and more like the Buscher portrait as he grows older. Watching the wagon train sequences, the scenes on the slave ship, the reconstruction of Sutter's adobe-walled fort, the battles with the Mexicans, and the first winter of the Gold Rush, one can see why the film cost so much, and why it represented the greatest loss Universal had ever sustained, wrecking a regime at that studio and ensuring that James Cruze would never be offered 'A' features again. Universal used some of the slave ship footage in an adventure film of the early 1940s, called *Mutiny on the Blackhawk*, and re-released *Sutter's Gold* in 1948 (to cash in on the centenary of the Gold Rush!) this time with saturation publicity — including a 'Gold Week' in Sacramento, and a special Gold Rush train from Los Angeles to take viewers to the première — but it still failed to recoup its enormous cost.

Another characteristic Cruze touch is the combination of a sentimental story (as *personalised* as the Nazi version) with scenes of epic grandeur. Sutter is hounded out of Switzerland because he has been *wrongfully* accused of a crime; he frees the slaves from the Sandwich Islands (despite the fact that Cendrars makes much play of his *enthusiasm* for, and exploitation of, the slave traffic); he shows his organising abilities fairly early on, by setting up the mutiny; he supports Fremont and Carson (there is no suggestion of opportunism here); and, most important of all, he disapproves of the Gold Rush — not because of his highly developed sense of property, or because he fears that the hard-earned rewards of New Helvetia will go to waste, or even because he is worried about his investment in expensive plant, but because, quite simply, he falls too easily for the charms of an evil Russian countess. (It is never quite clear what Elizabeth Bartoffski is doing in the story: at times she seems to have walked off the set of a horror movie, perhaps as a blood relative of that other evil countess, Elizabeth Bathory, or 'Countess Dracula'.) Thus each of the moral (and political) ambiguities of *L'Or* is neatly sidestepped, as we sit back to watch a series of spectacular 'episodes'. Critics at the time pointed out that 'one loses one's sympathy, when Sutter, too easily for a man of his character,

falls victim to the wiles of the Countess, who is too blatantly mercenary'; the *Kine Weekly* added that 'it is difficult at times to recognise and appreciate the story's moral objective'; the *Monthly Film Bulletin* felt that 'our sympathy merely becomes sentimental pity for a poor old man', and that, surely, was not right. Most of the critics singled out Harry Carey's performance as Kit Carson for special mention (and Carson, as we have seen, played no part at all in the original allegory).

The chief of the costing department at Paramount (refusing to itemise) had told Eisenstein that his version of *Sutter's Gold* was a three-million dollar picture, and that was 'too much'. James Cruze's version probably cost more than that. Ironically, Universal might well have done better if they had contracted Eisenstein to direct the picture. But if they had, they could never have persuaded him to present Sutter's dilemma as anything whatever to do with an evil Russian countess. Apart from anything else, the era of anti-Tsarist propaganda had ended with the tenth anniversary of the Russian Revolution, in February 1928.

A standard response to European Westerns of more recent times has been that in some sense they are not really 'Westerns' at all. They lack 'authenticity', we are told. They do not have any 'cultural roots' in the historical period depicted and can thus never aspire to a 'poetic vision' of the West. They have no 'feel' for the period. Their 'moral universe' is at odds with the ethical bases of the genre. And so on. These criticisms may seem rather strange in the light of the fact that critics have been arguing for over twenty years (ever since the Western became a serious object of study) about what exactly *does* constitute a 'Western' film, and about how we are to account for its enduring fascination once we have established what it is. But certain defining characteristics, or common internal characteristics, of the Western film have emerged from this debate, and it might help to clarify the issue if, before we look at the Italian and German Westerns of the 1960s and early 1970s, these are applied to all the different versions of *Sutter's Gold*.

For André Bazin, the Western is 'the American film par excellence'. By this he did not mean that Westerns have to be historically accurate: rather, they must be 'faithful to history', in the sense that specific events (and 'historical references') must provide the particular context within which 'the great epic Manicheism which sets the forces of evil over against the knights of the true cause' will be presented; more often than not, this 'epic' will deal in some way with 'the relation between law and morality'. The genre is thus 'historical at base', but 'epic art' may arise out of it: 'Westerns can turn the American Civil War into the Trojan War of the most modern of epics.' Bazin's thesis — which characteristically stressed that Westerns must have some point of contact with historical 'reality' — could not, of course, accommodate the European Western: 'if in fact Westerns have been shot in France against the landscapes of the Camargue, one can easily see in this an additional proof of the popularity and healthiness of a genre that can survive counterfeiting, pastiche, and even parody'. Films like Harry Watt's *The Overlanders* may have worked as 'Westerns', because the historical events depicted (pioneers in Australia) directly parallel those of American frontier history, but 'fortunately, no attempt was made to follow up this paradoxical achievement, whose success was due to an unusual combination of circumstances'. J.-L. Rieupeyrout, who extended Bazin's thesis about the historical 'realism' of the Western to include historical *accuracy* as a key criterion, also reckoned that the Western is a Hollywood product 'which has to perish under other skies': attempts to make Westerns in other countries (for example France) usually end up as 'heavy-handed parodies — whether explicit or not — of a genre which can only belong to one country, or at least to countries whose *topography* or *historical past* offer aspects in common with those of the American West, land or men'. Countries like Australia, which have a 'frontier' past, can at least produce Westerns where 'a plausible image' of frontier history emerges. Otherwise, the genre is 'very difficult to transpose and export'. (Rieupeyrout does not mention 'alien' Westerns which use American locations.) The third French critic to adopt a neo-realist stance *vis-à-vis* the Western, in the 1950s, was Jean Wagner, who related the origins of the movie genre to the same search for an American national identity as stimulated Frederick Jackson Turner's thesis about the cultural implications of the frontier: 'the Western was another expression of American national consciousness', a means of isolating exactly what 'America' was, at a time of mass immigration and the 'closing' of the frontier. 'Crises in America's national identity' — for example, 1910-20, the

early 1930s, the 1950s — were, in consequence, directly 'reflected' in the changing shape of the genre during these crucial periods. Wagner is less concerned about the historical bases of the Western than about the sensitivity of such a 'national genre' to crises in American society — but the defining characteristic of the Western was (and is) its attempt to define 'American-ness'.

The neo-realist critics at least drew attention to the Western as a legitimate source for academic study. More recently, however, critics have been less concerned about the *accuracy* of American Westerns, preferring instead to analyse the 'mythic' potential of the genre. For Jim Kitses, the defining characteristic is some account of the dialectical relationship between the opposing forces of Wilderness and Civilisation ('the contrasting images of Garden and Desert'): this account need not, however, be contained within a film which happens to have been made in America, by Americans. John G. Cawelti, following Kitses' analysis, has defined the Western as 'an epic moment in which savagery and civilisation stand against each other in a deadlock which is broken in favour of civilisation through the intervention of the Western hero who possesses qualities of both the savage wilderness and civilisation': the function of the Western is to 'resolve', in its own way, 'the conflict between key American values like progress and success and the lost virtues of individual honour, and natural freedom'. Colin McArthur also interprets 'savagery and civilisation' as key polarities within the genre, and relates the 'quintessentially American' conflict they represent to Turner's 'frontier' thesis, and Nash Smith's *The Virgin Land*: Westerns view the West as a (potential) garden, but also face up to the threat it poses as a desert. Other critics have added to Kitses' 'opposing forces' and Rieupeyrout's 'frontier past' a whole series of 'foundation myths' (allegedly exclusive to the 'Western' movie genre), including the inevitably 'progressive' effect of the colonisation and exploitation of the Western frontier; the 'manifest destiny' which greeted the native Americans; the 'rugged individualism' (preferably a Puritan type) which made the frontier possible; the 'cleansing' of the American paradise of sinful elements through the efforts of a saviour-hero, who is more violent than the traditional image of Christ because the savage American landscape calls for more violent solutions; and the myth of the 'last gentleman', who defines his life on the frontier by a strict code of honour. Fenin and Everson have attempted to deflate this 'mythic' approach to the Western by reverting to a neo-realist perspective: for them, 'the term *Western* is geographical, rather than dramatically descriptive — it refers to the locale of the story rather than to the content'. And Richard Collins has attacked the generic approach to the study of Westerns (the basis of the 'mythic' approach), on the grounds that the meanings we associate with locations, clothes, a specific historical period, and so on, do no more than establish a 'temporal and geographical context for the film': 'if genre exists as a distinct quantity it is in terms of a repertoire of stock situations, selected from the events of the American frontier, that are themselves unspecific, ambiguous and intrinsically without meaning'; a more useful approach might be to study the Western in terms of individual authors.

Will Wright, in his *Sixguns and Society*, has criticised both the 'mythic' and the 'literary' approaches to the Western genre — on the grounds that they both ignore or deny the fact that the Western, like other myths, is a *social* phenomenon. I will be looking at his criticisms in detail, as part of my analysis of Spaghettis and society (Chapter 1): for the moment, it is enough to outline the characteristics which Wright sees as exclusively belonging to the Western. One factor is the specific historical period: 'the crucial period of settlement in which most Westerns take place lasted only about thirty years, from 1860 to 1890. . . . Even if we include the period of the California gold rush and the first wagon trains to Oregon, the entire period of western settlement lasted less than fifty years.' Another factor is a series of 'basic oppositions' at work in the Western: these include 'inside society/outside society', 'good/bad', 'strong/weak', and 'wilderness/civilisation'. Wright goes on to subdivide Western stories into a set of episodes, whose presence in a given order may be said to constitute the Western genre. In other words, for Wright, the 'Western' consists of a series of narrative 'resolutions' of contradictions in American society — 'resolutions' which are presented within a specific historical time-scale, and which depend on some basic 'oppositions' normally associated with that time-scale. The Western stories he analyses are thus assumed to have 'cultural roots' in American society — for only if this assumption is accepted can the stories be expected to mediate, or 'resolve', social contradictions specific to America.

Despite Will Wright's tough analysis, less sociological versions of the 'mythic' interpretation are still very much alive. Recent criticisms have seen the Western as representing a legitimation of violence in the context of Puritan 'repressiveness' (the Western is 'a puritan morality-tale in which the saviour-hero redeems the community from the temptations of the devil' according to Peter Homans); a mythic version of the Voltairean prescription 'We must cultivate our garden'; and a nostalgic evocation of a world where words like 'honour' had some meaning, where grass-roots, participatory democracy seemed to be of benefit to both the participants *and* the community. The debate goes on . . .

All the versions of *Sutter's Gold* are, of course, concerned with 'the period of the California Gold Rush' (Wright): most critics would agree that this is within the correct historical time-scale. Sutter was a historical figure, and his actions took place during a crucial phase in frontier history (Bazin, Rieupeyrout, Wagner). The Sutter allegory is very much concerned with 'the relation between law and morality' (Bazin) — the individual versus the State, frontier conceptions of law versus 'Old World' property law, the 'morality' of Sutter's legal battle, and so on. Only the Hollywood version of the story attempts to sidestep these issues. The debate about 'progress' (Cawelti) lies at the centre of the Californians' quarrel with the obstinate Sutter, and one of the key ambiguities in Cendrars' *L'Or* is the strange opposition between the 'progress' which New Helvetia represents and the progressive implications of the Gold Rush: Sutter's problem is how to keep his 'honour' intact when caught in the crossfire. The Puritan aspects of the West (Homans) are represented by Sutter's strange brand of fundamentalist Christianity (especially strong in the novel, but referred to in the Soviet and German versions as well). His behaviour during the Mexican War would suggest that he wants to cultivate his own garden rather than anyone else's. And the grass-roots 'buckskin-and-flannel governments' which the forty-niners were seen to have set up spontaneously, constitute one of the much-vaunted 'benefits' which arrived in the wake of the Gold Rush ('benefits' we must bear in mind, if we are to make a balanced judgment of Sutter's behaviour). Kitses' (and Cawelti's) defining characteristic (like most other 'generic myths' studied from a 'Lit. Crit.' perspective) is isolated from Western movies by the rather tautological method of looking for recurring motifs in a few 'classic' films (or rather, for recurring motifs which coincide with the concerns of 'classic' commentators such as Frederick Jackson Turner and Henry Nash Smith), then seeing how many movies conform to this 'model'. Nevertheless, whatever the pitfalls of his method, both parts of the Sutter story are concerned with 'the contrasting images of Garden and Desert' (Kitses), and Eisenstein's version of Sutter's odyssey deals with the question of 'manifest destiny' as well; Sutter himself is an archetypal 'rugged individualist' (albeit of rather a flamboyant type — but that has seldom been seen as a disadvantage), and the whole story is a debate about the 'progressive' effects of westward expansion. Sutter clearly sees himself as 'the last gentleman'. As to the geographical location, Sutter's adventures were meant to be taking place (following Cendrars) in New York, the Missouri delta, Fort Independence, the Great American Desert, the Rockies, California and Washington (mainly frontier territory). If the term 'location' is extended to mean *cinematic* location (an extension which Fenin and Everson do not attempt), the assumption perhaps being that 'authenticity' has something to do with whether the rocks on the screen are the 'correct' rocks or 'representational' ones, all the films in question were to contain (or did contain) at least some footage shot on 'location'. In Eisenstein's version, 'Sutter's Fort' was to be the ranch belonging to Jesse Lasky, head of production at Paramount; 'the big trees' were to be filmed in the Yosemite (and transparencies were to be used for scenes which involved the actors); 'the shore of San Francisco' was to be found on the Catalina Isthmus; 'the desert' was to be a patch of arid land, with '3-4 gigantic artificial cactuses, and 6-7 small dogs "acting" Coyotes'; parts of San Francisco were to be used; the remaining set-ups (derived from Eisenstein's sketches done on the spot) were to be re-created in the Paramount studio. Luis Trenker wanted to film as much of *Der Kaiser* as he could on location in America, but there was a financial constraint: only $30,000 were provided for this purpose, most of which were spent on filming in Arizona (the desert and the Grand Canyon); the remaining exteriors were shot in Germany and Italy, and studio work was filmed in Berlin. The 'desert' sequences suffer more than the rest from the limitations of the budget: at one point, a speeding car is clearly visible in the background; at another, Trenker slips in a spectacular shot of a

wagon train (clearly from a different film, perhaps even *The Covered Wagon*), and the number of wagons in the 'pioneer' train continues to vary from shot to shot (sometimes one, sometimes three, sometimes six — the crew appears to have had access to only one). James Cruze filmed some of *Sutter's Gold* on location in California, and in the Sandwich Islands, but interiors, crowd-scenes, battle scenes, and sequences on board ship were all shot on the Universal backlot. Admittedly, all the 'Sutter' films were based on a French 'original' — but so was John Ford's *Stagecoach* (an adaptation of Guy de Maupassant's *Boule de Suif*). Perhaps the fact of being a 'Western' has something to do with the use of American actors. If so, Eisenstein's version was to have Francis L. Sullivan in the title role, Cruze inherited Edward Arnold as Sutter, while Luis Trenker at least had 'a screen personality somewhat like that of John Wayne in the United States'. The morality of the various 'Sutter' stories crucially depends on the 'basic oppositions' we expect to find in Hollywood Westerns, and the stories all explore the 'contradiction' in American society which the survival of the Gold Rush 'myth' may be said to represent. The Cruze version was not a popular success, and we may assume, I think, that the Eisenstein version would not have been a great box-office hit either. So, in Will Wright's terms, American audiences would not accept the presentation of social 'contradictions' within these particular films. But that does not alter the fact that Wright's analysis (and the definition of the 'Western' it assumes) can be applied to the 'Sutter' stories, without any substantial modification.

Who is to judge whether the two adaptations of *Sutter's Gold* made (or planned) by European filmmakers are 'Westerns' or not? In so far as any exclusively 'Western' characteristics have emerged from the twenty-year debate on the subject, these films seem to conform to them. Their ideological positions, their cultural points of reference, the European film techniques they epitomise, may all seem 'alien' to the traditions of the Hollywood Western, but no operational definition of the 'myth of the West' (in film terms — from a literary *or* a sociological perspective) can exclude them. They were made possible by film production contexts which favoured the use of recognisably Hollywood genres (as well as 'comments' on those genres). Clearly, before studying European Westerns, one must first analyse the studios from which they emerged (and the relationship — economic or cinematic — between those studios and Hollywood). They are not fully comprehensible without reference to the previous work of the individual directors concerned, and to the attitudes of these directors towards the Hollywood Western. A thorough analysis of them should be able to distinguish the specifically 'European' elements (technical, cultural or ideological) from the extensions of Hollywood 'forms' or 'dominant codes', the attempts to manipulate audience expectations about the Hollywood product, and the elements which are directly derived from the Hollywood originals. As we have seen, 'authenticity' (of costume, location or historical detail) is simply one strategy, which should be studied in terms of these analytical distinctions. In other words, the above discussion of the French, Soviet, German and American versions of *Sutter's Gold* has provided us with a critical frame of reference within which to look at the European Western.

Of the specifically European themes (presented from a European perspective) which have emerged during the course of this discussion, two in particular were to play a key role during the revival of the German (and thus the Italian) Westerns of the 1960s and early 1970s: the theme of the 'noble savage' (much loved by European artists who wrote about, or painted, American landscapes from the sixteenth century onwards, revived through the pulp novels of Karl May in late-nineteenth-century Germany - perhaps in part representing the 'awe' of a petty-bourgeois German in the face of wide open spaces which American writers could take more for granted — and featuring strongly in the 'odyssey' sequences of *Der Kaiser von Kalifornien*); and the theme of Gold, or the 'almighty dollar', as a neglected symbol of the implications of the 'myth of the West' (neglected, that is, by Hollywood). The various versions of *Sutter's Gold* emerged from very different institutional and cultural contexts — so the presence of specifically European themes common to all of them may seem surprising. The unifying factor, which to some extent explains the presence of these themes, was that each version adopted some kind of critical stance *vis-à-vis* the dominance of Hollywood 'codes', and they may thus all be read as 'European' commentaries on the film Western.

There had, of course, been European Westerns before these adaptations of *Sutter's Gold*. Some of the earliest American Westerns, filmed near New York, seem to have made more money in France than on the home market: they may even have been aimed primarily at European cinemagoers, rather than at customers who might know what the West really looked like. Gaston Méliès (brother of Georges) and his son Paul filmed a series of one-reelers, in Chicago and Texas, between 1909 and 1911, for their Star Film Company. Joë Hamman, a Gallic cowboy who had spent his youth in the West, appeared (often as 'Arizona Bill') in a series of twenty French Westerns (filmed in the Camargue and the suburbs of Paris) between 1907 and 1913. A still from one of Hamman's films (*Pendaison à Jefferson City*), made in 1910, has survived: it shows a 'saloon' (looking very much like a French café), complete with rows of Chianti bottles; a surly *patron*, hand on hip, with a pipe in his mouth; a travel poster ('Espagne') and a rodeo poster (for 'Bronco Buster' — perhaps a reference to Edison's 'Bucking Bronco', the first Western footage ever filmed, dating from 1894). In 1918-19, James Young Deer — a Winnebago Indian — made a series of Western shorts for the Pathé brothers in France. And there had been various other French, Italian and German Westerns, including Parisian shorts based on the 'Red Indian' tales of Gustave Aimard; a 'Spaghetti' filmed in Turin in 1909 by Aquila Films, starring Sergio Leone's mother (the silent star Bice Valerian) as the heroine, who in the climactic scene appeared on a white horse surrounded by Redskin warriors; and a silent German version of *The Last of the Mohicans* (presumably designed to appeal to Karl May readers), filmed in the forests of the Rhine, which starred the Hungarian actor Bela Lugosi in a pre-Dracula incarnation as the Indian hero Uncas.

Several Westerns were made in Europe immediately after these adaptations of *Sutter's Gold*, as well. Following the success of Trenker's *Der Kaiser* (which was partly filmed in Italy, had several Italians in the smaller parts, and boasted a musical score by Giuseppe Becce, another Italian), Westerns were produced in both Germany and Italy throughout the 1930s and early 1940s. Even before Trenker's film was made, August Kern had directed *Der Goldene Gletscher* (1932), a Western drama about the perils of gold-fever, set in the California of the forty-niners; and in 1939, Paul Verhoeven directed another Gold Rush adventure — this time a parody — entitled *Gold in New Frisco* (the title was in English, even for German distribution), which

20 (*Left*) Poster for the original Italian production of Puccini's opera *The Girl of the Golden West* (1911) – the first Spaghetti Western worthy of the name

21-2 (*Below*) The two faces of Maciste the muscleman in Pastrone's *Cabiria* (1913). He escapes from a heavily-guarded dungeon; and plays the pipes of Pan for the amusement of his master, Fulvius Axilla. Maciste (Bartolomeo Pagano) was not the first of the Italian muscleman heroes, but he was by far the most popular

23 Joë Hamman, the cowboy from the Camargue who made several Westerns for Gaumont-Paris between 1907 and 1913 under the name 'Arizona Bill'. Here he rides out of a Paris book shop, after signing his latest book. Jean Renoir may have had him in mind when he created the fantasy figure of 'Arizona Jim' for *Le Crime de Monsieur Lange*

24 The saloon sequence from *Pendaison à Jefferson City* (1910), which starred 'Arizona Bill'. Note the posture of the 'patron', the Chianti bottles, the travel poster, and the advertisement for a 'Bronco Buster' exhibition

starred Otto Wernicke and Annie Markart. Another parody Western, *Sergeant Berry* — like *Gold in New Frisco* based on a novel by Robert Arden — had been released a year before, as a starring vehicle for Hans Albers. This film begins in a Chicago setting, where Albers ('the terror of the Chicago underworld') routs a gang of hoods; the scene then shifts to the Mexican-American border (the Italian desert, actually), where Albers/Sergeant Berry — a master of disguise — deals with a band of Mexican smugglers. According to one critic, the baddies appeared to be an assortment of ruffians 'from south of every border in the Western hemisphere'. The lightweight tone of *Sergeant Berry*, and the fun the director evidently had at the expense of 'stock Western clichés', led William Everson to treat the film as a post-war movie — 'an antidote to morbid and defeatist films'; in fact, however, it was released in 1938 (again with an English title) and re-released in the late 1940s. Albers' other Western, *Wasser für Canitoga*, directed by Herbert Selpin, was a much more serious affair: it concerns the efforts of a group of pioneers, led by Albers, to pipe water to a Canadian mining community — and clearly aspires to the 'epic' quality of the Hollywood railroad-building (or Pony Express) sagas of the 1920s. At the end of the film, Albers (like Sutter) dies a martyr's death, destroyed by the crass materialism of his American (and English) employers, and the disloyalty of his former 'comrades'. William Everson thought this film was made in the late 1940s as well (probably because Albers dies in the final scene while saluting the Union Jack): in fact it was released early in 1939, and the reverence shown to the English flag (if not to the employers who colonised Canada in its name) *may* perhaps have had something to do with the political climate in which it was made — at a time of 'appeasement'. It is strange that no Westerns directly derived from the works of Karl May were produced in Germany during the period 1929-45: only one May adaptation (*Durch die Wüste*, 1936, directed by J.A. Hubler-Kahla) was released in this period, and that was based on his Oriental adventures. It was not until the early 1960s that the 'Winnetou' stories finally arrived on the screen.

If the Westerns of the Nazi era took the form of nationalist epics (*Der Kaiser*; *Wasser für Canitoga*) and parodies under 'American' titles (*Sergeant Berry*; *Gold in New Frisco*) — a fascination with the myth of the Gold Rush providing some sort of link

between the two very different types — the Westerns produced during the Fascist era in Italy seem to owe their origin to a source from another genre altogether: Puccini's opera *The Girl of the Golden West*. In 1942, Carl Koch (assisted by his wife, the famous silhouette animator Lotte Reiniger) directed *Una Signora dell'Ovest*, using the name Carlo Koch: the film starred Michel Simon, Rossano Brazzi and Valentina Cortese, and had a soundtrack score by Mario Nascimbene. *Una Signora*, the first feature-length Italian Western, tells of the adventures of an ex-music hall artiste and her lover Diego, in the golden West; they team up with a rich cattle-baron, William (played by Brazzi), who leads them to Butler (played by Simon), a strange old man who gives them the rights to an abandoned mine; but Butler kills Diego, making it look as if William is the real murderer; the signora believes Butler's story, and 'seeks consolation in his arms'; later, when she learns the truth, she rides off in search of William, finds him happily married, and asks his forgiveness. One critic of the time (Giuseppe de Santis, in *Cinema*, 25 February 1942) reckoned that Koch 'lacks the courage to set his film amongst our own Italian cattlemen, the *buteri*, and thus to transfer the action to a more realistic setting. The most irritating things about this film are the "cardboard" backgrounds, and a general atmosphere of the *baroque*. However, we cannot ignore Koch's serious commitment to his work.' De Santis' criticism founded a long tradition of attacking Spaghetti Westerns for their 'inauthenticity', their dependence on an alien genre (in this context an explicitly *political* judgment), and their 'baroque' exuberance; it is nevertheless odd to discover such a criticism as early as 1942, when 'more realistic settings' were so notably absent from other Cinecittà genres as well. *Il Fanciullo del West* ('Boy of the West', directed by Giorgio Ferroni) was released in the following year, 1943, and starred Giovanni Grasso and Nino Pavese: songs and 'musical comments' were provided by Amedeo Escobar. The story of this film (which was promoted by the ad-men as a remake of *Romeo and Juliet* in a Western setting) involves various attempts by a kind-hearted 'quack doctor' to put an end to the rivalry between two frontier families; although he has a personal interest in the rivalry, he eventually succeeds in patching up the differences between the 'two clans', unmasking the leader of a gang of bandits in the process; and, of course, 'like a latter-day Romeo, he wins the hand of his Juliet'. Giuseppe de Santis again reviewed this film for *Cinema* (10 February 1943), praising the 'inventive touches' which contributed effectively to the 'comic-paradoxical atmosphere'; these 'touches' apparently included 'a machine invented by the bandits to catapult their men into the air', 'an Indian who, having been trained to track his victims by following a few paces behind them, creeps along the ground all the time, as if unable to break the habit', and 'an old man who goes around in an invalid carriage which rears up like a horse during the final shoot-out'. The plot-line of Ferroni's film has a very familiar ring to it — part *Romeo and Juliet*, part *A Servant of Two Masters*. And his attempt to 'improve' on the more sentimental *Una Signora dell'Ovest* by adding 'inventive touches' of his own (bizarre machines, outrageous parodies of the American Western) also suggests that although men may come and men may go, in this sense Cinecittà goes on forever. De Santis may have disliked *Una Signora* (he would presumably have preferred an adventure set among the honest rustics of Tuscany, extolling the virtues of ruralism), but he has already begun to enjoy the excesses of the Spaghetti Western less than a year later.

Der Kaiser von Kalifornien was banned from West German cinemas by an allied military tribunal just after the war; but it was to be reincarnated — suitably modified, of course — in the 'Winnetou' films of the early 1960s. Ferroni's *Il Fanciullo del West* (as well as Koch's *Una Signora dell'Ovest*, of which it was an 'extension') emerged from a Cinecittà production system which is still very much in evidence today — only the scale of operations, and the financial structure, have significantly altered. Both films were box-office hits on domestic release, and may in consequence be said not to have offended the 'consensus of opinion' in their respective audiences; so, the Karl May Westerns of the early 1960s, and the Spaghettis of the mid 1960s, represent one important index of the changes in this 'consensus'

(among popular cinema audiences in West Germany and Italy) during the twenty-year period after the war. There were a few European Westerns produced between 1946 and 1960: in Italy, a series of Wild Bill Hickok adventures (carbon-copies of Hollywood 'B' features, with 'an emphasis on violent action' and very little else) appeared during the early 1950s, and the *influence* of American Western 'conventions' has been spotted (perhaps over-hastily) in the bandit films of Pietro Germi released at the same time — particularly *The Outlaw of Tacca de Lupo* (1952), set in Sicily just after Unification, but, according to Everson, 'trying to duplicate American Civil War stories'; in West Germany, Albers' two Westerns were re-released during the late 1940s, and Hollywood Westerns — some of them as old as *The Big Trail* — started to flood the market, often dubbed and partially re-shot (for close-ups and medium-shots) with German actors. But these examples are of little significance, from the point of view of the development of the genre — except in so far as they reveal how the popularity of Westerns (whether home-produced or imported) was sustained in Italy and West Germany. From that point of view, the defining characteristics of the *European* Western (as opposed to attempts at carbon-copies of the successful American originals) had already emerged clearly with the various versions of *Sutter's Gold*, and the two Cinecittà Westerns of the 1940s. Before these were released, there may have been a tradition of European Westerns in literature (Gustave Aimard, Karl May, perhaps Emilio Salgari), but the movies had yet to acquire distinctively European characteristics. It was not until the early 1960s that these defining characteristics were to be fully developed (as an Italian or German genre of Western evolved) — eventually having a significant impact on the Hollywood Westerns which these European Westerns had set out, directly or indirectly, to criticise.

The Context

John Ford: I love to make Westerns. If I had my
choice, that's all I would make.
Burt Kennedy: Have you seen any of these
Spanish or Italian Westerns?
John Ford: You're kidding!
Burt Kennedy: No, they have them and a few
have been popular.
John Ford: What are they like?
Burt Kennedy: No story, no scenes. Just killing.

> Burt Kennedy talks to John Ford,
> *Films in Review* (January 1969)

Several great Western directors come from
Europe: Ford is Irish; Zinneman, Austrian; Lang,
German; Wyler and Tourneur, French. . . . I
don't see why an Italian should not be included
in the group.

> Sergio Leone, interview in
> *Le Nouvel Observateur* (25 August 1969)

He goes to see his old pal, the one who had the
Marshal's job before him. He finds him on a
couch smoking an opium pipe, while the young
wet-back cat he is keeping sits in a corner
smoking sticks of pot. A great scene, in which
the former pigs tells our hero the real truth
about law and order. I think a great casting
coup for this role would be John Wayne,
especially now that he is playing character
parts. I realise Duke thinks that any picture
without a cattle drive is unAmerican, but
considering how much he liked High Noon
when it first came out, I think he could be
talked into this one.

> Carl Foreman, '*High Noon* Revisited' —
> dedicated, among others to 'S.L.',
> *Punch* (5 April 1972)

Spaghettis and Society

At last, a Fancy very odd,
Took me, This was *The Land of Nod*,
Planted at first when vagrant *Cain*
His brother had unjustly slain;
Then, Conscious of the Crime he'd done,
From Vengeance dire hither run,
And in a Hut supinely dwelt,
The first in *Furrs* and *Sotweed* dealt:
And ever since that Time, this Place
Has harbour'd a detested Race,
Who, when they could not thrive at Home;
For Refuse to these Worlds did roam,
In Hopes by Flight they might prevent
The Devil, and his fell Intent,
Obtain from Tripple-Tree Reprieve,
And Heaven and Hell alike deceive . . .

> Ebenezer Cook, *The Sot-weed Factor;
> Or a Voyage to Maryland, A Satyr* (1708)

A famous handbook on how to play *scopa*,
the most common Italian card game, written
in Naples by a Monsignor Chitarella, begins:
'Rule Number One: always try to see your
opponent's cards'. It is a good concrete
practical rule.

> Luigi Barzini, *The Italians* (1964)

From Europe's proud, despotic shores
Hither the stranger take his way,
And in our new found world explores
A happier soil, a milder sway,
Where no proud despot holds him down,
No slaves insult him with a crown . . .

While virtue warms the generous breast,
There heaven-born freedom shall reside,
Nor shall the voice of war molest,
Nor Europe's all-aspiring pride —
There Reason shall new laws devise,
And order from confusion rise.

> Philip Freneau, *On the Emigration to America*
> (1786)

I wondered why it is that the Westerns survive
year after year. A good Western will outdraw
some of the other subjects. Perhaps one of the
reasons, in addition to the excitement, the gun
play and the rest, which is part of it but they
can get that in other kinds of movies — one of
the reasons is perhaps, and this may be a square
observation, the good guys come out ahead
in the Westerns, the bad guys lose.

In the end, as [*Chisum*] particularly pointed
out, even in the old West, the time before New
Mexico was a state, there was a time when there
was no law. But the law eventually came, and
the law was important from the standpoint of
not only prosecuting the guilty, but also seeing
that those who were guilty had a proper trial . . .

> Ex-President Richard Nixon, from a speech at
> Denver (3 August 1970)

When the first Spaghetti Westerns began to arrive in the United States, critical comment was, to a large extent, confined to a sterile debate about the 'cultural roots' of the American/Hollywood Western. The fact that three of the founding fathers of the modern Western — John Ford, Fritz Lang and Fred Zinneman — were, respectively, Irish, German and Austrian by origin, was quietly forgotten (as was, presumably, the fact that an Italian 'discovered' America for the Americans, and another gave his name to the continent). Often, the debate centred on trivial questions about the 'poetry' and 'authenticity' of the Frontier *landscape*. Very few admitted, as Pauline Kael did in her review of a Japanese 'Western', Kurosawa's *Yojimbo* (the 'model' for Sergio Leone's first 'Dollars' film), that they were 'saddle sore', bored with an exhausted Hollywood genre:

> in recent years, John Ford, particularly, has turned the Western into an almost static pictorial genre, a devitalized, dehydrated form which is 'enriched' with pastoral beauty and evocative nostalgia for a simple, heroic way of life. The clichés we retained from childhood pirate, buccaneer, gangster and Western movies have been awarded the status of myths of our old movies. If, by now, we dread going to see a 'great' Western, it's because 'great' has come to mean slow and pictorially composed. We'll be lulled to sleep in the 'affectionate', 'pure', 'authentic' scenery of the West (in 'epics' like *My Darling Clementine*, *She Wore a Yellow Ribbon*, *Fort Apache*), or, for a change, we'll be clobbered by messages in 'mature' Westerns like *The Gunfighter* and *High Noon* (the message is that the myths we never believed in anyway were false).

Pauline Kael concluded that a film-maker like Kurosawa, because he was outside the Hollywood myth factory, could exploit the conventions of the Western genre, while debunking its morality. Just so Leone, or, indeed, any other talented director of Italian Westerns. I know of no Italian critic who complained that the image of Sicilian society presented in *The Godfather* and its derivatives was the travesty of the real thing it undoubtedly was.

More recent critical debates have again focused attention on Sergio Leone's Westerns. Using criteria which have been developed in the Film as Film versus Film as Montage versus Film as Art controversy (between those who maintain that film as a medium is best served by directors who make their points in the frame and relate them to the development of the narrative, and those who believe that points should be made by polemical use of cutting, and by self-conscious use of images), Leone can be castigated as a formalist of the most extreme kind, obtrusively 'stylish', a talented but undisciplined art director who breaks the golden rule 'If you notice it, it's bad.' Following on from discussions about 'film language' and semiology, and in particular about Christian Metz's 'grand syntagmatique' (a kind of 'syntax of the film'), Sergio Leone's use of the codes, syntagmas and visual clichés of the Hollywood Western can be placed in a fresh intellectual context: his manipulation of the audience's response to these codes suggests a clear understanding of what the codes have traditionally been held to imply — in other words, of their *resonance*. Perhaps the most obvious example of such a code or syntagma of the Western (and one which Leone indirectly exploits on various occasions) is the stock panning shot of a valley, showing a stagecoach (originally John Ford's *Stagecoach*) in the middle distance, and 'discovering' a group of waiting Apache warriors on a bluff overlooking the valley as the camera moves from right to left. The effect was one of John Ford's favourites, becoming a visual cliché in the heyday of the Cowboy and Indian film: the Indians are characteristically associated with the highlands, the 'above'; the settlers with the valleys, the 'below'. In Leone's hands, the valley becomes a desert, the stagecoach a lone rider, and the Apaches the barrel of a Winchester jutting into the far edge of the wide-screen frame. It is *because* we are so used to the visual cliché that we react to Leone's flamboyant variation -- either with laughter, or with a reassuring sense of recognition. Similarly, after recent critical debates about the relationship between auteur (director) and genre (Western), Leone's work can now be viewed (as I have already suggested) in terms of a form of 'critical cinema', utilising the internal conventions of the genre (and extending them), in order critically to examine not so much the mythology of the frontier itself, as a later cinematic mythology, debased but still producing 'infatuated tributes'. A form of 'cinema about cinema' — but one with the potential to 'comment' as well. In this study, I have tried not to adopt too doctrinaire a position *vis-à-vis* any one of these critical 'schools', but rather to reassess the Italian Westerns in the light of a series of continuing debates about film criticism. The section on critical reactions discusses the 'cultural roots' controversy, as well as the relationship of a group of particular Italian auteurs to the genre they chose to exploit for a while; my comments on Leone's visual 'style' take account of accusations of formalism in his use of composition, framing and cutting; and my analysis of Leone's redefinition of the iconography of the Western, and his use of visual clichés, owes much to the structuralists. This method of approaching the Italian Westerns, by using recent film theory as an 'arsenal of reference', was to some extent suggested by the fact that Sergio Leone himself is so very articulate about what it is (in terms of film theory) he is attempting to achieve in his work.

If there has been a radical shift in critical perspective since the Italian Westerns were first released, there has been an equally radical shift in attitudes towards the ideology of the 'classic' Western. In academic circles, the 'frontier' thesis of Frederick Jackson Turner was challenged nearly half a century ago: Turner's attempt to single out the 'idea of the frontier' as the key determinant of America's cultural and political identity was strongly criticised by those who held that European influences, via the Atlantic connection, were of far more significance. Crucially, the 'frontier' thesis had underplayed the role of the urban frontier (thus of immigrants from Europe), and the social impact of advancing technology: it was best interpreted in the light of other attempts to establish a 'national identity' for America, American agrarian democracy, and American 'individualism', at the turn of the century: amongst academics, the development of historical societies, research centres and journals; amongst consumers of popular entertainment, the development of dime novels, Western melodramas and Buffalo Bill's Wild West Show. The young lecturer from Wisconsin first presented his thesis to the American Historical Association at the Chicago Exposition of 1893, and while Turner was giving his paper Buffalo Bill's circus was in full swing just outside the Exposition grounds, since it had been refused official status as part of the Exposition proper. The academic seems to have known nothing about the circus; yet both, in their different ways, had helped to disseminate the national myth about the origins of 'rugged individualism', 'agrarian democracy', 'the classless society' and 'the new America'. Buffalo Bill Cody later took 'the frontier' to Europe. His circus — a mixture of military tattoo and live-action dime novel (complete with stagecoach robberies, scenes of taming the Indians, and colourful pop ethnography) — went down particularly well in the *Arena di Verona*, and after his first Italian tour Cody always featured a gondola prominently on his Wild West posters. In his stage performances, he preferred Italian or Spanish actresses to play the Indians. While Buffalo Bill was performing as unofficial ambassador, Turner was busy persuading the academics. Ironically, the Exposition where it all started had been a celebration of the *novelty* of precisely those developments which the nationalist myth sought to explain in evolutionary terms — technological advance, the economic exploitation of the West, the end of Edge City, and the rise of the great American metropolis: for Turner, the 'forces dominating American character' were above all the result of a *process*, a 'perennial rebirth of society', a series of recurring social evolutions as a people advanced to colonise 'the richest free gift that was ever spread out before civilised man'; now that the 'gate of escape' had been shut, he concluded, closing 'the first period of American history', some substitute for the frontier process had to be found. Another irony: did he but know it, several of Cody's dime characters were in fact of European origin: it was, for example, an Irishman (Mayne Reid) who had first exploited the stereotype of the lone cowboy with a mysterious past, the noble gunfighter; and the phrase 'a man's gotta do what a man's gotta do' seems to have originated in Tennyson's 'The Revenge' ('I have only done my duty/As a man is bound to do'). By the 1930s, Turner's thesis had already been challenged. At the more popular level of movie mythology, however, most of the 'classic' Westerns (and especially those by John Ford) still had their ideological base either in 'The Significance of the Frontier', or (later) in Henry Nash Smith's evocation of the 'desert into garden' myth, *The Virgin Land*. Today, in the disillusioned climate of post-Vietnam, post-Watergate America, Turner and Nash Smith — with their Puritan emphasis on 'rugged individualism', 'cultivating your own garden', and John L. O'Sullivan's concept of 'manifest destiny' as key factors shaping the evolution of American society — can have little credibility. At the level of movie mythology, their ideas are only kept alive in films starring John Wayne, in the 'twilight' Westerns of Sam Peckinpah, and in the Ford revivalism of Andrew V. McLaglen. Most directors of Westerns today prefer to show, in Pauline Kael's words, 'that the myths we never believed in anyway were false'.

Revising the traditional view of where America's political culture came from has involved challenging other aspects of the American (and, by extension, Hollywood) dream. Instead of paying lip service to the 'a man's gotta do what a man's gotta do' myth of frontier violence, American historians have been stressing for some time the more significant (and sordid) aspects of Eastern urban violence in mid- to late-nineteenth-century America. The emphasis has shifted from shootouts to muggings, for, between 1870 and 1885 (when, according to the cinema, the West was at its wildest) the grand total of deaths by violence in the infamous frontier towns of Abilene, Ellsworth, Wichita and Dodge City combined, came to 'a sleepy forty-five'. Economic historians (and especially those concerned with computer-based history) now deny that the coming of the railroads had such a 'progressive' effect on frontier society as the previous generation believed. Frontier newspapers were once thought to have been the main stimulus — with the dime novel (Erastus Beadle's 'new gold mine'), travellers' tales, saddle songs (mainly of European origin), melodramas, and the circus ring — to nascent mythologies about the West — 'on the spot' versions, as it were; but recent studies of these newspapers, the

Tombstone Epitaph, for example (a favourite of Hollywood), have shown that they were almost exclusively concerned with gold, silver, land deals, whisky profits, cattle fortunes, banks, etc., and that, in the words of one commentator, 'they had all the panache and excitement of a fertilizer company's annual report'. The headlines over the main story in the first issue of the *Epitaph* show well what residents in Tombstone wanted to read about: 'Millions in it', 'Bullion already Produced And Millions in Sight', 'Monthly Dividends Hereafter of $50,000'. Not such a surprising discovery, perhaps, since Tombstone was a mining town: but John Ford never gave that impression. The gripes of wrath have even encouraged an American television company to produce a mammoth reconstruction of the war crimes trial which followed the Civil War, concerning the atrocities committed at the Confederate concentration camp at Andersonville. Social historians (of the early 1960s) studying immigration to the United States came up with a new catch-phrase to apply to the phenomenon: immigrant societies on the East Coast used to be known as the 'melting pot'; today, they are known as 'vegetable soup' — with all the ingredients remaining separate. Of the two million Italians who migrated to America between 1900 and 1921, over half went back to Italy. Those who remained were often lampooned in popular magazines as illiterate organ-grinders.

So, on the question of whether Ebenezer Cook's *Sot-weed Factor* (1708) or Philip Freneau's *Emigration to America* (1786) represents the most valid interpretation of what Europeans were faced with when they arrived in America, Ebenezer Cook seems at the moment (and seemed at the time of the first Spaghettis) to be winning on points.

One such group of immigrants was the Italians. The biggest wave of Southern European immigrants in fact came after the West's wildest decade (which is one reason why Italian Westerns are more concerned with Irish settlers, Chinese laundry workers, Scottish cattle-barons, Polish mercenaries, and German arms dealers than with Italian immigrants). Luigi Barzini has described how they must have felt, in his study *The Italians*:

> [they] found themselves surrounded by an alien and hostile society. They had to cope with an incomprehensible language, puzzling customs, rigid laws, and what they considered an

oppressive regime. They felt cut off, for reasons they did not quite understand, from access to the good things of life, wealth and authority. They clung to what could give them protection and comfort, the Church, the family and their ways. They soon discovered that the arts their people had developed in the old country to neutralize alien laws were also useful in the new.... That they felt themselves a minority on the defensive is borne out by one of the names of their criminal organisation, Cosa Nostra. It means 'our own affair, something which must be guarded from intruders'. In fact, they discovered that the ancient arts were far more useful in America and went farther. The Americans were generally trustful, unprepared to defend themselves from guile, often unwilling to fight for what they considered small stakes.

According to Barzini, the Italians (and especially the Sicilians) reacted to what they thought at first was an 'alien and hostile society' by adopting the role of underground fighters in enemy-occupied territory. Among the European influences, mediated through the Atlantic connection, that were to shape modern American culture, this is clearly one to be reckoned with.

What are these sources of 'protection and comfort' for the Italian immigrants, and 'the arts their people had developed in the old country'? What, to put it another way, is the social, cultural and political context for the Italian Western? Luigi Barzini's elegant and cynical account (written for the benefit of American readers) provides some interesting answers: his choice of themes which exemplify Italian social life, past and present — among them 'pragmatism and guile', 'the trappings of chivalry', 'the power of the family', 'crypto-matriarchy', 'the mythology of individualism', 'the role of clans, extended families or consorterie' — parallel those recurring themes which I have considered most significant in the work of Sergio Leone. Indeed, if one accepts Barzini's account of these stereotypical themes at face value, one gets the unnerving (although not necessarily surprising) impression that contemporary Southern Italian society bears more than a superficial resemblance to the world of the Spaghetti Western. It is a society in which the strength of the family is not only a bulwark against disorder, but at the same time one

of its principal causes; in which the clan, cabala, camarilla, sect, or mafia commands more loyalty than official authority (which is considered hostile until proved friendly or harmless); in which the existence of two (sometimes rival) police forces (Polizia and Carabinieri) is considered an essential safeguard to liberty, since 'one always keeps watch on the other', the one which wins traditionally having to ally with a strong third party; and in which chivalry as a moral conception never deeply influenced social life, but was turned mainly into a polite pastime for the upper classes.

This is clearly an impressionistic, cavalier view of Italian life — which might explain why its emphases mirror so closely those of the Spaghetti Western. In turn, Barzini's account of how the Italian immigrants must have felt when they first arrived in the United States finds its counterpart in a popular American genre, the Mafia novel. The components of this genre, with its primary theme of the alienation of Italian immigrants from the legal processes of American society (and their consequent resort to, or rejection of, a different set of 'rules', epitomised by the *onorata societa* of Sicily) were recently synthesised in Puzo's *The Godfather*:

'No. Don't speak. You found America a paradise. You had a good trade, you made a good living, you thought the world of a harmless place where you could take your pleasure as you willed. You never armed yourself with true friends. After all, the police guarded you, there were courts of law, you and yours could come to no harm. You did not need Don Corleone. Very well.... Now you come to me and say "Don Corleone give me justice".'

During the era of the Italian Western, which predated the international fashion for Mafia films, this theme appeared in Italian popular films in a variety of guises. In *Sacco and Vanzetti* the prosecuting attorney (Cyril Cusack), when attacking the two heroes for their 'bolshevik' activities, accuses them of 'coming to our land of milk and honey — not for a dream, but for gain'; their alienation from American values in Montaldo's film apparently arises from the 'difficulty they find, in adjusting to our "superior" culture'. In those Italian Westerns which deal with the erosion of Southern chivalry during the aftermath of the American Civil War — and especially *The Tramplers* (Alfredo Antonini, 1966) and *The Hellbenders* (Sergio Corbucci, 1966) — this theme is implicit in the way the process of erosion is presented. In both these films, the Southern patriarch (played by Joseph Cotten) discovers that the ideals of Walter Scott can best be defended by methods which owe much more than a little to the Mafia: in *The Tramplers*, when the daughter of the family is thought to be consorting with an undesirable (played by Franco Nero), the patriarchal family group rapidly converts into a clan of a more modern kind; and the clash between the two sets of values eventually destroys the 'Cause' for which the patriarch thought he was fighting.

Barzini's view of the Italians cannot, of course, be treated as serious sociology: much of it simply reinforces stereotypes which American readers must have known about already from Barzini's sources — films, popular histories, and novels. So it is perhaps dangerous to generalise from *The Italians* to an analysis of the social bases of the Italian Western. The most recent serious attempt to treat Western movies as versions of social thought — not simply reflections of prejudice or fantasy, but narrative vehicles for the display, displacement and 'resolution' of what is on Americans' minds — Will Wright's *Sixguns and Society* (1975), attempts to find a more coherent method for looking at the relationship between the two (exclusively in terms of Westerns which were popular in the States). Wright begins by assuming that

> films are ideological productions — so that the popularity of the genre mainly depends on how well the ideology of the film fits the social experiences of its audience (rather than on 'the whims of a few powerful men in the industry'). In other words, the crucial variable would be the relation between the symbolic structure of the story and the basic social consciousness required by the institutional demands of daily life. This explanation is satisfying, I believe, because it does not assume that the audience is simply a passive receptacle of what is put in front of it. Instead, the audience is seen as an active participant in choosing, with regard to its own needs, which types of stories it will watch and enjoy. Of course, this choice is not exactly based on rational, conscious judgments; and it is made from a range that is limited by commercialism, industrial structure, and so on. But this approach has the merit of making the explanation take into account the social context of the films; to

recognise that to account for the significance of a myth or a genre, the nature of the society and the expectations of its members must be incorporated into the explanation.

Wright's analysis is thus limited to a study of only the most commercially successful Westerns (those which earned more than $4 million in the United States and Canada — sixty-four in total) and, specifically, to the plots, and plot structures, of these successful films. His main thesis is that there has been a development in the Hollywood Western, from a concern with solitary heroes fighting it out with villains (who usually go around in gangs) for the sake of the weak but growing community (and in defence of the family), to a concern with 'elite groups' of heroes, who have rejected the (still weak) community, and who fight simply to affirm their sense of themselves as professionals. In the former case (which Wright calls the 'classical plot'), the gunfighter tends to get the girl; in the latter (the 'professional plot'), he tends to be quite happy with his fellow gunfighters.

The 'classical plot' begins with the hero outside society, and shows his progressive integration into society; the 'vengeance variation' begins with the hero inside society, shows him going outside society for a 'job', and then returning to society (abandoning his 'job') because in the end he believes in the same values as the 'classical' hero; the 'transition theme' begins with the hero inside society, and shows his progressive disillusionment with society; the 'professional plot' begins with a group of men outside society — where they stay throughout the film. In this way, slight alterations in individual features of the plot ultimately result in a 'leap' — to a whole new plot variant (the 'professional plot'), where there is no individual hero, society is no longer seen as constructive (the 'classical plot') or even destructive (the 'transition theme'), but as irrelevant, and where group solidarity is all that is needed to provide the 'acceptance' that society once provided for the 'classical' hero. According to Wright, this structural progression in the Western is a response to a change in America from the ideology of a market economy (the gunfighter as *homo economicus*) to the ideology of a corporate economy (the gunfighter as the self-image of the technocrat). The old American small town ('society' for the 'classical' hero) gradually disintegrates as a credible narrative device, to be replaced by what Frederic

Jameson calls 'that suburban Los Angeles-type decentralisation, dominated by multi-national corporations and transcontinental networks of various kinds, in which only professional castes and individual networks of acquaintances are able to feel any kind of group identity'. The 'professional plot' also responds directly to another significant transformation — the emergence of a 'post-industrial media society', the most recent manifestation of 'late monopoly capitalism'. In this new context, the 'classical plot' — the last bastion of the rhetoric of 'possessive individualism' — can no longer have any credibility: even in its heyday, the inapplicability of 'individualistic thinking' to contemporary social realities (say, in the 1950s) had been explained away by the presence, 'alongside the hero', of 'society' as a separate entity (represented by the homesteaders or the townsfolk) to which this way of thinking was not expected to be relevant. Jameson continues: 'the final acceptance of the hero seals the narrative trick: we have been showing the ideology of individualism as still very much alive, but that it need not apply to us — so that its apparent inapplicability to the present-day world cannot amount to a disproof or refutation'. By the time of the 'professional plot', even this *rhetoric* of individualism has been definitively outmoded by the full development of a corporate kind of socio-economic organisation.

Will Wright's approach to the relationship between the Western and society, by taking as its prime object of investigation the *narratives* of a broad range of Westerns (for Wright, these narratives constitute 'forms of reasoning' about everyday life), and by drawing on the findings of structural studies of other 'bodies of texts', as well as on the methods of structural anthropology, aims to avoid the woolly-mindedness which has characteristically plagued surveys of the relationship between popular arte-fact (the Western film) and 'hidden history' (American values), in the past — surveys which have tended to chuck in words like 'reflection', 'analogy', 'correspondence', and 'parallel', with a marked absence of rigour, and have in consequence ended up simply 'raiding' Westerns for pithy quotations to support a general hypothesis about American history. As Wright's introduction points out, the traditional 'mythic' approach to the Western ('rugged individualism', 'the last gentleman', the 'frontier' thesis, 'the contrasting images of Desert and Garden', and so on) — an approach much loved by American Studies courses — has tended to fall back on rhe-toric, mystification, and above all ethical judgment, as a substitute for historical or structural analysis of the genre ('though these explanations contain valid insights into American culture, they cannot account for the *popularity* of the Western'). Those studies which attempt to explore the 'psychological needs' served by the Western (and especially the 'B' Western or TV series) have also tended to resort to fuzzy conjectures about 'human nature', 'our unconscious inner needs', 'the drive to violence' and 'the adolescent fear about adulthood' as a substitute for a *historical* view of reading (or viewing) publics ('the central problem with the psychological approach is that it either ignores or denies the fact that the Western, like other myths, is a social phenomenon'). Analyses of the Western which derive from old-fashioned studies of the novel (the Eng. Lit. approach), by laying emphasis on the point of view of the author (or director), have also, according to Wright, tended to deflect their findings about individual texts (rather than about a 'textual corpus' — which would be well beneath their visual threshold) in an ethical direction — and this approach may also involve upgrading a few individual Westerns by assimilating them to 'high culture' and insisting on their literary (or filmic) value, in a defensive way (where the Western in general is concerned, 'it is as though its mass appeal has made it unworthy of dignified scholarly research'). Let's give John Ford the *Good Housekeeping* seal of approval' by comparing his work to the 'great poets' of the pastoral (even if he would, as Andrew Sarris maintains, have been 'the last to admit it himself'). In consequence, there has been much talk of the 'vision' of individual Westerns (and the way in which this vision strikes a chord in individual members of the audience), as if an unlimited number of other 'visions' were available to the author (and the audience) at the time he or she was writing, or filming, or watching. What is needed, says Wright, is a study of the historical limits to a whole group of authors' 'choices' at a given time, and an analysis of the *historical* situation of the genre, as well as of the constraints operating upon the authors' 'visions' of that situation. Better still, why not make the whole notion of an 'author' (a hangover from Lit. Crit. days) redundant — it only raises more problems than it can solve (who *is* this theoretical construct called 'John Ford'?). And, paradoxically, there has been much stress on the general opposition between 'high' and 'popular' culture (a distinction which should, in Wright's terms, be purely methodological) rather than on the specific historical content of that opposition at a given time: some might oppose John Ford ('high') to the 'B' Western ('popular'), others might oppose Shakespeare to the Western in general, but in either case the contrast does not tell us very much about the Western (although it might tell us a lot about the academic background of the critic).

So Wright has tried all these 'literary' approaches and found them wanting. 'Analyses based on violence, or the Oedipus Complex, or the Garden and the Desert cannot increase understanding of real social conditions because they do not analyse those conditions and their relation to the Western.' He also seems to be taking issue with the traditional 'sociological' approach: for example, his introduction implies a rejection of the Frankfurt School model of 'mass culture' as 'culture industry'. If 'mass culture' is simply an 'industry', related to advertising techniques, and invested in by big business, then it must be about consumer brainwashing and very little else — by definition; so there cannot possibly by any intrinsic interest in its formal analysis. Yet Wright is primarily concerned to develop a coherent method of formal analysis, and he also believes that audiences vote with their feet, so he cannot be expected to find much common ground with these critical theorists. Some argue, says Wright, that

American tastes and preferences are not reflected but moulded in successful films by the powerful studio heads, directors, and movie stars. Successful movies, unlike successful tribal myths, are not determined by social acceptance but rather by the influence of big stars and big publicity. Thus, to understand the entertainment tastes of Americans, one must study not the films but the studio structure. . . . But within this well-known genre there have been many instances of films with star-studded casts and millions of publicity dollars that have been box-office disasters . . . most of them are interesting because they change and distort the standard images that define the Western myth. On the other hand, there are many examples of low-budget films, with few if any big stars, that become quite successful. . . . Significantly, [their] plot structure and setting are similar to the standard Western . . . it is essential to look at

the *genre itself* for a complete understanding of what makes for popularity.

For the same reasons, Wright's method implies a rejection of some more recent neo-Marxist criticisms of the Western — for example, the *Cahiers* collective text on John Ford's *Young Mr Lincoln* (1939). Any such attempt to 'read' a film scene by scene (as opposed to 'commenting' on it, 'interpreting' it, or 'dissecting' it), exclusively in terms of the apparent interests of the studio which produced it (20th Century-Fox), and the direct relationship of that studio to the power politics of the time (big business and the Republican Party, just before the election of 1940), will tend to limit the scope of questions we are permitted to ask about the 'choices' made by (and available to) film-makers, and can tell us very little about the ways in which these 'choices' might be built into the structure of a work: at most, Wright implies, such studios can elucidate one 'specific political meaning' which may have been intended by the makers (in so far as such intentions are recoverable from the available evidence). Since very few people went to see *Young Mr Lincoln* (it made far less money at the box-office than John Cromwell's *Abe Lincoln in Illinois* — also 1939 — and even this film did not earn enough to qualify it for the Wright hall of fame), Ford's Western does not, of course, feature in *Sixguns and Society*. Will Wright's rejection of the 'culture industry' model also implies a rejection of the classical Marxist concept of ideology in general — for this concept seems to underpin the position of the critical theorists. The 'culture industry' idea works if ideology is seen to be simply 'false consciousness', or 'collective error' (to be set against some scientific 'truth'); it does not work if one does not share this view of the nature of ideology, or of its function in the big-business end of culture. Will Wright's mode of analysis seems to be closer to Althusser's more recent definition of ideology as 'the representation of the imaginary relationship of individuals to their real conditions of existence' — a definition which, by stressing the 'quasi-narrative' function of ideology, perhaps reopens the way to a formal analysis of the relationship between the narrative bases of a given cultural formula, and the 'contradictions' these narratives may be said to resolve.

Some studies of these popular formulas (for example, John G. Cawelti's *Six-Gun Mystique*) have attempted to get away from both the 'point of view' approach (Henry James, move over) and the Frankfurt School's 'hypodermic' model, by adapting Northrop Frye's 'archetypal method' of literary criticism to the study of genre films; but the danger of this method (if Cawelti's book can be taken as a guide) is that, whereas Frye was trying to work towards some 'deep structure' of which his various 'archetypes' (in Cawelti's terms, 'formulas') were simply variants, it is all too easy to distinguish some 'formulas', and be happy to leave it at that, or, in other words, to deal only with superficial forms (which are presented as being both distinctive and dominating, almost by definition), and restrict one's analysis to the activity of classifying them. The net result may simply be to detach a 'body of films' from its historical context; to ignore the impact of film-texts on a specific viewing public. Will Wright has a far more ambitious aim: to explore the 'deep structure' of a 'body of films' (as social historian) at the same time as engaging in a 'formal analysis' both of the 'archetypes' *and* of the individual films (as structuralist). To do this, Wright has radically to modify Cawelti's concept of 'the formula': far from simply providing a means of differentiating and categorising a group of texts, the 'formula' becomes, in Frederic Jameson's words, 'a mediation between the structure of a text and its public', a key link between Wright's twin aims — to be both a social historian and a structural analyst at the same time.

Wright has been accused by critics of being a 'theoretical maverick'. Let's face it, his apparent attempt to synthesise the two main currents in structural analysis — Lévi-Strauss's structural study of myth (a synchronic, ahistorical account) and Vladimir Propp's analysis of narrative 'functions' in the Russian fairy tale (*by implication* a diachronic, historical account) — and then apply his synthesis to the films of John Wayne (among others) does at first sight smack of eclecticism for its own sake (*Sixguns and Society* started life as a university thesis). But by using Lévi-Strauss to lay the foundations for an account of how Westerns might be received, and then using Propp to provide a method of categorising these Westerns, Wright is actually fighting on two fronts at once: he wants to get away from the accusation, often levelled at formalists, that he is detaching films from their historical context, and he also wants to analyse the films in a rigorous, structural way — and, rather than mix the two traditions up in a (very) uneasy

synthesis, he does, in fact, hold to the position that one activity must always inform the other, or, in other words, that the social interpretation of a given text is integrally related to a structural reading of it, and vice versa. But you cannot do them both at the same time.

First, then, Wright's use of Lévi-Strauss. The structural anthropologist argues (and Wright quotes him) to the effect that 'the myths of totemistic societies serve to resolve conceptual contradictions inherent in those societies'; or, in other words, they provide an imaginary resolution of ideological (and, perhaps, social) 'contradictions', and, in the process, reassure the audience (the members of that society) that the 'contradiction' need not exist. If for 'myths' we read 'narratives' (as Wright seems to do), then Strauss's focus on the various 'codes' or 'signs' (expressed as binary oppositions) out of which these 'myths' are constructed, can be adapted to suit the basic oppositions at work in the Western: for Wright, these are 'inside society/outside society', 'good/bad', 'strong/weak', 'wilderness/civilisation' (although not the famous Straussian opposition between 'nature' and 'culture', which literally becomes part of the landscape). These 'codes' or 'signs' may then be used to evaluate the behaviour of the main characters in Western narratives ('Where does he stand *vis-à-vis* . . .?'), and can also help to decode the 'message' of a given sequence of episodes ('When are things getting dangerous . . .?'). The passage from Oedipus to John Wayne has not been as painful as it at first seemed, and Wright has his general frame of reference within which Western stories might be expected to be received by the public.

In order to subdivide Western stories into a set of episodes, narrative units, or 'functions' (whose presence in a given order 'may be said to constitute the Western genre', as Frederic Jameson puts it), Wright then adopts criteria gleaned from Vladimir Propp's method of analysing the production of narratives. The main focus of *Sixguns and Society* is on the permutations which have happened to these 'functions' since the arrival of the sound film. Wright's study of these permutations (or 'variations') is not restricted to a simple *categorisation* of narratives, however (as was Cawelti's analysis of changing 'formulas', and, perhaps, Propp's original study of the Russian folk-tale), for he is also concerned with looking at the relationship of his categories — once established — to the changing social context, or rather (in Frederic Jameson's words) to 'that external limiting situation or condition of possibility which accounts for the coming into being of a given variant and excludes the others'. For Propp, the meaning of individual 'functions' is recoverable by studying *only* the specific folk-tales of which they form a part: although he seems to have been aware that folk-tales could be 'transformed' by significant changes in 'practical life', he presented no sustained analysis of the relationship between the two. Towards the end of his *Morphology*, he stressed the need for a study which 'does not limit itself to the folktale. For the majority of its elements are traceable to one or other archaic, everyday, cultural, religious or other reality which must be enlisted for comparison'. In other words, certain questions could not be answered by formal narrative analysis alone — for example, why a given 'overall sequence of functions' came into being in the first place, and exactly how the 'combination' of functions came to be 'transformed' over time. But Propp only posed these questions: Wright attempts to extend the formal study of the changing role of narrative 'functions' to incorporate the social interpretation of texts as well, in a systematic way. He calls this extension 'a liberalised version of ... Vladimir Propp'. The passage from the Good Fairy to John Wayne has not been as painful as it at first seemed. Wright's fusion of structural anthropology and the 'formalist' analysis of narrative explicitly provides the basis for his method of approaching the problem of the American Western and its relationship to American society. We have already looked at both the more traditional modes of analysis against which Wright seems to be reacting, and the general conclusions about the Western and society which emerge from his extraordinarily rigorous theoretical framework. How have these conclusions been received?

Sixguns and Society has (as one might expect) been criticised from many different perspectives. From the point of view of film studies, Wright's emphasis on plot (and his method of analysing plot, which as we have seen derives from Vladimir Propp's formalist attempt to study the *narrative* sequences of Russian folk-tales), and consequent neglect of performances (stars, etc.), production structures (the studios), 'stylistic' considerations and technical developments, seems inadequate. Apart from anything else, most of the plots he schematises have been around for a very long time — at least since the days of Achilles and Perseus. Wright sometimes loses

sight of the fact that it is the *redefinition*, or 'transformation', of these plots (in Propp's terms) rather than their creation, that he is studying. And a big-budget Western has rather more to it, perhaps, than a fairy-story which is often communicated from one person to another, and which obeys a very rigid set of narrative conventions. Propp was studying a group of oral texts which had already been collected and set down on paper; thus he did not feel the need to incorporate the *act of communication* (tone of voice, emphasis, etc.) into his model. From the point of view of sociology, the breadth of Wright's social and political perspective has been seen as one of the reasons why so much of what he says verges on the tautological, and he has been accused of having a less than subtle sense of what 'society' (or the absence of it) means in Westerns. As Michael Wood has written, 'Westerns very frequently leave history and America behind, escape into those international regions of the imagination where society itself has been taken away, where revenge, for example, is still possible and honourable, where you might meet and kill your enemy with the ease and grace one knows only in dreams. Even *having* a single, identifiable enemy is a luxury which has been denied to serious literature since the Middle Ages.' Wood reckons that Wright 'might well have arrived at his conclusions without the application of all his critical apparatus ... since the films themselves are clear enough about where their values lie'. It may be, he adds, that Europeans react differently to Americans when they watch a Western ('an escape from society is inextricably caught up in the idea of America itself, while Europeans consider flight from society only after a very bad day or a lot of drinks'), but the Western — an *invented* moral and political landscape — can easily accommodate *both* sets of responses. From the point of view of this book, Wright's study can be severely criticised for the way in which he deals with the Italian Westerns: he refers to two of Sergio Leone's films, *For a Few Dollars More* and *The Good, the Bad, and the Ugly*. The latter film comes well within his $4 million bracket, and the former, as he admits, was also extremely successful in the States. Referring to the fact that big budgets have no direct relationship with big returns, Wright says: 'The Dollar films — *Fistful of Dollars, For a Few Dollars More, The Good, the Bad and the Ugly* — were just fill-in Italian Westerns until they caught on, became big money-makers, and made a superstar out of the virtually unknown Clint Eastwood.' 'Fill-ins' or not, he can only explain the success in the States of the second and third films of Leone's trilogy by stating that they are clear examples of the 'professional plot'. This plot is said to include the following list of (very broad) 'functions': the heroes are professionals; the villains are very strong; the job involves the heroes in a fight; the heroes form a group for the job; the heroes as a group share respect, affection and loyalty; the heroes fight the villains; the heroes stay (or die) together. Applying these 'functions' to the plot of *The Good, the Bad and the Ugly* (in so far as the film has one at all), it becomes apparent that something has gone very wrong: one of the heroes (Tuco) is not a professional; there are no villains outside the central 'group' (unless one includes *all* those who cross the 'group's' path — all far from 'strong'); the job (which is not in fact a 'job' in Wright's terms, but a treasure hunt) only involves the heroes in a fight when they stumble into the American Civil War by accident; the central characters do not form a group for the 'job' (they are at each other's throats throughout the film); they have no loyalty to each other, they do not fight the villains (unless one includes as a villain the one member of the 'group' who is *really* a professional) and they do not stay together at the end. By trying to relate Leone's most commercially successful films to *American* social and political values, Wright simply caricatures what the films are about (and, by extension, what American audiences must have made of them). Perhaps if he had treated them as the 'fill-in Italian Westerns' they apparently were 'before they caught on', he could have 'read' them in terms of the equivalent *Italian* values, and in the process made more sense of them. *Any* audience ('participant' or not) which comes out of *The Good, the Bad and the Ugly* thinking it had seen a 'professional' Western would have to have a very different notion of 'professionalism' to that provided by Will Wright's analysis.

Discussing Will Wright's adaptation of Vladimir Propp, and, specifically, the narrative 'functions' Wright lists to define his 'classical plot', Frederic Jameson has this to say about potential criticisms: 'At this point, no doubt, there will be room for useful and productive disagreement about the precise functions Mr Wright has defined: his final sequence (society accepts the hero, who loses his special status) will certainly be questioned by other students of the Western.'

Jameson is here referring to the radically different interpretations of the final sequence in *Shane* which are presented by Wright and John G. Cawelti. Both consider that George Stevens' film is *the* most perfect embodiment of the 'classical' Western: yet, for Cawelti, at the end of the film *Shane* remains a gunfighter who is no longer part of the community, and his ride off into the mountains symbolises the impossibility of his ever living in that community (as it clearly does in the original novel); for Wright, Shane could easily stay in the valley to enjoy his justly earned reward, or bask in the gratitude of the farmers, and this *possibility* suggests that he has really given up his status as a gunfighter (that he '*chooses instead* the dark night and cold mountains'). In other words, the two critics disagree about the final 'function' of the 'classical plot', if *Shane* may be taken as the most characteristic example of that plot. And Wright has the weaker case. Jameson continues:

> But to understand disagreement over various interpretations as an objection to Wright's method itself is to misconceive the very use of models in general. The reproach that the 'functions' are inaccurate would carry more weight against Propp than against Wright's modification of him, for the Russian theorist posited but a single sequence of functions for the fairy-tale in general. The use of his model thus encourages a primarily typological or classificatory activity, matching a given tale against the basic function to see whether it may be considered a folk-tale or not. Wright, however has used the concept of a sequence of functions to propose four fundamental variants, which he terms the classical, the revenge, the transition, and the professional plots respectively. For him, therefore, deviation from a given sequence is meaningful and can only lead to further analytical activity, where for Propp it is simply 'noise' and an aberration, something which cannot be accommodated by his system.

In other words, since Wright is discussing a series of permutations, his scheme can cope with conformity and variation alike. Since Propp is simply dealing with a mode of classification, important variations could prove fatal to his scheme: in the former case, deviations will prove productive; in the latter, they will be destructive. (The problem with this, of course, is that exceptions can always be 'explained away' by the simple expedient of adapting Wright's major variants *ad infinitum*: in this way, his schema can *always* be made impervious to factual criticisms — in theory, at least.)

But Jameson is here pointing to a disagreement about a film *within the genre*. *Shane* may have a 'classical' plot, or the ending of the film may place it in the 'transition' category; either way, there is plenty of room for it as one of Wright's four main variants. My point is that there is a world of difference between a squabble about the last reel of a specific Hollywood Western, and *an entire sub-genre* which fails to fit his model. This kind of exception goes well beyond 'mere nit-picking'. Perhaps because of its easily recognisable 'comments' on the whole history of the American Western, perhaps because of its specifically Italian ingredients, the Spaghetti Western tended to develop the characteristics it had hi-jacked from the American genre in several different directions at once: for example, *For a Few Dollars More* — one of the Spaghettis Wright mentions — contains strong elements of the 'vengeance variation' (Colonel Mortimer's motivation), the 'transition theme' (the rejection of society's law and order men, as cowards), and the 'professional plot' (the two bounty-hunters apparently working together — for a time); it is also a parody of the 'classical' Western (Mortimer riding off into the sunset, the 'saloon' sequences, and so on). Given the content of the most successful Spaghettis (part critique of the Hollywood 'originals', part attempt to get Italians to go to the cinema, both parts representing an investment by American subsidiaries in popular European cinema), it would be very surprising if Leone's films *did* fit unproblematically into Wright's schema. The films which American producers derived from the Italian Western — for example, *Hang 'Em High* (1968), a straightforward 'revenge' film — fit much more snugly, but that is a very different issue. The squabble about *Shane* is, in this sense, irrelevant: as Jameson points out, one can be sure the film will fit *somewhere* in Wright's analysis. One cannot be so sure about Spaghettis. This is not, of course, to attempt a critique of Wright's method in general (although, if Wright had taken more notice of the studio background to the making of Westerns, he might have noticed that Spaghettis had a different genealogy). His account of how to relate American formula films (treated as 'conceptual models for social action') to American society can only raise the tone of future debate

about the Western — and may (indeed, should) be applicable to other Hollywood genres, such as the gangster film and the police movie. If one were to set about seriously criticising this model, one would need a much more solid basis than the fact that a particular sub-genre fails to fit it. More devastating criticisms might, for example, be made as follows: (1) There is no *prima facie* reason why the starting-date of his history (the advent of the sound film) should coincide with any social or ideological change, or even with a significant change in 'forms of reasoning' about everyday life. (2) Wright's model seems to change its purpose at some stage during the transition from the 'classical' to the 'professional' plot. Whereas the 'classical plot' is said to 'resolve', through storytelling, an ideological contradiction (in essence, a concept of individualism which is in the process of becoming outmoded by developments in socio-economic organisations), the 'professional plot' is said to perform two very different functions: in the first instance, this narrative variant undertakes to 'present' a new ideology ('technocracy'), and, since that ideology is not yet felt to be contradictory, the variant then proceeds to 'reflect' or 'illustrate' both the new ideology and the new stage of social organisation which underpins it. (3) The sources Wright relies on for his social history (to test the 'hidden history' he first discovers in the Westerns) are not, perhaps, the most happy choices — MacPherson (for 'possessive individualism'), Galbraith (for 'the corporate economy'), Reisman (for 'the lonely crowd') and, at the last minute, Habermas (for 'rationality', brought in, as the author says, 'to the rescue' like the Seventh Cavalry) — and there is no sustained discussion of the model of historical development contained within these sources. (4) Since Wright is primarily concerned with 'the internal dynamics of superstructures' (narratives, 'structures of feeling'), he rather prematurely (and without adequate theoretical justification) attempts to relate these 'dynamics' to social and economic infrastructures, in the process having to fall back on precisely those terms ('reflection', 'correspondence', 'parallel') he seems to have set out to avoid. (5) Wright is *too* dismissive of the psychological approach to the Western myth (an approach he interprets as *necessarily* 'static' and 'ahistorical'). (6) Finally, Wright takes too little account of the studios and financial combines which produced his various hit Westerns (in other words, he does not devote enough space to the Frankfurt School model). Vladimir Propp's analysis may be 'congenial' to Wright's study of the Western film (as Frederic Jameson puts it, 'both fairy-tale and Western offer large bodies of texts which are relatively lengthy and episodic'), but one should, of course, remember that the Russian fairy-tales in question were not produced by giant Hollywood studios. Wright consistently holds to the view that 'big stars and publicity are neither necessary nor sufficient to create successful Westerns' and that consequently 'it is essential to look at the genre itself for a complete understanding of what makes for popularity' (incidentally, his concept of 'the genre' could be attacked, for ignoring the whole question of what a *dominating procedure* is). Despite all these criticisms, the misunderstanding of Spaghettis contained in *Sixguns and Society*, far from proving 'fatal' to Wright's scheme by itself, could well, as Jameson suggests, 'lead to further analytical activity' *within* that scheme. All Will Wright needs is another set of narrative variants — running parallel to the 'vengeance variation' and pre-dating the 'professional plot' (which was derived from it) — to be categorised under the general heading the 'Italian plot'.

Wright attempts to integrate the components of this 'Italian plot' into his overall schema; but there is, nevertheless, a strong case to be made for treating the plot as an entirely separate narrative development. It is never even suggested in *Sixguns and Society* that certain modifications of the American genre throughout the late 1960s (evidence for which is inscribed within some of the films listed, such as *The Wild Bunch* and *Big Jake*) might have something to do with the influence of the most successful European Westerns (which require a lot of pushing to fit into the 'professional' mould). Yet, using Wright's own list of top grossers, it is clear that the American Western was going through a bad time (comedies, parodies, spectaculars) in precisely the years (1964-7) when the best Spaghettis were beginning to earn a great deal of money internationally. In 1958, fifty-four Western feature films were made in Hollywood; by 1962-3, when Hollywood Westerns seemed to be suffering ideological traumas (Wright's 'transitional' phase), and when, as Pauline Kael pointed out, their appeal lay less in the Old West than in the old movie actors wheeled out to embody it, the total had fallen to eleven; but in 1967, annual production rose again to thirty-seven. Between these dates, there had been

times when, for the first time since Cecil B. De Mille sent his famous telegram asking for 'authority to rent barn in place called Hollywood', just prior to filming *The Squaw Man*, *no* feature-length Westerns were using locations in California. In 1958, no Western features were made at Cinecittà Studios, Rome; between summer 1963 and April 1964 (the date when Sergio Leone *began* shooting *A Fistful of Dollars*) twenty-five Western features were produced at Cinecittà; and by 1967, annual production had risen to seventy-two. According to John G. Cawelti, in *The Six-Gun Mystique*, the 'significant resurgence in popularity of the (American) Western film' revealed in the 1967 Hollywood production total, was largely due to the impact of the 'international Western', in particular the Clint Eastwood films made in Italy and Spain and directed by the Italian Sergio Leone'. By 1967, Hollywood too was investing heavily in Spaghetti Westerns. The popularity of Leone's Westerns not only created a commercial demand which made possible the production of large-budget Westerns in the post-1966 period, but also, as we shall see, may have influenced the content and style of several of the more successful Hollywood 'neo-Westerns' (some of which were shot in Mexico and Spain, rather than in Hollywood). If the Spaghetti 'originals' could be styled 'professional' Westerns, then this would not substantially affect Wright's analysis; but, as has been shown, if one accepts Wright's definition of 'professional', the schema does not work.

What would this 'Italian plot' look like? First, if we are to follow Wright's analysis, it would consist of a series of 'binary oppositions', or mechanisms for the production of meaning, out of which the narrative may be constructed and received. Wright's basic oppositions are moral ('good/bad') and ideological ones ('inside society/outside society', 'wilderness/civilisation'). More appropriate oppositions at work in the Italian Westerns, which can help us make sense of the genre, would be 'victim/executioner', 'Gringo/Mexican', 'inside the local community/outside the local community', 'pro-faction/anti-faction', 'family-oriented/self-oriented', 'amity/enmity' and 'money/commitment to a cause'. Still moral and ideological ones — but of a different order. Already, from these mechanisms for the production of meaning, we can see (following Wright) how the two decisive moments at which they intervene in the reception of the narrative of Spaghetti Westerns (helping the audience to evaluate the various characters' actions, or to decode the 'message' of a given sequence of episodes) both differ fundamentally from the equivalents Wright finds in the 'authentic' Western. In other words, the oppositions which form the basis for the analysis of American Westerns in *Sixguns and Society* simply do not work for Spaghettis: even in the most successful *early* Italian Westerns, society is virtually non-existent, all the protagonists are 'strong', the distinction between 'good', 'bad' (or, come to that, 'ugly') has been redefined, and the tension between 'wilderness' and 'civilisation' plays no part at all. The narratives which are constructed out of these specifically Italian 'oppositions' can be categorised into three main variants, each corresponding to a different phase in the Spaghetti boom. Since the Cinecittà production system is so geared to commercially successful 'formulas' (and to capturing audiences, rather than keeping them), it is relatively easy to extrapolate these variants from the (comparatively few) films which made a fortune on Italian domestic release alone: these include the Leone trilogy, Corbucci's *Django* (plus some derivatives), Tessari's 'Ringo' films, Lizzani's *The Hills Run Red*, Petroni's *Death Rides a Horse*, Valerii's *Day of Anger*, Damiani's *A Bullet for the General*, Corbucci's *Navajo Joe* and *A Professional Gun*, Sollima's *Big Gundown* and *Face to Face*, Parolini's *Sabata* and the first two 'Trinity' films.

The 'foundation' narrative variant (c. 1964-7) we might call (following Leone's suggestion) the '*Servant of Two Masters* plot':

a   The 'hero' rides into a shanty-town, on the Southwest border.
b   The 'hero' is established as being from a different culture to that of the 'Latin' inhabitants. He is usually a bounty-hunter.
c   The 'hero' is revealed to have an exceptional (not to say superhuman) ability — his technique (and knowledge of 'hardware') far outstrips that of his various opponents.
d   The society is divided into factions (or clans, mafias, camarillas): usually one is Mexican, one 'Gringo', and their economic power tends to rest on guns, liquor, gold or exploitation of the peons. These factions are not divided by values — simply by interests.
e   The 'hero' sells his services first to one clan, then to the other (no preference for the 'Gringos' — he exploits everyone); the plot

unfolds like a mathematical formula thereafter.
f   Apart from those involved in the clan rivalry, the society consists of peons, priests, whores and bartenders, and centres on the local church bell-tower (*campanilismo*).
g   The family is revealed both as a divisive force (the clans, or extended families), and as a guide to the morality of the protagonists (when the 'hero' has a past, it invariably involves the breakup of his family; and if he is not a bounty-hunter, he is out for revenge — to defend his family's honour).
h   The clans are stronger than the other groups in the society (which scarcely exist).
i   The leaders of the clans have much respect for the 'hero's' technical prowess, and attempt to buy his loyalty (without success).
j   The 'hero' plays one clan off against the other.
k   The clans endanger a friend (male or female) of the 'hero'.
l   The 'hero' watches the two clans destroying each other, then intervenes for the final showdown with the stronger leader; he invariably gets savagely beaten up by members of the stronger clan, then 'rises again' for this final showdown.
m   The 'hero' defeats the stronger villains, in an elaborate ritual.
n   The society is still not safe, but —
o   the 'hero' rides away, since, for the time being at least, there is no one left to exploit.
p   The 'hero' does not spend his dollars: he treats them strictly as 'prize', as 'something that must be grabbed, before the next man reaches them'.

The second narrative variant (c. 1966-8) we might call the 'transitional plot'. This is characteristically a variation on the '*Servant of Two Masters* plot', with two important extra 'functions', supplied by the two most successful Spaghettis on the home market in this period — Corbucci's *Django* (and derivatives) and Leone's *The Good, the Bad and the Ugly*:

a   One of the factions (or clans) consists of Mexicans who have stolen some gold, and are torn between using it to finance a radical group in the Mexican Revolution and stashing

it away for their own use. The hero (a 'Gringo')
— predictably, within the *Two Masters* formula — wants the gold for himself, and
usually gets it. But the dominant faction is
now torn between interests and values.

b   The shifts in loyalty occur within a clearly
defined historical context, such as the
American Civil War (presented in detail — the
result, perhaps, of increased budgets and more
ambitious   co-production   deals);   earlier
Spaghettis have a curiously 'disembodied' feel
to them (the 'shanty-town' being the only
set). This historical context provides a background against which the main characters'
actions can be judged (the Good to the Ugly,
after the battle for Langstone Bridge: 'I've
never seen so many men wasted so badly').
Again a new emphasis on values. The 'factions' walk in and out of this historical context, at various stages in the plot. This probably prepared the ground for the detailed
treatment of the Mexican Revolution in the
later, big-budget Spaghettis of the 'Zapata'
type.

The third narrative variant (c. 1967-71) we might
call (following Corbucci's suggestion) the 'Zapata-
Spaghetti plot'.

a   There are two 'heroes' — one a European
(Polish, Swedish, Irish) or American arms
dealer/mercenary, the other a Mexican peasant-
bandit.

b   The laconic, 'cool' style of the 'Gringo' is
contrasted with the flamboyant, talkative
style of the peon.

c   The 'Gringo' — a specialist in some form of
gunplay — offers to join the Mexican bandit,
in the hope of finding some gold, or of
arranging a 'hit' for which he has been paid
in advance. He is thus 'outside' the values of
the peons.

d   The 'society' is polarised into corrupt government   officials/brutal   army   officers,   and
oppressed, illiterate peons.

e   The Mexican bandit becomes a revolutionary,
through contact with a 'cell' of activists, and
through being cast in the role of 'hero' by the
peons (a role he feels obliged to keep up).

f   The 'Gringo' still tries to operate in partnership with the peasant revolutionary — offering
him technical assistance (guns, explosives) —

in the hope of finding gold, or being led to
his 'hit'.

g   The Mexican — now treated by the oppressed
peons as their saviour — tries to persuade the
'Gringo' to join the revolutionary cause.

h   The 'Gringo's' motives remain cynical — but
the Mexican nevertheless begins to warm to
him (in a suspicious sort of way).

Optional

i   The 'heroes' team up (form a group) briefly,
to fight a larger-than-life villain, who is trying
to exploit the chaotic situation in Mexico in
order to make money.

j   The 'heroes' defeat this villain — usually
during an elaborate showdown involving the
'Gringo'.

k   The Mexican bandit leads a successful guerrilla
raid against the corrupt Mexican authorities.

l   It is clear that this raid will result in more
(and better-equipped) counter-revolutionary
troops attacking the small revolutionary 'cell'.

Variant Endings

m   (early) The 'Gringo's' motives remain cynical
throughout, but the two 'heroes' go their
separate ways — with mutual respect and no
hard feelings.

n   (early) The 'Gringo's' motives remain cynical
throughout, and he is killed by the Mexican
bandit — who realises that no 'conversion' is
possible — in a final showdown.

o   (late) The 'Gringo' joins the Mexican bandit,
is 'converted' to the revolutionary cause, and
prepares to face the massed counter-revolutionary troops in a final, suicidal 'settling of
accounts'.

In the case of the *'Two Masters* plot', the role of the
'hero' remains constant, although there may be
changes in the context (one faction, two, even
three), and the 'problem' he has to resolve (to his
own advantage) may become more complicated. In
general, his motivation is either cash (the Leone
model), or revenge (the Corbucci model). Thus,
although the titles of individual films often contain
the name of the 'hero' (*Django*, *Ringo*) significant
differences between films within the general plot
variant are usually about his 'problem' or his 'context'. In the case of the 'Zapata-Spaghetti plot', the
'Gringo' figure clearly derives from the 'stranger' of
the foundation variant (prowess with a gun, cynicism, 'style'), but he is different to the extent that

he is now the *representative* of an alien culture, and the interest in his problems, or his relationships — especially in Westerns scripted by Franco Solinas — is sustained within a schematic 'political' context. The 'peon' figure is contrasted with the 'Gringo' in ways which derive from the 'Gringo-Mexican' conflict in the *Two Masters* variant, and from the Clint Eastwood-Eli Wallach relationship in the 'transitional plot': the contrast also prefigures the partnership between 'Terence Hill' (Northern Italian) and 'Bud Spencer' (Southern Italian) in the 'Trinity' formula, although the 'political' context again gives the 'Zapata' variant a more emblematic significance.

Of the films thus differentiated, some (such as *Fistful*) were made on a low budget, while others (such as *A Professional Gun*) had higher production values (in Leone's case involving a substantial American interest). If, like Wright, we base our analysis on a consumer sovereignty thesis, this consideration is important, for it suggests that far from being crudely stage-managed by the 'industry', Italian audiences voluntarily went to see those Western stories which corresponded 'most exactly' to their expectations, 'to the meanings the viewers demanded from the myth'. (The problem is, that the 'transitional plot' — an essential link between the two main variants — was entirely based on higher production values, and as the Spaghetti boom developed, the hit Westerns tended to be those which cost the most. This is not to say that all the expensive Westerns were successes (the fate of *Once Upon a Time in the West* is enough to disprove such an assertation), but rather that Italian audiences came to expect as much spectacle as Cinecittà (and friends) could offer them — an exogenous factor, involving an analysis of the studio's policy, which Wright's methodology cannot accommodate.) Again, if, like Wright, we assume 'myth' to represent a synthetic resolution of certain contradictions in society, which takes the form of a set of episodes presented in an 'expected' order (in other words, of a genre), we can sidestep the standard rhetorical assertions about the 'cultural roots' of the Western.

But there is a basic difference between the American Western and its Italian counterpart: the American Western has been around in film form since the origins of the cinema, and in recognisable literary form since the 1830s; the Italian Western captured Italian mass audiences in the early 1960s, and they were bored by it less than ten years later.

So, one question which Wright does not need to ask (and which is crucial for understanding Spaghettis) is 'How did they happen in the first place?' Another is 'Why did they only last eight or nine years?' (actually, it was something of a record by Cinecittà formula standards). Another is 'How were they sustained during these years?' And yet another is 'Why was a genre of American origins so successful in Italy at that time?' Our 'Italian plot' cannot help us find an answer to these questions: apart from anything else, Wright's formal analysis (the basis for our 'plot') crucially depends on the presupposition that the 'Western myth' is far more deeply rooted in the culture he is discussing than the Italian Western 'myth' ever could be, in Italian society. To answer these questions, we must look beyond the films — to the studios which produced them, to the expectations of those who enjoyed Italian popular genres *in general*, to the relationship between Cinecittà and Hollywood. It is not simply that I am asking different questions (or questions of a different order) from those Wright sets himself: on the contrary, we are both concerned to analyse the relationship between the Western and society. Nor am I making 'impossible' demands of Wright's thesis, in order to bring in the 'culture industry' model through the back door. The mode of analysis contained in *Sixguns and Society* in fact provides a useful means of *categorising* the main developments in the Italian Western genre. But in order to relate these developments to *Italian* society, the other questions — which Wright does not need to ask — must at some stage be asked. Attempts have been made, by Italian critics, to study the Spaghetti Western in terms of changes in *Italian* society, and their findings can perhaps help to illustrate just how far Wright's model can take us, or, in other words, how we can interpret our three main plot variants without bringing in other external factors (such as the studio, or its relationship with Hollywood).

Domenico Paolella, in an article called 'La Psicoanalisi dei Poveri' (written at the start of the Spaghetti boom, in May 1965) argues that the decline in popularity of the 'classical epic' (for Italian audiences), and the rise in popularity of the Western, can be related to significant changes in Italian society: whereas the 'epic' catered for 'infantile tastes' (the hero copes with a variety of obstacles by sheer muscle, he represents a force for 'good', and he does not have to rely on cunning, or technology), the Western caters for 'adolescent' tastes (the hero copes with a variety of obstacles by guile and 'technique', he is working for himself, and he must learn to dominate his instincts or he will be taken for a 'sucker'). The message of the 'classical epic' had been a simple one:

> The hero faces, in symbolic form, all the obstacles of everyday life. The monsters he meets are the workshops, the towns, the offices; the enemies are other people; the weapons of the adversary are the machines; the rivers of fire, the no less dangerous streams of traffic which choke our roads. And, in the middle of this hostile world, full of obstacles and traps, there is the man, the individual, with his extraordinary muscles.

Hercules was, of course, 'much more healthy and robust than the average Italian'. The message of the Western is rather more complex: the monsters are recognisable (if larger-than-life) people; the hero himself uses 'machines' (although he can easily dominate them) — muscle alone is clearly not enough; and the hero's cynicism is shared by everyone. How did this transition from the 'infantile' to the 'adolescent' come to be accepted (indeed, greeted) by Italian mass audiences?

> The 'mythological' film triumphed during a period of slow social evolution. We were actually living through a steady push to the left, with all that that entails in terms of social and cultural renewal. Then there was a government of the moderate left. Communist votes were on the increase. The President of the Republic, who was elected recently after a lengthy vote in Parliament, is a Socialist. In short, Italy is growing up. The consequences are felt everywhere — including in the tastes of the film-going public. And already we can see the signs of a decline in the 'mythological' film. Box-office takings are down. On the other hand, the takings of Westerns and police movies are up. A Western made in Italy, modelled on a Japanese film and camouflaged as an American one, has had an incredible success. . . . These symptoms ought to be considered as very comforting ones for the Italians.

Paolella — a veteran in the industry who had worked on Gallone's *Scipio Africanus* during the Fascist period, made Mafia films for American television, written with Pasolini in the 1950s, directed a few Totò comedies and, more recently, directed seven

'epics' featuring Maciste, Ursus, Hercules or Goliath — was convinced about one thing: in the near future, he would devote his energies to Italian Westerns. As 'Paul Fleming' he went on to make *Hate for Hate* (1967) with John Ireland and Antonio Sabato, and *Execution* (1968) with John Richardson. Paolella wrote his article — as a film-maker — in 1965. Looking back on the same phenomenon some ten years later, Lino Miccichè — as a film-critic (in *Il cinema Italiano degli anni '60*) — comes to a less optimistic conclusion.

Miccichè argues that one endemic disease in the Italian film industry is the absence of 'the average film', 'the product which constitutes the mainstay and the penetrating force of the Hollywood industry'. In cultural terms, this may well be a good thing, but

> the absence of a middle-of-the-road type of cinema becomes lethal in a market as large as the Italian one, which, throughout the 1960s, maintained the highest audience levels in Europe (and still continues to do so), the second highest (after the USA) in the so-called 'Western World'. In this situation, an industry such as the Italian cinema industry is in a state of perennial crisis and uncertainty. Unlike Hollywood, it has no dependable financial backing to allow for medium- and long-term planning, it is not structured for complete-cycle production (so companies have to depend on outside assistance) and it does not have a solid international distribution system which would mean that profits from the internal market would form only part of a production's total income. The net result of all this is that the industry seizes upon *any* immediately available consumer potential.

In the late 1940s and early 1950s, the genre of the moment was the 'film-fumetto', the sentimental 'weepy' culled from serials in women's magazines (in 1952, these constituted over 30 per cent of all films being made in Italy); in the mid-1950s, it was the farcical comedy (Totò being the most famous — and enduring — personality to emerge from this period); in the late 1950s — give or take about fifty costume dramas and the same number of opera films, both genres petering out for lack of funds — it was the 'mythological epics'; in the 1962-4 season, it was 'sexy' films of the *World by Night* genre; finally, in 1964, the Italian Western began to take off. Miccichè proceeds to relate both these attempts by the industry to 'seize' a 'mass audience', and the reactions of that 'mass audience', to significant changes in Italian social life:

The quantitative domination of the mass-market was sustained by the 'mythological' film from 1960-4, with the 'sexy' film running parallel for the last two years. Then the Italian Western, after a relatively limited impact in 1964, rose to prominence in 1966-8, and was only overtaken by the more recent police and spy films. So really, the passage from the 'mythological' film to the Italian Western as relatively stable popular 'genres' corresponded in 1964-6 to a precise phase in Italian society, during which the great expectations and the grand illusions of the early years of the decade were replaced by new frustrations and fresh delusions. The Italian Western is in its own way a typical by-product of mid-60s Italian society, and reflects, more or less unconsciously, some of the sociological data, some of the hidden history of those years. It especially betrays the ideological and moral confusion of that period, as well as the difficulty, which seemed to exist in a broad section of petty-bourgeois public opinion, of distinguishing 'who was guilty?', 'who was responsible?', 'who were the good guys?' in situations where, more often than not, old enemies were coming together and historic connections were being pulled in opposite directions. All this while the range of individual choices seemed to be restricted to forms of social conscience that were becoming more and more confined, because directed by 'external' forces. So it is that the Italian Westerner, far from reflecting the somewhat 'mystificatory' epic of the frontier, impersonates, in ways which are paradoxically entertaining (and too explicitly cynical to trouble the conscience) a commonplace of the everyday psyche of the 'average' Italian — the urge to overwhelm (or help someone else do it for you) in order not to be overwhelmed, the urge to guarantee that you will not become anyone's victim (using the only objectively recognisable 'values' — money and power, which go hand in hand). When he went to see a Western in the mid-'60s, which was really about the violence of a man who believes his only choice is violence, the Italian viewer could imagine himself shooting, wounding and killing the

puppets of the cinema's *kitsch*, identifying himself with the protagonist — who was not a hero, but a cynic in despair. Few at that time could foresee the crisis of 1968 towards which, in Italy as elsewhere, all the many strands of contemporary dissatisfaction were leading — a crisis in values which seemed to hit at everything that was certain in the past, made it difficult to define the present, and impossible to locate the future. The popular cinema in those years, whether 'sexy' or Western, in its ephemeral, mercenary cynicism reflected a state of mind on the one hand, and helped to 'fix' it on the other. It is one of the most significant records of the era, if studied with sufficient care and attention. Apart from anything else, it vividly reflected this blind social materialism because it wanted to survive: the corner reserved for finer feelings, for virtue rewarded, for heroism made worthwhile, for social respectibility, was occupied increasingly by the TV screen, through which the 'system' directly communicated its own ideology and culture.

Paolella interprets the rise of the Western in terms of Italy 'growing up' — the tastes of cinema-going audiences were becoming more sophisticated, more 'urban', as politicians faced up to the new possibilities of socialism. Miccichè also analyses the various popular genres which came and went during the twenty years after the war, in terms of a 'growing up': the 'film-fumetti' (despite their crass sentimentality) bore the influence of neo-realism (at least when compared with the equivalent product of 'white telephone' days); the 'sexy' films broke a few taboos ('they made no attempt to question the bases of a repressive morality . . . but had the same significance as could be attributed to the use of a dirty word'); and the Italian Westerns broke a few more (usually to do with violence), as well as catering for 'the most basic needs of the consumer' more directly than had ever been possible before. Paolella interprets the 'cynicism' of the Western as part of this growing-up process: Miccichè prefers to view it as an attempt by producers to find the lowest common denominator in the audience (money and power) at a time of political and social uncertainty; he adds that this same uncertainty resulted in the events of 1968 (with concomitant effects on the cinema — films of 'rage, scorn and iconoclastic violence' being much in evidence that year). And just as Paolella stresses the increasing 'urbanisation' of 'mass taste' in Italy, Miccichè provides figures to show how the urban middle class were, in fact, going to the cinema more often in the 1960s:

> The industry was trying to create an 'average' product for the 'first run' audiences and the urban middle classes, who, with increased income levels in the middle strata of society, constituted one of the main supports for keeping up levels of demand in the cinema. So, whilst box-office takings showed an increasing tendency towards the concentration of profits from first screenings, statistics also showed an increasing tendency towards the concentration of cinemagoing in urban centres. This was confirmed towards the end of the decade when it was seen that in 1963 there were 1,690 communes without a cinema, and in 1969 there were 3,399, whilst the number of cinemas throughout the country had not proportionately decreased; that the 18 Italian cities with a population of over 200,000 (Rome, Milan, Naples, Turin, Genoa, Palermo, Bologna, Florence, Catania, Venice, Bari, Trieste, Messina, Verona, Padua, Cagliari, Taranto, Brescia) accounted for over 33 per cent of tickets sold and over 41 per cent of takings; that the provincial capital/province ratio expressed in average annual per capita figures of cinema attendance was 14/9, whereas the same comparison made between numbers of TV owners was 250/194 (a much narrower gap); and that this was so in spite of the fact that, unlike the uniform cost of a TV set, a cinema ticket in towns with over 200,000 inhabitants cost on average twice as much as in towns with under 50,000 inhabitants.

(Paolella, however, makes a distinction — omitted in Miccichè — between the cost of tickets for 'art films', and the 'sword and sandal' epics: the latter could, not surprisingly, cost a great deal less at the box-office, particularly if they were given saturation distribution.)

If we examine the relationship between these two accounts of social change in Italy and the 'Italian plot', we can perhaps work towards some observations about 'the external limiting situation or condition of possibility which accounts for the coming into being of a given plot variant and excludes the others'. The trouble is that both Paolella and Miccichè are writing less about 'objective' changes in Italian society than about possible 'changes of attitude' in the Italian cinema-going public, and their approach to the problem (part pop psychology, part sociological generalisation) too often becomes just plain woolly-minded. They tend to chuck in words like 'reflection' and 'parallel' with rare abandon, and (in Miccichè's case especially) tend also to deflect what 'findings' they provide in a decidedly ethical direction (it is clear that Miccichè is out of sympathy both with Italian Westerns and with the social symptoms he takes them to represent).

Nevertheless, it is worth briefly attempting a social interpretation of our three plot variants, on the basis of what they have to offer. Clearly, the 'Servant of Two Masters plot' represents a symptom of the increasingly 'urban' sophistication of the audience: the complexity of the plot, the divisions in society which the 'hero' exploits to his own advantage, the reaction against sentimentality, the stress on interests rather than values, the 'control' over hardware, and so on. And the fact that the 'hero' never commits himself to any one 'cause' is perhaps symptomatic of the uncertainties (and disillusionments) Miccichè outlines. The phenomenon may represent a 'growing-up', but it is clear that the stage of 'adolescence' brings mixed blessings with it: films like A Fistful of Dollars are there to 'resolve' the contradictions. The 'transitional plot' is symptomatic of the increasing expectations of an expanding urban audience, while the appearance of 'values' (albeit in subplot form) reveals a search for a 'cause' — a way out of the impasse: perhaps there is more to life than the 'guarantees' of money and power, but no one is quite sure what; these 'values' may also be symptomatic of Cinecittà's attempt to 'capture' a more international audience (in order to recoup more international investment in the films). The 'Zapata-Spaghetti plot' (at its peak popularity in 1968) derives a clear political stance from the 'Transition plot', and represents the first explicitly political form of popular cinema in Italy since the Mussolini era. This 'political' stance may be interpreted in terms of the shaky relationship between Italy and the Superpowers: a relationship which is 'resolved' in favour of the 'peons'.

Unfortunately, the shortcomings of our two sources are reflected in these rather bland generalisations about the 'Italian plot' — generalisations which tell us very little about the Spaghetti Western, and which run the risk of becoming tautological (or self-fulfilling). The only substantive data Miccichè provides is about the studio and its market research — and these are considerations which the Wright model does not permit us to use; for example, the central role given to the 'peon' figure in the 'Zapata-Spaghetti plot' may simply reflect the increasing success of Cinecittà Westerns in Third World markets. (Tomas Milian, who played several of these 'peons', reckons that he became a 'symbol of poverty and revolution' to Third World viewers — and this may have helped to expand the Cinecittà sphere of operations considerably.) What is needed, for a thorough analysis of the Spaghetti Western phenomenon, is a conceptual model which can take account of commercial imperatives of this kind, and which does not necessarily need to argue a 'consumer sovereignty' thesis: changes in the formula often occurred simply because the vast majority of Westerns were going in a certain direction (not just those which did well internationally), and the model will need to cope with the Cinecittà production system in order to explain this. If it is true that Spaghetti Westerns faced up to the 'realities' of Italian society more than any previous popular genre, after the ground had been prepared by the 'taboo-breaking' genres which preceded them, then what order of 'realities' may we expect to find within the Western genre, and what particular sections of 'Italian society' are we discussing? One thing is certain: the social changes noted by Paolella and Miccichè do not take us very far. And even when such issues have been discussed, that still leaves the question 'Why the Western?' In the rest of this chapter, and in the sections which follow, I have attempted to address all these questions. But, for the moment at least, it is clear that we will have to abandon the Will Wright model.

One of the key problems (and it is not, of course, confined to film studies) is how to analyse artefacts such as Westerns *symptomatically* (to use the current term), while at the same time treating them as artefacts. The decipherment process this entails should ideally involve looking at films as ideological *productions* (with that emphasis), rather than as purveyors of raw ideology. Of course, unless one adopts a crudely 'reflectionist' position (looking at plots in isolation, as direct 'reflections' of social and political structures), the problems of studying performance, 'style', derivations, images, production values, and so on, within this context, are immense.

But if one ignores these problems one cannot hope to do justice to the films in question. Barry King has suggested one possible line of approach. He argues that Wright's 'attempt to connect genre change with social change is perfunctory and mechanical to the point of mere juxtaposition': this is, he adds, because Wright leaves most of the important questions unanswered. 'Given that American capitalism has changed (or rather popular awareness of its form has changed) and that the Western has changed, it is still necessary to show how Hollywood mediates this change and why. But since Wright argues a consumer sovereignty thesis, the influence of Hollywood must accordingly be played down. Apart from the circularity of claiming that box-office Westerns are popular because they have a plot structure Wright detects, there is the practical evidence of Hollywood's efforts to influence popular opinion.' Since the change in American society from a market economy to a corporate economy did *not*, of course, take place during the brief forty-year period (1930-70) with which Wright is concerned (and since generalisations about 'popular awareness' of this change would require a great deal more proof than Wright offers), it might have been more useful to relate the shifting values he isolates to changes within *Hollywood*: 'In the period in question, it is Hollywood — not American capitalism — that moves from an individual (star, director, etc.) versus society (studio) opposition to a conflict between teams (independent production company) and society (distribution finance) ... these and other issues are masked by a preference to discuss myth — "a communication from society to its members" — instead of ideology — a communication from professional communicators to their audiences.' Wright's use of the $4 million category as an index of participation (he omits, incidentally, to allow for changes in the value of money), thus crucially ignores the *production context* of each individual film. (One does not, of course, necessarily have to accept King's definition of 'ideology', in order to accept this.) So, if we are fully to discuss Spaghettis and society, in addition to looking at the *social* context, the Cinecittà *production context* must also be borne in mind. And unless we distinguish between the *general* social context, and the specific reasons why the Spaghetti Westerns were first made at the time they were, we are likely to come out with a thesis which is as circular as Wright's.

First, then, the general social context. Barzini's study *The Italians* may not be good sociology, but it is interesting that its emphases mirror so closely those of the Italian Western. Popular Mafia novels may not be serious literature, but it is interesting that their view of American life mirrors the view which Barzini attributes to Italian immigrants. Although it is impossible to justify in terms of method, putting the two side by side does seem to tell us as much about the films (or books) themselves as Wright's elaborate structural study of the Western (the artificial rigour of which suggests that it started life as a dissertation) — perhaps because both Barzini and the films are dealing with a series of popular mythologies, and crudely defined self-images. In other words, both can be related to the internal dynamics of 'superstructures' alone. If we look at the Italian Westerns in terms of more serious sociological analyses of these 'superstructural' phenomena (mythologies, self-images, etc.) in, for example, Southern Italy, the results seem to be remarkably similar. Perhaps this is because, as Michael Wood suggests, broad studies of this kind are by definition tautological (Will Wright accuses those who interpret the American Western in terms of a series of all-embracing 'foundation myths' of the same thing). But, until a more complex method has been suggested (a method which can go beyond a schematic analysis of plot to a fully contextual reading of style and performance as well), or until elaborate surveys of a broad sample of cinema-goers' responses to specific artefacts have been mounted, less methodical studies can at least provide a general context within which to view the films.

It may be, for example, that the popularity of the Western among Italian audiences (especially in Rome and points south) has something to do with an urge to 'escape from society' that is analogous to the 'flight' which Michael Wood sees as 'inextricably caught up in the idea of America itself'. Perhaps the hostility to codified law (and to the encroachments of central government) which is often enshrined in Hollywood Westerns (of both the 'classical' and 'professional' types) *and* which was to become central to the Spaghetti Westerns, finds a parallel (albeit arising from a different set of traditions) in the equivalent hostilities of Southern Italian society. After all, the Italian Westerns were not made by the Northern intellectuals of the film world. They were made, on the whole, by a group of youngish film-makers (mostly in their late thirties or early forties) who had found themselves in Rome (as college students, journalists, production assistants, assistant directors, film reviewers on popular magazines, film critics in serious journals) during the American invasion of Cinecittà Studios, in the mid-1950s. Largely as a result of this invasion, in Geoffrey Nowell-Smith's words, Cinecittà became to Rome 'what Hollywood is to Los Angeles', and the Via Veneto came to resemble Hollywood's Sunset Strip. The ensuing boom in film production had given these budding cinéastes an opportunity to make their mark in the industry (in the first instance as assistant directors on American-financed spectaculars, or, more commonly, as assistants on Italian derivatives of the 'sword and sandal' epics), and by the time of the 'peplum' boom of 1960-3, most of them were either co-directors, or directors, of their own films. There were exceptions to this, of course: Carlo Lizzani, for example, a veteran film director who had been making films about bandits of all descriptions since 1951, and who had written a full-length study of the Italian cinema in 1953, made two Spaghetti Westerns (also about bandits and rebels) in the 1960s under the pseudonym of 'Lee Beaver' — *The Hills Run Red* (1966) and *Requiescant* (1967). But the most prolific and influential Italian Western directors (such as Sergio Corbucci, Sergio Sollima, Duccio Tessari, and Sergio Leone) all more or less fit this pattern. Many of these hardened Cinecittà professionals (whose training in the 1955-62 period included some script-writing, as well as the experience of 'assisting' or co-directing) came from Rome and further south. Sergio Leone, for example, was from a Neapolitan family, and was studying at the Lycée in Rome (at the same time as Ennio Morricone, who was two years his junior) when the post-war boom in the Italian cinema began. According to Domenico Paolella (who, like Lizzani, was of an older generation), as 'professionals' they were looked down upon by the Northern intelligentsia of the film world, not only because of their training in 'pulp' films (often co-productions) but also because as a result of their training (or their 'occupational ideology', perhaps) they tended to make 'pulp' films themselves, usually pitched at the home (Southern) market. Paolella himself made his name with 'sword and sandal' epics, then went on to direct Italian Westerns for the same audiences — which, according to him, characteristically consisted of those who felt most alienated 'by the dominance of modern technology'. At the time he first started making Westerns, he sadly recalled that his work was often treated as an object of 'derision', that his films were scorned as 'committee projects', and that he was often told by Northern intellectuals 'the only people who could be remotely interested in your form of cinema are the simple-minded and the crudest members of the audience'. 'This tendency only to praise forms of "culture" which are *detached* from popular interests', he concluded, 'is one of the most dramatic aspects of our country's artistic life. It goes back several centuries.' Paolella was writing in 1965, but Francesco Rosi, in an interview recorded in 1978, restated the problem — albeit from a very different point of view: he was talking about his latest film, *Christ Stopped at Eboli*, which concerns the experiences of a Northern intellectual in a community of Southern peasants.

> Even the best of bourgeois intellectuals and artists, who are quite happy to live amongst these people, with whom they feel a real brotherhood, end up leaving them to it. I'm all too familiar with the problem. I had the same experience when I was Visconti's assistant on *La Terra Trema*. I get on well with these people, but I know that at a certain point I'll be leaving them — to carry on buying expensive clothes and shoes, travelling around, while they have to stay there and face their problems. . . . The film is about an encounter between a bourgeois intellectual representing a refined Northern culture and a completely different, distant world, the world of the peasant in one of the most neglected regions of the south.

Rosi's remarks suggest that the North-South differential in Italian cultural life is still most often seen as one between 'the intellectuals' and 'the crudest members of the audience'; unlike Paolella, however, he reckons that Cinecittà 'popular culture' does little more than provide bread and circuses for the oppressed classes. Indeed, he is convinced that the Southern *contadini* have been 'dispossessed of their culture by the arrival of a new one via the mass media and TV which has superimposed itself on their own ancient culture': in other words that Cinecittà formula films represent a type of cultural imperialism, with the Romano-American mass media dominating Southern peasant culture. Whether or not this is true of the Italian Westerns (they seem

to have been most popular with mass *urban* audiences), both Paolella and Rosi provide evidence, from very different perspectives, of the ways in which Northern intellectuals continue to sneer at 'Southern culture' (whether ancient *or* modern). The most famous 'art film' directors we associate with Italy in the 1960s all originated from the same region in the North: Antonioni (Ferrara), Bertolucci (Parma), Fellini (the Romagna coast), and Pasolini (Emilia-Romagna). According to Don Ranvaud, in his article on Pasolini, Italian film-makers 'are inevitably affected by the determining conditions of their regional . . . origins to a far greater extent than their European counterparts'. The fact that these film-makers have all returned to their home landscapes (and to the provincial societies from which they came) to use them as settings for their films, provides interesting evidence of this. By contrast, as we have seen, many directors of Spaghettis tended to come from further south: of the most well-known, Corbucci (Rome), Leone (Naples), Lizzani (Rome), and Paolella (Foggia). Sergio Leone's films do not appear in the standard serious histories of the Italian cinema (or even of the Western) which have been written by Italian film critics, but Leone does make an appearance in the Michelin *Green Guide* to Rome — as a tourist attraction!

Most of the comments from Barzini's *The Italians* which I outlined above are more specifically about the Southerners. Clearly this is one social context that must be borne in mind, if we are to understand the Italian Westerns: although some of these films (about 20 per cent, in fact) were to be released internationally, at first nearly all the Spaghettis seem to have been intended for the home market, and until the Italian Western became established as a genre, Italian members of the cast and crew hid behind American pseudonyms (usually derived from Westerns, with a preference for what they thought were 'Texan' or 'Californian' names) in the hope that gullible audiences would take these Westerns for a new brand of their favourite Hollywood product. (For horror films, by contrast, Cinecittà directors hid behind English pseudonyms in the hope that their work would appear to have emerged from the house of Hammer.) In America, directors such as John Ford and actors such as John Wayne had adopted monosyllabic pseudonyms in order to appear as WASP-like as possible; in Italy, for less social and more economic reasons, suntanned Roman Catholic Latins did the same thing (with results ranging from the derivative — 'John Fordson'/Mario Costa — to the bizarre — 'Helen Wart'/Anna Miserocchi, 'Humphrey Humbert'/ Umberto Lenzi). After the genre had gained in self-confidence, most of the Roman producers were to be if anything even more opportunistic about relating their films to the known audience expectations of the Southern Italians, and of those Northern Italians who enjoyed watching stereotypes of their Southern counterparts.

In 1958, Edward C. Banfield, an American political sociologist, wrote a study of a small town he called 'Montegrano', in Southern Italy, after living there for a year. This study was concerned with the political culture of a poor community 'in the pre-industrial sector' of Italy. Banfield labelled this culture 'amoral familism': *Maximize the material, short-run advantage of the nuclear family; assume that all others will do likewise*. One whose behaviour is consistent with this rule will be called an "amoral familist". The term is awkward and somewhat imprecise (one who follows the rule is without morality only in relation to persons outside the family — in relation to family members, he applies standards of right and wrong; one who has no family is of course an "amoral individualist") but no other term seems better.' This study of the 'Montegrano' region goes on to explain exactly what 'amoral familism' means, with reference to a series of axioms for the conduct of a successful life with other 'amoral familists': 'no one will further the interest of the group or community except as it is to his private advantage to do so'; 'only officials will concern themselves with public affairs, for only they are paid to do so'; 'organisation (i.e. deliberately concerted action) will be very difficult to achieve and maintain ... for it is a condition of successful organisation that members have some trust in each other and some loyalty to the organisation'; 'office-holders will not work harder than is necessary to keep their places'; 'the law will be disregarded when there is no reason to fear punishment'; 'office-holders will take bribes when they can get away with it ... whether they take bribes or not, it will be assumed by the society of amoral familists that they do'; 'the claim of any person or institution to be inspired by zeal for public rather than private advantage will be regarded as fraud'; 'there will be no connection between abstract political principle (i.e. ideology) and concrete

behaviour in the ordinary relationships of every day life'; 'it will be assumed that whatever group is in power is self-serving and corrupt'; 'there will be no strong or stable political machines in a society of amoral familists'. Each 'axiom' is illustrated by interviews with locals from various social groups, or by discussion of some local issue. At one point, Banfield writes about the small-time entrepreneur who is building a cinema in 'Montegrano': 'Before the cinema goes into operation, he must have a permit from the proper authority. After months of waiting, his request for a permit had not been acted upon. "If I took an envelope with 160 dollars and slipped it into the right pocket, I would have my permission right away" he told an interviewer. "Its the little yellow envelope that gets things done. Big and small, they all take bribes". "Why don't you do it, then?" "Because I don't have 160 dollars to spare".'

The conclusion is that, in the spectrum of political and social culture, 'Montegrano' represents a model example of non-participation, and of the primacy of parochial (or family) over national considerations. Barzini's more entertaining (if even less systematic) account comes to strikingly similar conclusions about the South of Italy in general. Banfield's thesis has been attacked by Italian sociologists (such as Gilberto Marselli and Alessandro Pizzorno), and an attempt to apply it to a village of Western Sicily has drawn further attention to some of its inadequacies: Banfield, as an American observer, was apparently not familiar with the more general aspects of Southern culture; he confused his description of a concrete case with the presentation of a theoretical model; he failed to understand the traditional relationship between the Southern Italian peasant and the provincial or national government; he did not give enough emphasis to the *clientela* (or patronage) system, which would stretch *beyond* the citizens of 'Montegrano'; perhaps 'Montegrano' was not the community Banfield expected it to be at all, but simply an aggregate of families, he neglected the role of *extended* families (again, this would have taken his study beyond 'Montegrano'). The key questions raised by this type of criticism are whether or not Banfield over-stretched his rather limited data, and how his concept could be extended (or adapted) to apply to the whole of Southern Italy. Attempts to extend Banfield's analysis have suggested that, if anything, he *underestimated* the role of clans, sects or extended families, and his main error of judgment was to expect Southern Italians to behave like his image of the grass-roots American democrat. But, from the point of view of Italian political sociologists, a more significant criticism of Banfield is that, in failing to understand the *structural* problems of Southern Italian communities, he had written about phenomena which were really superficial (or 'superstructural') while thinking that he was getting to the root of the matter. All of the participants in this debate accept that the concept of amoral familism 'has some points of reference in reality' (Pizzorno). But few think that the phenomena Banfield was studying actually *explain* anything. From the evidence of the Italian Westerns, the Cinecittà producers clearly did their market research, into areas these political sociologists deem 'superstructural' (rather than those areas Will Wright deems 'structural'), very thoroughly indeed. Unlike Banfield, they were not likely to be concerned with passing judgment on the Southern Italians (or on the Northerners who believed all the stereotypes); they simply wanted them to go to the cinema more often.

For example, the three main characters who owe the *least* to Hollywood conventions or to Hollywood stereotypes, in Sergio Leone's films — Tuco in *The Good, the Bad and the Ugly*, Cheyenne in *Once Upon a Time in the West*, and Juan in *A Fistful of Dynamite* (or *Duck, You Sucker*) — are all prime examples of amoral familism. They have a strong loyalty to their families (the only man who can *really* upset Tuco is his brother, Padré Ramirez; Cheyenne recalls wistfully how 'fine' a woman his mother was; and the destruction of Juan's grotesque extended family alters the whole course of his life), but they cannot be trusted completely by *anyone else*. And in most Italian Westerns, loyalties to those outside the family change as often as the reels. This does not mean that the family is *necessarily* the great standard of right and wrong in these films: on the contrary, extended families or clans wreak havoc in many Spaghettis (Leone's included), and, in Barzini's terms, the strength of the family in the Italian Western tends to be one of the principal causes of disorder (at the same time as being an important safeguard against it). Many of the Italian Western heroes (particularly if they are Gringos, and if the stories were designed to cash in on the success of *A Fistful of Dollars*) tend rather to be 'amoral individualists'. But when standards of right

and wrong do feature in these films, the standards are usually associated with loyalty to the family — more specifically, loyalty of the Latin 'social bandits' to their families and communities: Banfield's thesis about 'bell-tower patriotism', for example, can help us locate functions d, f, g, h, n, and perhaps p of the *Servant of Two Masters* variant. That the recurring themes in Italian Westerns which relate most closely to those aspects of Southern Italian life observed by Banfield and others (amoral familism, cynicism about priests, disregard for codified law, and so on) should be thought 'superstructural' by Italian political sociologists (especially Marxist ones) is not really surprising. What is more surprising is that a critic like Will Wright should attempt to relate Westerns (including Spaghettis) *directly* to the 'base', or 'structure' of a society.

The heroes and villains of Spaghetti Westerns are almost invariably obsessed by 'style', 'image', 'ritual', and their confrontations or interactions are, typically, symbolic ones: one of the trademarks of the Spaghetti (especially after *A Fistful of Dollars*) was to become the extended face-off, or duel, or settling of accounts; and the hero-figures are usually identifiable by a collection of external gestures, mannerisms, 'stylish' articles of clothing, or even motifs on the soundtrack, rather than by anything remotely to do with the 'inner man'. We know that Clint Eastwood is about to intervene, for example, because we can see some cigar smoke being puffed into the frame, or because a pair of suede boots has suddenly appeared in the foreground, photographed from ground level, or because we have seen a series of extreme close-ups of frightened (or impressed) faces. This obsession with style, ritual or external gesture — with Latin *machismo*, rather than American *toughness* — perhaps explains why the very 'superficiality' of studies like Banfield's makes them such appropriate sources for the social context of the Spaghetti Western.

One of Jean-Luc Godard's criticisms of the Italian Western (contained in his film *Wind from the East*, 1969) seems to have been precisely that, by exploiting 'superstructural' phenomena of this kind, and by reinforcing the Southern Italians' crudest image of themselves for the benefit of both Northerners *and* Southerners, the genre (like most popular genres) did not allow for criticism of the status quo (political or aesthetic), or for *any* kind of political statement about *structural* problems in society. Those early Spaghetti Westerns which simply pandered to this (exclusively male) self-image were scarcely likely to 'challenge' the consensus of political and social opinion in any other way. Godard would probably go further, and add that the part-government-owned studio at Cinecittà was exploiting these phenomena with the *intention* of anaesthetising criticism, sponsoring an elaborate dream-world — a *Commedia dell'Ovest* — to divert the attention of the gullible from the more fundamental anomalies which exist in everyday life. Bread and circuses for fans of the Wild West. And a mindless exploitation of the 'dominant codes' of Hollywood. But one of the strangest aspects of Cinecittà formula cinema (Godard might say one of the in-built contradictions in capitalism) is that it very often has the capacity to criticise itself. After the 'rules' of the Italian Western genre had been established (and proved to be commercially viable), a group of writers (and especially Franco Solinas, as we shall see) managed to *use* the genre for overtly political purposes, manipulating audience expectations while putting over their ideas about American interventionism, particularly the role of the CIA in Latin America. Godard would, of course, consider this use of *lumpen* cinema for political purposes as ensuring a very low level of political debate, if not a complete dilution of the political message in a sea of gimmicks derived from the formula which is being exploited. Sergio Sollima, for example, has agreed with the suggestion that his Italian Westerns were 'disguised' political parables — so 'disguised', maybe, that the parables were unlikely to be understood by those who were expecting yet another remake of *A Fistful of Dollars*. But the films written by Franco Solinas, and directed by Sollima, Corbucci or Damiani, at least show that Cinecittà producers *were* prepared to invest in genre pictures which were more or less critical of the *status quo* (and, indirectly, of the genre itself) — so long as people continued to go and see them. Some of these genre pictures even contained stylistic 'experiments' which may be interpreted as a *challenge* to the 'dominant codes'.

Whatever the drawbacks of Will Wright's analysis in *Sixguns and Society* (and there are many) it does make the crucial point that 'to account for the significance of a genre, the nature of the society and the expectations of its members must be incorporated into the explanation' and (on more shaky ground) it also permits the critic to see the audience as 'choosing . . . which types of stories it will watch and enjoy'. By studying only those films which were spectacular box-office hits, Wright at least ensures that they are ones which were *chosen* (for whatever reason, by active participants *or* passive recipients) from the many available. Having looked briefly at some studies of the nature of Southern Italian society and the expectations of its members, and having discussed the validity of this type of evidence, it is worth examining which Italian Westerns were *chosen* (again, for whatever reason) from the vast number (well over 400) distributed on the home market. This is not to suggest that 'consumer sovereignty' is *the* index to the social significance of films. But commercial success (whether or not prompted by the gigantic publicity machines of the large studios) is a key factor in the development of *formula* cinema, so the figures are worth looking at. Sergio Leone's 'Dollars' trilogy made it into Wright's $4 million category by a fairly wide margin (with a much smaller market than America and Canada, of course). *A Fistful of Dollars* grossed $4,600,000 in Italy alone, between October 1964 and February 1968; *For a Few Dollars More* grossed $5 million in Italy, between 1965 and February 1968; and *The Good, the Bad and the Ugly* grossed $4.3 million on the home market, between December 1966 and February 1968. Enzo Barboni's second 'Trinity' film (starring the Venetian superstar 'Terence Hill' and with a strong emphasis on comedy), *Trinity Is Still My Name*, was the only other Italian Western to make quite as much money at home (outgrossing two of the three Leone films). None of the other Spaghettis qualify for Wright's hall of fame, although some starring Franco Nero (*Django*; *A Professional Gun*) and Giuliano Gemma (the 'Ringo' films; *Day of Anger*) were in the millions — as were Sollima's two 'political' Westerns and some Hill and Spencer comedies. The Italian Westerns which were released internationally did wonders for the rocky finances of Cinecittà Studios. In 1958, Italian film exports earned $14½ million: ten years later, the figure was $50 million. A fistful indeed.

Of the ten Italian films which made the most money at the box-office, internationally, between 1956 and 1971, Sergio Leone's 'Dollars' trilogy came second, third and sixth: *For a Few Dollars More* made 3½ billion lire, *A Fistful of Dollars* $3\frac{1}{5}$ billion, and *The Good, the Bad and the Ugly* $3\frac{1}{5}$ billion. Others on the list include *Trinity Is Still My Name* (which out-grossed all Leone's films on the international market); *La Dolce Vita*; *The*

Decameron; and *The Bible*. In the same years, the number of co-productions, based in Italy, increased dramatically, until in 1970 (the peak year), for every film financed entirely by Italian producers, there was a co-production — although a small majority of these co-productions still involved an Italian commitment of over 50 per cent.

When interpreting these international figures, it is as well not to lose sight of the fact that most Italian Westerns were in the first instance aimed at the home market. One way of relating the expectations of this audience to the films themselves is always to imagine how Spaghettis would have been received in the 'Roxy, Calabria' (or equivalent movie palace in the South).

Luigi Barzini aptly describes the Italians' (specifically the Southern and Central Italians') self-image as that of 'soldiers in a solitary outpost surrounded by the enemy, who grumble, shirk unnecessary dangers, make their dug-outs comfortable, adorn them with pictures and flowers, hoping for salvation but also resigned to death'. Some of these 'pictures and flowers', he continues, have traditionally taken the form of 'cynical comedies of intrigue and deceit', based on ancient Roman models and updated by Machiavelli, in which the author takes care not to make a fool of himself by praising honourable ideals, for he feels much more secure believing that 'all sovereigns were cruel, crafty and ruthless; that all priests and monks were libertines, whoremongers, gluttons and rapacious money-grabbers, and all women harlots'. This tradition lives on, he adds, in the work of 'a few famous Italian writers of today (and some of the best films, which are partly inspired by them) who have paid as much attention as their forefathers did to the solid aspects of life and have shown the old familiar suspicion of the ideal and noble. Some of these men have described the pleasures of lust, greed, and ambition with the ancient gusto, sometimes reaching daring refinements which even the Renaissance had not known.' Other 'pictures and flowers', dating from a later, superficially more heroic (and, as Gramsci reminds us, superficially more democratic) time of Risorgimento in the mid to late nineteenth century, have taken the form of magnificent operas. Gramsci reckons that the Risorgimento had few points of contact with 'the great popular masses' in the South, 'who actually stood quite apart from that cultural tradition and did not care about it, even when they knew of its existence'. Nevertheless, it was Giacomo Puccini who wrote the first horse opera worthy of the name, in *La Fanciulla del West* (*The Girl of the Golden West*), just after the turn of the century. This opera, first conceived in New York in 1907, when Puccini went to see David Belasco's four-act melodrama of the same name, was premièred at the New York Metropolitan in December 1910 (with Caruso as the hero), then performed at La Scala, Milan, and Covent Garden, London, in the following year. Puccini had been particularly impressed by Belasco's elaborate stage-devices — which almost had the impact of 'cinematographic' effects (combining as they did tricks of the light with moving curtains) — used to re-create blizzards, mountain panoramas, and the 'exteriors' of a Californian Gold Rush town: *The Great Train Robbery* had opened in New York four years before. Although the libretto, by Carlo Zangarini, Guelfo Civinini, and above all Puccini himself, was derived from an American 'original', the operatic version remains unmistakably Italian in style. The librettists added two extra scenes (a man-hunt and a lynching), while Puccini rewrote a series of American folk-tunes (including 'The Old Dog Tray', and 'Doodah Day') as well as inventing some new ones of his own: he even introduced a *bolero* theme, to accompany the arrival of the bandit Ramerrez with his Mexican heavies. In the draft version of Act III of *La Fanciulla* (which was almost entirely written specially by the Italians), the main Red Indian character, Billy Jackrabbit, was shown to be the leader of a lynch-mob: this had to be changed for the New York première, because it was thought that the American public would not accept a non-white character in that role. Clearly, the Italians had at some stage strayed a long way from Belasco's script. In the opera, each main character has a distinctive *leit-motif* — lyrical (for Minnie, the saloon-girl), wistful (for Ramerrez, or Johnson, the romantic bandit) and brooding (for the real villain, who turns out to be Sheriff Rance) — and Puccini attempted to re-create some of the 'cinematographic' spectacle of the original melodrama, in the scene where Ramerrez is hunted by the miners through a Californian forest, and in the climax, when there are no less than eight horses on the stage. Perhaps because it is so difficult (and costly) to stage, the opera is rarely revived: it only reaches its full, epic potential in a setting like the Arena di Verona. The connections between the music of Ennio Morricone and the tradition inspired by Puccini (or, less flatteringly perhaps, Menotti) were immediately apparent in the first of Leone's Westerns, *A Fistful of Dollars*. (David Belasco's melodrama, *The Girl of the Golden West*, was, incidentally, filmed four times by Hollywood — in 1915, 1923, 1930 and 1938 — but Puccini's music was never featured: the 1938 version, with Nelson Eddy and Jeanette MacDonald, boasted a score by Sigmund Romberg instead!)

But the optimistic, heroic phase in Italian literature and music which had accompanied the Risorgimento did not last — particularly when it gradually became apparent that unification would not lead to economic and social integration, and that the North-South differential might, if anything, have suffered as a result of Count Cavour's underhand diplomacy. In the life and work of Gabriele d'Annunzio — poet of the radical right — patriotism and 'spiritual renovation' became an excuse for gory, ornate and decadent adventures. D'Annunzio's most recent biographer, Philippe Jullian, has shown how the 'curious gusto' with which the poet and playwright described 'brutal scenes, revolting infirmities and degrading superstitions' foreshadows the film works of Visconti, Pasolini and even de Sica. 'The world of d'Annunzio the realist was a *mondo cane* both comic and primitive.' In 1913, d'Annunzio rewrote the subtitles and gave some coherence to the story of Giovanni Pastrone's epic silent film *Cabiria* (the Greek word means 'born of fire'). Apart from being the first film to make extensive use of the tracking shot on static scenes, a technique which was still being given extraordinary prominence in Italian popular films of the 1960s, this classical extravaganza introduced the muscleman Maciste to Italian audiences — and it was Sergio Leone's father who 'discovered' the original Maciste in the person of Bartolomeo Pagano, a Genoese docker. Maciste was not the first muscleman to appear in an Italian 'epic': the huge success of *Quo Vadis* (Enrico Guazzoni, 1912) had made *Cabiria* possible, and the character of Ursus in *Quo Vadis* provided a 'model' for Fulvius Axilla's giant, trusty slave in Pastrone's follow-up. (In *Quo Vadis*, for example, Ursus performed the amazing feat of rescuing a virgin tied to the back of an enraged wild bull.) But d'Annunzio did manage to inject some humour into the formula role (almost sending up the character of Ursus): as Maciste bends the solid metal bars of his prison, at one point, a title reads 'Maciste meanwhile is whiling away the hours.' Perhaps this explains why Pagano proved to be the most popular of the early muscle-

men, appearing in over fifteen sequels during the next ten years.

Are Sergio Leone's invincible Western heroes the spiritual descendants of d'Annunzio's proto-Fascist superman? Maciste went on to exemplify the triumph of the torso during the successful revival of the Italian 'epic' in the early 1960s, just before the Spaghetti Western boom. Certainly, Philippe Jullian's description of d'Annunzio's early style, a weird fusion of the 'gaiety of Goldoni' with a decadent fascination for the morbid, could well be applied to Leone's first Western, *A Fistful of Dollars* — an exuberant, brutal reworking of the '*Servant of Two Masters* plot'. But an equally convincing case could be made, stressing the connections between the 'Gringo/Mexican', 'Anglo/Greaser' theme in Leone's work, and the analysis of the conflict between the 'splendidly isolated life of the proud man' and the clan mentality of the Italians, which is contained in the writings of Antonio Gramsci, secretary general of the Italian Communist Party in the 1920s; the evident relish with which Leone treats the earthier aspects of Italian peasant culture could also, perhaps, be related to this tradition. Some of the later Spaghetti Westerns, as we shall see, make much of the theme of an agrarian *rivoluzione mancata*. But it is, in fact, extremely difficult to locate Leone's 'Dollars' Westerns in the Italian *political* spectrum (from the evidence of the films alone) and to give them catch-all labels. He often said at the time he was making these films that 'as men working in show-business, we have no right to prick the political conscience of our contemporaries. We are not *magisters*. The films we make ought to make people think. We are professional "exciters". But we are not directors of conscience. The audience should be allowed to draw their own conclusions.' Other, more engagé directors and scriptwriters of Italian Westerns are more easy to label politically as men of the Left; their relationship *vis-à-vis* what Geoffrey Nowell-Smith calls 'the two main cultural forces' in Italian political life — 'Marxism (and its penumbra) and Catholicism (and its penumbra)' — is a flexible, though clearly articulated one. But Leone's stance — as a conjurer 'presenting' his tricks to the public — makes him more difficult to locate, in these terms (unless the stance itself is interpreted as a political act of sorts). His family background is one of resistance to Mussolini's regime: in contrast to film-makers such as Mario Bonnard, Mario Camerini and Riccardo

Freda (all of whom, incidentally, were still making popular films in the early 1960s), Roberto Leone Roberti fell foul of the regime (specifically, the Institute of Enlightenment) and was forcibly prevented from making films after 1941. Both sides of Leone's family were deeply involved in the Italian film industry — his mother, Bice Valerian, as a popular star, his father, 'Roberto Roberti', as a less popular director specialising in sentimental, dialect comedies with a 'message': in other words, as professional entertainers who started working well before the rise of Fascism, in the silent era, but, in the case of Roberto, who also attempted to communicate ideas which were opposed to the regime, in the period 1938-41. This background, this combination, explains a lot about Sergio Leone's films. Yet, from the evidence of these films alone, Sergio's position *vis-à-vis* the 'two main cultural forces' in Italian political life is a complex one. His interpretation of history (like Bertolucci's in *1900*) is populist rather than materialist. He seems to be anti-clerical, yet all the ritual confrontations in his films are presented as if they were part of the liturgy. He is clearly critical of a society based on 'amoral familism', yet he *celebrates* the duplicity and double-dealing which that society engenders. In the 'Dollars' trilogy, his attitude towards Catholicism (or towards the iconography of Catholicism) represents one of the key 'hidden structures' which make the films comprehensible — as we shall see; and in his last three films (roughly from 1967 onwards), he seems to recognise that 'Marxism (and its penumbra) and Catholicism (and its penumbra)' are both cultural forces which he must, at some level, address. But the specific tradition within which his films operate *could* derive from either d'Annunzio or Gramsci. And it is even possible (some would say likely) that Leone is simply having a good time at everyone's expense. In short, the films alone do not provide us with enough interpretable evidence to answer questions of this kind. They need to be contextualised, so that the channel of communication between film and audience can, as far as possible, be recovered. Consequently, more useful ways into the politics of Leone's films in particular (and of Spaghetti Westerns in general) can be found in contextual accounts of Italian social and cultural development (such as Barzini's), in sociological surveys (such as Banfield's), and in recent debates about 'frontier mythology' (debates which were mirrored in, and foreshadowed by, Leone's

'vision' of the Wild West): his treatment of this mythology, and of related issues such as violence, the role of the 'almighty dollar', the impact of the railroads, the American Civil War, and immigration, may account for the revival of interest in Spaghetti Westerns, in post-Vietnam, post-Watergate America. Perhaps it is politically significant (as Andrew Sarris has suggested) that Italy, like Japan and Germany, should produce 'Westerns' in which the hero lives on his wits, prefers survival to 'honour', revenge to social morality, and has little faith in the 'progressive' aspects of the era in which he lives — this in an atmosphere of extreme brutality: for all three were defeated nations in the Second World War. 'Axis Westerns', so to speak. Sergio Leone has recalled his first encounter with the Americans:

> In my childhood, America was like a religion. Throughout my childhood and adolescence (and I am by no means sure that I have grown out of that stage even now, although I passed the age of forty a long time ago), I dreamed of the wide open spaces of America. The great expanses of desert. The extraordinary 'melting-pot', the first nation made up of people from all over the world. The long, straight roads — very dusty or very muddy — which begin nowhere, and end nowhere — for their function is to cross the whole continent. Then real-life Americans abruptly entered my life — in jeeps — and upset all my dreams. They had come to liberate me! I found them very energetic, but also very deceptive. They were no longer the Americans of the West. They were soldiers like any others, with the sole difference that they were victorious soldiers. Men who were materialist, possessive, keen on pleasures and earthly goods. In the GIs who chased after our women, and sold their cigarettes on the black market, I could see nothing that I had seen in Hemingway, Dos Passos or Chandler. Nor even in Mandrake, the magician with the outsized heart, or Flash Gordon. Nothing — or almost nothing — of the great prairies, or of the demi-gods of my childhood.

Mussolini and the Institute of Enlightenment had built up the Italian film industry into a powerful propaganda force: the post-war neo-realist boom, for example, would not have been possible without such a well-established 'home-grown' industry. But Anglo-American military occupation policy also ensured that free flow of 'democratic' films, from Hollywood to Rome, became a crucial component in the post-war Italian industry. According to Jeremy Tunstall (in *The Media Are American*, 1977), 'the longer-term position of Rome as the major foreign bastion of Hollywood was soon foreshadowed by the enormous strength of American films in the Italian market. In 1948, only 11 per cent of all films exhibited in Italy were Italian products, while 73 per cent were American or British products.' By the 1950s, this domination of the Italian film industry was accompanied by the arrival of Hollywood film crews in Rome (to take advantage of the Cinecittà production system, already a 'mini-Hollywood', for the making of classical 'epics'): a standard joke at the time, first told by a Paramount executive of course, was 'A Dino de Laurentiis Production is a Hollywood team on location in Rome.' The Westerns made in Italy date from a time when the sun had just set on the Samuel Bronston empire — the second American media invasion of Italy: American producers had just pulled out of Cinecittà, because of rising costs, and because the craze for classical 'spectaculars' — 'conspicuous production' — had passed. Shortly after the Americans left, some of the larger Italian companies (such as Titanus) went spectacularly bust. The Westerns were mostly directed by men who had first entered the industry during the post-war neo-realist period (see my Filmography), had gained their first experience with important productions (as co-writers or assistants) just after Marshall Aid ceased, and who were young enough to be a generation away from the actual fighting in the war: they had learned their trade, Hollywood-style, side by side with American directors, and characteristically, on films which were directly derived (in the first instance) from the Hollywood originals. Some of them had written about Hollywood films in popular magazines and critical journals, before the American invasion of the film capital began in the mid to late 1950s. Others had first made their reputations writing manifestos in favour of neo-realism, in the late 1940s. The more seasoned contributors to the genre had already made (or written) films which dealt with the impact of the Americans on Italian political or social life. Franco Solinas, for example, later to become scriptwriter of the most successful political Spaghettis, had launched Francesco Rosi's quartet of films about political corruption in post-war Italy, with his script for *Salvatore Giuliano*

(1961); Rosi's *Lucky Luciano* (1973), the fourth film of the cycle, was to deal specifically with the relationship between the invading American forces and the Neapolitan Mafia in 1943-4. Carlo Lizzani had already directed several films which were concerned with the use of 'bandits' (American or Sicilian) for a variety of political purposes.

The relationship between the rising generation of film-makers at Cinecittà, and 'Hollywood', then, provides one *specific* context for the making of the first Italian Westerns, and to some extent explains the form they took. A combination of professional expertise in Hollywood film techniques, and cynicism about the values which the 'classical' Hollywood Western had epitomised, is apparent not only in Leone's films (the most obvious example) but in the whole Spaghetti Western cycle as well. By the early 1970s (when the boom was beginning to slow down), the Italian film industry was, after the American, the world's second largest exporter of feature films; but, as Jeremy Tunstall has pointed out, this export performance can be interpreted, paradoxically, as 'an indirect extension of Anglo-American influence.... The countries which are strong regional exporters of media tend themselves to be unusually heavy importers of American media.' Such an economic context, Tunstall continues, often results in hybrid cultural forms. As we have seen, the Italian Westerns were characteristically directed by film-makers whose training included work on both 'neo-realist' projects (a 'realist' aesthetic, and, as Bazin so often stressed, 'authentically Italian'), and Hollywood classical epics (a 'fantasy' aesthetic, based on the primacy of Hollywood visual 'codes'): perhaps for this reason, many of the Spaghettis use 'realistic' backgrounds (a 'peep-show' view of history) as a *strategy*, in their attempt to redefine the language of the Hollywood Western.

Jeremy Tunstall concludes his analysis of 'media imperialism' with the suggestion that such hybrid cultural forms should be the subject of very detailed study: 'In many countries there are older cultural forms which continue in vigorous existence, although modified by western influences. Pop music often takes this form; "eastern westerns" or the Latin American *telenovelas* are other examples. The debate should, then, be about whether such hybrid forms are primarily traditional and "authentic" or whether they are merely translations or imitations of Anglo-American forms.' The fact that Cinecittà produced Westerns at all may signify the impact of Hollywood on the Italian film industry; but the form these Italian Westerns took — redefining the dominant 'codes' of Hollywood within an authentically Italian cultural context, and questioning the values which these 'codes' had traditionally been held to represent — places any study of them within the terms of reference which Tunstall outlines. That is one of the purposes of my analysis.

The Studio

Cinecittà Studios, like Hollywood (and like some studios producing films for popular consumption in Brazil, Mexico, Egypt, Hong Kong and Bombay), had a *tradition* of producing mass-appeal films (some innovative, some repetitively formula) within a variety of genres, in the years before the Italian Westerns. Between the early 1950s and the mid-1960s, Italian (and, later, Spanish) producers working at Cinecittà Studios had made various attempts to anticipate (or exploit) the taste of Italian urban cinemagoers, by hi-jacking entire film genres — the most notable being the 'film-fumetto' (1948-54), the farcical comedy, often of a dialect kind (1955-8), the 'sword and sandal' epic (1958-64), the horror film (1959-63), the *World by Night* or *Mondo Cane* genre (1962-4), and the spy story derived from James Bond (1964-7). Many of these Cinecittà films were made in assembly-line circumstances which resembled those of Hollywood 'B' features, or even TV series: shooting schedules which seldom over-ran a five- or six-week norm; budgets averaging below $200,000; the more solid sets used over and over again; only two or three 'takes' per shot; post-synchronised sound and dialogue tracks (even in the Italian versions); and the same pieces of action footage frequently turning up in 'disguised' form. It has been said of Hollywood 'B' Westerns that the acting talent of the cowboy-hero never extended beyond the ability to say 'heck' with his hands tied behind his back, and that, where the Indians were concerned, if they were hostile they were expensive, so there were an awful lot of friendly Indians. The assembly-line products of 'the belching stomach of Italy' (as Pasolini christened the Roman film studios) have often been associated with similar limitations.

William Price Fox, a reporter on the *Saturday Evening Post*, visited Cinecittà in the spring of 1968, to watch a Spaghetti Western being made; and his comments, although more than a little 'Hollywood-centric', give a rough idea of the studio's production methods. Fox starts by interviewing an expatriate Hollywood film-producer, who works at Cinecittà and who prefers to go by the name of 'Jennings Clayton'. As the two men sit in the Café Doney on the Via Veneto, watching all the extras go by, the producer reveals some tricks of the trade. He explains that the Roman producers of Cinecittà formula films often have only enough cash to film for a few days. By showing the first week's shooting to the distributors, they may be able to finance the second week — and so on. 'The pressure', says 'Jennings Clayton', 'is incredible.' He continues: 'Check the names on the marquees and the bill-boards. Lot of them are look-alikes. Damn promoters think some sap will read Warren Beatton and pay his money thinking it's Warren Beatty. I heard one was trying out Clark Grant.' ' "Clayton" hitchhiked his thumb at some ex-gladiators from the old muscle pictures, sitting behind us with their biceps bunched and straining against their shirt sleeves. "Few years back, anyone with a good set of pectorals and a fifty-five-inch chest was a star. Now all that's being shot is Westerns. The muscle boys are dead. Hell, you put two guns, a pair of chaps and a belt of ammo around one of them, and he photographs like a heavy cruiser." '

Next, Fox interviews 'Rod Dana', another American expatriate, who originally went to Rome to study singing and who wound up carrying a spear in *Cleopatra*. 'Rod Dana' now earns his living in Spaghetti Westerns. He takes the interviewer to the Fono-Roma dubbing studios. 'Rod explained that actors don't like to spoil their images by taking bit roles, but they can and do take dubbing jobs. The jobs pay well, and the audience doesn't know or care whose voices are being used.' He shows off the new electronic equipment that can 'split a word in half and slug in a syllable', and explains how the dubbing track can be made to match the filmed lip movements. The obvious advantage of this process is that, since a picture can be shot virtually as a silent film, there are no problems either with noise or with actors speaking different languages.

The projection room was dark. Rod and a tall cowboy actor stood at two lighted podiums, facing the screen. The cowboy had a hangover and was gripping the stand, trying to steady his nerves while he looked at the script in front of him. At the side of the room, with his dog at his feet, sat John Gayford, the dubbing director. Gayford's job is to help the dubbers synchronise their speeches with the lip movements on the film, and he is allowed to make on-the-spot changes in the script when necessary. In the scene they were doing that morning, a man about to be shot was digging his own grave. In the script, the gunman about to kill him said, 'OK, half-breed, you'd better say your prayers.' Watching the film closely, Rod tried the line. It didn't work. It was too short. The lips on the screen were still moving after Rod stopped talking. Gayford said, 'Change the "OK" to "all right". And try a chuckle on the end.' They ran it once, twice. The third time it was perfect.

Eventually, Fox gets to interview an American actor, Hunt Powers, on the set of a Spaghetti Western being shot at Cinecittà. It is called *The Greatest Robbery in the West*.

The director, Maurizio Lucidi, who got his movie training cutting film for Orson Welles, speaks English, Spanish, Italian, French and German. When I explained my assignment, he looped his arm over my shoulder, gave me a script to read and told me to talk to anyone I wanted. Said the movie was going to be great — a combination of *Desperate Hours* and *High Noon* — a sure sale to America. . . . I went out behind the set with the script. Strange choppy story, strange bad dialogue. A sample of Italian 1880 — Western conversation: 'As soon as the guide comes, we *cut* out.' When Lucidi asked me what I thought of the script, I told him I didn't like it much. 'Don't worry. We'll change it as we go along. You won't recognise it when we're through.' I asked him why have any script then? 'We need an idea of where we're going. Watch a few shots. You'll understand.' A scene was set up. The camera, the arc lights and the reflectors were pointed at the porch of the general store.

Leaning and sitting on the porch rail and steps were Erika Blank from Trieste, who speaks Italian; George Hilton from Uraguay, who speaks Spanish; Katia Christine from Holland, who spoke French on the set; and Hunt Powers and Walter Barnes, another American, who spoke English. As the reflectors were jockeyed to catch the sun and kill the shadows, Lucidi shouted '*Silenzio!*' Then, '*Luci!*' The lights came on. '*Azione!*' The scene began. Lucidi was everywhere, begging for more enthusiasm, more humour, pathos, understanding. The actors' different languages mixed in the air. Checking the Italian version of the script, Lucidi moved his hands apart and together, indicating how long or short each speech should be. Between takes, I asked him who would be starred. 'We have three stars', he said. 'In Germany, Walter Barnes gets the top billing. He has a big following up there. If the film goes to Spain, George Hilton becomes the star. If America, Hunt Powers. It's really up to the distributors; they decide who will bring the public in.'

During the siesta time between scenes, Hunt Powers, a member of the Actors' Studio since 1957, reminisces about his experiences at Cinecittà:

He told me about a sensitive American 'method' actor who came over to play 'meaningful' roles. After learning his own lines and those of everyone else in his scenes, the actor was ready for the first day's shooting. It was a Western. In his first scene, he was to rush into the colonel's office and describe a massacre. The colonel, played by one of the biggest stars in Rome, was supposed to calm him down, tell him that his wife was safe, and then give him instructions about how to protect the fort. The camera began rolling. The actor raced into the office, delivered his breathless report in fine dramatic style, and waited. The colonel, in full-dress uniform and standing before the American flag and a photograph of Lincoln, snapped to attention, looked him dead in the eye, and then slowly and expressively began counting to ten.

The implication of this story is that the Roman actor knew his job a great deal better than his American, 'method' counterpart.

Hunt Powers then talks about a scene in which he had appeared the day before. Although he is playing a gunfighter, for some reason Powers wears a Franciscan monk's robe for the role throughout the film. In the scene he is discussing, Powers

> spread his monk's robe out near a church altar and made love to an actress named Sonia Romanoff. He said it was an Italian first, but Lucidi and the producer Mr. Mattei were playing it safe; they had taken away the monk's robe and the altar for a second shooting. Powers said Italy was tame compared to Spain. In Spain, horses are actually blown up, their entrails thrown at the camera for close-ups. . . . 'I'll tell you the clincher,' he said. 'They were doing a scene about a man shot with a gold bullet. The doctor was probing for it, and the guy was sweating and biting down on a piece of rawhide. All of a sudden the director had a brainstorm. He had the doc find the bullet, hold it up, and shout 'Gold!' Then someone else shouted it, and nine men stampeded over and started clawing at the poor guy's stomach looking for more.' 'You're kidding!' 'I'm not. I think they finally cut the scene for export, but they like plenty of blood over here.'

When Hunt Powers and William Price Fox finally see the rushes of the 'love-scene' mentioned above, they discover that 'there was no sign of either the monk's robe or the church altar. Lucidi and Mattei had apparently decided to go for the Vatican Seal of Approval.'

If one ignores the obvious 'asides' about the crudities of Italian popular film-making (and Spanish audiences), Fox's article on the making of a Spaghetti Western points to several important facets of the Cinecittà system: the need to attract co-production money, if possible; the key role played by Spanish producers and audiences (and cheap Spanish labour on location work); the hasty shooting schedules and the necessity of dubbing (more up-market products, by contrast, being shot in various foreign-language versions); the use of pseudonyms (a relatively recent phenomenon — most directors of muscleman epics worked under their own names); the flexibility about scripts, and the strange compulsion to make this film more bizarre than the last one. This system — evidence of the tendency of Cinecittà producers to capture audiences rather than to keep them, to seize on any immediately available consumer

potential — has been interpreted by Lino Miccichè as 'in many ways typical of the popular cinema of underdeveloped regions — the *comedieta populachera* of Mexico, the Egyptian *song-film*, the Brazilian *chanchada*, the Indian "picturised song", the South American *telenovela*, and Italy's film-fumetto'. By the time of the Spaghetti Western boom, this 'capturing' of audiences (Miccichè calls it 'rape'), this pitching of a fresh 'genre' at (predominantly Southern) Italian urban audiences when the products of the assembly-line ceased to get top figures on the home market, had been a characteristic of the Cinecittà production system for over ten years. In 1952, out of 134 films made, over 30 per cent fall into the category of the 'film-fumetto', or the sentimental tearjerker. The next genre to achieve the same *scale* of success was the 'sword and sandal' epic: before 1957, only about ten of these films had been made at Cinecittà (although, as we have seen, the tradition goes right back to the origins of Italian cinema); between 1958 and 1964, over 170 were produced (about 10 per cent of all Cinecittà films, including co-productions). After that, it was the turn of the 'World', 'Night' and 'Sexy' films to be made in assembly-line circumstances — a 'genre' initiated (in all innocence, if that is the correct word) by Alessandro Blasetti's *Europe by Night* (1959): the extraordinary success of this, and, later, of Jacopetti's *Mondo Cane*, opened the flood-gates — *World by Night*; *World by Night No. 2*; *Hot World by Night*; *World on the Beach*; *Sexy World by Night*; *World by Night No. 3*; *Forbidden World*; *Mad World by Neon*; *Naked World*; *Sweet Night*; *Naked Night*; *Hot Night of the Orient*; *America by Night*; *Sexy*; *Sexy by Neon Lights*; *Sexy by Neon Lights No. 2*; *Sexy in the Sheets*; *Mad Sexy*; *World of Sexy*; *Naked Sexy*; *Forbidden Sexy*; *Very Forbidden Sexy*; *Africa Sexy* . . . And when the fee-paying customers had become tired of glimpses into forbidden 'worlds', of living vicariously 'by night', and of staring at 'sexy' antics (the films were nearly all shot in Roman studios, in fact), these 'last decaying dregs of what had once been neo-realism' (as Geoffrey Nowell-Smith puts it) made way for the James Bond derivatives and the Spaghetti Westerns. Between 1964 and 1967, Cinecittà produced about fifty films (in parallel to the Westerns) chronicling the adventures of spies with all kinds of license to kill: after 007, Agents *777*, *Sigma 3*, *S53*, *S03*, *3S3*, *X77*, *X1-7*, *Z55*, *A077*, *A009*, *A008*, *A001*, *2+5*, *OSS117*,

OSS77, S2S, S-007, 7X3, 00, and 002 — and those were just the agents with no names. Ironically, back home in England, when Ian Fleming became tired of writing James Bond thrillers, he turned to books about *Thrilling Cities* (numbers 1 and 2).

The genre which seems to have had the most direct connection with the Spaghetti Western was the 'sword and sandal' epic (christened by French critics 'les pepla', after the Latin plural of 'peplum', a typical garment worn in ancient times). Some of the directors of Westerns, as we shall see, first made their names in this genre: Sergio Corbucci made three, Domenico Paolella made seven, Mario Bava made four and Sergio Leone made two. Other directors (the most prolific) included Pietro Francisci (eight), Riccardo Freda (five), Vittorio Cottafavi (seven), and the veteran Carmine Gallone (four).

(Gallone had made his first epic in 1937, *Scipio Africanus* — one of the purposes of which was to 'legitimise' Mussolini's activities in Africa.) The best-known stars of the 1960s 'peplums' were Steve Reeves, Mark Forest, Reg Park, Kirk Morris, Ed Fury and Dan Vadis ('brother of Quo?' asked Raymond Durgnat), and some of these, for example Steve Reeves, attempted to transfer their talents to Spaghetti Westerns. The trouble was that, as ex-Mr Universes, they tended to 'photograph like heavy cruisers'. Many of these Cinecittà mini-epics featured the four muscleman heroes Hercules, Maciste, Ursus and Samson: of the two 'home-grown' heroes, Ursus had begun his cinematic career in *Quo Vadis* (1912), Maciste in *Cabiria* (1913). The accompanying chart, showing all the films in which these heroes appeared (between 1958 and 1965), will

	HERCULES	MACISTE	URSUS	SAMSON
1958	*Hercules*			
1959	*Hercules Unchained*			
1960	*The Loves of Hercules* *The Revenge of Hercules* *The Strength of Hercules**	*Maciste in the Valley of the Kings*	*Ursus*	
1961	*Hercules at the Centre of the Earth* *Hercules Conquers Atlantis* *Ulysses Against Hercules*	*Maciste in the Court of the Great Khan* *Maciste Against the Vampires* *The Triumph of Maciste* *Maciste — Strongest Man in the World* *Maciste in the Land of the Cyclops* *Totò Against Maciste*	*The Revenge of Ursus* *Ursus and the Tartar Girl*	*Samson*
1962	*The Fury of Hercules*	*Maciste Goes to Hell* *The Gladiator of Rome* *Maciste Against the Monsters* *Maciste Against the Sheik* *Maciste — Strongest Gladiator in the World*	*Ursus in the Valley of the Lions* *Ursus in the Land of Fire* *Ursus, Terror of the Khirghiz* *Ursus — Rebel Gladiator*	

1963	Hercules Against Moloch	Maciste Against the Axe-Men** Maciste — Greatest Hero in the World Zorro Against Maciste	Samson Against the Pirates Samson And the Black Pirate
1964	Hercules Against the Sons of the Sun Hercules Against the Tyrant of Babylon The Gladiator from Messalina Hercules Against Rome Hercules Versus Samson The Triumph of Hercules	Maciste in the Court of the Tsar Maciste Against the Men in the Moon Maciste Against the Mongols Maciste and the Queen of Samar Maciste, Gladiator of Sparta Maciste in the Hell of Genghis Khan Maciste in King Solomon's Mines	Samson and the Treasure of the Incas Samson against the Seven Saracens Samson Against Hercules***
1965	Battle of the Giants The Magnificent Gladiator Hercules the Invincible	The Invincible Brothers Maciste	
TOTAL:	19	23	7	6

These titles have, in most cases, been translated from the Italian. The films which were exported often underwent title changes in the process — in particular, Maciste's name was often removed since he was a little-known muscleman outside Italy.

* The original title, Le Pillole di Ercole, seems to contain an untranslatable pun — Pillars, Pills, Balls.

** Literally, Maciste Against the Men Who Chop Heads Off.

*** This seems to be a different film to the 'Hercules' item in the same year: Ercole Contro Sansone, as opposed to Ercole Sfida Sansone.

Ursus (1960) was the most successful of these films on home release, followed closely by the two Pietro Francisci 'Hercules' films (1958, 1959), both starring Steve Reeves. Late in 1965, the four heroes all joined forces for Hercules, Samson, Maciste and Ursus the Invincibles — a final attempt to recapture audiences to the genre, which, however, took less than a quarter of the receipts of these 'Ursus' and 'Hercules' films. Cinecittà producers had to learn the hard way that dynamic tension was no longer enough.

perhaps help to clarify the dynamics of the Roman production system.

Having established these characters as popular heroes — and having centred the genre on the need for muscle-power to resolve almost any problem (including, in one film, the thermo-nuclear bomb), in contrast to the 'film-fumetto', where it was always virtue that triumphed after a long and melodramatic struggle — the producers, scriptwriters and directors then used their ingenuity to invent ever more bizarre adversaries for their fabulous strongmen. At first, these adversaries were Greeks and Barbarians: it was the American producers and scriptwriters working in Cinecittà at this time who inherited the mantle of Mussolini's 'Roman grandeur' epics; the Italians preferred Greek mythology, or comic-strip mythologies of their own concoction. But unlike the Hollywood producers, who often featured eminent American historians in their souvenir brochures, the Italians did not feel in any way bound by considerations of 'authenticity', or by the 'lessons of the past'. So they were free to set their heroes against assorted Atlanteans, Tyrants of Babylon, Vampires, Shieks, Tsars, Men in the Moon, Pirates, even popular comedians of the day, as the cycle progressed. Mario Bava (a horror director) explored the possibilities of challenging Maciste against the Vampires. Riccardo Freda, in *Maciste Goes to Hell*, began with a horror film setting (an eighteenth-century Scottish mansion), then used clips from three previous 'Maciste' films (including *Maciste in the Land of the Cyclops*) to fill out the story. In *Zorro Against Maciste* and *Samson and the Treasure of the Incas*, the strongmen found themselves in Western stories, and several of the 'gladiator' variants were derived from *The Magnificent Seven* (1960). Reviewers often pointed out the connections between even early examples of the genre and 'Western' plots: for example, Georges Lenglet (in *Midi-Minuit Fantastique*, November 1962) referred to Mario Caiano's *Ulysses Against Hercules* as 'a mythological Western', in which 'Hercules-Sheriff-Olympian leads Ulysses-bandit to Jupiter, as if he was a horse rustler who ought to be lynched'. So, out of the strong, came forth . . . Westerns.

Most of the products of this rapid rhythm of production were aimed, in the first instance, exclusively at the home market. Italian directors and scriptwriters may have learned much from the American companies which moved to Rome and Spain to shoot Samuel Bronston-style epics in the early 1960s, but they seldom intended to pitch their work directly towards the American market. The Americans had other, more immediate uses — at the production end. Since the money which American companies earned in Europe had to be spent in Europe (for tax reasons), there was always the chance of negotiating co-production deals, or of finding work for Cinecittà extras and technicians on American productions based in Rome. Bronston's *King of Kings*, for example, one of the more tedious examples of a Hollywood epic with 'cultural' pretensions (directed, alas, by Nicholas Ray) was originally planned (and promoted) as a 'creative' way of using up American companies' frozen dollars in Spain and Italy. And American impresarios were, of course, sometimes quick off the mark when it came to spotting the investment potential of the Italian product. Whether or not the more elaborate 'peplums' were originally intended for home consumption only, they were ready for distribution very soon after completion, they cost a fraction of their American counterparts, and it was far cheaper to buy the rights (both at home and abroad) — as Joseph E. Levine discovered to his profit. In 1958, he bought the rights to Pietro Francisci's *Hercules* for $35,000, spent a million advertising his product, and still made a clear $4 million on the deal. Francisci's follow-up, *Hercules Unchained* (1959 — originally called *Hercules and the Queen of Lidia*), made even more money by the same process. When it came to the Westerns, United Artists bought the rights to Leone's first two 'Dollars' films (American domestic release) for $35,000 and $70,000 respectively (we have already seen how good an investment these proved to be).

Perhaps the most crucial side-effect of this Cinecittà production system, from the point of view of this study, was a certain *competitiveness* between rival production companies working within a given genre, which in turn sometimes led to a type of internal pressure towards bizarre experimentation (and may even account, to some extent, for the wilder excesses of, for example, horror masters such as Mario Bava, or 'peplum' masters such as Vittorio Cottafavi). Having described the effects of this *competitiveness* where Hercules, Maciste, Ursus and Samson were concerned, it is time to relate it to the assembly-line genre which took off after the success of *A Fistful of Dollars* in the 1964-5 season — the Spaghetti Western.

25-7 Some Cinecittà muscleman heroes, 1958-62: Ursus (Ed Fury) in *Ursus in the Land of Fire* (1962); Hercules (Steve Reeves) in *The Labours of Hercules* (1958); and a less muscular Hercules (Reg Park) in *Hercules Conquers Atlantis* (1961), an inventive send-up of the whole genre

Umberto Eco, the semiologist, has provided a useful model for analysing the relationship between commercial imperatives (in our case, represented by the Cinecittà mode of organisation) and formula artefacts (in our case, represented by the Spaghetti Western): Eco produced this model from his structural reading of DC Comics' 'Superman' stories ('The Myth of Superman', *Diacritics*, Spring 1972), but, as we shall see, it can be applied — suitably modified — just as aptly to the heroes of the Italian Western. The conclusion reached at the end of the 'Superman' article is that in a comic-strip genre of that type, which has 'mythological' pretensions, the possibilities for character and plot development are extremely limited — by definition. Any development of the formula will thus tend to take the form of new settings (more spectacular, more bizarre, more fetishistic — although bearing some relationship to 'everyday life'), and varied treatments of Superman's technological problems (how will he do it? will he be resourceful enough to solve *this* one? etc); so long as Superman retains all his 'familiar gestures' and behaves in his stock way (above all, he must *never* form lasting relationships), the demands of the readership will be constantly satisfied. If the comic-strip hero is placed in settings which are too bizarre, too early, he is likely to die the death — Dick Tracy perhaps being an example of this process. Before applying Eco's conclusions (and, with them, his model) to the Cinecittà Western formula, it is worth looking more closely at the main stages in his argument.

Umberto Eco begins by outlining the characteristics of the 'mythological hero' in an industrial society: 'Often the hero's virtue is humanised and his powers, rather than being supernatural, are the extreme realisation of natural endowments such as astuteness, swiftness, fighting ability, or even the logical faculties and the pure spirit of observation found in Sherlock Holmes. In an industrial society, however, where man becomes a number in the realm of the organisation which has usurped his decision-making role, he has no means of production and is thus deprived of his power to decide. Individual strength, if not exerted in sports activities, is left abased when confronted with the strength of machines which determine man's very movements. In such a society, the positive hero must embody to an unthinkable degree the power demands that the average citizen nurtures but cannot satisfy.' Having established 'the undeniable mythological connota-

tion' of Superman, in these terms, Eco proceeds to examine the narrative structure through which the myth is offered daily or weekly to the public, in order to analyse the 'fundamental difference between the figure of Superman and traditional heroic figures of classical and nordic mythology': he concludes that, whereas the classical hero had an irreversible destiny, and a *story* (a well-known story, which characterised his heroic features, and made the mythical hero come alive), the modern popular hero (for example, the hero of a best-selling novel) is part of a story 'in which the reader's main interest is transferred to the unpredictable nature of *what will happen* and, therefore, to the plot invention which now holds our attention'; so the (classical) mythic potential of the character — his predictability — must to some extent be sacrificed to 'this new dimension of the story'. 'The mythological character of comic strips finds himself in this singular situation: he must be an archetype, the totality of certain collective aspirations, and therefore, he must necessarily become immobilised in an emblematic and fixed nature which renders him easily recognisable (this is what happens to Superman): but since he is marketed in the sphere of a "romantic" production for a public that consumes "romance", he must be subjected to a development which is typical of novelistic characters.' The problem is compounded by the fact that Superman, by definition a character whom nothing can impede, finds himself in the 'worrisome narrative situation of being a hero without an adversary and therefore without the possibility of any development. . . . Aesthetically and commercially deprived of the possibility of narrative development, Superman gives serious problems to his scriptwriters.' The solution — or synthesis — occurs, by the simple expedient of putting Superman to the test of various obstacles which are exciting because they are unforeseen by the audience, but which are, however, always surmountable by the hero: 'first of all, the reader is struck by the strangeness of the obstacles — diabolically conceived inventions, curiously equipped apparitions from outer space, etc . . . second, thanks to the hero's unquestionable superiority, the crisis is rapidly resolved, and the account is maintained within the bounds of the short story'. But this raises another problem: if Superman succeeds in conquering these obstacles (as he always must) he has *accomplished something*, and this means that 'he has made a gesture which is inscribed in his past and weighs on his future'; in other words, by his actions, Superman has 'consumed' himself. Since Superman is not a god (one condition of his acceptance by the public is the fact that he is 'immersed in everyday life', even if endowed with superior faculties), he must be 'consumed' according to the ways of everyday life; yet Superman *cannot* be allowed to 'consume himself', since, as a mythic hero of sorts, he is 'inconsumable' — another problem for the scriptwriters. The solution is to break down all sense of the passage of time *between the stories*, and to present the actual stories in a dream-like climate 'where what has happened before and what has happened after appears extremely hazy'. 'In the sphere of a story, Superman accomplishes a given job (he routs a band of gangsters); at this point the story ends. In the same comic book, or in the edition of the following week, a new story begins. If it took Superman up again at the point where he left off, he would have taken a step towards death. On the other hand, to begin a story without showing that another had preceded it would manage, momentarily, to remove Superman from the law which leads from life to death through time. In the end (Superman has been around since 1938), the public would realise the comicality of the situation.' So the narrator is forced to pick up the strand of a given event again and again, 'as if he had forgotten to say something and wanted to add details to what had already been said'. One example: Superman can never be allowed to develop permanent relationships (or be saddled with 'irreversible premises'), so emphasis must be placed on 'the platonic dimension of his affections, the implicit vow of chastity which depends less on his will than on the state of things, and the singularity of his situation . . . this is one of the conditions that prevents him slowly "consuming" himself, and protects him from the events, and therefore from the passing of time, connected with erotic ventures'. A confused notion of time is thus the main condition which makes the stories credible. 'Superman comes off as myth only if the reader loses control of the temporal relationships and renounces the need to reason on their basis, thereby giving himself up to the uncontrollable flux of the stories which are accessible to him and, at the same time, holding on to the illusion of a continuous present.' One side-effect of this is that the reader forgets about the problems we normally associate with the dictates of time — such as the possibility

of planning, the necessity of acting on plans, the unpleasantness that such planning may involve, and the personal responsibility that it implies — perhaps a key ingredient in the enduring success of the Superman myth.

In resolving these two problems (Superman as mythic character, who is nevertheless presented to a public which expects to be excited by *what will happen*; Superman as 'inconsumable' hero), the scriptwriters fall back on two of the staple devices of formula fiction: first, the story tends to take the form of 'a series of events repeated according to a set scheme (iteratively, in such a way that each event takes up again from a sort of virtual beginning, ignoring where the preceding event left off)' — a 'set' which structures more than just the 'plot', however (after a time this ceases to sustain any interest in itself), eventually becoming 'a fixed schematism involving the same sentiments and the same psychological attitudes' as well; and second, the writer 'introduces a continuous series of connotations, to such an extent that their reappearance in each story is an essential condition of its reading pleasure' — these will characteristically take the form of recognisable personality traits, idiosyncrasies, or 'tics', which 'permit us to find an old friend in the character portrayed', and they will in time become 'the principal conditions which allow us to "enter into" the event'. This repertoire of stock gestures ultimately becomes far more important to the reader than what may *appear* to be a new situation, or a new variation on the usual plot: 'we say *appear*; the fact is that the reader is never brought to verify the extent to which something new is told. The noteworthy moments are those when the hero repeats his usual gesture . . . the attraction of the book, the sense of repose which it is capable of conferring, lies in the fact that the reader continuously recovers, point by point, what he already knows, what he wants to know again: that is why he has purchased the book. He derives *pleasure* from the non-story; the *distraction* consists in the refutation of a development of events, in a withdrawal from the tension of past-present-future to the focus on an *instant*, which is loved because it is recurrent.' If we take the example of the formula detective story — in pulp novel or film form at least, and arguably in 'classic' form as well — at first sight the story seems to appeal to 'a taste for the unforeseen or the sensational', or even to a crossword-puzzle mentality: in fact, it is probably read 'for exactly the opposite reason, as an invitation to that which is taken for granted, familiar, expected: not knowing who the guilty party is becomes an accessory element, almost a pretext'. The *distraction* derives from following certain 'topical' gestures of 'topical' characters whose stock behaviour we already love. So long as Sherlock Holmes scrapes carelessly at his violin, Poirot worries about his appearance, Nero Wolfe looks after his orchids, and Maigret keeps puffing on his pipe, the reader's 'hunger for redundance' is satisfied. According to Eco, it does not really matter what the detectives actually *achieve* (we know they are going to crack the case). (A more recent and clear-cut example, that of the American TV cop show, illustrates his point even more directly. We have been encouraged to get to know cops who are bald, blind, fat or crippled, cops in dirty raincoats, cops with back trouble, cops who ride horses, and the main distinguishing feature about the mysteries in which these cops appear is the amount of violence — or the attitude towards violence — the stories contain. After an evening's viewing of their various exploits we may feel punch-drunk rather than relaxed, but it does nevertheless appear that, individually at least, these bundles of familiar characteristics or gestures are presenting us with 'an indulgent invitation to repose'.) Eco's insight can perhaps explain those extraordinary occasions when the reading public invents 'connotations' for popular heroes (or villains) which are not 'recognisable' enough in the original texts: Sherlock Holmes' deerstalker (mentioned only a couple of times in Conan Doyle's stories, when the detective is travelling through the countryside), Fu-Manchu's moustache (which does not feature in Sax Rohmer's original stories at all), and Jack the Ripper's top hat and Gladstone bag (for which there is no evidence) are good examples of this phenomenon. One can only assume that both Conan Doyle and Sax Rohmer were in this respect unaware of the popular impact of their own formulae: in addition, they both made the mistake of attempting to 'kill off' popular myths.

By placing so much emphasis on a 'hunger for redundance' as the key to explaining the enduring success of formula heroes, Eco seems to be suggesting that both the narratives in which these heroes operate and the 'ideological contents' of these narratives are of secondary concern: 'the problem is not to ask ourselves if different ideological contents conveyed by the same narrative scheme can elicit different effects. Rather, an iterative scheme becomes and remains that *only* to the extent that the scheme sustains and expresses a world: we realise this even more, once we understand how the world has the same configuration as the structure which expressed it. The case of Superman confirms this hypothesis. If we examine the ideological contents of Superman stories, we realise that on the one hand that content sustains itself and functions communicatively thanks to the narrative structure; on the other hand, the stories help define their expressive structure as the circular, static conveyance of a message which is substantially *immobilistic*.' Not surprisingly, Eco starts with the 'hidden' structures in *Superman*, and only then asks questions about the ideological contents of the stories: for these contents are, to him, inseparable from the structures, and vice versa; they help to define each other.

Superman, like his colleagues in DC Comics' 'Justice League of America', is 'gifted with such powers that he could actually take over the government, defeat the army, or alter the equilibrium of planetary politics. . . .' Batman's powers are the result of training while Superman's come from the planet Krypton; but both engage in activities which are superhuman, and, for our purposes at least, they are indistinguishable. However, Superman carries on his *earthly* activities at the level of the small community where he lives, and 'if he takes trips to other galaxies with ease, he practically ignores, not exactly the dimension of the "world", but that of the "United States" '. In the sphere of his own little town, he restricts his activities to combating a very specific form of evil — that of organised crime ('the only visible form that evil assumes is an attempt on private property'), organised that is, by villains who will *always* remain recidivists. 'Superman is thus a perfect example of "civic consciousness", completely split from "political consciousness". His civic attitude is perfect, but it is exercised and structured in the sphere of a small closed community.' And just as evil is represented only by offences against private property, good is represented only as charity (lending a helping hand to those in need, organising benefit performances to raise money for orphans, etc). Superman must always operate on this small scale (within this very limited moral frame of reference); his 'adventures' must always remain static, repetitive — both for precisely the same reason: if Superman started exercising 'good' on a cosmic scale (for example, creating work for the unemployed, or creating wealth for capitalism), this would 'draw the world, and Superman with it, towards final "consumption" ' (perhaps this is why the caped crusader is told by his father 'never to interfere in human history'). Superman's limited sphere of operations depends on the structure of his 'plots' (that is, on 'the need to forbid the release of excessive and irretrievable developments'): conversely, the 'plots' will remain static, and undeveloped, because Superman *must* make 'good' consist of many little activities on a small scale, 'never achieving a total awareness', because that is the particular kind of teaching which represents the adaptation of the authors 'to a concept of "order" which pervades the cultural model in which the authors live'. To write of the authors' 'ideological preferences' (Superman as ideological state apparatus, perhaps?) is thus — according to Eco — to ignore the dialectical relationship between formula, plot and action which has lain at the root of the Superman myth ever since 1938.

The reason I have discussed Eco's model of the Superman formula in such detail is that it seems to provide a set of criteria for analysing popular genre films — without resorting to elaborate discussions of narrative motifs, without having to argue a consumer sovereignty thesis, and without categorising the sponsoring bodies as 'Ideological State Apparatuses'. The 'commercial imperatives' in Eco's model are to do with *quantity* (several short stories a week, each featuring the same hero), rather than with specific *qualities* in the narrative (the Will Wright thesis); thus Eco does not have to prove that specific Superman stories were box-office hits (an index, if we are to believe Wright, of narrative 'resolutions' which especially appeal to the public) — simply that the conveyor-belt keeps moving. The analysis which follows is based on *all* the films within one sub-genre — successful or not. Of course, even comic-strip heroes respond to the dictates of fashion (witness the changing values of *Marvel* comics, since the late 1960s), but, in Eco's model, that is not the prime consideration. The commercial imperatives at Cinecittà were of a rather different order (for two or three stories a week, read sixty-six Westerns a year, in the peak production year of the Spaghetti Western, 1967; between 1964 and 1972, the *average* number of Cinecittà Westerns produced annually was over thirty); and, as we shall

see, the formula played itself out relatively quickly (it is as if Superman faded away just after the Second World War): but there is still enough in Eco's analysis to provide a frame of reference for our study of the relationship between film studio and formula product. The kind of internal pressure exerted by the Cinecittà system (a system built around formula products) on a genre which, after the commercial success of *A Fistful of Dollars*, centred on the activities of a different type of superman, may perhaps be interpreted in the light of Eco's distinction between 'romances' and comic-strip 'plot schemas'. The superman of the Italian Western does not come from a different planet (rather, from a different culture), does not lead a double-life or rely on superhuman feats of toughness (using agility and muscle-power to fight on the side of the angels): he openly leads the life of a super-efficient trickster, and relies on a superhuman endowment of *machismo* (using dexterity and fire-power to fight on the side of those who pay him best). But, according to Eco's criteria, he is still a superman. He always surmounts a series of unforeseen obstacles (as the formula developed, these were to become more spectacular, more bizarre, more fetishistic — especially where the technology of death was concerned — in the end, constituting the only important variations on the 'plot'). He never 'consumes himself', yet he operates in a setting which is crammed with details of 'everyday life' on the southwestern frontier. The films rely on a confused, dream-like treatment of time (this has less to do with the specific period in which they are set — it may be during the American Civil War, it may be during the decade afterwards — than with the absence of any temporal development *between the stories*). The hero — a product of the 'continuous series of connotations' which had proved so successful with the Man With No Name — becomes involved in a story which is 'a series of events repeated according to a set schema' (in fact, as we shall see, two distinct set schemas which are distinguishable from, though related to, our *three* variants of the 'Italian plot'); as the formula evolved, the stories may have appeared to vary significantly, but the noteworthy moments became those when the hero repeated his usual gestures (the 'suspense' arising from the question 'When will he repeat them?'). And if the hero committed himself to any one cause (banditry, revolution, law and order), or actually *spent* his dollars, he would soon cease to be a 'wandering vagabond': instead, each of the separate stories tells of how the arrival of this impoverished superman in a small town escalates tensions which were there already. Superman's moral universe may have changed (the hero characteristically works for money, and does not seem to be unduly concerned about offences against private property), but the choices which are open to his Italian Western counterpart (violent revenge, bounty-hunting) may still represent 'the scriptwriters' adaptation to the particular concept of "order" pervading the cultural model in which they live': as I tried to point out in the 'Spaghettis and Society' chapter, the parochialism of the American hero (civic consciousness divorced from political consciousness) becomes the 'amoral familism' of the Italian hero (revenge, or playing one side off against the other, without any reference to the role of the State or central government).

At the end of *A Fistful of Dollars*, Silvanito asks the Man With No Name if he would like to extend his activities beyond small-town politics, and the gunslinger replies, 'You mean the Mexican government on one side, the American government on the other, and me in the middle? . . . too difficult!' The *Fistful* formula had involved this superman with no name in a rivalry between two powerful factions — one (the stronger) Mexican, the other Gringo. In the series of Westerns featuring another hero, Django, and derived from the *Fistful* formula, the inflation or complication of 'unforeseen obstacles' which the hero will surmount takes the form of more bizarre settings, and an almost fetishistic emphasis on the hero's technological resourcefulness. Sergio Corbucci's *Django* (the film which launched the series in 1966) again locates the superman in a rivalry between two factions, only this time he has to contend with 'the Fanatics' (red-hooded Ku-Klux-Klansmen led by Major Jackson) and 'the Bandidos' (comic-opera Mexicans led by General Hugo Rodriguez, whose joviality masks an extraordinary penchant for sadism). Sergio Leone's town of widows in *Fistful* becomes a ghost-town populated only by out-of-work whores, a bartender, and a preacher who collects protection money from the brothel before roundly condemning the whores for immorality. The Man With No Name's prowess with a gun (and dramatic use of dynamite) becomes Django's machine-gun (fired from the hip), which he keeps hidden in a coffin. The comic-strip violence of *Fistful* (and especially the scene where the Rojos beat up the Man With No Name and Silvanito the bartender) becomes the comic-strip mayhem of *Django*: Maria (one of the whores; and later the hero's girl) is brutally whipped by the Bandidos, and the preacher has his ear cut off; Major Jackson shoots the peons from the surrounding countryside, for fun, and the Bandidos are sucked into the quicksand; whores wrestle in mud, and Django has his hands crushed (deliberately) by horses' hooves. The two main 'set-pieces' in *Fistful* (the exchange of hostages, and the final gundown) have their counterpart in two sequences which are located at exactly the same points in the story of *Django*. During the first, Django (Franco Nero) waits in the main street (a sea of mud), near a tree stump, his coffin by his side, with the whores looking on, as the Klansmen formally parade into town; the tension is broken as he whips open the coffin, brings out his machine-gun and opens fire. In the second, Django arranges to meet Jackson and the Fanatics for a final showdown in the cemetery at Tombstone Hill (this setting was to find its way back to Leone's trilogy, in *The Good, the Bad and the Ugly*); Django's hands have been crushed, so he rests his gun on a metal cross, and pulls back the hammer with his bloody stumps ('In the name of the Father and of the Son and of the Holy Ghost . . .'). The success of *Django* on domestic release (the film was banned outright in England) encouraged producers to extend the story by the Corbucci brothers and Franco Rossetti in even more outlandish directions. Three motifs from *Django* were to have a particularly varied life: the anti-clericalism, the emphasis on elaborate weaponry, and the 'Bandidos' subplot (which involves a conflict between those who want to use some gold to finance a revolution and those who want it for more selfish purposes). In *A Bullet for the General* (1966) the bandit/priest (Klaus Kinski) lobs grenades at the Federales 'in the name of the Father . . .'; in *Dead or Alive* (1967), after a shootout in the belfry of a church, one of the bounty-hunters looks at a priest who has died in the cross-fire, and comments, 'It is bad luck to plug padrés — they are not worth a cent . . . I will have to excommunicate him, and ordain myself'; in *Find a Place to Die* (1968), the priest turns out to be a sex maniac; and in *No Room to Die* (1969), the bounty-hunter is himself a Bible-reading preacher. Django's original way of transporting his machine-gun was to spawn a whole series of elaborate gadgets for secreting firearms:

28 German publicity for Sergio Corbucci's *Django* (1966), starring Franco Nero as the brutal anti-hero

29 Django (Franco Nero) waits in a graveyard for the final showdown

30 (*Below*) Two scenes from Corbucci's *Django*: a Mexican heavy, accompanied by a dwarf, prepares to show the town who is boss; and Klansmen bite the dust as Django lets them have it 'in the name of the

Father, the Son and the Holy Ghost'. The film was banned outright in England on account of what was considered to be its excessive brutality

GOLDEN ERA FILM DISTRIBUTORS
present
"DJANGO KILL"
'X'
TECHNICOLOR · TECHNISCOPE

1 (*Above left*) Tomas Milian (the Stranger) arrives in a shanty-town at the beginning of Questi's *Django, Kill* (1967)
2 (*Above right*) Zorro (Roberto Camardiel) parades through town with his friendly black-clad muchachos: 'You
on't know how much my muchachos mean to me, in their shiny black uniforms . . . '
3 (*Below left*) Survivors from Django's gang are hanged in the main street by the 'respectable' townsfolk, led by the
torekeeper and the hotelier
4 (*Below right*) The Stranger (Tomas Milian) is tortured and crucified by Zorro's men, in an attempt to find out where
he gold is hidden: the 'muchachos' try everything, before the Stranger finally breaks down under an attack by vampire
ats . . .

LDEN ERA FILM DISTRIBUTORS
present
"DJANGO KILL"
'X'
ECHNICOLOR · TECHNISCOPE

between 1966 and 1969 (roughly between Corbucci's *Django* and the Tony Anthony 'Stranger' series), these gadgets were to include crutches, banjos, toys, specially designed clothes, a church organ and elaborate saddle-cloths. By September 1968, Andrew Sarris was (justly) complaining that 'the Italian Western has already escalated violence and viciousness to the point of self-parody. Tony Anthony rides around in the "Stranger" series like a portable ammunition dump financed by the Warsaw pact, and just when American Westerns had become reasonably frugal with fire-arms in the workaday West. . . . The old joke about firing 20 bullets from a six-shooter without reloading is irrelevant to a genre in which gunpowder seems as plentiful as dust. How do the spaghetti sharpshooters pay for their bang-bang? The screen is seldom quiet enough for the question to be asked, much less answered.' The third motif from *Django* which was to be inflated by later Cinecittà derivatives (the theme of gold stolen for the Revolution — in *Django*, Franco Nero has his hands crushed because he has double-crossed the Mexicans over this gold), we will be encountering again when we discuss the more political Spaghetti Westerns (including those made by Sergio Corbucci). It constitutes the third variant of our 'Italian plot'. Perhaps the ultimate extension of the *Fistful* formula (mediated through Corbucci's *Django*) came in 1967, when Giulio Questi (a veteran who had been working in the industry since 1954 and who had been an assistant on Fellini's *La Dolce Vita* in 1960) made his one and only Western, *Django, Kill*. In this film, the Django character (played by Tomas Milian) finds himself unable to cope with the two rival factions who are ruling the town — the Mexican faction, which consists of black-leather-clad homosexual 'muchachos', who ride around on snow-white horses and are led by a larger-than-life bandit called Zorro ('You don't know how much my muchachos mean to me, with their shiny black uniforms'), and the puritanical townspeople (led by a storekeeper called Hagerman, who is extremely fond of his pet parrot). The climactic shootout (during which the parrot comments on the action) ends with Hagerman being drowned in molten gold. In the original Italian print of this film (which was, perhaps understandably, cut to pieces by the English censor), the violence was of an extraordinarily savage kind: murderers were roasted over a slow fire, animals disembowelled, men blinded, children shot, and

bits of human anatomy were strewn all over the dusty main street. Questi's bizarre vision of cowboys and bandits as very nasty children going through a homosexual phase may perhaps be taken as his comment on the development of the formula Spaghetti Westerns up to that time. In *Django, Kill*, the 'plot' ceases to sustain any interest at all — the film may be made up entirely of 'unforeseen obstacles' of the most outlandish kind, but the viewer still recovers, over and over again, 'what he already knows'. One Italian critic, Oreste de Fornari, has called *Django, Kill* 'a cross between the films of Jansco and an equestrian circus'. By 1967, when Questi made the film, things were beginning to get a little out of hand: an Italian magistrate seized all the copies of *Django, Kill* he could find, and a Cinecittà producer dragged Tinto Brass out of the cutting room of another Spaghetti Western, *Yankee*. It was ironic, wrote Fornari, that of all films these two should receive 'the stigma of artistic martyrdom'.

Between the production of Corbucci's *Django* in 1966 and the arrival of 'Slim Alone's' *Django Always Draws Second* (the last of the series) in 1974, twenty features chronicling the adventures of the character Django were released in Italy; several features about other Italian Western heroes (such as Sartana, Gringo, Joko, and just plain Bill) were retitled to cash in on the name Django, for French distribution, and if we include these, the total number of 'Django' films rises to over thirty. Since Django was the first of the named heroes created especially for the genre (Arizona and Ringo were inherited from the Hollywood Western, Sartana made his first appearance two years and Trinity four years later), and since Corbucci's baroque variation on the Leone formula was unusually enduring by Cinecittà standards — lasting, in one form or another, for eight years — it is worth looking briefly at the 'unforeseen obstacles' introduced in *all* the films of the series (not just the most successful), also the 'plot schemas' and the changing 'connotations' of the central hero, in the light of Umberto Eco's observations about the Superman myth. Although Corbucci's 1966 film was never shown in England, it was extremely successful both on the European market and in some Third World countries (in the Jamaican feature, Perry Henzell's *The Harder They Come* (1972), a showing of *Django* at the Kingston Rialto leads the hero to a life of violent crime, and in the last reel, when the hero is faced by impossible odds, he compares the indestructibility of his Western 'model' with the tragic (and destructive) showdown forced on him by the corrupt representatives of authority in society), encouraging Cinecittà producers constantly to reinvest in their 'phantom vagabond' formula. In *Django*, as we have seen, the hero pits his wits against two rival gangs — Major Jackson and the Ku-Klux-Klan, and General Hugo Rodriguez with his 'revolutionary' bandits. Django, a tramp with a mysterious coffin in tow, first deals with Jackson's men, then joins forces with Rodriguez to steal some government gold. After being double-crossed by the Mexicans, he runs off with the gold, but is caught and savagely mutilated. Rodriguez is then trapped and killed by Jackson and the remains of the Klan. Django returns to the village, and succeeds in defeating Jackson during a final show-down in the cemetery; his revenge is complete (throughout the film, he has been trying to settle an old score, which has something to do with the death of his wife), and he gets the girl as well (having saved her from both gangs). *Django* is thus partly a revenge film (involving the family's honour) with a 'populist' subplot, and partly a remake of *Fistful*.

Alberto de Martino's *Django Shoots First* (1966), with Glenn Saxon as the hero, tells of Django's attempts to avenge the death of his father. The culprit is a banker named Kluster, but when Django tries to take revenge, he finds that another murder has been pinned on him. The rest of the film involves Django's attempts to prove his innocence (with the aid of 'Doc', his friend), and his developing relationship with Jessica, Kluster's mistress; Kluster eventually kills Jessica, and Django shoots Kluster in a cemetery, on the grave of his father. *Django Shoots First* is again a revenge film (involving the family's honour) but he now has a sidekick ('Doc'), and he is only pitting his wits against one gang (the complications of the plot emerge more from the wrongful arrest theme). This time, the girl is killed (her main function being to complicate the plot). Only in the final scene, at the cemetery, does de Martino attempt directly to emulate Corbucci's 'style'. The 'populist' connotation is still there (the banker's control over the authorities, and his confidence that he can make the charge stick), but it has been more thoroughly integrated into the main story.

In Osvaldo Civirani's *Son of Django* (1967) — known outside Italy as *The Return of Django* — Tracy, the son of Django, is on the trail of his father's murderer. During his search, he teams up with Logan (a gunfighter) to fight against Clay, a rich industrialist whose gang is terrorising Topeka City. Eventually, Tracy discovers that Clay is the man he is looking for; but one of Django's old friends (the Rev. Fleming, a gunslinger-turned-priest) persuades him of the futility of his revenge, and Tracy rides out of town, having decided to spare Clay's life. *Son of Django* is again a revenge film (involving the family's honour), and the hero again has a sidekick (Logan). The hero pits his wits against two gangs (back to the *Fistful* formula) — in the first instance, against Logan's men, then, having joined forces with Logan, against Clay — and the 'populist' theme is completely integrated into the main plot; but this time the hero is persuaded of the immorality of his revenge, and (implicitly) of the futility of using violence against men like Clay. The second generation (represented by Django's son) thus seems to be rejecting the motivation of earlier Italian Western heroes, and the conversion is shown to be a religious one. The deus ex machina (Fleming — played by Guy Madison — the first of many gunslinger/priests in the genre) represents another new departure: in later variations on this theme (such as *Reverend Colt*, Leon Klimovsky, 1971, in which Guy Madison again plays the role), a more characteristic 'conversion' was from priest into gunslinger.

Romolo Guerrieri's *10,000 Dollars Blood Money* (1967, with Gianni Garko — later of Sartana fame — as Django) begins with the kidnapping of Mendoza's daughter, Dolores, by a Mexican bandit, Manuel Cortez. Mendoza is a rich landowner, and can afford the services of Django, a bounty-hunter, to get her back. Django, however, is reluctant to take on the assignment, and names a price that is so high ($10,000) that Mendoza refuses to hire him. Manuel Cortez bushwacks Django, but with the help of a young girl named Myanou the hero manages to escape. Hoping that this experience will have chastened Django, Mendoza renews his offer, increasing his original fee; but Django is still not keen, and when he meets Manuel Cortez readily agrees to join forces with the bandit in an attack on a stagecoach carrying gold — provided there is no killing involved. Cortez then double-crosses him, kills all the passengers and rides off with the gold. Eventually, Cortez takes refuge with his father, a man named Stardust, and it is there that Django finds him; after a complicated series of fights Django succeeds in killing Cortez. In *10,000 Dollars Blood Money*, Django is no longer out for revenge to protect his family's honour — he is now a professional bounty-hunter. He works on his own (although he is prepared to team up with Cortez for a complicated job), but he is also choosy, both about his employers and his assignments: he prefers not to work for a rich landowner, and if he is going to break the law he tries to restrict his activities to attacks on property. The 'populist' theme has thus by now become part of Django's motivation, but, as in *Son of Django* (albeit for different reasons), his ambitions are not realised: Mendoza wins in the end, for Django finds himself obliged to kill Cortez, by force of circumstances, and the attack on the stagecoach involves a great deal of violence. The female interest (Dolores, Myanou) is simply there to help along the plot.

Django the Condemned, also known as *Django, Honourable Killer* (1967), directed by American veteran Maury Dexter and starring George Montgomery, again supplies the hero with a career. This time he is a lieutenant in the Mexican army, under General Miguel Camargo, and his job is to protect the General's property against Espada's bandit gang. Django is accused of killing the nephew of a rich landowner, Cristobal Riano, and when General Camargo begins to show interest in Francesca, a young widow living in Riano's house, he also finds himself accused of the murder. After extensive inquiries, Django manages to piece together the story of the nephew's death, and discovers that Riano himself is the culprit. Espada's bandit gang strikes again, and Django succeeds in killing most of them during his defence of the General's property. Finally, Django gets the woman (Francesca) with whom he has fallen in love, and General Camargo is left to look after himself in future. *Django the Condemned* takes up many of the themes of earlier examples of the genre — false accusation, the influence of the rich landowner over the authorities, the hero falling for the woman he has saved — but the central character is no longer either a violent avenger (Corbucci) or a scrupulous bounty-hunter (Guerrieri): he has become a stock figure of the Hollywood 'B' Western, the young lieutenant whose prowess saves his commanding officer — the main change being that the army is now Mexican.

Giulio Questi's *Django, Kill* (also known as *If*

You're Alive, Shoot!, 1967), with Tomas Milian as Django, we have already discussed. The hero pits his wits against homosexual bandits, puritanical towns-folk, and the Gringo bandits who were once his friends, but who left him for dead. The Django formula becomes the excuse for a surreal, brutal phantasmagoria, in which the plot stubbornly resists any categorisation.

A Few Dollars for Django (1968), made by Leon Klimovsky, with Antonio de Teffé as Django, presents the hero as a bounty-hunter employed to find out about the man responsible for a hold-up of a few years before — Jim Norton, who is rumoured to have since died. Django tracks down Norton's twin brother, George, who lives happily in Main City with his niece Sally. Although the town is torn apart by the struggle between the local magnate's gunmen (Logan's gang) and the peasant cultivators, George Norton has resolved to keep out of the struggle, and has up to now succeeded in leading a peaceful life; but two of Logan's hit-men (ex-members of Jim Norton's gang) inform Django that George and Jim Norton are in fact the same person. The bounty-hunter is reluctant to arrest a man who has managed to go straight for so long. Eventually, Norton finds it impossible to sit back and watch the cruelty of Logan's men, so, with help from Django, he takes up the defence of the peasant cultivators; Logan's gang is wiped out — but at the cost of Jim Norton's life. In Leon Klimovsky's film, Django is again a scrupulous bounty-hunter: although his prime motivation is assumed to be cash, he also makes moral choices about the type of criminals he is prepared to turn in. He has to use his guile in two ways: first to deduce (detective fashion) who the real Norton is, then to combat Logan's tyranny. The 'populist' theme is strongly present in the Logan sections of the film, and has an interesting (almost subtle) impact on the main plot: Norton has managed to go straight for some years, but it is only when Django reminds him of his past that the ex-bandit fully realises how detached he has become from any commitment to a 'cause'. Django's arrival thus directly stimulates Norton's decision to defend the cultivators in an active way; and, ironically, Django ends up having 'seen his job through', for Norton sacrifices his life to the cause. The female interest (Sally) is simply there as a symbol of Norton's peaceful family life.

Ferdinando Baldi's *Django, Get a Coffin Ready* (1968), with Mario Girotti/'Terence Hill' — later of

'Trinity' fame — as Django, is much closer in plot and detail to the original *Django*, partly because it was written by Franco Rossetti, who had co-scripted Corbucci's film. Django makes the acquaintance of Martin, a senator who has ambitions to become governor of the State. Martin is prepared to use fair means or foul to achieve his ambition: he employs Lucas and his gang to kill and rob, and then uses his authority to find an innocent fall-guy to arrest for his own crimes. Eventually, Martin kills Django's wife, and the hero swears to avenge her death: the first step is to kill Lucas and his gang — which he duly does. But when Django arranges to meet Martin in the cemetery, he falls into a trap: Django is forced by Martin to dig his own grave; he digs until he finds a coffin; in the coffin is a machine-gun (which he has hidden earlier), and Django uses it to wipe out Martin and all his men. *Get a Coffin Ready* is a revenge film (involving the family's honour), with a 'populist' plot (Martin's control over the authorities, and his use of banditry to support his political ambitions): the final scene looks like a parodic version of Corbucci's original. The main box-office stimulus seems to have been *The Good, the Bad and the Ugly* (rather than *A Fistful of Dollars* or *For a Few Dollars More*), and elements of comedy are unusually predominant (Terence Hill's 'lightweight' persona, comic-strip cutting, and so on). Eduardo Mulargia's *Don't Wait for Django, Shoot* (1968), with Ivan Rassimov/ 'Sean Todd' as Django, begins with the robbery and death of Burke, an old farmer, by Navarro and his son Chico; the two killers are in the pay of Don Alvarez, a rich landowner. Burke's brother Pitt and his daughter Mary persuade Django to avenge the old man's death, but Chico has made off with the money, with his father Navarro in hot pursuit. Django, helped by his friend Diego, starts tracking them both down; he kills Navarro, but learns that Chico has by now been robbed by José, who has disappeared with the loot. Eventually, the trail leads Django and Diego back to Don Alvarez, and after a gun battle they succeed in defeating the Don's men, and in recapturing Burke's money; but Diego discovers that Pitt has been killed, and that Mary is Don Alvarez's prisoner. Meanwhile, the Don has been killed and robbed by Nico, a Mexican bandit. Django finally succeeds in rescuing Mary, as well as killing Nico and his entire gang. *Don't Wait for Django, Shoot* is a revenge film of sorts (although Django is 'employed' to take revenge),

and the villain is, predictably, a rich landowner. The plot is really a series of disconnected episodes, linked together by a kind of 'pass the parcel' game involving Burke's gold (shades of Leone?). Django has a trusty sidekick (Diego), who plays a key role in the story. Since the central character lacks any coherent motivation, the main dynamic of the plot is the complicated way in which the links in the chain of subplots are forged together. Mulargia does not emphasise the parodic aspects of the story, although the choice of names (Burke, Pitt) suggests an attempt to set 'emblematic' Englishmen against histrionic Mexicans. The female interest (Mary) is simply there to help along the story.

Sergio Garrone/'Willy S. Regan's' *Django the Bastard* (1969), with 'Anthony Steffen', who wrote the screenplay under his own name, Antonio de Teffé, as Django, opens in an American Civil War setting. Three Confederate officers, Murdock, Ross and Hawkins, betray their own unit, and cause the soldiers to be massacred. Fifteen years later, one of these soldiers reappears — Django; he kills Ross and Hawkins, then sets out after Murdock, who is by now a rich and influential landowner. Murdock lives with his brother (who is mad) and his sister-in-law. Having heard of his fellow officers' deaths, and having deduced that Django is responsible, Murdock has hired a gang of Mexican bandits to defend him. Although Django is alone, his strange appearances and disappearances begin to un-nerve the bandits. Then one terrifying night, Django succeeds in wiping out most of the hired killers; he seems indestructible, and Murdock has been left alone to deal with him. Eventually, the two men meet, and Murdock is killed in a duel; afterwards Django disappears as mysteriously as he first appeared — like a ghost. *Django the Bastard* is a revenge film (with the central character avenging *his own* death). He works alone, and most of his time is spent fighting one gang (Murdock's body-guard). The enemy has, predictably, become rich and powerful as a result of his crimes (although the 'populist' theme is not strongly in evidence). The character of Django represents the (il)logical extension of Corbucci's 'phantom vagabond' formula: in the original film, Django's *prowess* is 'fantastic'; in *Django the Bastard* (as in Clint Eastwood's later *High Plains Drifter*) he really is a ghost, and succeeds in frightening his enemies as often as killing them. The Civil War setting owes much to *The Good, the Bad and the Ugly*, and there are parodic references to many films (including Eisenstein's *October*, at one point!). The female interest (Murdock's sister-in-law) is simply there to enhance the 'Gothick' atmosphere.

In Julio Buchs' *Django Does Not Forgive* (1969), with John Clark as Django, the setting is Canada in 1885. Django swears to avenge the death of his sister, who killed herself after being raped by an officer of the Mounted Police. He starts asking questions at a local army depot, during a campaign against the Indians: at first treated with suspicion, Django finds himself facing a firing squad, but he is saved in the nick of time by an Indian attack. Later, during another engagement with the Indians, an officer in the Mounted Police admits to him that he was responsible for the girl's death: the officer asks Django's forgiveness, and subsequently saves his life — stopping a bullet which was intended for Django — whereupon our hero is forced, reluctantly, to give up his revenge. *Django Does Not Forgive* is a revenge film (involving the family's honour). As in *A Few Dollars for Django*, the hero discovers that his 'task' is not as simple as he had hoped (but he is not persuaded to forget about his revenge. Despite the officer's change of heart, Django is furious that he has been beaten to it). Again as in *A Few Dollars*, Django has to play the detective. He does not have to pit his wits against any gang, and the 'populist' theme is non-existent (the army versus Indians plot resembles that of any low-budget Hollywood cavalry picture). The female interest (Django's sister) is there to set the revenge theme rolling.

The next two 'Django' films (1970) teamed the central character with Sartana (by now another successful Italian Western hero in decline): Diego Spataro/'Dick Spitfire's' *Django and Sartana Are Coming* (also known as *Sartana, If Your Left Arm Offends, Cut It Off*, with 'Chet Davis' as Django), and Demofilo Fidani/'Miles Deem's' *Django and Sartana* (with Hunt Powers, an American actor, ex-Actors' Studio, as Django). Fidani, a prolific director of (very) low-budget and low-quality Spaghettis, who made his name at the tail-end of the 'Sartana' craze (after 'Jeff Cameron' had taken over from Gianni Garko in the leading role) was really responsible for both films: he wrote and co-directed the first, and was writer-director on the second. In *Django and Sartana Are Coming*, both the heroes are bounty-hunters ('the most famous in the West'), who are employed to find the kidnapped daughter of a rich landowner. Their methods (and weapons) differ, but together they find the girl and kill all the kidnappers. Sartana is happy to see justice done; Django is happy to take the reward. In *Django and Sartana*, Sartana is again concerned about justice (he is the 'enlightened' sheriff of Black City), while Django is a bounty-hunter who insists on doing the sheriff's job (for the reward). Eventually, Sartana loses face so much that he is tempted to leave town; but Sartana succeeds in locking Django up, leaving him the time to deal (alone) with a gang of Mexican bandits, led by Sanchez. The townsfolk are satisfied; Django the bounty-hunter and Sartana the sheriff are reconciled — and Black City is peaceful at last. In both films, Django has become an unscrupulous bounty-hunter (to set against the character of Sartana, the angel of justice). He is dressed like Franco Nero in the Corbucci film (as a tramp), while Sartana is dressed in a black frockcoat (like Gianni Garko in Parolini's *Sartana*, 1968): the contrast works almost entirely at the level of such visual 'connotations'. Django has become the weapons expert, Sartana the negotiator. In the second film, it is suggested that *both* methods are essential, if Black City is to be tamed.

After B. Ron Elliot's *Nude Django* (1971), a sexploitation film with Donna West, Django made his reappearance, as an older man, in 'Lucky Dickinson's' *Django Story* (1971), also known as *Reach, You Bastards*, with Hunt Powers as Django. Fidani again had a hand in the screenplay, which is focused on a saloon chat between the young Bill Hickok, and 'the most famous hero of the Far West — Django'; Django, it appears, was Hickok's childhood hero, and Wild Bill wants to hear all about the ageing bounty-hunter's most memorable exploits. The rest of the film links together these reminiscences: the destruction of the terrifying Sanchez twins, a duel with the infamous criminal O'Neil, which takes place during a tornado, and the slaughter of Buck Bradley with his gang. Hickok wants to join forces with Django, but Django refuses the offer, saying that he prefers to work alone. Eventually, a punch-up starts in the saloon, and the two heroes sort it out, together. In *Django Story*, the hero is again a bounty-hunter, and Fidani's anecdotal screenplay suggests that he always was. He is still active, but clearly enjoys reminiscing over a drink. The *Story* is really an excuse to present a few short episodes which are alleged to have occurred earlier in the saga; the 'populist' theme is non-existent, there is no female interest, and the film clearly owes a lot to Penn's *Little Big Man*. The confrontation of a character from American Western mythology with a Spaghetti hero was to occur again — to greater effect — at the end of the Leone cycle, in *My Name Is Nobody*.

Pasquale Squitieri/'William Redford's' *Django Defies Sartana* (1971), with José Torres and George Ardisson, again links the two characters, only this time they are both bounty-hunters on the trail of Huston, his desperadoes, and thousands of dollars. Django and Sartana clash, join forces for the battle with Huston, then go their separate ways with the loot. Although the two characters are dressed distinctively (as in *Django and Sartana*), by now their motivations and actions have become indistinguishable.

In Eduardo Mulargia's *Viva Django* (1971), again with Antonio de Teffé/'Anthony Steffen' as Django, the hero spends the film trying to avenge the death of a young woman: she is killed on her farm by three men, and Django tracks them down one by one — Gomez and Thompson, associates in the arms trade, and Jeff, a bandit. He then learns that Carranza, his informant throughout the story, was also involved in the killing. After the inevitable duel, Carranza is shot. *Viva Django* is a straightforward revenge film (although it is never made clear exactly *why* Django is taking all this trouble); the 'populist' theme is not emphasised (by now, we *expect* the rich arms salesmen to be baddies); the story is a belated remake of Petroni's *Death Rides a Horse* (1967), with the added 'twist' that Django's assistant turns out to be one of the murderers.

'Slim Alone's' *Django Always Draws Second* (1974), with Frank Jeffries as Django, takes itself less seriously: since Django is always slow on the draw, he is being wounded in duels throughout the film. Frank Jeffries does a passable imitation of Franco Nero, and Juan Maria Sabatini, as the lead Mexican heavy, does a good imitation of Fernando Sancha (the villain in two 1966/7 contributions to the series).

It will have become clear, from this survey of the 'Django' formula (which inevitably makes for rather strange reading), that the plots may *appear* to vary significantly, but the 'noteworthy moments' are really those when the hero repeats his usual gestures (his prowess with an assortment of guns, his cunning manipulation of one side against the other, and so on). Basically, the 'plots' conform to two main schemas (both of which operate *within* the

variants of our 'Italian plot'): in the first, Django is out to avenge a member of his own family, or clan, and the films show how, despite distractions, he is able to achieve this (Will Wright's distinction between 'inside society/outside society', a crucial component in his 'vengeance variation', seems of little use here); in the second, he is a bounty-hunter, and the films show which assignments he is prepared to accept, and the methods he uses to 'see his job through'. Given these two basic motifs (revenge, bounty-hunting), the variations are characteristically introduced as part of the question 'How will he do it?' Sometimes Django pits his wits against one gang, sometimes two; he may require a sidekick, he may not; he may be employed by someone, he may be working freelance; he may develop a relationship with a woman, but he is unlikely to saddle himself with any 'irreversible premises'; the villain is probably a rich landowner, or influential politician, but the 'populist' connotation of Django's quest (if such it can be called) may or may not be strong; Django will lack commitment to any cause (except his own), but may stimulate such a commitment in others; he may have to play the detective, or he may know the villain from the outset; he may be arrested on a trumped-up charge, but he will always find the man who nailed him; he will usually see his job (or revenge) through, but he may be dissuaded from revenge, or someone may reach his target before him; his sidekick may turn out to be a villain, he may not; the story may contain overtly parodic elements, or it may take itself seriously — and so on. Occasionally, the influence of films from *outside* the formula, or the impact of changing fashions, will be apparent, especially at moments when Cinecittà producers seem to be running out of ideas: if *Django* owes much to *A Fistful of Dollars*, *Django the Bastard* and *Get A Coffin Ready* have an equal debt to *The Good, the Bad and the Ugly*, while *Django Story* seems at times like an Italian remake of *Little Big Man*; in *Son of Django*, the hero temporarily becomes a hippy. During his declining years, Django will team up with another hero (Sartana), will become the excuse for a sexploitation film (*Nude Django*), and will, like Trinity, feature as a comic character in a live-action cartoon. In short, like Superman, he will join a 'Legion of Super Heroes'; and *Django Story* may perhaps be seen as the equivalent of Superman's *Untold Tales* — stories that concern events already told, but in which 'something was left out'. What is significant, throughout the cycle, is the increasing complexity of the obstacles the hero has to surmount, and the 'continuous series of connotations' which enable us to recognise the Django figure as an old friend: the growth of beard, the shabby clothes (as distinct from Sartana's 'specialist' outfit), the coffin, the penchant for firing a machine-gun from the hip. The rest, as Umberto Eco has pointed out, does not really matter.

In a sense, the 'Django' series represents the 'foundation formula' of the Italian Western genre: several actors, such as 'Terence Hill', 'Anthony Steffen', and Gianni Garko, first learned their trade working in the formula, and were later to become the heroes of more successful variations (such as the 'Trinity' series); several stock characters (such as the gunslinger-priest) were to emerge from the series, the result of scriptwriters' frantic attempts to find yet more 'unforeseen obstacles'; what looked for a time to be a separate formula (Duccio Tessari's 'Ringo' films — featuring a sympathetic hero who even achieves a kind of nobility) based on more gentle parodies of the Hollywood 'originals' (in particular of Westerns by John Ford and Howard Hawks) eventually came to be incorporated in the 'Django' cycle — with far less subtlety. And the films I have described in such detail are, of course, far more *characteristic* of the genre than the few high-budget co-productions which were exported to England and the States. As such, they elude Will Wright's schema for analysing the narratives of successful American Westerns — for many of the 'Django' films were not commercial successes: and neither Wright's 'basic oppositions', nor the 'plot functions' he isolates are of much use in analysing them — we have seen how his 'vengeance variation' is of a very different order to the 'revenge' variant in the 'Django' formula. However, since the film which originally sparked off the formula was Leone's *A Fistful of Dollars*, most of the developments *within* the 'Django' series between 1966 and 1974 fit broadly into the variants of our 'Italian plot'.

The internal pressure exerted by the Cinecittà system (once the genre had been proved commercially successful on domestic release) does seem to conform neatly to Umberto Eco's model. In addition, this model helps to explain why so much emphasis is given to functions c, d, e, f, h, i, m and n in the *Servant of Two Masters* variant. Once the *Fistful* schema had played itself out (in the 'Stranger' series launched by the 1966 *For a Dollar in the Teeth*, and in Questi's *Django, Kill*), other formulae were tried (including the blind gunslinger, the mercenary caught up in the Mexican Revolution, and, after the success of the 'Trinity' series, the freewheeling, lazy hero who punches his way through a variety of slapstick situations), until the genre itself had no mileage left. By the time Sergio Leone began shooting *For a Few Dollars More*, at least ten features derived from *A Fistful of Dollars* were being made simultaneously. It may be that some of Leone's extensions of the more successful script ideas and visual effects contained in his first Western are directly related to this pressure on the formula: the character of Colonel Mortimer in *For a Few*, for example, owes much to motifs which Corbucci's *Django* had made popular for the first time — he is introduced to us in the guise of a Bible-reading cleric, and he is later shown to be riding around with a 'portable ammunition dump' strapped to his saddle-cloth (as well as a derringer up his sleeve). The famous cemetery scene in *The Good, the Bad and the Ugly* may have originally come from the same source. By the same token, other aspects of the genre which Leone first introduced in *Fistful* were to be remoulded and extended over the next five years. These include the use of music to heighten the tension during shootouts, and the self-parodic elements: in the comedy Western *Seven Guns for the MacGregors* (1965), which launched a series of its own, a bar-room fight is accompanied by renditions of Chopin and Liszt on a honky-tonk piano, and the films 'in which gunpowder seems as plentiful as dust' are satirised by a running gag about the Scotsmen's proverbial meanness with ammunition (this gag was to reappear in Joseph Losey's *Modesty Blaise*); in *Revenge at El Paso* (1968) a hotel orchestra is made to play a full-length waltz, as Eli Wallach faces the combined might of Kevin McCarthy's gang (while the terrified hotel residents lie flat on the floor); and in *Dead or Alive* (1967), two bounty-hunters wait outside the town of Escondido, to shoot bandits with prices on their heads *before* they can reach the centre of town to sign their amnesty papers — 'A price on a man's head makes it legal instead of just fun'; eventually, having shot the hero *after* he has signed his papers, the bounty-hunters leave in disgust — 'If this amnesty keeps up, I'm going to turn to buffalo hunting.' After 1967 (and the success of *The Good, the Bad and the Ugly*) a whole series of

Italian Westerns extended Leone's use of a symbolic *corrida* as the location for the climactic gunfight, by actually setting this gunfight in a bullring. As we have seen, not only does the Eco principle apply to Westerns which were derived from successful Italian *Westerns*, but it also applies to Westerns which were derived from successes in other Cinecittà genres. During the Spaghetti boom, there were to be various comedy Westerns (starring Rita Pavone, or Franchi and Ingrassia), spy Westerns (such as *The Price of Power*, 1969), horror Westerns (such as *Django the Bastard*, 1969), circus or acrobatic Westerns (anything directed by Gianfranco Parolini/ 'Frank Kramer') and even a 'sword and sandal' Western (*Samson and the Treasure of the Incas*). A more recent example of the Cinecittà producers' penchant for saturating the market with remakes or derivatives of money-making genre pictures was prompted by the phenomenal success (on domestic release) of Pasolini's earthy social comedies *The Decameron* and *The Canterbury Tales*. In the latter case, hastily compiled rip-offs were in production even before Pasolini had finished shooting his version. Scriptwriters worked so fast that they did not have time to discover that Canterbury was the destination of the pilgrims rather than the author of the *Tales*; so a series of films with titles on the lines of 'More Tales by Canterbury', and 'Canterbury Rides Again' were unleashed onto the Italian market. These were, of course, retitled for international release on the plastic raincoat circuit.

This Cinecittà system is similar in many respects to that masterminded in the last fifteen years by Run Run Shaw, in Hong Kong. In the mid-1970s, Shaw's Kowloon studio managed to produce forty assembly-line films a year (many of them shot in Shawscope): it was not unusual for seven films to be made simultaneously, using the same crews and sets. Run Run's brother Runme looked after the Singapore side of the business. The Shaws' empire was built up mainly on action films: 'In the mid-60s,' explained Run Run, 'it was sword-fighting films, then after some years the audience gets tired and likes fist-fighting films. And as long as they remain popular they will be 50 per cent of our production': thus kung-fu adventures appeared in various guises — costume kung-fu, ghost kung-fu, contemporary kung-fu, and so on. Already (since Run Run Shaw said this) martial-arts spectaculars have died, as a popular genre, both here and in the Far East, and slapstick comedies have taken over: but both the 'fist-fighting' and 'sword-fighting' films probably had their cinematic origins in the Hong Kong/ Chinese swashbuckling and fantasy epics of the 1930s — the 'classic genres'. Run Run Shaw explained the amount of stylised brutality contained in his kung-fu pictures by referring to the specific example of the Cinecittà Westerns (many of which were immensely popular in Hong Kong): 'It is like Italy making Westerns more violent than Hollywood makes.' Bruce Lee's *Way of the Dragon* actually used (uncredited) themes from Morricone's soundtrack album of *Once Upon a Time in the West*. And the wheel came full circle with the Run Run Shaw-Carlo Ponto co-production of *Blood Money* (starring Lee Van Cleef, or 'Li Yun Ch'i-li-fu') and the kung-fu spectacular *For a Fistful of Yen*.

There are similarities, also, with the pattern of production at studios in Bombay (the products of which are aimed at the vast Hindi market): compared with these studios, which are responsible for over 400 feature films a year — most of them mimed 'song-films' — Cinecittà is almost a small-scale operation! Superstars like Shashi Kapoor find themselves making four or five films *simultaneously* in this assembly-line production system, and, with 75 million Indians going to the cinema every week, there seems to be an insatiable market for all-singing, all-dancing movies (very few of which are exported) set in night clubs or ornate gardens. According to Shyam Benegal, one of the 'New Wave' directors who is attempting to break into the Hindi market, 'many Indian films take their plot lines from American cinema', although these plot-lines have up to now always been re-defined to take account of the more 'traditional moral attitudes' of Hindi society: 'these films uphold traditional values, whatever else they may do'. The products of this mass-production industry may lack the sophistication of their Cinecittà counterparts, but the context is certainly comparable — and the charge that has been levelled at the 'song-films' by left-wing critics, that they really represent a kind of 'opiate' for the people (a dream-world actively sponsored by the authorities), has, as we have seen, also been levelled — in different terms — at Cinecittà formula films. 'New Wave' directors in India are currently exploring the possibilities of *using* this production system, to put over less traditional ideas to Hindi-speaking filmgoers. It is, as Benegal says, a question of testing how far a critical film-maker may go without alienating either the authorities or the audience.

Some Italian Western heroes
and villains

35-6 (*Above left and right*)
Ringo (Giuliano Gemma) faces
the evil Sancho (Fernando
Sancha) in Duccio Tessari's
A Pistol for Ringo (1965)
37 (*Right*) The Mexican Mendez
(Henry Silva) enjoys a shootout
in the saloon, during Carlo
Lizzani's *The Hills Run Red*
(1966)
38 (*Below right*) Sabata (Lee
Van Cleef), with a gun from up
his sleeve, in Gianfranco
Parolini's *Return of Sabata*
(1971)

(*Above left*) Trinity ('Terence Hill'), the footloose hero of a series of slapstick Westerns directed by Enzo Barboni, attempts to thumb a lift
39-40 The series began with *They Call Me Trinity* (1970, *above left*) and continued with *Trinity Is Still My Name* (1971, *right*). Part of the fun derived from the contrast between the agile Trinity and his huge, bear-like brother Bambino ('Bud Spencer')
41 (*Left*) Sartana (Gianni Garko), the mysterious avenger, in the film which launched another series, Gianfranco Parolini's *Sartana* (1968). Garko had acted in several of Visconti's stage productions before playing Sartana in six films (1968-72)
42-3 (*Below left and right*) Many Italian Westerns were, of course, parodic in the first place. But by the late 1960s they had begun to parody themselves. (*Left*) Two gunslingers, one of them called Mortimer — who lose their trousers in *They Call Me Trinity*. (*Right*) Three men ride into town, in Enzo Castellari's *I go, I shoot, and I return* (1967); they look suspiciously like Lee Van Cleef, Clint Eastwood and Franco Nero

At Cinecittà, by contrast, this 'testing' seems to have become a possibility well over fifteen years ago.

While the early Italian Westerns were being shot, Cinecittà still produced films about the adventures of Dick Malloy, Agent 077; Dick Smart, Agent 2/007; Walter Ross, Agent 3S3; George Collins, Agent X-1-7; Bond Callaghan, Seventh Earl of Moreston ('The Ace of Spades'), and many others. Hercules, Maciste, Ursus and Samson still tried to impress audiences with their feats of strength (sometimes, in their declining popularity, all in the same film). Sandokan (in the person of Steve Reeves or Lex Barker) still worked on behalf of the British colonial regime, in a series of Indian jungle adventures freely based on the novels of the Italian fantasy-merchant Emilio Salgari. Two of Mario Bava's Westerns — *Arizona Bill* and *La Strada per Fort Alamo* — were released in the same year as Bava made *Blood and Black Lace* and *Night Is the Phantom*. And Italy's resident clowns — particularly Totò, and the Sicilian double-act of Franco Franchi with Ciccio Ingrassia — continued to send up the more successful genre films in innumerable pick-up-and-throw-away items such as *Totò by Night, No. 1*; *Whatever Happened to Baby Totò?*; *Totò of Arabia* — and, with the Franchi-Ingrassia team, *The 00-2 Secret Agents*; *Two Mafiamen in the Far West* (co-starring Aldo Guiffré, of *The Good, the Bad and the Ugly* fame); *Ringo's Two Sons* (a parody of Leone's first two Westerns); and, inevitably, *The Handsome, the Ugly and the Stupid*, with a plot evidently intended to comment on Leone's 'episodic' presentation of dramatic climaxes. During the mid-1960s it was not unusual to discover Franchi-Ingrassia films showing at twenty different Roman cinemas simultaneously. And there were, as we have seen, attempts to fuse successful Western formulae with other Cinecittà genres. Piero Pierotti's *Samson and the Treasure of the Incas* (1965), which must have one of the most bizarre plotlines in the history of narrative cinema, begins, simply enough, as the story of Sheriff Alamo's journey by stage-coach to Silver City, bringing a suspected murderer to justice. One of the stagecoach party — Jerry Damon, the real murderer — for some reason suddenly decides to set off in search of the famed treasure of the Incas, which is buried in the Pallidi mountains. Meanwhile, the other members of the party are captured by the Incas, who are on the hunt for victims to sacrifice to their Sun-God: Mysia, Queen of the Incas, recognises the suspected murderer as the man who once saved her life, and promptly falls in love with him — a sin apparently punishable by death in Inca circles. The imprisoned travellers' situation seems hopeless — until Samson turns up in the last reel and 'causes the temple of the Incas to collapse, rescuing his friends from a cruel fate'. *Samson and the Treasure of the Incas* was not billed as a comedy.

Other aspects of these Cinecittà genres of the 1960-3 period inevitably influenced the form and shape of the Italian Western. From the spy film, perhaps, the Westerns inherited an emphasis on the technology of death, on the anonymity of the central character (in the case of the spy films, lost in a vast bureaucracy), on the money-power equation (characteristically represented by 'The Organisation' our hero is sent to infiltrate) and on flip 'asides' which release the audience's laughter after a sadistic interlude. (Sergio Leone has attributed the commercial success of the Bond films to the fact that 'out of sixty scenes, at least fifty ensnare the audience in suspense': the low-budget Spaghettis were to rely even more on the impact of successive, noisy climaxes, usually taking the form of gun battles.) From the horror film, perhaps, the Westerns inherited the use of garish colour filters (later to introduce violent flashbacks in the Westerns), shock zooms, as in Mario Bava's *Black Sabbath*, cluttered 'period' décors, and an unusual directorial emphasis — even with Bava and Freda — on elaborate (or fussy) visuals rather than performance or plot. Giulio Questi's surreal *Django, Kill* includes a scene — shot from a variety of 'disturbing' angles — where the hero (Tomas Milian) is locked up in a cell full of all manner of fearsome beasts, including vampire bats. From the comedies, perhaps, Spaghettis inherited the occasional appearance of *Continuo*-type humour (if that *is* the Italian word for 'Carry On'), and the tendency of Mexican heavies to indulge in operatic bouts of wheezy laughter.

But, as I have already suggested, the genre which seems to have had the most direct influence on the Western, was the 'classical' epic. For example, in the parodic relationship between musical sound-track and action, best illustrated by a 'peplum' such as Duccio Tessari's *Sons of Thunder* (1962), which cleverly uses, among other themes, the 'Colonel Bogey' march for a bridge destruction sequence, 'Anchors Aweigh' for the arrival of the

Titans, and 'Deutschland über Alles' for a battle scene, to 'punctuate' the action. As a bonus, *Sons of Thunder* also includes a neat John Ford parody. Tessari and Ennio de Concini (the co-writers) even managed to incorporate a few 'political' comments along the way: when Crios, the youngest of the Titans, shouts 'Long Live Freedom!' at the Theban populace, the Thebans reply with a chorus of 'What is Freedom? ... Long Live Freedom? ... Long Live Freedom!!' As was pointed out at the time, *Sons of Thunder* owes as much to *Père Ubu* as to classical mythology.

Another link might be the almost slapstick choreography of violence in some of the more inventive 'peplums'. A notable example is the riotous tavern punch-up which opens Vittorio Cottafavi's *Hercules Conquers Atlantis* (co-scripted by Tessari). Cottafavi's Hercules (Reg Park) does not believe in exerting himself, and always waits until the last moment before using his muscles. As Charles Barr wrote in *Movie*, the humour of this was 'perfectly consistent with the film's presentation of heroism. Hercules would rather finish a meal than join in a brawl, he'd rather sleep than fight, he wants to stay at home instead of joining the King of Thrace's expedition against Atlantis. The king has to drug his wine to get him on board ship. They all watch him apprehensively as he sleeps on. But when he wakes he just looks round, sees what has happened, and smiles: "Lovely day, isn't it?" He will only fight under provocation, in defence of himself and his friends. Atlantis has to be destroyed since otherwise it will destroy Greece.' Atlantis is morally doomed anyway, because the 'expropriated peasantry' (in Raymond Durgnat's words) have been forced into the role of fanatical warriors, and because such a totalitarian system is 'inimical to democracy and the dignity of the individual'. Cottafavi's *Hercules* showed that, despite (or perhaps because of) the pressures of the Cinecittà system (which can be aptly compared with those of the comic-strip), and despite the related tendency of Cinecittà genres to parody themselves, in the hands of an intelligent artist these genres could become a positive inspiration. As Charles Barr wrote, 'it is true that there is no exhaustive "characterisation"; but in this the strip-cartoon differs little from the fable. By going back into the past, the artist *can* recreate a simpler, purer world free from mundane associations. A parallel that suggests itself is Yeats' adaptation of Irish myth in his early

poetry.' Cottafavi's debate on heroism, on totalitarianism, and on myth revealed that films which transcend the Cinecittà formulae (at the same time as deriving from them) were well worth the attention of the critics.

Other possible influences on the Western, mediated through these 'epics', include, on a technical level, the use of unusual framing and 'impossible' camera angles, as, for example, in Cottafavi's *Goliath and the Dragon*. In this film, the camera is placed *beneath* Goliath (Mark Forest) as he purposefully strides across the screen. Perhaps the slow, ritualised confrontations which tend to occur in the last reel of most early Italian Westerns have their origin in the ways that the mighty feats of strength performed by Hercules and Maciste were characteristically edited (sometimes accompanied by triumphant music). And there were plenty of plots concerning 'mercenary' gladiators, such as in Michele Lupo's *Death in the Arena*, and the Tony Russel vehicle *The Invincible Seven*, both made in the same year, 1963. These gladiators were forerunners of the bounty-hunters in Spaghettis: the sons of *The Magnificent Seven*, and the fathers of *The Five Man Army*. The Italian Westerns continued the practice of casting Hollywood 'veterans' as the not-so-muscular co-stars: in Cinecittà epics, these had included Alan Ladd, Broderick Crawford, Orson Welles, and Stewart Granger. They inherited, too, the formula of the strong-man hero who, by more or less successful manipulation of special effects, performs superhuman physical actions, such as destroying buildings, wrestling with monsters, or simply sending innumerable Atlanteans/Barbarians/Vampires flying out of every available 'window'. This strong man could be a gentle giant, a mindless thug, or a brawny confidence trickster. He characteristically acts as an apparently unmotivated 'Avenger', utterly detached from the baffling events he feels impelled, for some reason, to resolve. Even in more sophisticated examples of the genre, the lead actors usually behave with the same kind of pre-Freudian simplicity as (not surprisingly) characterised the muscleman heroes of Italian spectaculars produced before the First World War, such as Ursus in *Quo Vadis* and Maciste in *Cabiria*. Political motivation is normally on the level of the gladiator's credo in Cottafavi's *The Warrior and the Slave Girl* (Cottafavi did not always transcend the formula): the gladiator will only lay down his arms 'When Armenia has won its freedom, and all its slaves have lost their chains'. And, as Harmonica informs Cheyenne in *Once Upon a Time in the West*, 'they didn't have dollars in them days'.

Finally, continuity at Cinecittà is more specifically illustrated by the use of acrobats such as Crios (Giuliano Gemma) in *Sons of Thunder*, and at least one character in all the films directed by Gianfranco Parolini (alias 'Frank Kramer'), whether 'epics' or Westerns, *Revolt of the Gladiators* or *Sabata*. The films of Parolini, like those of Tessari and Cottafavi, show how unimportant was historical accuracy, or any sense of 'period', in most 'peplums'. As Richard Whitehall noted, the climax of *Pirates of the Black Hawk*, one of the less significant examples of the genre, depended on 'the presence of Chinese pirates in Central America during the eighteenth century'. Shortly after Duccio Tessari's *A Pistol for Ringo* was released, Giuliano Gemma compared Tessari's direction of his performance as Ringo, and as Crios in the earlier *Sons of Thunder*. 'For this film, I acted a character who was a little like the one I had played in *Sons of Thunder*. Quite simply, I was in a different costume and a different setting.'

Raymond Durgnat has analysed the appeal of the Cincittà 'mini-epics', comparing them to early Hollywood Westerns:

> In some ways the muscleman epic takes us back to the early days of cinema. Only now (1965) are the peasant and the poorer classes of Italy confronting industrial democracy, with its new work-rhythms, new complexities and patterns of ideas. The change is traumatic (as *Rocco** shows), and the muscleman epic owes its immense popularity to being a relaxation to a relaxed, physical, simple world, where muscles meet magic. The escape from the new semi-feudalism isn't to the old, presumably because that was a harshly stagnant one; the escape is into a pagan world, where the hero is personally free and chats with Kings and Goddesses. Through its very simplicity, the genre offers the possibility of international lowbrow appeal, corresponding to the Western's. But, in fact, most muscleman films are so simple as to correspond, not to the modern Western, which is often morally complex and embittered, but

---

*Visconti's *Rocco and His Brothers* (1960) was the story of a peasant family that migrates to the big city from the more primitive, poverty-stricken South of Italy.

to the silent Western, when Rin-Tin-Tin did all the thinking. Hence few muscleman films earn circuit release, and here their spiritual home is the kids' Saturday morning sixpenny scramble. Domenico Paolella sees the decreasing popularity of muscleman films with Italy's masses, as compared with the rise of Westerns . . . as a sign that the peasants are acquiring a 'city' sophistication.

The connections between the classical 'epic', Greek and Roman literature, and the Renaissance implied by the Italian Western movement go deeper than this might suggest. Several Spaghettis, such as *Minnesota Clay*, some of the 'Django' series and *Blindman*, seem to owe much to the Oedipus motif. Other Italian Westerns owe as much to Petronius (via Fellini) as to Zane Grey. More significantly, in an interview in *Bianco e Nero*, Sergio Leone has commented on the relationship between classical and Western mythology, while explaining why he approached his first Western 'like an epic':

> 'for me, and I say this with a smile, the greatest screenwriter of Western films was Homer, because Achilles, Ajax, Hector and the others are the archetypes of Western characters'.

Leone characteristically stresses that the Western may well have originated in *European* mythological archetypes. But, despite such comments about Homer, it is no surprise to discover that the studio which produced de Martino's *Perseus Against the Monsters* also produced Leone's *A Fistful of Dollars*. Homer can scarcely be styled the *spiritual* father of the Italian Western:

> 'The Americans', Leone adds, 'have always depicted the West in extremely romantic terms — with the horse that runs to his master's whistle. They have never treated the West seriously, just as we have never treated ancient Rome seriously. . . . Perhaps the most serious debate on the subject was made by Kubrick in the film *Spartacus*: the other films have always been cardboard fables. It was this superficiality that struck and interested me.'

One school of American thought also holds that the traditional Western (on film and in literature) has its origins in classical mythology. The most recent expression of this thesis occurs in Cawelti's *Six-Gun Mystique*:

If we look for mythical archetypes for the Western hero, we might compare the Lone Ranger type with Perseus or Bellerophon, dragon-slaying bravos who have been provided with magical steeds and other aids by the gods and whose problems in accomplishing their missions are purely strategic or technological. Once they have managed to acquire the appropriate silver bullets or magic helmets they are able to move directly and without ambiguity to the destruction of the savage monster. The archetype of the more complex Western hero would have to be Achilleus, that great warrior torn between his loyalty to the Achaeans and his transcendant sense of personal honour. When he is finally drawn into the conflict that will destroy him, his former joy in violence and war become a bitter and resigned acceptance of fate ... this more complex Western hero is rather elegiac than tragic, and he does not reach the profound depths of grief and knowledge that Achilleus does, but the similarity is unmistakable.

Cawelti goes on to explain that one of the reasons why the 'complex' Western hero never achieves the tragic power of an Achilleus, is that 'in the Western story ... the hero's situation is linked to a particular period of history with its limited way of life'. The Man With No Name clearly belongs to the Lone Ranger category.

Many of the directors of the most successful Spaghettis managed to adapt their talents from genre to genre with remarkable ease: the early experiences of film-makers such as Sergio Sollima, Duccio Tessari, Sergio Corbucci, and Sergio Leone were, as we have seen, gained either in genres derived from Hollywood originals, or while working with American production crews, based in Rome. Sergio Sollima (or 'Simon Sterling') — a late arrival — co-scripted Parolini's *Revolt of the Gladiators* (1963), and three of Paolella's epics, before directing two 'Agent 3S3' films (1965/6), and a film with Stewart Granger about an embittered English spy, *Requiem for a Secret Agent* (1966). He went on to direct his two political 'cat and mouse' Westerns, *The Big Gundown* and *Face to Face*, in 1966 and 1967, but switched to the urban crime thriller with the magnificent *Violent City* (1970), set (and partly shot) in New Orleans. This starred Charles Bronson as a hired assassin, and featured the inevit-

able Jill Ireland. Duccio Tessari had co-scripted three of Cottafavi's 'spectaculars', and one of Freda's, before directing his first solo effort (*Sons of Thunder*) in 1962. The similarities between Tessari's 'parody' epics and his two 'Ringo' Westerns — *A Pistol for Ringo* and *The Return of Ringo* — have already been noted; but in the same year as the Westerns, Tessari directed a spoof spy thriller *Kiss Kiss ... Bang Bang* (1965) starring a bowler-hatted Giuliano Gemma (who looked understandably bewildered wandering around London locations), and in 1966 co-scripted Prosperi's *Dick Smart 2/007*. Tessari's other contributions to the Italian Western genre included co-scripting *A Fistful of Dollars* (unsigned), and *Seven Guns for the MacGregors*, an unusually action-packed Spaghetti concerning two elderly Scots pioneers, and the adventures of their seven sons against a gang of Mexican heavies. Ennio Morricone wrote the music — trombones blowing raspberries accompanied by electric organ, doubling for bagpipes. One of Tessari's more recent films, made in 1972, is a parody post-Western entitled *Et Viva la Révolution*. Franco Nero stars as a renegade priest, Eli Wallach as an unscrupulous bandit (who, after being mistaken for a revolutionary saviour, eventually sides with the oppressed peons), and Lynn Redgrave as a tough Irish journalist sent to cover the Mexican Revolution. The film contains a wild send-up of the climax to *Two Mules for Sister Sara*, and was the product of the same phase in the (late) Spaghetti cycle as Corbucci's *Compañeros*, or Leone's *Duck, You Sucker* — which we will be discussing when we look at the politics of the Italian Western.

Before 'specialising' in Spaghettis, Sergio Corbucci co-scripted two Totò films, *Totò Against Maciste* and *Totò of Arabia*, and one parody of Leone's films (*For a Few Dollars Less*), as well as directing *Totò, Peppino and ... la dolce vita*, and a variety of 'epics', including the Steve Reeves *Son of Spartacus*. Corbucci's Westerns with Franco Nero — *Django*; *A Professional Gun*; and *Companeros* — all reflect the director's earlier experience as a hard-working studio gag-writer. To take one example: a sequence in *For a Few Dollars More* where Colonel Mortimer coolly strikes a match on a hunchback's braces, recurs, in different settings, but in even more surreal circumstances, throughout *A Professional Gun*. The mercenary Sergei Kowalski demonstrates his cool by striking matches on any rough surface that happens to be handy — whether it be a hanging man's boot or a Mexican heavy's beard.

Of the post-Leone Spaghettis, Enzo Barboni's 'Trinity' Westerns have proved by far the most popular in Italy, making the Venetian actor 'Terence Hill' (Mario Girotti) into something of a superstar. Trinity is a footloose layabout, always busy doing nothing, who tends to team up with his brother Bambino ('Bud Spencer'). Wherever he goes, he causes trouble: 'One store destroyed, three heads split like overripe melons, one man wounded and one castrated — all in two hours,' moans Bambino, the brawny one; 'Well, you asked me to give you a hand,' replies blue-eyed Trinity with a smile. He drives his horse like a Lamborghini, is incredibly quick on the draw, eats an extraordinary amount of baked beans, and is handy with his fists as well: at one point in *They Call Me Trinity*, he bangs a baddy's head against a cash register, until it rings up the message 'Thank You'; at another, he forces a black-clad hired gun (inevitably called Mortimer) to rush out of town in his red long-johns. The 'Trinity' films are loosely constructed comedies, with an emphasis on slapstick bar-room brawls in which stunt-men hurtle across the screen from every direction. Unlike Corbucci's Westerns, the comic scenes of which reveal the director's earlier experience cobbling together popular Cinecittà farces, Barboni's Westerns seem to take their inspiration from Hollywood slapstick of the Mack Sennett era. *They Call Me Trinity*, for example, opens with a long sequence showing Terence Hill lazily sunbathing on a horse-drawn travois: the sequence is clearly inspired by Laurel and Hardy's *Way Out West* — with Bambino standing in for Ollie and Trinity for Stan.

Tonino Valerii — a more recent arrival on the Spaghetti scene — learned his trade later than the others we have looked at, working as Leone's assistant director on *For a Few Dollars More*. He went on to make *Day of Anger*, a pedestrian 'young-man-meets-veteran-gunfighter' story with Giuliano Gemma and Lee Van Cleef, and the extraordinary *Price of Power*, a retelling of the Kennedy assassination story set in post-Civil War Dallas, which uses many of the sets and some of the Italian cast (Frank's men) from *Once Upon a Time in the West*, and stars Van Johnson as the (Northern) President who is destroyed by Southern political corruption during the Reconstruction era. The President's train ride to Texas recalls Anthony Mann's compact thriller about Lincoln, *The Tall Target*. In 1973,

Valerii was chosen by Leone to direct *My Name Is Nobody* — a film which, as we shall see, does not resemble Valerii's earlier work at all, but in places looks like a carbon-copy of Leone's films.

After Peter Bogdanovich and then Sam Peckinpah had been approached, Leone's other assistant director, Giancarlo Santi, was originally scheduled to direct the post-Western *Duck, You Sucker* (with Leone supervising proceedings — 'The actors demanded my presence'), and in fact started shooting (for ten days). Because of producers' pressure, and because the lead actors, James Coburn and Rod Steiger, preferred to work with the maestro alone, Leone took over the direction once the project had got under way.

Leone himself was unusual in this company, since much of his formative experience was gained in the second unit of *American* production companies. His father, Vincenzo Leone, who acted with Eleanora Duse in 1904, was the man who 'discovered' the screen's first Maciste, in the person of Bartolomeo Pagano, a Genoese docker. After the success of Pastrone's *Cabiria* (1913), Pagano went on to play Italy's most famous muscleman in a whole series of Maciste epics, produced over the next twelve years. Leone's father also 'created' the silent vamp star Francesca Bertini, and directed nearly fifty of her films (under the pseudonym 'Roberto Roberti' — as Sergio recalls, 'so that my grandfather would not be ashamed of him'). He acted with Pola Negri. Sergio's mother, Bice Valerian, was a minor star of Italian silent films, and appeared in what must have been one of the earliest Spaghetti Westerns, shot in Turin in 1909. Under Mussolini, during the era of 'white telephone' comedies, and of 'Roman grandeur' epics (bitterly christened 'the African disease' by some Italian film-makers at the time), Vincenzo Leone was, briefly, president of the Italian Directors' Guild. He had directed the first version of *Fra Diavolo* in 1930. In 1939, he made and co-wrote, under the pseudonym 'Roberto Leone Roberti', *Il Socio Invisibile* (*The Invisible Partner*), a film which tells of what happens when a poor man invents a well-off partner, to obtain the financial credit which has up to now been denied him. Eventually, the invisible partner becomes an obsession with him, so he decides to reveal the truth. The trouble is, no one will believe him; so, in the end, he burns down his office, passes himself off as dead, and starts all over again. Giuseppe Isani, in *Cinema* (23 December 1939) observed that 'the fairly high level of the story, in which the moral implications go well beyond the specific plot, is badly served by the actors and the general interpretation'; however, it was good to see that Leone Roberti 'has resurfaced after a gap in his work of nine years', and the scenario deserved 'full marks for good ideas'. Two years later, 'Roberto Leone Roberti' made *Mouth on the Road* (*La Bocca Sulla Strada*), from a screenplay by Guglielmo Giannini. This film is about the illegitimate daughter of an aristocrat, who after her father's death is brought up by the porter employed in the ancestral home ('in accordance with the nobleman's wishes'); an industrialist and his family move into the chateau, and eventually the son and heir marries the girl. Diego Calcagno, in *Film* (27 December 1941) thought that the 'obscurely symbolic' title was a mistake, but that the film was 'crisp, and enjoyable. The action takes place in the porter's lodge of one of those huge, grey, sleepy Neapolitan mansions. The atmosphere is extremely well conveyed. And "Armando Falconi" (Gennaro Cuoco), in the porter's livery, gives a fantastic performance.' Filippo Sacchi, in *Corriere della Sera* (18 October 1941) reckoned that the film was 'daring in its imagery' (especially the image of the mouth on the road, an emblem which is proudly displayed on the gateway of the huge mansion — symbolising the feudal relationship between the aristocrat and his vassals) and that it abounded 'in the things our cinema does *best* — especially Neapolitan dialect comedy'. According to Oreste de Fornari, at the time it was first released this film was thought by many to be 'very impolite to the Fascists and the police spies'. And, for some critics, the obvious social implication of the story (the industrialist becomes a bourgeois version of the aristocrat) was not sufficiently obscured by the 'fumetto' story which surrounded it. Just after this, according to Sergio Leone, 'Mussolini's entourage had written a screenplay, and summoned my father to give his honest opinion of it. My father was honest . . . and his career was ruined.' Vincenzo Leone only escaped exile because 'one of his friends had a ministerial post'. But he was forced to retire to the countryside near Naples (where he was born), at first under constant police surveillance. Sergio was thirteen years old at this time. A footnote to this story: after he had completed *Duck, You Sucker*, Sergio Leone was scheduled to make a film about the last days of Mussolini, but a rival production company

acquired the rights to the property on which Leone's screenplay was to be based and the project was abandoned. The film was eventually made by Carlo Lizzani, with Rod Steiger in the lead role, in 1974.

After a period at law school in Rome, Sergio Leone began as an assistant director, working for Mario Soldati, Mario Camerini, Carmine Gallone, and Vittorio de Sica (he played the part of a German priest in de Sica's *The Bicycle Thieves*, as well as being a 'voluntary assistant'). He worked in the second unit of various American production companies making Hollywood 'epics' in Rome during the 1950s. The directors of these films included Mervyn Leroy (*Quo Vadis*, 1952) and Robert Wise. Leone began working with Raoul Walsh's second unit, responsible for the battle sequence of Wise's *Helen of Troy* (1955), but was later promoted to the main unit (perhaps having a hand in the two spectacular 'duels' between Achilles and Hector, Paris and Menelaus). Before William Wyler would agree to direct *Ben-Hur*, released in 1959, he apparently made it clear in his contract that he was to have nothing to do with the chariot race: Andrew Marton's second unit was to continue shooting the race until he was satisfied with it. Leone was senior assistant in this second unit, with responsibility for retakes: 'we had more than two months to prepare the horses, and more than three to shoot the actual race. During that time, I must have seen the first *Ben-Hur*, made by Fred Niblo, one hundred times, for there was a screening of the film every evening, and the whole unit had to go and watch it.' In fact, when *Ben-Hur* actually opened, all showings of the original version were ruthlessly suppressed: Forrest J. Ackerman, the distinguished film historian, tried to organise a rival première of the Niblo film (the abridged, sound version), but was raided by the FBI. The action sequences in the Wyler film were, apparently, no improvement on those of the original. Ironically, William Wyler himself had worked as assistant director on the chariot race sequence of the Fred Niblo version. An assortment of young Cinecittà extras (among them Giuliano Gemma) who were later to make their names in Italian 'peplums' and Westerns are briefly to be seen, sitting in the background of the Wyler *Ben-Hur* Roman baths sequence.

Also in 1959, Leone worked as assistant on Zinneman's *The Nun's Story* (which starred Audrey Hepburn), in the unit partly responsible for the

44-7 Sergio Leone served his apprenticeship working for several Hollywood directors at Cinecittà: these included Robert Wise (*Helen of Troy*, 1955) (*top*) and William Wyler (*Ben-Hur*, 1959). A particularly memorable experience was working as assistant with responsibility for re-takes, on the unit which filmed the chariot race sequence of *Ben-Hur* (*below left* — Leone is somewhere in this picture). The other stills show the shooting of the actual race, and the casting of Italian extras for crowd scenes

48-9 (*Above left and right*)
Leone directs his own 'peplum',
The Colossus of Rhodes, in
1960. This story of a slave-
uprising, Spartacus-style,
featured Rory Calhoun as Dario
and Lea Massari as Dalia
50-1 (*Below and right*) After
Colossus, Leone directed the
Italian version of *Sodom and
Gomorrah*, in 1961-2, and
assisted Robert Aldrich on the
American version. (*Below*)
Sodomite patrols charge into
battle. (*Right*) Astaroth
(Stanley Baker) administers
'delightfully imaginative'
tortures to Scilla Gabel

'Congo' scenes.

Leone summarises the experience he gained as assistant director on some fifty-eight Italian and American films, from the standpoint of a hardened Cinecittà professional:

> If you are an assistant with your own ideas, it is better to work with several directors — for, if you work with one, and particularly if he is one you admire, you eventually lose your ideas. I cannot say that working with the great American directors was a dazzling experience: for one thing, the Italians I worked with were old professionals who knew their job very well; for another, it is easy to make films as the American directors do, if you have vast budgets, kilometres of film footage, several cameras, and several crews who often do all the hard work.

He also relates this experience to his subsequent stylistic development:

> If the critics write that Leone resurrects the old myths and makes them even larger, that's true; but there has to be a biographical reason for that. I made 58 films as an assistant — I was at the side of directors who applied all the rules: make it, for example, a close-up to show that the character is about to say something important. I reacted against all that and so the close-ups in my films are always the expression of an emotion. I'm very careful in that area, so they call me a perfectionist and a formalist because I watch my framing. But I'm not doing it to make it pretty; I'm seeking, first and foremost, the relevant emotion. You have to frame with the emotion and the rhythm of the film in mind. It takes on a dramatic function.

But the experience of working with a variety of directors 'from the best to the worst, from the mediocre to the talented, from the genius to the idiot', although a useful course in Hollywood methods of film-making, was not always a happy one:

> I was a great admirer of Raoul Walsh, one of the masters of the Western. When we were shooting *Helen of Troy*, I asked him all about this genre: he always replied, 'the Western is finished'. I insisted that the Western had been killed off by those who had maltreated the genre; but he still replied 'the Western is finished; the public

does not want it any more!' So I saw all these cinéastes, like William Wyler, sacrifice themselves to the taste of the moment by making 'peplums'. And I was their assistant, the victim of some curse. I was more in love with the idea of America than anyone you could imagine; I had read everything on the conquest of the West, building up a vast archive on the subject, and I was obliged to spend my time directing Roman circuses in papier-mâché Colosseums. While I organised chariot races, battles between triremes, and explosions on galleys, I was silently dreaming about Nevada and New Mexico.

In 1959, just as the 'peplum' craze was beginning to dominate production at Cinecittà, Sergio Leone took over the shooting of *The Last Days of Pompeii* in Spain, after the scheduled director, the aged Mario Bonnard, had retired because of illness. Steve Reeves (the man of the moment, with *Hercules* recently released) was the star. Leone was called in (because of his reputation as an assistant) the day before filming was due to begin, but refused to associate his name with the finished product, since 'it was not my film': most of the work consisted of supervising three men who were later to become the other founding fathers of the Spaghetti Western — Duccio Tessari (scriptwriter), Sergio Corbucci (assistant director), and Enzo Barboni (assistant director of photography). Today, *Pompeii* seems like a tired carbon-copy of the 1952 *Quo Vadis*, with unconvincing special effects and without Peter Ustinov to liven up the proceedings. But in 1959, it made 830 million lire (only 150 million less than Francisci's *Hercules*) and provided Leone with the opportunity to direct Rory Calhoun in *The Colossus of Rhodes* eighteen months later. Without a fully-worked-out script from which to shoot *The Colossus*, Leone 'amused' himself 'technically, with little ideas': 'I agreed to do it, hoping to treat the subject in an ironic way, without telling the producers at MGM.' But he still does not consider *Colossus* to have been a 'personal' film. It was an Italian-Spanish co-production, shot in Spain, starring Rory Calhoun and Angel Aranda as two leaders of a slave uprising against King Serse, on the island of Rhodes (it was to star John Derek, of *Ten Commandments* fame, but he refused to take part in the action sequences and so fell out with the director). Despite the slave uprising theme, this 'peplum' cannot be said to reflect the admiration for Stanley Kubrick's

Spartacus which Leone has so often professed since; rather, it shows the director's ability closely to control and manipulate the pace of action sequences (the uprising, the earthquake in the last reel), to invest a thin story-line with a feeling of scale and grandeur (by use of formalised compositions, rather than expensive set-ups) and, at the very least, it is the work of a talented art director with a highly developed sense of 'irony'. Some of the Italian critics complained of 'the excessive realism of the torture and battle scenes'. Perhaps this contributed to the film's success — it made 657 million lire at the box-office, which puts it well below the first two 'Hercules' movies, and the first *Ursus* (released in the same year), in terms of popularity, but still among the top grossers which earned international release at this time.

'I never wanted to make films in the "epic" genre, and, after the commercial success of *Colossus*, I had to turn down a dozen *Maciste* or *Hercules* films.' Instead, in 1961-2, Leone worked as Robert Aldrich's assistant on *Sodom and Gomorrah*, and directed the Italian version (under Aldrich's 'super-vision'). His unit was responsible for the action footage, in particular the battle and flood scenes which were shot on location near Marrakesh. The Italian print of *Sodom* is more explicit in the two 'court entertainment' sequences, which show how the Lesbian-dominated Sodomites like to be amused. Certain aspects of *Sodom and Gomorrah* seem to relate to Leone's subsequent work, and in particular to later applications of his bizarre sense of humour. For example, the establishing shots of the market-place in Sodom show slaves being casually thrown on to farm-carts, doubling as 'death-wagons', after they have been whipped to death by a leering Gary Raymond (compare the final 'joke' in *For a Few Dollars More*). 'Delightfully imaginative,' murmurs Anouk Aimée (Queen of the Sodomites), as she watches Scilla Gabel being hugged to death by a blind man who is (unwittingly) wearing a jerkin studded with sharp spikes (compare the more elaborately Machiavellian 'tortures' devised by Clint Eastwood and Eli Wallach in *The Good, the Bad and the Ugly*). But *Sodom and Gomorrah* cannot be classified as a Leone film. Raymond Durgnat has shown how the central tension in the film's story between the virtuous, hard-working, patriarchial Hebrews who control the salt market, and the rich, sybaritic Sodomites whose ethic of conspicuous consumption is challenged by Lot's

more austere version of capitalism, is essentially based 'on the contrast too often made by old-fashioned American puritans, between rural America (hardworking, frugal, virtuous) and the big city (rich, pleasure-ridden, corrupt)'. Leone's version of the American pastoral was to be based on a less simplistic set of antinomies.

By the time that the Aldrich-Leone *Sodom and Gomorrah* was released, Samuel Bronston's Spanish empire was in decline, and Cinecittà 'peplums' were ceasing to make money at home or abroad. Robert Aldrich remembers the time just after the completion of *Sodom* as very tense: 'the Italians were ready to kill all of us. . . !' Sergio Leone has often talked about the unstable circumstances existing in the Italian film industry, in the year before the shooting of *A Fistful of Dollars*: 'Economic conditions made it virtually impossible to shoot a film in Italy in 1964. In 1962, the "epic" craze had come to an abrupt end. In 1963 the gigantic "Titanus" crash took place, and all the banks stopped credit.' Titanus had, in fact, co-produced *Sodom and Gomorrah* — one of the company's last projects at this time. Leone also recalls that the great studios at Cinecittà were 'like deserts', surrounded by unemployed technicians and extras. The executives on the Via Veneto were casting around for any idea that would attract co-production money. As we have seen, the usual response of the part-government-owned Cinecittà production machine to such recurring crises was to switch genres (using many of the same actors, production crews, and sets as before) and then saturate the market with a new 'craze', hoping to force the commercial pace. The Spaghetti Westerns became viable in the first instance because of the commercial success of some German films which Sergio Leone thought were 'like very, very bad television . . . . But they showed that the West still had some magic left in it, and that the frontiersman was a hero who still lived in the hearts of cinema audiences. This idea gave me confidence in the future.' A group of young film-makers had learned their trade with the neo-realist 'masters', and, later, with Hollywood actors and production companies. The Italian film industry had fired their enthusiasm; Hollywood had provided them with jobs. Most of them were film buffs -- some with a special interest in Hollywood, others in post-war 'realist' experiments. A few had developed a technique which was readily adaptable to any popular genre they might be commissioned to work in. When the Americans retreated (because of rising costs, and public rejection of the last variations on the 'peplum' formula), all their jobs were at risk. The first consideration was to find a genre which would recapture the home market, thus stimulating the industry in a small way. The first Spaghetti Westerns were, in fact, carbon-copies (with a 'made for TV' look) of the American versions, dealing with the adventures of well-known characters such as Buffalo Bill, or with battles against the warlike Apaches. (Ironically, the original Buffalo Bill had been in the vanguard of the first American cultural invasion of Italy — with his Wild West Circus.) In the early 1960s, the way to recapture an Italian mass market that had been saturated with Hollywood or ersatz-Hollywood products was thought to lie in distributing home-made films that looked like traditional Hollywood ones: as 'Terence Hill' has recently recalled, 'To sell a Western in Italy, you had to have American names.' But the genre which finally succeeded in recapturing the home market was far from a carbon-copy: it was almost a revenge on Hollywood, a commentary on 'the dreams about Nevada and New Mexico' which seemed so far removed from the concerns (and behaviour) of the Hollywood producers and directors who had just left the popular Italian cinema for dead. When the earliest Spaghetti Westerns began to fail at the box-office it was a sign that the second American invasion (the first had begun in Sicily in 1943) was well and truly over.

Karl May and the Noble Savage

The immediate stimulus, in 1963, and the reason why Italian and Spanish producers became interested in backing the Italian Western, was the unexpected financial success of Harald Reinl's 'Winnetou the Warrior' films, made in West Germany and Yugoslavia. Of the German production companies involved in these Karl May adaptations, Constantin was the most spectacularly successful, and it was Constantin that later agreed to co-produce *A Fistful of Dollars* with Ocean and Jolly Films, splitting the risk three ways. The addition of a popular German actress to the cast of *Fistful* (as Marisol) secured Constantin's interest in the film. Marianne Koch had been voted the most popular actress in West Germany by the *Film Echo* in 1960.

Out of the (approximately) thirty-five 'Western' novels which chronicle the adventures of 'Old Shatterhand', the Teutonic pioneer, and 'Winnetou the Warrior', chief of the Apaches, not one has ever been translated into English; and only a few of the 'Winnetou' short stories have been made accessible to English-language readers. Before briefly discussing the impact of the Harald Reinl 'Winnetou' films, it is worth looking at the bizarre life and work of the first (and still most widely read) creator of European Westerns.

Karl May was born near Chemnitz, Saxony, in February 1842, the fifth of seven children. His father was a weaver (Karl was later to be accused, by representatives of the various pressure groups he had alienated, of being 'a little weaver's lad, with a weaver's morality'). His mother was a professional mid-wife. Up to the age of ten, Karl May was a very sickly child — for a time, he was completely blind. In his youth, he later recalled, he spent as many leisure hours as possible losing himself in *Pfennig-dreadfuls* (if that is the correct term) — such as *Himlo Hinlini — the Noble Robber Chief*. At the age of twenty-three, just after he had graduated from the Plauen Seminar, May began serving his first term in Zwickau prison: he had

been given five years for masterminding an insurance swindle, and for fraudulent sale of medicines. Less than six months after his release in the winter of 1868, Karl May was back inside again for another four-year stretch. His crime: impersonating a police lieutenant (or was it a civil servant? — the accounts differ). He was later to claim that he spent the year of the Franco-Prussian War in America, researching for his 'Winnetou' books. It was, in fact, during the eight years that he actually served in Zwickau that May (who had rapidly been promoted to prison librarian) first began to read (and plan) adventure novels — as many as the authorities would permit. Evidently the library was well stocked with the works of Fenimore Cooper, and early-nineteenth-century German travellers' tales about life in the West. There may also have been more serious anthropological studies of the American Indian way of life, for, at some stage, May seems to have researched Apache lore in detail. Winnetou's life, for example, was probably based on that of Cochise, the Apache chief. Some of May's material was also gleaned from encyclopaedias. Perhaps he read, or saw references to, John Heckewelder's *Account of the History, Manners and Customs of the Indian Nations* (1819) — Fenimore Cooper's primary source. While he was serving his second term in Zwickau (1869-72), May is thought to have sent some of his early attempts at writing Western stories, as well as 'Arabian' tales, to popular German periodicals (although this is disputed by some commentators): what is certain, is that shortly after his release, publishing houses were competing for the rights to print them.

Clearly, the compensatory fantasies which May evolved — a substitute, perhaps, for feeling impelled to behave in anti-social ways, and for adopting fictitious 'establishment' roles — had provided him with an opportunity to 'belong' in German society (almost on his own, weirdly romantic, terms) and, even more crucially, to be noticed, for the first time. For 'Dr' May cunningly encouraged his public to associate the wanderings of Old Shatterhand around the American Frontier, and of Kara-ben-Nemsi around Arabia, with his own early life: he had been Shatterhand, he had also been Kara-ben-Nemsi, and now he was Dr Karl May.

When it was suggested, in 1899, that the years supposedly spent in America and Arabia had in fact been served in Zwickau, and that May's much-vaunted doctorate had been bought from an organisation known as 'The German University of Chicago', run by an ex-barber, there was a public outcry. Hounded by the press — partly because of a divorce and over-hasty remarriage to an old friend's widow, and partly because he had alienated various political pressure groups, on both Left and Right, as well as representatives of the Catholic church and the teaching profession, with his curious brand of 'harmonious' Christian democracy — May suffered a nervous collapse. His fantasies and projections had enabled him to go straight for the second half of his life — but at the cost of a dangerous dependence. After the revelations of 1899, the *Übermensch* had few props left. During the public inquiry, at which (apparently) a Mohawk Indian who worked at a travelling circus was roped in to testify about the accuracy of the 'Winnetou' stories, the *Berlin Post* ran the headline 'Old Shatterhand Scalped'. Some West German scholars still maintain that May must have spent part of his early life in America (the evidence for this being May's extraordinary use of English expletives 'as used in the West', such as 'thounderation', 'the deuce', 'zounds', 'heavens', 'hum', 'hello', 'hang it all', 'the devil', 'lackaday', 'hihihihi', and 'the favourite word of the frontiersman — pshaw'). But the general consensus seems to be that May only visited the United States once, in 1908, four years before his death in Radebeul.

Hans-Jürgen Syberberg's recent film biography *Karl May* (1974) — part of a trilogy exploring (or 'exorcising') the roots of German cultural mythologies, the other two films dealing with the relationship between Wagner and Ludwig of Bavaria, and 'the leading figures of National Socialism' — cleverly re-creates May's fantasy world (while suggesting why his stories should have had such a wide appeal at the time) by use of obviously artificial, and consciously *kitsch*, images to illustrate it: postcards, a toy steamer called the *Kaiser Wilhelm* with which May plays in the bath, crude forward and back projection (for May's 'journeys' — a characteristic

Syberberg technique); a greenhouse, a stuffed lion, a wigwam in the garden, a showing of Méliès' *Voyage Across the Impossible*, and a fairyland Saxon village (complete with snowstorm), which appears as May reminisces about the heart-rending stories his grandmother used to tell him (for the *kitsch* world of May's dreams). In one sequence, Karl May appears, improbably dressed in the outfit of a frontier scout, and clutching his trusty *Bären-töter* (with studs on the stock to represent the number of people he has shot) to lecture a group of school children on Indian lore: when quizzed about the forty languages he claims to speak, May proceeds to recite the first chapter of Genesis in Hebrew. In another sequence, Syberberg shows how the illustrations for the 'Winnetou' series were prepared: an Aryan muscle-man poses, uncomfortably nude, while the illustrator attempts to translate this image into the picture of an Indian brave. The illustration is for *Winnetou II*, and the artist is Sacha Schneider. In fact, the cover designs for the first three 'Winnetou' books all featured nude figures, with 'classical' physiques, in melodramatic postures — appropriately enough, looking very like the posed figures in the opening sequences of Leni Riefenstahl's *Olympiad* (1938): Schneider's vision of the 'West' seems to have stemmed in the main from Old Testament stories, William Blake, and turn-of-the-century 'decadent' French book illustrations. In his correspondence, he addressed Karl May as 'My dear Old Shatterhand'! Much of Syberberg's film concerns the clash between Karl May's fairground world (especially the curious brand of anti-militarist, 'harmonious' Christian democracy he thought it represented) and the political pressure groups which could not cope with May's spectacular success. Karl May is presented as an almost unwitting accomplice in the popular success of his fantasies: when his first wife asks him to 'admit it — now and again you lie', he simply replies, 'What do you mean?' To some, May incarnates 'the true heroic vision of the age of Wilhelm'; to others, he is responsible for an extremely dangerous type of 'opium for the proletariat'. Towards the end of the film, we are shown Karl May addressing a pacifist conference (in Vienna, two and a half years before the outbreak of the First World War): one of the students in the audience is the rather Chaplinesque figure of Adolf Hitler. In this and other ways, Syberberg hints at the relationship between the success of May's synthetic mythologies and the rise of Nazism. Most of the actors and actresses in *Karl May* were in fact former stars (or affiliates) of the Nazi cinema: leading roles are taken by Kristina Soderbaum, the ex-wife of Viet Harlan, the director of the notorious *Jud Süss* (1940); Mady Ruhl, said to have been one of Dr Goebbels' mistresses; Lil Dagover, the female lead in *The Cabinet of Dr Caligari*, as well as the star in numerous romantic comedies of the 1930s; and Helmut Kautner, who plays Karl May (and looks like John Carradine), began his career as a director of Max Ophuls-style films under the Third Reich. Syberberg chose these people because 'I had to find actors who could easily identify with the reality of the period I was showing'. At the end of *Karl May*, the author is shown dying shortly after the pacifist conference (two days before Good Friday, 1912). The final sequences of the film represent a synthesis of the artificial images of fantasy that have punctuated the main body of the narrative: he dies in a snow-covered wigwam that has been erected in the garden of the Villa Shatterhand, Dresden.

Karl May's stories have sold over 26 million copies since first publication and have been translated into sixteen languages. In Germany, their success was assisted by the fact that Fenimore Cooper — the most obvious rival — translated very badly into the language: today, the German versions of the 'Leatherstocking Tales' seem to be, if anything, even more ponderous than Karl May's 'adaptations'. He was not the first European to write popular novels in which the hero allies himself with the Redskins, against the villainous 'Americans of the North': between 1850 and 1870, for example, the French novelist Gustave Aimard published nearly fifty stories for children about French heroes and their Indian friends — usually set in the 1790-1840 period, with titles like *Les Outlaws du Missouri* and *Les Trappeurs de l'Arkansas*. (Before May's death, one or two French films — single-reelers — which emerged from this tradition had already been made about the Red Indians). But Karl May was by far the most successful.

Klaus Mann, in an article published in November 1940, was the first to reveal to non-German readers that May was the 'Cowboy Mentor of the Führer' — it appears that Hitler was very fond of reading the 'Winnetou' books, from his youth in Austria right up to the war years. A.J.P. Taylor has more recently (*Observer*, 12 June 1977) gone so far as to suggest that the Führer may even have thought of himself as 'the Last of the Mohicans'! It seems that Taylor was

satirising the wilder excesses of the recent spate of psycho-biographies — nevertheless, he might have got his facts right: Winnetou was, of course, an Apache. After the disaster of the Russian campaign in 1943, Hitler *did* apparently order his General Staff to read the 'Winnetou' books as part of a morale-boosting exercise. And he is known to have presented his nephew, Heinz, with a collected edition, when the young man first entered the National Political Education Centre. According to Syberberg, 'Hitler appreciated May's work enormously. He was fascinated by these upright, noble heroes who came up with strategy after strategy for avoiding bloodshed and doing away with the evils of the world. Hitler quickly understood how he could draw useful elements from May's work.' The two men never met, but Hitler was, it seems, at Karl May's pacifist conference in January 1912. We have already noted, when discussing Luis Trenker's version of *Sutter's Gold* (*Der Kaiser von Kalifornien*) how easily the specifically German attitudes towards the 'noble savage' could be adapted to suit Nazi ideology: during Sutter's odyssey to the West, he has much more in common with the Indians than with the vicious, money-grubbing Americans (in Trenker's film, the Indians speak English, the Americans low German). These attitudes towards the 'noble savage' had originated with German travellers and painters from the sixteenth century onwards. But they were associated with a very different set of values when they reached a mass audience through the work of Karl May: Trenker was simply exploiting these values, just as Hitler was to draw 'certain useful elements' from the 'Winnetou' stories. That May's works need not *necessarily* have been used in these ways is shown in George Grosz's reminiscences about his favourite boyhood hero: 'The reading of these books awakened in the youngster a yearning — that secretly exists in practically every German — for distant lands and exotic adventures. (These books could well have been the result of the ardent propaganda of the time for German colonial expansion.) Yes, indeed, we certainly had a warm place in our hearts for our great, blond German-American hero, Old Shatterhand, who with one blow of a clenched fist could lay low a horse, not to mention a contemptible betrayer. . . . Winnetou was one of the ideals of the German youth of my day. He actually became a national figure, even more famous than his renowned colleagues, Uncas and Chingachgook, because there was something "German" about him.'

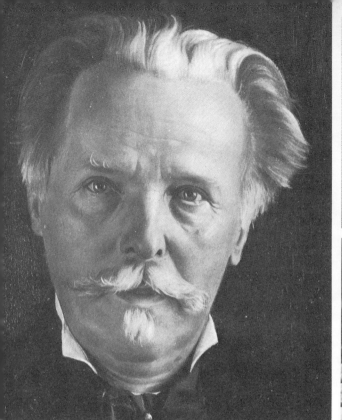

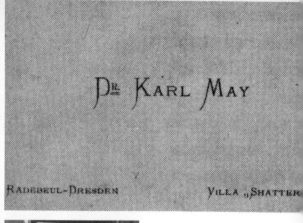

WINNETOU·I

52-4 Karl May (1842-1912), creator of 'Winnetou the Warrior'. Although May lived near Dresden in his later years, a facsimile of his Villa Shatterhand now forms part of the Karl-May-Museum, Bamberg, West Germany, together with his collection of 'Wildwest' guns — including the *Bärentöter* and the *Henrystutzen* (*above*)

55-6 (*Left and below*) Sacha Schneider, a symbolist painter, designed some of the original covers for Karl May's stories, including the 'Winnetou' novels and the surreal epic *Ardistan and Djinnistan*

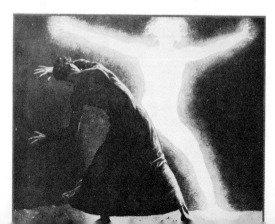

57-9 Hans-Jürgen Syberberg's film biography *Karl May* (1974): Karl May (Helmut Kautner) discusses why his fantasies should appeal so much to German readers; a Mohawk Indian testifies at his trial in 1899; and one of his fans, an art student in Vienna, attends May's lecture on 'Toward a World of Grace' in 1912

60 (*Below*) Handouts for the annual Karl May Festspiele, which still take place at Elspe and Bad Segeberg: since 1978, Pierre Brice has acted the part of Winnetou in these open-air productions

Grosz (who would surely have been more critical of May's stories had he seen any *direct* connection between them and the revival of German nationalism) remembered Shatterhand and Winnetou as fairly innocent boyhood heroes. Others preferred to think about May's fantasies in terms of the author's yearning after 'class harmony', and, specifically, his Christian stance of anti-militarism: Albert Einstein, for example, considered them 'in occasional hours of doubt, of great worth to me'. Hermann Hesse professed to be 'astounded by May's great sincerity.' Many commentators today reckon that the most significant thing about the 'Winnetou' books is the 'fight against race hatred' they represent. Karl May himself always claimed that his ideas about ecology, Christian fellowship, and agrarian populism were at right angles to the usual left-right political axis. Whatever German readers made of these books in the past, according to Richard Cracroft American State Department personnel in Germany are *still* being asked to read Karl May's stories, for the historical insight they give into German attitudes towards the United States; and Mormon missionaries still complain about the abuse they sometimes get from over-zealous readers of these tales of *der Wild West*. In Germany, Karl May remains best known for his stories about Winnetou the Warrior.

About halfway through *Winnetou I* (1893), we are told that the young hero's real name is Karl (his close Indian friends come to call him 'Sharlih', or Charlie). It also becomes clear as the long narrative unfolds that, even before he sets out for America from Germany, Karl has read so much about the *Wild West* and the Red Indians that he knows as much about them as some pioneers who have spent the best part of their lives actually living in the wilderness: this must have come as something of a relief for Western buffs living in Germany who could not afford the fare. Karl serves his apprenticeship in what May calls 'the science of the *Wild West*' under two 'tutors' — Mr Henry, an American gunsmith in St Louis, and Sam Hawkens, another German immigrant who has become one of the most 'famous hunters and scouts between the Mississippi and the Rocky Mountains'. But Karl is already a very proficient *Westmann*: he can ride, shoot, swim under water, and stalk his prey; he claims to be a specialist in zoology, ecology and anthropology; and, above all, he is committed to the idea of learning from '*life* — the real university where students

have to undergo fresh examinations all the time'. After our hero has delivered a lecture to Mr Henry on the ecology of the frontier, the famed gunsmith is, predictably, astounded:

> 'Good Lord! Have you really only just arrived from Europe?'
> 'Yes'
> 'And you've never been to the *Wild West*?'
> 'Never'
> 'Well, well . . .'

Sam Hawkens, who reckons — after a difficult lesson in the art of the lassoo — that 'no one I've taught has ever taken as much trouble as you', is equally astounded by the amount Karl already knows from books:

> 'I see', said I, 'you intend to capture a mustang.'
> 'How on earth do you know that?' replied Sam, looking amazed.
> 'I've read somewhere that when horses are not securely tied, they try to join any wild mustangs that may be in the vicinity.'
> 'Devil take you! You've read everything and there seems to be no way that I can surprise you.'

And the apprentice is keen to experience danger face to face (to be fully 'challenged', as he puts it) even if the master-craftsman urges caution ('challenged? — a true hunter thinks only of the *practical* side of things'):

> 'When you are warned of danger, instead of holding your ground, you throw yourself right into the middle of it. . . .'
> 'I did not come to the *Wild West* to run away from danger,' I said.
> 'A good reply. But why did you choose to attack the bull buffalo — the most dangerous of the animals?'
> 'Because it was more of a challenge. . . .'

The long first section of *Winnetou I* is structured around a series of elaborate *rites de passage*, which Karl must undergo in order to be fully initiated into the esoteric 'science of the *Wild West*'. Sam Hawkens tells him of some danger that may be lying in wait for him (buffaloes, wild horses, grizzly bears, Kiowa Warriors), and in the ensuing discussion the young hero takes the opportunity to show off his zoological, ecological or anthropological knowledge. The next stage involves Karl actually encountering the danger (shooting an angry bull buffalo, stopping a stampede of wild horses, wrestling with *der Grizzlybär*, mediating with the warlike Kiowas), and saving Sam's life in the process. Finally, Karl tells the reader all about the lessons he has learned so far, and complains that trigger-happy hunters, horse-traders, trappers, railroad scouts or Indian fighters are wrecking the balanced ecology of the Western frontier.

'There's only one animal more dangerous than an angry buffalo,' said Sam.

'Which animal is that?'

'The bear.'

'Surely you don't mean the black bear, the one with a yellow muzzle . . . ?'

'Of course not. He's quite inoffensive — and so tame you could teach him to do your laundry. No, I'm talking about the *grizzly*, the grey bear of the Rocky Mountains. I expect you've read books about that animal, as well. . . .'

'Correct.'

'Well, thank your lucky stars that you have never met one face to face. When the *grizzly* rears up on his hind legs, he's taller even than you, and can cut your head open with his razor-sharp teeth. Once he is angry, he will not stop until he's torn his victim to pieces.'

'Unless the "victim" beats him first.'

'There you go again. You seem to be very keen to look for trouble.'

'Not at all. Its just that I do not believe the *grizzly* is more invincible than any other wild animal.'

'You must have found that phrase in one of your books.'

'Quite possibly.'

'Then I understand. The books must have turned your mind. Were it not for that, you'd be no more stupid than the next man. But, with your mind warped by stories about hunting in the *Wild West*, you fancy that you are capable of facing a *grizzly* single-handed — just as easily as you faced that buffalo yesterday.'

'Certainly, if I have to.'

'What do you mean? You never *have* to do such foolhardy things.'

'Foolhardy is the wrong word. Human beings always have the means of saving themselves, if the occasion demands. . . .'

And, of course, the hero *does* meet a grizzly face to face, and *does* manage to outwit him single-handed (even if the small-minded Yankees who have fled in terror at the mere sight of the bear are not prepared to give him the credit he deserves).

The relationship which Karl May seems to have been attempting to establish between himself (as Shatterhand) and his readers throughout the first half of *Winnetou I* is nicely captured in the opening words of the introductory chapter, 'Ein Greenhorn':

Have you any idea, dear reader, what the word *greenhorn* really means? No? Well — it is a very disrespectful word, which has even been known to make men come to blows. *Green* as in green, *horn* as in the horns of a snail. So, a *greenhorn* is a man who is 'green' in the sense we give to that word when we speak of fruit which has yet to ripen — in other words, a man who has just arrived in the country, a novice who must have very sensitive attennae if he is not to run the risk of making a fool of himself. A *greenhorn* is a man who does not speak English at all, or else who speaks the language *too* eloquently: the Yankee version of English, or the *argot* of the *Wild West*, is not easy on the ears. A *greenhorn* smokes cigarettes, and dislikes the kind of gentleman who chews tobacco. A *greenhorn* rushes off to the local judge to file a complaint, when he has been punched in the face by a *paddy* [footnote: Irishman], instead of standing his ground and fighting back, as a true-born Yankee would do. A *greenhorn* does not dare to rest his muddy boots on his travelling companion's knees, or to savour his soup with a noise like a dying buffalo. The *greenhorn*, who cares a great deal about hygiene, packs a sponge as big as a pumpkin, and ten pounds of expensive soap, when he sets off for the *Prairie*; he also loads himself up with a bulky compass, which, from the third day onwards, indicates every possible direction except North. A *greenhorn* jots down a selection of useful Indian phrases, but when he actually meets a Redskin for the first time, realises that he has sent his precious notes home to his family by mistake, instead of the letter which is still in his pocket. . . . When he is in the *Wild West*, a *greenhorn* lights an enormous camp-fire, the flames from which leap up as high as a tree, then proceeds to be amazed — as he is discovered and dragged away by the Indians — that they have managed to find out where he was. In short, a *greenhorn* is a greenhorn — and I was one of them at the time my story begins. Don't imagine, however, that I thought for a moment that this nasty epithet could be applied to *me*. Far from it, say I, for another characteristic of the greenhorn is that he applies the term to everyone else except himself.

At the beginning of *Winnetou I*, Karl visits St Louis, to work as tutor to an immigrant German family. But a certain Mr Henry *the gunsmith* (a historical figure — and the designer, incidentally, of the rifle favoured by the Man With No Name in Leone's 'Dollars' films) thinks Karl would make an ideal *Westmann*, kits him out with a heavy double-barrelled *Bärentöter*, and arranges a job for him as part of the surveying team hired by the Atlantic and Pacific Railroad Company (needless to say, Karl is an authority on surveying techniques). Mr Henry ('a real craftsman') is putting the finishing touches to his *Henrystutzen*, an early automatic rifle which will fire twenty-five rounds rapid, and Karl debates with him at length the ethics of producing such a weapon, given 'the nature of man'. Very soon after he has set off from St Louis, the 'sun-bronzed, fair-haired' hero becomes disgusted by the vulgarity of his colleagues on the surveying team ('they were true Yankees, who insisted on reminding me that I was still a *greenhorn*, an inexperienced foreigner'). So, together with Sam Hawkens (who comes as welcome comic relief — his name probably originating with the Hawken rifle, the mountain man's trusty flintlock) Karl resolves to teach them a few Teutonic manners. Throughout the 'Winnetou' series, when they are in the company of 'true Yankees' such as these, the German heroes insist on drinking German beer, reading German newspapers, and singing German songs — just to make their feelings crystal clear. Karl's particular brand of muscular Christianity prefers the use of fists to guns, and he will not shoot to kill (his speciality with firearms being what we would today call 'kneecap jobs'). He thus spends most of the later 'Winnetou' adventures avoiding enemies he has wounded in previous episodes. In *Winnetou I*, after a violent fist-fight with Mr Rattler (one of the more unpleasant of the 'crafty Yankees' on the surveying team), Karl is christened 'Shatterhand' by Mr White, a nice Yankee and the chief engineer on the neighbouring sector:

'Its incredible. Frankly, I would not relish the prospect of being involved in a fight with you. You deserve to be called "Shatterhand". . . . To knock out a bruiser like that with one blow. No mean achievement. . . !'

'Shatterhand!' cried Sam. 'Not bad! Our *greenhorn* has a *nom de guerre* at last. And what a *nom de guerre*! Shatterhand. How about *Old* Shatterhand? Like Old Firehand, the strongest hunter in the *Wild West*. . . .'

. . . So there I was, baptised with the *nom de guerre* that I have borne ever since — without my consent. Such is the custom of the West.

Other 'customs' of this kind which are mentioned in *Winnetou I* include the baptism of firearms (Sam's is called Liddy) and also of horses (Sam's is called Mary).

After fighting hand-to-hand duels with Tangua, chief of the Kiowas, and Metan-Akwa, his most invincible warrior, Shatterhand has to undergo yet another trial of strength — this time among the Mescalero Apaches (who are at war with the Kiowas): the hero has to swim (underwater) to a totem pole in the middle of a lake, while the Mescalero chief Intschu-tschuna hurls tomahawks at him. Having passed this test, Shatterhand is at long last accepted as worthy of the title 'white Apache', and as a suitable blood-brother to Winnetou the Warrior, the chief's son. He is also given an Apache hunting costume — a symbolic gesture in more senses than one: 'it fitted me exactly; the best tailor in New York could not have done better'. From the moment Shatterhand sets eyes on Winnetou, it is clear that they are going to make sweet music together:

His bronze-coloured face bore the imprint of a very special nobility. We seemed to be about the same age. He immediately impressed me as being endowed with an exceptional mind, and an exceptional character. We looked each other up and down. His eyes shone with a dull fire, and I thought I could detect in them the faint light of sympathy. The others told me that Winnetou has accomplished more, though still in his youth, than ten other warriors could hope to accomplish in a whole lifetime. I believed them. One day, his name would be famous through all the plains, and in all the mountains.

Later, Winnetou reveals — in a less flamboyant way

— that the feeling was mutual: 'I admired his courage and strength. His face seemed sincere. I thought I could love him.' After *der Zweikampf*, the young warrior grudgingly admits that there is something else special about Shatterhand: 'the Great Spirit has endowed you with an extraordinarily robust body ...'

Winnetou's first task is to teach Karl about the Apache way of life: as a methodical ex-tutor in languages (and avid reader of books about the Redskins, including those by Fenimore Cooper, back home in Germany) Shatterhand has no problem at all learning all the various Apache (and Navajo) dialects. He has more of a problem explaining to Nscho-tschi ('Spring Day' — Winnetou's beautiful sister, an *Indianermädchen* who instantly falls for our Aryan hero) that 'if she wishes to marry a white man, the Chief will have to arrange for her to be civilised'. But Big Chief Intschu-tschuna is sufficiently impressed by Shatterhand's missionary sentiments to persuade his daughter to go to a Christian school in St Louis:

> 'She will live in a town built by the Pale-Faces, and stay there until she becomes the equal of the white squaws. Do you think that Nscho-tschi will be able to find people who are prepared to look after her, and teach her?'
>
> 'Certainly,' I replied. 'I will make it my business. However, the Apache chief ought to bear in mind that the Pale-Faces are not, in general, as hospitable as the Indians.'
>
> 'I know. I know. When the Pale-Faces come to our wigwams, we willingly give them all they need, without asking anything of them in return. But when we go to them, we have to pay twice as much as a White Man would pay — and even then, they only give us poor quality goods. I know that Nscho-tschi will have to pay.'
>
> 'Unhappily, that is true.'

Shatterhand is convinced that 'Spring Day' will make an ideal pupil — 'she had a good memory, a keen gift for observation, and she was prepared to listen ...': sadly however, as the party travels towards St Louis, Nscho-tschi and her father are both brutally killed by Santer, the Yankee villain ('with a sneaky look about him') who was to reappear in two 'Winnetou' sequels. Santer is after some gold that the Apaches have discovered in Nugget-Tsil (the 'Hill of Gold') nearby: although the existence of this gold is fairly common know-

ledge in Mescalero circles, only on very special occasions are the Indians even tempted to use this 'dust of death' — as Shatterhand has been proudly informed.

> I must confess that a feeling of admiration — mixed with a little jealousy — came over me when I heard these words. These Indians were the possessors of untold treasures. But, instead of using these treasures, they lived a way of life that could scarcely be called civilised.

The education of Nscho-tschi was to have been one of those very special occasions ...

After writing this episode, Karl May made no further attempt to introduce a romantic interest into the 'Winnetou' books — unless one counts the healthy 'outdoor' relationship between Shatterhand and his new blood-brother, a distinctly Teutonic variation on Leslie A. Fiedler's 'Myth of the two Good Companions in the Wilderness'. Nscho-tschi had been expected to go to the white man's school: as Shatterhand gets to know Winnetou, he gradually comes to realise that he is dealing with someone who, in spirit at least, has already been to one.

> [Winnetou] held a book in his hand. On the cover of the book, in large golden letters, was the word 'Hiawatha'. This Indian, this son of a people that many call 'wild', could, apparently, not only read, but possessed a mind and taste for culture. Longfellow's famous poem, in the hand of an Apache Indian ... !

This 'mind for taste and culture' seems to be shared by all the members of Winnetou's family:

> [Intschu-tschuna] amazed me. I had read many books about the Redskins, but none of the characters in these novels even approached this Indian. He spoke English well — although in a slightly *recherché* manner. The logic of his reasoning, and the way in which he expressed himself, were those of a man of culture. ....

If Nscho-tschi was dressed in European clothes, she would have created a sensation in any *salon*. In contrast to other Indian women, who liked to cover themselves with glass beads and cheap baubles, she wore no ornaments at all. Her thick, heavy plaits, which were black (and which shone blue in the light), fell almost to her knees. Her hair reminded me of Winnetou's — and so did her eyes. Her eyes were soft, and velvety, shining through from under thick, black eyelashes. The perfect, delicate shape of her face was not spoiled by the prominent cheekbones which are such a common feature among the Indians. Her nose made her profile seem more Greek than Redskin. She must have been about eighteen years old.

(In *Christmas in the Wild West* (1897), Winnetou is described in remarkably similar terms, except that *his* profile seems more 'Roman': 'the cut of his earnest, beautiful face, the cheekbones of which barely stood out at all, was almost Roman' — 'Greek', 'Roman', it seems to have been all the same to Karl May, provided the Indians in question passed the 'cheekbone' test.)

Other members of the tribe may speak the Apache language, but Winnetou and Intschu-tschuna usually talk in High German, with a tendency to end their long speeches on the portentous line 'Howgh, Ich habe gesprochen' — at which point the other Apache warriors animatedly reply, 'Uff, Uff'. According to Karl May, 'Howgh is an Indian expression which reinforces the sense of a phrase, and it is more or less the equivalent of "amen", so be it, that is my last word, etc.', while 'Uff' is an all-purpose word, intended to convey 'admiration, scorn or surprise — depending on context'. After Shatterhand has been fully accepted by the Apaches, his pronouncements tend to be greeted with 'a general Uff'.

As Richard Cracroft has noted, it is precisely *because* Winnetou can appreciate European culture, as defined by Shatterhand, that he can become an *Edelmensch*. And the same can be said of his dynasty. So when May writes of the 'degeneration of the Indian nation', and complains that 'the red race is dying ... crushed by a remorseless destiny that knows no pity', he is clearly using very different criteria to those of Fenimore Cooper, his most obvious literary model. The more 'cultured' Indians in the 'Winnetou' stories (the chosen ones) are aware that the Twilight of the Gods is approaching, that they are 'The Last of the Tribe'. Intschu-tschuna, for example, is resigned to the fact that 'we cannot stop the white men from coming here and stealing our land. First, the scouts and the pioneers. Then, if we resist, the army. It is our destiny'; and Klekih-Petra (the 'white father', a crippled missionary who has lived with the Apaches most of his life) shares the Chief's pessimism:

'Winnetou is my spiritual son. He has a noble soul. If he was the son of a European monarch, he would become a great leader in battle — better still, a prince of peace. But as heir to an Indian Chief, he will die — perhaps miserably. For that is the destiny of his race.' In May's vision, the myth of the noble savage has less to do with 'back to human nature' than with 'forward to European culture' (or, to put it another way, 'away from both primitive *and* Yankee cultures'). But the noble savage is doomed (and knows it), and there is nothing that the Siegfried of the Sagebrush can do about it, except convert him to Christianity before he goes: when Winnetou finally does die (at the end of *Winnetou III*), his last words to Shatterhand are 'I believe in the Saviour; Winnetou is a Christian. Farewell!'

Throughout the 'Winnetou' stories, Shatterhand and his blood-brother represent a type of 'racial purity' in the face of May's favourite villains — half-breeds, Mormons and Yankees. As Cracroft — a graduate of the University of Utah — recalls, the Mormon Elder in *Among Vultures* (1888), Tobias Praisegod Burton, is a murderer and a hypocrite, while Elder Harry Melton in *Mountain Stronghold* (1893) smokes, drinks and shoots people. Santer ('skinny, tall and thin-necked ... with genuine crafty Yankee features') we have already seen in action. Against these, in a last-ditch attempt to save the values of 'civilisation' and 'culture', stand Shatterhand and Winnetou: it is as if Gene Autry's cowboy code has been rewritten by Kaiser Wilhelm. When the Italian Westerns came to be made, they often featured Mormons, Samurais, circus people, dwarfs, cripples and a gallery of grotesques who might have walked off the set of Fellini's *Satyricon*, but this was usually a reflection of the film-makers' sense of the bizarre or the surreal, and was seldom used to make a critical point. When a critical point *was* being made (as, for example, in Sergio Sollima's films), the Mormons were characteristically presented as outcasts — kindred spirits to the Mexican heroes. In the case of Karl May, the distance between Shatterhand *Westmann* and *Hans Westmar* was not too great (as Hitler himself seems to have realised), giving the series a mythical/ideological slant which was far removed from the concerns of Cinecittà directors and writers.

Pio Baldelli's article on the Italian Westerns (*Image et Son*, 1967) quotes Duccio Tessari as saying, 'We have banished the blonde who ... falls in love with the sheriff, the village dance, with its

sentimental dialogue on the verandah which is interrupted by gunshots, and also the Indian who insists
on saying "Ough, J'ai parlé" — because the Indian
who speaks like this, is part of the very worst
"Western" literature.' Clearly, Karl May's particular
brand of Western cliché (in the original books) had
little to offer where the Italian Western was concerned. On the rare occasions that Indians play an
important role in Spaghettis (*Navajo Joe*; *Captain
Apache*), they may be corrupted through contact
with American values ('Teach me the ways of the
White Man'; 'Well — first you steal a horse'), but
they are not exactly *noble* savages even before they
leave the reservation.

In 1962, Rialto Film of Hamburg (who owned
the rights to the 'Winnetou' stories — which had,
for some reason, never been filmed before) joined
with Jadran Film of Zagreb in a co-production of
Der Schatz im Silbersee (*The Treasure of Silver
Lake*), directed by Dr Harald Reinl, a veteran from
'mountain film' days. At a time when the popular
German cinema relied almost exclusively on Edgar
Wallace thrillers, erotic melodramas, fearsome sex
education films, and Rider Haggard-type adventure
stories for its daily bread, this represented something of a gamble. But, with Lex Barker (a one-time
Tarzan and a Sandokan of Cinecittà formula films)
as Shatterhand, and Pierre Brice (a French actor) as
Winnetou, the film was a box-office hit, and was
soon followed by *Winnetou the Warrior*, made by
the same team. Stewart Granger took over from Lex
Barker in 1964, playing Old Surehand — with a fine
sense of self-parody — in *Among Vultures* ('Why are
we all "Old" — Old Shatterhand, Old Surehand?'
asked an understandably bemused Stewart Granger
in an interview in 1965). Other actors to play in
'Winnetou' films, or derivatives, included Herbert
Lom, Rod Cameron, Klaus Kinski, Peter van Eyck,
Charles Aznavour and Anthony Steel. At the height
of the new Karl May craze, German pop singers
were to be heard offering 'Der Wind der Prairie',
and a newspaper featured a 'Wildwest ABC', the
glossary of which tried to explain what the words
'Grizzly', 'Paddy', 'Howgh', 'Uff Uff' and 'Zounds'
meant. Also, Karl May's misogynist vision of the
West was enlivened by the presence of Elke Sommer
as One Gun Annie the frontier hellcat (in *Among
Vultures*). Lex Barker was later tried out as Kara-
ben-Nemsi in May's *Der Schut*, directed by the
veteran Robert Siodmak. (In contrast to the
Westerns, May's Oriental adventures *had* already

been filmed, in the 1920s and in the Nazi period.)
But this could not compete with the 'Winnetou'
films by the mid-1960s. Nor could Dr Harald
Reinl's *The Last Tomahawk* — a German-Italian
co-production based on Fenimore Cooper's *The
Last of the Mohicans*.

Most of these German Westerns were shot on
location in Yugoslavia, with the unit based at Split
on the Adriatic. At the height of their popularity,
according to Stewart Granger, they made $2 million
profit each out of German, Austrian, Dutch and
Scandinavian markets alone. The most interesting
example is Reinl's *Winnetou the Warrior*, which
featured Mario Adorf, the Italian villain from the
James Bond epic *Thunderball*, as the evil Santer.
Reinl's *Winnetou* was based (loosely) on the early
part of Karl May's *Winnetou I* — chronologically
the first of the cycle, although not the first to be
written. May's story of the meeting of Shatterhand
(Lex Barker) and Winnetou (Pierre Brice), their
developing friendship (after saving each other from
warlike Kiowa Indians, buffalo hunters, or Frederick
Santer's men), and Shatterhand's growing affection
for Nscho-tschi (Marie Versini) is used in the film
to link together (jigsaw-fashion) a series of very
lively action sequences. These include: a Kiowa
attack on a wagon train; an exploding wagon, left
behind by the settlers; a mass gunfight in the main
street of the town of 'Roswell'; the building of
the 'Great Western Railway'; a canoe race; a buffalo
stampede; and a spectacular climax in the mountains, which ends with Santer falling over a precipice,
to the amplified sound of vultures. The screenplay
(by Harald G. Petersson) retains some of the *kitsch*
romanticism of the original ('Winnetou — his name
lived in every tent, and at every campfire') but
seems most at ease when injecting a little humour
into scenes which the original had taken *im Ernst*:
Sam Hawkens (the Gabby Hayes or Arthur Hunnicutt
part, played by Ralf Wolter) christens Lex Barker
'Shatterhand' as a joke, after Barker has sent three
of Santer's heavies sliding along the bar, during a
tavern brawl; and Shatterhand's interview with Big
Chief Intschu-tschuna (Yugoslavian actor Mavid
Popovic) about Nscho-tschi's future is also played
tongue in cheek:

'She go to school, then she will be smart.'
    'Well, that's a fine idea. Your tribe will
benefit, you'll see. . . . She's a bright girl.'
    'But she may learn too much the ways of the

white man.'
   'At a girl's school?'

Petersson also emphasises the contrast between the Kiowas (as painted savages) and the Apache warriors (as noble red men) which appears so forcefully in May's original novel — but this is probably because the contrast conforms to Hollywood stereotypes as well. The original story seems to have been less important to Reinl than the two main action plots — the building of the 'Great Western' on Indian land, and the hunt for buried treasure at Nugget Tsil. The climax to the railway plot — which involves Shatterhand's friends laying tracks through the night, and driving a locomotive through the middle of Santer's hideout first thing in the morning — is cleverly handled, and the treasure hunt gives Ernst Kalinke the opportunity to do some stunning location photography (of the Yugoslavian country-side): in particular, the canoe ordeal (will Shatterhand beat Winnetou to the sacred statue in the middle of the lake, when his canoe has been sabotaged?), filmed at a large inland lake surrounded by sheer cliffs, combines the best of Kalinke's work with some lively action cutting. Peterson's screen-play makes the most of sequences in the novel which have action potential: in *Winnetou I*, Karl and Sam Hawkens *pretend* that a covered wagon is about to explode (to keep the Kiowas at bay), they fight it out with a single bull buffalo, and Shatterhand *swims* to the sacred statue; in the screenplay, the wagon does explode, the two heroes have to face a buffalo stampede, and the trial of strength turns into a tense canoe race. Reinl's speciality seems to be directing stuntmen in these fast-moving action sequences; Kalinke's photographing panoramic views of rocky terrains, with isolated riders (usually Winnetou, arriving in the nick of time to save his blood-brother) on the horizon. In the dialogue sequences, Reinl's 'style' — an attempted *re-creation* of traditional Hollywood set-ups — tends to be far less imaginative. It is clear that little attention was given to questions of detail in *Winnetou the Warrior*: Apache extras pick their noses in the background, and the 'Great Western Railway' is represented by a modern Yugoslavian locomotive. The production company also made the mistake of killing off too many leading characters at one go (Santer, Nscho-tschi), leaving the scriptwriters of sequels with the problem of inventing a new set of squaws and villains from scratch. (Eventually, they had to resurrect Nscho-tschi.) But the death of Nscho-tschi in *Winnetou the Warrior* did at least ensure that Winnetou and his smiling, white-clad blood-brother were left alone for the traditional fade-out: 'I loved her, Winnetou — now I know it, she's gone,' says Shatterhand. 'Manetou watches over her,' Winnetou assures him, and they ride off together into the sunset.

Robin Bean has analysed the appeal of these simplified adaptations of Karl May's novels. He sees them as

> a rejection by German audiences of moralists, sociologists and cynics; a return to the child's world in which everything is just good or bad, black or white, no shades of grey, no conscience. At least as far as their own problems, their own country, are concerned. No past, no present, just a dream world. The films are not completely faithful to the spirit of May — if they were, they might be too sentimental even for a German audience. So to lift the emphasis away from Winnetou . . . one is presented with as much physical action as possible.

He concludes:

> The straight-backed, noble figure (of Winnetou) astride a horse, hair blowing in the wind, so full of goodness that one might squirm, has brought a new romanticism.

It is precisely this form of 'romanticism' that has more recently been criticised by contributors to the renaissance of the *independent* German cinema. Wenders, Herzog, Fassbinder and Syberberg, have all, at one time or another, reacted against the *international* aspects of the German cinema from the mid-1950s onwards: to these film-makers, a reliance on international co-productions, made to appeal to a world market, and with an emphasis on 'dreams of a better world' (in Wenders' words) has done little else but symbolise the loss of con-fidence of the *German* cinema (and the dominance of American values or 'American friends') since the Nazi trauma. If an authentic, *critical* form of German cinema is to be re-established, it must make a start at a parochial level, and strive to recapture the identity of 'a legitimate German culture', thus have more confidence in the home market than international co-productions would allow. The punch-line to Wim Wenders' *Kings of the Road* (1975), a film which confronts most of these issues head-on, is 'nearly all of the films we see, are made by Constantin and the big American studios. Better no cinema at all than that'. (Jeremy Tunstall's figures, in *The Media Are American*, tend to support Wenders' assertion.) The same director's *The American Friend* (1977) plots the gradual seduction and destruction of a Hamburg picture-framer by an American con-man, Tom Ripley (Dennis Hopper in a cowboy hat). 'Do you wear that hat in Hamburg?' asks Nicholas Ray, who plays a New York forger: to which Ripley replies, 'What's wrong with a cowboy in Hamburg?' The film is crammed with images of American popular culture — the *General* (Buster Keaton's locomotive), a Red Indian canoe by a waterfall, a juke box, pool table, pin-ball machine, even Samuel Fuller muttering something about 'German co-productions' — and Ripley's colonial-style house seems to be decorated throughout with props from 1950s Hollywood movies. The West German craftsman, of course, sells himself to the cowboy — but the main point of the film seems to be that even the cowboy does not know what to believe in any more: 'I know less and less about who I am, or who anybody else is — even this river reminds me of another river'; 'I would like to be your friend, but friendship is not possible . . .' Ripley tries to hide all this confusion behind self-consciously 'tough' dialogue — 'Freeze, Mister, I got a gun' — but to no avail. The cowboy is genuinely envious of the craftsman's skills, of the life he manages to lead in his period house surrounded by impersonal sky-scrapers: 'I've always wanted to do something with my hands'; but his enjoyment of 'the smell of paint and wood' seems highly incongruous. 'What do you make?' asks the craftsman. 'I make money,' replies Ripley; 'I'm bringing the Beatles back to Hamburg'. *The American Friend*, among other things a parody of the Western 'buddy movie', reveals a fascination with the aesthetic of Hollywood films, combined with a revulsion against the society that produced them — in practice, a distinction that is very difficult to draw. A work like Syberberg's *Karl May* may be interpreted, in this context, as a double exorcism: a critique of the type of 'anonymous' cinema represented in the 1950s and 1960s by the work of Dr Harald Reinl, and an analysis of the reasons why Karl May's stories (or derivatives) have had such a lasting success in Germany, and in Europe.

In one sense, these criticisms of the implications of the Karl May revival in the early 1960s have been less than fair: *Winnetou* does represent, in diluted form, the culmination of a specifically German tradition of attitudes towards the Western. But in all other respects, the analysis of independent German film-makers remains substantially correct: for the 'Winnetou' series also represents a loss of confidence *because* the emphasis has been lifted 'away from Winnetou . . . with as much physical action as possible'; 'physical action' (on Reinl's scale) necessitated a series of co-production deals (to split the expensive risk several ways) and also showed that producers were not prepared to be 'faithful to the spirit of May'. If Constantin was concerned that straight adaptations of May's stories 'might be too sentimental even for a German audience', then why did they bother to pillage these stories to provide the basis for a series of action movies? Even the 'dream world' (Robin Bean), or the 'dreams of a better world' (Wim Wenders) were sent up, presumably because the adapters were frightened that this aspect of May's work might be scorned (or even thought to be ideologically unsound) by international audiences. The apparent rejection 'by German audiences of moralists, sociologists, and cynics', represented by the success on the home market of these bland, non-committal adaptations of the 'Winnetou' stories (whatever their technical qualities), was thus seen by the new generation of German film-makers as a key factor militating against the development of 'a legitimate German film culture'. To put it another way, perhaps the American friends were not friends after all.

The Karl May films created a commercial context which made the Italian Westerns possible: Sergio Leone is in no doubt about this — 'it was because of the success of the German "Winnetou" series, directed by Harald Reinl, that the Western began to interest Italian producers'. In the first instance, it was the success of the series with *Italian* audiences that encouraged producers to invest in Westerns (about cowboys and Apaches) for the home market. After the Spaghetti Western genre had gained in self-confidence, however, it was clear that the Cinecittà product would be very different, in tone and style, from the 'Winnetou' films: the best Spaghettis were to demonstrate that, even within a co-production context, it was possible to retain some vestiges of a cultural identity, and to criticise what had up till then been accepted internationally as *the* context within which to make Westerns, and

61-3 The location for
Dr Harald Reinl's 'Winnetou'
films (1962-5), at Split in
Yugoslavia, near the Adriatic
coast. Pierre Brice (ex-
Zorro) played Winnetou, Lex
Barker (ex-Tarzan) played
Old Shatterhand
64 (*Below*) By asking the
question 'What's wrong with
a cowboy in Hamburg?'
Wim Wenders' *The American
Friend* (1977) was implicitly
criticising the values of
Reinl's films

the Protestant-liberal tradition which Westerns were expected to represent. As Leone points out, Italian popular literature had its equivalent to Karl May's novels in the work of 'Emilio Salgari, whose fiction excited Italians once upon a time': and during the early 1960s, Salgari's work resurfaced (minus the colonial propaganda, plus a lot of action) in the Cinecittà 'Sandokan' films. Leone now sees this genre (together with the 'peplums') as part of a craze for 'simple spectacle' against which those directors of Italian Westerns who were brought up 'in the hard school of neo-realism' were reacting.

The Critics

No doubt Sir Launcelot bore himself with a grace and breeding of which our unpolished fellow of the cattle trail has only the latent possibility; but in personal daring and in skill as to the horse, the knight and the cowboy are nothing but the same Saxon of different environments, the polished man in London and the man unpolished in Texas; and no hoof in Sir Thomas Malory shakes the crumbling plains with quadruped sounds more valiant than the galloping that has echoed from the Rio Grande to the Big Horn Mountains.

Owen Wister, author of *The Virginian* (1902), on 'The Evolution of the Cowpuncher'

If in relationship to the Old World, those first Americans were patricides, regicides, in the last analysis, deicides, in their relationship to the new, they were genocides, destroying the original inhabitants of the land they took for their own, the Indians.

Only after the Anglo-Saxon founding fathers of the White New World had given way to a generation of effete sons, who snubbed and patronized the more recent immigrants from the Mediterranean South or the Slavic East of Europe, and a generation of earnest daughters, who schooled the children of these immigrants to believe that there were real men out there once in the West, was the real damage done. At that point, no one in the East seemed any longer to remember, and no one in the actual West (just beginning to contemplate tourism as a major industry) cared to remind them, that it was gunslingers and pimps, habitual failures and refugees from law and order, as well as certain dogged pursuers of a dream, who had actually made the West — not Ivanhoes in chaps, desexed and odourless, though still lethal to cross and quick on the draw. Careful men,

if violent ones, real Westerners preferred to gun their enemies down with a shotgun from behind some convenient shelter; but in fantasy they walk towards each other for ever, face to face, down sun-bright streets — ready for the showdown, which is to say, the last form of chivalric duel. No wonder the myth had to be immunized against reality, more and more narrowly localized in time and space — to keep anyone from making comparison with a world he knew at first hand. The decade just after the Civil War becomes the mythological time, the 'Far West' . . . the mythological place in which Indians are subdued, or Mormons (anti-Mormonism being the anti-Semitism of the West), or outlaws.

Leslie A. Fiedler,
The Return of the Vanishing American (1968)

[In Italian conversations] the emphasis is always on the solid, the down-to-earth, the material, with a wealth of precise and substantial details. The people they describe are seldom virtuous, disinterested and generous; the loves, seldom pure and spiritual. The characters they mention, living politicians or dead historical figures, are always blandly accused of all sorts of crimes, homosexuality, adultery, the seduction of minors, corruption, nepotism, treason, cowardice, the plundering of public funds, or the worst crime of all, stupidity. Why was a certain man appointed to a certain post? The last explanation they accept is that he may be capable of fulfilling some of its functions. It pleases them to think that it is because he is somebody's brother-in-law, has come across documents which would ruin the man who appointed him, belongs to an all-embracing secret society, or made love to a powerful man's mistress. After the war, for instance, everybody tried hard to find a suitable answer (in these terms) to the puzzling problem: why was the United States showering billions of dollars on their country?

Luigi Barzini, *The Italians* (1964)

The man of the West bore no resemblance to the man described by Hollywood directors, screenwriters, cinéastes. The whiter than white redresser of wrongs did not exist, any more than the bandit leader without any scruples, or the always warlike Indian. One could say that all the characters they present to us come from the same mould: the incorruptible sheriff, the romantic judge, the brothel-keeper, the cruel bandit, the naive girl, and so on. And the women — those inevitable women . . . ! All these moulds are mixed together, before the happy ending, in a kind of cruel, puritan fairy-story. It is the Far West reinterpreted by Frankenstein and Disneyland.

The real West was a world of violence, fear and instinct — a world of men. . . . Me, a pessimist? Whenever people accuse me of that, I cite the case of one of the most famous heroes of the West, a man called Wyatt Earp. This individual was responsible for the deaths of over 150 people — most of them shot in the back! In the vast majority of cases, that was the way people were killed in the West. If you were honourable — like the heroes of traditional Westerns — you would find yourself in the cemetery in no time at all. When he was nominated sheriff, Wyatt Earp decided to go and provoke one of his friends into a duel. This was a duel which obeyed the rules — a rare thing. The friend found himself in the dust. But, wait a moment! At the end of the duel, hearing a sound behind him, the new sheriff thought that one of the dead man's friends had come for his revenge. He turned round, drew his gun and fired . . . at his own deputy, a man he had appointed the same day. Life in the West was not pleasant or poetic, at least not in any direct sense; this must be admitted. . . . The arrival of the railroads did, however, transform the conditions of life, and people's attitudes. But, up until then, the law belonged to the most hard, the most cruel, the most cynical. After that one form of violence was replaced by another: the killers of the West were succeeded in America by those of the Mafia, by the anonymous society of crime. And you can see all this in Vietnam. Who can possibly claim that my vision of America is pessimistic? My vision of man is, perhaps.

Sergio Leone, in an interview (1973)

. . . he fights not for advantage and not for the right, but to state what he is, and he must live in a world which permits that statement. The Westerner is the last gentleman and the movies which over and over tell his story are probably the last art form in which the concept of honour retains its strength.

Robert Warshow, on the role of the Western hero, in *The Immediate Experience* (1964)

Just how *did* you kill a dragon? I could bury the axe in his belly. That would be fun, all right. Stick it right in the middle of his skull and it would look a lot better. They wouldn't come fooling around after seeing pictures of that. How about the neck? One whack and his head would roll like the Japs used to do. But nuts, why be that kind?

This guy was *really* going to die . . .

Mickey Spillane, *The Girl Hunters* (1962)

The 'Cultural Roots' Controversy

When the Leone Westerns — *A Fistful of Dollars*; *For a Few Dollars More*; *The Good, the Bad and the Ugly*; and *Once Upon a Time in the West* — were first released internationally, they were almost invariably panned by reviewers. The argument, repeated with monotonous regularity, went roughly as follows: given the fact that the Westerns made at Cinecittà Studios, Rome, had no 'cultural roots' in American history or folklore, they were likely to be cheap, opportunistic imitations. The detachment with which directors such as Sergio Leone, Sergio Corbucci and Sergio Sollima characteristically treated their Westerns seemed to confirm this initial prejudice. The films were 'gratuitously' violent, and 'obsessively' concerned with American currency; the soundtracks were too loud and the lyrics usually indecipherable; budgets were clearly low — indicated by flimsy sets, variable colour matching and the inadequacies of the Techniscope process; the acting of the Italians was crude and histrionic, and of the Americans 'laconic', 'wooden' or, quite simply, non-existent; in short, audiences were to be subjected to the same kind of cheap and nasty cinematic hyperbole as had become the trademark of the Cinecittà 'sword and sandal' epics. If any Italian Westerns transcended this formula, they had, as the *Monthly Film Bulletin* put it, 'attempted to rise above their station'. The Italians had their own real-life cowboys, the *buteri*, who were currently dying off with the Tuscan buffalo herds they tended. Perhaps Tuscan lore explained why the gunman hero in Spaghetti Westerns usually pitted his wits, fists and gun against packs of Sicilian-style bandits draped in ponchos. The films were often concerned with brutal vendettas and sometimes ended up with the main characters facing each other in a large arena, resembling the Spanish *corrida*. So, why could Italian film-makers not leave American mythology well alone?

When the posters for *A Fistful of Dollars* proclaimed, 'This is the first motion picture of its

kind. It won't be the last!' the reviewers groaned. Some thought that the crudity of this 'peculiar and unlovely genre' made the films unwatchable (there were numerous references to 'the shadow of the Colosseum'); others, that such appalling taste was a lot of fun (for best results, watch at an all-nighter, preferably stoned); most agreed with David McGillivray of *Films and Filming* that

> we are accustomed, however imperfectly, to a sense of poetry — from John Ford via Martin Ritt to Andrew V. McLaglen — bred by an ingrained tradition. In the European Western, this tradition is non-existent, so that all the films produced in this genre are nothing more than cold-blooded attempts at sterile emulation.

On the rare occasions that critics treated the first showings of Leone's films seriously, they felt obliged to compare them — unfavourably as a rule — with the American originals:

> *Per un Pugno* is not, let's face it, Ford at his best. But it's certainly preferable to Ford at his worst. . . . The film is almost an anthology of every Western one has ever seen. Yet Leone has directed it with that European flair, the worldly-wise attitude of 'Yes, public, I know you've seen all this before, but let's have a laugh at Hollywood's expense and show that we can do this sort of thing just as well.' Naturally, violence is laid on thick . . .

wrote John Francis Lane, before the films had been internationally distributed. Leslie Halliwell's guide simply categorised these films as 'savage Westerns on the American pattern'. Those critics who asserted that there was a 'given' relationship between Western stories and the landscapes within which these stories were played out objected strongly to the Spanish locations used in Spaghettis: films made in and around Hollywood had at least captured 'the look of the Old West', and some had even succeeded

in achieving the status of 'documentaries' (of sorts).
But any 'sense of poetry' was bound to be lost if
the desert was not *really* the Southwestern desert.
Somewhere along the line it had been quietly
forgotten that John Ford (real name: Sean Aloysius
O'Fearna) was an Irishman (like many of the
founding fathers of the genre, a second-generation
immigrant), and that *Stagecoach* was stated by Ford
himself to have been based on Guy de Maupassant's
Boule de Suif. Ford buffs were particularly enraged
by Leone's *Once Upon a Time in the West*, which
not only included a scene shot among the giant red
buttes and mesas of Monument Valley ('Ford
country', as Peter Bogdanovich christened it, which
'has become so identified with him that other
directors feel it would be plagiarism to make a picture here'), but also cast Henry Fonda — Ford's
Wyatt Earp, his General Custer (in all but name),
and the actor who was on record as saying that 'the
idea of playing *Young Mr Lincoln*, to me was like
playing Jesus' — as a smiling, blue-eyed child-killer.
In *Once Upon a Time*, the combination of epic
grandeur and wilderness hostility represented by
Monument Valley was used in a way which fans of
Stagecoach and *Cheyenne Autumn* were not likely
to appreciate.

Recent criticisms of the Italian Western have
been less stereotyped. English university film
periodicals provide an interesting cross-section. The
Brighton Film Review (January 1969) considered
that their interest is 'with the James Bond films,
purely sociological'. *Kinema* (Nottingham, Autumn
1971) suggested that 'if the element of stylization
in the Western is important, the image of life which
it seeks to evoke should stay essentially true to
frontier experience, or at least to what we imagine
frontier experience to have been, as it does in much
of John Ford's work.... In contrast, ersatz Westerns
made in Europe lack this intimate conviction....
A piece of merchandise like *A Fistful of Dollars*,
with its ritual slaughter, protracted silences, and
chinking background score, has solidified more or
less into parody.' Trevor Blount, the *Kinema* critic,
added that Leone's films were 'full of contrived
ironic reversals', and revealed a 'rootlessness that
dehydrates what we see'. In the same issue of
Kinema, an 'ABC of the Western' (under 'D for
Dollars') concluded that in the Italian Westerns
'panache was confused with over-acting, over-
directing and over- just about everything else....
The complaint isn't that the films are not the same

as the Hollywood product — the most successful
ingredients are always the unfamiliar locations and
art direction — but that they're debased versions of
it which fail to seize a unique opportunity to take
the genre in fresh directions.' *Cinema* (Cambridge,
August 1970) included an 'Italian Western Supplement' consisting of a 'Concordance' by Mike
Wallington — designed to sketch 'the *substantive*
area for future debate on the Italian Western' — and
an article on Leone by the present writer, which
attempted to discuss critically various recurring
motifs in the 'Dollars' trilogy, and to analyse
Leone's style without resorting to loaded asides
about the American old masters. *Cinema* paved the
way for more detailed retrospective analyses of both
form and content in Spaghettis, and, incidentally,
stimulated the National Film Theatre to mount a
short season of Italian Westerns in their 'New
Critical Magazines' survey in the summer of 1971.

The latest criticisms of Leone's films have tended
to become involved in, and confused with, wider
problems of film theory — for example, notions of
'genre'. Andrew Tudor in *Theories of Film* suggests
that 'the best evidence for the widespread recognition of [the conventions of the Western film] is to
be found in those films which pointedly set out to
invoke them ... obvious examples are provided by
the series of Italian Westerns'. Leone's direction of
Lee Van Cleef's performances in *For a Few Dollars
More* and *The Good, the Bad and the Ugly* 'depends
very much on the *image* he [Van Cleef] has come to
occupy over two decades of bit part villains'. Other
actors in Leone's films — Clint Eastwood, Eli
Wallach, Jack Elam, Charles Bronson — 'perpetually
verge on self-parody'. Tudor concludes of *Once
Upon a Time in the West* that it is a 'fairy-tale
collection of Western conventions'. Notions of genre
may be difficult to pin down, but without 'clear,
shared conceptions of what is to be expected from
a "Western" ' the full impact of Leone's films is
incomprehensible. So, whether or not a concept
such as the 'Western genre' is useful, the 'Dollars'
trilogy provides a key example of what a mass
audience may be expected to think a 'Western' is.
Philip French, on the other hand, in *Westerns* (1973
edition), excludes 'European Westerns, whether
German, Italian or British, and ... American
Westerns filmed in Spain' from his (unashamedly)
personal definition of what constitutes the 'Western
genre'. To French, a filmography of the most
important Italian Westerns up to 1971 'reads like a

brochure for a season in hell', but he does concede that some would argue 'this disqualifies me as a true student of the genre' and directs the reader to the two *Cinema* articles. In the latest edition of *Westerns* (1977), however, Philip French describes his own earlier remarks about Italian Westerns as 'patronizing and unduly dismissive' — an interesting index of the shift in critical opinion during the last seven years. Jim Kitses, in his introductory notes to *Horizons West*, on the 'constituent elements of the form', suggests that 'first of all, the Western is American history': but he hastily dismisses the 'cultural roots' school of Leone critics by adding 'needless to say, this does not mean that the films are historically accurate or that they cannot be made by Italians. More simply the statement means that American frontier life provides the milieu and mores of the Western.' This milieu, according to Kitses, creates a specific frame of reference for a more nebulous set of conventions — the idea of the West — which Henry Nash Smith has studied in terms of an ideological struggle between progressives and anti-progressives: a conflict within American society between the drives to turn the desert into a garden, and the garden into a desert. Kitses' neat definitions of the 'Western form' ('genre' is perhaps too specific a term usefully to be applied here) — whatever their shortcomings — seem at least to provide an answer to those who employ the 'cultural roots' (as opposed to the 'social roots') argument in support of their personal distaste for Italian Westerns. Nash Smith's 'desert into garden' mythology may have been hi-jacked by nineteenth-century American intellectuals, but it goes back at least as far as the Bible, if not further (in Ford's *Three Godfathers*, 1948, the West becomes the 'New Jerusalem'), and even has its parallel in ancient Chinese mythology ('out of the dung-heap grows the lotus-flower'). There is little that is significantly transatlantic about the 'idea of the West', and John Ford's key icon for communicating this 'idea' — the cactus rose — has its counterpart in most European cultures.

Rémy G. Saisselin, in his article on 'The Poetics of the Western' (*British Journal of Aesthetics*, 2, 1962) has explored in a fairly systematic way the interconnections between types of European iconography and 'the myth of the West' (as represented in some historical paintings of the nineteenth century and some movies of the twentieth). 'No wonder', he concludes, 'that the genre given birth by the remembrance of the process of European civilisation should combine elements which are the expression of this drama of developing civilisation, but should also renew art forms and techniques proper to early societies, such as the European Middle Ages.' In particular, Saisselin explores the role of the traditional Western hero ('the Westerner') in terms of the icons we associate with medieval conceptions of nobility — for example, with the Knights of the Romances: icons connoting 'honour' (the code of the duel, the relationship between hero and trusty steed), emblems of 'one dominant character trait' (easily recognisable, and only tangentially associated with 'credibility' — 'Roland est brave, mais Olivier est sage'), the conventions of the 'epic journey' or the 'return' (emigration, the cattle drive, the Civil War, or personal revenge), the image of 'the lady' (an idealised image, if she is to serve as a reward for heroism, a more down-to-earth image if she is to be taken through violence — the blonde Isolde and the dark-haired Isolde) and the creation of legends (dime-novel writers standing in for minstrels).

Saisselin continues:

> The techniques of the *trip* and the *return* might be supplemented by others; but are themselves sufficient to allow full exploitation of the themes treated in the Western and within these themes to exploit stock scenes which are inseparable from this art form. We may find in the Western the stock scenes reminiscent of classical European drama: reversal of situation, recognition scenes, *malentendu*, etc. But in addition to these stock scenes the Western has several which are proper to it; these are the gun-duels, the hold-ups, the horse chase, the bar-room brawl, the hangings, etc. These create the atmosphere of the West, the tension and the drama. Of special consideration is the duel, which in terms of style is as formalised as any classical duel, almost as formal as a bull-fight. . . . Recently, Westerns have suffered from an addiction to technical proficiency in gun duels. This may be due to the various shooting schools in Hollywood. In any case it is apparent that the duellists are too good and they tend to become technicians.

If Saisselin had extended the range of his study to include biblical imagery, he could have found many other examples to support his thesis about the *synthetic* nature of 'the myth of the West': in nineteenth-century frontier paintings, for example, Daniel Boone leading the settlers through the Cumberland Gap characteristically bears more than a passing resemblance to popular images of Moses leading the chosen people through the desert, while family groups of homesteaders often tend to look more like Joseph, Mary and the infant Jesus than rough-and-ready settlers. In general, however, Saisselin's point follows from the evidence he presents — the point being that the 'cultural roots' of the Western were firmly planted in European (or at least extra-American) soil. And his conclusion seems to turn the whole 'cultural roots' controversy on its head: by making Western duellists into mere 'technicians', the Italians are in these terms debasing the *European* roots of 'the myth of the West'! Whatever the specific application to Spaghettis, 'The Poetics of the Western' points to one basic flaw in the 'authenticity' argument — that is, its disregard for what the function of myth-as-ideology really is, and for how the component parts of a myth historically come together.

But, in coffee-table surveys of Westerns, the 'cultural roots' criticism of Leone's films still persists. The Parkinson and Jeavons *Pictorial History of Westerns* defines Spaghettis as 'violent, amoral, surrealistic, noisy, naive, pretentious, ridiculed, revered and astonishingly popular and lucrative pastiches of the hallowed American Western'. Directors such as Leone are simply snipping away 'the strands of myth and honest recreation which connect the American Western to the real American West'. It soon becomes apparent why the two compilers of the *Pictorial History* overreact in this way: basically, they have got it in for the Italians. For example, one of their major criticisms of Cinecittà Westerns is that they often include 'a singularly Italian emphasis on gross eating habits'. In *Western Movies*, Walter Clapham reckons he is making a significant critical point about Italian Westerns when he tells us that a representative of the Italian government does not consider them good public relations for his country's culture.

Such views are by no means restricted to English critical circles. Jean-Louis Leutrat, for example, in his analysis of *Le Western* (1973), concludes of the Italian Western:

a few enthusiasts have launched themselves into 'appreciations' which are both very detailed and very self-indulgent, on the most recent

manifestations of their favourite genre. It is difficult to understand the recent enthusiasm for the Italian Western phenomenon, if one does not take account of the cinematographic myth which has been created in this way. The Italian films, basing themselves on this myth, have created a universe which is *parallel* to that of the American Western, without ever identifying themselves with it. This process, operating as it does in a limbo, could never be expected to last very long.

The suggestion is that Italian Western directors represent the worst kind of Western buff, and that critics who enthuse over their films should be tarred with the same brush.

Lino Miccichè, in the '. . . et Circenses' section of his *Il cinema Italiano degli anni '60* (1975) presents the same argument, rather more subtly: 'Whereas in the classic Westerns, the point of reference on which to construct a myth is provided by the historic past, in the Italian Western, the point of reference is that same myth (a cinematic myth) seen in the grim light of the present.' Given the basically 'abstract' nature of this type of cinema, which is indicative of 'a notable impotence in the perception and definition of "what is real"', most Italian Westerns are bound to be 'parasitic' — inert, passive re-readings 'of the myth via the "myth"'. Miccichè is convinced that this is a recipe for an uninteresting set of ersatz films, which will, by definition, never manage to challenge accepted ways of seeing in any significant way.

As part of a 'postscript' to a series of 'Notes on the Western', published in the Parisian journal *Cinéma* 71 (March 1971), Gaston Haustrate had gone a great deal further, by asking the question 'Must we burn the Italian Westerns?' (The question was phrased in imitation of Simone de Beauvoir's celebrated essay on the Marquis de Sade.) The answer was 'yes'. According to Haustrate, the Italian Westerns revealed the worst excesses of the 'Mediterranean temperament'. Since the Cinecittà directors were clearly unable or unwilling to appreciate the 'soul' of the 'authentic Western', they had decided to 'deform' certain formal aspects of the genre: whereas in American Westerns violence had always been 'historically placed', in the Italian versions it was 'gratuitous'; the historical context was non-existent, becoming an 'object of derision' in the Civil War sequences of *The Good, the Bad and the Ugly*; the characteristic presence of *commedia dell'arte* grotesques revealed how Spaghettis belonged more to the world of the Borgias and Machiavelli than to that of the American pioneers; Hollywood Westerns had eulogised those positive human qualities which contributed to the American democratic idea, while their Cinecittà counterparts 'despised' such a view of human nature; according to the Italians, those who decided to 'Go West Young Man' were 'unbalanced, twisted and paranoiac'. Haustrate concludes his extended comparison between the sane 'classicism' of the American Western and the manic 'exuberance', too superficial to be categorised as 'baroque', of Spaghettis, by suggesting that the whole movement represented the revenge of Europe on her bastard children, who had succeeded (socially and economically) where Europe had failed. Thus the Cinecittà counter-mythology was based on a profound jealousy, and the 'shadow of the divine Marquis' could clearly be discerned presiding over the comic-strip 'fêtes sanglantes' of the Italian Western.

Some of Haustrate's detailed critical points — when separated from his eulogies to the American (or Hollywood) dream — are actually quite helpful to us, particularly since he assumes such a *direct* connection between the traditional Western and its historical base. The Italian Westerns, because they were made from *outside* the Hollywood system, had no such direct connection with a 'real history', and thus had no obligation to justify themselves with reference to that history. The heroes did not *have* to represent a self-image of 'the American way', or indeed *any* moral lesson which was recognisably 'Western' in the traditional sense. Haustrate reckons that the Spaghettis 'despised' the American democratic idea: it may be that they were in a position to do so precisely *because* they were so 'inauthentic' (in his terms). In a sense, the *rhetoric* of the Italian Westerns — an *extension* of themes, situations, 'décors and details' which audiences already knew and loved — represents a kind of 'free code' (in Sylvie Pierre's words, 1970), 'free' because borrowed from a context where it once had a firm ideological and historical base. This 'free code' could be rearranged and transcribed in ways which the mainstream Hollywood Western, by definition, could not consider — and aspects of frontier history which had been ignored, or evaded, could be introduced, via this rearrangement, for the first time.

As Haustrate suggests, Sergio Leone *does* seem to have a cavalier view of American history, and is evidently fascinated by the more bizarre aspects of the West. His history is not *invented* — that would defeat the purpose of the exercise. But the fact that his Westerns were made in Italy enabled him to indulge in this taste for the bizarre *while still making 'Westerns'*. The milieux and décors of the first two 'Dollars' films were based on research into over fifty eye-witness accounts of what it was like to live in growing frontier towns, particularly in the Southwest, but certain colourful incidents, such as the story of Joseph Alfred ('Jack') Slade, stuck in Leone's mind. Mark Twain, in *Roughing It* (his memories of Virginia City), described Slade as 'so friendly and so gentle spoken that I warmed to him in spite of his awful history'. Buffalo Bill apparently shared Twain's opinion. But Jack Slade was better remembered for a series of incidents which occurred in or near Julesburg, Colorado, in 1863. He had been sent there by his employers, the Overland Stage Company, to get rid of another employee of the company, René Jules (after whom the place had been named), who was suspected of being in league with a band of horse thieves. Slade was ambushed, and shot in the back with a load of buckshot. Having miraculously survived this, Slade tracked Jules down, tied him to a fence-post and tortured him to death. Then he cut off both Jules' ears and nailed one to the post; the other he used as a watch fob. The following year — before Jack Slade was lynched in Virginia City, Montana — he was to be seen using Jules' ear in various bars as 'mock payment for a drink'. Sergio Leone has often referred to this story in interviews. ('A sadist? A madman? Not at all. A man just like any other, who was scared — like everyone around him. For the West was dominated by fear. . . . The ear signified, for all to see, "careful, leave me alone, I am dangerous" '.) Perhaps the story's appeal lies in the obvious bull-fight analogy. The elaborate tortures devised by Tuco and Blondy throughout *The Good, the Bad and the Ugly* (set in the same historical period) certainly seem puny by comparison.

'Sweetwater' may have been chosen as the location for the McBain family massacre in *Once Upon a Time in the West* with reference to an incident which occurred near the Sweetwater Valley, Carbon County, Wyoming on 20 July 1889. It was there that a lynch mob of prominent cattle-barons and businessmen strung up Jim Averell and his former mistress, the ex-prostitute Ella Watson (thought to be 'Cattle Kate', a lady who had often accepted livestock as payment for services rendered) — apparently because their small properties were on land coveted by the giant Wyoming Livestock Association. A noose was tied around Averell's neck, the rope thrown over a nearby pine branch, and the other end tied around Cattle Kate's neck. Then the buckboard on which they were both standing was driven away. Both dropped about two feet in the air. At a token court hearing, the verdict was that the two had 'met their death at the hands of unknown parties'. The incident has obvious parallels with the McBain massacre in *Once Upon a Time* (for Wyoming Livestock Association read A. and P.H. Morton Railroad Company), including the involvement of an ex-prostitute in the person of Jill McBain. The irony of the name 'Sweetwater' has a similar impact whether one is reading about Cattle Kate or watching the first part of the film. In fact, the most recent researches suggest that the Sweetwater lynch mob did not even hang the person they were after: Ella Watson was probably *mistaken* for Cattle Kate. So the Sweetwater affair represents an historical variant on the *Ox-Bow Incident* (Walter Van Tilburg Clark's fictionalised statement about the dangers of 'vigilante justice').

If Leone's interest in weird anecdotes about the American West (such as the more than slightly dubious story of Wyatt Earp shooting wildly in the direction of a footstep behind him, and accidentally killing his deputy) is clearly apparent in his films, so is his 'neo-realist' attitude towards the *details* of everyday life on the frontier. Leone often bases his characters' appearance on nineteenth-century photographs, and he takes personal responsibility for staining, or 'ageing', the costumes his actors wear. The Man With No Name, like most of the principals in the 'Dollars' trilogy, never shaves, and he goes to bed fully clothed. The main streets in 'Leone towns' — San Miguel, White Rocks, Tucumcari, El Paso, Agua Caliente, Flagstone, Sweetwater — bear little resemblance to the traditional Hollywood film set. They usually consist of a few white adobe huts, a church with a bell-tower, and a mansion built in Spanish style dominating the main square, or else a selection of half-built wooden huts. But it is as well to bear in mind Joseph G. McCoy's famous description of early days in the cattle-town he founded — Abilene, Kansas (the location, incidentally, where *Once Upon a Time in the West* was originally to be situated) — before

asserting that Leone is pointlessly flouting Hollywood conventions while at the same time saving money on flimsy Cinecittà sets. Abilene was, according to 'the real McCoy',

> a very small, dead place, consisting of about one dozen log huts, low, small, rude affairs, four-fifths of which were covered with dirt for roofing; indeed, but one shingle roof could be seen in the whole city. The business of the burg was conducted in two small rooms mere log huts, and of course the inevitable saloon, also a log hut, was to be found.

When, in Sergio Sollima's *The Big Gundown*, the main street of a small Western town appears as a sea of mud, with townsfolk wading to the shops, one suspects that this must have been what it was like at the time. In this, as in so much else, the Italian Westerns owe a great deal to those scenes in George Stevens' *Shane* which take place outside the Grafton Store. According to Leone these sequences were the first to show 'what really happens when a bullet hits someone'.

This is not to suggest that Leone is in any significant way a 'neo-realist' director (even if, as he says, he *was* trained 'in the hard school of neo-realism'). Far from it. But apparent authenticity of background is one strategy he uses, in his attempts systematically to deconstruct one mythology and reconstruct another: to demythologise, rather than to demythicise. In general, the Italian Westerns do not represent a movement towards demythicisation: many of them, for example, resemble parables. But they often criticise the mythology of the Hollywood Western, as a prelude to using its 'syntax' for specifically Italian purposes. In this type of *critical* cinema (dealing as it does with genres, 'formulas', 'codes' and audience expectations), 'neo-realist' backgrounds are a crucial component. Other directors of Spaghettis, such as Sergio Corbucci and Giulio Questi, with less interest in detail than Leone, tend to use landscapes — such as snow flats, salt pans, 'glorious sun-baked sands' — expressionistically, in ways which American film-makers had seldom attempted up to the mid-1960s.

Henry Fonda has commented on Sergio Leone's unusually enthusiastic interest in the tiniest detail of setting and props. Charles Bronson was surprised to discover that Leone 'knows more about the Western than most American directors'. Clint Eastwood has described how Leone 'lives' the parts he is directing: 'He is a short, heavy fellow, but when he acts out his roles you can see what he wants and you know that he really feels himself tall and lean, a gunfighter.' This identification with the main characters is illustrated by the opening sequence of *For a Few Dollars More*: on a ledge overlooking an expanse of desert, an unseen bounty-hunter waits. He is *heard* lighting a cigar, cocking his rifle, and casually whistling. Leone himself did the whistling.

Describing the way he shot *Duck, You Sucker*, Leone has said:

> It's the two characters in the film that are making it, so in fact I have two directors with opposing conceptions as to the staging. They have the camera in their hands. While shooting, I just put myself in their place, and their two fantasies co-exist and meet within me.

This process has its clearest expression during the closing moments of the duel between Bronson and Fonda in *Once Upon a Time in the West*. Bronson recalls (in flashback) the death of his brother, and, for a brief moment, Fonda *shares* the memory, at last discovering who Harmonica, played by Bronson, is.

Throughout Leone's films (and the derivatives they inspired, particularly those by Corbucci, Damiani and Sollima) it is clear that he is concerned with aspects of American history in which Hollywood had rarely shown interest — aspects which could only achieve prominence once the genre had been divorced from its traditional historical base:

1 *The Southwestern frontier* According to Professor Eugene Hollon in *Frontier Violence*, 'violence associated with the cattle industry on the northern plains was fairly tame stuff compared to what went on in New Mexico and Arizona in the 1870s and 1880s'.

2 *Confrontations between Anglos and Greasers* (Gringos and Mexicans) rather than Cavalry and Indians, or Homesteaders and Ranchers (Washington land treaties with the Indians had often contained the phrase 'as long as the grass shall grow and the rivers run': in the Spanish desert there is very little grass, and most of the rivers seem to have dried up). Other Spaghetti directors — such as Corbucci and Damiani — were to give these confrontations a more overtly *political* resonance, often relating them to the concerns of Third World (specifically Latin American) politics.

3 *The relationship between Mexican bandits and peasant communities* Just as the small ranchers had their folk-heroes in Billy the Kid and the James brothers, the Hispanos of New Mexico hero-worshipped Elfego Baca and Juan José Herrera, who protected Mexican farmers and sheepherders from Texan landowners in the 1880s. Herrera first came into contact with Anglo violence when he saw some of the methods used by railroad and mining unions in Colorado, and Leone may well have had him in mind in his creation of characters such as Tuco Ramirez in *The Good, the Bad and the Ugly* (particularly during the scene in which Tuco meets his brother Padré Ramirez and explains that, from their social background, their choice of career is limited to bandit or priest); Cheyenne in *Once Upon a Time*, a man who was originally to be called Manuel 'Cheyenne' Gutierrez; and Juan, the peasant bandit who becomes a political hero as a result of his ambition to rob the bank at Mesa Verde, in *Duck, You Sucker*.

4 *The significance of the bounty-hunter* — a character who seldom appeared in 1950s mainstream Hollywood Westerns, the few examples including Anthony Mann's *The Naked Spur* (1953) and the TV series which made Steve McQueen's name, *Wanted, Dead or Alive* (1958). In the 'Dollars' films, the bounty-hunter becomes a key symptom of violence in the history of the American West. *For a Few Dollars More* begins with the words 'Where life had no value, death, sometimes had its price. That is why the bounty-hunters appeared.'

5 *The significance of the hired gun* employed by giant commercial companies to 'remove small obstacles' — perhaps Leone was thinking of the twenty-two gunfighters hired by the Wyoming Livestock Association ($5 a day, expenses, and a bonus for every homesteader killed 'resisting arrest') during the Johnson County War in January 1892, who arrived with a trainload of horses, tents, ammunition, dynamite and strychnine. Since 1968, this theme has often been exploited by Hollywood, for example in *Butch Cassidy and the Sundance Kid*, and *The Wild Bunch*, but never to such telling effect as in the Morton-Frank subplot of *Once Upon a Time in the West*. John Sturges' *The Magnificent Seven*

(known in Europe as *The Seven Mercenaries*, and based on Kurosawa's *Seven Samurai*) — which grossed over three times as much money in Europe and Japan as it had in America — had encouraged American producers to think more in terms of the European market. Clearly, stories about hired guns, or mercenaries, operating near the Mexican border (albeit, in the case of six out of the Seven, mercenaries with their hearts in the right places) were great box-office in France and Italy. Other aspects of *The Magnificent Seven* — the semi-parodic, 'hard', dialogue ('We deal in lead, brother'), the idea of a group of 'specialists' in killing and of their relationship with a Mexican peasant community, the Boot Hill sequence — may have influenced the form and shape of the Italian Western movement. Four stars of *The Magnificent Seven* subsequently featured in Spaghettis, three of them in films by Leone.

6   *The status of immigrant or minority groups in growing Western towns* — particularly 'John Chinaman', Irish navvies, Scottish cattlemen, Polish or Swedish mercenaries, and Mexican 'Greasers': less a 'melting pot', than a 'vegetable soup', with all the ingredients remaining separate. In Sollima's films, the Mormons are usually seen as social outcasts (soulmates of bandits on the run). Other Spaghetti directors were more concerned with the relationship between freed slaves and Mexican bandits during the Reconstruction era. The role of the 'outsider' in the community is, of course, a key feature of most Italian Westerns.

7   *The symbolism of the cemetery, and of death icons in general* The fact that cemeteries were customarily called 'Boot Hill' says a great deal, according to Leone, about the cheapness of human life during the period: those who died with their boots *off* had no graveyards named after them.

8   *The significance of internment camps*, and, of course,

9   of *The needless brutality which accompanied the Civil War* Leone's Northern camp, Betterville, in *The Good, the Bad and the Ugly*, made its appearance at a time when American historians were reappraising documents about the Andersonville atrocities in the South (which included slaughter, starvation, and even cannibalism.) In a sequence cut from the English release print, Il Cattivo (Lee Van Cleef) justifies his treatment of Southern prisoners to the Betterville camp commandant by specifically referring to the Andersonville example. But Leone's version is associated with the *winning* side. As much screen time is devoted to Betterville as to the spectacular battle, and the film abounds in brief visual references to overcrowded 'hospitals', crippled war veterans (the one-armed Union soldier, the legless Confederate 'half-soldier'), and disposal of the dead. John Ford may have shown Civil War field surgery in *The Horse Soldiers* ('Can I have some of that liquor to swallow, Doc ...?'), but he never attempted to create an atmosphere of decay and death as pervasive as Leone's. However, to suggest, as Haustrate does, that the Civil War is treated as an 'object of derision' is to misunderstand Leone's polemic. As we shall see, Leone deliberately blurs the traditional distinction between North and South, and introduces obvious anachronisms, in order to make the war seem more real to his audience.

10 *The corruption of some law-enforcers in frontier towns*, and

11 the *neo-feudalistic ways in which Spanish/ American towns may have been run* Baxter in *A Fistful of Dollars*, the sheriff of White Rocks in *For a Few Dollars More*, and the sheriff of Flagstone Territory (Keenan Wynn) in the shooting-script of *Once Upon a Time in the West* (see Appendix 2) are inept, scared, or on someone's payroll. In *For a Few Dollars More*, the Man With No Name asks the Sheriff of White Rocks (who has tried to warn 'Red' Cavanagh's men that the Man is on their trail) whether a lawman is supposed to be 'courageous ... and, above all, honest'. 'That he is,' replies the Sheriff. The Man then pulls the tin star off the lawman's chest, throws it into the street, and tells the townspeople, 'You need a new Sheriff.' The Baxter-Rojo rivalry in *Fistful* illustrates another way in which towns just south of the border may have been administered. Leone seems to be suggesting that it is dangerous to be oversentimental about grass-roots, 'democratic' notions of frontier justice. Hollywood Westerns may have featured the occasional corrupt sheriff (or, more characteristically, banker/mayor) but there is the suggestion in most Italian Westerns that such corruption was a structural problem.

12 *The role of women in the West* Just as Italian Western towns tend to consist of *only* a church, a barber's shop, a hotel, a saloon/brothel, a general store and a bank (the inhabitants all providing services, rather than producing anything), so the role of women in the community is restricted to whores, hotel receptionists, or Mexican peasants who live just out of town: schoolmarms, judges' daughters, ranchers' wives or wealthy Eastern girls trying to make a go of it out West would seem very out of place in this setting. Grace Kellys, Rhonda Flemings, and Inger Stevenses ('those inevitable women', in Leone's words), for most Spaghetti directors constitute 'the shame of the traditional Western'. As Leone has put it,

Even in the greatest Westerns, the woman is imposed on the action, as a star, and is generally destined to be 'had' by the male lead. But she does not exist *as a woman*. If you cut her out of the film, in a version which you can imagine, the film becomes much better. In the desert, the essential problem was to survive. Women were an obstacle to survival! Usually, the woman not only holds up the story, but she has no real character, no reality. She is a symbol. She is there without having any reason to be there, simply because one must have a woman, and because the hero must prove, in some way or another, that he has 'sex-appeal'.

More than one critic has noted that Leone's films (and derivatives) have made the old-style Western heroine redundant. But some critics, in Andrew Sarris' words, have interpreted the role of women in Italian Westerns ('realistic' or not) as revealing 'an astonishing hatred of the female':

the thin veneer of Madonna worship has been scraped away in the Spaghetti Western to reveal . . . a hatred never remotely approached even in the wildest of the Freudian Hollywood Westerns. . . . The Freudian Western amplified the mythology of the male by giving him a female partner. By contrast, the Spaghetti Western has reduced the female partner to a mindless, helpless victim, a mere detail in the bloody decor. Yet the most 'realistic' Italian films are relatively squeamish about abusing the Madonna principle lurking even in the boldest whore. Consequently, the Western provides the necessary distancing for Italian

directors to abuse a species they at least subconsciously despise. The Western for the Italian director is thus comparable to the French bedroom farce for the American director of yore in that only by the distancing represented by gay Paree could adultery achieve the necessary lightness for an artist and audience of Puritans.

Simone de Beauvoir, in *Tout Compte Fait*, 1972, seems implicitly to disagree:

some adventure films have kept me in suspense — some westerns, for example, including films made by the Italians such as *The Good, the Bad and the Ugly*. Stories that I should think ludicrous if they were written down can enchant me on the screen. . . . There is an odd shift, a difference of phase, between the immediate evidence of one's eyes (the indestructible illusion of reality) and the unlikelihood of the facts. If a director uses this shift intelligently, he can make it produce the most delightful effects. That is the basis of the humour of the Italian westerns. But it has to be used intelligently.

Clearly, Ms de Beauvoir did not think these films *too* ideologically unsound for comfortable viewing. Whether or not one accepts Andrew Sarris' view, it is clear that a distinction must be drawn between the attempt by some Spaghetti directors to criticise the role of women in the traditional Western, and the (Italian) stereotype of women which may have been substituted. One of Leone's criticisms was precisely that 'the Freudian Western amplified the mythology of the male by giving him a female partner', and that the Hollywood heroine did not even exist *'as a woman'*. But the criticism may well have been, at base, a historical rather than an ideological one. 'In the desert', Annie very seldom got her gun.

Another, less direct way in which Leone reveals his interest in the more bizarre aspects of American history, and at the same time his intention to demythologise the Hollywood West (as a prelude, or even backdrop, to the creation of a new mythology), is by redefining his characters' relationship with the landscape. In the 1950s Hollywood Western (and especially Will Wright's 'classical plot'), the good guys the hero is eventually persuaded to defend tend to have some commitment to the land — as farmers, community-builders, law-enforcers, ranchers. Even the lone gunman archetype in *Shane* fights on the side of the homesteader, and will help out with domestic or farming chores. In Leone's films, the bounty-hunters have no such commitment to rural values, or to the development of the community. Since they have no intention to settle, they use locations as means to their own ends. This is well illustrated by the scene in *The Good, the Bad and the Ugly* where Clint Eastwood and Eli Wallach shoot down the members of Lee Van Cleef's gang. They start at one end of the main street and walk slowly to the other end, picking off the gang one by one; they then ride away, on the next stage of their journey to Sad Hill cemetery and the gold. Mike Wallington, in *Cinema*, has neatly pinpointed this curiously modern relationship between character and landscape: 'the gringos treat landscape with an urban sensibility — it's like a block of apartments, somewhere to move through'. Brutality in Leone's films often has the quality of urban violence, of the *film noir*, rather than of pioneering violence in defence of a threatened rural existence. (As Professor Hollon has recently observed, in *Frontier Violence*, it was in the Eastern cities rather than on the Western plains that most of the violence occurred in nineteenth-century America.)

Leone's films seldom dwell on the more constructive aspects of frontier 'mythology-as-ideology' — the implications of starting a new life out West, the building of a community (schools, chapels, courtrooms, banks), the resource shown by some early entrepreneurs, transporting cattle from Texas to beef-starved Northeastern towns after the Civil War, the 'improving' effects of such developments as the railway revolution, and the conversion of arid land. As Franco Ferrini has observed, Sergio Leone's West is 'a world irredeemably condemned to immobility, somnolence, to the lack of all resource and development'. If in Sam Peckinpah's films the characters' odysseys take the form of a quest for self-knowledge, a final attempt to 'enter my house justified', Leone's odysseys (if that is the appropriate term) are more concerned with vengeance (*For a Few Dollars More*; *Once Upon a Time in the West*), treasure-hunting (*The Good, the Bad and the Ugly*), or blood-money (*A Fistful of Dollars*). The Man With No Name may tell Colonel Mortimer that he intends to buy a ranch 'and possibly retire' on his bounty, but when, in the final shot of *For a Few Dollars More*, he drives a farm-cart into the hills,

it is full of valuable corpses. The Clint Eastwood character has no intention of joining the ranks of the Cincinnati — those figures in classical and American mythology who perform good deeds and then disappear from public life, to work on their farms. To the oppressed local communities he unwittingly serves, he may appear to combine the selflessness of a Garibaldi with the idealism of a Mazzini, but in fact he is more likely to use the methods of a Cavour, or a Premier Depretis.

Apart from anything else, the Man With No Name seems to be operating as a completely marginal figure *vis-à-vis* the various social groups he encounters. Each of the films in the 'Dollars' trilogy shows him on some kind of journey — but it is a journey that begins nowhere and ends nowhere. The Man arrives in a town with a whole series of options open to him, and leaves when all these options have been used up: it is not barbed wire, or the railroads, or the big ranchers, or a call to 'Go West, Young Man' that impels him to move on: it is simply that the various groups he has tricked cannot be exploited any more. The explanation of his marginality may perhaps be a 'historical' one — that he comes from a different culture: but, against that, he seems to be equally 'marginal' to both the Gringos and the Mexicans (for example in *A Fistful of Dollars*). It is almost as if his adventures in society — which, despite Leone's attention to detail, have a strangely 'disembodied' feel about them — represent the exposition and working out of some economic theorem (perhaps concerned with the relative effect of monopoly, bilateral monopoly, duopoly, and oligopoly . . .). The 'collage' structure of the films is built around the Man's successful attempts to sell himself (or seem to commit himself) first to one bidder, then to another: the value of his services (or those of his rivals) inflates as he walks through a series of adventures which keep moving (jigsaw-fashion — far from the unambiguous, linear development of most Hollywood Western narratives in the traditional mould) largely because of ever more extraordinary shifts in loyalty. As the Man flits from one antagonist (a bandit gang, a rival, an army) to another, as the antagonists change their uniforms (from Federales to bandits, from bounty-hunters to bandits, from the North to the South and vice versa), and as the Man manages to shut off all his various options (for example, by damaging one party, in order to enhance his value to another), the complex antagonisms are gradually (and progressively) pared down to a simple resolution — in the form of a face-off, or settling of accounts, where all the various plots and subplots are more or less balanced up. The theorem (what would happen if a Man with his abilities as a 'performer' and his 'style' were to be placed in the middle of this or that set of antagonisms?) seems to be much more important than the story, or the motivations of the various characters.

Given this schematic quality in the 'Dollars' films, it comes as no surprise to learn that one of the main inspirations for Sergio Leone (after *Fistful*) was 'the Puparri — marionettes of the traditional Sicilian theatre. I reread all the "arguments" of these puppet shows, the canvases on which the Sicilian puppeteers had embroidered their stories: and I discovered a strange fraternity between the Puparri and my friends of the Wild West. Their adventures were identical. Of course the décors and details were different — in other words, all the *external* things. But the motivations of human beings are simple, and the situations do not change. One is working within a fairly restricted margin.' The development of Leone's narratives is usually labyrinthine, based on a series of almost self-contained episodes, each of which builds up to a climax which, in a more traditional Western, would be big enough to carry the whole movie. As Noel Simsolo has noted, the puppet stage is a main street (or a series of main streets), the scene-changes involve the Man going in and out of doors or through 'barriers' (either belonging to the various bidders, or else representing neutral territory), and the curtain which reveals his journey to us is a curtain of dust. In the first film, the Man negotiates with two rival factions; in the second, two rival bounty-hunters negotiate with one faction; in the third, three rival bandits negotiate with two armies in the American Civil War. The puppet-show form seems to lend itself well to the exposition of fairly intricate theorems (Karl Marx, for example, is alleged to have explained his ideas about class warfare to his daughter 'Tussy' by telling her a series of stories about a Magic Toyshop.) But it does not really work (as Leone himself suggests) unless the characters are emblematic or symbolic ones. Eastwood, the man who leads the audience, like a mercenary version of the traditional 'trickster' figure, from one group or 'enclosed' space to another, is the most marginal of Leone's characters. In the second and third films

of the trilogy (the ones partly based on the 'arguments' of Sicilian puppet plays), he has no past, no relationships (his 'friendships' are in fact competitions with other tricksters), and he sees no need to make any political or social choices. Most of the other main characters in the trilogy seem to relate more to Hollywood/Western stereotypes which we can recognise. Colonel Mortimer, an ex-soldier and a technical 'specialist', is fundamentally an honourable man whose revenge is legitimised by Hollywood (and Sicilian) convention. Like Indio, he has a past. Indio is a psychotic baddy — more baroque in presentation than the villains of the complex Freudian Westerns of the 1950s (he smokes pot, and, in the Italian version, baptises his gun with holy water before shooting people), but still recognisable. The Bad (played by the actor who was the Good in the previous film) is less anarchic (more systematic) than the Good and the Ugly: when he is paid, he can be relied upon to see his job through; he enlists on the Union side in the Civil War, and is duly promoted to the rank of second-in-command to the officer in charge of an internment camp. His two rivals are also bad — but there is a cinematic justice in his death (where there would not be with the other two) since he is a *conventional* baddy who should meet a conventional baddy's end. As Sylvie Pierre has suggested in *Cahiers du Cinéma* (no. 200-1), the levels of irony which can be applied to the three main characters in *The Good, the Bad and the Ugly* vary between Lee Van Cleef and the others:

This lack of symmetry is the most interesting invention of the film. The irony of the label [the Bad] which is applied to Lee Van Cleef denounces the cinema as conventional fiction, *by making that convention function*. On the other hand, the irony of the labels applied to the other two *undermines* the cinematic convention of the good and the bad by *preventing it from functioning*: neither the good, nor the ugly proves that there is an absolute goodness or badness. The one closes the eyes of a dying man, gently; the other steals his watch, vindictively. So, if in the end the bad is the only one killed, this does not follow entirely from a taste for 'pure spectacle'. It is necessary for the two survivors to emancipate themselves from conventional western fictions: to become two ordinary individuals in time of war; whose gold helps them to shed the need for further adventure. The bad does not die so that good may triumph: he dies for the safeguard (and the peril) of the western.

Just as in *For a Few Dollars More* the Leone character (Eastwood) finds himself at odds with the Hollywood character (Van Cleef) — one of the more interesting antagonisms which run through the film, as Noel Simsolo points out — so, in *The Good, the Bad and the Ugly*, the two Leone characters (Eastwood and Wallach) find themselves at odds with a different type of Hollywood character (again Van Cleef). This antagonism is a constant, amid all the false identities, changes of uniform and the extraordinary duplicity. Whereas the Bad enlists with the Union, the Good and the Ugly stumble into the war by accident (and are prepared to force the pace of military strategy, to further their own ends). The Ugly is a peasant bandit — raucous, unsubtle (except in the sense that a rat is subtle), and from a background which polarises young people into bandits or priests: like Cheyenne (Jason Robards) in *Once Upon a Time in the West*, and Juan (Rod Steiger) in *Duck, You Sucker*, he is an 'amoral familist' (to use Banfield's term) — and his character represents one of the distinctively Italian additions to the genre. For example, the figure of Judas is often celebrated in Latin cultures, for his function of focusing and channelling aggression: as we shall see, the Ugly is celebrated in a similar way, and frequently associated with the figure of Judas; his untrustworthiness is thus based on a very different set of values to that of the Bad.

In short, Eastwood's journeys are not 'odysseys' in the Hollywood sense at all. Since he is such a marginal figure, it is, in fact, extremely difficult to relate him to any of the cherished myths of frontier society. He plays the emblematic role of the trickster, just as the Ugly plays the emblematic role of the peasant bandit. Other antagonists in the trilogy — Mortimer, Indio, the Bad, for example — are emblematic for different reasons, since they can be located within the formulae of the Hollywood Western. The Man With No Name, and Leone's social bandits, illustrate well the 'strange fraternity between the Puparri and my friends of the Wild West': they represent one of the strategies Leone uses, to give life to well-worn Western situations. Mortimer, Indio and the Bad represent another (which is comprehensible in the terms of reference

of the conventions which are being deconstructed). In general terms, Leone's updated marionettes of the traditional Sicilian theatre (the trickster, the bandit) help us to relate his Spaghetti Westerns to surveys of Southern Italian society such as Banfield's, for their functions within the stories relate to symbols and myths which are special to that society. The other main characters (from a different puppet show) help us directly to understand Leone's critique of the Hollywood Western and its values.

And this is where Leone's cavalier view of history becomes interesting. The characters who are to a great extent Italian by origin, and their 'adventures', may belong to some timeless Sicilian puppet tradition, but 'the décors and details' are different ('in other words, all the *external* things'). The settings for the escapades of characters from *both* traditions, the clothes the antagonists wear, the weapons they use, the context for their business activities, are all based on a 'peep-show' type of historical research. Those aspects of frontier history which Hollywood has traditionally ignored, and which, as a result of the commercial success of Leone's films, were to become standard ingredients in the Spaghetti Western, serve the function of 'décors and details' in Leone's fusion of two traditions in popular culture. Sometimes, these 'décors and details' (and the history) are manipulated to suit the demands of an Italian tradition; sometimes, they represent a 'neo-realist' background, which locates Leone's critique in a specific context; sometimes, they appear to have been included (as 'digressions'), simply because Leone is so enthusiastic about the Wild West. Whether or not Leone thinks he is setting the historical record straight, by removing Robert Warshow's 'concept of honour' (see page 120) from the picture — a doubtful proposition, if one accepts that much of his critique (however 'authentic' it may look), and the 'concept of honour' which is substituted for the final 'settling of accounts', are both to some extent based on specifically Italian values and traditions — it is clear that he is criticising *Hollywood's* version of frontier history. In the process, many aspects of that history (those which can best be fused with, say, the 'arguments' of the Puparri), and especially the most cavalier ones, were *emphasised* in Western movies for the first time.

But the Sicilian puppet shows were also morality plays. And, as we shall see when studying the

'Dollars' films in greater depth, there *is* a clear morality running through them. The Man may always be a marginal figure *vis-à-vis* society, and his journeys may not be odysseys in any accepted sense, but he is not operating in a *moral* vacuum. Other Spaghetti Westerns sometimes came to resemble biblical parables. Leone's 'Dollars' films do not (at least, not in a direct way), but they still owe a lot to the Italian morality play. *Once Upon a Time in the West*, on the other hand, confronts some of the cherished myths of the Western more directly and (perhaps because of Bernardo Bertolucci's contribution), a clearer view of the Hollywood interpretation of history emerges. As Leone has said (about *Fistful*),

> naturally, it was not my business to write or make history — in any case, I had neither the inclination nor the right. So I made the film starting from *my own* history — a fantastic history — seeking also to say some things about the precise links with the men of today. . . . It was necessary to present a very *precise* historical debate — thoroughly documented — in order to address this problem — with the infusion of a large measure of fantasy as well; within this debate, I could look at human values which are no longer around today. It was a little as though one was going *à la recherche du temps perdu*.

It is apparent in *Once Upon a Time* (as it is in the 'Dollars' trilogy, for different reasons) that Leone would not consider himself one of the 'progressive' school of commentators on Western mythology: at the beginning of the film, as the train pulls into Cattle Corner station, the words 'directed by Sergio Leone' drop into the frame, and land just in front of the locomotive's cowcatcher, to act as a buffer. The scenario of *Once Upon a Time* is full of *reversals* of 'classical' Hollywood plots: the opening sequence (where three gunslingers wait for the good guy, who is arriving on the train) reverses the equivalent situation in *High Noon*; the massacre of the McBain family reverses the 'idyllic' scenes involving the Starrett family in *Shane* (with little Timmy McBain behaving exactly as little Joey Starrett does in George Stevens' film); and the Frank-Morton plot (which is used to comment on the implications of the arrival of the railroad) reverses the morality of the *Iron Horse* or *Union Pacific* sub-genre. The cavalry, the Indians ('manifest destiny' as

natural right), the cowboys, the prospectors, the mountainmen ('rugged individualism') seldom appear in Leone's films, and when they do, it is simply as local colour. In another scene cut from the English release print of *The Good, the Bad and the Ugly*, Tuco tests the accuracy of the new Colt revolver he has pieced together from parts of the latest models on show in the gunsmith's shop (a bizarre celebration of the development of interchangeable parts for firearms) by shooting at (and knocking down) three life-sized wooden Indians. A weird (and irrelevant) example of 'manifest destiny' is thus enacted in a 'tuppence coloured' shooting gallery.

Lack of reference to the 'foundation myths' does not, of course, necessarily mean that the stories develop in a historical vacuum. As we have seen, Leone's knowledge of the more bizarre aspects of the West is unusually thorough. And the 'local colour' is detailed. In *Once Upon a Time in the West*, as the train arrives at Flagstone station, an aged prospector ('Gramps'), plus burro, a few disgruntled 'Redskin warriors' (who have travelled with the cattle), a cattle-baron, a cripple, some black servants, and a finely dressed child all appear briefly, each with different motives for visiting Arizona. Leone's personal copy of the script includes a subsequent and related scene (shot, but cut from the final version) which reveals his interest in the wider implications of such background details:

> Scene 35. Railway Carriage, Interior. Day.
> . . . The Man [Charles Bronson] . . . looks around, inside the carriage. Panning shot of the interior, which is crowded with passengers. The people who set out from a town like Abilene [later changed to Flagstone], are different from those who arrive there. On one side, the 'victorious', those who have 'tamed' the West, with brains, a whip and a pistol. And those who have not succeeded. Others have had their first 'victories', have managed to make good money, even become rich, and are now going to enjoy themselves in one of the cities of the East, which resemble Europe, and which seem so far away. Also present are those who are responsible both for such riches and such misery — the businessmen, the commercial travellers, the technicians, so used to the train, that once inside, they settle down and fall asleep immediately, without even looking around them.

The ambivalent attitude towards the 'significance of the frontier' which runs through *Once Upon a Time in the West* is well illustrated by the dialogue between Frank (Henry Fonda) and Harmonica (Charles Bronson) just before the final showdown:

Frank: Surprised to see me here?

Harmonica: I knew you'd come.

Frank: Morton once told me I could never be like him. Now I understand why. Wouldn't have bothered him knowing you were around somewhere alive.

Harmonica: So you found out you're not a businessman after all.

Frank: Just a man.

Harmonica: An ancient race. (*Pause*.) Other Mortons'll be along, and they'll kill it off.

Frank: Future don't matter to us. Nothing matters now — not the land, not the money, not the woman. I came here to see you. 'Cause I know that now you'll tell me what you're after.

Harmonica: Only at the point of dyin'.

Frank: I know.

This dialogue, which forms part of the most stylish passage in the whole of Donati and Leone's screenplay, is punctuated by shots of the railroad gang laying tracks — and has its visual counterpart in the twin images on which the full-length version of the film ends: as the train pulls out of Sweetwater (a town which is no more than a series of flimsy, 'film-set' frontages, hastily erected so that there can be a station ready by the time the railroad gang arrives), Harmonica rides off into the hills, with the corpse of Cheyenne slung over the bandit's horse — and both images are contained within one long panning-shot. So, *Once Upon a Time in the West* opens with death at Cattle Corner station, and closes with death at Sweetwater station — perhaps the inevitable result of technological progress. Turner's 'frontier' thesis (and the films which had their ideological base there) stressed that this progress 'evolved naturally' from the very origins of the frontier, and from the frontier *process*: after the explorers came the fur traders; after the pioneers came capitalist free enterprise — and all these different 'phases' contributed, in their own ways, to the building of the new America. As Jefferson might have said, 'I was a warrior so my son could be a farmer so *his* son could have the choice of being a poet or going to Harvard Business School.' *Once Upon a Time in the West* seems to be challenging this evolutionary

model ('the perennial rebirth of society') in two ways: by showing how radical was the break which occurred in the frontier process with the arrival of the capitalist barons, and by indicating how those whose destiny it was to make way for technological advance (the heroes of an earlier phase in frontier history) could foresee their own fate — and resent it. In the light of this, the parallel between the Frank-Harmonica dialogue and the famous dialogue which concludes chapter 4 of Giuseppe Tomasi di Lampedusa's *The Leopard* (1958) can scarcely have been accidental:

Chevally thought: 'This state of things won't last; our lively new modern administration will change it all.' The Prince was depressed. 'All this shouldn't last; but it will, always; the human "always" of course, a century, two centuries . . . and after that it will be different, but worse. We were the Leopards and Lions; those who'll take our place will be little jackals, hyenas; and the whole lot of us, Leopards, jackals and sheep, we'll all go on thinking ourselves the salt of the earth.' They thanked each other and said good-bye.

Chevally, the representative of Northern Italian 'progress', is a Piedmontese bureaucrat: Don Fabrizio, the apologist for the traditional Southern mentality, is Prince of Salina in Sicily. The Prince resents the Northern notion of 'progress' which will undermine the feudal, Southern way of life of his dynasty, but he is aware that he must make way for it. Frank, the representative of Eastern technology, is attempting to become a businessman: Harmonica, the apologist for frontier individualism — for exorcising *his own* memories, is 'the last gentle man'. Both accept the inevitability of the process which will bring other 'jackals' like Morton along when it gains momentum, and which will 'kill off' what they have in common. In other words, both see this process as something very new — even revolutionary. If the American Civil War theme in *The Good, the Bad and the Ugly* occasionally looks like a transposition of the North-South struggle during the equivalent period of *Italian* political history, the cynicism of that film (in which the heroes see the struggle as at best a distraction) is a long way from the nostalgia for 'the world we have lost' which lies at the heart of *Once Upon a Time in the West*. Harmonica may not be an aristo-crat, and his lament may not take such a reactionary form as Don Fabrizio's in *The Leopard*, but the two characters share an awareness — and a resentment — of their own destiny, an awareness which belies any attempt to frame a progressive, evolutionary account of the process which is destroying them both. From this perspective, the critique of Turner's thesis contained in *Once Upon a Time* is a great deal less radical (if more explicit) than in the 'Dollars' films: despite Bertolucci's contribution to the story, Leone seems to be veering more towards Visconti territory. But at least the film is confronting Hollywood head-on, by laying bare what are seen to be contradictions in the 'progressive' aspects of movie frontier history, and, in the context of 1967-8, when the Turner thesis was providing a justification of sorts for the South East Asian frontier, the position of *Once Upon a Time* may perhaps be interpreted as an overtly critical one. The parallel with Lampedusa's *The Leopard* shows again how complex is the relationship between Leone's films and the history of the Wild West: the films may be commenting, implicitly or explicitly, on that history (as seen by Hollywood) but the comments are likely to be couched in terms which can be located within an *Italian* cultural context. According to Leone, his interpretation of frontier history (which some critics have called 'deeply pessimistic') represents 'the essential difference between me and John Ford'.

> As Romans, we have a strong sense of the fragility of empires. It is enough to look around us. I admire very much that great optimist, John Ford. His naiveté permitted him to make *Cinderella* — I mean, *The Quiet Man*. But, as Italians, we see things differently. That is what I have tried to show in my films. The great plains — they are very beautiful, but, when the storm comes, should people bury their heads in the sand of the desert? I believe that people like to be treated as adults from time to time. Because a man is wearing a sombrero, and because he rides a horse, does not necessarily mean that he is an imbecile. . . .
>
> Ford, because of his European origins — as a good Irishman — has always seen the problem from a Christian point of view . . . his characters and protagonists always look forward to a rosy, fruitful future. Whereas I see the history of the West as really the reign of violence by violence.

In the 'Dollars' trilogy, there are no good-natured

brawls: when people hit each other, they mean it to hurt (or else they mean onlookers to *think* that it hurts). Leone was particularly delighted when a Jewish-American businessman came up to him and suggested, 'Signor Leone, you should make the story of the American constitution, which appears to be so democratic, but which in fact is tremendously evasive. In the first place, it was drafted by criminals . . .'

So the criticisms of Gaston Haustrate (in 'Must we burn the Italian Westerns?') — essentially an emotional reaction against the political implications of Leone's films, with 'Mexico' and 'the Southwest' being read as a synonym for 'Italy', perhaps — at least suggest how far the Italian's version of frontier history can provide us with a way into his films. Leone may admire Hollywood Westerns, but he does not believe in the dreams they embody: the historical bases of the 'myth of the West' may not be central to his concerns (after all, *Aida* is not a documentary about Egypt), but they do provide one point of reference.

Since Haustrate published his article, and since the heyday of the 'cultural roots' school of critics of the Italian Western, much interesting work has been done on Leone's work in particular, and Spaghettis in general. We have already referred to Noel Simsolo's article in *Image et Son* (September 1973). In the same year as Haustrate's article appeared (1971) *Cahiers du Cinéma* featured an analysis of 'The Ideology of the Italian Western' by Pierre Baudry: this study of the 'second phase' (in our terms, the third variant) of the Spaghetti Western relates to the politics of the genre, and will be dealt with in a later chapter on that issue. Like Sylvie Pierre's articles (1968-70), it shows that the *Cahiers* school were beginning to take Italian Westerns seriously. In America, Andrew Sarris had devoted two pieces to 'Spaghetti and Sagebrush' (in *The Village Voice*) as early as September 1968: although these were based on an extended comparison between developments in the American and Italian genres (a comparison which at times encouraged Sarris to caricature the Italian films he was studying), they at least attempted to locate Spaghettis — whatever their *cinematic origins* — in a specifically Italian context. Also in America, *Film Comment* (March 1973) published a useful general survey of Leone's films by Richard Jameson, and in Canada, *Take One* (May 1973) featured a patchy analysis of 'The Grotesque West of Sergio Leone' by Stuart

Kaminsky, rewritten for *The Velvet Light Trap* (Spring 1974) under the ambitious, if misleading, title 'The Italian Western Beyond Leone'. Perhaps the most significant indication of a general shift in critical approach to Italian Westerns occurs in the Italian film journal *Bianco e Nero*. In the issue for January 1968, Tullio Kezich concluded a survey of recent American Westerns with an attack on the home-grown product for its emphasis on sado-masochism, its crude soundtrack music, its pretentiousness, its monotonous and heavy-handed sensationalism. A film like Questi's *Django Kill*, wrote the baffled and faintly embarrassed Kezich, owed more to Edgar Allan Poe and Roger Corman than to Bret Harte and John Ford. The issue of *Bianco e Nero* for September 1971, by contrast, is entirely devoted to 'Leone and the Anti-Western'. Apart from script extracts, and an interview, the journal includes a penetrating analysis of Leone's *critical* type of cinema, by Franco Ferrini — an analysis which owes a lot to the *Cahiers* collective text on *Young Mr Lincoln* (1970). Ferrini's article examines in depth a series of icons, indices, visual signs and themes in Leone's films — some prominent, some peripheral — as representative of the director's redefinition of traditional Western iconography: the analysis is structured under the (apparently random) headings 'Drinks', 'Names', 'Weapons', 'Banks', 'Cattle', 'Laws', 'Cemeteries', 'The Dance' and 'Duels'. Sometimes, the semiological aspects of Ferrini's method lead him to strain the evidence: Leone's whistling, at the beginning of *For a Few Dollars More*, is compared with Hitchcock's celebrated personal appearances (as if the audience *knew* it was Leone!); the shot of Jill McBain throwing earth into an open grave (filmed from the 'coffin's point of view') is likened to an equivalent shot in Dreyer's *Vampyr*, and a critical point is based on the similarity. But, despite such over-enthusiasm, Ferrini's article contains the most useful insights of all the more recent Leone studies.

Ferrini's study attempts to isolate the specifically European, or Old World, aspects of Leone's 'Anti-Westerns'. Such studies render 'cultural roots' criticisms of Spaghettis almost redundant. Leone's films are of interest partly *because* they attempt to criticise and redefine the 'rules' of the Hollywood Western genre — an attempt which could only have come from *outside* the Hollywood system. Leone's intellectual position is not particularly sophisticated (witness his interpretation of American social

history). And we have seen how difficult it is to label his films politically. But Leone's response to European cinematic 'vibrations' is both sensitive *and* sophisticated: for example, the visual (cinematic) exploration of spatial relationships, fluid camera-work, and quasi-abstract settings of *The Good, the Bad and the Ugly* seem to owe a great deal to the Hungarian Miklos Jancso's *The Round Up* (1965); parts of *Once Upon a Time in the West* seem calculated to illustrate Pasolini's (then) recently expressed ideas on semiotics, the 'language of the visual sign'; and Leone had evidently noted and appreciated visual qualities in the work of American directors — such as Robert Aldrich, Budd Boetticher, Sam Fuller and Nicholas Ray — around whom European 'cults' had developed. Perhaps in retrospect, Leone's Westerns will be seen as part of a significant European cinematic movement — the other contributors being Bertolucci, Chabrol and Pasolini. Claude Chabrol's films of the period *extend* the archetypal characters and situations of the bourgeois thriller (using Hitchcock's work as a starting-point) into a type of melodramatic expressionism: the films first arose from Chabrol's interest as a critic in the work of the cinéaste he most admired, Alfred Hitchcock. Bernardo Bertolucci, in his version of Moravia's *The Conformist* at least, attempts a similar process with the political thriller, using characters who *conform* to (or who would like to conform to) political stereotypes (whether cinematic or literary) — the hit-man, the street agitator, the humane academic, the blind propagandist, the middle-class woman, and so on — and filming their activities in ways which manipulate the clichés of the genre (a *Third Man*-type chase, complete with expressionist camera angles, for example) — the overall effect being to capture the 'bored, estranged style' of Moravia's original novel. In the 'Dollars' trilogy, Leone applies this method to the Hollywood Western, and in particular to the work of John Ford (a cinéaste he admires 'very much'): again, his films can be interpreted as a type of European genre cinema, which extends and manipulates the clichés of the equivalent Hollywood genre. Bertolucci was commissioned to draft the original 'story' for *Once Upon a Time*: more recently, with *1900*, he has again realised that a vast historical extravaganza, pitched at a popular audience, is a useful vehicle for social and political ideas, and that his low-budget parables may simply have preached to the converted. Bertolucci's lengthy 'story' had been abandoned when shooting began on *Once Upon*. But Morricone's music had all been recorded. Leone improvised a 'ballet de mort' around the 'structure' of Bertolucci's contribution, and around the Morricone score which had been written for it. *Once Upon a Time* seems not only concerned with Hollywood Western stereotypes, all of whom have 'something to do with death' from the moment the film begins — the avenger, the hired gun who aims to become a businessman, the railroad boss who uses a hired gun's methods, the whore with a heart of gold, the romantic bandit — but with less genre-oriented, if equally schematic, sexual archetypes as well (the comparison with *1900* is striking, so perhaps Bertolucci's influence is apparent here); these archetypes — dream lover (Harmonica), father-figure (McBain), rootless sinner looking for a home (Cheyenne), dominating sadist (Frank) — are all defined in their relationships with Jill McBain. A stock figure in the Hollywood Western is the dance-hall girl who has fled out West to escape her past: she is usually alienated from the rest of the towns-folk and thus more willing (and able) to understand the hero's moral conflicts, to offer sympathy and to revive the hero's flagging commitment to his 'cause'. Yet (and in this respect she is often unlike the hero), she is committed to town values. Leone and Bertolucci simply adapted this stock figure, in order to highlight and comment on the established bases of the formula, and in order to enhance her emblematic status. In this and other ways, the stereotyped characters and situations of *Once Upon a Time* are extended into an almost Chabrolian melodramatic expressionism: in *Ten Days' Wonder*, Chabrol pays visual homage, in turn, to the railway station scenes of *Once Upon a Time*; and in the more recent *Nada*, the character of Diaz is presented (and criticised) as a combination of the Man With

No Name and Che Guevara. Pasolini was the intellectual of this group — explaining the role of popular myth (from a recognisably Marxist *and* a recognisably Roman Catholic perspective); discussing what Gramsci had to say about Northern and Southern Italian culture; and analysing the contribution of semiology to the study of both Italian cinema and Italian poetry: also exploring the social/psychological bases of archetypal myths (and their modern resonances) in films such as *Oedipus*. As we shall see, Pasolini was interested enough in the Spaghetti Western phenomenon to consent to play the part of a revolutionary priest, in Carlo Lizzani's *Requiescant* (1967).

Perhaps Leone will eventually be promoted by critics into this pantheon.

The visual inspiration for the firing-squad sequence in *Duck, You Sucker* came from Goya: Leone showed some of the 'Disasters of War' series to Giuseppe Ruzzolini (also Pasolini's director of photography), in order to get the lighting and colour effects he wanted. 'For *Once Upon a Time in the West* I showed the cameraman, Tonino Delli Colli, a series of Rembrandt prints. I was after that monochrome colour. We often failed despite my demands'.

When John Ford was asked by Peter Bogdanovich which of his cavalry films most pleased him, he replied 'I like *She Wore a Yellow Ribbon*. I tried to copy the Remington style there — you can't copy him one hundred per cent — but at least I tried to get his colour and movement, and I think I succeeded partly.' Another visual inspiration for Ford (as well as for Andrew V. McLaglen) was the frontier paintings and illustrations of Charles M. Russell.

The fact that Rembrandt and Goya had never been to the Wild West seems rather beside the point.

65-8 Clint Eastwood, the
smiling ramrod in tele-
vision's *Rawhide*, becomes
Clint Eastwood, the brutal
bounty-hunter in Leone's
'Dollars' films. The Italian
script for *A Fistful of
Dollars* calls him 'Joe, the
stranger', but American
and English cinemagoers
were to know him as the
Man With No Name

The Films

In the re-allotment of fiefs after Sekigahara a great many warriors were left without an overlord. Some became farmers, others took service under new masters, but large numbers became what were known as *ronin*, literally 'wave men', namely masterless warriors. Throughout the Tokugawa period the *ronin* were a distinctive element in society, and we shall meet them again, for they projected into the twentieth century a tradition embraced by many adventurers, notably on the Asian continent. The *ronin* in history and legend appears in many guises: as a gallant freelance, jealous of his honour; as a brawling swashbuckler ready for any deed of violence; as a bully; as a social nuisance.

> Richard Storey on the 'samurai without an overlord', from *A History of Modern Japan* (1960)

The appeal of the indestructibility of a good many heroes is obvious enough; it is partly what has made the *Odyssey* so perennially enjoyable. It is always enjoyable to be able to identify with someone who is skilful, clever, and above all lucky, especially when the skills displayed by him are indeed convincing (as with Hammett's Continental Op, and Modesty Blaise and Willy Garvin, and several of the samurai played by Toshiro Mifune) and sometimes even when they are preposterous (as in Leone's 'Dollar' Westerns, and Chinese 'sword' movies, and Douglas Fairbanks' costume adventures). This kind of invulnerability is generally vicious only insofar as a seriously-minded crusading element is involved.

> John Fraser, *Violence in the Arts* (1974)

I see him . . . a little man going forward day after day through mud and blood and death and deceit — as callous and brutal and cynical as necessary — toward a dim goal, with nothing to push or pull him to it except he's been hired to reach it.

> Dashiell Hammett on the Continental Op, the man who is hired to 'clean up Poisonville', in *Red Harvest* (1927)

He is a paradox of virtue and vice: a man who, as he trims his rose garden, avoids stepping on a caterpillar, while at the end of the garden one of his victims is being consumed in an incinerator. The story contains diabolic humour, bitter satire and social criticism.

'Verdoux's claim is, derivatively, that it is ridiculous to be shocked by the extent of his atrocities, that they are a mere "comedy of murders" in comparison with the legalized mass murders of war, which are embellished with gold braid by the "System".'

> (A letter to Chaplin from the Breen Office — a branch of the Legion of Decency — explaining why they could not pass the script of *Monsieur Verdoux*)

> Charles Chaplin, *My Autobiography* (1964)

For Italians, few decisions are allowed to be influenced by sentiments, tastes, hazards or hopes, but usually by a careful valuation of the relative strength of the contending parties. . . . This is one of the reasons why, when negotiating even the smallest deal, Italians must always look at each other's faces. They read in their opponent's eyes the signs of his stubborn decision or hidden timidity. They can thus decide when it is safe to increase one's demands, when to stand pat, and when it is more prudent to retreat and accept the other man's decisions. Capitulation must, of course, be done with *garbo*, the retreat (for which a door has always been kept ajar) disguised with ingenious and flattering explanations. People are so unconsciously expert at this difficult art that few describe it.

Luigi Barzini, *The Italians* (1964)

The Good, the Bad and the Ugly could never have been made in America. For one thing, it is too long and plot-heavy for the generally single point-of-view Hollywood Westerns. Leone, far from being glossy, seems to revel in the texture of Death Valley dustiness. When Eli Wallach (the Ugly) drags Clint Eastwood (the Good) across a desert, the suffering becomes so intensely vivid and the framing so consciously poetic that the audience is subjected to a kind of cactus Calvary. No American Western would ever wallow so ecstatically in pain and privation worthy of the most masochistic Messiah. But Clint Eastwood is more a mercenary than a Messiah, and he will be rewarded in this world long before the next. Leone knows this, and Leone's audience knows this. Then why is the mercenary's reward so long deferred? Simply because the sheer duration of the suffering makes Eastwood a plausible lower-class hero whose physical redemption is the contemporary correlative of Christ's spiritual redemption. Leone's longueurs are thus part of a ritual alien to the American's traditional confidence in his ability to conquer Nature. Leone's characters require more than strength and determination to survive. They require also a guile and reason more European than American.

Andrew Sarris, 'Spaghetti and Sagebrush',
Village Voice (26 September 1968)

I forget who wrote the script, but they had to invent many things because, in reality, nothing happened during the entire building of the line except that they ran out of wood for the telegraph poles . . . the only other thing that disturbed the laying of the line was the ticks on the buffaloes: the buffaloes got itchy and rubbed themselves against the poles and the poles tumbled. And that was *all* that happened. . . . When the film was finished I found out that the laying of the line did not take half as long as the shooting of the picture!

Fritz Lang on the filming of *Western Union* (1941)

. . . . I returned to visit my dear mother, but finding the house watched, I left after only two hours. From there I was on my way to the Sierra de Menores; to make it, I had to pass by the Rancho de Valdés, owned by Don Eulogio Veloz. Since everyone there knew me, I crossed a pasture some distance from the house. Before I got back on the road a man rode up and in an insulting tone accused me of trespassing and said he was going to take me before the owner. I answered, 'I am doing no harm.' He rode his horse against mine and struck me twice. My anger boiled up. I spurred my horse, drew my pistol, fired and killed him instantly. I dismounted for his pistol and cartridge belt. Looking at the body a moment, I thought to myself, 'If he had given me no cause, I would not have killed him.' I remounted and followed the dead man's horse, which had run off and stopped behind some rocks. It would not let me catch it so I shot it, took the saddle and rifle, and went on toward the Hacienda de Menores.

The Memoirs of Pancho Villa,
collated by Martín Luis Guzmán (1965)

The enemies of the country and of freedom of the people have always denounced as bandits those who sacrifice themselves for the noble causes of the people.

Emiliano Zapata, quoted in Robert P. Millon,
Zapata (1972)

Sergio Leone's Films — The Sources

When deciding whom to cast in his Westerns, Sergio Leone always aimed high — even in low-budget days. For *A Fistful of Dollars*, he originally wanted Henry Fonda to play an older Man With No Name, but Fonda 'was too expensive for the Italian cinema at that time'. So was James Coburn. Colonel Mortimer — the character who represents the Man With No Name at the age of fifty, in *For a Few Dollars More* — was again to be played by Henry Fonda, but he was busy shooting another film, so Leone tried for Lee Marvin, who had unfortunately just signed the contract for *Cat Ballou*. 'Then I remembered Lee Van Cleef — an actor I had often seen in fifties Westerns. When I went to see him, he had been very ill for three years; he had come out of hospital, and was not working any more. I saw him from some way away, and was struck by his silhouette, his extraordinary attractiveness: he was perfect for my character'. (Van Cleef had, in fact, been unable to get any film work for some time: when Leone found him he was working as a freelance painter.) In this way, Lee Van Cleef, who had featured in countless Hollywood Westerns — among them *High Noon*; *Gunfight at the O.K. Corral*; and *The Man Who Shot Liberty Valance* — as a walk-on 'heavy' (and who had played a few character parts, such as a Chinese general in Fuller's *China Gate* and Smitty in Fleischer's rodeo picture *Arena*), became an international star. *Once Upon a Time in the West* was originally to open with a scene containing Leone's farewell to the 'Dollars' trilogy. The three main characters from *The Good, the Bad and the Ugly* — Clint Eastwood, Lee Van Cleef, and Eli Wallach — were to play the three gunfighters who wait for the train to arrive at Cattle Corner, and who are killed by Harmonica just after the end of the credits. But 'this proved impossible' (although the others agreed, Eastwood refused), and Leone eventually killed off two of his guest stars — Jack Elam and Woody Strode — instead. United Artists were willing to spend more money

setting up *Once Upon a Time* than Paramount, but Leone 'would have been obliged to cast Kirk Douglas, Charlton Heston and Gregory Peck'. So he made the film for Paramount — which enabled him to cast Henry Fonda — at last — as the villain: 'Fonda asked to see my three other Westerns; he saw them one after the other on the same day, and, as he came out, asked to sign the contract. The idea of playing a "baddy" did not frighten him.' (He had, in fact, already played a kind of baddy, one with a heart of gold, in *Firecreek* — a geriatric version of *High Noon* made in 1967.) Henry Fonda recalls:

I went to the studio and I sat by myself at Goldwyn for three and a half hours and I watched all of *Fistful of Dollars*, all of *For a Few Dollars More*, and about half of the third one. I had a lot of fun, all by myself. I thought they were very funny and entertaining in every possible way. I called Eli Wallach, who was in the last one and who is a friend of mine, and he said 'Don't miss it. You will love every minute of it. You'll love Sergio . . .' So I accepted. Now I read the script again and I know that the guy he wants me to play is a heavy. I've got several months before I have to go over there to report and I'm thinking about playing this guy. So I went over to a guy in the Valley, an optometrist, and I had myself fitted for contact lenses that would make my eyes dark because I didn't think my baby blues would be the proper look for this heavy character. I grew a moustache which was a little bit like John Booth's who shot Lincoln. I was trying every way that I knew to look like a period heavy. I arrived in Rome and went on the set and Sergio took one look at me and said 'Off!' He wanted the baby blues: he wanted the Fonda face. If you remember my first scene . . . the camera comes round very slowly until you can recognise the killer — and Sergio Leone was waiting for

69-70 Charles Buchinsky, in *Vera Cruz*, becomes
Charles Bronson, in *Once Upon a Time in the West*
71-2 Gian Maria Volonté, in *A Fistful of Dollars*,
and (with marijuana) in *For a Few Dollars More*

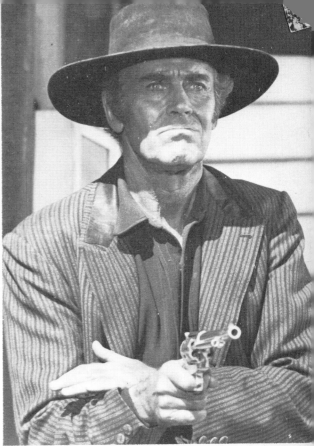

73-4 (*Above*) Henry Fonda, the blue-eyed sheriff in *My Darling Clementine*, becomes Henry Fonda, the blue-eyed killer in *Once Upon a Time in the West*

75-7 (*Below left to right*) Lee Van Cleef, who had walked on to be shot in *High Noon*, hanged in *The Tin Star*, knifed in *Gunfight at the O.K. Corral*, and pushed over a cliff in *China Gate*, becomes Lee Van Cleef, the sinister co-star, 'Il Colonello', in *For a Few Dollars More*

78-81 Many historical details in Sergio Leone's Westerns were gleaned from archive photographs of the period. These examples -- taken in 1862, 1885 and 1864 — show the origins of the Civil War sequences in *The Good, the Bad and the Ugly*, and the opening sequence of *Once Upon a Time in the West*

the audience to gasp 'Jesus Christ, it's Henry Fonda!' It was all fun. I loved every bit of it.

Leone's direction of Henry Fonda's performance shows exactly why he had been so keen, since *Fistful* days, to use him, and neatly illustrates Leone's relationship with the films of John Ford: the *hardness* which lay behind the appealing blue eyes, the toughness which had always been belied by the 'open' smile, even in Fonda's most humane characterisations, were cunningly exploited. Wyatt Earp, the friendly neighbourhood Marshal of *My Darling Clementine*, had also kicked Indians out of the saloon — 'What kind of a town is this — selling liquor to Indians? Indian, get out of town.' Leone cast Charles Bronson as Harmonica, because of his face: 'it is the face of destiny ... a sort of granite block, impenetrable, but scarred by life'. He had already offered three parts to Bronson (including the Eli Wallach role in *The Good, the Bad and the Ugly*!), but Bronson had turned the scripts down, thinking they were terrible (he has since judged the original script of *Fistful* to be the worst he had ever read — 'what I did not know, was what Leone would do with it'): for *Once Upon a Time*, Leone's persistence at last paid off. But Paramount executives thought this choice very risky, since Bronson was not a big enough star to carry the film — even if he did look like something from Mount Rushmore. At one time, Robert Hossein was to play the Sheriff of Flagstone Territory (a part later taken by Keenan Wynn).

When Leone was considering the *Giù la Testa* (*Duck, You Sucker*) project he set his heart on 'Jason Robards for Juan, and the young actor from *If*, Malcolm McDowell, as Sean, because the men of the I.R.A. were very young. I wanted thereby to show two generations — father and son — in opposition and unity. At the end, we were to have realized that the boy was wiser and more mature than the man of 50.' But United Artists insisted on better-established stars — Rod Steiger and James Coburn — so the original Brechtian theme of education of the old by the young had to be shelved. At first, Steiger 'thought of the film as very serious and intellectual and had a tendency to come off in the style of Zapata or Pancho Villa. Once he understood his mistake, everything went very well. Coburn, that's something else. With him, it's the star system: you explain the scene to him, he says "yes, sir" and off he goes and does it.' Leone modified the script

(through improvisation) as he went along; since *Giù la Testa* had originally been set up to be directed by Peter Bogdanovich ('with whom I did not have a constructive debate') or Sam Peckinpah (who accepted the project, before the backers eventually insisted on Leone), he found himself in 'a situation conceived for an American filmmaker'. As we have seen, Leone's assistant, Giancarlo Santi, was in charge for the first ten days of shooting. Leone still does not think of the project as completely his.

When he finally cast *A Fistful of Dollars*, Leone can have had no idea of how lucky he was, in 'discovering' Clint Eastwood. Since he could not offer the part to Fonda or Coburn, Leone tried various American actors living in Germany and Italy, and one of these — Richard Harrison, who had already appeared in *Gunfight at Red Sands*, directed and scripted by Riccardo Blasco, and who was later to star in numerous small-budget Spaghettis such as *100,000 Dollars for Ringo* (de Martino) and *El Rojo* (Leopoldo Savona — a *Fistful* derivative) —suggested the clean-cut, thirty-four-year-old co-star of the CBS TV series *Rawhide*. Clint Eastwood had played a few small film parts — for example, he was the pilot who dropped napalm from a B52 onto the gigantic Tarantula in Jack Arnold's classic chiller of that name — and had appeared as a cop on television in *Highway Patrol*. He had joined the *Rawhide* case (as Rowdy Yates, the 'ramrod') to play opposite Eric Fleming's Gil Favor, trail boss, in winter 1958. Eastwood was signed by Leone to play The Man With No Name in spring 1964. The salary was $15,000, and the total budget for the film was $200,000. After the seven-week shooting schedule in Spain and Italy was over, Clint Eastwood returned to the cast of *Rawhide*, soon to be promoted to solo billing as trail boss on the death of Eric Fleming, before the series folded early in 1966.

On Richard Harrison's recommendation, Leone had watched an episode of *Rawhide*:

Clint Eastwood did not say a word, but he was good at getting on a horse, and he had a way of walking with a tired, resigned air. . . . However, he was a little sophisticated, a little 'light', and I wanted to make him look more virile, to harden him, to 'age' him for the part as well — with that beard, that poncho which made him look broader, those cigars. When I went to find him, in order to offer him the part, he had never smoked in his life; this posed problems, for, to have a cigar constantly in one's mouth when one does not know how to smoke . . . ! Before the second film, he said to me 'Listen, Sergio, I'll do everything you want, except smoke!' — but this was impossible, since the protagonist was the same.

(Clint Eastwood still refers to the debate about his cigars, in interviews: 'I didn't really like them, but they kept me in the right kind of humour — kind of a fog . . .')

Rowdy Yates was a long way from the Man With No Name — even in Leone's original conception of the part: the novelisation of *Rawhide* (Frank C. Robertson, 1961) describes him as 'a little over six feet, a good-looking kid, mature beyond his years, with a shock of tawny hair that seemed habitually in need of cutting, and honest, sometimes challenging, blue eyes'. His image in the series was like that of a tear-away Pat Boone or Ricky Nelson, only he did not sing. When he took over from Gil Favor as trail boss, the tone of *Rawhide* changed dramatically: while Favor had been a stern, demanding boss, Yates was easy-going, more willing to listen to his men, more liberal (he even employed a black cattle-driver on the crew). Since viewers were used to seeing Rowdy Yates as a bit of a hell-raiser (though still 'a good ramrod, probably the best'), this change of regime was perhaps inevitable.

But Leone's original characterisation of the Man With No Name altered substantially when Eastwood took over the part. Leone recalls: 'In real life, Clint is slow, calm, rather like a cat. During shooting he does what he has to do, then sits down in a corner and goes to sleep immediately, until he is needed again. It was seeing him behave like this on the first day that helped me model the character.' Eastwood also recalls how the central character in the final version of the film resulted from negotiation between himself and the director: 'Italian actors come from the Helzapoppin' school of drama. To get my effect I stayed impassive and I guess they thought I wasn't acting. All except Leone, who knew what I was doing . . .'

The original script of *Fistful* was, according to Clint Eastwood (and Charles Bronson), extremely wordy and long — 'a strange Italian version of the Western dialect'. But it contained some good ideas, especially in the opening scene when the 'hero' first sets eyes upon the attractive 'heroine': in the traditional Western, says Eastwood, we would

know immediately from this scene that 'two people are going to get together, and it isn't the guy and the horse . . . !'; in the *Fistful* script, by contrast, our 'hero' has the door slammed in his face even before he has time to smile. The American actor negotiated with the Italian director about the *longueurs* of the script (a tedious process, since he only spoke two words of Italian when he arrived) throughout the shooting, and his part was gradually made less and less verbal. Eastwood also recalls that more 'black humour' was added after the shooting-script stage. When the production of *Fistful* was first announced in the Italian trade journals, the star of *Rawhide* was billed as both actor and 'Western consultant'.

Leone cast Gian Maria Volonté — a young stage actor who had played Romeo at the Arena di Verona in 1960, and subsequently appeared in two films, *The Man Who Burned* (1962) and *The Terrorist* (Gianfranco de Bosio, 1963) — to play opposite Clint Eastwood, as Ramon Rojo. The producer, Giorgio Papi, thought this casting insane, and at that point said he never wanted to see the finished film. For the American version, Volonté dubbed himself; for the Italian version, Eastwood was dubbed by Enrico-Maria Salerno, one of the better-known Italian actors of the day. In 1967, Salerno was himself to star in a Massimo Dallamano Western entitled *Bandidos*. Volonté was subsequently to become more deeply involved in Italian political cinema, and now talks of Westerns as 'a tiring genre in which I personally do not have much interest': he prefers to remember the Westerns of Damiani and Sollima to those of Leone, because they had more explicitly political connotations. But he recalls that in 1963, it was almost impossible for a young actor to reach a wide public, unless he appeared in a film which appealed to the 'mono-polistic controllers of distribution' in Italy. Thus, Westerns provided a useful launching pad. Sergio Leone has not talked much about what it was like to work with Volonté, but J.-P. Melville (who directed him in *Le Cercle Rouge*) was fairly outspoken on the subject. Melville first saw Volonté in Carlo Lizzani's *Banditi a Milano*: 'an instinctive actor, and he may well be a great stage actor in Italy, he may even be a great Shakespearean actor, but for me he was absolutely impossible in that on a French set, in a film such as I was making, he never at any moment made me feel I was dealing with a professional. He did not know how to place himself for the lighting. . . . I also think the fact that he is very involved in politics (he's a Leftist, as he never tires of telling you) did nothing to bring us together. . . . For him, everything Italian was marvellous and wonderful and everything French was ridiculous.' Melville found the whole experience 'very wearying'. It is likely that Leone had an easier time, since he was filming in Italy, and since Volonté had yet to become what Noel Simsolo has called 'a one-man political myth'.

So that *Italian* audiences would not think that *Fistful* was home-made, the distributors made most of the cast and crew hide behind pseudonyms. Leone became 'Bob Robertson' (he chose the name in homage to his father, Roberto Leone Roberti), Volonté became 'John Wells', and the Conservatory-trained composer Ennio Morricone — who had scored *Mad Desire* (directed by Luciano Salce) in 1962, *Gunfight at Red Sands* (the Richard Harrison film, Morricone's first Western) in 1963, and was currently working on the music for *Pistols Don't Argue* — became 'Dan Savio'. From the distributors' point of view, these pseudonyms were important, since it was thought that the (unashamedly) Italian Western craze of the previous year had blown itself out. Leone recalls:

> before *Fistful*, twenty-five Italian Westerns had been made. When I finished the film, a Roman businessman who owned a chain of at least fifty cinemas didn't even want to see the private screening, because it had already been established that the Western genre in Italy was completely finished. These Westerns had been released, but the critics had not noticed them. . . . They had been doing the rounds for second and third showings. Nobody had noticed, because they all had 'stolen' titles, because they were thought to be 'B' films, re-releases of American TV films.

Films such as *Massacre at the Grand Canyon* (co-directed by Sergio Corbucci); *Gunfight at Red Sands*; *Buffalo Bill, Hero of the Far West*; and *Two Twins in Texas* (which featured the US Cavalry riding picador-style, fifty stars on their flag), had already been parodied by Franchi and Ingrassia — a sure sign that the 'craze' existed, but also that it would have to change course if it was to survive. The same co-production team as backed *Fistful* — Jolly Films (Rome), Ocean Films (Madrid) and Constantin Films (Munich) — was simultaneously shooting *Pistols Don't Argue* (directed by Mario

Caiano, alias 'Allan Grunewald' or 'William Hawkins'), using identical locations, and *Pistols* took up the lion's share of the budget. Rod Cameron, the American star of the 'A' feature, was paid more than the whole cast of *Fistful* put together; Leone's Western was shot 'to use up waste material'. But at least this gave the director 'complete autonomy'. The street scenes were filmed in a small village called Colmenar, near Madrid: a 'Western town' had been built there two years before (for some of the earliest Spaghettis), but Leone recalls that by the time *Fistful* was shot, 'the town had the abandoned look of a ghost town' (that was just the effect he wanted). Other exteriors were shot in the villages and desert of Almeria, southern Spain.

The story-line of *A Fistful of Dollars*, written — with help from Tessari and Catena — in three weeks at Leone's apartment in Rome, was taken from Akira Kurosawa's samurai film, *Yojimbo* (1961): Leone had just seen the film (as *La Sfida del Samurai*) in Rome. In Kurosawa's version, a footloose samurai (Toshiro Mifune) offers his services as Yojimbo, or bodyguard, to two rival factions — the silk merchants and the saké merchants. He plays one faction off against the other — largely out of boredom — and watches the gory result from a wooden fire-tower overlooking the main street. Having started the trouble in the absence of anything better to do, the Yojimbo gradually becomes committed to ending the feud once and for all: in a final confrontation, he wreaks havoc on both houses, finally having a showdown with the villainous Unosuke (Tatsuya Nakadai in a striped kimono) who possesses the only firearm in the neighbourhood — a Smith and Wesson no. 2.32 rimfire. *Fistful* closely follows the same pattern — so closely, in fact, that the published novelisation of Leone's film claims to be 'based on the screenplay of a Jolly film, Rome . . . by permission of Kurosawa Productions Ltd, Tokyo': the authors of *Yojimbo*, Kurosawa and Kikushima, were compensated for the obvious resemblances between the two stories, by being granted exclusive rights to distribute *A Fistful of Dollars* in Japan, Formosa and South Korea, plus 15 per cent of the worldwide box-office takings. Leone's defence was that the author's rights for both films should be paid to the estate of the late Carlo Goldoni, who originated the idea with *Arlecchino Servo di due Padroni* (*The Servant of Two Masters*).

Leone, Tessari and Catena had invented two

important new scenes — the massacre of the soldiers, and the trick in the cemetery — and had cut out some sequences in which the central character does not appear (for example, those showing the intervention of a government agent) but the main lines of the story still read like a simplified version of *Yojimbo* — dollar-book Kurosawa — the most crucial change, at a script level, being greater emphasis on the stars and on a series of spectacular climaxes. The saké merchants' henchmen in *Yojimbo* are a grotesque rogues' gallery who bear more than a passing resemblance to the Rojo gang. The Yojimbo, like the Man With No Name, helps a peasant and his wife to escape from the warring factions. At the end of Kurosawa's film, only those who have taken no part in the conflict remain sane and alive (apart from the Yojimbo): the saké-seller, the coffin-maker, and the watchman. In Leone's film, the sole survivors (apart from the Man With No Name) are the bartender, the coffin-maker and the crazy bell-ringer. But similarities of script do not, of course, necessarily mean similarities in the finished product. The legal argument seems to have been mainly about the script.

At the beginning of Kurosawa's film, as the Yojimbo arrives in the town, he sees an Alsatian dog walking briskly past him, with a human hand in its mouth. At the beginning of Leone's film, as Eastwood arrives in San Miguel, he sees a few black-clad widows scurrying across the street, and is passed by a dead man propped upright on a horse, with the words 'Adios Amigo' pinned to his back; he turns, acknowledges the 'greeting' by lightly touching his hat, and rides on. Throughout the two films, Leone and Kurosawa use such images in very different ways, to different purposes. In the former example, Kurosawa is trying to create a pervading atmosphere of grotesque brutality, and linking this to imagery associated with the sword. In the latter, Leone is attempting to show how powerless the San Miguel peasants have become (scurrying widows, like beetles or ants; a human 'envelope'), how inhospitable the 'bosses' are (even their 'greetings' are based on violence and death), and how the Man With No Name comes from a different culture (touching his hat in acknowledgment). Kurosawa's image is economical, austere; Leone's is more humorous, flamboyant and easily accessible. If the use of imagery differs, so does the use of dialogue, characterisation, and camera work.

The Yojimbo tries to provoke a fight with the saké merchants' gang. He is smiling, and, as usual, chewing on a matchstick. In the previous scene, he has told the watchman and the coffin-maker, 'I like it here. I'll stay . . . I get paid for killing. It would be better if all these men were dead.' He ambles pensively over to the saké merchants' men.

Mifune: What gentle faces.

The henchmen begin to look furious.

Mifune: When you're angry you look even nicer.
    Man: Look here. See this tattoo? I wasn't in prison for nothing.
    Another man: The law's after me. I'll hang if they catch me.
    Mifune: No objections to fighting, then.
    Man: You just try and kill me.
    Mifune: It'll hurt a little.
    Man: Bad men like us can't be cowards.
    Mifune: Then it can't be helped.

Mifune whips out his sword, cuts an arm off and punctures a gut, then formally replaces the weapon in its scabbard — all in a few seconds. He walks over to the coffin-maker and orders two coffins. On reflection, he says, 'No, maybe three.' Virtually the whole scene is filmed in medium-shot, with the occasional brief close-up of both parties.

The Man With No Name tries to provoke a fight with some of the Baxter clan (to impress Don Miguel Rojo, his future employer). He has just been insulted by the Baxters, who also 'spooked' his mule, causing him to grab hold of a wooden beam outside the Cantina (a mock 'crucifixion') to save himself from falling out of the saddle.

The Man stands near the Rojo residence.

Eastwood: Don Miguel Rojo, I want to talk to you. Don Miguel, I hear you're hiring men. Well, I might just be available. I gotta tell you before you hire me (*pause, as he removes the cigar from his mouth, and spits into the dust*) I don't work cheap.

He slowly walks towards the Baxters (high-angle shot, from the Cantina — 'neutral' — balcony). He passes the coffin-maker, who is humming loudly to himself as he planes a piece of wood. (Side view of Eastwood in the foreground, with coffin-maker and his wares in the background.)

Eastwood: Get three coffins ready.
    Coffin-maker: Uh . . . ?

The Man continues walking, as 'soothing' music on the soundtrack — solo oboe, with Spanish guitar — reaches a crescendo. He reaches the Baxter residence, where the same group as insulted him earlier is still sitting around on the corral gate.

Member of the gang: Adios, Amigo.

Another: Listen, stranger. Did you get the idea? We don't like to see bad boys like you in town. Go and get your mule. (*Laughs.*) You let him get away from you? (*The others start laughing.*)

Eastwood: (*in extreme close-up with his head down*): See, that's what I want to talk to you about. He's feelin' real bad.

Member of the gang: Huh?

Eastwood: My mule. You see he got all riled up when you went and fired those shots at his feet.

Another: Hey! You making some kind of joke.

Eastwood: (*lightly*): No. You see I understand you men were just playing around . . . but the mule, he just doesn't get it. 'Course if you were to all apologise. (*Much laughter from the Baxters, partly shot in individual close-ups. A brief 'trill' on the soundtrack.*)

Eastwood: (*in extreme close-up, his face slowly rising to stare meanly at the gang; no more joking*): I don't think its nice, you laughing. (*Faint electronic 'whirr' begins to build up on the soundtrack.*) You see my mule don't like people laughing. Gets the crazy idea you're laughing at him. Now if you'll apologise, like I know you're going to . . . I might convince him that you really didn't mean it.

(Close-ups of Baxters' faces, as they begin to get apprehensive. One of them spits. The electronic 'whirr', now with feedback, gets louder and it 'punctuates' a series of extreme close-ups of Eastwood, his eyes narrowing. As the Baxters go for their guns, we see Eastwood draw — filmed from behind — and fire five rounds. The Baxters fall off the gate, as a horse whinnies: the sound is heavily amplified. Eastwood turns, as John Baxter storms out of his house.)

Baxter: I saw the whole thing. You killed all four of them. You'll pay all right. You'll be strung up.

Eastwood: (*looking really mean*): Who are you?

Baxter: Don't fire son. (*He fumbles in his waistcoat, to find his tin star.*) I'm John Baxter. Sheriff.

Eastwood: Yeah? Well, if you're the Sheriff, you'd better get these men underground.

(He turns and walks away. A 'trill' on the soundtrack, this time accompanied by guitar, 'whip' sound and bell. He reaches the sidewalk outside the Cantina, where he sees the coffin-maker.)

Eastwood: (*side view again*): My mistake. Four coffins. (*Music swells to become a 'square-dance' on solo violin.*)

This scene from *Fistful* is, apparently, a 'remake' of the *Yojimbo* scene. But Leone's direction (extreme close-ups, rapid cutting from face to face in order to build tension, use of music and amplified 'natural' sounds), together with the quasi-parodic dialogue, make it (except at the most superficial narrative level) utterly different. The dialogue of *Yojimbo*, by Kurosawa and Ryuzo Kikushima is *staccato*, economical: Mifune never for a moment seems to be taking things seriously; there is no sense of menace; the emphasis is on comedy, although the violence is (if anything) more sudden and shocking than in the Leone film. And the camerawork is more 'objective', less obtrusive. Part of Leone's intention is to *extend* the visual conventions normally associated with Western confrontations. We notice the technical effects because we are clearly supposed to.

In addition, the acting styles contained in *Fistful* and *Yojimbo* differ significantly. In *Yojimbo*, there is a family conference (or 'sodan') scene, where the bodyguard's present employers are discussing how to get rid of him. Again, the emphasis is on comedy and satire: the family group is sitting in a circle, chatting amiably; there are no pauses between question and answer. If one of the group gets angry he begins to speak even more quickly, his voice rising in pitch. The equivalent scene in *Fistful* (a discussion between Esteban and Don Miguel Rojo on what to do with 'the Americano') is acted in full melodramatic style, complete with long pauses during one of which Esteban sulkily stamps around the room. Esteban suggests that he could creep up on the Americano, to 'snuff him out' from behind. 'You're stupid, Esteban,' shouts Don Miguel, throwing his crumpled serviette onto a wooden table, 'even if you are my brother.' At this point, Esteban grabs a knife and rams it hard into the table. The two men stare at each other. If, throughout the 'Dollars' trilogy, there is a deliberate tension between the acting styles of the Americans (laconic, cool) and the Italians (flamboyant, operatic, external), particularly if one classifies 'surrogate Mexicans' (Actors' Studio graduates like Eli Wallach, Jason Robards and Rod Steiger) as Italians, neither style has any point of contact with the actors in *Yojimbo*.

Finally, the social contexts of the two stories are, quite literally, worlds apart. After the final bloodbath, Yojimbo sees the farmer's son, dying and calling for his mother. 'Yes,' says Mifune 'a long life eating rice-gruel is the best. . . .' At no time in the 'Dollars' films does the Man With No Name indulge in anything remotely resembling this type of homespun philosophy. Kurosawa has firmly stated, in interviews, that the social 'message' contained within his films is impossible to transpose to other contexts. Asked what he thinks about the 'Western' adaptations of two of his films (*The Seven Samurai*/ Sturges' *Magnificent Seven* (1960); *Rashomon*/ Ritt's *The Outrage* (1964)), Kurosawa replies: 'I've got nothing against adaptations of my films. But I do not think they can succeed. The basic context is so very different. And, whatever my views, pastiche films, of a premeditated kind, can never be good films. . . . It is, for example, ridiculous to imagine me directing a Hollywood Western. For I am Japanese . . .'

The *Servant of Two Masters* story of both *Yojimbo* and *Fistful* does originate — albeit very indirectly — with the Italian Carlo Goldoni. But the *Two Masters* idea had been updated in the late 1920s by the most successful of the 'Black Mask' school of American thriller-writers, Dashiell Hammett, as the basis for his first full-length book, *Red Harvest*. In this novel the 'Continental Op' (the original Man With No Name) visits the mining town of Personville, known locally as 'Poisonville', and discovers that it is being run by rival gangster factions. He plays one faction — run by Noonan, the corrupt police chief (shades of Baxter?) — off against another, run by the hood Max 'Whisper' Thaler. The Op seems to be immune from the temptations put in his way by the gangsters, and even keeps his distance from Dinah Brand, the local call-girl. By the end of *Red Harvest*, the most Jacobean of all Hammett's 'Black Mask' contributions (at times it

reads like an updated version of *The White Devil* or *The Duchess of Malfi*), twelve of the nineteen main characters, including Noonan and 'Whisper', have been killed. At one point in the story, the Continental Op is informed about how the burg came to be run by rival gangs of hoods. Old Elihu Willsson, the 'baron' who controlled most of the business enterprises in Personville, had been faced with a strike in 1921:

> The strike lasted eight months. Both sides bled plenty. The wobblies had to do their own bleeding. Old Elihu hired gunmen, strikebreakers, national guardsmen, and even parts of the regular army, to do this. When the last skull had been cracked, the last rib kicked in, organized labour in Personville was a used firecracker. *But old Elihu did not know his Italian history*. He won the strike, but he lost his hold on the city and the state. To beat the miners he had to let his hired thugs run wild. When the fight was over he couldn't get rid of them. . . . They had won his strike for him and they took the city for their spoils.

Hammett had obviously made full use of his Burckhardt. André Gide found this particular red harvest 'the last word in atrocity, cynicism and horror'. But he thought it was a fine novel. In *Red Harvest*, like in the three more famous novels which followed it, the basic rule of life for the detective is 'I trust no one.' As Steven Marcus has pointed out, 'society and social relations are dominated by the basic principle of mistrust'. Personville is Hobbes' 'artificial man' in action.

> For forty years, old Elihu Willsson had owned Personville, heart, soul and guts. He was president and majority stockholder of the Personville Mining Corporation, ditto of the First National Bank, owner of the Morning Herald and Evening Herald, the city's only newspaper, and at least part owner of nearly every other enterprise of any importance. Along with those pieces of property he owned a United States senator, a couple of representatives, the governor, the mayor, and most of the state legislature. Elihu Willsson was Personville, and he was almost the whole state.

And the Continental Op, the private eye who has to set both ends against the middle in order to survive, is one symptom of such a society: as Hammett put it, 'he's more or less of a type and I'm not sure that he's entitled to a name . . .' The Op works on his own — always keen to 'see his job through' — his relationships are instrumental, calculated to serve his own interest, and he never gives anything away about himself: partners, emotional involvements, or wearing his heart on his sleeve would all make him vulnerable. For him, each job is like a poker game. The Op With No Name has been called the first of 'the modern existential anti-heroes': however, unlike the Man With No Name, he finds this job turning sour on him. At the beginning of the story, he enthusiastically admits, 'Poisonville is ripe for the harvest. It's a job I like, and I'm going to do it.' By the end, he discovers that 'this burg's getting me. If I don't get away soon I'll be going blood-simple like the natives'. But he leaves the survivors in Poisonville with a characteristically cynical thought: 'You'll have your city back, all nice and clean and ready to go to the dogs again.' The connections between Leone's Westerns and the American *film noir* have already been mentioned. According to Leone, 'Kurosawa's *Yojimbo* was inspired by an American novel of the "série noire" so I was really taking the story back home again.'

Significantly, George Orwell's famous *Horizon* article on 'Raffles and Miss Blandish' (1945) — an attack on a *European* version of Hammett's early 'Black Mask' stories by the Englishman 'James Hadley Chase' — criticises *No Orchids for Miss Blandish* using criteria which the 'cultural roots' school of Leone critics would find most congenial. Orwell is amazed that Hadley Chase has 'made a complete mental transference to the American underworld' ('with technical errors, perhaps, but certainly with enormous skill'), using only films and books as his sources, rather than personal experience.

> Raffles . . . has a set of reflexes — the nervous system, as it were, of a gentleman. Give him a sharp tap on this reflex or that (they are called 'sport', 'pal', 'woman', 'King and Country', and so forth), and you get a predictable reaction. In Mr. Chase's books, there are no gentlemen and no taboos. Emancipation is complete, Freud and Machiavelli have reached the outer suburbs.

The more traditional mystery story may occasionally seem to be challenging accepted morality (although it is clearly understood that Raffles' crimes must be expiated sooner or later, according

to Orwell), but in *No Orchids*, an English rewrite of the American 'hardboiled' genre, the only morality is 'Might is right: vae victis.' It is perhaps not too far-fetched, in the context provided by Orwell's article, to compare the golden age of crime stories (most of which obeyed strict rules) with the era of the classic Hollywood Westerns. The English version of Hammett's tough stories seems to have been viewed by Orwell in much the same terms as some critics viewed Leone's films. But Orwell also sees *No Orchids* as symptomatic of an increasing tendency, in American-influenced books and films, to blur the distinction between right and wrong, or between crime and crime-prevention. In these terms, being a criminal is only reprehensible because it does not pay. Being a policeman pays better, but there is no moral difference, since the police use essentially criminal methods. The American 'log cabin to White House' myth can easily be transposed to apply to a criminal's biography:

> Switching back eighty years, one finds Mark Twain adopting much the same attitude towards the disgusting bandit Slade, hero of twenty-eight murders, and towards Western desperadoes generally. They were successful, they 'made good', therefore he admired them.

Leone's attitude to Jack Slade, as immortalised by Mark Twain, we have already discussed. The methods of the freelance 'police' (bounty-hunters) in the 'Dollars' films are distinguishable from those used by the bandit clans they destroy simply by virtue of the fact that the 'police' work alone (or, uneasily, in pairs). Leone's view of American history does not lay stress on the 'log cabin to White House' aspects of his criminal characters' biographies: he does not seem to be particularly interested in the 'success ethic', or, indeed, in motivation of any sort — except at the crudest level. Only in *Once Upon a Time in the West* does Leone explore the implications of this myth, in the wider context of 'progressivism'. Nevertheless, the parallels between Orwell's critique of Hadley Chase, and the 'cultural roots' critics of Leone's 'Dollar' Westerns, are striking. The English film version of *No Orchids for Miss Blandish*, written and directed by St John L. Clowes and released three years after Orwell's article was published, attempts (unsuccessfully) to comment on the American *film noir*, by highlighting the tension between the violent exploits of the Grisson gang and the Hollywood myths associated with gangsters of the 'Black Mask' type. The final, bloody shoot-out occurs immediately after a sequence showing the cabaret mimic Jack Durant taking off Peter Lorre and Sidney Greenstreet in *The Maltese Falcon*; Eddie, a member of the gang, comments on the way that 'broads' like to dress in styles 'they've seen in the movies'; and the dialogue tries hard to parody the 'hardboiled' original ('This will put years on my life'/'Learn to grow old graceful'). Perhaps the cultural shock of seeing English character actors (such as Sidney James and Michael Balfour) in an apparently American gangster picture is similar to the effect created by early Spaghettis, when seen by Italian cinemagoers for the first time. The *Manchester Guardian*, in April 1948, was content to categorise *No Orchids* as 'un-British'. One thing is certain: George Orwell would have *detested* Italian Westerns.

Another literary antecedent to both *Yojimbo* and *Fistful* is Mark Twain's short story 'The Man That Corrupted Hadleyburg' (1899). In this story — which is plotted like a mathematical formula — a mysterious stranger, who has been wronged, vows that he will corrupt Hadleyburg, a town which prides itself on a reputation for being 'honest and upright'. He does this by depositing a large sack of gold in the town, leaving a note with it which says that the citizen who did him a good turn a year or two before is entitled to claim the gold if that citizen can remember the 'remark' he made when he was being so generous. The sack, and the envelope containing the correct 'remark', is not to be opened for a month, at which time the lucky citizen is to report to the Town Hall. 'This is an honest town, an incorruptible town,' the stranger adds just before he leaves, 'and I know I can trust it without fear.' Gradually, as the weeks pass by, the town 'takes on a sick look'; then, when the month is nearly up, the nineteen notables of Hadleyburg *all* receive a letter telling them the gist of their 'remark', and 'reminding' them of the particular good service they performed. (Each individual recipient, of course, keeps this information to himself — and plans how he will spend the gold.) Eventually, the great unveiling takes place, in the Town Hall — as the local minister reads out all the versions of the 'remark' which have been handed in to him by the nineteen: each notable, in turn, claims the sack — a violent argument ensues — and the 'honest, upright' town is revealed before the assembled press-men, to be full of complacent hypocrites. Even the oldest inhabitant, who was thought by all to be above temptation, finds himself compromised. The mysterious stranger has been fully revenged.

> By act of the legislature — upon prayer and petition — Hadleyburg was allowed to change its name to (never mind what — I will not give it away), and leave one word out of the motto that for many generations had graced the town's official seal . . .
> *Former Motto*
> Lead Us Not Into Temptation
> *Revised Motto*
> Lead Us Into Temptation

The fragile 'decency' of the citizens of Hadleyburg, the ways in which the stranger plays one party off against another in order to show up that 'decency' as a mask for hypocrisy, the almost mathematical precision with which one 'fall' follows on from another — all these aspects of 'The Man That Corrupted Hadleyburg', filtered through Hammett's man that cleaned up Poisonville, provide one model for all the various 'anonymous stranger' Westerns from Leone's *Fistful of Dollars* to Eastwood's own *High Plains Drifter*, where traditional small-town morality is deliberately turned inside-out. Carl Foreman has used the town of Hadleyburg, or Hadleyville — to similar effect — in two of his Western stories, *High Noon* (1952) and *MacKenna's Gold* (1968).

Kurosawa and Leone, not surprisingly, stress that their main inspiration came from Hollywood films. Just as *The Magnificent Seven* was based on Kurosawa's rather more magnificent *Seven Samurai*, so *Yojimbo* was originally born out of a love for the Hollywood Western, and in particular for *Shane*, an incredibly popular film in Japan. As Kurosawa has said:

> Good Westerns are liked by everyone. Since humans are weak, they want to see good people and great heroes. Westerns have been done over and over again and in the process a kind of grammar has evolved. I have learned from this grammar of the Western.

But, Kurosawa hastens to add, he had no intention of making a 'pastiche' version of George Stevens' movie.

Sergio Leone has said that *Shane* was the major influence on his early Westerns, and it is easy to see why: George Stevens was explicitly using the conventions of the Western to stress the mythic, universal qualities of Jack Schaefer's story. The presentation of Jack Palance as Wilson, the hired gun, the 'specialist', seems particularly to have impressed Leone. When Wilson enters the saloon, in his tall black hat, wearing one black glove, accompanied by the amplified jangle of spurs on the soundtrack, we see a bedraggled dog in the foreground get up, and walk across to the other side of the saloon in fear and disgust. This sequence, and the later scene outside the Grafton Store where Wilson shoots 'Stonewall' Torrey (Elisha Cook, Jr, the archetypal 'fall-guy'), are filmed *rhetorically*, to heighten the mythic qualities of the conflict. Other aspects of *Shane* — the use of amplified natural sounds, of formal groups of figures, and of music to reinforce climaxes (for instance in the tree-chopping sequence and in the fight between Starrett and Shane), as well as the central theme of a 'Stranger' who rides into the neighbourhood from nowhere, helps the family, and 'moves on' to nowhere having done good by evil means (there are cryptic references to his past, as a gunfighter) — also have obvious connections with Leone's 'style' and intentions. The presentation of the 'holy family' in *Shane* (Joe, Marian and Little Joey — a family of Protestant homesteaders) may have suggested the idea for Leone's very different (and very Italian) 'holy family' (Julian, Marisol and Little Jesus) in *Fistful*: by the time he made *Once Upon a Time in the West*, Leone was explicitly criticising the presentation of the family in *Shane* (in the sequence showing the McBain family preparing their wedding feast) — his 'ballet de mort' is, perhaps, a 'pessimistic' version of the family dance enjoyed by the rugged homesteaders on Independence Day.

While the homesteaders wear everyday farming clothes, Shane wears a buckskin outfit which instantly 'places' him: he is a loner on the frontier, as much at home among the Indians, or as a scout, as he is among the farmers, or in the town. In *Fistful*, the Man With No Name wears a poncho and rides into San Miguel on a sleepy mule, while the townspeople (apart from the two rival gangs) wear sombreros and white farming smocks. The Man is clearly at home in a Mexican setting, but his sheepskin waistcoat, tight-fitting trousers and suede boots suggest he is an 'outsider' in San Miguel — a 'specialist' who wears his gunbelt in traditional gunslinger fashion.

As we have seen, Leone's last project before preparing *Fistful*, was to co-direct *Sodom and Gomorrah* with Robert Aldrich. Aldrich had just finished shooting *The Last Sunset* (1961) — a Western, mainly set in Agua Caliente, Mexico — which was to become something of a cult film in Italy, championed by the journal *Bianco e Nero*. The gunfight which climaxed this film — involving a black-clad Kirk Douglas, and a wholesome Rock Hudson who has been on his trail throughout the movie — was so elaborately staged (and cut) that some critics at the time likened the final scene to 'a synthetic Greek tragedy': Douglas walks to his death packing an empty pistol, for he has just discovered that he is in love with his own daughter. Dalton Trumbo's self-consciously Freudian story seems to have appealed to Bertolucci, for, as Philip French points out, he featured *The Last Sunset* in the open-air cinema sequence of *Spider's Stratagem* (1970) — but it is the final scene that is more likely to have impressed Leone. The duel is, of course, a *linear*, as opposed to a *circular* one, but the formalised way in which it is presented (rhythmic cutting, matching shots, extension of 'real' time, and so on) was to be copied in many of the more confident Italian Westerns — as was the theme of a duellist with an empty gun, which reappears in (among other films) Petroni's *Death Rides a Horse* (1967).

Aldrich's earlier film *Vera Cruz* (1954) had an even more significant influence on the Spaghetti Western in general, and on Leone's *For a Few Dollars More* in particular. This film, set in Mexico at the time of Maximilian (1866), and telling of the adventures of a couple of freewheeling American mercenaries who have been hired to escort a wagonload of the Emperor's gold through territory controlled by followers of the revolutionary leader Juarez, seems today to be almost a prototype for the more 'political' Spaghettis, while the central relationship between an ex-Major from the South (Gary Cooper) and an agile confidence trickster of a gunslinger (Burt Lancaster) prefigures the equivalent cat-and-mouse relationship, based on mutual distrust and wary admiration, between Colonel Mortimer and the Man With No Name in Leone's second Western. Aldrich's film is full of noisy climaxes (horse-stealing, a shootout in a village square with children used as 'cover', chases, an attack on a fort — with the Major wielding a mean machine-gun, a final duel to the death, as

82-3 (*Above left and right*) Toshiro Mifune watches
the two rival factions fight it out, before facing
Tatsuya Nakadai in a final duel between the sword
and the pistol: scenes from Kurosawa's *Yojimbo*
(1961)

84-5 (*Right and below*) The success of Sturges' *The
Magnificent Seven* (1960) in Europe encouraged
producers to invest in Westerns about hired guns and
bounty-hunters, set on the Mexican border: four of
the stars were subsequently to appear in Spaghettis,
three of them (Eli Wallach, Charles Bronson and
James Coburn) in films by Sergio Leone. Direct
'quotes' from Sturges' film were included in
Bertolucci's script of *Once Upon a Time in the West*,
and in the credits sequence of *My Name Is Nobody*

86 Alan Ladd arrives
from nowhere, to
defend the holy
family in Stevens'
Shane (1953)
87 Kirk Douglas
and Rock Hudson
meet for the final
settling of accounts
in Aldrich's *The Last
Sunset* (1961)
88 An earlier
Aldrich film, *Vera
Cruz* (1954), set the
pattern for many
Spaghetti Westerns
by placing the
adventures of two
gunfighters (cynical
Burt Lancaster and
honourable Gary
Cooper) in the noisy
and confusing
context of a
Mexican revolution

89 (*Top left*) The 'moral' of Charles Chaplin's comedy of murders, *Monsieur Verdoux* (1947), was to influence Sergio Leone as he prepared *The Good, the Bad and the Ugly*

90 (*Top right*) Bertolucci structured the story of *Once Upon a Time in the West* around 'quotes' from his favourite Westerns ··· among them *The Magnificent Seven*, *Shane*, *The Searchers* and *The Last Sunset*. Perhaps the most explicit 'quote' comes from Nicholas Ray's *Johnny Guitar* (1954), 'the first of the baroque Westerns'. Here, Sterling Hayden tries to get Joan Crawford to admit that she has missed him

91-2 (*Above left and right*) One of Fred Zinnemann's sketches for the final shootout in *High Noon* (1952), and the beginning of that same sequence in the finished film. Note the name of the town, Hadleyville, and the first appearance in a Western of Lee Van Cleef, as Jack Colby.

93 (*Below*) Samuel Fuller, together with several directors of 'marginal' Westerns in the 1950s, became something of a cult-figure among European cinéastes at the time of the early Spaghetti Westerns. His *Forty Guns* (1957), in particular, was to have a major impact

many corpses as the Superscope process could cope with, and so on) and sudden visual surprises (for example, the appearance of Juaristas at strategic points in the village square). It even boasts a *corrida*, laid on for the amusement of Maximilian's lancers who have captured a terrified Juarista. For the mid-1950s, Aldrich's film is remarkably cynical: all the main characters, with the possible exception of Gary Cooper, are out to double-cross each other. Although Maximilian has hired the two mercenaries, he has no intention of paying them — 'If they are not shot by the Juaristas, our bayonets will do the job . . .'; he compliments Burt Lancaster on his choice of 'cause', to which the gunslinger replies, 'Let's put our cards on the table, Your Majesty — our services are being well paid for.' Lancaster himself, whose cynical pronouncements are always accompanied by a very broad grin, believes one should 'never trust anyone . . . never do any favours'. For this reason he finds it difficult to cope with Gary Cooper: 'He likes people, and you can never count on a man like that.' In the end, Cooper's morality wins the day, and the gold is presented to the revolutionaries. The setting of *Vera Cruz* (the desert, cactus, crucifixes), and the sympathy shown for the Juaristas (as opposed to Maximilian's over-dressed, decadent court) makes the film a direct ancestor of Solinas' 'populist' Westerns. Only the final showdown (in which the Burt Lancaster character has to die) sets the film apart from the morality of Leone's later, even more cynical, variations. Two specific features of *Vera Cruz* were to feed into the Spaghetti Western genre in a more definite manner: the way in which Lancaster dresses (in Civil War surplus clothes — exactly like *Django*), and the presence of an actor named Charles Buchinsky who plays a walk-on part (as 'Charles Bronson', he was to star in *Once Upon a Time in the West*).

By the time he made the third film in his trilogy, *The Good, the Bad and the Ugly*, Leone was less interested in the idea that one man (like Shane, Major Benjamin Trane or the Man With No Name) could help the community by using violent, anti-social means, and instead explored the more general notion that any individual's egotism could some-times lead to 'good deeds'. The curious morality of Chaplin's *Monsieur Verdoux* has influenced the presentation of such themes in Leone's work, by his own admission: he finds fascinating the idea that a lady-killer of Bluebeard proportions can stand up in

court and say, 'I am just an amateur compared to Mr Roosevelt and Mr Stalin, who do such things on a grand scale.' Many aspects of Chaplin's 'Comedy of Murders' were adapted by Leone to suit his Westerns (and particularly *The Good, the Bad and the Ugly*): the idea that killings could be organised as 'a strictly business enterprise'; the humour of confusing the language of business with the language of murder ('You must have made a killing . . .'); the changes of dress and uniform (to infiltrate the 'enemy's' camp); the structure of the film (built around Verdoux' train journeys from wealthy victim to wealthy victim); the ways in which Verdoux' activities are located in a broader political and economic context (the Spanish Civil War, the stock market crash, the rise of the dictators); the association between Verdoux' business interests and his financial support for his crippled wife. And so on. When Verdoux is asked if crime pays, he replies, 'No, sir, not in a small way — it needs to be organised.' He calls himself an 'amateur' in comparison with those who make weapons which 'blow innocent people to pieces': 'Wars, conflict — it's all business. One murder makes a villain; millions, a hero. Numbers sanctify!' The comic (and chaotic) warfare of Charlie the Tramp against society becomes, in *Monsieur Verdoux*, a cool and calculated exploita-tion of society's own weapons. As Leone has said, 'Verdoux is the model for all the bandits, all the bounty hunters. . . . Put him in a hat and boots, and you have a frontiersman.' The dialogue which accompanies the battle of the bridge sequence in *The Good, the Bad and the Ugly* can almost be interpreted as a critique of the final part of John Ford's *The Horse Soldiers* (1959) from the moral perspective of Chaplin's *Verdoux*.

Perhaps, as well as such diverse film sources as *Yojimbo*, *Shane*, *Vera Cruz*, *The Last Sunset*, and *Monsieur Verdoux*, the 'Dollars' trilogy owes something to Nicholas Ray's *Johnny Guitar* (1954), a Western which attempts to use Hollywood verbal and visual clichés to comment on the *vulnerability* of the main characters. These clichés take the form of rock-hard dialogue (spoken by a less than rock-hard character) — 'What's eating the fancy man?'; 'I never shake hands with a left-handed draw' — and static, formalised, almost theatrical composi-tions (for example, when Vienna, played by Joan Crawford, first faces the townspeople, led by John McIvers and Emma Small, in her saloon). André Bazin wrote of *Johnny Guitar* that Nicholas Ray was 'no less aware of the rhetoric of the genre than the George Stevens of *Shane*', and Bernardo Bertolucci has called the film 'the first of the baroque Westerns'. Bertolucci's observation is particularly interesting, since, as we have seen, he contributed the original script 'structure' to *Once Upon a Time*: for Leone's film contains a series of direct references to *Johnny Guitar*. The wooden model of a railway depot, with surrounding town, which Vienna displays in her saloon, has its counterpart in McBain's wooden models at Sweetwater, the symbols of his 'dream of a lifetime'. Vienna refuses to be driven out of her saloon, because she knows that when the rail gangs arrive (they are just the other side of the mountains) she will see a whole community develop around her valuable site. She thus reluctantly enlists Johnny's help. Jill McBain (another ex-prostitute) stays at Sweetwater because the Man has warned her, 'This isn't the time to leave.' In *Once Upon a Time* the models play a more central part. For example, after the McBain family massacre, while Cheyenne is looking for 'the why', we see Brett's wooden train in the foreground, reminding us that Cheyenne's hunt for gold is fruitless. After Jill has collected Brett's mysterious order of timber, she recalls the model 'Station' sign — she rummages through Brett's suitcases, but Frank has reached Sweetwater before her, and, in an extraordinary moment accompanied by 'sinister' music, the tiny wooden 'Station' sign apparently floats into the frame, through the air; Jill registers shock, and the camera slowly pans up from the sign to a hand, from the hand to Frank's mean face. This kind of effect had been used by Ray in *Johnny Guitar*: at one point, a whisky glass rolls precariously near the edge of the bar, but a 'mysterious' hand stops it from falling off, and coolly places it upright again; the camera slowly pans up to show Johnny (his first appearance in that scene). Perhaps — in the schematic pattern of relationships represented by both films (based on the dance, in one case a square-dance, in the other a slow 'ballet de mort') — the two characters John McIvers (Ward Bond) and the Dancing Kid (Scott Brady) have their counterparts in Mr Morton, another big businessman, and Cheyenne the bandit.

The late 1950s Westerns of Samuel Fuller (another 'cult' director in Europe at the time, as 'an American Primitive') may also have influenced the development of Leone's early 'style' — in particular *Run of the Arrow* (for its visual exploration of shapes, and fluid camera-work in set-pieces), and *Forty Guns* (for its use of extreme close-ups, for the presentation of Griff Bonnell's 'walk', and for the ways in which the ballad comments on the action). References to the credits sequence of *Forty Guns* abound in *My Name Is Nobody*.

Budd Boetticher was a bullfighter before he became involved in film-making, and several of his films are concerned with that sport. But the basic situation of the bullfight is made more abstract in his Westerns. The circular pans which sometimes describe the 'arenas' in which Boetticher's trapped heroes must outwit their opponents perhaps provided one 'model' for Leone's use of the *corrida* — although the positioning of the protagonists themselves, during the climactic confrontations in Boetticher's films, is more traditional, and thus *linear*. The final shootout in *A Fistful of Dollars* extends this technique. The Man With No Name faces Ramon Rojo, in the main street of San Miguel. It looks as though this will turn into a traditional, linear confrontation. But, as the Man stumbles from side to side of the main street (purposefully advancing, then retreating as bullets hit his metal chest-shield), Leone intercuts with close-ups of Ramon's gang, one by one. An entire circle is thus described; and as Ramon dies, a series of 'subjective' shots perform circular motions against the sky. In this way, what Leone calls the 'arena of destiny' is defined. At the climaxes of Leone's later films, this arena becomes a circular flagstone *corrida*, in which the Man, Mortimer and Indio, or the Good, the Bad and the Ugly, must finally meet. When Harmonica and Frank take up their positions for the final duel in *Once Upon a Time*, the camera takes first Harmonica's then Frank's point of view, as Frank walks around the perimeter of the yard, and as Harmonica advances from a tree-stump to stand before him: the camera lingers on this confrontation in the centre of a circular arena. A subtitle hi-jacked from the 'sword and sandal' epics would have been singularly appropriate at this moment: 'Those about to die salute you.'

Boetticher's handling of the climactic duel may have suggested the theme of the *corrida* to Leone: we have seen how Aldrich's handling of a similar scene may equally have influenced the way in which Leone presents his various *corridas*. But another aspect of the gunplay in Leone's films — the gundown in the main street, the gunfighter stalking his prey, the gunfighter being stalked by his enemies —

seems to owe as much to Fred Zinnemann's choreography of a gunfight at the end of *High Noon* (1952), where the layout of the street — shops, stables, balconies — plays a crucial role. Certainly, *High Noon* is referred to, explicitly, in *Once Upon a Time in the West*: in Zinnemann's film, it is Lee Van Cleef who plays the harmonica, but the chief baddy is known as Frank, and as Frank's three henchmen wait by a water-tower for the arrival of the train, or walk along the rails (filmed from a low angle), they could be walking towards the opening sequence of Leone's film.

In interviews, Sergio Leone particularly stresses his debt to Charles Chaplin and George Stevens. He has also mentioned his admiration for the *aesthetic* (as opposed to the complex plots) of several 'cult' directors of unusual Westerns — Ray, Fuller, Boetticher — and described the popularity of Sturges' *Magnificent Seven* in Italy. If we add Kurosawa and Aldrich to this list, it is clear that Leone is nothing if not eclectic. Individual scenes from his films seem to come from the most unlikely sources: for example, the scene where Eli Wallach selects his gun and turns it on the shopkeeper, in *The Good, the Bad and the Ugly*, comes straight out of the James Cagney gangster movie *Public Enemy*; and the scene where the Old Prophet's house is shaken up by a passing train, in *For a Few Dollars More*, is filmed like the equivalent sequence in an old Goofy cartoon about going on vacation. For those who like playing the 'sources' game, the list is almost endless — perhaps because Leone himself is such a movie buff, and such a *detached* anthologist of favourite Hollywood moments. Meanwhile, as Leone never tires of reminding us, the essential point of reference is the West as interpreted by John Ford: if the 'Dollars' films represent a form of critical cinema (rather than simply a passive rereading of the Western via the Western), then we may expect the criticisms to be levelled in the direction of 'that great optimist', rather than in the direction of cinéastes who were already associated with the making of anti-Westerns.

The 'Dollars' Trilogy — Décors and Details

Sergio Leone's 'Dollars' trilogy comprises a two-level detachment from the Hollywood Western genre. Firstly, as a type of European critical cinema which, using an established cinematic tradition, and without shedding its popular character, can deconstruct and rearrange the images and themes which exemplify the *reverence* of puritan-liberal Hollywood Westerns, the established bases of the genre. Thus Leone can go beyond merely *interpreting* the West in a critical sense; he can re-create it: as Silvanito (the bartender) says to the Man With No Name in *A Fistful of Dollars*, 'It's *like* playing cowboys and Indians.' As we have seen, since the 'Dollars' films were made *outside* the Hollywood production system, they could involve a transcription of the traditional Western 'codes' — without being subject to the usual ideological constraints. Secondly, Leone makes no attempt to engage our sympathy with the characters, but watches the brutality of his protagonists with a detached calm: they are brutal because of the environment in which they exist. And they make no attempt to change that environment. They accept it, without question.

We have seen how Leone's view of American social history (*and* his enthusiasm for Sicilian puppet plays) informs his presentation of the West (or, in this case, the Southwest). The primary motivation is money, the dollar. Not so much money as usable for ready cash, but, as one critic has put it, 'money as *prize*, as something that must be possessed'. In more traditional Westerns, *il denaro* might be invested (in livestock, real estate), used for protection (against Indians, or rustlers) or quite simply spent on weekly provisions and household goods (at the Grafton Store). It might even be won at cards, although the figure of the *professional* gambler — with his sneaky derringer in his waistcoat — is likely to be a marginal one, and, as often as not, this professional will eventually be asked to leave town. In the 'Dollars' films, *il denaro* is not to be invested, or spent on day-to-day living: it is, as

Oreste de Fornari puts it, to be worshipped. When the Man With No Name is asked, 'Why are you doing this for us?' he is liable to answer, 'Five hundred dollars . . .?' and extend an open hand. But he never seems to spend his dollars. In *A Fistful of Dollars*, he collects from both the Baxters and the Rojos before initiating a series of incidents which cause both clans to be wiped out. Silvanito warns the Man that a town with two bosses is not a place to stay: San Miguel is a town of widows, where only the coffin-maker earns a steady living, and where a dried funeral-wreath lies on the disused roulette table. But the Man will not listen: 'The Baxters on one side, the Rojos on the other, and me in the middle . . . that crazy bell-ringer was right. There's money to be made in a town like this.' Consuela Baxter tells him that at the rate he is going, he will soon be a rich man: 'Yeah,' he replies, 'and that won't break my heart.' But in the next film, *For a Few Dollars More*, he is still on the move, still killing for profit, and still dressed in poncho and tatty sheepskin waistcoat. Ramon Rojo massacres a detachment of cavalry at the Rio Bravo canyon and rides off with their consignment of gold, but his clan's life-style does not alter at all. Indio robs the El Paso bank, in *For a Few Dollars More*, and works out an elaborate scheme whereby his gang will kill each other off, leaving him to spend the money. But there is no suggestion that he *will* spend the money. Dollars are not currency, not associated with conspicuous consumption — but something that must be grabbed before the next man. Leone is more interested in the price that society places on a man's head than in the value of the man or the money: 'Where life had no value, death, sometimes, had its price . . .' This may explain the references to Judas throughout the trilogy: 'Even when Judas hanged himself, there was a storm too,' says Tuco in *The Good, the Bad and the Ugly*, as he prepares to shoot the legs off Blondy's stool; Harmonica reluctantly turns

Cheyenne in, to raise money for Sweetwater, in *Once Upon a Time*:

'Judas was content with $4,970 less.'
    'They didn't have dollars in them days.'
'But sons of bitches, yeah.'

(We have seen how this strange *celebration* of the Judas theme relates to a distinctively Latin cultural context.) At the end of *For a Few Dollars More*, Indio opens the chest which once contained the booty from El Paso: all he finds is a 'wanted' poster showing his own laughing face. The dollars do not really matter, once they have been grabbed. But the 'wanted' poster does. Some time later, after the final showdown, Colonel Mortimer rides off into the sunset, leaving the Man to collect the reward money on the whole of Indio's gang. The Man heaves the corpses on to a farm-cart, but finds that the total prize is a little short of expectations. There is a noise behind him, so he wheels round and fires. Mortimer shouts, from the distance, 'Having trouble, boy?' 'No, old man,' replies Eastwood, removing a cigar from his mouth. 'Thought I was having trouble with my adding.' Mortimer smiles benignly, and continues to ride off.

In the elaborate game which the treasure hunt by the Good, the Bad and the Ugly represents, no one protagonist can trust the other two. Much of the violence has a cartoon quality about it, and the relationship between Tuco and Blondy bears more than a passing resemblance to that between the Cat and the Fox, Gideon and Honest John, in Disney's *Pinocchio*. Tuco has a price on his head, so Blondy coolly turns him in, collects, and shoots through the rope before Tuco can be hanged (shades of W.C. Fields and Mae West in *My Little Chickadee*?), then they both ride on to the next town, to repeat the process. Il Cattivo (Lee Van Cleef — the Hollywood character) has a strong — and rather unimaginative — sense of honour where money is concerned: he is paid to kill one man, but before doing this job he is paid by the victim to kill the original employer; he returns to do this, justifying his action with the words 'You know when I'm paid I always see my job through.' The two characters for whom we develop a measure of sympathy as the film progresses, (the 'Italian' characters) Blondy and Tuco, never behave with this type of 'honour' — the honour of the businessman, the principle of the perfect employee — 'I don't make the rules, sir, I just obey them.' Their greed is more anarchic,

and unprincipled. Not for nothing was the film originally to be entitled *Two Magnificent Rogues*. In *The Good, the Bad and the Ugly*, loyalties change as often as the reels. In their quest for the gold, Blondy and Tuco first wear Confederate uniforms, then, after escaping from Betterville, enlist with the North — on both occasions because they have no choice.

The surroundings may be squalid, but dollars are the prize, and the gun the arbiter. So there is no peace. In *A Fistful of Dollars*, the Man is asked by Ramon whether he appreciates peace: 'It's difficult to appreciate something you've never had,' he replies. Later, when the Man has been paid for telling the Rojos about the two 'surviving' soldiers holed up in the cemetery, he refuses to ride with them, saying, 'When a man has some dollars in his pocket, he begins to appreciate peace.' But the peace which the Rojos offer is simply a breathing-space, to put the authorities off the scent. In *For a Few Dollars More*, Indio's gang acts peacefully, so as not to cause suspicion before the bank raid. As the bartender in El Paso observes, if a man wears a gun, but will not use it when provoked, 'you can be sure he's got a pretty good reason'. And there is no trust. The Man tells Mortimer that he will persuade Indio's gang to ride in a certain direction, which will set them up for an ambush. In the event, they ride in a different direction, towards Agua Caliente. But Mortimer is there to meet them. When asked how he figured out which way they would go, he replies (with extraordinary logic) that he could be sure the Man would do the opposite of what he said, and equally sure that Indio would not take the Man's advice: 'Since El Paso's out of the question, well, here I am!' In *The Good, the Bad and the Ugly*, the only workable relationship between two men after the same gold is if one knows the general area where the gold is hidden, and the other the specific part of that area. When both agree to reveal their secrets, it is the Good who lies. The one way a man can be persuaded to threaten his own self-interest by revealing some information is to beat him up. And the question whether a man talks or not is not a question of toughness, or of 'honour'. Blondy asks Il Cattivo whether he is to be given the 'same treatment' as Tuco:

'Would you talk?' replies Il Cattivo.
    'Probably not.'

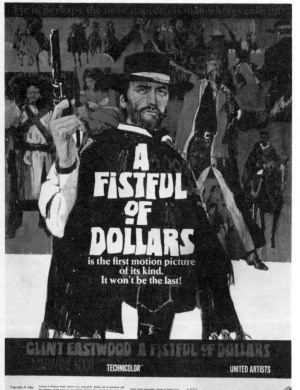

94-6 (*Top and above left*) Italian, French and American publicity for *A Fistful of Dollars* (1964)

97-8 (*Left an opposite*) Italian and French publicity for *For a Few Dollars More* (1965) — note the rising production values

'That's what I thought. Not that you're any tougher than Tuco, but you're smart enough to know that talking won't save you.'

When Tuco tries to persuade the dying Carson to tell him about where the gold is hidden, he first of all roughs the man up, then refuses to give him any water until he has talked. 'My name's Bill Carson,' groans the dying man, 'and ...' 'Yeah, Carson, Carson,' replies Tuco testily, 'glad to know you. I'm Lincoln's grandfather. Now, what was that you said about the dollars?' A little later, when it is clear that Carson will die without water, Tuco rushes off to fetch some, shouting, 'Don't die till I come back. I'll get you water.'

In *The Good, the Bad and the Ugly*, this atmosphere of brutality, gold-digging and mistrust is enshrined in a series of maxims for the conduct of life:

'There are two kinds of people in the world, my friend, those with a rope around their neck and the people who have the job of doing the cutting. Listen, the neck at the end of the rope is mine. I run the risks. So the next time I want more than half.'

'You may run the risks, my friend, but I do the cutting. If we cut down my percentage . . . Cigar? . . . It's liable to interfere with my aim.'

'But if you miss, you had better miss very well. Whoever double-crosses me and leaves me alive, he understands nothing about Tuco. Nothing.' (*He eats the cigar.*)

'There are two kinds of spurs, my friend. Those that come in by the door' (*Tuco makes sign of the cross*) 'and those that come in by the window. Take off that pistol belt.'

'You see, in this world there are two kinds of people, my friend. Those with loaded guns, and those who dig. You dig.'

In this kind of atmosphere, the basic need is to survive: if life is 'nasty, brutish and short', relations between individuals are judged as much in terms of efficiency as in terms of any more traditional values. The Man With No Name enters no relationships at all — except perhaps the contractual. He is a *ronin*, a masterless samurai, who can free the 'holy family' in *A Fistful of Dollars* (offering as motivation 'I once knew someone like you, and there was no one to help'), and *still* ride away with some of the money he has collected from the two clans who were oppressing them. He cannot afford to believe in fair play. Nor does he wish to slow down, get a stake in the community and start cultivating his garden. When he confronts himself twenty years on, in the person of Colonel Mortimer, he asks, 'Tell me, Colonel, were you ever young?' The Colonel replies, 'Yes, and just as reckless as you . . .' But the *ronin's* aim to 'settle down, and possibly retire' is never achieved. The heroes of the 'Dollars' trilogy are not the law-enforcers, but the bounty-hunters, the specialists in killing.

By *celebrating* the place that the 'almighty dollar' holds in the capitalist West, and by showing how frontier towns may really have been run (usury, economic terrorism, neo-feudalism) Leone seems, in his strange way, to be *criticising* the ideology by showing it at work as the central axis of his plots — as Mike Wallington has pointed out. This process is aided by his bizarre sense of humour, and rhetorical use of time-worn cinematic devices.

Into this critical vision of the American West, Leone infuses more comedy *and* more history as the trilogy progresses. Various jokes recur in his Westerns: a gunslinger bursts into a hotel room, and discovers a naked woman in a bath (*For a Few*; *Once Upon a Time*); guns are fired from unexpected places (up a sleeve, over a shoulder, in the bath, in a boot; later Italian derivatives were to extend this gag: for example, a gun is secreted inside a banjo in *Sabata*; inside a church organ in *Sartana's Coming*; and inside a cripple's crutch in *The Price of Power*); fun is made of the heroes' undressing habits ('Don't worry, I didn't dirty the sheets,' says the Man to Silvanito in *Fistful*, as he gets out of bed fully clothed; 'I don't wear 'em,' he shouts as he throws a pair of long-johns to the terrified resident he has just 'ejected' from a hotel, in *For a Few*; 'Put your drawers on, and take your gun off,' he tells the naked Tuco in *The Good* . . .); dotty old men are gently ridiculed (Piripero, the coffin-maker, in *Fistful*, and the Old Prophet, driven mad by the noise of the 'damned trains' in *For a Few*, both played by the German actor Josef Egger as an aged version of the 'B' Western character Fuzzy); very fat (and lethargically brutal) bandits are the target for rougher humour (Chico in *Fistful*, Nino in *For a Few*, Wallace in *The Good* . . . , all acted by another member of Leone's stock company, Mario Brega — alias 'Richard Stuyvesant'); and much emphasis is laid on the bodily functions (all the films include lurid close-ups of people messily eating; in the original cut of *The Good* . . . , Tuco pisses over the parched Blondy, as they trek across the desert; later, he escapes from a train by pretending to piss over the side of a moving truck; and in the original cut of *Duck, You Sucker*, Juan opens the film by pissing over an ants' nest, in the hollow of a tree). This style of humour, in recent years a standard feature of Italian popular cinema, recurs with a vengeance in Fellini's *Satyricon*, and Pasolini's *Canterbury Tales*. Other jokes are more understated: the hotelier's vast wife, standing beside her tiny husband ('He's tall, isn't he?' — 'You're just dirty'); the chickens of Santa Cruz, and the hundreds of eggs in the telegraph office; the 'smoking' incident involving Mortimer and the Hunchback (Klaus Kinski) (all from *For a Few Dollars More*). In the same film, the Man arrives in Alamogordo: since that desert town was the site of the first atomic bomb test, in 1945, the Man heralds his arrival with — what else? — a large stick of dynamite. Of the jokes about illiteracy in Leone's films, the best occurs in *The Good* . . . , when Tuco struggles with the words 'See you soon, Idi . . . Idio . . .' 'Idiots,' suggests Blondy. 'It's for you!'

Perhaps the most successful gags involve Ennio Morricone's caricatural soundtracks. (Leone recalls how unnerving it was to watch Morricone in the viewing theatre, as the 'Dollars' films were run through: for he roared with laughter at *everything* — not just the comic sequences.) In *A Fistful of Dollars*, the Man's actions and 'hard' dialogue are complemented by high-pitched trills or single notes on a jew's-harp. In *For a Few Dollars More*, the same trill (and harp note) complements the Man, a lower-pitched trill Colonel Mortimer, and a chord on Spanish guitar El Indio. Whenever Indio lights up a joint, we hear en electronic whirr on the soundtrack — the only indication that he is not just a compulsive cigarette smoker. In *The Good, the Bad and the Ugly*, each of the characters ironically categorised by the title has a distinctive 'insignia', such as a trill or whine (sung, whistled or played) taken from the opening bars of the main title theme. Sometimes these sounds are the only indication we have of what a character is thinking (as when a trill tells us that the Man is not really drunk, in *Fistful*). Sometimes they are a cue for the audience to laugh, after a tense confrontation (as in the scene with the Baxters from *Fistful*, quoted earlier). Since the characters are so emblematic, the

sounds used to 'illustrate' their presence help the audience to recognise them, even when they are just off the screen (for example, the trills or whistles heralding most of Clint Eastwood's first entrances).

Morricone uses 'sounds' and snatches from main themes to represent characters, loud orchestral passages for action sequences or panoramic landscape shots, and formal trumpet solos (with syncopated chord backing), often reminiscent of triumphant bullfight music, for 'set pieces', such as an exchange of hostages or the climactic duels. Morricone himself is a trumpeter. The main title themes usually consist of a simple electric guitar line (sounding rather like 'Riders in the Sky'), made more appropriate to the tone of the film, by the addition of yells ('Quick, get back'), shrieks, gunshots, rifles being cocked, church bells, whipping sounds, trills, whines, rhythmic jew's-harp and other assorted electronic effects, to 'punctuate' the basically traditional Western score. His music often contains long sustained pedal-points — with these unusual sound-effects going on in the melody line.

When Morricone was approached to write the music for *Fistful*, he was working on Caiano's *Pistols Don't Argue*. The *Pistols* soundtrack is not particularly interesting: a fully orchestrated main theme, based on a four-chord structure, with a French horn taking the tune, backed by insistent 'hoofbeat' drums — all reminiscent of the Hollywood equivalent. *Pistols Don't Argue* even has a traditional ballad entitled 'Lonesome Billy', sung by Peter Tevis. Sergio Leone thought Morricone's early film scores terrible — and Morricone (who, it transpired, had been at the lycée in Rome with him) apparently agreed. But Morricone had produced (anonymously) a strange arrangement of the American folk-song 'Pastures of Plenty': Leone found this more interesting; and they worked together on the *Fistful* soundtrack. This soundtrack turned out to be unlike anything Morricone (or anyone else, for that matter) had scored before. The tunes were not particularly original (in fact, one can often recognise phrases from other Western themes, or from popular tunes of the moment, in Morricone's scores, and he is especially fond of hi-jacking 'quotes' from Beethoven and Bach): but the arrangements were extraordinarily appropriate. It was as if Duane Eddy had bumped into Rodrigo, in the middle of a crowded Via Veneto. Since the 'Dollars' trilogy, Morricone's work for other directors — over thirty-five Westerns, and many more soundtracks in

99-101 Italian, American and French publicity
for *The Good, the Bad and the Ugly* (1966)

102 Some of Ennio Morricone's many soundtracks
for Cinecittà films in the 1960s and early 1970s

other genres — has seldom matched up to his Leone scores, in either invention or appropriateness — notable exceptions being the Pontecorvo films *The Battle of Algiers* and *Queimada*, and Bertolucci's *1900*. In fact, some of Morricone's musical themes and ideas, after rejection by Leone, tend to turn up — re-arranged by Bruno Nicolai — in other Italian Westerns where they simply become obtrusive. Although more than one music critic has categorised Ennio Morricone as a ' "B" feature musician', it seems clear that the relationship between director and composer in this particular case proved unusually fruitful, on a par with the relationships between Franju and Jarre, Truffaut and Delerue, Fellini and Rota, or Demy and Legrand.

Morricone's original use of the human voice as just one other musical instrument, and experiments with 'concrete' sounds, are sometimes used by Leone to link otherwise unrelated picaresque episodes (this is particularly noticeable throughout the first half of *The Good, the Bad and the Ugly*). Heavily amplified background noises, in particular animal sounds, are used to dramatic and humourous effect. A cock crows loudly before a man is betrayed (*The Good . . .*) and before violence suddenly erupts (*Once Upon a Time*). A cat mews just before a gunflight (*Fistful*; *For a Few*). A dog howls mournfully (the opening shot and Tuco's arrival at Sad Hill in *The Good . . .*). Crows caw, as the three protagonists meet in a flagstone circle, at the climax of *The Good, the Bad and the Ugly*. And throughout the trilogy, Leone lovingly evokes the mechanics of loading, cocking and firing a pistol or rifle by electronically simulating the sounds these processes make. In *For a Few Dollars More*, a crescendo of gunshots is used to emphasise the rivalry between the Man and Mortimer: as they each stand looking at the 'wanted' poster for El Indio, Leone cross-cuts closer and closer to their faces (face, mouth, nose and eyes, eyes) in rhythm with 'expressionistic' gunshots on the soundtrack. In long scenes where there is little or no dialogue, amplified 'natural' sounds help to create an atmosphere of mounting tension: for the opening sequence of *The Good, the Bad and the Ugly*, these include the wind whistling, rustling canvas (a derelict wagon), a dog howling, boots crunching on gravel, followed by a sudden silence; for the credits sequence of *Once Upon a Time*, the soundtrack provides a variety of effects, including a metal door slamming (electronically simulated), wooden doors creaking, knuckles being

pulled, water dripping on to a bald pate, a fly buzzing, a telegraph receiver tapping, and, most of all, a water-wheel, in much need of oiling, inexorably turning round; when Jack Elam gets fed up with the tapping of the telegraph, he violently wrenches it from its shelf — at that moment, the sound of the squeaky water-wheel abruptly ceases, leaving a long silence, which will only be broken by the buzzing of a fly. The lazy but enervating atmosphere of this opening sequence is shattered by the deafening shriek of a train whistle as a locomotive hurtles over the camera. Perhaps Leone's finest use of 'simulated' sound-effects occurs later on in the same film, in a scene where Frank returns to the train, to find that Mr Morton and his cronies have been wiped out by Cheyenne's gang: throughout the sequence, the stationary locomotive coughs, wheezes and puffs like a bursting lung. These sounds are not always just part of the décor, part of Leone's *rhetoric*, however: in both *Once Upon a Time* and *For a Few Dollars More* musical instruments play a key role in the plot, symbolising as they do the traumatic memories of the protagonists. Mortimer's chiming watch and the Man's harmonica both introduce the flashbacks which provide missing pieces in the puzzle of each story, and the ways in which these musical themes are woven into other motifs on the soundtrack indicate the importance of these vague, unfocused memories at key moments in the development of the plot.

Clearly, Leone could afford to be more careful about details like this as the budgets for his Westerns increased. Other Italian Westerns, which did not have such international success, had to stick with more parochial production values — successive shootouts, each of which is intended to carry the dramatic force of a 'climax' to make up for deficiencies in the budget (a kind of ersatz 'spectacle'); small groups of noisy bandits (instead of large groups of extras — again, to create an atmosphere of 'big spending'); and décors which look authentic, but which in reality cannot hide the inadequate research that must, of necessity, have gone into them: often the American flags are the big giveaway: in one low-budget Spaghetti, the US cavalry (vintage 1870) rides into battle with fifty stars on the unit's flag; in another, the flag has thirteen stripes and only seven stars (apparently the research for this one came from a World War Two photograph of 'Old Glory' shot to pieces). Leone's films represent a gradual shedding of these parochial production values (and a gradual incorporation of concessions to the international audience), as American and Italian investors poured capital into his projects. *A Fistful of Dollars* was commercially the most successful Italian film ever made up to 1964 (in terms of the cost/profit ratio), but *For a Few Dollars More* made more money than *Fistful* in under twelve months. So Leone had little problem attracting investors: *Fistful* cost $200,000 (of which Eastwood's salary accounted for $15,000); *For a Few Dollars More* cost $600,000 (Eastwood earning $50,000 and a percentage); *The Good, the Bad and the Ugly* cost $1,200,000, half a million of this advanced by United Artists, in exchange for half the box-office takings outside Italy (Eastwood's cut being $250,000 plus 10 per cent of the European and American profits — a sum considerably in excess of both Blondy's *and* Tuco's 'prize' at the end of that film). As Clint Eastwood remarked after finishing the third film in the trilogy (a film in which he had less to do than the other big star, Eli Wallach), 'I'm probably the highest paid American actor who ever worked in Italian pictures.' *The Good, the Bad and the Ugly* marked Leone's definitive break with Cinecittà formula Westerns: instead of the small, shouting rabble of bandits in the 'Django' films, we see two armies of extras dressed in blue and grey; instead of one 'B' feature American actor living in Europe, the names above the title include Eastwood (by now a top international star with his television career behind him) and Eli Wallach (ex-Actors Studio, *The Magnificent Seven* and *How the West Was Won*, with an acting *style* to set against the underplaying of the other American stars, a style to represent the Latin quarter of the film); instead of the unmitigated cynicism of the first two 'Dollars' films (which, if we are to believe Lino Miccichè, was calculated to appeal to the lowest common denominator in Italian urban cinemagoers), Leone introduces a series of 'edifying' moments into his historical epic — the camp commandant claiming that there is still honour in the Union ranks, Tuco suddenly becoming articulate as he blames the environment into which he was born for his anti-social behaviour as an adult, the Man With No Name showing sympathy for a dying Confederate drummer (not 'paternal' sympathy as in *The Horse Soldiers*, admittedly, but even John Wayne would have had difficulty getting away with that in 1967). Oreste de Fornari interprets these 'edifying' moments as *intrusions* on the 'timid

amorality' of the previous two films — 'slipped in, for the intercontinental market'.

The success of *Fistful* encouraged the original Italian co-production company, Jolly Films, to buy two episodes from the TV *Rawhide* series, splice them together, arrange for some extra footage to be shot, and reissue this 'collage' under the title *Maledetto Gringo* (or *The Magnificent Stranger*, as it was to be called for other markets), starring the man with the cigar, Clint Eastwood. After a legal action, the film was withdrawn. Soon after this, Lucas Film tried a similar trick, this time calling the result *El Gringhero* (which they claimed was 'directed by Clarence Brown', no less). Again, Eastwood took the matter to court, and won his case. It was, he maintained, a question of protecting his image. In the excitement following the success of the 'Dollars' films, it was even announced (erroneously) that Leone was working on a remake of *Gone with the Wind*!

As the production values soared, and as the audience became more intercontinental, so Leone was able to indulge his almost obsessive interest in the tiniest details of Western life. *Fistful* was clearly made on the cheap: the townsfolk only appear in two short scenes, colour matching is poor (particularly for dusk or night-time sequences), and the interiors are decorated in a (minimally) functional way. *For a Few* is full of closely observed details: cluttered bar-rooms; townspeople inquisitively gathering round the El Paso bank, after Indio's raid; Confederate banknotes found in the safe; the honky-tonk piano-player who (of course) stops playing as Colonel Mortimer pushes open the saloon doors. And this film gave Leone the opportunity to linger over Colonel Mortimer's armoury: in an extraordinary moment, Mortimer casually unbuckles his saddle-cloth (accompanied by a 'twang' on the soundtrack), to reveal a Buntline Special (Uberti reproduction model, with detachable shoulder-stock), a Colt Lightning pump-action rifle, a Winchester '94 (genuine), and a double-barrelled Lefaucheux action pinfire! The Man With No Name favours his simple '45 (with snakes on the grips), and a Winchester, or Henry '66 (Uberti reproduction, with forestock removed). In *For a Few* and *The Good, the Bad and the Ugly*, there is an unusually detailed emphasis on gun lore: Blondy takes his Navy Colt to pieces, cleans and reassembles it, then loads; Tuco (in a scene cut from the English release print) visits a gunsmith's shop, browses around the case of Colts and Remingtons, then pieces together his own 'custom-built' model from various parts — choosing these by *listening* to the sound they made (the hammer clicking back, the chamber revolving etc.), in much the same way as Indio *listens* to the action of the Colt he is given when he is sprung from jail in *For a Few*. Now, it may simply be that Leone and other Spaghetti directors (in particular Corbucci and Sollima) emphasise these details *because* the Cinecittà context is so 'inauthentic': Hollywood directors would not need to 'impose' details they take for granted, or to adopt such a 'peep-show' attitude to social context, for, if one accepts Will Wright's thesis, Hollywood Westerns are *themselves* 'documents' of a kind — 'documents' representing a position *vis-à-vis* the continuing re-interpretation of American history for the benefit of American audiences.

But, in Leone's case at least, this 'neo-realist' attitude towards 'décors and details' (of which the firearms are perhaps the most striking example) is, as we have seen, an essential strategic device in the criticism of one (historical/cinematic) mythology, the re-creation of another (cinematic) mythology. The 'décors and details' must not be invented, for the film-maker is playing on the audience's recognition of them. In Leone's terms, the guns his characters use represent some of the 'external things' which constitute the specific contribution of the Western to 'adventures' which are timeless. So 'external' (in Leone's case) that he is not really concerned about accuracy of detail at all (despite appearances). His interest in firearms is as much aesthetic as technical or historical. Blondy may use a Colt Navy Model, but he wears .45 cartridges around his gunbelt. Anachronistically, his Navy has been converted for centre-fire cartridges — this makes him quicker on the draw, and he can load faster. If he looks good, it does not matter that the details are wrong, even if the details *are* uncharacteristically emphasised. For the scene where 'Shorty' gets hanged, Blondy has a Henry '66 rifle (Uberti reproduction) *with telescopic lens*!

The battle for Langstone Bridge in *The Good, the Bad and the Ugly* seems at first sight to involve an extraordinary array of authentic Civil War weapons: Gatling guns, mortars, Whitworth field guns (all borrowed, in fact, from the Army Museum in Madrid); but metallic-cartridge Gatlings had not been invented by that stage in the Civil War. Again,

a general atmosphere of authenticity is being created (witness the number of shiny Whitworths and Gatlings which stand prominently in the foreground during dialogue sequences), and even if the details are wrong, Leone clearly takes great pleasure in photographing such a stockpile of archaic destructive technology: as the rhythm of battle accelerates, he zooms in on mortars and Gatlings, then pulls back to show their effects. The Civil War sequences in this film may be crammed with 'peep-show' details (Matthew Brady even makes a fleeting appearance), but these details make possible what are evidently intended to be deliberate anachronisms. Whereas the Hollywood Western had traditionally made a clear distinction between the two sides in the war (the aristocratic, patriarchal Confederacy, the liberal, pragmatic North), whichever side the scriptwriters were backing, Leone purposely blurs this distinction to create a more up-to-date, living picture of war. In *The Good, the Bad and the Ugly*, there is no attempt to present the Confederacy as a 'stage' in history out of which the new North developed (or even as an economic satellite of the North — a more cynical interpretation which might make the parallel with Italy even more explicit): from the point of view of the protagonists (and the film), there is no difference between the two sides, just a lot of dust to make recognition of uniforms very difficult. Leone's model for the Civil War is derived from more recent conflicts in which Italy was involved — the trenches of the First World War (Langstone Bridge), the concentration camps of the Second (Betterville). It may be that there is a historical justification for this (the Civil War seen as the first recognisably modern war), but that is beside the point: Leone's 'peep-show' makes his deliberately anachronistic, critical interpretation a possibility, providing a visual context for the disillusioned speeches of the Northern Captain (whose attitudes are more traditionally given to the meanest private) and the Man With No Name (who is disgusted by the 'waste'). In the case of the battle for Langstone Bridge, these 'décors and details' must have cost a fortune to set up: according to both Clint Eastwood and Eli Wallach, the bridge was blown up prematurely, before the cameras were rolling, and had to be rebuilt — a classic example of the 'Ready when you are, Cecil B.' gag. Recalling the incident, Leone simply shrugs it off: 'Bridges tend to get blown up in my films . . .'

According to the Italian arms magazine *Diana*

Armi (May 1969), the Spaghetti Westerns did wonders for the Lombardy-based replica firearms industry: 'the single-action pieces used in the various films shot in Italy, Spain and Yugoslavia are identical to those we can buy from any respectable gunsmith, except for the barrel, which is faked — it is a simple tube, without rifling'. The article encourages those who enjoy collecting 'Wild West' pieces to go and see some of the films. Apparently, some gunsmiths in the replica trade were even beginning to *specialise* in the restoration of firearms damaged during the filming of Spaghetti Westerns — one particular skill, much in demand, being the straightening of rifle-barrels which had been bashed against rocks by over-enthusiastic heavies. Reading a magazine like *Diana Armi* (indeed, thinking about the title alone, with its association of mythology, sex and guns) helps to locate the Italian Westerns within a gun culture where 'the persuasive lips' seem to turn people on every bit as much as in the States: perhaps the fetishistic emphasis on detail in some of these films only makes real sense in such a context.

Leone's Westerns also had a considerable spin-off effect on the model railway trade in Italy: Rivarossi, for example, started bringing out hand-made wooden models of the buildings and accessories which could be seen in *The Good, the Bad and the Ugly*, and *Once Upon a Time in the West*. But, again, emphasis on detail should not be confused with authenticity of detail. Many of the Leone buildings in *Once Upon a Time* (and especially the McBain place) have the look of Northern Italian Alpine chalets. Rivarossi's quarter-inch scale models also had this look — as hardened railway buffs in Italy were, apparently, quick to point out. The A. and P.H. Morton Railroad Company starts laying tracks in sight of the Atlantic, and Morton himself hopes to see the Pacific before he dies; but no *single* railway company was, in fact, responsible for laying tracks across the whole continent. As to the locomotives which Morton uses, most of them are thinly disguised Spanish shunters (which postdate the period in question by a *very* long time) — the giveaway being the positioning of the exterior boilers and of the 'fake' smokestack: one way to tell which parts of *Once Upon a Time* were actually filmed in America is to look for the genuinely American locomotives (they appear twice, in the English release print). It says much for the success of Leone's attempt to re-create a 'peep-show' of the Wild West (by piling on detail after detail, simply for visual effect) that critics have so often praised him for his *authenticity*. By the time of *Once Upon a Time*, the 'peep-show' was getting extremely expensive: the main street of Flagstone, for example, which was constructed at Guadix, Spain, cost considerably more than the whole budget for *Fistful* - $250,000.

Since Leone seems to be so interested in problems of communication and categorisation (how easily identification is achieved; what a man is like when divested of the things by which we normally recognise him, such as his name, his past, his conversation, even his complexity), external details such as clothes, and personal props are given unusual emphasis in his films. When Tuco is 'hanged' for the first time, in *The Good, the Bad and the Ugly*, the camera pans along a row of depressed peasant faces watching the execution. Later, when he is 'hanged' again, we are shown a row of eager, expectant faces, well-groomed and evidently wearing Sunday-best clothes for this spectacle: the town is more prosperous, the inhabitants have a more *bourgeois* attitude towards the death of a bandit and rapist. Like most of Leone's details, these provide well-observed (sometimes caricatured) social background, against which the picaresque, surreal adventures of the central characters can more effectively take place. In a sense, the Civil War sequences (injected into the narrative of *The Good, the Bad and the Ugly* with a splendid sense of construction) serve precisely this function: perversely, the war intervenes to *save* the lives of Blondy and Tuco on several occasions. A mysterious Confederate death-wagon appears from nowhere, in the middle of the desert, and distracts Tuco's attention, thus saving Blondy from being shot. A mortar shell breaks the beam from which Blondy is about to be hanged, and gives him the chance to escape. As Tuco is about to be thumped by Wallace, at the railway station near Betterville concentration camp, a Northern train pulls into the station, and Wallace spares Tuco for the time being. Later, Tuco manages to cut through the handcuffs chaining him to Wallace, by placing the chain on a railway line: a Northern troop train does the rest (shades of Aldrich's *Apache*, perhaps, where Burt Lancaster does the same thing). Finally, Southern mortar fire provides a smoke-screen, from behind which Blondy and Tuco can systematically pick off the members of Angel Eyes' gang. But the war also defines the morality of the film, in terms of the model provided by Chaplin's *Monsieur Verdoux*. Il Buono, Il Brutto and Il Cattivo may be self-centred bastards, but the Civil War is an inferno of death, needless destruction and mutilation. An army thief is briefly shown carrying his coffin to the foot of a nearby wall, standing up against the wall, and being hastily shot; the sequence lasts a few seconds, and we scarcely notice it. A Confederate spy is shown strapped to the cowcatcher of a Northern troop train: again, the incident is scarcely noticed. But these details build up into a collage of day-to-day violence: Blondy stands watching the battle for Langstone Bridge (itself a monument to human folly), and comments, 'I've never seen so many men wasted so badly.' The events leading up to the destruction of this bridge, based on a situation 'borrowed' from an earlier European (French) Western, Robert Enrico's *Incident at Owl Creek*, (also owing something, perhaps, to the equivalent sequences in Buster Keaton's *The General* and John Ford's *Horse Soldiers*) provides the film with its one main moral contrast.

Leone has described why he made the picture:

I began *The Good, the Bad and the Ugly* like the two previous ones, this time with *three* characters and a treasure hunt, but what interested me was on the one hand to demystify the adjectives, on the other to show the absurdity of war. What do 'good', 'bad' and 'ugly' really mean? We all have some bad in us, some ugliness, some good. And there are people who appear to be ugly, but when we get to know them better, we realise that they are more worthy. . . . As for the Civil War which the characters encounter, in my vision, it is useless, stupid: it does not involve a 'good cause'. . . . I show a Northern concentration camp, but was thinking partly about the Nazi camps, with their Jewish orchestras. All this does not mean that there is nothing to laugh at in the film. Across all these tragic adventures, there runs a picaresque spirit. . . . The picaresque and the Commedia dell'arte genres have this in common: they do not have true heroes, represented by one character.

Certainly, the episodic structure of the narrative, based as it is on a series of chance encounters between cunning rogues, recalls the picaresque novel — a Latin literary tradition. Two of the scriptwriters, Age and Scarpelli, had already made a

name for themselves with a series of witty, picaresque historical epics — such as (most recently) Mario Monicelli's *L'Armata Brancaleone* (which starred Vittorio Gassman, as the head of a gang of roguish crusaders). The most oft-repeated line in *The Good, the Bad and the Ugly* is 'Let's get the hell out of here.' And Il Buono is not a 'hero': in a Hollywood Western, he might even be categorised as a baddy. After he has become fed up with his business deal with Tuco (turning him in, and shooting through the rope), he rides off, taking all the money instead of just his cut. Tuco shouts after him, 'If I ever catch you, Blondy, I'll rip your heart out and eat it.' Blondy reins in his horse, and slowly turns round. 'Such ingratitude,' he spits, 'after all the times I've saved your life.' The frame is frozen, and the words *Il Buono* appear beneath Blondy's face.

There is plenty to laugh at in the film. A gunslinger (who appeared in the opening sequence) surprises Tuco while he is having a bath. 'I've been looking for you for eight months . . . now I find you in exactly the position that suits me . . .' There are four spurts of flame from beneath the suds. The gunslinger falls back. Tuco slowly gets out of the bath, clutching a soapy Navy Colt. 'When you have to shoot, shoot, don't talk!'

Even the war is used as the situation for a gag. Blondy and Tuco see a detachment of seemingly grey-clad troops in the distance. 'Blue or grey?' asks Blondy. 'They're grey like us,' replies Tuco, looking at the uniform he has stolen from Carson. 'Let's say hello to them and then get going.' As the troops draw nearer, Tuco shouts, 'Hurrah for the Confederacy. Hurrah. Down with General Grant. Hurrah for General . . . what's his name?' 'Lee,' prompts Blondy. 'Lee . . . Lee. God is with us because he hates the Yanks too . . .' 'God's not on our side,' says Blondy, looking more closely at the now stationary troops, ' 'cause he hates idiots also.' We then zoom in on the sleeve of the troop commander — being brushed; as the desert dust comes off, it is clear he is wearing Blue. Leone immediately cuts to a shot of marching feet, on their way to Betterville concentration camp. The feet march over a rickety bridge; like the bridge over which Tuco staggers after his ordeal in the desert, the river underneath has long since dried up — another symbol of nature's cruelty.

Leone may have 'begun the film like the two previous ones', but, in terms of stylistic self-assurance, and the performances he could get out of his actors, *The Good, the Bad and the Ugly* is streets ahead of the two 'Dollars' films. *Fistful* concerns one man's fight against two rival factions. Its success had encouraged Leone to make a sequel. We have seen how the various derivatives of the first film may, by the usual Cinecittà process, have encouraged Leone to *extend* his style, to experiment. 'I wanted to prove — to myself above all — that this success was not a question of luck, as people had said.' 'It was', he continues, 'with *For a Few Dollars More* that I directly grappled with my theme for the first time: the friendship that can spring up between two men. Remember, there were, in that film, two generations which opposed one another before uniting.' In *For a Few* Eastwood's performance as the Man With No Name (whose motives by now were far more ambivalent) began to become overtly self-parodic; Volonté's performance as Indio was played with all the stops out, and the raucous enthusiasm of the Mexicans was contrasted (more effectively than in *Fistful*) with the staccato curtness of the Gringos; Lee Van Cleef managed to convey an almost paternal authority (to embody the running gag about 'old man' and 'boy') instead of his customary menace. But Van Cleef's very different performance as the Bad (a younger man) was altogether more convincing: the narrowing 'Angel Eyes', the empty smile, the slow, punchy delivery. In the first dialogue scene of the film, this sinister delivery was particularly effective: 'Is that your family?' he asks the farmer (Fernando Rey), indicating a photograph on the wall. 'Nice family.' As the Good, Clint Eastwood managed to send himself up in a more stylised (and self-effacing) way than the previous films had suggested he could (Leone recalls that Eastwood was at first reluctant to share the billing with *two* other protagonists). Eli Wallach's portrayal of Tuco, a loud, self-indulgent, agile, and extraordinarily effective performance, complete with Chico Marx accent, was clearly based as much on improvisation as script — at one point, he loses his words completely. Wallach's infectious enthusiasm — the Method gone wild — dominates the entire film. He represents 'the word' — just as of the other players, or rather underplayers, Eastwood represents 'cool', and Lee Van Cleef 'menace'.

If the performances reveal a development in Leone's technique as a director, so do the visuals. Odd moments in *Fistful* had suggested the shape of things to come: in *one* shot, he shows the arrival of Silvanito and the Man at a ledge overlooking Rio Bravo canyon, adjusts the focus as the two men dismount, then cranes up and over the ledge, to reveal a group of wagons (Ramon's gang) and a detachment of cavalry riding across the river beyond. But this kind of expansiveness is rare in *Fistful*, only recurring during the final shootout (already described in detail). Other photographic effects suggested that Leone had still retained the interest in art direction (framing, colour) he had first shown in *The Colossus of Rhodes*: when Ramon (in a milk-white shirt) first meets the Man, white pieces of fluff float across the scene, almost suggesting a crisp snow effect; during the exchange of hostages, this white gives way to a softer autumnal brown (leaves on the street, sand, dust, horses, costumes) against which Ramon's dark, formal outfit, and the child's white smock stand out. Leone retained the cameraman from *Fistful*, Massimo Dallamano, on *For a Few Dollars More*. In this film, Leone's penchant for *rhetorical* cinematic effects became more apparent — a *rhetoric* operating within the 'codes' of the traditional Western, 'transcribed' and extended but still easily recognisable. The montage, punctuated by gunshots, showing the rivalry between Mortimer and the Man for Indio's blood; the rhythmic cutting of the duels between Tomaso and Indio in a church, and between Mortimer and Indio in a symbolic *corrida*, with the Man acting as referee; the less staccato cutting of the lazy, relaxed confrontations between Calloway and Mortimer, the Man and Mortimer; the crane-shot as Calloway leaves a hotel bedroom, jumps from the roof, and makes off down the street; the use of extreme close-ups, and of recognisable guns or hands suddenly appearing at one side of the frame (the introduction of 'characters' iconographically); the delayed-action 'expressionist' rain, which pours down as the Man passes under the White Rocks town sign; the increasingly characteristic filming of confrontations — matching pans in rhythm, the marking of areas by tracking round and by showing a 'circle' of faces in close-up; crosscuts to dreamlike flashbacks, 'shared' by the two interested parties (and of psychological, as well as narrative, significance); the main story delayed until at least twenty minutes into the film, to give time for a series of self-contained episodes which introduce us to the 'style' of the two protagonists individually, before they join forces, with a climactic confrontation to round each episode off — all these revealed a new assurance and individuality in

A Fistful of Dollars

103-5 The Man With No Name (Clint Eastwood) escalates the rivalry between the two clans, b shooting a few of Baxter men

106 The Last Supper: Ramon, Esteban and Benito Rojo entertain th Man With No Name *inset*; Madonna and child Marisol (Marianne Koch) protects her son Jesus

Leone's approach, and showed him to be a director who was sensitive to current cinematic vibrations, at the least. Those critics who said of directorial effects, 'If you notice it, its bad,' began to fear the worst . . . For, as *Cahiers* pointed out, Leone's films were becoming a clear case of 'cinematographic narcissism'.

From the rack-focus shot which opens *The Good, the Bad and the Ugly*, of Al Mulock's gnarled face rocking into frame in extreme close-up, to the closing long-shots which show Clint Eastwood riding off into the geology of Spain, Leone explores shapes and spatial relationships in an expansive way which makes his previous work seem almost understated. For much of the film, the camera will simply not keep still. If a man walks out of a house towards a team of horses, the camera starts tracking at the far end of the team, and reaches the wagon at the same time as the man, thus describing two sides of a triangle. In order to show the relationship between a Northern camp guard and the orchestra he is forcing to play, the camera starts tracking past the various dejected instrumentalists, eventually reaching the guard, who is briefly held in close-up as he spits in the dust. If a man runs around a circular area, the camera films him every step of the way, in a series of sweeping circular pans. To show some characters' arrival at a battlefield, Leone films them in medium-shot, then cranes over to a high-angle shot, which reveals a community of entrenched soldiers on the other side of the hedge. As gun-slingers get off their horses, the camera starts below their stirrups, and *rises* to be level with their faces when they reach the ground. Panning shots slowly explore horizontal shapes — a Navy Colt's barrel, a Henry rifle — jutting into frame from the side: Fritz Lang is on record as having said that the wide screen is only useful for snakes and coffins; Leone has certainly added the rifle to that list. Objects appear from out of frame, originating *beneath* the camera's field of vision: Angel Eyes'

spade, Northern sentries' bayonets, rifles threatening Tuco. In *For a Few Dollars More*, Leone had experimented with this technique, during the final *corrida* sequence, when a pocket-watch 'floats' up from beneath the frame, held by the Man's outstretched hand. When the camera is not exploring shapes in *The Good, the Bad and the Ugly*, it ostentatiously emphasises spatial relationships on the wide screen by use of uncomfortable close-ups, and of unusually high (or low) angles. At times, the framing recalls the more zany moments in Dick Lester's *Running, Jumping and Standing Still Film*. Subjective shots proliferate: as the death-wagon is stopped by Tuco, the camera is placed in the driver's seat, and bounces with the vehicle; when Blondy makes Tuco stand on a rickety wooden cross, with the gold scattered beneath his feet, the camera provides a Tuco-eye view of the proceedings. The visual similarities between ugly, pock-marked physiognomies and rugged desert landscapes are frequently exploited. This type of camerawork, possibly inspired by Miklos Jancso's *The Round Up*, and executed this time by director of photography Tonino Delli Colli, finds a grand synthesis in the two formal 'set-pieces' which climax the film — Tuco's search for Arch Stanton's grave in the vast circular area of Sad Hill cemetery, and the duel between the Good, the Bad and the Ugly. Together with the silent opening sequence, these two 'set-pieces' account for nearly twenty minutes running time. The whole of *The Good, the Bad and the Ugly* can be interpreted, or 'read', in terms both of the cinematic exploration of spaces or shapes, and of experimentation with a form of pure iconography: icons of death, the church, the war, and icons normally associated with the traditional Western — redefined in this 'free' context. It is as if Machiavelli has rewritten the screenplay of *Helzapoppin'*. Leone's cinema is looking at itself more closely than ever.

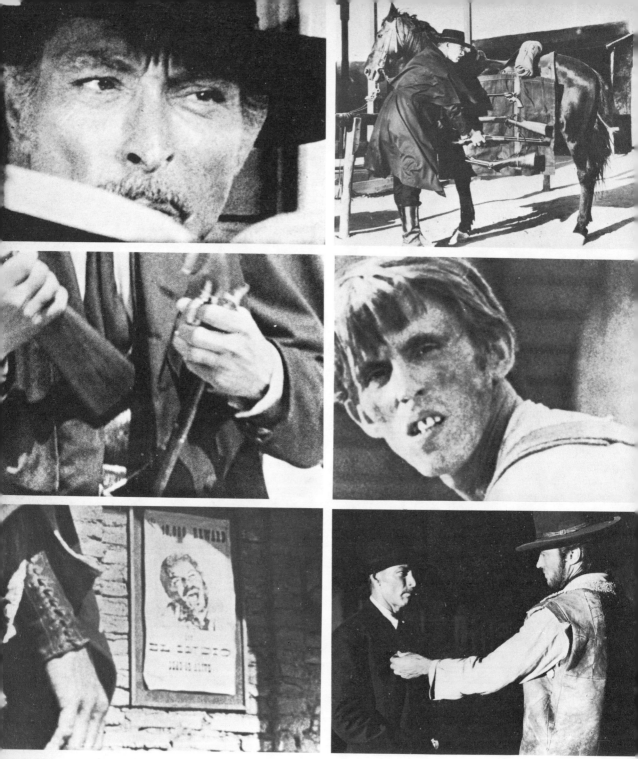

For a Few Dollars More
108-13 The 'Reverend' (Lee Van Cleef) selects
a weapon before gunning down his prey.
Reward money brings the two bounty-hunters
together

114-19 The Man With No Name referees the *corrida*
between Colonel Mortimer and El Indio.
As the 'old man' rides off into the sunset, his revenge
complete, the 'boy' piles all his assets onto a farm-cart

The Good, the Bad and the Ugly

120 (*Above*) The Good (Clint Eastwood) rescues the Ugly (Eli Wallach) so that *he* can hand him over to the authorities and claim the reward money

121 (*Above right*) This time Tuco has the advantage over Blondy when their paths cross again

122 (*Below*) The two 'magnificent rogues' have stumbled into the American Civil War by accident. They watch the battle for Langstone Bridge from the safety of a Union Captain's shelter: 'I've never seen so many men wasted so badly.'

123 (*Right*) 'Blue or Grey?': whichever uniform they happen to be wearing, the troops are an unwelcome distraction from the more important business of finding the gold

24-31 The Good, the Bad and the Ugly finally meet in a giant flagstone *corrida*
at Sad Hill cemetery: 'It's a lot of money . . . we're going to have to earn it.'

The 'Dollars' Trilogy — Analysis

The easiest critical response to Leone's 'Dollars' trilogy is to condemn (or praise) the films for their destructive view of the West, for the detachment with which Leone treats brutality, and for their excessively rich 'visual style' — an overdose of formalism. Because Leone seems to be commenting on the ways in which 'classic' Western situations were traditionally filmed, his technical effects are often deliberately overstated. Because he is engaged in what I have called a form of *critical* cinema, and is a film buff as well, many of these effects may tend to seem imposed on the action — a cinematic firework display, having no point of contact with a 'Realist' aesthetic. But his emphasis on external ritual, and on *style*, may also be seen as a key part of both the action and the technique: just as Leone is not interested in the 'inner man', or in the finer points of motivation, he is not particularly concerned with making subtle points by use of cinematic technique; most of the points (in his mature films) are made through shock editing, fluid camera movement (with the camera often participating in the action), the placing of objects in unusual relationships with each other, careful framing, and a self-conscious emphasis on iconography. Just as most of the interactions between his characters tend to be symbolic ones, so the ways in which these characters are presented to us tend also to be 'stylish', rhetorical, flamboyant — a good example of the inseparability, the interconnectedness, of form and content *as a process*, and of the dangers inherent in a critical approach which insists on interpreting form *per se* as a series of 'superficial tricks' (as Eisenstein put it). Take the case of Leone's emphasis on spatial relationships (at its most ostentatious in *The Good, the Bad and the Ugly*). Sometimes, Leone is not so much concerned with spatial depth, with depth of field, or the spatial relationships between his characters (although these are, of course, exploited as well): in parts of *The Good, the Bad and the Ugly*, and in all of *Once Upon a Time in the West*, he uses space geometrically, operating in terms of the possibilities of the wide screen; in other words he manipulates spaces *cinematically* — a technique which reveals a profound knowledge of the possibilities of cinema (and of the uses to which the wide screen can be put), at the same time as a *celebration* of the 'codes' of the Western. Often, the flattening effect of the wide screen image, and the emphasis on the geometry of spaces, rather than their depth, achieves a kind of unity with the action itself — where a set of cinematic mythologies are being acted out (Italian mythologies side by side with Hollywood ones). The protagonists are 'other-regarding', and so is Leone. In a sense, Leone's particular brand of formalism thus cuts across the terms of the debate between those who reckon that the possibilities of cinema are best served by cinéastes who make their points *in the frame*, and those who prefer self-conscious use of editing, montage and so on; for Leone not only edits ostentatiously (for example, in his use of close-ups to show a character's reaction, rather than to show him as he speaks), he also fills the frame ostentatiously (for example, in his stress on geometric relationships, his placing of key icons, etc.). Hollywood fantasies are re-enacted in neo-realist settings. An interesting example of all this occurs in the flashback sequences of *For a Few Dollars More*. These sequences (which show the rape of Mortimer's sister by Indio) are shot through a red filter, and appear for most of the film as the violent, erotic, pot-induced fantasy of Indio: but, at the climax of *For a Few*, when the flashback is 'explained' for the first time, the fantasy seems to be *shared* by Mortimer (still the same violent, sado-erotic dream). In terms of plot, this *sharing* simply tells us that the girl is Mortimer's sister, and that Mortimer thus has a score to settle with Indio: it could, however, also be read as a criticism of the apparently 'paternal' persona of Mortimer — for if Mortimer shares the flasback, then he was also there at the time (as a voyeur watching his sister's rape), and if he recalls the events in the same way as Indio (red filter, distorting sounds, sado-eroticism), then he is enjoying the fantasy as well. Those critics who look for subtle points being made in the frame, within a 'Realist' aesthetic, would presumably opt for the latter interpretation. In fact, in the terms of reference of the film, this is the least likely interpretation: what is more likely is that Leone was concerned about the most 'stylish' way of presenting his flashback, and that he was simply making a point about the plot (retrospectively explaining Mortimer's motivation throughout the film, and showing him to have been a Hollywood-type 'goody' all along — rather than either a callous bounty-hunter or a psychopathic nut). By the time Leone made *Once Upon a Time* (a more mature work), he seems to have become more aware of the ambiguities of *shared* flashbacks, so he filmed the flashback (which this time tells us something about *both* protagonists simultaneously) from *two points of view*. In *For a Few*, the 'dream' is stylish, and very cinematic; but it does not tell us as much about the characters as at first sight might appear — it simply serves a narrative function (where Mortimer is concerned), and adds to the 'baroque' presentation of the larger-than-life baddy (where Indio is concerned). The key point to be made about Leone's formalism is that the style is *so seldom* at odds with the action (Indio's 'dream' perhaps being a rare exception): it is not that the obtrusive technique has a jarring effect — the *cinematic* effects suit the cinematic mythologies which are being manipulated, laid bare, and transcribed; the rhetoric of the image is consistent with the rhetoric of the whole exercise. Leone's Westerns constitute a form of cinema about cinema: it seems churlish to complain that they do not make very profound points about the human condition, just as it may seem trivial to complain that his emphasis on detail is no substitute for getting these details right.

The 'Dollars' trilogy has also been criticised for the destructive view of the West which the films apparently represent ('only an Italian could do this . . .'), and for the detachment with which Leone treats brutality. Yet certain central motifs in the trilogy indicate that Leone has substituted through his Catholicised iconography, his juxtaposition of music and image, his manicheistic moral ambivalence, and his belief in certain positive forces in society, a new ethical frame of reference within

which his successive climaxes have a clearly articulated structure. The Man With No Name has been consistently misinterpreted by critics as a brutal existentialist living in a *moral* vacuum. We have seen how many of Leone's ideas for his mature Westerns came from Sicilian morality plays. His new ritualism bears some relationship to American historical myths — and at the same time echoes Italian values. Leone did not set out to make carbon-copy Westerns: the Spaghettis which predated *Fistful* had attempted that, and, inevitably, failed (Leone does not even see the *attempt* as worthwhile). Rather, he utilised his cultural background to help give life to what he saw as a dying cinematic genre. Leone's emphasis on the value of family life, and on positive community values, is a *substitute* for Nash Smith's evocation of the 'garden' or 'agrarian' ideal; this is not, of course, to say that Leone is a 'progressive', in more traditional terms. The 'Great American Desert' (another basic aspect of the myth), finds its *substitute* in Leone's orchestration of images, his close-ups of faces against a rocky or barren topography: apart from two sequences in *For a Few Dollars More* (the flashback, and Eastwood's entry into White Rocks), the sun always shines in the trilogy. And the traditional Western theme of ambivalent attitudes towards technological advance, as represented by the railroads (the central problem in Leone's thematically isolated *Once Upon a Time in the West*) plays an important part in Colonel Mortimer's motivation throughout *For a Few Dollars More*. Mortimer travels on the train to Amarillo at the start of the film, when he is 'posing' as the Reverend, but the fact that he stops the train at Tucumcari (not a scheduled stop) by pulling the emergency chord, to an extent indicates his distaste for that kind of technology. We later learn from the Old Prophet that Mortimer was an efficient soldier from Carolina, until the 'damned trains' came, when he had to earn his living as a bounty-hunter.

So those aspects of the Hollywood dream which Colin McArthur has styled the 'quintessentially American qualities of the Western genre' are used by Leone in ways which incorporate concepts and themes of Italian origin. For example, the link between the twin images of family life and the community symbol of the church bell (campanile) gives a clear definition to the term *campanilismo* ('bell tower patriotism'), or loyalty to the family, clan, church and local authority — a historically Italian concept. The desert backdrops have an almost Dali-esque sense of unworldliness about them: the environment could be Western (and Leone carefully uses realistically Mexican/frontier locales to justify his use of landscape, to provide a context for his catholicised iconography, and dramatically to oppose two different modes of life — Anglo and Greaser) but somehow it remains international. Perhaps the clearest example of how Leone unites two distinct periods of history, and fuses the Old World and the New, occurs in the Langstone Bridge sequence of *The Good, the Bad and the Ugly*. The lines of soldiers, with their mortars, Whitworths and Gatlings before the battle, and the rows of dead afterwards, seem to recall Matthew Brady's Civil War photographs: in the American print of the film, Brady himself makes a brief appearance, photographing a formal group of immaculately dressed officers, near the platform of Betterville station — a striking contrast to the sordid rubble of war just outside his field of vision. Yet, as we have seen, Leone's presentation of the battle also recalls trench warfare in Europe, 1914-18 (just as his scenes in the concentration camp relate to Nazi Germany): the stagnant, impersonal aspects of the battle are emphasised, and the moral stances of the two central characters relativised against this background.

The family as a central, positive force

In *Fistful*, the Man With No Name helps the 'holy family' (Julian, Marisol and son) to escape the brutality of the Rojo clan, itself a grotesque extended family, and also helps them out of their incidental involvement in the Baxter-Rojo rivalry. The Baxter clan is mother-dominated (by Consuela Baxter), the Rojo clan run by three delinquent brothers, one of whom (Ramon) is smarter than the others ('Is it possible, my brothers, that you will never find anything out for yourselves . . . ?'). The 'holy family' is more balanced — although, inevitably, Marisol/Mary gets the lion's share of screen time and of the audience's sympathy. The Man falls to the ground to pick Marisol up, after he has slugged her by mistake (one of his few expressions of emotion in the film). Later he admits that he has never known peace, and thus betrays his fear of the situation which Wyatt Earp describes in Sturges' *Gunfight at the O.K. Corral* (1957): 'All gunfighters are lonely. They live alone and they die without a dime, a

woman or a friend.' By the end of *Fistful*, the Man has a great deal more than 'a dime', but Leone hints at a lack of emotional self-sufficiency, particularly when Eastwood is asked by the Rojos to make himself at home and replies: 'Well, I never found home that great, but let's go.' In *For a Few Dollars More*, the Man With No Name claims that he wants to settle down and 'possibly retire' with his reward. Mortimer looks at him in disbelief. At the end of the film, he rides off into the hills with his farm-cart, but, as we have seen, he must always keep moving on. As Cheyenne says of Harmonica in *Once Upon a Time in the West*, 'people like that have something inside, something to do with death'. In *The Good, the Bad and the Ugly*, Tuco says to his brother, Padré Ramirez (Luigi Pistilli), that from their family background one had to become a bandit or a priest, and judges his own actions retrospectively by the extent of his contribution to the family. 'You chose your way and I chose mine. Mine was harder.' When Padré Ramirez accuses Tuco of neglecting his family ('Only now do you think of them'), Tuco replies that when 'Pablito' went off to study for the priesthood, he stayed behind; but it just did not work out. Characteristically, when the priest is accused of neglecting the family, Leone makes him resort to violence. As Tuco leaves the monastic cell, Padré Ramirez pleads '. . . please forgive me, brother'. But Tuco — although moved — keeps on the way he's going. (It may be, as Oreste de Fornari has suggested, that this 'edifying' scene represents a concession to the international market — but the specific form it takes seems to relate directly to Leone's concerns in earlier films and that, surely, is what requires explanation. In general, de Fornari *misplaces* the cynicism of the first two 'Dollars' films). In an earlier sequence, Tuco cunningly uses the 'family' strategy as a means of ingratiating himself with the convalescing Blondy: 'Do you have parents, Blondy, . . . a mother . . .? Not even a mother . . . No, you're all alone . . . like me, Blondy . . . we're all alone in the world . . . I have you and you have me, . . . only for a little while, I mean.' As we have seen, Tuco is the first of Leone's 'amoral familists'.

The family as a paradigm for assessing motivation

In *Fistful*, Eastwood explains his action in helping the 'holy family': 'I once knew about someone like you, and there was no one to help.' The opening images of a maltreated family give some idea of the Man's attitude (he *expects* a smile from Marisol), yet the personal nature of his motives also makes his gesture of help an egotistical gesture: he seldom thinks beyond himself. The 'holy family' symbolism is extended by the presentation of the Man With No Name (in Leone's estimation, 'an incarnation of the Angel Gabriel'), and by the mocking attitude of the Baxters: Eastwood is 'crucified' on a Cantina sign almost as soon as he arrives in San Miguel. During the exchange of hostages in *Fistful*, Leone cuts from a shot of Consuela Baxter 'welcoming' back her prodigal son (by slapping him hard), to a zoom-shot of Marisol warmly embracing her child. But Eastwood does not intervene until Silvanito has taken the initiative: after that, the help he offers the 'holy family' is almost inseparable from his intention to escalate the Baxter-Rojo rivalry. In *For a Few Dollars More*, Indio's killing of Tomaso and family, including a small child, while the soundtrack plays the film's main theme on a church organ, exemplifies the intensity of his urge for revenge — as does his pot-smoking after the killing. Colonel Douglas Mortimer's motive for killing Indio (as symbolised by the musical watch) is a family affair. Mortimer is presented as a 'goody' *because* he has such a motive. Thus he refuses any reward money: he has avenged his sister, yet there is a curious moral ambivalence in his final line, 'Perhaps next time' (unless Leone was simply leaving his options open for a sequel). The family symbol (watch) is used to extend the climax of the final gunfight almost to breaking point. 'Time-games' (usually relating to some brutal destruction of a member of the protagonist's family, in the distant past) were to play an increasingly significant role in Leone's films. Even in *The Good, the Bad and the Ugly*, the soundtrack during the final shoot-out refers to the chiming watch theme of *For a Few*: in this climactic confrontation, each of the characters is at last meeting his destiny (although each has his eyes on the gold, as well). At Agua Caliente, in *For a Few Dollars More*, Mortimer and the Man With No Name shoot some apples off a tree, to help a small child: Leone uses this gesture to illustrate the motivation of his characters, if such it can be called. Eastwood is eager to show his prowess with a gun both to the three bandits and to Mortimer. He wishes Indio to hear the shots. But some form of useless target practice would have served these purposes equally well; instead, he helps the child gather his apples. Mortimer wants to surprise the Man, to show his prowess, and to make the shots sound more fearsome for Indio's benefit. We can sympathise with the 'old man' and the 'boy', but Indio never makes a gesture of this kind to help us choose our loyalties.

In Leone's post-Western, *Duck, You Sucker* (also called *A Fistful of Dynamite*), the anarchic, gutsy form of peasant banditry of Juan (Rod Steiger) is exemplified by the family 'clan' he tries to control: the 'clan' consists of his six bastard children — each from a different mother ('I never counted them,' he says). Sean (James Coburn), an Irish revolutionary and explosives expert, realises that Juan's banditry can be harnessed to the revolution in Mexico, Juan responds by imagining that Sean's expertise can be harnessed to the robbing of banks ('It takes one bandit to know another'). His father had tried unsuccessfully to rob the bank at Mesa Verde when he was a child, so the robbery has become a matter of family honour. Throughout the first section of the film (a direct commentary on the more political Spaghetti Westerns) this cat and mouse game, if anything, enhances Juan's cynicism about political commitment. He robs the bank at Mesa Verde (with the aid of a toy train — called *John and Johnny USA* — crammed with explosives, and pulled by one of his more 'angelic' children), thinking that the vaults are full of gold; in the event, they turn out to be full of political prisoners, and Juan, despite himself, is fêted as an instant political hero. But Sean is still unable to persuade him that commitment to the revolutionary cause is a worthwhile activity. 'Don't talk to me about revolution,' says Juan — those who read books tell those who can't read what to do, and the peasants are the ones who die for the 'cause'. Pancho Villa, for example, was a man of the people once (with 'balls like a bull') — but he is now a high-ranking general, and has allowed himself to be corrupted by power ('My land? My land is me and my family'). Juan's inflexible views have two main effects: they encourage Sean to have less and less faith in intellectuals' writings on revolution (he throws Bakunin's *Patriotism* in the mud); and, by *seeming* to lead to acts of political violence, they escalate Juan's own involvement in the cause. Before he meets Sean, Juan's peasant anarchism has been symbolised by his stagecoach ride in the desert. While the bourgeois travellers (civil servants, an American businessman, a priest) eat well — and with disgusting manners, for we see them eating from Juan's point of view — the peasant has to grovel in the mud for a crust of bread. Juan robs these representatives of the bourgeoisie (with the aid of his 'clan'), makes them strip naked, and rapes the only woman in the party: 'Can you make a baby?' he asks one of the stagecoach travellers; the man shakes his head, so Juan proceeds to rape his wife ('Thank you — for *everything*'). Clearly, Juan is endowed with the *cojones* which Villa once had — before the revolution emasculated him. After the bank raid at Mesa Verde (and the 'Don't talk to me about revolution' speech) Juan still seems to be impervious to Sean's influence. Sean's own commitment — symbolised by his expertise (dynamite), his cavalier attitude towards the law (an addiction to marijuana), and his past (half-remembered dreams of a *menage à trois* during the Irish revolution) — is also becoming increasingly ambiguous as the relationship develops. But Juan's anarchic gestures (blowing the bank vaults, destroying a bridge — because he is conned into it) inevitably lead to reprisals from the authorities in the form of the massacre of his entire family. He may never have counted his children before, but the impact of this massacre on Juan's behaviour is profound. What started out as a simple treasure hunt ('I don't want to be a hero. I want the money') becomes a brutal vendetta. When Juan has to decide between accepting a substantial bribe and shooting the Governor (a 'test' set up by Sean), he does the revolutionary thing, and is again fêted as a hero, but he still dreams of robbing banks in America (*John and Johnny USA*). This choice (despite mental reservations) paves the way for Juan's final acceptance of the revolutionary struggle as a worthwhile activity (subsuming Sean's enigmatic motivations — a reverse mirror image of his own — by appropriating the Irishman's memories of the revolution back home, in the form of the final, shared flashback). Sean's attitude to the Mexican Revolution is coloured by these memories (a strange *menage à trois*, in which the other man is executed, through Sean's efforts, as an informer, and in which the woman seems to represent Sean's youthful vision of the Irish revolution). Juan's attitude to the Mexican Revolution is directly related to the state of his family, or 'clan': when the 'clan' works together, Juan is in no doubt about what he considers the 'moral' thing to do; when the 'clan' falls apart, his motivations become much more complex — a

traumatic interlude, during which he learns to think beyond his own interests. At the beginning of *Duck, You Sucker*, Juan seems to be behaving like Tuco; in the second section of the film, he resembles Mortimer (or Harmonica, in *Once Upon a Time in the West*); in the final sequences, an overtly political component has been added to the dollars (pesetas)/ vengeance schema. Sean (a more complex version of John Ford's 'optimistic' Irish gunmen) gradually has his view of revolution *humanised*, through contact with Juan in all his various incarnations.

On the face of it, the story of *Duck, You Sucker* resembles that of all the best 'populist' Spaghettis (see chapter 9): the central relationship (between an 'outsider' who offers technical assistance to a peasant bandit, and a peasant who realises that his heart is in the right place after all — in de Fornari's terms, between James Bond and Antonio das Mortes) seems to be a characteristic one, and the context (a *Viva Maria* view of the revolution — full of bizarre explosions and larger-than-life villains) is predictably baroque. But there are basic differences: the 'outsider' is not a mercenary, and his relationship with the peasant is an explicitly 'paternalistic' one, at least to begin with; the dialectic (between pesetas and revolution) is far from straightforward; the view of professional revolutionaries (epitomised by the character of Doctor Villega, played by Romolo Valli) is unusually cynical; and the high-cost spectacle (battles, explosions, firing squads, etc.) becomes a distraction — almost an end in itself. The cynicism (and the international production values) of Leone's film led some of the Italians involved in it to object strongly to the original title — *Once Upon a Time, the Revolution*. Oreste de Fornari's criticism is characteristically severe:

Leone was a latecomer in the field of the 'populist' Western, and had to be noticed at all costs. His production was an international one — involving Rafran, San Marco, Miura and United Artists. . . . The film was not written for the director, and had no claims to originality. . . . The stars seem to have persuaded the director to push the central characters to crude caricature, avoiding any of the complexities which may originally have been there. All these things point to a not-very-ambitious work, a follower on a well worn path. But the structure of the film is almost diametrically opposed to the 'populist' Westerns of Damiani and Corbucci. Corbucci, for example, concentrates his revolutionary message on the relationship between the two protagonists — and chucks in his massacres simply as *largesse* granted to the less 'spiritual' tastes of the Italian public. Leone, showing less provincialism, downgrades the psychological aspects to comedy and melodrama — and instead *elevates* the scenes of action to the level of 'historical spectacle'. What emerges from this is the most falsely humble, the most solidly international of all the Italian 'populist' Westerns. Part of his de-provincialising strategy is to move towards a strengthening of stereotypes (while other film-makers were challenging them), and towards a moralising paternalism which governs their reciprocal relations. . . . Revolutionaries and counter-revolutionaries are distinguished only by the colour of their uniforms, and by the eagerness of the authorities to kill prisoners. The Mexican Revolution was about taking land from the *latifondisti*, not just about defending oneself against the violent henchmen of Huerta and Diaz.

We have seen how Leone does not consider *Duck, You Sucker* to have been fully 'his' film — the script was written before he arrived on the scene, the stars were not of his choosing, and some footage had already been shot by someone else. Clearly, he was not at home in Corbucci or Damiani territory — apart from anything else, the Hollywood 'Mexican Revolution' genre did not provide him with recognisable enough 'clichés' or 'codes' to transcribe in his characteristic way. So his 'criticisms' (by now almost a trade-mark) seem to have been pointed in the direction of the 'Italian' genre instead. And the result — if compared with the *clarity* of Solinas' scenarios, or if related to the concerns of the 'populist' directors — is a strange blend of comedy, spectacle, and cynicism about the development of the Italian Western. But de Fornari's main critical point — that Leone's film represents a *rejection* of the Italian audience, and of the themes which appealed to that audience in his earlier Westerns — seems to me to be more questionable. One difference between *Duck, You Sucker*, and the other 'populist' Westerns, a difference which locates Leone's post-Western firmly within the overall development of his work, is the central emphasis on Juan's 'family' or 'clan'. Of all the examples of 'amoral familism' in Leone's films,

Juan is perhaps the clearest.

Throughout the 'Dollars' trilogy, Leone's citations of Renaissance paintings and icons (the Last Supper set-up for the Rojos party in *Fistful*; the pulpit from which Indio tells his parable in *For a Few*; the effigy of Christ to which Tuco prays in *The Good, the Bad and the Ugly* and the clutter of statues in Padré Ramirez' cell) emphasise Catholic family traditions and undercut the moral values of the bandit clans. In *Fistful*, a suit of armour from a former age of Italian chivalry and military prowess is used for target practice. The Man With No Name uses armour at the end, to protect his heart, and relies on Ramon's pride in his aim. However unscrupulous the bandit leader may be, the Man can assume he will not aim for the head: Ramon has said that 'When a man with a Winchester meets a man with a pistol, the man with a pistol is a dead man,' and he has been challenged to 'aim for the heart'. The confrontation is a matter of pride: 'The heart, Ramon — don't forget the heart. Aim for the heart or you'll never stop me!' (by aiming for the heart Ramon is actually giving the Man the opportunity to get into pistol range). Typically, when the Man gets hold of dynamite from Piripero, he does not use it to blow the Rojos up, but rather to herald his return in as dramatic a manner as possible. Certain other responses can be relied on, in dealings with the rival gangs — a paternalistic set of values, a form of clan chivalry (the Spanish *hidalguià*), pride in efficiency, a quick reprisal for any outrage (a distinctly Sicilian variant on the samurai values represented by Kurosawa's *Yojimbo*) — and it is only the central family group which, thanks to Silvanito rather than the Man, realigns the tension in the hostages scene. When Indio is sprung from jail in *For a Few Dollars More*, the gang complains of the difficulty of planning without him: he is the only man with control over the easily aroused youth in the clan. Indio lets one prison guard go free, but cautions him to 'remember this day'. He inspects Eastwood's neck wound after the El Paso robbery (in fact the result of Mortimer's foresight), and concludes, 'You did your part.' When Indio breaks down after emptying his gun into Cuchillo ('the Knife'), he claims that the man was trying to break up the clan: although the motive is self-created, Indio loses control of himself at the thought of this disunity from below. The El Paso bank is known as a 'fortress', and Colonel Mortimer discovers which bank Indio's men will try to break by checking which one has the reputation for being the strongest: he can rely on Indio's pride, as well as his 'madness'. When Indio opens the chest which once contained the booty, all he finds is a 'wanted' poster with a grotesque laugh on his photographed face: legend is here confronted with the reality of Indio's rapidly disintegrating gang.

Leone links the family motif with his attitude to the church (as centre of the community) by the 'bell' image, and by his emphasis on *campanilismo*: it is the 'crazy bellringer' who greets Eastwood on his arrival at San Miguel in *Fistful*, and who warns him that he will wind up 'rich or dead'. There is a church bell in the background during the Man's final shootout with Ramon Rojo. The townsfolk of San Miguel are twice alerted by the ringing of the church bell, once when the Rojos' houses are on fire, once in the closing moments, when 'peace' seems to have been restored to the 'town of widows', albeit at a fearful cost. In *Fistful*, Leone substitutes the church-tower and bell for Kurosawa's wooden watch-tower in *Yojimbo*. The final bell image of *Fistful*, because of its dual association with family and clan, helps to undercut an apparent sense of normality and 'peace' in the community. The mission bell is used for target practice by members of Indio's gang, to herald their arrival at the church hide-out (after Indio has killed Tomaso and family in *For a Few Dollars More*). In the same film, the wooden safe at the El Paso bank is first presented as an 'altar' (complete with tall candlesticks on either side of it), accompanied by an amplified bell on the soundtrack. The scenes at Padré Ramirez' mission, in *The Good, the Bad and the Ugly* (where, as we have seen, notions of family loyalty are discussed at length), are 'punctuated' by the rhythmic tolling of a mission bell.

The church

Church buildings play an important part in Leone's version of the Western landscape: the adobe walls of the church or mission represent a centre of the community. The church provides a respectable 'front' for Colonel Mortimer — who reads his Bible, dresses formally in black, and is mistakenly called 'Reverend' (although his pipe, frock-coat and black boots also have obvious non-religious connotations: he is the fastidious 'specialist', the collector of 'specimens'). The mission serves as a hide-out for Indio and his gang: in this case, it houses an 'anti-State'. In *The Good, the Bad and the Ugly*, the value of Ramirez' monastery as a place for looking after the sick and wounded is emphasised by a series of 'peep-show' establishing shots accompanied by an elegiac 'war' theme on the soundtrack: given the pervading atmosphere of decay and casual brutality, this seems, in the context, to be the only positive contribution made by any community in the Civil War years (analogous, perhaps, to the contribution of the Belgian nuns, at the outbreak of the war, in *The Nun's Story*). There are not enough beds, and the facilities are clearly inadequate for coping with war casualties, but some gesture is being made. This, despite the fact that Tuco's brother is accused of neglecting his family duties by studying for the priesthood, and despite a socio-economic environment which polarises families into bandits or priests. But Leone's implicit comments on the social function of the church (an institution which might, perhaps, have been expected to bear the brunt of his crude satire on double-dealing — as it does in many Spaghettis by other directors in the period — but which plainly does not) are less important than his use of the iconography of that institution to establish various levels of irony, and apply these to his characters.

When Ramon leaves his clan to 'have a good time', the resulting banquet recalls Leonardo's version of the Last Supper — only this time the 'Angel Gabriel' is present, to feign drunkenness in an attempt to slip away and save the 'holy family'. Indio's villainy goes beyond usual cinematic convention by achieving an almost religious intensity. In the Italian print of *For a Few*, he baptises his Colt in holy water, before shooting people. He delivers his 'parable of the carpenter' (which explains how to blow the El Paso safe) from the pulpit of a mission, accompanied by the soft strains of a church organ; his twelve followers slowly begin to understand the point of the parable, and the camera lingers on their faces as they see the light. Il Cattivo (also known as 'Angel Eyes') observes at Tuco's second 'hanging' that 'a golden haired angel watches over him': the camera picks out Blondy, sitting on his horse at the end of the main street and aiming his Henry rifle at the rope; an angelic choir bursts into song on the soundtrack, to reinforce the gag. These jokes help to establish the irony of Leone's (and Hollywood's) moral labels — Good, Bad and Ugly. Blondy (Il Buono) helps a dying Confederate drummer in a ruined chapel, makes him comfortable and offers his cigar, then steals the soldier's poncho after he has died. The brother of a monk prays at a crucifix (for the benefit of passers-by) to give thanks for Blondy's salvation, then turns his back on the effigy and takes a swig of whisky, with a look of malicious glee on his face. The Italian script of *For a Few Dollars More* christens the Man With No Name 'Il Monco' (the Monk): on one occasion, in the international print, Indio refers to the bounty-hunter by that name.

Duck, You Sucker takes this process one stage further: the peasant Juan christens Sean 'Holy Water' — because he is an IRA man and a nitro-glycerine expert; Juan has a votive altar in his caravan, with the sacred words 'National Bank of Mesa Verde' inscribed above it; during his first meeting with the IRA man, Juan imagines that Sean has developed a 'halo', with the same sacred words written around it. Juan even expects the National Bank to have golden doors, 'like the gates of Paradise'. In fact, there is no gold in this celestial palace, since it has been taken over to house political prisoners: nevertheless, as we have seen, Juan is hailed as a peasant hero for having unwittingly 'sprung' these prisoners. In *Duck, You Sucker*, the association between Juan's simple religious beliefs and his ultimate ambition is particularly telling, since, without its customary barter value as *currency*, the gold can never serve the 'civilising' function attributed to it in classic Hollywood Westerns. After the slaughter of his 'clan', Juan throws away his rosary: its association with his former way of life will no longer hold true. But the rosary is returned to him (by Sean) at the very end of the film, just before the Irishman's death. It says much for the consistency of Leone's use of iconography that we can 'read' this gesture to mean that the Revolution has taken the place of gold, as the prime mover in Juan's life.

Iconography of death

Leone's self-indulgent use of death symbols — part of his increasingly *rhetorical* technique — almost mocks the half-heartedness of Hollywood Western symbolism. Traditional icons, such as Baxter's tin star in *Fistful*, the White Rocks sheriff's badge in *For a Few*, the 'uniforms' worn by local law-enforcers in *The Good, the Bad and the Ugly*, are all shown to be empty symbols of authority, rendered almost irrelevant by the brutality of the social context. But, in Leone's vision of blood and sand, death icons play a more central part. In *Fistful*, the coffin-maker plays Chorus — he is the only character to give the Man With No Name some identity, as 'Joe'. The Man's first action on deciding to stay in town is to order three coffins. After his brutal beating-up (and before his miraculous 'resurrection') he can only escape from the Rojos by hiding in a coffin: we thus get a coffin's-eye view of the ensuing holocaust. Two dead Federales are used as a decoy, to set the rival gangs against each other, and placed against a tombstone in a large cemetery (ironically, a memorial to 'the only man who ever died of pneumonia in these parts'). Leone cross-cuts from the cemetery sequence to the Man's hunt for Ramon's gold. One of the running gags in the film is derived from the coffin-maker's thriving industry in such an economically depressed town: the final sequence shows the coffin-maker scampering around the town square with his tape measure; he has never seen so much business, but there is no one left to pay for it.

On arriving at Agua Caliente, in *For a Few Dollars More*, Indio observes, 'This place looks like a morgue: be careful, it could so easily become one.' And, of course, it does become a morgue. As the gang is wiped out, Leone cuts from the slaughter outside to a squashed beetle on the table in front of Indio: like the beetle, the clan is in the process of losing its 'wings'. Throughout the film, close-ups abound of faces scarred from previous gunfights — mangled eye-sockets, gashed cheeks, syphilitic noses, nervous tics. Appropriately, since many of the characters have 'something to do with death', their names often have a deathly ring about them: the coolly efficient bounty-hunter is called Mortimer, the brothers whom the Man With No Name has recently killed are (according to the front page of an El Paso newspaper) the Morton brothers. In *Once Upon a Time in the West*, Leone again christens a character Morton — only this time he is the railroad businessman who leaves a trail of death behind him, in the form of 'two beautiful shiny rails'. After Indio has shot Tomaso, the victim is unceremoniously dragged out of the 'arena', like a bull after the toreador's triumph. *For a Few Dollars More* closes on a shot of the Man's farm-wagon, crammed with dead bodies — a favourite Leone motif and a fitting image of a society where 'life had no value' but 'death, sometimes, had its price'.

In *The Good, the Bad and the Ugly*, Leone handles iconography in general, and icons of death in particular, with a new assurance. A driver-less hearse appears from nowhere, in the middle of the desert. A soldier prepares his own coffin, just before he is shot. Tuco is twice told that the Lord will have mercy on his soul, just before he is to be hanged. His brother repeats this good wish. Cripples with arms, legs and eyes missing struggle through the Civil War sequences. The captain at Langstone Bridge may die with a smile on his face, but he is covered with blood-soaked bandages: to him, 'the most potent weapon in war' had been a bottle of whisky. Blondy and Tuco wade through the dead and dying, to place their explosives beneath the bridge. The gold is buried inside a grave at Sad Hill, and the wrong coffin is dug up by mistake. During the final shootout, Leone cuts to the stub of Lee Van Cleef's finger, creeping towards his gun; 'Angel Eyes' falls into a grave as he is shot, and his gun and hat are shot after him in a parody of traditional Western 'respect for the dead'. Tuco is ordered to stand on an unwieldly wooden cross, a rope around his neck and his share of the gold scattered at his feet. It is 'quite like old times' again when Blondy finally shoots through the rope.

The desert

The opening shots of *Fistful* establish the desert landscape as a central motif. The camera is held into the sun, followed by a close-up of sand and stone, then a medium shot of the Man on his mule in the desert. His first action is to stop at the well. At the end of the film, he unhitches a mule from the shafts of a nearby wagon, and rides from San Miguel into the desert wilderness again. *For a Few Dollars More* opens with a red background and an orange sun; the sun blurs and changes into a far-away rider. The rider is shot by an unseen rifle (off-screen to the right) and falls from his horse in the distant desert. The final shots are of Mortimer riding into the desert sunset, and the Man driving his death wagon off into the desert hills. *The Good, the Bad and the Ugly*, as we have seen, begins with a register-ing shot of the desert, then a man's pock-marked face abruptly appears against this parched back-ground. Topographical details, usually of the desert, are emphasised throughout, only to be obscured by close-ups of faces. The camera picks

out details of landscape, such as a tombstone, a hedge, a ridge of sand, then cranes out into a long-shot of a cemetery, a battlefield, or a desert expanse: in this way, a sense of relative space and scale is created (an example of Leone's exploitation of spatial *depth*, as opposed to the geometrical presen-tation of spaces in other parts of the same film). The effects of intense heat on Blondy's face are shown in detail. The final long-shot of *The Good, the Bad and the Ugly* gives symmetry to the begin-ning: even before the opening rack-focus shot, the credits begin with two moving 'suns' against a coloured background, 'suns' which unite into one circle.

Sergio Leone's picture of blood and sand re-creates 'a world irredeemably condemned to immobility, somnolence, to the lack of all resource and develop-ment', in Ferrini's words: the characters seem mar-ginal to everyday social and political events. In *The Good, the Bad and the Ugly*, Tuco cannot remember General Lee's name; Blondy, when asked where he is headed, by a Northern captain, can only think of Illinois (Lincoln's state). The Civil War enters their lives because of Carson's gold — stolen army money. Throughout the trilogy, characters often change sides, unable to be *interested* in any one cause except their own. The Man With No Name joins the Rojos, the Baxters, Indio, Mortimer, the North and the South; his identity is defined by the self-interested moves he makes. As we have seen, the stories in the trilogy have the schematic quality of an economic theorem. The parched desert provides a suitable backdrop for a world based on brutality, apathy, and callousness. Yet this picture of the Southwestern frontier — where icons of death supersede traditional icons of author-ity — is not purely destructive: by substituting themes and images taken from an Italian historico-cultural context for the traditional bases of the Western genre, Leone creates a fresh cinematic mythology, critical but clearly located, crude but visually sophisticated. Gunfighters no longer stride towards each other down the main streets of Lordsburg, or during the Last Sunset, but instead face their destiny in a *corrida*, set within a vast graveyard: the linear confrontation has been redefined as the circular. And the duel is filmed as if it is part of the liturgy. The centre of the com-munity is no longer the sheriff's office, the bank, the schoolhouse, or the building where claims are staked, but rather the bell-tower — symbol of *campanilismo* — above the church: the iconography of Catholicism is superimposed on the iconography of the popular Western. Banks are not symbols of the civilising function of capitalism or of a progressive, developing community: they are places to rob — where the 'prize' is stored. Lassoos are not used to rope in steers: they are thrown over a safe, to drag away the dollars after a successful bank robbery. A man's loyalties do not depend on his political views, his attitude to property, his interest in economic development, his relationship with native Americans, or his obsession with doing 'what a man's gotta do': in Leone's West, they depend on considerations of family, clan or tribe. The characters' odysseys are no longer quests for self-knowledge: they are treasure hunts, endless hedonistic Gold Rushes. These odysseys take place in a landscape which is a long way away from the blue grass of Kentucky, the lush plains of Wyoming, or even the majestic splendour of Monument Valley — just miles and miles of 'sun-baked sand'.

Many other Spaghetti Westerns (made after *Fistful*), and 'Paella' derivatives, utilise the iconography of Roman Catholicism: for example, in Vic Morrow's *A Man Called Sledge*, the anti-hero (James Garner) straps a crucifix to his broken arm, in preparation for the final shootout (which takes place during a religious festival). We have seen how various directors exploited the iconography of the church in increasingly bizarre ways — responding to internal pressures from within the Cinecittà system. When Fellini wanted to satirise this system (in *Toby Dammit*, his contribution to the anthology of *Histoires Extraordinaires*, 1968), he imagined an enthusiastic priest telling Toby (Terence Stamp) about his latest brain-child, 'the first Catholic Western. The return of Christ to a desert landscape — the frontier'. The film is to be shot in the styles of 'Dreyer, Pasolini, with a touch of Ford'. And it will be in colour, 'a mixture of Piero della Francesca and Fred Zinneman'. The early part of *Toby Dammit* (Toby's arrival in Rome as a fallen angel) can be read as a very perceptive critique of the direction Italian *lumpen*-cinema was taking at the time. The *substitution* of Catholic icons for more traditional symbols of the West (which Fellini seems to be satirising) is, perhaps, hardly surprising. Spaghetti Westerns were, after all, pitched at the 'Roxy, Calabria' in the first instance, and visual references might be expected to be recognisable to that audi-

ence. But Leone's films attempt more than this. Not only does his emphasis on Roman Catholic iconography (particularly in *The Good, the Bad and the Ugly*) provide a *fusion* of the 'rules' of the Hollywood Western with a Latin-Italian cultural context (rather than simply imposing spurious connections on carbon-copy remakes of American films) but it also plays a key role in challenging the *universal* moral implied by the classic Hollywood contributions to the genre. This, perhaps, is the 'hidden order', the 'deep structure' of his films. Leone is less interested in the opening of a new frontier, than in the closing of a more 'ancient' one. His heroes and villains are not the pioneers of a new West, but the temporary leaseholders of a static, immobile Southwestern frontier. The actions of his heroes, as we have seen, have nothing to do with the traditional quest for self-fulfilment (supported by frontier notions, of law and order): the Man With No Name's dream of settling down to retire on his own ranch is shattered by his own greed, his obsessive urge to grab (rather than spend) in excess of a few dollars more. The quest for the Holy Grail has become a brutal hunt for blood-money, or revenge. And the settings for this hunt bear little *direct* resemblance to Nash Smith's Virgin Land. Leone's landscapes are presented expressionistically, as *appropriate* (rather than *authentic*) extensions of events happening in the foreground — a type of detailed 'creative geography' (to hi-jack Vertov's concept). Monument Valley is a *very* long buggy-ride away from Flagstone (or rather Flagstaff), Arizona Territory, but the dreams which that location has traditionally come to embody, and the location's *cinematic* resonance, seem somehow *right* in the context of Jill's odyssey to Sweetwater in *Once Upon a Time in the West*. Throughout the 'Dollars' trilogy, the action shifts from New Mexico to Texas, as if territorial boundaries did not exist: the Southwestern frontier remains a constant, static netherland.

The *profanations* of Roman Catholic icons, the weird associations Leone makes between symbols of the church, the monastery, the cemetery, on the one hand, and symbols of greed, self-seeking and neo-feudalism, on the other, should be interpreted in these contexts. In his first two Westerns, as we have seen, *campanilismo* represents some kind of positive social force. In *The Good, the Bad and the Ugly*, the monks manage (in impossible conditions) to help casualties of the American Civil War. But

132-3 (*Top*) Sergio Leone directs *Once Upon a Time in the West* (1968), in America and Italy

134-5 (*Above*) French and Italian publicity for *Once Upon a Time in the West*: the leather 'dusters' worn by the three gunslingers became an instant hit in Parisian menswear shops, no doubt helping the film to run for several years in Paris

Leone can still debase the iconography of the church (as distinct from the institution itself) as part of his assault on the moral implications of the frontier myth. Throughout *The Good, the Bad and the Ugly* and *Once Upon a Time in the West*, most of the characters with whom we can sympathise exemplify Leone's distrust of 'progressives', and are clearly intended to *celebrate* a 'lack of all resource and development'. These two films challenge the implication (present in the classic Hollywood Westerns) that 'inevitable processes' are at work as the frontier is ploughed westwards, that the colonisation of the Virgin Land is somehow 'predestined' — and the profanations of, or weird associations with, Catholic icons play their part in this challenge. Leone's films contain no *universal* moral messages (as many Hollywood Westerns have claimed to), and his heroes are not intended to set an example for today. The traditional 'inevitable processes', whether represented by 'manifest destiny', 'rugged individualism', 'making the desert into a garden', or, more generally, 'the evolution of the frontier', are by these means reappraised, and, in Leone's terms, criticised. It is this critical perspective which takes the 'Dollars' trilogy beyond a mere 'passive rereading of the myth via the "myth"' to a coherent position *vis-à-vis* the Westerns of 'that great optimist', John Ford. Oreste de Fornari, questioning the conclusions to my article on Leone in *Cinema*, has written that 'the Catholic imagery in the "Dollars" films has no equivalent in the moral ardour of the hero, or in the diabolical perversion of the villains, who are many and colourless'; he accepts that the imagery of the family in Leone's early films is associated with a positive morality, but cannot see any relationship between the Catholic iconography and the morality of the protagonists. That, of course, is the whole point — and it constitutes the basis of Leone's strange form of critical cinema.

The emphasis, in the 'Dollars' trilogy, on amoral familism; families, clans and *camarilla*; Latin conceptions of chivalry (more conspicuous leisure than moral law); *campanilismo*; plots involving crosses and double-crosses (often taken from Sicilian puppet plays); and, perhaps most important of all, the profanation of Catholic icons — the emphasis on all this firmly locates Leone's rearrangement of the 'codes' of the Western within the context of Southern Italian society, and shows exactly the terms on which he has chosen to address the 'cultural force' of 'Catholicism (and its penumbra)'. But Leone has also studied closely these 'codes' of the Hollywood Western — characters, themes, variations, situations, settings, décors and details, clichés of all descriptions — 'codes' which had in the past proved extremely popular at the 'Roxy, Calabria', and the resulting fusion of a *rhetoric* gleaned from the Western with Italian cultural values, seems a world away from the traditional, 'historically-based' image of the frontier — based as it was on a combination of Social Darwinism and the Protestant ethic.

Once Upon a Time in the West

Once upon a time . . .

Wild Bill Hickok was shot in 1876 — shortly after playing the part of himself in a three-act entertainment entitled *Scouts of the Prairie*, compiled by E.Z.C. Judson (better known as 'Ned Buntline'). Throughout the rehearsals for this play, Wild Bill insisted on wearing dark glasses — like many a Hollywood star fifty years later. But Hickok did not wear shades in order to promote his inscrutable star appeal: he wore them because the stage lights were too bright for him, and because he was rapidly losing his eyesight, from glaucoma. When Buffalo Bill Cody (Hickok's co-star in *Scouts of the Prairie*) died in 1917, he had acted the part of himself in several short films designed to spread his own legend — in addition to becoming famous as the great impresario of the West as circus. Wyatt Earp died in 1929: his pallbearers were Tom Mix and William S. Hart (like the other famous US marshals Bat Masterson and Bill Tilghman, he had had a brief career in the movies shortly before his death). One of Earp's side-arms had been a twelve-inch-barrelled Buntline Special, presented to him by the dime-myth-maker, 'Ned Buntline'. Until he lost this weapon in 1901 (it was accidentally dropped in a river), Earp always insisted on wearing it in public. However, he seldom used it, except to club drunks over the head with its foot-long barrel. 'Buntline' also gave presentation Specials to lawmen Bat Masterson and Bill Tilghman, during a visit to Dodge City in winter 1875: with each weapon came a demountable stock, buckskin sling and hand-tooled holster. Masterson and Tilghman publicly accepted their gifts, then, shortly after 'Ned Buntline' had left Dodge, filed the barrels of their Specials down to eight inches, so that they were of some practical use. Wyatt Earp, like most Western lawmen, preferred a double-barrelled shotgun crammed with buckshot for both long- and close-range work. He died in bed, with his boots off, at the ripe old age of eighty-three. John Ford kept a pair of gloves, worn by Buffalo Bill in his Wild West circus, by his bedside. As Eric Mottram reminds us, they were found there when he died early in 1974.

The most famous heroes of the West, on both sides of the law, exploited the potential of their own myths to the full. William Bonney seems to have been aware of the Eastern dime novels and 'authentic' sagas of Billy the Kid which were published after his jailbreak from Lincoln, New Mexico, for after that incident he began publicly to claim a 'dead list' of twenty-one — a figure taken from such opportunistic accounts, compiled by New York journalists, as *The Authentic Life of Billy the Kid*: in fact, only three or four of his killings can be authenticated from historical records. Emmett Dalton, the last surviving member of the Dalton gang, specialists in great train robberies, actually collaborated on a book in 1937 (subsequently filmed) entitled *When the Daltons Rode*. This book told the story of how Emmett Dalton had died a romantic death at Coffeyville, Kansas, forty-five years previously, while attempting (with the help of his three brothers) to rob two banks, on opposite sides of the street, at the same time. Even when bandits did not 'ghost' their own memoirs, Emmett Dalton style, or actually appear in the movies, Al Jennings style, they sometimes contributed to the Robin Hood legends with which poor farmers liked to associate them. Jesse James is a good example of this type of self-glamorisation (he apparently got many of his ideas from Jacobean tragedies — his favourite reading). The exploits of the 'Hole in the Wall' gang were romanticised in the first adventure Western, *The Great Train Robbery*, at the same time as more factual reports of these same exploits were appearing in the newspapers. For a brief period in American history (roughly 1875 to 1920), folk-myth and actuality existed contemporaneously, with the 'heroes' contributing to both. Hollywood continued to single out the exploits of these individuals, bandits or lawmen, while taking the melo-dramatic potential of their careers several stages further than dime novels or Wild West shows could possibly have done. Thus, the James and Younger brothers were honest rustics until forced, by corrupt officials, to become criminals; William Bonney became unhinged when his much-loved father-substitute was shot during a range war; Wyatt Earp and Doc Holliday were defending family honour, and protecting the community, when they shot down the Clantons at the O.K. Corral. In the hands of film-makers such as Ford, King, Penn, Ray and Sturges, these characters were moulded to personify aspects of Wild West mythology. They became parts of the terminology of popular frontier history — albeit parts which were responsive to the dictates of fashion. During the late 1950s, they began to reflect on their own legends: in Nicholas Ray's *The James Brothers* (1957), Jesse reads a 'penny dreadful' account of his own exploits; in Arthur Penn's *Left-Handed Gun* (1958), Billy the Kid is hounded by a dime-novelist and souvenir hunter, who eventually betrays him. More recently, films concerned with demythologising the West have often chosen the same characters and incidents as a starting-point: examples include Marlon Brando's *One-Eyed Jacks* (1961), John Sturges' *Hour of the Gun* (1967), Philip Kaufman's *Great Northfield Minnesota Bank Raid* (1971), Frank Perry's *Doc* (1971), Stan Dragoti's *Dirty Little Billy* (1972) and Sam Peckinpah's *Pat Garrett and Billy the Kid* (1973). The song may be different, but there is still a characteristic emphasis on the singer — the singer who now *knows* he is becoming a star. And there is a characteristic concern with 'getting back to the historical characters as they really were' in many of these remakes. Or rather, a concern with making the characters look like the sepia photographs.

When dealing with historical folk-heroes and their adventures, Hollywood has traditionally been less concerned with the socio-economic contexts which gave rise to them, or with the interplay between these contexts and the resulting escapades (except in so far as these can be expressed in terms of a clash of personalities), than with the ways in which maximum audience identification (Marcuse's 'voluntary servitude') can be achieved. Even if Will Wright's thesis is accepted — that Westerns represent the enactment of a variety of social choices, the most commercially successful being the most 'appropriate' at a given time — it says more about the *ways* in which frontier mythology (and Western formulae) can be manipulated, than about specific treatments of cherished historical myths. More, in other words, about the socio-economic contexts which continue to sustain the mythology, than about the historical analysis which is contained within Hollywood Westerns ('classical' *or* 'profes-sional') — if such a distinction can be drawn. The rule in these films, predictably enough, has been 'When the facts don't fit the legend, print the legend.' And make the legend accessible to American cinema-going audiences. The first mechanical reproduction of a photograph appeared in the New York *Daily Graphic* in 1880: it was a scene in a frontier shanty town. If there were criticisms of the legend (for example, in *The Man Who Shot Liberty Valance*), they derived not from any analysis of history, but from a story about an individual living a lie. Stories about post-Civil War unemployment (Jesse James — who oscillated between ex-Yankee and ex-Rebel factions, using the Civil War 'as an excuse'), the economic implications of the range wars (Billy the Kid — who hired himself out to *both* the sides fighting for social and economic power) and Wyatt Earp's family vendettas (the O.K. Corral — where the Clantons were shot, either to protect the Earp family investments, or else to silence those who could make a charge of robbery with violence stick against the 'fighting pimps', as they were called) do not make good box-office in the States. At least one assumes they do not; no one seems actually to have tested the hypothesis. Eric Mottram has described the Billy the Kid legend as 'a cover for social fact, enabling us to watch the legendary figure fusing politics and economics and the desire to be freed from their necessity.... The Western hero emerges at the intersection of the economy and popular media in America, themselves already permeated with the belief in permissive conquest as *laissez-faire* policy and lawlessness as natural birthright.'

Sergio Leone would agree with the punch-line to Ford's *Liberty Valance*. But his films (after *Fistful*) were to become increasingly concerned with relating the legend to the socio-economic context from which it evolved — precisely during the dying moments of the civilisation and values which the legend sought to enshrine. We have seen how, in Leone's early films, the relationship bet-ween the romantic bandit and the local peasant community he unwittingly protects is a recurring theme (having its most complete expression in the Padré Ramirez sequence of *The Good, the Bad and the Ugly*). When Leone decided to produce 'a fresco on the birth of a great nation', in *Once Upon a Time in the West*, he did not base the film on historical incidents or folk-heroes — attempting to reinterpret the 'great moments' to which the Hollywood genre had often returned. Rather, he chose to 'portray America's first frontier using the most worn-out of stereotypes: the pushy whore, the romantic bandit, the avenger, the killer who is about to become a businessman, the industrialist who uses the methods of a bandit'. These stereotypes, which, in Leone's and Bertolucci's hands, become fictional 'emblems' of a sort, are taken from the dime novel, the Wild West show, the Hollywood film, the pulp magazine, the comic-strip, rather than from American history — parts of the 'fixed terminology' or 'code' of the fictional genre. Yet they are used to explore the relationship between frontier history and the dreams embodied in the fiction. 'To narrate great events, as Chaplin has taught us, it is always necessary to take as subjects humble, insignificant characters. For example, it is extremely difficult faithfully to re-create the great Napoleon on the screen. But the little character always becomes more human, and more real, *because* he is anonymous.' Audiences share preconceptions about famous historical characters, according to Leone, and these preconceptions give the characters too much specificity to allow audiences to sympathise with, or try to understand, the problems posed by relationships in the story. Leone's masterpiece is intended to 'recount, through small characters, usual characters, taken from American traditions of fiction, the birth of a nation. . . . Before they come onto the scene, these characters know themselves to be dying in every sense — physically and morally — victims of a new era which was advancing; the new, unpitying era of the economic boom.'

The main theme of *Once Upon a Time in the West* — the impact of technological developments on the Western frontier — raises questions about myth and history which had been peripheral to the 'Dollars' trilogy. It was, of course, a standard theme in Hollywood Westerns, from *The Iron Horse* to the Richard Widmark and Henry Fonda subplot of *How the West Was Won*: Frank Gruber categorises the *Iron Horse* story as one of the seven basic plots in the genre. But in the context of the 'personality' view of history represented by traditional Hollywood Westerns, criticisms associated with technological advance tended to take the form of stories about corrupt railroad agents — perhaps in conflict with soft-spoken frontier scouts, whose job it is to negotiate with the Indians, settlers, or any others who have no channel of communication with the railroad agents' superiors. Hollywood was not likely to criticise technological progress *per se*, for the socio-economic values it represented, or for its *disjunction* with the fiction — even from a romantic, individualistic standpoint. John Ford, then a socialist of sorts, seems to have had few qualms about putting his name to a piece of merchandise like the *Iron Horse* (1924).

From the point of view of plot, Leone's use of the *Iron Horse* formula marks a break with his previous Westerns — for we know the story already (more or less), so the *distancing* effect of his work (attenuated in the 'Dollars' films by the need to extract a coherent plot from the collage of episodes) becomes even more apparent. Since the story is 'given', Leone seems to be more concerned with exploring variations on a theme (and manipulating expectations) than with 'laying bare' or redefining the genre from its base. (In this sense, *Once Upon a Time* constitutes Leone's *support* for the Hollywood Western.) That is perhaps why so many people (in Paris, particularly, according to Noel Simsolo) have seen the film over and over again. To know the story is simply to *start* appreciating *Once Upon a Time*. The plots of the 'Dollars' trilogy may have been schematic — in the sense that a Sicilian puppet play is schematic; but the schematism of *Once Upon a Time* is of a very different order. Each of the main characters in the story 'moves' like a chesspiece, the chessboard being, in William Burroughs' phrase, 'the mythological system, that is, the cycle of conditioned action'. It is the ways in which Leone presents these 'moves', describes the 'cycle of conditioned action', and explores the implications of each 'move' for the other important 'pieces', that constitute the main interest of *Once Upon a Time*. The *Iron Horse* formula (or rather its reversal) provides a historical context of sorts for the chess-game. Since Leone was for the first time presenting a discourse on the Western from *within* the terms of reference of the Hollywood system, it is not surprising that *Once Upon a Time* had little or no impact on the Cinecittà production of Westerns — despite the fact that the film was very successful in Europe: products of the home industry could not hope to copy, or reapply the techniques of, Leone's most mature transcription of the 'codes' of the Western genre. *Once Upon a Time* was to open with a farewell to the 'Dollars' trilogy: of the main characters/stereotypes, only Cheyenne (like Tuco, the man with the words) seems to relate closely to Leone's previous characterisations. And the use of the *Iron Horse* formula (together with the historical questions this raises) constitutes another significant 'break' with the concerns of the trilogy. Also, *Once Upon a Time* was the first of Leone's films, since *Fistful*, in which there was no reference to the American Civil War.

The production of low-budget Italian Westerns at Cinecittà had slowed down considerably by the time Leone's 'fresco' was released: in 1969, fewer than twenty came off the assembly-line. *Once Upon a Time*, by contrast, was another international co-production, involving San Marco, Rafran (Leone's own business), and Paramount, a Gulf and Western company. The story 'outline' was by Leone, and two younger Italian directors — Bertolucci and Dario Argento (who was later to specialise in thrillers, then horror movies). The screenplay was by Leone and Sergio Donati (who had scripted two of Sollima's 'populist' Westerns). Four Italian intellectuals, two of them known to be left-wing, and 2,000,000,000 lire, to remake *The Iron Horse*, to challenge the Turner thesis, to explore the relationship between popular fictions (once upon a time . . .) and their historical base (. . . in the West). Looking back, it seems like a very strange investment.

I recently (January 1980) had the opportunity to ask Bertolucci in person about why he became involved in *Once Upon a Time*, and exactly what the extent of his contribution was. After talking about the comparison between John Ford's use of Monument Valley and his own use of the landscape around Parma ('it is *not* just topographical narcissism'), he replied:

> In the first place, I got involved because I did not have any lire. Also because, in the late 1960s, I liked the way some popular Italian films were going. I thought that Sergio Leone was brilliant — brilliant and vulgar at the same time. But I did not know him. On the first day *The Good, the Bad and the Ugly* was shown in Italy, I met Leone — in the projection booth. The day after, he called me and asked me to write the movie. I wrote a huge treatment — about three hundred pages long, full of 'quotes' from all the Westerns

> I love. Some of the 'quotes' even Leone did not recognise . . . And I wanted to write the whole script, but I didn't, so I lost most of the money.

Bertolucci's 'huge treatment' seems to have survived only in the 'outline' from which Leone worked during the shooting. The final version of the film is so crammed with 'quotes' from Hollywood Westerns that it is difficult to imagine how many more Bertolucci could have fitted in. But it seems likely that the critical perspective of *Once Upon a Time* originated with the director of *Partner*.

Throughout *Once Upon a Time in the West*, most of the main characters have no respect for the railroad. Frank stops and starts the train as he pleases, sits in the rail boss's chair, and is constantly helping himself to the boss's cigars — he is visually associated with the railroad from the first scene, when a mention of his name is illustrated by a screenful of railroad tracks. Cheyenne casually enters Morton's carriage by using a lavatory chain as a stirrup, and travels either by clinging to the underside of the carriage or by sitting on the roof. To Harmonica, Morton's train represents just another vantage point from which he can observe Frank's movements. Only Jill McBain seems at ease travelling in the normal way on a passenger train, and she is visiting the West (from New Orleans) for the first time: in a sense, she represents 'civilisation'.

Morton, of course, is committed to technological progress, represented by his dream to lay tracks across America: but he is too physically weak to cope with Frank, Harmonica or Cheyenne. And he, more obviously than the other main characters, is slowly dying — only kept alive by his dream, when 'any normal man would have put a bullet in his brain'. Throughout the film, the 'dry rot' of tuberculosis of the bones steadily creeps through his body. Morton represents an essential, but self-destroying, 'stage' in capitalist economic development. He is the entrepreneur who will be made redundant by the technological imperatives he plays a key role in unleashing. Perhaps for these reasons, as Frank begins to realise that he is 'not a businessman after all', he treats Morton with less and less sympathy. 'Don't play the sick man with me, Mr Morton,' he warns, and later threatens to crush Mr Morton (having kicked his walking frame away), 'like a rummy apple'. This time Morton plays for Frank's sympathy — but as Frank reverts to his role as gunfighter (with the strict code of 'chivalry' that role implies), he sees his relationship with Morton purely in terms of physical power, forgetting Morton's advice about the more effective power of the dollar.

Frank, Harmonica and Cheyenne belong to an 'ancient race', which will inevitably be 'killed off' by 'other Mortons'. Morton unsuccessfully uses Frank's methods: he buys off Frank's men, in the hope that they will kill their boss. Frank enjoys sitting in Morton's chair — 'It's almost like holding a gun, only much more powerful' — but instinctively goes for his gun when he hears Morton opening a drawer behind him. Morton calmly explains that there is one thing Frank will never really understand — the supreme power of money, even over the gun. Later, as Harmonica watches Frank's men deploy themselves in hiding places around the main street of Flagstone, he compares Frank's methods to those of the businessman ('You sound like a real businessman, Frank; being with Mr Morton's done you a lot of good . . . you've learned some new methods . . . Easy, Frank, easy. You've got to learn not to push things. Taking it easy is the first thing a businessman should do. I got an idea Mr Morton can teach you a lot more . . .'). As he prepares for the final confrontation with Harmonica, Frank discovers that he's 'not a businessman after all' — just a man. The corollary to this realisation is Morton's use of a gunfighter's techniques to mortally wound Cheyenne: in a scene cut from the non-European release print, Cheyenne explains why he has to 'stay here' (just out of sight of Sweetwater) to die: 'I ran into Mr Choo Choo . . . I didn't count on that.' Just as Frank understands for the first time that Morton was right in saying 'You'll never succeed in being like me,' Cheyenne brutally discovers that he cannot live in a world of 'beautiful, shiny rails'. The 'worn-out stereotypes' of fiction have played out their roles, only to be destroyed, or absorbed, by history: they are either eliminated or, like Harmonica, deprived of any further function.

If the intricately constructed sequences dealing with the gunfighter-businessman dialectic hinge on the two key icons, the dollar bill and the Colt .38, in the shooting-script of *Once Upon a Time* this theme is anthropomorphised in a series of short scenes involving Sam (Paolo Stoppa) and his horse, Lafayette. The horse ('a bag of bones') is frequently compared with the new, efficient 'iron horse' (again, the theme comes over, in the end, as a *comment* on the opening sequences of Curtiz' *Dodge City* (1939),

in which a stagecoach loses a race against a locomotive, and Colonel Dodge concludes, 'Iron men and iron horses — that's progress'). In *Once Upon a Time*, as Sam pulls up his buggy outside a ramshackle bar located in the middle of the desert (in another sequence cut from the English-language prints), he is asked by Jill why he is stopping: 'Don't the trains stop?' he replies; Lafayette needs some water, and Sam needs some whisky. The railroad surveyors' gang learns to its cost that Sam and Lafayette have no intention of making a detour, just to avoid disrupting the gang's work. The icons representing this conflict — money/gun, horse/iron horse — are present in the twin images on which the original version of *Once Upon a Time* closes. But in the American print, the final images suggest a very different (and more 'progressive') conclusion to the saga: the arrival of the railroad, and the assumption by Jill of her new role as mistress of Sweetwater and 'mother' to the hardworking rail gangs, become the twin climaxes.

When Leone was raising money for *Once Upon a Time*, he insisted that he had no intention of making a follow-up to *The Good, the Bad and the Ugly*. He had originally gone to the States to discuss plans for a film saga about American gangsters in the 1920s, provisionally entitled *Once upon a Time, America*. He talked about this project to Warren Beatty (who came up with the *Bonnie and Clyde* package a few months later). But United Artists wanted another Western. Obviously expecting to repeat the commercial success of *The Good, the Bad and the Ugly*, they offered him expensive stars (Kirk Douglas, Charlton Heston, Gregory Peck) and an overall budget to match. Leone preferred a measure of 'autonomy', no pressure to make another film of the 'Dollars' type, and Henry Fonda — so he made the film for Paramount. It is ironical that Leone's masterpiece was prepared more hastily than his previous two films — and that at first, he did not really wish to make the film at all. A 'story' was commissioned from Bertolucci, but this had been abandoned by the time shooting commenced. Leone had a definite 'structure', but he no longer had 'a precise scenario': 'I shot *Once Upon a Time in the West* (contrary to the practice of my previous films) when Morricone had already composed his music. Throughout the shooting schedule, we listened to the recordings. Everyone acted with the music, followed its rhythm, and suffered with its "aggravating" qualities, which grind the nerves.' The pace and construction of scenes representing the four main 'moods' in the film are direct reflexions of Morricone's four basic musical themes: the comic (Cheyenne's theme — whistling, electric piano and banjo), the expansive (the main title theme — richly orchestrated, with solo female voice), the brutally jarring (Harmonica's theme — harmonica and amplified guitar, backed by syncopated violin chords), and the hopeful, with sinister undertones (Morton's 'Pacific' theme). Leone had helped to draft Bertolucci's 'very provisional scenario', but he retained 'only its basic outline', preferring to 'work on the inspiration of the moment'. The fly incident, involving Jack Elam, in the credits sequence, was originally the result of a chance happening, and such an 'inspiration'.

In this way, Leone's 'dance of death' came to be improvised — the interplay (almost 'symmetry') between music and image representing perhaps the most memorable technical achievement in the film. *Once Upon a Time in the West* gives a new meaning to the phrase 'horse opera' — a phrase first coined, appropriately enough, by William S. Hart. As one critic has put it, 'it may be described as an opera in which arias are not sung but stared'. From the point of view of the Paramount executives who viewed the finished product, this was just the trouble. Leone had created a 'dance of death' which was intended to 'make the audience feel, in three hours, how these people lived, as if they had spent ten days with them — for example, with the three killers at the beginning of the film, who are waiting for the train and who are tired of the whole business. I tried to look at the characters of these three men, by showing the ways in which they live this boredom.' The director had obviously enjoyed *dilating* the audience's sense of time, exploiting, in his ostentatious way, the *rhetoric* of the Western, and dwelling on the tiniest details to fulfil his intention — in scenes such as the credits sequence he here describes. Preview audiences in America, and those who went to see the film during the first weeks of its release, just thought the film was too long and too slow. In one of the most brutal acts of vandalism in the history of modern cinema, Paramount cut nearly half an hour out of the original three-hour film, leaving the action sequences intact, but ignoring the dual climax to which the whole film had pointed. At least cinemas could now squeeze an extra performance into the daily programme. Although *Once Upon a Time* now made

little sense (characters greet each other as if they have met before, when we have not seen them do so; for no apparent reason, Cheyenne begins to look pale and tired towards the end of the film, because in the original he is dying; Jill and Frank suddenly appear to be in a strange room — it is, in fact, Frank's hide-out in the mountains, the exterior of which features as the backdrop to a long scene in the original), it did have a massacre, a gunfight, and a duel to commend it. In France, Italy, Switzerland, Germany and Japan (where the film was distributed more or less intact), *Once Upon a Time* was a box-office smash. In Paris, it ran continuously for nearly six years. But in America it continued to flop. Only now, with the revival of interest in Leone's films on campuses and in film clubs, is it proving a success in the States. Clearly, both United Artists and Paramount had expected a remake of *The Good, the Bad and the Ugly*; in fact, as we have seen, Leone originally wanted to symbolise his departure from 'the rules which I had imposed', and wave goodbye to the 'Dollars' trilogy, by showing the death of these three characters in the credits sequence, before the main story had actually begun.

Although set in locations where the Spanish cultural influence was historically of little or no significance, *Once Upon a Time* again refers at times to the central motifs which were used by Leone in the trilogy to 'rearrange' the bases of the Western in an Italian context: the plot hinges on the massacre of a family (Irish Catholic) and the destruction of their 'dream of a lifetime' (thematically, Leone's definitive reply to John Ford's — and George Stevens' — interpretation of the West); throughout the film, the inexorable advance of the railroad is evoked by long-shots of Morton's locomotive ploughing its way through the desert landscape; the unprincipled bandit's relationship with the church is much the same as Tuco's (he will, he says, kill anyone except a child or a priest, 'a Catholic priest, that is'); the motivation of the Avenger is again to do with the violent death of a relative, an event recalled in a climactic flashback; and this flashback shows Harmonica's brother being hanged from a bell, attached to a red-brick and sandstone arch, incongruously placed before a backdrop depicting the rugged majesty of Monument Valley — Leone's clearest synthesis of Italian *campanilismo* and the West of John Ford. A bell chimes as little Timmy McBain is shot; it does so again as Harmonica's brother kicks the support from beneath him and is hanged. The flashback also highlights one of the differences between *Once Upon a Time* and Leone's three preceding Westerns. Shooting for the film had started in Arizona, but because of difficulties with American technical crews, and because there were too many telegraph poles almost wherever the crew went, Leone filmed most of *Once Upon a Time* in the Spanish desert, with interiors shot at Cinecittà. The only two studio 'exteriors' contained in the film represent attempts to integrate American with Italian footage: after Jill McBain and Sam have been shown, in an expansive panning shot, driving a buggy through Monument Valley, there follows a sequence in which Morton's railroad surveyors try to flag the buggy down, and prevent Sam from disrupting work; this sequence is played before a painted backdrop of desert buttes and mesas — as is the final flashback. The one Western location which Leone wanted to keep on film (for obvious reasons) was re-created on a Cinecittà backlot.

Leone's concern with the minutest details of dress, firearms, décor, personal mannerisms, and so on, is still very much in evidence: the camera lingers on, and explores the shape of, Frank's Silver Colt .38 (reproduction), Harmonica's Colt Peacemaker (genuine, with the frontsight removed, and the hammer smoothed down to improve speed on the draw), and Stony's (Woody Strode's) Winchester (with a very short, sawn-off barrel, and an enormous loading arm, both stuffed into a long and ridiculously slung holster). Again, Leone seems to be concerned more with the 'look' of such details than with their function. The clutter inside Sweetwater creates an atmosphere of both domesticity and 'authenticity'. The plush interior of Morton's personal railroad carriage, which contrasts sharply with the simplicity of the desert landscape seen through the window, contributes to our understanding of the type of 'civilisation' Morton's dream represents. Frank feels more at home back at his private army's hide-out — a few holes carved in a red sandstone rock face: here, it is Mr Morton who looks out of place ('like a turtle out of its shell' as Frank puts it). As Jill walks away from Flagstone station, the camera picks out and lingers momentarily on the details of life in a busy, growing community: the Chinese laundry, the horse-drawn omnibus, the half-built theatre.

But, in *Once Upon a Time in the West*, the set-ting is no longer a surreal desert netherland in which the picaresque adventures of a Blondy or a Tuco can credibly take place. The setting is Arizona during the railway boom, and Leone is, for the first time, transcribing the Hollywood Western on its own ground. Perhaps this explains why there are more *specific* references to Hollywood Westerns in *Once Upon a Time*, than in the 'Dollars' trilogy: the parody *High Noon* opening; the *reversal* of the Starrett family scenes from *Shane*; 'quotes' from *Johnny Guitar*; an explicit verbal reference to the *3.10 to Yuma*, the names McBain and Sweetwater from the gun-running subplot of *The Comancheros*; the 'dusters' worn by Frank's men from the first flashback sequence of *The Man Who Shot Liberty Valance*; the visual references to Ford's *Iron Horse*; and so on. Leone's casting for *Once Upon a Time* suggests an attempt to comment on — or even parody — the established images of Western actors. The character of Frank, and his relationship to the flawed 'innocents' played by Fonda in Ford's *My Darling Clementine*, and *Young Mr Lincoln* we have already discussed. Jack Elam ('one-reel Jack', the expendable, wall-eyed heavy of countless Hollywood Westerns) and Woody Strode (John Ford's noble black cavalry sergeant, and, later, his Uncle Tom) are both shot dead before the story begins: the most memorable characteristics of these two much-loved faces (Elam's eye, Strode's fine baldness) literally fill the screen, and feature in two elaborate gags. Elam's eye rolls, to catch a glimpse of an irritating fly which attaches itself to his stubble and then buzzes around the side of a wooden bench: he draws his gun, not to shoot the fly (a rerun of the Buster Keaton butterfly gag from *The Paleface*), but to trap the creature in the gun's barrel. Strode's shaven pate shines, as water drips on to it from above, until 'Stony' decides to catch this water in his hat: too much dripping wears away a stone. In *Once Upon a Time*, more screen time is devoted to this fly, and this dripping water, than to the massacre of Mr Morton's entire staff (an event of which we only see the results — a suitable backdrop to the death of Morton himself). 'Heavy' Lionel Stander plays a jovial bartender, who drools over the arrival of Claudia Cardinale in the middle of the desert. Charles Bronson ('Bernardo', the gentle mercenary who becomes a hero and an example to the Mexican children in *The Magnificent Seven*) is cast as an almost supernatural Avenger in *Once Upon a Time*, *all* of whose actions are calcu-

36-40 Some of Bertolucci's written 'quotes' which ⟨w⟩ere made visual in *Once Upon a Time in the West*: ⟨l⟩⟨e⟩*ft*) the laying of the railroad tracks in John Ford's ⟨T⟩*he Iron Horse* (1924), and the funeral sequence in *Shane* (1953); (*right*) equivalent scenes in *Once Upon a Time*; and, of course, the appearance in Leone's epic of 'Ford country' (*below*)

lated to provide a suitable setting for his revenge: he has no identity apart from this quest; when asked 'Who are you?' by Frank, he replies with a list of dead men — 'all alive until they met you'; Cheyenne knows him as Harmonica (the musical instrument which plays a key role in the death of his elder brother, and which, after the final flashback *shared* by Harmonica and Frank, tells Frank who the Avenger is, without a word being spoken). The massacre at Cattle Corner station, which opens the film, ends with four bodies lying near the railroad line — Harmonica on one side of the line, Frank's reception committee on the other: but, some hours later, one of them rises from the dead, with work still to be done. Harmonica represents no recognisable moral lessons, since, with his almost supernatural command of time and space, he exists in a different dimension to the rest of the characters — an inscrutable version of Sturges' Bernardo with no attachments to anyone living (just to his own family memories). He only kills Frank's men, while Cheyenne deals with Morton and employees.

By changing the location from Abilene to Flagstone, Arizona, Leone was presumably justifying the use of Monument Valley (and, perhaps, the absence of cattle). Yet the central themes are treated in a characteristically Italian way. *Once Upon a Time* is concerned with 'the end of a world' — this 'in contrast to that great optimist I admire, John Ford': 'His naiveté and openness allowed him to make *The Quiet Man*, that is to say, Cinderella. He has the sentimentality of the Irish living in the United States, who still believe in green prairies extending into the future. Me, I'm a Roman, therefore fatalistic and pessimistic.' For example, John Ford's version of the dance in his classic Westerns — a formalised expression of incipient community feeling, a ritual which will usually be shattered by the intrusion of violence or stupidity — becomes redefined, in Leone's hands, as a 'dance of death'. Ford's folksy dancers enact in mime the social harmony on which they hope to build their community: but the measured steps of the square-dance are not a true reflection of the harmony regulating social relations — rather, as has often been pointed out, they represent an ideal expressed in ritual. In the very first narrative Western, *The Great Train Robbery*, a square-dance was used to symbolise the kind of society to which frontiersmen ought to belong. Leone's 'dance' represents no such ideal. It is a dance of destiny, usually performed in a flag-stone *corrida*. The rituals of violence associated with this dance 'resolve' themselves in a series of external gestures (perhaps the 'punch-line' to a digressive subplot, perhaps the meeting of two interconnected destinies). These external gestures are inseparable from Leone's (by now characteristic) stress on spatial relationships (defined by the rectangle of the wide screen), and on the *dilation* of time. His effects, like his characters, are consistently other-regarding. Such a dance has more of an aesthetic than an ideological resonance, and, as an exercise in 'style' achieves a universality to which Ford's community rituals never aspire — as Franco Ferrini has noted. Within this aesthetic, Leone's 'danse macabre' invariably ends in death, or 'sacrifice'. The McBain wedding feast becomes a massacre (rather like the equivalent sequence in *1900*): the idea of death subtly intrudes on the festivities. The sequence begins with a glimpse of the double barrels of Brett's shotgun, pointed at a flying partridge; later, Maureen McBain will smile as she sees some partridges in flight, the moment before she herself is shot; little Timmy 'mimes' the shooting of another partridge (just as little Joey 'mimes' the shooting of a deer, in *Shane*); Patrick is surly with Brett, on the subject of his new 'mother' Jill — 'our mother died six years ago'; Brett responds to this mention of death by slapping Patrick, hard — but a moment later this is forgotten, as Brett sentimentally reads out Jill's letter. Throughout the wedding-feast sequence, these suggestions of the slaughter to come are reinforced by the use of amplified natural 'sounds': the chirping of cicadas, which unaccountably ceases, then as suddenly starts again; the flapping of wings; the excited squawking of turkeys; the gunshot which kills Timmy, instantly blending with the shriek of a train whistle (to accompany an out-of-focus shot of a smokestack belching steam) — the result visually linked to the cause, the 'small obstacle on the track' to the locomotive itself. 'We're going to be rich, Pa?' asks Maureen, just before the balletic holocaust. Brett pauses, then cautiously murmurs, 'Who knows?' Quien Sabe? 'Me, I'm a Roman, therefore fatalistic and pessimistic,' says Leone. Wyatt Earp's community dance in *My Darling Clementine*, and the Starrett's fourth of July celebrations in *Shane* were never like this.

But, as Leone continues, *Once Upon a Time* is also concerned — as a parallel development to the end of one world — with 'the birth of matriarchy and the beginning of a world without balls'. This theme is exemplified by the character of Jill McBain, in her relationship with the other protagonists. She is cast in a variety of roles — most of them passive. As Frank discovers, she comes from the finest whorehouse on Bourbon Street, New Orleans, to start a new life at Sweetwater. At first, she reacts to the 'threat' of Cheyenne by behaving as she would back in New Orleans: 'I'm here alone in the hands of a bandit who smells money. If you want to, you can lay me over the table and amuse yourself — and even call in your men. Well, no woman ever died from that. When you're finished, all I'll need will be a tub of boiling water and I'll be exactly where I was before — with just another filthy memory.' To which Cheyenne (suitably chastened) replies, 'You make good coffee at least . . .?' (a quotation, incidentally, from the last scene of the Dick Powell *Farewell, My Lovely*: 'She made swell coffee, anyway'). Later in the same scene (which takes place at *precisely* the same time as the Morton-Frank discussion about businessmen and gunfighters, after which Frank decides to try a new role), Jill begins to warm to Cheyenne, and confides her disappointment to him. Immediately after Frank has told Morton that 'pretty soon, the widow McBain won't be a problem no more', Leone cuts to Jill confessing her faith in Brett McBain: 'You wake up one morning, and say "World, I know you. From now on there are no more surprises" and happen to meet a man like this, who looked like a good man — clear eyes, strong hands — and he wants to marry you, which doesn't happen often, and he says he's rich — which doesn't hurt. So you think, "Damn you, New Orleans. Now I'll say yes and go live in the country. I wouldn't mind giving him half a dozen kids after all. Take care of a house. Do something, what the hell" . . . Well, God rest your soul, Brett McBain, even if he's going to have a job pulling you out of the Devil's grip . . . Mrs McBain goes back to civilisation, minus a husband, and plus a great future.' 'You deserve better,' replies Cheyenne. 'The last man who told me that is buried out there,' Jill warns. And, of course, Cheyenne does end up 'buried out there'.

During the same scene, it becomes clear that Cheyenne would like to treat Jill as some kind of mother-substitute. As he prepares to leave, he sentimentally observes, 'You know, Jill, you remind me of my mother. She was the biggest whore in Alameda and the finest woman that ever lived. Whoever my father was, for an hour or for a month, he must have been a happy man.' At their last meeting, he approvingly recalls, 'My mother used to make coffee this way — hot, strong and good.' By this time, Jill has got over her initial disillusionment, ceased to look for 'the why' Brett and family were killed, and decided to stay, having accepted Harmonica's almost supernatural control of her destiny: 'You don't look at all like the noble defender of poor, defenceless widows, but then again, I don't look like a poor, defenceless widow . . .'

Allied to her role as Cheyenne's 'mother', Jill becomes matriarch to the hot and tired railroad gangs, working just outside her new home. She has been prepared for this role throughout the film. Cheyenne helps her light a fire. Harmonica stops her from packing her bags and returning to New Orleans: he strips her of the city frills on her costume, leaving her with more practical clothes in which to fetch water from the Sweetwater well: 'Get me some water. From the well. I like my water fresh.' This extraordinary sequence, which starts brutally ('Cheyenne's right. Once you've killed four, it's easy to make it five'), seems to be about to involve rape (which, in a weird way, it does), and ends with Bronson calmly stripping Cardinale for her role as water-bearer (the well being the pivot of the whole story), has both narrative and thematic significance. For the stripping serves another function — to remove all traces of white lace from her dark costume, so that she will not become a sitting target for Frank's men. Cheyenne, who at first seems to Jill a predator (she suspects him of the massacre, despite his anxious attempts to convince her that she 'ain't caught the idea', and she expects to be gang-banged by his men at any moment), later casts himself in the role of her grateful son (and protector), and takes his final leave of Jill by gently patting her behind ('Make believe its nothing'): this gesture associates him with the workmen outside (her 'sons'), who, he has sheepishly warned her, may occasionally try to do the same thing ('You can't imagine how happy it makes a man feel . . . Make believe its nothing'). As the train pulls in, during the final sequence, the rail gang gathers around the universal provider and matriarch, and the 'world without balls' is born. Richard Jameson has suggested, correctly I think, that this is at the same time a critique of American

'Momism' (from a European perspective), and a celebration of the great Italian earth-mother, who nevertheless signals, in both roles, the departure of a rugged, independent 'ancient race'. Fritz Lang, talking about the Hollywood Western, has asserted that 'the development of America is unimaginable without the days of the Wild West — when a dance-hall girl was placed on a pedestal because she was the only woman among a hundred gold miners. The American woman today is still on a pedestal — I don't think she likes it. . . . I once said, "in America sex is preached, in France it is done".' His views can be interpreted, perhaps, as another perspective on Leone's 'world without balls'.

Although Jill hopes that Harmonica will stay, it is inevitable that he has 'gotta go' once his task is done. He looks out of the door, approvingly, and notes, 'It's going to be a beautiful town, Sweetwater': but his vague hint that he will return 'some day' has an empty ring about it. While Harmonica stands at the door, Jill's face registers, by turns, expectation, hope, bewilderment, anxiety, then resignation. Cardinale's performance at this moment (despite Charles Bronson's comment that 'she is no Anne Bancroft') seems utterly convincing. Cheyenne leaves more reluctantly. Just before the climactic duel at Sweetwater, he asks Jill to place a bowl of water near the window 'so I can watch the railroad go by while I shave'. He does not watch the duel between Harmonica and Frank, and cuts himself as the fatal shot is fired. After the duel, Jill observes, 'You're sort of a handsome man.' 'But,' he replies, 'not the right man.' Throughout the final sequence of events, he has acted as Jill's (and the audience's) interpreter or 'Chorus'. When asked what Harmonica is 'waiting for out there, what's he doing?' Cheyenne turns to the camera to tell Jill (and us), 'He's whittling on a piece of wood. I've gotta feeling when he stops whittling, something's going to happen.' After the shot has been fired, he tells Jill that whichever man comes through the door, that man will pick up his things and 'say adios'. 'People like that have something inside, something to do with death.' After Harmonica has coolly left, with the parting words 'some day' (not bothering to say 'adios'), Cheyenne reluctantly follows: 'Yeah, I've gotta go too.' With both men out of her life (one a stage-manager, the other a dependant), Jill is ready to assume the role for which both have groomed her.

Whereas the behaviour of all the other main characters has some impact on events (within the 'cycle of conditioned action'), Jill McBain is a *reactor*, a character who only makes sense, is only defined, with reference to the male protagonists. At least, until the final sequence. She wants to leave Sweetwater, but is told 'Now isn't the time to leave': later, she is told 'It's time to go home'. She is stripped (by Harmonica), raped (by Frank), protected (by Cheyenne), bargained for (by Morton), and she adopts the successive roles of whore, adoring wife, mother, whore again, and matriarch — one of the side-effects of her final role being to have her bottom pinched by the sex-starved workmen. At no stage in the story, until the very end, does she take the initiative for herself; she is always being prompted or prepared by others. Yet her function in the film is a crucial one. Not only does she bring together, or bring into focus, all the other 'worn-out' stereotypes — but she is the *only* character who is not destroyed when history bursts in on the fiction: whereas the others play their parts, then bow out, she at last has a useful, purposeful role to fulfil when the railroad finally arrives. As the 'myths' dissolve, she comes into her own. Leone and Bertolucci may be misogynists — but Jill McBain is the only one to survive.

Leone creates the impression throughout the film that Harmonica is always there, just out of frame, ready to step in and help Jill when he is needed: Harmonica is forever eavesdropping (on Cheyenne's conversation, or Frank's meeting with Wobbles), watching (Frank's movements in town, Jill's behaviour after leaving the Chinese laundry), or warning Jill that she is about to hear 'that sound' of a rifle being cocked. At one point, Leone cleverly suggests that Harmonica is watching in two places at once: he cuts from the sequence showing Frank and Jill in bed to the auction sequence in Flagstone, splicing in a brief shot of Harmonica peering through some lace curtains, as a 'bridge' between the two scenes. Cheyenne's entrances are usually framed by the Sweetwater doorway, and immediately followed by the amplified sound of a door slamming. He first appears (after sounds of shooting off-screen, signifying his escape from a prison escort) framed by a bar-room door. Next time, the camera dollies round the open door of Sweetwater, as Jill is about to leave, to reveal Cheyenne's face, again framed by a wooden doorway. 'Did you make coffee? Make it.' When he returns to Sweetwater (after another, less successful escape from a prison escort), he dramatically enters through the doorway, slamming the door at the precise moment Jill does the same with the back door. Cheyenne's arrivals are frozen 'portraits', the romantic bandit coming home. Henry Fonda's first appearance is shot as if the camera is seeking out his face — from over his shoulder, to a side view of those well-known features, rendered almost unrecognisable by an uncharacteristic suntan, a few days' stubble, and a wad of tobacco puffing out his cheek. 'Jesus Christ, it's Henry Fonda!' It is only when he smiles, in extreme close-up, just before he shoots little Timmy McBain, that we notice the blue of his eyes: 'What shall we do with this one, Frank?'/'Since you call me by name ...' Later, Frank usually enters by striding into the centre of the frame (loosely and youthfully in the recurring flashback sequence, stiffly and formally when he opens the saloon doors at Flagstone, or comes out from behind the bushes outside Sweetwater). Frank is attempting to adopt a new role (the smartly-dressed businessman), but the anxious look in his eyes, during his walk along the main street of Flagstone, belies the new role his formal posture implies. He is 'not a businessman after all'. In contrast to these two characters, Harmonica *slides* into the frame from the side, usually photographed in extreme close-up. On the shooting script of *Once Upon a Time*, Leone simply writes of his appearances, 'The Man enters the scene in his usual way.' Apart from his first entrance (discovered standing the other side of the railroad tracks, after the train has pulled out), Harmonica always 'enters the scene' as if he has been standing just out of frame all along, only making an appearance when he is needed. He slides into the frame from behind a post, from the bottom of the stairs in the Sweetwater stables, or viewed through a window. More characteristically, he just *appears*. Cheyenne rides away from Sweetwater at a gallop, the horse bolting before he is fully in the saddle: he is always on the run, and in a hurry. Frank rides more coolly, in full control: two of Delli Colli's most rich compositions show him stiffly riding back to Morton's train, across the desert (in rhythm with Morricone's music), and purposefully riding past the railroad gangs, to meet his destiny at Sweetwater. Both sequences (the first a long-shot, the second a panning-shot with the blurred bustle of the gangs in the background, the grey dappled horse in crisp focus, 'bobbing' past them) are 'punctuated' by a slow funeral dirge, played on the trumpet and backed by a string quartet. In the

American release print, Harmonica is never shown riding a horse. In the full-length version, he rides off into the hills at the end of the film, past the railroad gangs, with the body of Cheyenne slung over a second horse. But during the action, he does not need to ride — for he is always in the right place at the right time.

To achieve these effects, Leone shows more confidence (or flamboyance, perhaps) in his visual 'style' than he had in the first two 'Dollars' films, and develops technical ideas with which he had first experimented in *The Good, the Bad and the Ugly*. He again uses expansive crane-shots (Jill's arrival at Flagstone), sweeping pans (Jill in Monument Valley), rhythmic cutting to music (the final duel), extreme close-ups (Harmonica's eyes, during the face-off), matching pans in rhythm/symmetry (Harmonica watching Frank's movements in Flagstone, the duel), and intercut subjective shots (particularly effective for showing both Brett's and Timmy's first views of the massacre). The McBain massacre sequence is, in fact, constructed entirely around fluid camera movements which follow the characters around, broken only by subjective shots from the point of view of each character in turn: the camera *participates*. During the duel sequence of *The Good, the Bad and the Ugly*, Leone had cut in various shots of the three protagonists' eyes: 'Angel Eyes', the eyes of the rat, the steely eyes of the 'protecting angel'. 'If I include so many extreme close-ups in my Westerns,' Leone explains, 'it is largely because I want to show that the eyes are the most important feature. Everything can be read in the eyes: courage, menace, fear, uncertainty, death.' In *Once Upon a Time*, close-ups of eyes serve a variety of purposes: they reveal Morton the visionary, the dreamer, as he stares at a picture of the sea; they reflect Frank's anxiety as he walks to his horse in Flagstone, and after his men have been killed (with Harmonica's help); they show that *nothing* matters any more, except to find out who the Man is; they show that Harmonica and Frank are *sharing* the final flashback. The use of soundtrack to 'punctuate' such effects again shows the development of Leone's ideas since *The Good, the Bad and the Ugly*. The 'symmetry' between music and image we have already discussed: each character has his own 'insignia' (plucked banjo for Cheyenne, harmonica wail for the Man, electronic whine or amplified guitar for Frank), and each main theme in the film has a direct musical inspiration. By this stage,

Once Upon a Time in the West
141-8 (*Above and opposite*) Frank's men (Jack
Elam, Woody Strode and Al Mulock) wait for
Harmonica (Charles Bronson) at Cattle Corner station

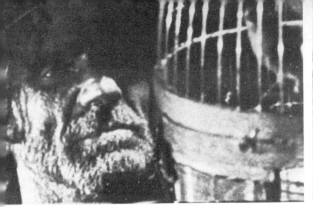

149-56 (*Below and opposite*) Brett McBain (Frank Wolff) and family are massacred by Frank (Henry Fonda) and his gang outside the Sweetwater farm

157-60 (*Above and opposite*) Jill McBain (Claudia Cardinale) and Sam (Paolo Stoppa) arrive at Sweetwater, expecting a wedding reception

161-4 (*Above and opposite*) Mr Morton (Gabriele Ferzetti) talks business with Frank, while Jill adjusts to 'a quiet, simple country life', with assistance from Cheyenne (Jason Robards) and Harmonica

165-72 (*Below and opposite*) Frank and his men try to shoot Jill's protector, before persuading her to sell Sweetwater to the lowest bidder

173-7 (*Above and opposite*) Frank walks the streets of Flagstone, then rides back to the train, to discover that Morton and his employees have been massacred by Cheyenne's men

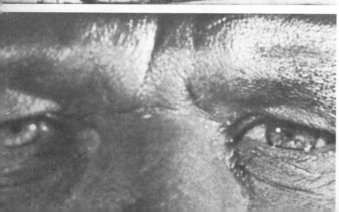

178-97 (*below and opposite*; *overleaf, top and opposite*) The final settling of accounts: Frank at last gets an answer to his question 'Who are you?' but it is 'only at the point of dying'

198-9 (*Below and opposite*) The train arrives outside the makeshift station at Sweetwater

Leone knew how to exploit his sense of 'style' and 'gesture' to the full: the 'fashionable' clothes of *The Good* ... (Eastwood's high-waisted coat, Tuco's bell-bottom trousers) have their counterpart in the 'dusters' worn by Frank's men — and these long suede and leather coats (only distantly related to the smoked and greased hide coats worn by the genuine frontiersmen) started a 'craze' in Paris menswear boutiques. The presentation of the flashback in *Once Upon a Time* is far more subtle (and unambiguous) than in *For a Few Dollars More*. Shot out of focus and in slow motion, it impinges on Harmonica's consciousness three times: on the first two occasions, Harmonica cannot quite recall the incident with clarity; the third time, Frank continues to walk towards the camera, and Harmonica's motives are at last revealed — the recall is total, when *both* characters are shown to have been participants in the incident.

Despite its length, *Once Upon a Time in the West* consists of only about twenty scenes (the first three of which take up over a quarter of the screen time). Leone's 'debate' takes place in four main settings: (1) *Sweetwater*, scene of the McBain massacre, the funeral, Jill's search for 'the why' and meeting with Cheyenne, the incident at the well, building a station, and the final shootout; (2) *Flagstone*, scene of Jill's arrival at the station, Wobbles' Chinese laundry, the Man's 'shadowing' of Wobbles, the auction and subsequent events in the saloon, and Frank's walk to his horse; (3) *Morton's Train*, scene of the discussion about businessmen and gunmen, the Man's capture and Cheyenne's destruction of Morton's men, Morton's decision to buy off Frank's men, and Morton's death; and (4) *Monument Valley*, scene of Jill's buggy ride, the laying of railroad tracks, and the final flashback. The isolated farm, the developing town, the railroad, the desert — these are the four contexts for Leone's 'mosaic'. Each setting is associated with a series of key icons: the well, the McBain graves, the kettle, the rosary, the model train, the family photographs, the mirror, the lace above the bed, the checked table-cloth — Panofsky's icon of 'domesticity' (Sweetwater); the theatre frontage, the half-painted clock-face, the horse-drawn omnibus, the station clock, Jill's watch, the ornate, empty saloon (Flagstone); Morton's walking-frame (symbol both of Morton's own 'dry rot' and of the 'slime' he leaves behind him, in the form of 'two beautiful, shiny rails'), the picture of the Pacific Ocean, the portrait of George Washington,

the 'executive' desk, the silver model locomotive, the cigars (railroad); the cathedral rocks, unforgettably linked with the films of John Ford (Monument Valley). Leone links his long sequences with 'bridging' images: Harmonica getting up/McBain's shotgun; Timmy's death/the locomotive's smokestack; Jill making coffee/Morton 'removing a small obstacle'; Harmonica peering through some lace curtains (to link Frank's bedroom with an auction); Morton 'dealing' five $100 bills/'$500' bid at the auction. These are supported by 'bridging' effects on the soundtrack: respectively, a gunshot, a scream, 'You make good coffee at least?'/'Not bad', a wooden hammer banged on a table (recalling Harmonica's aim to 'build a station'), the sheriff telling us, '$500.' Such linkages are immaculately constructed. And within each sequence, Leone continues to indulge his ostentatious visual 'style', lingering on the tiniest details and dilating our sense of time and space by means of his extraordinarily *controlled* use of every inch of the wide screen. Again, the director is looking at himself looking at the Western.

When the film first appeared most critics of *Once Upon a Time in the West* suggested that it simply revealed Leone's talent as an art director. The sequence showing Claudia Cardinale lying on a four-poster bed, shot from above through the canopy of black lace, was 'stunning', as were the panning-shots showing Frank riding back to the train, and, later, past the rail gangs, but these were also thought to be empty flourishes, devoid of any thematic significance. The basic plot was that of a Z feature Western (but at least it *had* a plot which was recognisable, in the full version); the script was too schematic; Leone was too *conscious* of 'making a Western for Art' (the *Monthly Film Bulletin* complained) and, as a result, the film was like poor man's Visconti. What started out as cinema about cinema, ended up trying to take refuge in Art — a classic admission of impotence in the face of anything 'real'. Leone's emphasis on detail, said others, was somehow *external*, or imposed, a well-photographed and scored peep-show. Leone's formalism had become much too much of a good thing. The Italian Western had risen 'above its station'.

There is, perhaps, some truth in these criticisms. As has already been pointed out, Leone seems to be a director whose forte is keeping up with European *cinematic* vibrations. Many of his effects (and in particular his use of iconography) seem to be too 'conscious', and too obviously 'arranged' for some critics — especially if they have read and enjoyed V.F. Perkins' *Film as Film*. These effects are seldom economically achieved. But to divorce Leone's 'formalism', his 'rhetoric', completely from the content of his films is radically to misinterpret what he is trying to achieve. (As Eisenstein wrote in 1925, 'it is time some people understood that form is determined at a very deep level and not through some superficial little "trick" that is more or less successful'.) Roland Barthes has suggested that a reluctance to *display* codes is a mark of bourgeois society and the 'popular culture' which has developed from within it: both seem to require 'signs' which do not look as though they *are* signs — probably because these 'signs' mask the ideology which informs them. Leone's flamboyant *display* of the 'codes' of the Western shows how well he had digested the implications of the early writings of semiologists on *Mythologies* — and it is this *display* which has been treated by many critics as an (empty) exercise in 'formalism', an over-indulgent use of the medium. Leone's self-conscious use of iconography, the care he takes over framing (often a commentary on the 'codes' of the Hollywood Western), and the primacy of montage in his mature work, may seem to amount to a highly incestuous form of cinema about cinema — at its most pretentious in *Once Upon a Time in the West*. But, to my mind, it is precisely the *unrestrained* quality of Leone's *display* in *Once Upon a Time*, which sets the film apart as the finest synthesis of his attempts to transcribe the Hollywood Western. As we have seen, *Once Upon a Time* is concerned as much with the fictional stereotypes, as with the history of the West — specifically, the divorce between 'myth' and socio-economic context, a cinematic study of fictions as distinct from (and, finally, destroyed by) history. *Once Upon a Time* is also concerned with the 'language' and 'syntax' of the Western (in a different way from the 'Dollars' trilogy, since Leone here uses a cliché Hollywood plot as a starting point, and explores variations from that 'received' base) — an unmasking or 'display' of the terminology of the genre. William Burroughs again: 'None of the characters in my mythology are free. If they were free, they would not still be in the mythological system, that is, the cycle of conditioned action.' In *Once Upon a Time*, not only the characters and contexts, but the technical effects (the 'syntax') as well, are part of that cycle. The visual correlatives of the basic themes,

the interplay between music and image, the construction of 'set-pieces' — all seem to achieve a 'control' which leaves most American directors of Westerns (even the formalist ones) standing — albeit with a very different intention, which could only be realised from *outside* the Hollywood system. In particular, the creation of a pervading atmosphere of pessimism — the destruction of comfortable fictions, when faced with the objective realities of technological advance — while still in a strange way *celebrating* the Hollywood dream, is a spectacular achievement.

In Costa Gavras' *Z*, a sequence showing well-dressed crowds going to watch the Bolshoi Ballet is intercut with scenes of violence and demonstration outside the theatre: such rarified art forms (even if they do symbolise 'cultural exchange') have no place, it seems, in the development of political consciousness. As the demonstrators surge forward to confront the police, they pass a film poster, and tread it into the ground. The poster shows Clint Eastwood as the Man With No Name in one of Leone's 'Dollars' films: Gavras seems to be saying that 'fantasy' films (represented by Eastwood) are nearer to the concerns of the demonstrators, but that 'fantasy' violence has no point of contact with the *act* of violence (and 'consciousness-raising') in a political confrontation. In *Once Upon a Time in the West*, a sequence shows Frank (with Harmonica's guidance) shooting one of his own men, who has positioned himself on the roof of the Flagstone theatre. The gunman slides down the roof, ripping through the paper-thin theatre banner: the Wild West show, and the dime novel (like the Street of Pleasure in *My Name Is Nobody*) have their place in the development of frontier mythology, but they must be 'read' in the context of the brutality which inevitably accompanied proto-capitalist development. 'Fantasy' violence (and the fantasy self-images of men of violence, the roles they see themselves as playing), Leone seems to be saying, have in this sense a more direct relationship with 'political' or 'economic' violence (on which frontier mythology was built) than Costa Gavras would allow. Only when the theatre banner has been torn (and shown to be paper-thin, 'laid bare', as it were) can this relationship be explored, or, in other words, can the relationship between the mythology of the West and its objective history (or the conditions which sustain the mythology) be 'unmasked'. And that, after all, was what the semiology of cinematic mythologies — so trendy in the late 1960s — originally set out to achieve.

If this interpretation is correct, *Once Upon a Time* represents a form of 'intellectual cinema', not unlike Sergei Eisenstein's. Sometimes, Leone *links* images in order to *expound* an abstract idea (for example, Brett's wooden model train, representing 'the dream of a lifetime', linked with Morton's metal model train, complete with removable 'small obstacle'). Sometimes, he *collides* images, in order to *create* such an idea — relying on the audience to make the connection (for example, his shock cut from the barrel of Frank's silver Colt .38 to an out-of-focus shot of a locomotive's smokestack). In both cases, the images are clearly intended to function as abstractions — but with a grammar of their own. Eisenstein's *October* (his finest experimental example of 'intellectual montage') opts almost exclusively for the *collision* method (as opposed to the *linkage* method, represented, for example, by Esther Shub's compilation, *The Fall of the Romanov Dynasty*, which was released to commemorate the same series of events): after *October*, Eisenstein, too, was to be accused by the authorities on cinema of 'excessive formalism' (by then a cardinal sin). Whether or not such parallels can be convincingly drawn in general terms (although he challenges accepted cinematic norms, and 'dominant codes', by laying them bare, Eisenstein was not, of course, concerned with *genre-conscious* cinema), it is evident, more specifically, that Leone owes a great deal to the techniques used by Eisenstein to sustain and extend dramatic climaxes. When Eisenstein wishes to show the 'conversion' (by Bolshevik agitation) of Kornilov's 'Savage Division', he rhythmically intercuts shots of faces, eyes, hands on swords, swords slowly being drawn ('in the name of God'), eyes, swords slowly being returned to scabbards. The 'conversion' is in this way presented ritually. Sergio Leone's equivalent method of filming climactic duels as if they were part of the liturgy, we have already discussed. Which brings us back to *Sutter's Gold*, the first attempt to cinematically criticise the bases of the 'epic' Western (represented by *The Covered Wagon*), way back in 1930. And to Eisenstein's remarks on the determination of form, written five years earlier.

By the end of *Once Upon a Time*, the 'worn-out stereotypes' which Leone and Bertolucci used to perform their 'dance of death', have no further use — all that is, except 'the pushy whore', who at last

has found a role. Mr Morton never sees the Pacific: instead, he dies, crawling like a snail towards a puddle in the middle of the desert — the urine of his own puffing and wheezing locomotive. Frank never makes the transformation from gunman to businessman: 'at the point of dying', he discovers who the Man is, and the Man's harmonica, stuffed into his mouth, plays his death rattle. Cheyenne asks Harmonica to turn away, as he dies just out of sight of Sweetwater: 'Mr Choo Choo' and his 'slime' have destroyed him. The Man rides off into the hills, leaving behind him an empty promise to return 'some day', and taking with him the body of Cheyenne: as the train pulls into the facade of a station, he 'gotta go'. Jill finally takes the initiative, by adopting the role of matriarch to the thirsty workmen, ushering in a 'world without balls'. She is now, as Sylvie Pierre puts it (1970), part of history. The others have been operating in a domain — a fictional, rhetorical domain — which is presented as *separate* from that history, and which is finally absorbed by it.

Once upon a time, according to Leone's story, these characters lived and died in a world of simple icons, where they enacted a series of rituals in which even life and death became external, melodramatic gestures — and these gestures were codified, as the story was retold, to become a fully-fledged myth, a myth which should not be confused with a moral code, but which belongs entirely in the realms of fiction.

If Sergio Leone expresses all this by indulging in extreme stylistic formalism, it is clearly because, in his terms, the melodramatic gestures or poses (visual and verbal, in a word *rhetorical*) are inseparable from the relationships (mythic and historical) he wishes to explore. Leone's treatment of these relationships is intended both to help elucidate the meaning of the West, and to reappraise its trace — the Hollywood Western, a global text. For, unlike in the 'Dollars' films, the codes are no longer 'free' — they are still separate from Turner's history, and separate from the morality of Hollywood, but *Once Upon a Time in the West* reveals Leone's inevitable realisation that the historical bases of the genre must, at some level, be confronted.

Nevertheless, like all Sergio Leone's films, *Once Upon a Time in the West* views the American frontier myth from an Old World, European cultural perspective. A Shakespearean fool introduces the action of *A Fistful of Dollars*. The scenario of

Once Upon a Time stresses the Brechtian (or perhaps Chaplinesque) analogy between businessmen and gunmen, capitalists and bandits: like *Arturo Ui* and *Monsieur Verdoux*, the film seems to be as much concerned with an unending struggle in capitalism between victims and predators, as it is with the specific 'Western' conflict between barbarism and civilisation. The 'Dollars' trilogy, as we have seen, had as much to do with Sicilian puppet plays, as with the Hollywood Westerns it was criticising. John Ford had characteristically used American folk-tunes, for example 'Dixie' or 'She Wore a Yellow Ribbon', as musical themes for his Westerns: Leone and Morricone prefer a Bach Toccata (as a prelude to the death of Tomaso in *For a Few Dollars More*), Mozart's 'Eine Kleine Nachtmusik' (as a 'bridge passage' in the 'Marcia degli Accattoni' from *Duck, You Sucker*), or Wagner's 'Ride of the Valkyries' (fused with variations on the *Fistful* title theme, to punctuate the ride of the phantom Wild Bunch across the desert, in *My Name Is Nobody*.) When a German arms-dealer confronts a Mexican bandit at the climax of Sergio Sollima's *The Big Gundown*, Morricone uses Beethoven's 'Für Elise', with Spanish guitar accompaniment, musically to illustrate the ensuing duel. Many points of reference in the genre remained distinctively European — even when the productions became multi-national, and seemed to be veering away from Cinecittà towards Hollywood.

In *Once Upon a Time in the West*, Leone is not trying to *compete* with Ford — just as, in his thrillers, Claude Chabrol is not trying to compete with Hitchcock: both are using works by directors they understand and admire as *points d'appui* from which to explore emblematic characters and situations or codes, excavated from the Western and thriller genres, the resulting extensions of both form and content being presented in a melodramatic, expressionistic style. In general, as Sylvie Pierre concludes (1970), Leone seems to be less interested in history or ideology *per se* than in a cinematic *rhetoric* which is a product of them both. *Once Upon a Time* is beginning to appear on American critics' lists of 'the ten best Westerns of all time'. References to Leone's 'masterpiece of rhetoric' should also, perhaps, appear in surveys of the types of European *critical* or *genre-conscious* cinema represented in the work of Chabrol and Bertolucci and in both films and theoretical writings by Pasolini. A type of 'cinematographic narcissism', which *also* has a critical intention.

When *Once Upon a Time in the West* was released, Sergio Leone admitted, 'I have finished, for the time being at least, with Westerns. . . . I no longer love the things associated with the West as I used to — the horses, the firearms, and so on.' Since then, he has taken over one film — the post-Western *Duck, You Sucker*, also known (in England) as *A Fistful of Dynamite* and (in France) as *Once Upon a Time, the Revolution* — both alternative titles suggesting direct connections with his previous films which are rather contrived. He has 'supervised' two Westerns — Tonino Valerii's *My Name Is Nobody* (1973) and Damiano Damiani's *A Genius . . .* (1975). And he has abandoned two major projects — one of which was to have been based on Céline's *Journey to the End of Night*, the other on the last days of Mussolini. He has also talked a great deal about *Once Upon a Time, America*, his long-planned saga of the Roaring Twenties: this film is to be about the 'war' between Jewish and Irish gangsters, *before* the arrival of the Sicilians, the central character being a Jewish gangster (an avid reader of Lenin's works) who returns to New York after thirty years' absence, to discover it is no longer like his home town any more — 'politics has taken over'. (Leone was offered *The Godfather* as a project, but turned it down, since he wanted to make *Once Upon a Time, America*. He now regrets it.) And Leone has mentioned a version of *Don Quixote*, set in present-day America, in which 'America would be Don Quixote, while Sancho, a European finding out about that country, would be the only positive character in the film'. 'What a pity Gérard Philipe is dead. He would have made an exceptional "baddy" in that film.' He has expressed interest in directing a Soviet-financed film about the siege of Leningrad, structured around the Shostakovich 7th Symphony. But all his attempts to 'change to a completely different genre' have so far come to nothing.

Perhaps Sergio Leone's narcissistic cinema *only* works when he is dealing with 'the most cinematographic genre of all', as Jean-Luc Godard has christened the Western. For this genre, with its clearly defined 'codes', provided Leone with the opportunity, and the frame of reference, to make four films from a consistent standpoint — oppositional films, 'films' as he puts it 'which are *against*'. Certainly, Leone's contribution to the Western both elucidates and challenges André Bazin's famous assessment of the genre: 'The Western is

American cinema *par excellence*.' As such, his films are likely to have a particular appeal for movie buffs who, like the director, can recognise and enjoy the many references to other films. Certainly, *Once Upon a Time in the West* would, I imagine, make little sense to anyone who has never seen a Hollywood Western. As Oreste de Fornari concludes, perhaps somewhat cynically:

> 'I don't want state finance to be used up on *Once Upon a Time in the West*.'
>   'And I don't want it to be used up on *Partner*.'

Mino Argentieri's harangue, and Vinicio Marinucci's reply, at the Conference on Cinema held at Coppola Pineta Mare in October 1968, seems to sum up an old dispute. Not just art versus industry, hermeticism versus popularity, but state cinema versus American capital, and even Molotov Cocktails thrown at the Union Pacific. But the reality is more subtle than these slogans might suggest. Bertolucci collaborated on the story of *Once Upon a Time in the West*, and the cultural terrain of *both* films is not just Imperialist America, or the Vietnamese Revolution — about which Bertolucci's film has very little to say — but above all, the world of the Paris cinéphiles, with their never-ending search for minor classics, and with their avant-garde which was seeking to understand, and sabotage, the 'syntax' of these minor classics. Not for nothing did *Cahiers du Cinéma* eulogise both Leone's metaphysical pistoleros, and Bertolucci's psychoanalytical 'barricades' — and not for nothing did the *new cinema* reject both films out of hand. 1968, as Helmut Berger said in a Visconti film, was a very difficult year.

One thing is certain: *Once Upon a Time in the West* proved a very bad investment.

Spaghettis and Politics

A famous passage in *Insurgent Mexico* describes the reactions of American journalist John Reed while watching Pancho Villa receive a medal for devotion to the Revolution, at the splendid Governor's Palace in Chihuahua City, in March 1914:

Villa entered the aisle between the rigid lines of soldiers, walking a little pigeon-toed, in the fashion of a horseman, hands in his trouser pockets. He seemed slightly embarrassed, and grinned and nodded to a *compadre* here and there in the ranks. . . . Finally, pulling his moustache and looking very uncomfortable, he moved towards a gilded throne, with lions-paw arms, raised on a dais under a canopy of crimson velvet. He shook the arms violently to test the throne's dependability, then sat down. There followed six speeches extolling Villa's bravery on the field. Through it all, Villa slouched on the throne, his mouth hanging open, his little shrewd eyes playing around the room. Once or twice he yawned but for the most part seemed to be speculating with some intense interior amusement, like a small boy in church, what it was all about. . . . Finally, with an impressive gesture, an Artillery officer stepped forward with a small cardboard box. The officers applauded, the crowds cheered, the bands burst into a triumphant march.

Villa put out both hands eagerly. He could hardly wait to open the box and see what was inside. He held up the medal, scratched his head and, in a reverent silence, said clearly, 'This is a hell of a little thing to give a man for all that heroism you are talking about.' They waited for him to make a conventional address of acceptance. Puckering up his face, as he always did when he concentrated intensely, Villa leaned across the table in front of him and poured out in a voice so low that the people could hardly hear, 'There is no word to speak. All I can say

is my heart is all to you.' Then he sat down, spitting violently on the floor.

This passage seems to represent the *point d'appui* for most Hollywood films — good, bad or ugly — about Pancho Villa and the Mexican Revolution of 1911-19. In Jack Conway and Howard Hawks' *Viva Villa* (1934), Wallace Beery plays him as a scruffy, ruthless bandit with a heart of gold; in George Sherman's *The Treasure of Pancho Villa* (1955), Villa works with unscrupulous killers, bank robbers and gun-runners, but somehow (the fact is never explained) inspires the love that asks no question; in Buzz Kulik's *Villa Rides* (1969), he is randy and impulsive (there is a running gag about his many marriages), with a disregard for all types of red tape — and with a preference for followers like Rodolfo Fierro (Charles Bronson), who gets a kick out of executing 300 prisoners in one session, pausing only to lubricate a badly bruised trigger finger. In all these films, and many others besides, the image of the colourful 'primitive rebel' is set against that of a taciturn, detached American observer, who becomes increasingly (though sometimes reluctantly) loyal to the rebel as the story progresses. In *Viva Villa*, the American is supposed to be John Reed himself, and one of the central scenes of the film shows how uncomfortable the bandit feels at a banquet in the grand setting of the Presidential Palace: watched by all the dignatories, the dirty, unshaven Villa sits on an ornate desk and proceeds to take his boot off in order to massage his foot. In *The Treasure of Pancho Villa*, the American is a black-clad mercenary (Rory Calhoun) — armed with a prized machine-gun which he has christened 'La Cucaracha' — who robs banks and trains apparently on behalf of Villa, but in fact out of loyalty for his friend Gilbert Roland, and who is finally persuaded by a schoolteacher in sympathy with the Revolution (Shelley Winters) to donate all his treasure to the peasants' cause. In the final scene, the mercenary takes on a whole army of

200-1 (*Above and top right*) Italian and English publicity for *A Fistful of Dynamite* (1971; also known, in America, as *Duck, You Sucker*, and, in France, as *Once Upon a Time the Revolution*)

202-3 Juan (Rod Steiger), with his grotesque family, and Sean (James Coburn) with his motorcycle, in *A Fistful of Dynamite*. Leone's film can be read as a cynical commentary on the development of the 'political' Spaghetti Western in the late 1960s

Rurales single-handed, to prove his new point. In Richard Fleischer's *Bandido* (1956), the American is a cynical arms dealer (Robert Mitchum), an outsider who becomes increasingly impressed by the commitment of the revolutionaries. In James B. Clark's *Villa!* (1958), the American journalist is played, in characteristically wholesome style, by Brian Keith (while Villa himself is played by a real live Mexican — a unique occasion in Hollywood's history). In *The Wild Bunch*, the well-meaning chaos of the Revolution (represented by a brief appearance of the Villistas, and by the character of Angel, an idealist) is contrasted with the cool efficiency of Pike Bishop's gang: the American bunch are, however, sufficiently impressed by Angel's commitment to his local (colourful) peasant community to put aside for him a box of arms and ammunition (provided he sacrifices his cut of the proceeds). Before the final curtain, four of the Americans wipe out a large, faceless army of Northern Mexicans, partly to honour Angel's memory, partly because they do not like German armaments experts and partly because they want to go down fighting ('Why not?'). And in *Villa Rides* (co-scripted by Peckinpah), the American is a footloose aviator (Robert Mitchum again — the part seems to suit his image as an outsider without a cause) who teams up with Villa and Fierro: in one sequence, the illiterate bandit (Yul Brynner) asks the American to teach him how to fly a bi-plane with the words, 'Teach good . . .!' The Mexican needs the technical assistance, the American enjoys being asked.

Other adventure films dealing with revolution and bandit warfare in Mexico have also featured sophisticated American mercenaries, soldiers of fortune or 'observers' — modelled on the Gary Cooper character in *For Whom the Bell Tolls*, perhaps — whose function is to intervene (with their superior fire-power or expertise) when the going gets rough. In Aldrich's *Vera Cruz* (which, as we have seen, is set during an earlier period of Mexican history, when Juarez was mounting a republican rebellion against the emperor Maximilian), the standard conflict in the genre between the lure of the dollars and the (easy) attractions of commitment is represented, uncharacteristically, by *two* Americans — one (Burt Lancaster) an unscrupulous but lovable gunman, the other (Gary Cooper) a Southern gentleman. These two heroes are easily identifiable; the Juaristas, by contrast, appear in their hundreds, as an undifferentiated mass — their function being simply to help us decide which of the Gringos we like best. Of *The Magnificent Seven* (1960), only one of the seven turns out to be mercenary to the core — the rest offer their versatile services free of charge to the poor villagers who are being terrorised by a local warlord (Eli Wallach). 'You *stayed* . . . why?' *The Professionals* (in Richard Brooks' film, 1966) also realise that there is more to life than the almighty dollar, when they refuse to shoot it out with the Mexicans on behalf of their employer, an Eastern businessman: as Lee Marvin breaks the news of their change of heart, the railroad magnate can only say, 'You bastard . . . !' — to which Marvin casually replies, 'In my case an accident of birth, but you, sir, are a self-made man.' Again, the specialists are prepared to offer their services to the Mexicans, even if it means working at a loss or challenging their ethic of professionalism: the message may be more sympathetically presented than in *The Magnificent Seven*, but the 'hidden' theme of paternalism is as strong as ever. Andrew McLaglen's *The Undefeated* (1968) reverts to the *Vera Cruz* formula, by exploiting the notion that a Southern gentleman (Rock Hudson) might wish to fight against dictatorship in Mexico after the American Civil War: on this occasion, however, John Wayne tries to dissuade him from doing such a foolish thing (Wayne's own *The Alamo* (1960) had been one of the few films of this type in which neither cash *nor* sympathy with the Mexicans came into it — the prime motivation throughout was patriotism, expressed as the urge to kick the nasty greasers out of Texas). Don Siegel's *Two Mules for Sister Sara* (1970, written by Budd Boetticher) contrasts the cool efficiency of the mercenary (played by Clint Eastwood, 'a sparkle of all-consuming awareness in his eyes') with the well-intentioned, but amateurish commitment of the Juarista captain. Eastwood can even blow up a bridge when he's had too much to drink: it is clear that the Mexicans are incapable of doing it for themselves when sober (shortage of equipment being only part of the explanation).

In short, John Reed's famous description of the scene in Chihuahua City could quite easily have been slipped into most Hollywood accounts of revolution and bandit warfare in Mexico. The passage contains all the staple ingredients of the genre: the American 'outsider' watching Villa's behaviour from a distance, at the same time as being strangely impressed by the man's personal mag-

204-5 The changing face of Pancho Villa, Hollywood-style: Wallace Beery in the Howard Hawks/Jack Conway *Viva Villa* (1934), and Yul Brynner in Buzz Kulik's *Villa Rides* (1969)
206-7 (*Below*) John Wayne defends the lone star state in *The Alamo* (1960), armed with the legend of Davy Crockett, and his own manifesto

"The Alamo" had to be made into a motion picture. It has the raw and tender stuff of immortality, peopled by hard-living, hard-loving men whose women matched them in creating a pattern of freedom and liberty.

"The Alamo" is a story that happened—only 125 years ago, on March 6, 1836. It is the story of 185 men joined together in an immortal pact to give their lives that the spark of freedom might blaze into a roaring flame. It is the story of how they died to the last man, putting up an unbelievably gallant fight against an overwhelming army; and of the priceless legacy they left us.

Their crumbling little fortress fallen, strewn with their own corpses and 1,700 of the enemy, these martyrs snatched victory out of disaster when 46 days later General Sam Houston vanquished the dictator Santa Anna at San Jacinto and won the independence of Texas.

However, this is not a story that belongs only to Texas; it was filmed to convey to Americans and people everywhere a sense of the debt they owe to all men who have died fighting for freedom.

Some very astute people in our business who have seen this film prophesy that "The Alamo" will outgross any other motion picture. This is very important to me, naturally, since it was made for commercial reasons, but I am desirous that something more than profits will result from "The Alamo." I hope that the battle fought there will remind people today that the price of liberty and freedom is not cheap.

Making this picture has given me great satisfaction because, paraphrasing Crockett, it gave me the privilege "of feeling useful in this old world." If there is anything better than that, I don't know what it is.

John Wayne

208-11 Missionaries for the gospel according to Monroe: *The Magnificent Seven* (1960) (*top left*); *The Wild Bunch* (1969) (*top right and above*); and *The Professionals* (1966) (*left*)

netism; the contrast between the revolutionary bureaucracy (often represented in the movies by a colourful gang of comic-opera generals, but in Kazan's thematically isolated *Viva Zapata*, 1952, represented instead by 'the Communist mentality' in the shape of Joseph Wiseman clutching a typewriter, 'the sword of the word') and the grass-roots 'primitive rebel'; the issues of the Revolution symbolised by the *personalities* of the main protagonists; 'exotic' local colour, the main function of which is to provide a series of spectacular backdrops; and so on. By emphasising this aspect of *Insurgent Mexico* to the exclusion of all others (Reed's own position *vis-à-vis* the Revolution, for example), the directors and writers of these 'Mexican' adventures may have been attempting to create a generic figure (the 'outsider') with whom audiences could identify, or implicitly stressing the role of 'invisible' dollar imperialism during the period when the movies were released — either way, it came over as if a series of action-packed films about the Soviet Revolution were telling the story of an American journalist's developing friendship with one of the 'army of the unfed' (who is tempted to join the Red Army) during the civil war of 1918, *and* paying lip service to the notion that the events described (perhaps a train robbery, perhaps the blowing up of a palace) really 'shook the world'. Even in the late 1960s, when the number of Hollywood adventure films set in Northern Mexico significantly increased (partly as a result of the fortunes of some Spaghettis on the American market), the narratives of the most successful ones seldom made explicit critical reference to the parallel with contemporary events (for example, in South East Asia): instead scriptwriters spiced the traditional formula with extra ingredients such as a lot of blood (after all, both portable machine-guns and barbed wire had been invented by 1911) and new-look stars with new-look images (Clint Eastwood or Charles Bronson as opposed to Robert Mitchum or Rory Calhoun). It was a case of 'chili con carnage', in Jenni Calder's phrase. The action set-pieces — a train robbery (*The Wild Bunch*), the destruction of a bridge (*Two Mules*), a cavalry battle (*Villa Rides*) — remained distinctively 'Western' in character. Mexico simply provided colourful exteriors, cheap extras and a fashionably 'Third World' atmosphere — it had become ideologically unsound to slaughter Red Indians, so now it was the turn of Mexicans, in their hundreds. The Conway and Hawks *Viva Villa* had been criticised,

on first release, in *Cinema Quarterly Review*, for conceiving 'the Mexican fight for independence on the lines of a Western with all the attendant plot circumstances we know so well. ... The only way they could avoid the great social issues involved was to convert the revolution into cowboy fights and to concentrate on personalities.' Kazan's *Viva Zapata* had also been criticised, by the *New Yorker*, for being simply 'an old-fashioned Western'. The criticism could be applied, with more solid foundation, to all the 'Mexican' Westerns produced by Hollywood in the late 1960s which, implicitly or explicitly, made American intervention the excuse for a lot of target-practice with the latest line in firearms. The American gunmen, mercenaries, soldiers of fortune or journalists, the hawks who flew through the open door from Hollywood to Mexico all seem to have borne a distinct family resemblance to Dorfman and Mattelart's Donald Duck — even if they *were* sometimes converted into doves. First of all, in their perception of 'the picture-postcard Mexico: mules, siestas, cactuses, huge sombreros, ponchos, serenades, machismo and Indians from ancient civilisations. The country is defined primarily in terms of this grotesque folklore. ... This is Mexico recognisable by its commonplace exotic identity labels, not the real Mexico with all its problems.' The 'dislocated prejudices proclaimed by tourist-posters' provided the context for their missionary activities, their 'invisible imperialism' — the second resemblance to Unca Donald: 'The good foreigners, under their ethical cloak, win with the natives' confidence, the right to decide the proper distribution of wealth in the land. The villains, coarse, vulgar, repulsive, out-and-out thieves, are there purely to reveal the ducks as defenders of justice, law, and food for the hungry, and to serve as a whitewash for any further action. Defending the only thing that the noble savage can use (their food), the lack of which would result in their death (or rebellion, either of which would violate their image of infantile innocence), the big-city folk establish themselves as the spokesman of these submerged and voiceless peoples. ... In order to assure the redemptive powers of present-day imperialism, it is only necessary to measure it against old-style colonialism and robbery.' The third resemblance concerns the contrast in the comics between city and country — a contrast which, according to Dorfman and Mattelart, tells us a lot about the intended audience for the comics: 'while the city-folk are intelligent, calculating, crafty and superior; the Third Worldlings are candid, foolish, irrational, disorganised and gullible (like Cowboys and Indians)'. The heroes tend to have the city virtues, the villains tend to be brutal or militaristic (this displaces any charges of overt imperialism against the heroes), and the victims tend to be infantile, unable to look after themselves, and living in a state of mindless pastoralism: if stories about Turner's frontier no longer pulled in the paying customers, then perhaps stories about the open door, or reciprocity, would do the trick. In this way, the Mexican Revolution Hollywood-style (complete with 'authentic' Westerners) came to be about goodies and baddies we could all recognise — in much the same way as the implications of President Polk's annexation of California from the Mexicans had been displaced in James Cruze's film about Sutter and the Russian countess.

Only two Hollywood movies had really attempted to come to grips with the issues raised by the Mexican Revolution — and of these, one (Eisenstein's *Que Viva Mexico*, 1931-2) was shelved, while the other (Kazan and Steinbeck's *Viva Zapata*, 1952) eventually turned into an anti-Communist polemic. The circumstances in which *Que Viva Mexico* was planned, and partly shot, have been fully covered elsewhere. The fourth 'novel' of Eisenstein's scenario (a novel which was never filmed) describes an incident in the Revolution from the point of view of a *soldadera*, one of the soldiers' female camp-followers ('a machine-gun ribbon hanging across her shoulder, a big sack containing household utensils weighing heavily on her back'): although the story is sentimental and melodramatic (the girl gives birth to a child, loses her man in the Revolution, and finds another protector in time for the fade-out), the 'novel' was to end on a musical tableau representing the triumph of revolution against the forces of dictatorship, a tableau which only makes full sense in the context of the other 'novels' — the second of which deals with the expropriation of peasant land under the Porfiriato.

'The brass band discovers a new source of strength that enables it to play *Adelita* stoutly, solemnly and triumphantly. Like peals of thunder roll the triumphant shouts above the heads of the soldiers. The armies are fraternizing. One might decipher on the banner — the last word of its device. Towards Revolution. Towards a New Life ... says the voice of the author. Towards a New Life! ...'

Kazan's *Viva Zapata* is also structured around a series of sentimental and melodramatic incidents — Zapata's wedding, Zapata's quarrel with his brother Eufemio, his relationship with the inhuman bureaucrat Fernando, his abdication of power ('I'm going home') — none of which had been given prominence in Steinbeck's main source, Edgcumb Pinchon's fictionalised *Zapata the Unconquerable* (1941): but the main theme of the screenplay, the distinction between a harmless rebel (a 'man of individual conscience', in Kazan's words) and a harmful revolutionary (who can say 'I'm a friend to no one — to nothing except logic. This is a time for killing!') locates the film firmly within the consensus of political opinion in early-1950s America. In order to make Zapata seem more like a 'man of individual conscience' (Actors' Studio variety), Steinbeck presents him as an illiterate peasant on a white horse (he was, in fact, a literate tenant-farmer who rode a sorrel) and sets him against a 'Communist' intellectual (Fernando), a semi-alcoholic brother (Eufemio), and a sincere liberal politician (Madero); as a matter of historical fact, however, intellectuals played little part in framing Zapatista policy, Eufemio was not a heavy drinker at that time, and Madero betrayed Zapata on several occasions. (John Womack is clear on all these points). The central moment of the film — Zapata's abdication of power — was also made more 'nakedly dramatic' than could ever have been the case. This should not, of course, matter very much — were it not for Steinbeck and Kazan's almost exclusively anecdotal approach to the issues of the Mexican Revolution, an approach which looks as though it has significance beyond the story in question, and were it not for the insistence of both artists that they did not in any significant way falsify the historical record. (Eventually, Kazan did admit, 'I thought John's angle had great value for *our thinking today*, and I was proud to direct it'). As Peter Biskind concludes: 'revolution had occurred a long time ago in backward peasant societies like Mexico, and it could with safety be exhumed and examined for lessons applicable to the present'. There was no American character, of the John Reed type, with whom audiences could identify: but the director's own point of view ('our thinking today') more than made up for his absence. In *Viva Zapata*, Pablo (the spokesman of the peasant revolution) reminds us that 'up there (in the USA) they are a democracy'; even Fernando has a grudging admiration for the country where 'the Government governs, but with the consent of the people'. It is strange to hear this from Fernando, since to some extent he represents a *reversal* of the role usually given to the American 'outsider': he is cool and efficient (despising all those who would make revolution with silk gloves), but he is also Mexican and a representative of 'the Communist mentality', both of which make him especially dangerous. This presentation of Fernando, a fictional character, does, however, ensure that we identify with Zapata and his personal problems.

Lester Cole, later to be one of the Hollywood Ten, was asked by MGM to adapt Pinchon's book about Zapata in 1947, well before Steinbeck and Kazan took over the project. In 1975, he recalled what happened to his script:

> After perhaps three months work on the treatment, the producer submitted it to Eddie Mannix, the general manager of the studio, and he was horrified. 'Get rid of this fuckin' script,' he said, 'this bastard Zapata's a goddam commie revolutionary!' But the producer would not give up, and together we went to Mexico and sought help from the government. They were so pleased with the script's portrayal of Zapata they offered MGM fifty percent of the costs of the film if the studio would make the film as written! They expected nothing in return! When the producer brought this news back to Mannix (the offer of over a million and a half dollars in services gratis), he thought for a moment and said, 'A million and a half! How can we lose?' and he added to justify his decision, 'What the hell, Jesus Christ is called a revolutionary sometimes, ain't he?' So it was all ready to go when the Un-American Activities Committee handed me a subpoena. This identification of Cole the revolutionary and Zapata scared MGM and they quickly unloaded the script to 20th Century Fox, and gave it to Elia Kazan to direct. . . . Mexico was so angry that . . . they wouldn't let him come into the country to shoot the picture.

(Shortly after the film was released, Kazan explained the reaction of the Mexican film industry to his treatment of the life of their 'national hero' with equal simplicity: 'John said, "I smell the party line." I smelled it too.')

In the light of both Lester Cole's and Elia Kazan's reminiscences about the circumstances in which *Zapata* was made (which differ on every single point of detail), it is worth looking at Zapata's own view of what the Revolution is all about, in a screenplay which is freely adapted from the 'folkways' and songs of the Morelos peasants 'by a wandering poet named John Steinbeck':

> Our cause was Land — not a thought, but corn-planted earth to feed the families. And Liberty — not a word, but a man sitting safely in front of his house in the evening. And Peace — not a dream, but a time of rest and kindness. The question beats in my head. Can a good thing come from a bad act? Can peace come from so much killing? Can kindness finally come from so much violence . . .?

When Zapata reaches a position of power, he realises that he must either renounce this power or renounce his pre-political attitude towards the Revolution. But, as incarnated by Marlon Brando, he has a further problem: at the very moment when he is telling the peasants that they are *all* leaders ('There's no leader but yourselves'), we see a group of well-scrubbed extras looking up, in awe, at the superstar. In other words, Zapata would like to be a Cold War liberal but since he is played by Brando he is almost tempted, momentarily, to become a genuine social revolutionary. The extent of his subversive activity — as for so many bandits in the traditional Western — is to cut through some barbed wire.

So, although there is no John Reed figure, the Mexican Revolution was redefined in *Viva Zapata* to emphasise precisely those issues which could be related most closely to the concerns of the American cinema-going public of 1952: families, homes, peace and quiet (as if the peasants were in a position to relax in front of their houses in the evening!); a dislike of bureaucracy in public life, and a proud fidelity towards one's wife and children in private life (this last represents the most extraordinary of all Steinbeck's inventions — Zapata continued to father bastards all over the place). Again uncharacteristically for the genre, the spectacle of Mexico was played down in Kazan's film — the horses and the armoured cars, the machetes and the machine-guns, the deserts and the barbed wire, the *hacendados* in their splendid charro costumes, the comic-opera generals, the fiestas, with guitars, fireworks and beautiful peasants dancing in the village square, all these 'exotic' backgrounds which Hollywood had traditionally exploited to the full were, it seems, not important to either Steinbeck or Kazan. This, at least, sets them apart from the other contributors to the genre I have been discussing, and shows the *New Yorker* review to have been a little unjust. To expect some analysis of (or even reference to) the wider causes of the Revolution as well — the accumulation of racial, social and economic discontents under the dictatorship of Diaz, the interests of classes as well as individuals — would, of course, be asking far too much.

Sergio Leone has said of his post-Western *Duck, You Sucker*, 'the Mexican Revolution in the film is only a symbol and not *the* Mexican Revolution, only interesting in this context because of its fame and its relationship with cinema. Its a real myth. . . . To avoid misunderstandings, I rejected the romance of the sombrero, preferring to deal with the theme of friendship which is so dear to me.' As a European looking at another American genre, Leone was evidently attempting once again to make rhetorical use of material from earlier Hollywood films, in order to revitalise the tired clichés of the genre by appropriating and 'transcribing' them. As we have seen, two crucial aspects of the particular cinematic 'myth' to which he refers were (1) the relationship between an 'outsider' and a 'primitive rebel', and (2) the exotic 'romance of the sombrero'. Obviously the treatment of the 'outsider' was likely to be very different if the film was not being pitched exclusively at an American audience — and if the central character was an Italian/Spanish/Mexican peasant. In Leone's case, this 'outsider' is not a soft-hearted American mercenary but an Irish Catholic who has already experienced another form of revolution. And the treatment of the Mexican Revolution was also likely to differ significantly in the hands of an Italian: John Steinbeck, writing in 1963 about the ways in which contemporary parallels with the Mexican Revolution had been misunderstood when *Zapata* was first shown in America, added that 'in Europe, where people knew about revolutions, there were not these problems'. In the event, Leone's treatment of this 'symbol' is far more cynical than had been the case in any of the 'Villa' films which constituted the bases of this genre. Given his concerns, Leone was more likely to 'transcribe' these popular adventure films than the more 'difficult' works by Eisenstein or Kazan; by the same token, he was more likely to be interested in Villa than Zapata: but the eventual commitment of the 'outsider' to a cause, one of the crucial components in

the 'Villa' formula, Hollywood-style, would have been very out of place in Leone's 'fatalistic, pessimistic' interpretation of the Revolution which Hollywood had pillaged, the Revolution by means of which Hollywood had sought to justify itself. 'I chose to oppose an intellectual, who has experienced a revolution in Ireland, with a naive Mexican. . . . You have two men: one naive and one intellectual (self-centred as intellectuals too often are in the face of the naive). From there, the film becomes the story of Pygmalion reversed. The simple one teaches the intellectual a lesson. Nature gains the upper hand and finally the intellectual throws away his book of Bakunin's writings. You suspect damn well that this gesture is a symbolic reference to everything my generation has been told in the way of promises. We have waited, but we are still waiting! I have the film say, in effect, "Revolution means confusion".' In short, the relationship between outsider and rebel was to be redefined from an entirely 'alien' perspective — a characteristic rejection of the politics of the American genre, at the same time as a utilisation of its aesthetic (a distinction which can, in practice, give rise to all sorts of ambiguities). Since Leone was also keen to reject 'the romance of the sombrero' (the other crucial component in the 'Villa' formula), and since most of the 'codes' in the genre were derived from the Hollywood Western anyway, the 'symbol' he was attempting to transcribe turned out to be a fairly uninteresting one. (Leone did spend much of his multi-national budget on what he calls 'the spectacular setting of a civil war' — for which he was strongly criticised by left-wing critics in Italy — but it was all a far cry from the 'romance' of the Cisco Kid and Pancho. The stock set-pieces were carefully presented with the usual emphasis on 'décors and details' — several firing squads, a bridge demolition sequence involving an antique armoured car and a lot of dynamite, a head-on collision between *two* locomotives travelling at full speed — all of which, according to some Italian critics, tended to distract attention from whatever interest there might have been in the relationship between the two protagonists. But the main purpose of these set-pieces, unlike the equivalents in Hollywood Westerns, seems to have been simply to contribute to the prevailing atmosphere of 'confusion'.)

More interesting was the Italian sub-genre which had emerged in the years before 1971, in the form of the political Spaghetti Western. As we have seen,

212 (*Above*) A Mexican bandit tries to make
coherent criticisms of 'the communist mentality':
Marlon Brando in Elia Kazan's *Viva Zapata* (1952)

213-14 (*Above and below*) The brutality of
Porfirio Diaz' dictatorship, and the celebration
of a modern 'death day': 'novels' from
Eisenstein's unfinished *Que Viva Mexico* (1931-2)

5-18 (*Above and below*) Frantz Fanon, Spaghetti-
~~le~~. Lou Castel (as the Gringo agent) and Gian
~~aria~~ Volonté (as the Mexican bandit/revolutionary)
~~n~~ Damiano Damiani's *A Bullet for the General*
~~(1~~966)

the cynicism of *Duck, You Sucker* sets the film apart from previous Italian accounts of the Mexican Revolution — indeed, it can be read as a belated attack on the parochialism of the 'populist' Western (the third variant of our 'Italian plot'). Leone recalls that 'it was difficult to say "Revolution means confusion" — so difficult, in fact, that the Italian partners rejected my title in Italy. I had to change *Once Upon a Time, the Revolution* to *Giù la Testa*, which means, in Italian, "duck", but also "get out of the way", so that the title takes on a very precise social connotation.' So in this film, as in *Once Upon a Time in the West* (though for different reasons), Leone was isolating himself from the direction that the Spaghetti Western had taken — and if *Duck, You Sucker* seems to lack the coherence of his previous two films, it may be because Leone was attempting to comment on a Hollywood genre *and* a Cinecittà critique both at the same time. The result, another oppositional film which can be interpreted at many levels, looked suspiciously reactionary in the context of what had been happening at Cinecittà since Clint Eastwood days.

In the same year as *Giù la Testa* was made, Pierre Baudry noted in *Cahiers du Cinéma* that certain contributors to the Italian Western genre had for some time been introducing a type of 'discourse on revolution' from within the main currents of the genre:

> We know the Italian Westerns are almost without exception built around the principle of variations (epitomised by the names of the characters, the décors, the faces, the recurring motifs in scenarios) on a schema which distributes fixed symbolic-fictional roles among groups of characters; what one might call the first phase of the Italian Western usually represented the following distribution: Gringo/Mexican bandits/ Mexican victims (Type A). But it seems that more recently, this schema has been modified by the addition of an extra set of roles — the 'Mexican Revolutionaries'. Now the distribution looks more like: Gringo/Mexican revolutionaries/ Mexican counter-revolutionaries (/victims) (Type B). This development from within the structure of the genre points to a desire on the part of certain Italian film-makers to conjugate commercial considerations with progressivism.

Baudry goes on to analyse the ambiguities inherent in such a 'conjugation': popular, formula cinema,

because it is genre cinema, and thus has the illusion of autonomy, usually tries hard to escape from the region of *precise* ideologies (being by nature a kind of 'pure spectacle', it can be in some sense *outside* the realms of ideology, or, on the other hand, it can be included in the undifferentiated mass of 'Opiates for the People'). . . . In the transition from Type A to Type B of the Italian Western, Mexico is still a metaphor for Italy, but in Type B this is less because 'Mexico' makes possible the use of a 'latin folklore' in these films, than because this 'folklore' can *hide* its sphere of influence under the illusion of autonomy. When the Gringo abandons his mercenary or pecuniary aims, and 'puts himself beside' the revolutionaries, he is showing how bourgeois discourse can no longer deny the existence of revolutionary discourse; it is thus no longer a question of ignoring revolutionary discourse, or even of overtly criticising it, but of producing a double, a *faux-semblant* which, by 'miming' it, destroys it. This process can be described as the appropriation by one ideology of the *terms* of a contradictory ideology. . . . In a film like Corbucci's *Compañeros*, there is much talk of revolutionary ideals, but only at the level of a mention of their existence . . . for the 'detached' hero, the outsider, the Gringo, the revolution is there for enjoyment.

In other words, the appearance of a 'discourse on revolution' from *within* a popular genre of the moment is seen (from a Marxist, *Cahiers* perspective) as a sinister development — a process of anaesthetising genuine revolutionary commitment, by subsuming that commitment into a type of cinema which relies on set formulae. From this point of view, Baudry's Type B is not really very different from his Type A: and Baudry interprets the phenomenon specifically in terms of what he sees as the *authoritarian* relationship between Cinecittà producers and *Italian* society. A colonial ideology is being used to 'criticise' a colonial reality — a dangerous game to play — and, in the process, all we get is a repetition of nineteenth-century stereotypes (the dignified poor versus the immoral rich).

Jean-Luc Godard's film *Wind from the East* (which was released the year before Baudry's article), adopted a similar position *vis-à-vis* the use of popular genres to put over 'revolutionary' ideas. *Wind from the East* was first planned just after the 'events of May 1968' in Paris: in its original conception, the film was to be a Western in colour, scripted by Daniel Cohn-Bendit, produced by an Italian, Gianni Barcelloni, shot in the countryside near *Cinecittà* ('near Dodge City'), and starring Gian Maria Volonté (of *Fistful of Dollars* fame). Cohn-Bendit has described what *he* thought the film was going to be about:

> My idea was to make a political Western, a left-wing Western. I had in mind a story about miners on strike, who fight against their 'masters', about the boss with his gang of thugs who attacks the workers, the workers who take over the mine, and so on. At one point, there was to have been a duel. In Rome, we tried to make this film, but it did not work out at all. Godard had his own ideas . . . the film never got off the ground. He had been told that we wanted to make a Western, but I think there must have been some misunderstanding about every word we said . . .

By the time Cohn-Bendit dropped out of the proceedings, Godard's express intention was to engage in a far less 'populist' activity, to 'draw parallels between the repressiveness of traditional political structures and the repressiveness of traditional film structures; particularly those of the Western'. The finished film was, according to Godard, nothing less than an all-out attack on 'the bourgeois concept of representation'. In it, the relationship between the standard film Western and its audience is used to symbolise the ways in which the bourgeois cinema manipulates the desires and emotional inadequacies of its *clientele* while deliberately ignoring their critical intelligence. This manipulation is seen by Godard to constitute a political act on the part of producers and distributors (and, further, a political act, of an unconscious kind, on the part of the audience which 'shares' the experience). Thus popular Westerns which look as though they are about revolution are in fact 'smokescreens' which divert attention from any serious critique of the status quo. Godard uses one sequence in particular in *Wind from the East* to illustrate this idea. An American cavalry officer (Gian Maria Volonté) — whom we have seen taking up guard duty, at the beginning of the film — is beating up a girl revolutionary (Anne

Wiazemsky). First we briefly see the officer trying to strangle the girl, while some red liquid is thrown from off-screen, staining both the girl and the officer. Later on, we see the same scene, expressed through extreme close-ups of the two characters' faces (without any tomato ketchup). (According to Peter Brooker, in *Monthly Film Bulletin*, January 1972, these sequences of 'stock Western characters acting out skeletal Western scenes' are 'rife with latent imperialism'.) Later still, we are shown the same cavalry officer beating up some political prisoners, from horseback, and the scene is filmed in a stylised way which is intended to draw attention to the *form* which such a scene would normally take, if the director wanted the audience to consider the scene as 'realistic', in other words, if he wanted the audience to identify emotionally with the oppressed (through identification with the 'realistic' plight of the prisoners). We have already seen the 'political prisoners', and the 'Indians', applying their make-up. Another section of *Wind from the East* is devoted to a critical (and auto-critical) survey of the history of revolutionary cinema: in this survey, Godard points out that Eisenstein (whose style was derived from D.W. Griffith) found it all too easy to slot into the Hollywood system, when he was commissioned to make a 'bourgeois' film about the Mexican Revolution. The (rather laboured) point of all this seems to be that a genuine *critical* cinema must evolve a form which does not confirm the audience's expectations, which keeps their critical intelligence on the *qui vive*, and which does not use the standard techniques of bourgeois cinema to instil an emotional identification with the 'heroes' (or an emotional hatred of the villains): the device must always be explicitly 'laid bare'. 'The bourgeois concept of representation', on the other hand, because it encourages the view that what is happening on the screen is a 'heightened' version of reality, and because it does not allow the audience to be *distanced* from the events depicted, relies on a mindless acceptance of its own techniques and 'codes'. It is part of an *authoritarian* relationship between film and audience. Thus, applying the criteria of *Wind from the East* to Baudry's critique of the Italian Western, it is impossible for popular genres to make a truly revolutionary statement (which would imply participation on the part of the audience), since the viewers (expecting Type A, but getting Type B, which in fact is only a variant on Type A, however different it looks) have all sorts of preconceptions about the style and content of the formula before the curtain even rises (preconceptions which film-makers may try to transcend, but because they are working from within a fairly rigid set of commercial conventions, they cannot).

James Roy MacBean, in his Marxian analysis of the films of Godard (*Film and Revolution*, 1975) singles out the series of popular political films written by Franco Solinas as examples of the fallacious application of this 'bourgeois concept of representation' to the cinema of revolution: as we shall see, Solinas was to play an important part in the development of the political Spaghetti Western (Baudry's Type B), so MacBean's comments are of some interest:

> These films are useful in stirring up emotional support and sympathy for the revolutionary cause, as well as in stirring up a healthy sense of revolutionary outrage at the paramilitary machinations the ruling class uses to maintain its power and privileges. But *The Battle of Algiers*, *Queimada* and *State of Siege* (to name only the best of such films) do not go very much beyond the emotional level; and we have seen from Leni Riefenstahl's *Triumph of the Will* just how frighteningly easy it is to use the emotional power of the cinema to arouse masses of people to support even the most unjust and ignominious causes. If revolution is to be truly liberating, it must be much more than just the emotional revenge of the oppressed. And if a film-maker's commitment to revolutionary liberation is more than just an emotional identification with the oppressed, then his cinematic practice must address itself to the viewer in a way that calls forth *all* his human faculties, rational and emotional, instead of relying on the emotional manipulation of the viewer's tendency to *identify* with the characters on the screen.

Jean-Luc Godard expressed similar views, in an interview of April 1970. Films like *Z* or *Battle of Algiers* could, he conceded, 'help certain people in a certain way', but he doubted it: 'there is nothing but feelings, an opposition of feelings, but not a dialectic. It's metaphysical, not dialectical. . . . A film like *Z* is an objective ally of Hollywood.' Jean-Pierre Gorin, Godard's comrade, added: 'A film like *Z* can be helpful in a very precise circumstance: if

you don't know *anything* about Greece, maybe you learn that somebody was murdered whose name was Lambrakis. But the film is a flop unless you have a political friend sitting by your side, explaining to you what the real situation was in Greece, and why the colonels took power. The film explains nothing about the Greek situation.' Where *Z*, or the *Battle of Algiers* went wrong, Godard continued, was in attempting to deal with political issues from within a Hollywood frame of reference: 'it is necessary to stop making movies on politics, to stop making political movies, and to begin making political movies *politically*. It means maybe taking a gun one day, and the next day going back to a pen or the camera.' 'Hollywood is more powerful than ever before: they don't even need to make movies themselves anymore, they have found slaves everywhere to make the movies they want. In Yugoslavia, Spain — everywhere. You know, the only tank we could find in Czechoslovakia was a United Artists tank, from a Russian-American co-production!' (Presumably, for Godard, Italian Westerns would epitomise this process.) Gorin added that 'many political film makers think about audiences the same way Hollywood thinks about audiences. They may go to the masses, but they don't see that the point is to go to the masses *politically*. . . . You can't show your film to more than a few people who are involved in the same political process as you, because political films are made to be shown politically.' A film, concluded Gorin, 'is no more than a leaflet, and a leaflet is just shown to the people it's addressed to'.

When Bernardo Bertolucci (having contributed to *Once Upon a Time in the West*) was given the chance — and the multi-national budget — to express his ideas about the development of Italian rural communism through the medium of a blockbusting historical epic, *1900*, he found himself arguing with the Italian Left in precisely the terms outlined above. The main criticism was that the two main characters — a landowner and a peasant labourer — had been used to symbolise the dialectic at the heart of the film: this was considered too 'sentimental', thus revisionist. In a recent reply, Bertolucci has criticised much of the political Italian and French cinema of the late 1960s (his own films included), for being *too* concerned about 'experiments with the form and style of cinema'. 'This was a non-communication model . . . a cinema for the elite': it may have been 'right for the late 1960s', but circumstances have changed a lot since then. What emerged from this movement, he says, was a kind of Brechtian cinema (constantly commenting on its own form, attempting to keep the audience at arm's length) and, ultimately, a type of Marxism which had no dialectic with the audience: 'I ended up talking to myself . . .' His answer to the accusation of manipulating the viewers' emotions, by using lyrical photography, character stereotypes (even sex-role stereotypes), and the conventions of opera in his *1900*, has consistently been that political cinema *must* find some point of contact with popular cinema, if it is to achieve anything more than simply preaching to the converted. 'I no longer believe, as many did in 1968, that the camera can be used as a machine-gun': even in Brechtian cinema, there is a place for 'emotions as well as ideas'.

Sergio Leone (who is clearly less committed to the idea of political cinema than Bertolucci and who attempted to *satirise* political Spaghettis in *Duck, You Sucker*) nevertheless holds an analogous position *vis-à-vis* popular cinema. We have seen how he refuses to label his films politically in a formal sense (especially the 'Dollars' trilogy), and how he does not wish to be cast in the role of *magister* in political matters. But he has strong views about what he calls the 'sad paradox' on which sixties political cinema was based:

> I think that Mister Chaplin did more for socialism forty years ago than Togliatti has done here in Italy. My friend Francesco Rosi makes only political films. He has a thousand spectators who come to see his films, talk about them, and that's all. These spectators are already aware of the problem. I believe, on the other hand, that we have to inject today's political problems into the spectacular entertainments of the people. . . . Politics no longer make any sense in Italy! That's why I make the films I do. We believed in mankind, and mankind has let us down. Of course, the situation is the same in other countries, but somehow we are the most unlucky. Our hypocrisy and our 'politics of compromise' have pitched us into a crisis. As intellectuals, we have resigned ourselves, tired of the battle. What else can we think of but death? After twenty years of Fascism, we are going to have to face it again. Isn't that the most unbelievable thing in the world? We are the only country in the world to live this absurdity. They

are going to win and we act like the man who cuts off his own balls to punish his wife. Its the purest madness! Given this situation, I am trying to create fables, epics. Our political cinema, after all, is too national; its meaning can only be appreciated in Italy. That doesn't interest me as much.

Hence his reaction against the *parochialism* of the more radical Spaghetti Westerns.

Pierre Baudry's 'Type B' of the Italian Western (represented by his schema Gringo/Mexican revolutionaries/Mexican counter-revolutionaries (/victims)) is best exemplified by works of Damiano Damiani (*A Bullet for the General*, 1966), Sergio Sollima (*The Big Gundown*, 1966; *Face to Face*, 1967) and Sergio Corbucci (*A Professional Gun*, 1968; *Compañeros*, 1970). These films (the best of the political or 'populist' Spaghetti Westerns) are all concerned with the relationship between an 'outsider' (in Corbucci's case a Pole or a Swede, in the others an American) and a bandit who is also involved in some revolutionary activity. (There were strong precedents for this, as we have seen.) They are all set either in Mexico or on the frontier. The 'outsider' is usually a mercenary, a contract killer (or, in the case of Sollima's films, a sheriff and a college professor respectively), the bandit/rebel invariably an energetic, but illiterate Mexican peasant (played by Tomas Milian, a popular Cuban actor, Tony Musante or Gian Maria Volonté). The humour in this relationship characteristically derives from the contrast of acting styles (and attitudes to 'style' in general) between the 'Gringo' (who is cool and laconic, even when played by an Italian such as Franco Nero) and the 'peon' (who is noisy and flamboyant): musical motifs (in four of the five cases supplied by Ennio Morricone) tend to reinforce this contrast, and thus add to the humour. The 'outsider' teams up with the bandit/rebel for his own purposes, offers him technical assistance (guns, expertise), helps in the revolutionary struggle in some way, then has to make one of three decisions: to abandon his mercenary trade and throw in his lot with the Revolution (*Compañeros*); to abandon the Revolution, his real aim (which he has managed to hide from the bandit/rebel throughout the film) achieved (*A Bullet for the General*); or to split with the bandit/rebel, while retaining a respect for his revolutionary commitment (*A Professional Gun*; *The Big Gundown*). The development of the relationship between the 'outsider' and the bandit/rebel (and thus of the story) is usually similar to the equivalent scenes involving Clint Eastwood and Eli Wallach in *The Good, the Bad and the Ugly* — it is a cat-and-mouse relationship, and this provides the opportunity for a series of apparently self-contained, picaresque adventures. Unlike the many derivatives of *A Fistful of Dollars*, in which all the focus of attention is on the self-sufficient hero and his problems (films with *titles* which almost invariably relate less to the story than to the central character — 'My Name Is . . .', 'They call me . . .' Django, Sabata, Sartana, Ringo, Gringo, '. . . Is Still My Name', and so on), the films in Baudry's 'Type B' make their political points through the various ways in which this relationship is presented — specifically, through the revolutionary *strategies* this relationship comes to symbolise.

Sollima, Damiani and Volonté have all stressed, in interviews, that the Westerns in this sub-genre were intended to be read as parables about the relations between the Third World (represented by 'Mexico') and the capitalist countries of the West (represented by 'the outsider'): the unstable relationship between bandit/rebel and 'Gringo' was apparently meant to illustrate 'the difficulty of sustaining a dialogue between the Third World and the industrial world'; the 'outsider' was meant to 'reveal the pretensions of Euro-American culture to represent the culture of the whole world'; and the treatment of the Revolution was meant to 'recall the anti-colonial struggles of the peoples of Latin America, of Vietnam, and of minorities within the United States'. These Westerns were also, apparently, intended to present a *critique* of Hollywood versions of the Mexican Revolution — redefining the 'codes' of Hollywood as part of that critique. Whether or not these film-makers succeeded in their stated aims (and Baudry, for example, would claim that such a 'conjugation of commercial considerations with progressivism' was doomed from the outset, however explicit the political intentions), certain recurring themes of a political kind (often derived from the work of Frantz Fanon — especially if the screenplays have anything to do with Franco Solinas) *are* apparent in the 'Type'. Oreste de Fornari reckons that, despite this obvious presentation of Fanonist themes, 'the confrontation between the two main characters seldom develops into a conflict of interests. Most of the film-makers were content to note from time to time that the

heart is more human than the robot.' He goes on:

> The mythology of the Mexican Revolution provided a good context for transplanting a progressive ideology into a plebeian genre: this mythology, however, was a fixed module which subordinated the triumph of the Revolution to the difficult comradeship between Anglo-Saxon technology and Latin sentiment. . . .
> Fortunately, in some of the Italian Westerns, the terms of this alliance between brain and brawn were far from obvious. . . . Born with the intention of breaking the bread of socialism on the plate of the humble, the Italian 'populist' Western eventually fulfilled the opposite and complementary function of providing the blueprint for more ambitious experiments, such as those by Pontecorvo. . . . In Italian cinema, many directors are well versed in the art of describing the *strategy* of revolution — some of them in hagiographic terms, some by investigating the psychology of the militant — but nearly all of them neglect to explain the reasons for the Revolutions, or even the issues that need to be taken into account. And the public prefers not to pay any attention to these issues, naturally. The danger is that these films, like *Allonsonfan* and *Novecento*, will trivialise matters.

Whatever the terms of the Italian and French critical debate on these Westerns, the frequent appearance of Fanonist themes clearly locates them in a very different tradition to the most famous Hollywood treatments of the same 'fixed module' — despite the many resemblances. As we have seen, the treatment of the Mexican Revolution, Hollywood-style, usually represented either a 'missionary' reformulation of the Monroe Doctrine, with American 'specialists' helping out defenceless peasants (whose sole function is to look oppressed, or to pat tortillas photogenically in the background), or else a redefinition of the struggle in terms of American ideas about what constitutes a rebellious hero. The Revolution was part of the décor (so it did not merit any significant comment), and audience sympathies were displaced in the direction of engaging American gunmen (against nasty bandits, Stalinists, or German armaments experts). 'The American presence' was invariably a matter of individual choice. In more mainstream Hollywood Westerns (from which the 'Mexican' genre was derived), the term 'desperado' (a Spanish one) was traditionally taken as a synonym for 'bandit' or 'outside the law'. When Hollywood products took account of the expectations of Mexican audiences — for example in the early 1930s — they simply reshot the WASP versions of Westerns, using more 'Latin'-looking American actors than the original stars. (One is reminded of Jack L. Warner's comment on *Objective Burma* (1945): 'I like the idea of having a Jewish officer in Burma. See that you get a good clean-cut American type for Jacobs.')

By contrast, the more obvious political themes of the Italian 'Type B' include: the decadence of provincial military governors (who take conspicuous consumption to bizarre extremes — Corbucci's speciality); the weakness of local administrations (Mexican skin, Gringo masks); a graphic presentation of the plight of the wretched of the earth, who cannot get a fair hearing in the courts (*The Big Gundown*); who have to work as miners in revolting conditions (*A Professional Gun*); and who can only find one literate man in the entire community to stand as mayor, after liberation (*A Bullet for the General*); the difficulties of setting up a post-colonial regime (a key theme in *A Bullet*, and *A Professional Gun*); the need to believe in a 'social bandit', which is often seen as an indicator of a community's state of consciousness (especially prominent in *Face to Face* and *A Bullet*); a detailed presentation of violent counter-insurgency measures (Sollima, in particular, is concerned with this theme — *The Big Gundown* being the clearest example); and a strong streak of anti-militarism or anti-clericalism (which is shared, in one form or other, by all the films in question).

The most important figure in the development of this sub-genre was probably the writer Franco Solinas. Solinas' stories provided the basis for works by Damiani (he wrote the dialogue for *A Bullet for the General*), Sollima (the story of *The Big Gundown*), and Corbucci (the story of *A Professional Gun*, written with Giorgio Arlorio, the same team that created the screenplay of *Queimada*). Solinas — an extraordinarily prolific writer of popular political scenarios — had worked on *Salvatore Giuliano* for Francesco Rosi, wrote *State of Siege* for Costa Gavras, and contributed to Gilberto Pontecorvo's two films, *The Battle of Algiers* and *Queimada*. *Queimada* represents the finest achievement of this stage in Solinas's career, and relates closely to his work on the Italian Westerns (to

this extent, de Fornari's observations seem valid): in particular, the central relationship between Sir William Walker (Marlon Brando) and José Dolores (Evaristo Marquez), which is used as a peg on which to hang a whole series of Fanonist themes, resembles the equivalent relationships in the Westerns he wrote for Damiani, Sollima and Corbucci — while the various allegorical 'stages' of this relationship (the 'outsider' helps to raise the 'bandit's' racial consciousness for his own purposes, seems to be friendly with the 'bandit', rejects him, plays 'cat and mouse' with him, then discovers that his own techniques are being used against himself) seem close (considerations of genre notwithstanding) to the permutations of Baudry's 'Type B'.

At the beginning of *A Bullet for the General*, the Gringo Bill Tate (Lou Castel) is asked by a Mexican child 'Do you like Mexico?' He replies, 'Not very much,' as he buys a ticket for a train out of town. But Tate manages to persuade a bandit leader El Chuncho (Gian Maria Volonté), and his brother Santo (Klaus Kinski), a priest-turned-bandit, that he also is wanted by the authorities (back in the States) and as a result is permitted to ride with them as they steal arms to sell to General Elias (Jaime Fernandez), a leader of the revolutionary army. At this stage, Santo is a much more committed revolutionary than his brother: when asked by one of his victims how he can wear the cloth and be a bandit/rebel at the same time, he replies, 'Between two bandits Jesus died on the cross'; unlike the American, he is not aware that Chuncho is going to *sell* arms to the revolutionaries. Gradually, El Chuncho becomes fascinated by the Gringo's cool efficiency, his knowledge of firearms, and lack of passion for anything except money, and, almost despite himself, he begins to strike up a friendship with him. 'You don't smoke, you don't drink, you don't like pretty girl — what the hell do you like?' 'Money!' On arrival in the town of San Miguel, Chuncho is persuaded by the oppressed peasants to help them kill Don Felipe, the local landowner, rather than continue his journey to General Elias. Why do they want to kill Felipe? 'Because we are poor people, and he wants us to stay poor people.' During the ensuing carnage, Chuncho kills one of his own men, after an attempt on the life of the Gringo. Having helped to elect a mayor for San Miguel (the only man who can read and write), Chuncho begins to understand why the peasants are so keen

219-20 (*Above*) An American history professor
(Gian Maria Volonté) finds himself *Face to Face*
with a Mexican bandit (Tomas Milian) in Sergio
Sollima's film of 1967

221-2 (*Right, above and below*) The first of Sergio
Corbucci's bizarre 'proletarian fables': *A Professional Gun* (1968), with Franco Nero as 'the
Polak', and Tony Musante as the Mexican peasant
he 'assists'

223 (*Below*) Tomas Milian as a Mexican revolutionary who begins to look more and more like Che
Guevara, in Corbucci's *Compañeros* (1970)

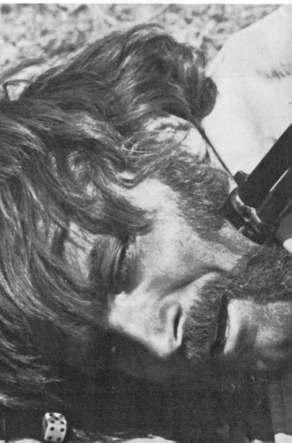

to treat him as a revolutionary hero: the Gringo is less understanding, and sets off with the guns to General Elias, leaving Chuncho to train the peasants of San Miguel (ill-equipped, but keen to learn) for the inevitable clash with the military. Eventually, Chuncho deserts these peasants, and catches up with Tate. ('Why did you leave with the guns? The people may not wear perfume, but they are men like you and me'). On the way to General Elias, Tate contracts malaria, and Chuncho carefully nurses him back to health. 'Why do you spend so much time worrying about others?' 'I don't like to be loved, I like loving.' When the two reach Elias' camp, Chuncho is sentenced to death for deserting the peasants of San Miguel. Tate meets the child again: 'Now do you like Mexico?' 'No.' It transpires that Tate's purpose all along has been to assassinate General Elias (with a golden bullet he keeps in his briefcase), and that he has been using El Chuncho to lead him to his victim. Chuncho is saved, but both Santo and the General are killed. We then see Tate being paid in gold by American agents of the Mexican government 'for services rendered'. Chuncho meets the Gringo at Ciudad Juarez (as previously arranged) and is given half the blood money as a token of friendship. Tate calmly admits that he engineered his original meeting with Chuncho, simply in order to gain access to the General's camp. Chuncho is shattered by this news, and, as the Gringo is boarding a train out of town, he shoots him. The 'bandit' (now a 'revolutionary') then tears off his city clothes, gives his share of the reward to a peasant, and tells him not to buy bread, but dynamite.

In Sollima's *The Big Gundown*, the central theme is again the developing friendship between a Gringo (Texas lawman 'Colorado' Corbett — Lee Van Cleef) and a Mexican bandit/rebel ('Cuchillo' Sanchez — Tomas Milian), but this time the American has been commissioned to track down and arrest the Mexican, for the rape of a white girl. Cuchillo has been accused of this by Brokston (Walter Barnes), a successful speculator in railroad stock, and Corbett agrees to take on the assignment when Brokston hints that he will support the lawman's ambition to start a political career. As Corbett doggedly pursues Cuchillo (and as the wily Mexican successfully outwits him on various occasions), he begins to understand the way his opponent thinks. Eventually, they both find themselves sharing a jail in Mexico: Cuchillo explains that he once fought with Juarez, the revolutionary leader, and that because of

his earlier association with the struggle to liberate oppressed peasants, he has become the innocent victim of Brokston's prejudice. Corbett sees what he means when Brokston, his German bodyguard (an armaments expert), his son-in-law Chet, a group of trackers and a pack of hounds all arrive in Mexico, to 'hunt' Cuchillo through the cane-fields. Gradually, it dawns on Corbett that the real rapist is Brokston's son-in-law Chet. During the inevitable gundown, in the Mexican desert, Cuchillo (with his bare hands and a knife) faces the combined might of Brokston, Chet and the German bodyguard. He succeeds in killing Chet, but at that point Corbett intervenes, shooting both the German and Brokston (after he himself has been shot at): at last he has realised that the institutions of 'law and order', to which he has devoted his life, in fact belong to a class of people like Brokston, who manipulate them to protect their economic interests. Sanchez — 'the knife', the guerrilla, the man who works with his hands — parts company with Corbett — 'the red', the man who was once associated with the power of the railroad barons — on the best of terms.

In *Face to Face* — Sollima's next Western to be released internationally — the central relationship, between a New England professor of history dying of tuberculosis (Brad Fletcher — Gian Maria Volonté) and a half-breed outlaw leader (Beauregard Bennett — Tomas Milian), is more complex. Fletcher has dismissed his class back East (at the start of the American Civil War) and travelled to the Southwest in order to convalesce. There, he saves the life of 'Beau' Bennett, an outlaw on the run, and strikes up a strange friendship with him: as Fletcher watches the outlaw leader and his gang in action, he develops an obsessive intellectual interest in their 'instinctive reactions' and their brutality, eventually deciding to try and imitate them, hoping to get the same results by use of intellect alone. In the brutal environment of the Southwest, he has every chance to try out his scheme. But, as Fletcher becomes more and more ruthless, Beau begins to recoil from those aspects of his friend's character he can see as potential in himself. Soon Brad takes over the leadership of the gang, still convinced that his cold, methodical ruthlessness is part of an elaborate intellectual game: 'To kill alone, is murder; to kill with ten men is an act of violence; but to kill with a thousand men — that is an organised act, a war ... a necessity!' (In this and other ways, the parallel with European Fascism is stressed throughout.

Cahiers 215, christened Brad 'a Nietzchean of the Sierra'). Fletcher's first major robbery is sabotaged from within the gang by Charly Siringo (William Berger — posing as a bandit, but really the infamous Pinkerton man), and Beau is captured when he stays behind to look after a lonely Mexican child — a victim of the townspeople's prejudice. He escapes, to lead the rest of his gang, with a group of outcast women and children, into the desert. A vigilante committee from the town sets off in hot pursuit. As the pilgrims struggle through the desert (to the accompaniment of 'biblical' music on the sound-track), they are joined by Charly Siringo (who keeps the vigilantes at bay). Eventually, Beau, Brad and Siringo find themselves face to face, for the final settling of accounts. After Brad has wounded the Pinkerton man, he is shot by Beau. Siringo, realising that Beau's transformation is complete, lets him escape, although he knows that he was once a brutal outlaw. Brad Fletcher, the man who had been fas-cinated by the 'instinctive forces' he saw at work in Beau's earlier behaviour, and who had tried to appropriate them, dies alone in the desert.

In Corbucci's *A Professional Gun*, the Gringo is Sergei Kowalski (a 'Polak' mercenary, played by Franco Nero), the bandit/rebel Eufemio, played by Tony Musante. (Eufemio was not only the name of Zapata's brother; it is also a town in Southern Italy.) Kowalski has been hired by Alfonso Garcia, a mine-owner, to ride shotgun on a con-signment of silver which is being transported to Texas, during the Mexican Revolution. He discovers that the workers have taken control of the mine, and teams up with Eufemio, the workers' spokes-man, hoping to make some money out of the Revolution. Under Kowalski's guidance, Eufemio gains a reputation as a revolutionary liberator (comparing himself at one point to Simon Bolivar), and the Polak gets rich. They both cross the path of Curly, a homosexual mercenary (Jack Palance). Eventually, Eufemio begins to understand why the peasants wish to cast him in the role of social bandit, and what the Revolution is all about: he confiscates the Polak's wealth, and turns him over to the authorities. But Kowalski escapes, meeting Eufemio (now a rodeo clown) and Curly for the final show-down. Eufemio kills Curly, rejoins his revolution-ary band, and refuses Kowalski's offer to work with him. Although it is clear that Eufemio still needs Kowalski's help, they part company — Eufemio to join the Revolution, Kowalski to remain a mercenary.

In the sequel, *Compañeros*, Franco Nero again plays the mercenary (Yod, a Swede, also known as 'the penguin' because of his spats) and Tomas Milian the bandit/rebel Basco (dressed in the style of Che Guevara). The plot involves an attempt to rescue Professor Xantos (a pacifist — Fernando Rey), and his Marxist students, from the hands of the Americans in Texas: Yod joins the rescue party in the hope of finding some gold (only Xantos knows the combination of the safe). They both cross the path of John (a pot-smoking villain with a wooden hand and a pet falcon named Marsha — played by Jack Palance), who has an old score to settle with Yod. Eventually, Basco loses patience with Yod's opportunism, and challenges him to a duel. But the showdown is interrupted by the arrival of the counter-revolutionary army, and this time Yod decides to ride back to his companeros, joining the revolutionaries (who are about to fight against impossible odds).

In many ways, Corbucci's two films represent the most extreme examples of the problems facing those Spaghetti directors and scriptwriters who tried to infuse populist themes into the genre (or 'Type'). We have seen how Corbucci was a prolific director of 'peplums' and comedies (he was even involved in a send-up of *The Leopard*) before the Western boom: he was to make more than ten Spaghettis between 1963 (before *Fistful*) and 1971. His comic-strip style, his undisciplined use of every possible gag, and his susceptibility to pressures from within the Cinecittà production system (in *whatever* genre he is directing) tend to swamp whatever 'disguised' political themes there are, in, for example, Solinas' stories. In *A Professional Gun*, he cannot resist yet another satire on the church's role (Nero and Musante dressed up as angels in a religious pro-cession), and the fashionable flashback which frames the main story (it begins and ends with the climactic shootout) has as much to do with Corbucci's urge to parody the most successful Spaghettis, as it does with the story in question: Jack Palance, in a white suit, with a carnation in his buttonhole, minces into a circus ring, to face Tony Musante, who is still dressed as a rodeo clown; as Palance is shot, blood begins to trickle from his carnation. The sequence is stylish, in a bizarre way, but works more as a parody (or extension) of the way Leone films *his* climactic confrontations, than as a resolution of the political themes in Solinas' screenplay — yet Corbucci is on record as having suggested that Curly represents 'the calamities which capitalism brings to the Third World'! At other moments in the film, Corbucci's undisciplined direction seems to suit the story more (for example, when staccato camera movements are used to show how the revolutionaries become accustomed to firing a machine gun). In *Compañeros* (the story of which is again 'framed' by a climactic duel), the presentation of the villain is even more bizarre. John (Jack Palance — completely out of control) has a wooden hand, because Yod once nailed him to a cross:

'How did you get down from that cross?'
'It was Marsha!'
'She pulled out the nail?'
'No, she ate my hand!'

Throughout the film, John feeds tasty chunks of his Mexican victims to his beloved falcon. The political symbolism is clear (American eagle feeding off the riches of the Third World), but a combination of Corbucci's evident relish for such bizarre touches, and Palance's over-acting, rather kills the message. At another point in the story, Corbucci even manages to include a visual parody of the head-crushing sequence in Eisenstein's *Que Viva Mexico*: in the original, this sequence was intended to show, in graphic terms, the ritualised brutality on which Porfirio Diaz' dictatorship rested; in *Compañeros* (and also *A Professional Gun* — for Corbucci always repeats an effect), it becomes the excuse for an extended gag. This (consistent) pattern in Corbucci's work almost locates his films among the *send-ups* of 'Type B' — of which there were, inevitably, many. During the final phase of the Spaghetti Western boom, for example (when the emphasis shifted to comic-strip stories, slap-stick comedy, stuntmen, and 'engaging' heroes — the model being the 'Trinity' series), Tomas Milian, of all actors, was to appear in the burlesque *They Call Me Providence*. And Tessari was to parody Solinas' screenplays in *Et Viva la Révolution* (also known as *Long Live Death . . . Preferably Yours*).

Damiani (a veteran, from neo-realist days) and Sollima seem to have been less concerned with parodying, or extending, fashionable gimmicks of the moment. Sollima saves up his more rhetorical effects for elaborate set-pieces, such as the manhunt through the cane-fields in *The Big Gundown*, and both these directors were prepared to use traditional Hollywood techniques to tell their simple stories when need arose (a cause for complaint, in Leftist critical circles). Pasolini certainly thought that *A Bullet for the General* represented an authentic form of political cinema (one which reached the displaced peasantry, perhaps), for it was as a result of this film that he agreed to appear (as a revolutionary priest, again with Lou Castel) in Lizzani's *Requiescant* (1967), which concerned the struggle against foreign financiers who were propping up the counter-revolutionary federal government. Critics have called Sollima's two Westerns 'disguised anarchist cine-texts'. But, quite apart from the question (posed by Baudry, Godard, MacBean and de Fornari) whether the relationship between audience and film in this type of popular, genre cinema can *really* allow for a raising of political consciousness (or, indeed, to re-pose the question, whether *any* film alone can succeed in doing that, except at the most vicarious level) another, equally important question is prompted by these films: given that the directors and writers claim to have set out with the intention of making political films, and given the kind of audiences at which they were aimed (the 'Roxy, Calabria'), how far were they successful on their own terms? The set of oppositions which the central relationships in the Westerns of Damiani and Sollima represent, are, of course, very simple ones: the 'outsider' often owes as much to the Man With No Name as he does to any thoughts about the role of American capital (or the CIA) in Latin America, and the bandit figure tends to show a marked lack of political responsibility, even after his 'conversion'. In most of these films, the conflict is only peripherally one between class interests. The type of 'technical assistance' the Gringo offers (diffusion of capitalism?) too often becomes an excuse for a strange kind of fetishism about elaborate firearms (the quick-firing rifle in *A Bullet for the General*, the German bodyguard's equipment in *The Big Gundown*). The dialectical aspects of the Gringo-Mexican relationship usually become over-schematic at some stage in the plot, involving a sudden Damascus Road experience on the part of one or other of the protagonists (this is especially true of Beau in *Face to Face*). Because of this, the plots seem to work best when the bandit on the run is associated in some way with a minority group *outside* the central relationship — the Mormons who look after Cuchillo in *The Big Gundown*, the peasants who want to kill Don Felipe in *A Bullet for the General*, the Mexican child and the outcast women in *Face to Face*.

But perhaps the difficulties these directors faced, when trying to 'conjugate commercial considerations with progressivism' (assuming their statements of intent may be taken at face value) are best illustrated by the various adaptations of screenplays by Solinas. These screenplays all share a loose allegiance to Fanonism, which means that the targets they attack are at least underpinned by a coherent social and political analysis; this takes Solinas' work (on paper) well beyond what Andrew Tudor has called 'the *diffuse* unease' of mainstream American political cinema — and means that even when incidents or moments from Hollywood films are 'transposed', they tend to take on a radically different meaning. The Don Felipe incident in *A Bullet for the General*, for example, includes a series of direct quotations from *Viva Zapata*: but, within Solinas' frame of reference, the incident appears as part of a thoroughgoing critique; in Steinbeck's screenplay, and Kazan's film, it had merely functioned as a colourful anecdote. And Solinas is evidently concerned about the strategy and organisation of revolutions (raising a set of issues in which Hollywood cinema of the 1950s and '60s had seldom if ever shown interest): there are even meetings to discuss guerrilla tactics and the consolidation of power. The problem is, that this basis in a coherent analysis (one of the defining features of the Solinas adaptations and derivatives) can too easily become masked (or 'disguised' completely) when the medium (the 'style' of Cinecittà Westerns, and the associated expectations of the audience) is at odds with the message. There was a distinguished precedent for this problem. Eisenstein discovered the attractions of the Mexican tradition of *vacillada* while he was filming *Que Viva Mexico*, and his response to this *vacillada* shows clearly in the surviving fragments of the film: the intense political commitment which informs parts of the first four sections of *Que Viva Mexico* gives way to the exuberance and *joie de vivre* of the epilogue — a death-day pageant in modern Mexico, the only part of the film Eisenstein was determined to have sent back to the Soviet Union. But *vacillada*, expressed as a turned-on vision of a pageant of death, can take very different forms in the hands of a Damiani, or a Corbucci: in *A Bullet for the General*, it takes the form of an exuberant, loud 'reply' to Kazan's *Viva Zapata* (a 'reply' about which both Damiani and Pasolini

obviously felt strongly); in *A Professional Gun*, it takes the form of an exuberant, loud reworking of the clichés of the most commercially successful Italian Westerns, with passing reference to Sturges' *Magnificent Seven* (an enterprise which Corbucci seems to have enjoyed a lot). The original title of *A Bullet* (*Quien Sabe* . . .?) was probably taken from the fourth 'novel' of *Que Viva Mexico*, a film which Corbucci *parodies* in *A Professional Gun*. The result is that in Damiani's case the message comes over loud and clear — the exuberance serves his political purpose. In Corbucci's case, the exuberance smothers Solinas' words, and we are left with a bizarre version of Robin Hood: only the director's evident distaste for hippies and yippies (as opposed to political activists) survives the struggle.

Noel Simsolo, in *La Revue du Cinéma* (September 1973), is more harsh: he does not distinguish between these various directors at all. For him,

> the political Italian Westerns were all aimed at a mass, popular audience — which explains why there is usually a contrived sympathy for the Mexicans who represent 'the people', and always . . . an overdose of violence, destruction and vulgarity. The virus of superficial 'politicisation' infected Italy, and the Western caught the germs. Among the reasons why the Italian Western should prove a good breeding ground for these germs was the fact of 'the Mexican presence' — which was often dictated by geographical considerations (exteriors) and by the social situation. The Italian people — as well as Puerto-Ricans, Africans, all the representatives of the Third World, and all the marginal groups of the capitalist system, could easily identify themselves with a 'Mexicanised' hero. The 'revolutionary' Western was thus only a way of getting substantial returns on money invested — not an attempt to disseminate a productive political discourse.

Perhaps Simsolo has a point — after all, the Italian Westerns were the favourite form of entertainment of the King of Morocco.

Jeremy Tunstall, like Noel Simsolo, has suggested that the impact of the Spaghetti Western on 'the typical consumer of imported media' in the Third World — 'a young white-collar worker or a factory worker — not an elderly peasant in a remote rural area' — resembles that of the Anglo-American product. 'Many of these urban consumers will themselves have a personal history of social and geographical mobility, and may respond to these themes in American media.... The appeal of stylized violence to the frustrated urban youth of many lands cannot be better illustrated than by the many imitations of the American Western. Some of the most obvious are the Italian and Spanish, Spaghetti and Paella, Westerns.' But Tunstall adds that one of the key factors paving the way for 'cultural imperialism' is the political instability of Third World countries which import such 'imitations': 'Not only peasants' rebellions, guerrilla uprisings and palace revolutions but large-scale civil wars are a recent experience or an immediate realistic prospect in many lands. In the many countries where the prime object of policy is to reduce the threat of armed conflict, the need to strengthen "authentic culture" may not be seen as primary.' The assumption that *all* the 'many imitations of the American Western' will take consumers' minds off revolution and rebellion is unwarranted: as we have seen, many of the more successful Spaghettis were concerned (for whatever motive) with the role of revolution (and social bandits) in Latin countries — a concern which was far removed from the ideology of the 'Anglo-American product'. If the prime object of policy in Simsolo's 'Third World' market is to 'reduce the threat of armed conflict', then it seems rather eccentric (not to say dangerous) to import a film like Damiani's *A Bullet for the General* (which was a great hit, for example, in the West African market). Tomas Milian reckons that he became a 'symbol of poverty and revolution' to 'Third World cinemagoers', providing opportunities for audience identification well beyond the stock 'oppressed' characters in more traditional Hollywood Westerns — scarcely a 'symbol' calculated to take the heat out of an explosive political situation.

The most significant thing about some of these political Italian Westerns' is that anyone allowed them to be made in the first place. Take the example of *Trinità Voit Rouge* (*Trinity Sees Red*), 1972, an Italian-Spanish co-production, directed by veteran Mario Camus (and unfortunately not released in this country). In this film (which had a last-minute title change, to cash in on the phenomenal success of the 'Trinity' series of Westerns — it was originally called *The Anger of the Wind*), Trinity (Terence Hill) is employed by an Andalusian landowner (at the turn of the century) to destroy an anarchist cell which has sprung up in the Andalusian countryside. As the

story develops (in fits and starts — since the producers seem to have taken fright, and cut the film to ribbons) it becomes clear that Trinity has taken on not just one anarchist cell but a full-scale revolution against the aristocrats who own the vast *latifundia* in Southern Spain. Although *Trinity Sees Red* is a characteristically episodic 'Western' adventure (despite the location!), Mario Camus manages to devote a substantial part of the film to the organisation of strikes, the seizure of landowner's property, and the details of the Andalusian peasant revolution. As in Sollima's *The Big Gundown*, the freelance 'lawman' begins to realise that the bandit/rebels are not as fearsome as his employer originally told him they would be. One scene in particular makes Trinity unsure about what he has been employed to do. An old man is addressing the inhabitants of an Andalusian village. He has been an anarchist all his life, and he tends to talk in parables. But it soon becomes clear what his political programme entails. Eventually, he spells it out in these terms:

'We want a classless society — no more exploiters, no more exploited. We should no longer accept injustice — we should rise up, and fight for our liberty, our dignity, and our rights. We bear within ourselves a new world, a world full of promise. Ruins and destruction do not frighten us, for we have built everything with our own hands — palaces and churches, roads and bridges; *we will destroy them all if need be, to rebuild a more beautiful world.*'

Although, like the other 'Trinity' films, the emphasis of *Trinità Voit Rouge* is on Terence Hill's talents as an 'engaging' hero who moves from adventure to adventure without batting an eyelid, Mario Camus also ensures (even in the cut version) that due emphasis is given to the brutality of the latifundian aristocracy, the success of the anarchists' strike, and the solidarity of the revolutionaries. In the same year that Salvador Puig Antich, the militant anarchist, was executed in Barcelona (garrotted, in fact) a Spanish film director was able to include the above words in an anarchist leader's speech. The film was partly shot in Spain, and Spanish producers were involved. It was distributed by Inter-Film (Rome), co-starred Fernando Rey, and was publicised by a poster which featured (prominently) a cowboy brandishing a large red flag — watched by an unusually pensive Terence Hill. Because *Trinità*

224 From the same team as wrote *A Professional Gun*, Giorgio Arlorio and Franco Solinas: Gillo Pontecorvo's *Queimada* (1969), with Marlon Brando as Sir William Walker of the Antilles Sugar Company, and Evaristo Marquez as José Dolores, a slave who becomes first a bank robber, then a revolutionary, under 'guidance' from Walker

225 (*Right*) French publicity for Mario Camus' *Trinity Sees Red* (1972), with 'Terence Hill' in unusually pensive mood as he contemplates the red flag

UNIVERSEL EXPORTATION présente

TERENCE HILL

mise en scène de
M. CAMUS

avec
FERNAND REY

MARIA GRA
BUCELL

TRINITA VOIT ROUGE

26-7 Daniel Cohn-Bendit thought he was writing a 'political' Spaghetti Western; Jean-Luc Godard and his collective thought they were making a film about the bourgeois concept of representation': the result of this confusion was *Wind from the East* (1969) with Gian Maria Volonté as a US Cavalry officer. Glauber Rocha stands at the crossroads

228 (*Above*) The bandit who was originally a Western hero, in Glauber Rocha's *Antonio das Mortes* (1967)

Voit Rouge was only an Italian Western ('not an attempt to disseminate a productive political discourse'), as far-fetched as the rest, it passed through the Spanish censors (after the producers had cut some of it).

An attempt to 'anaesthetise' genuine political commitment? 'The appropriation by bourgeois ideology of the terms of a contradictory ideology?' *Trinità Voit Rouge* is not a politically sophisticated film; it unashamedly manipulates the emotions of the audience. In MacBean's terms, because the film does not 'call forth *all* the human faculties, rational and emotional' it cannot possibly have raised the consciousness of the audience. But it *is* a stirring film about an anarchist uprising in Andalusia, and it *was* seen by cinemagoers in Franco's Spain.

Gillo Pontecorvo (ex-Communist Party, now a 'left-wing independent') sees the function of his type of cinema in precisely these terms: films like *The Battle of Algiers* and *Queimada* may have been criticised explicitly in Godard's *Wind from the East*, and may be theoretically unjustifiable from the 'more radical than thou' perspective of a critic like James Roy MacBean, but they have one thing going for them which Godard, in his present incarnation, must always despise: they are seen by an enormous number of people, in many countries.

> You must not overrate the importance of cinema on politics. Cinema is one of various means which contribute to the advancement of certain ideas. Lenin used to say that from among all the arts film is the most important for the oppressed classes — but from among *all the arts*. The experiences that really matter are those the masses live directly. This seems self-evident, yet not all 'committed directors' appear to be convinced about it. I believe film's limitation lies in its not being able to penetrate deeply. Instead, it 'communicates'.

When asked about the polemic against the political film which runs 'You can't make a politically serious movie with capitalist money', Pontecorvo replies:

> The polemic is the result of 'political infantilism'. They should remember what Lenin said about the inner contradictions of capitalism that take place at every level, even the very low one we are now considering. I think a producer would back a movie that slanders both his mother and father if he knew it would make a profit. You see, I am deeply convinced that the establishment fully understands the limitations of political films. As we said before, a film is not a revolution. . . . The main difference between political novels and political films is the film's larger circulation. Otherwise the differences all weigh against cinema because its communication is only skin deep. . . . But cinema can be a way of revitalizing a people's deadened responses. We have been conditioned to absorb a false vision of reality that is dominated by the tastes, morals, and perceptions of the 'establishment'. To forego the possibility of opposing the *fictions* diffused by this establishment is in the least irresponsible. That is why I believe in a cinema which addresses itself to the masses and not a cinema *d'élite* for an elite.

Franco Solinas (still a member of the Italian Communist Party) also maintains that the creator of political films faces a choice between sharing his commitment with 'an elite', and ensuring that his ideas reach 'the largest possible audience', if necessary through the medium of a popular genre:

> Let us first say that movies have an accessory and not a decisive usefulness in the various events and elements that contribute to the transformation of society. It is naive to believe that you can start a revolution with a movie and even more naive to theorize about doing so. Political films are useful on the one hand if they contain a correct analysis of reality and on the other if they are made in such a way as to have that analysis reach the largest possible audience.

Solinas recalls that he has written 'some more commercial products for survival or just for fun' (he is presumably referring to his work for Corbucci here), but that his screenplays 'usually begin with a political topic'. And he outlines the political context out of which his work for Pontecorvo (as well as his Spaghetti Westerns) emerged in 1966-8:

> They were times when European politics were stagnating for two main reasons. First, the working class was thought of as completely integrated, it seemed non-existent in relation to the revolutionary cause. Second, a deep analysis of the political situation had completely ruled out the possibility of a revolution on our continent. You can understand how the

explosions of colonial contradictions, the revolutions, the armed struggles that then were erupting in the entire geography of the Third World stirred up hope as well as interest. You had come to believe that capitalism seemingly undefeatable at home could have been defeated once and for all in its supplying bases. In a way it was the same hope that was to be theorized on the one hand by Lin Piao with the strategy of 'the country and the city', and on the other by Frantz Fanon's proposal to abandon the traditional models and means in the construction of a different civilization.

(Solinas' political concerns, and especially those derived from Fanon's work, are apparent in functions d, e, f, g, k, l, o and p of the 'Zapata-Spaghetti' variant to our 'Italian plot').

So, in reply to the criticism that their work made opportunistic use of fashionable subjects such as Vietnam, the CIA, Che Guevara, and Third World revolutions — in typical Cinecittà style, too much of an historic compromise — both Pontecorvo and Solinas would reply that it was quite possible to make sensible films on these subjects which opposed the fictions of Hollywood, but which *at the same time* aimed to be successful with regular cinemagoers.

In *Wind from the East*, there is a scene which shows the Brazilian film-maker Glauber Rocha standing at a crossroads; his hands are pointing in two directions. A girl comes up to him and says, 'Excuse me for interrupting your class struggle, but could you please tell me the way towards political cinema?' Glauber Rocha replies, singing the words at one point, 'That way is the cinema of aesthetic adventure and philosophical enquiry, while this way is the Third World cinema — a dangerous cinema, *divine and marvellous*, where the questions are practical ones like production, distribution, training three hundred film-makers to make six hundred films a year for Brazil alone, to supply one of the world's biggest markets.' The girl hesitates, then chooses the road of 'aesthetic adventure'.

Glauber Rocha had met Godard, in Rome, just as *Wind from the East* was being filmed: he was visiting Cinecittà, trying to arrange some distribution deals for Brazilian films. Godard was to reproach him for having such a 'producer's mentality', for worrying about mere practical matters while there were urgent theoretical questions still to be asked

about the very bases of Third World cinema; Rocha was later to reproach Godard for spending so much time and energy worrying about the usefulness of art, and for making a film which attempted to 'destroy' art, both of which were senseless, politically negative occupations. The crossroads sequence reflects this dispute, and, in our terms, reflects the dispute between critics such as MacBean or film-makers such as Godard, and film-makers such as Pontecorvo, Bertolucci, Damiani, or writers such as Solinas. Godard goes down the road of 'aesthetic adventure'; Pontecorvo goes down the road of 'a dangerous cinema'. According to *Wind from the East*, it is a choice which must be made by all those involved in films which call themselves political.

When he set out to make *Antonio das Mortes*, Glauber Rocha was originally attempting (among other things) to 'recover the atmosphere' of the American Westerns which had made the most profound impression on him — among them, Peckinpah's *Guns in the Afternoon*, and three of the Howard Hawks and John Wayne films. In particular, the critical exploration of 'myth and reality on the frontier' which these films contained, provided a starting-point for Rocha. But, as shooting progressed, this theme apparently faded more and more into the background, eventually to be replaced by a strong critique of American imperialism. In an interview published just as he was about to appear in *Wind from the East*, Rocha explained why the Western had provided such an essential starting-point for him, and why he subsequently rejected the genre:

> Antonio is a killer — tied to his own cultural tradition; but he also relates to another tradition — that of the Western. Everything that makes him seem to resemble a hero of the Far West 'works' in all sorts of countries — Japan, Brazil, America, Sicily. . . . This mystique associated with the heroes of the Far West is a tradition of a special kind. In American films, there is always the reality, and a kind of questioning of the myth that reaches beyond it. For us, it is more complicated. In an American Western, there is already an established language: when the hero arrives, we know who he is by his horse, or by his clothes: he carries all kinds of information around with him. In our films, he cannot carry this information around with him because we have no cinematographic tradition of this kind.

Perhaps this is a limitation on the development of our cinema.

He continued:

Every film that is made has found the money from somewhere. A cinéaste, even if he thinks of himself as an artist in the traditional mould, or as an intellectual, has to understand that he is also associated with the cinema as an economic phenomenon. Either he makes *auteur* films, very stylish, very political, films which can be shown in the big cinemas while discussing the principles of commercialism at the same time. Or he makes more marginal films, in which case he has to organise a more clandestine distribution. . . . If you make films against the system which are never shown, the system does not give a fuck about them. The cinema is about 'mass communication' in the most open sense possible, not about secret societies. If you want to confront the system, you must operate through some kind of organisation. And a journal like *Cahiers du Cinéma* has an important role to play, in clarifying these things. . . . Abroad, *Cahiers* has helped to develop a cinematographic culture, but has also been responsible for a certain alienation among young and independent cinéastes. They often swear by *Cahiers*, and make their first films as if they were aimed exclusively at *Cahiers*. This is the origin of a sort of academicism, in criticism and in film.

Some of the better Spaghetti Westerns seem to me to be going down the path signposted 'a dangerous cinema . . .' Ironically, *Cahiers* liked them too.

Epilogue
Spaghettis in the
Looking-Glass

'. . . Just look along the road,' the King said,
'and tell me if you can see either of the two
Messengers.'

'I see nobody on the road,' said Alice.

'I only wish *I* had such eyes,' the King
remarked in a fretful tone. 'To be able to see
Nobody! And at that distance too! Why, it's as
much as *I* can do to see real people, by this
light!'

All this was lost on Alice, who was still
looking intently along the road, shading her
eyes with one hand. 'I see somebody now!' she
exclaimed at last. 'But he's coming very
slowly . . .'

. . . 'Who did you pass on the road?' said the
King, holding out his hand to the Messenger . . .

'Nobody,' said the Messenger.

'Quite right,' said the King: 'this young lady
saw him too. So of course Nobody walks slower
than you.'

'I do my best,' the Messenger said in a sullen
tone. 'I'm sure nobody walks much faster than
I do!'

'He can't do that,' said the King, 'or else
he'd have been here first . . .'

Lewis Carroll, *Through the Looking-Glass*,
chapter VII (1868)

A cock crows. A dog howls. Three gunslingers ride into a shanty-town in the West. They dismount and go into a barber's shop. After menacing the barber (and his little son) they bind and gag them. Meanwhile, further down the street, an elderly gunfighter named Jack Beauregard is asking the local telegraph operator when the next ship leaves New Orleans for Europe; it leaves, he is told, in eleven days' time. Beauregard walks purposefully back towards the barber's shop. One of the gunslingers has dressed up in the barber's overall and is waiting for his customer, while the other two are trying to look occupied in the street outside — one sitting on a stool milking a cow, the other brushing down a horse. Jack Beauregard sits in the barber's chair and asks for a shave. The gunslinger approaches him, cut-throat razor in hand. As the razor is about to touch Beauregard's throat, the gunslinger abruptly stops short; there is a loud click, as of a pistol being cocked. Beauregard has quietly unholstered his pistol, and is pointing it right between the gunslinger's legs. This strange shaving ritual continues — only now the gunslinger is shaking. Outside, the cow continues to be milked, the horse to be brushed. Just as Beauregard's shave is over, violence erupts — suddenly. The 'barber' is shot, and falls back into the chair — outside, we can see (reflected in the barber's mirror) the other two gunslingers biting the dust. Beauregard calmly leaves some compensation for the damage he has done, and leaves. When the barber (and his little son) have managed to free themselves, they survey the scene in awe:

'How did he do it, Pa?' asks the child. 'I only heard one shot.'

'It's a question of speed, son,' replies the barber.

'Pa — ain't nobody faster on the draw than him?'

'Faster than him? Nobody.'

Abruptly, we cut to a river, where a tall, blue-eyed youth rises up to his full height, from under the water. The title fills the screen: *My Name Is Nobody*.

This scene is full of references to Sergio Leone's previous Westerns — and the technical effects are unmistakably Leone. The three gunslingers could have appeared in the opening sequences of either *The Good, the Bad and the Ugly* or *Once Upon a Time in the West*. The barber's shop setting is straight out of Leone's full version of *Once Upon a Time* (and the Agua Caliente scenes of *For a Few Dollars More*). The barber behaves exactly as the stationmaster behaved in *Once Upon a Time*. The child's response to the gunplay comes from *For a Few*. The *mistrust* symbolised by the relationship between Beauregard and the 'barber' could have come from any of Leone's mature films, as could the bizarre comedy of the gunslingers' behaviour — strangely rural occupations in such an urban setting. Later in the film, direct references to Leone's films will abound: two gunfighters will take pot-shots at each other's hats, as part of a competitive ritual (*For a Few*); an old prophet will be gently mocked, as he rails against progress (also *For a Few*); a duel will take place during which Henry Fonda's behaviour will exactly match the equivalent scene in *Once Upon a Time*; this time, it is Fonda who is out to avenge his brother's death. And so on. The technical effects in the opening sequence are also instantly recognisable. The film opens with an elaborate camera effect — a shift of perspective — which at one moment makes it look as if the three gunslingers are very close to the camera, at the next makes it clear that an expanse of dusty main street lies between us and the three riders. Amplified sound effects (mainly 'natural' sounds) help build up the tension in the barber's shop sequence: the razor grating over Beauregard's chin, the cow's udders being pulled, the brush being run through matted horsehair — all this accompanied by the sound of an alarm-clock ticking away. It seems scarcely necessary to add the words on the screen 'Sergio Leone presents . . .'

But *My Name Is Nobody* is not a Leone film. Apart from the opening sequence which, according to Oreste de Fornari, was directed by Leone himself, the film was directed by one of his protégés — Tonino Valerii — in a style which looks at times like a parody of Leone's, and at other times like a second-rate attempt to emulate his success. In the central section of the film (which takes place at a fairground, and in a saloon), scenes are held for far too long, and Terence Hill is given his head (allowed to indulge the virtuoso brand of amiable, freewheeling humour he evolved in the 'Trinity' series) too often. The screenplay is uncharacteristically wordy (the last ten minutes of the film being an elaborate explanation of what the story has been all about), and the loose, episodic structure for once lends an air of needless digression, or lack of control, to the proceedings. The climax of the film (characteristically, a shootout, in which various key themes find their resolution) does not really work, partly because Henry Fonda's adversaries ('150 pure-bred sons-of-bitches on horseback' — the Wild Bunch out of Sam Peckinpah and Fuller's *Forty Guns*) have been introduced to us twice before (the same piece of film clearly being used over and over again) and partly because Valerii attempts to 'freeze time' at the actual moments of shooting (rather than during the preliminaries, which is Leone's style). There are sequences in the film — the opening, a scene in an Indian graveyard (which Leone himself also 'assisted'), the final duel — when Valerii is covering ground which Leone had already trodden many times before, that achieve the kind of controlled rhetoric for which Leone had by then become justly famed. But when Valerii is trying to apply Leone's techniques to original material (the fairground sequences, Nobody stealing a train, the confrontation with the Wild Bunch), his performance too often seems like that of an understudy who is out of his depth.

So, the reasons why the film is interesting (and why an analysis of it seems an appropriate epilogue to this book) have little to do with authorship. Some critics have treated the film as Leone's fifth Western. It clearly is not. The interest of the film lies less in the execution of Leone's/Gastaldi's/Valerii's ideas than in the reasons why Leone felt drawn to the project in the first place (as producer and supervisor of the editing): 'For me, the interesting thing about *My Name Is Nobody* was that it confronts a myth with the negation of that myth. I do not see this as *destructive* at all. On the contrary. The moral of this adventure attempts to show that people never attack a nobody: in the West as in life, the only person who is taken into account is the man who is thought to be unbeatable.' Leone sees the central antagonism in the film — between an ageing gunfighter who refuses to accept his mythic status (not considering that he deserves to 'get into the history books'), and a younger man who hero-worships him, and is determined to engineer the confrontation which will ensure that the gunfighter becomes a living legend (so that he can then be seen to step into the older man's shoes) — as locating *My Name Is Nobody* among those European Westerns which set out to comment directly on the values of the Hollywood 'originals', as well as pointing a clear 'moral' about the perils of fame. This central antagonism can be (and has been) interpreted in many ways: Tony Rayns (*Monthly Film Bulletin*, February 1977) has analysed the film as 'an explicit, thoroughgoing critique of Sam Peckinpah's work up to 1970'; others have seen it as yet another 'death-of-the-West-and-Western movie', with Henry Fonda, appropriately enough, incarnating a 'national monument' in decline; Tony Williams (*Italian Western*, 1975) has written of *My Name* as 'a gentle send-up, not only of the "Trinity" films, but also of key elements of Leone's own Westerns'. There is enough in the film to sustain all these interpretations (except, perhaps, the second). But Leone's comment — that 'it confronts a myth with the negation of that myth' — points to a wider interpretation.

The central antagonism between Nobody and Beauregard seems to me to represent three main themes. First, that every mythic hero needs a good scriptwriter. Not only does Nobody constantly remind Beauregard of his own past ('rewriting' it), but he also stage-manages the *context* for Beauregard's final, 'legendary' gesture. When he was a child, Nobody admits, he used to look up to Beauregard as a just and invincible hero ('People need something to believe in'): Beauregard, however, simply wants to retire to Europe while he is still in one piece, and read some books. He complains when Nobody keeps insisting that he should follow through his revenge to its logical conclusion by shooting it out with the entire Wild Bunch: the trouble with young hot-heads like Nobody, he says, is that they see revenge as something *inevitable*, and are prepared to go around killing people for just a fistful of dollars: 'People like you think that if a man's older than you, he'll go along with old-fashioned notions like blood's thicker than water. Sure Nevada was my brother — he was a Grade A skunk who shot people in the back ... I ain't risking my life to avenge him. My destiny's to get out of here — I've got an appointment with a ship that's sailing for Europe.' So Beauregard decides to leave, and (in the most elegiac section of the film), rides off into the sunset. But, as Nobody has already told him, 'Sometimes you run smack into your destiny on the very road you take to get away from it,' and, sure enough, the climactic encounter with the Wild Bunch *does* take place, with Beauregard's last stand being frozen on to the pages of a history book at the very moment it takes place.

But if every mythic hero needs a good script-writer, he also needs an audience. And one of the most consistent features of the film is its use of a series of images which explore *reflections* of Beauregard's or Nobody's deeds. The opening moment of violence ('I only heard one shot,' says the child, and so did we) is reflected in the barber's shop mirror: the camera is placed at an 'expressionist' angle, as the two gunslingers waiting outside are seen to die, in slow motion — a mirror-image which the child will recall a little later on. Nobody's extraordinary prowess with a gun is reflected in a mirror at the saloon. On two occasions, Nobody admires *himself* in a small pocket-mirror, as his 'scriptwriting' for Beauregard is beginning to pay off: on the first, he has been given Beauregard's hat, in the Navajo cemetery, and wants to see how he looks in it; on the second, he has 'set up' a confrontation between Beauregard and Sullivan's men, in the main street of Cheyenne, and acts as the older man's 'guardian angel' (much as Harmonica did with Frank in the main street of Flagstone), by spotting snipers lurking in the shadows — with the aid of his mirror. Nobody further torments Sullivan's hit-men, by shooting it out with them in a Hall of Mirrors (*Lady from Shanghai* style). As Beauregard's confrontation with the Wild Bunch becomes the stuff of history (fulfilling Nobody's promise) we see the pages of a history book filling up with pictorial 'evidence' of the event. And when Nobody decides that the next move is to 'kill' Beauregard (ensuring that *his* status as myth will be

fixed) — a duel is 'set up' in the main streeet of New Orleans: this duel is transmitted to us (upside-down) through the viewfinder of the official photographer's camera, and both parties carefully position themselves, so that the image will not be spoiled. Nobody is Beauregard's scriptwriter — apart from the decision to sail to Europe, Beauregard does not make up his own mind about anything throughout the action of the film — and we watch 'reflections' of the ensuing scenario:

'Well, now you got me in the history books — how do I quit?'
　'There's only one way.'
　'How's that?'
　'You've got to die.'
　'Where?'
　'Where there's lots of people.'

Not since Arthur Penn's self-regarding *Left-Handed Gun* (1958) had there been so many mirror-images in a Western.

The second main theme, to which Leone's comment refers, is the difficulty of being a hero and anonymous. A series of (Lewis Carroll-inspired?) gags about Nobody's anonymity run through the film — 'Who are you?' 'Oh ... Nobody'; 'Nobody was faster on the draw'; and so on — and it is clear that Nobody will only make a 'name' for himself, if he can persuade Beauregard to act out his legend to the full. The Beauregard of legend implies the need for a Nobody (who can look up to him, and remind him of his 'obligations' as a mythic figure), just as a Nobody needs a Beauregard to give him some purpose in life. 'In the West as in life, the only person who is taken into account, is the man who is thought to be unbeatable.' As Beauregard reminds Nobody, after the 'showdown': 'You gambled too big this time, and there's too many people know you're somebody after all.' The man with no name must achieve some sort of identity, if he is to 'go down in history'. The setting for Nobody's quest — which, after Melville, could have begun with the words 'Call Me Nobody' — although specifically Western (turn of the century), is also a baroque netherland, consisting mainly of a bizarre Street of Pleasure (where a giant turns out to be a dwarf on stilts, Negroes are used as targets for custard pies, a saloon is the setting for elaborate machismo games, and a ghost train becomes the 'reflection' of a gunfight): Nobody must establish his prowess, by cutting these 'penny dreadful' effects down to

229-30 French and Italian publicity for *My Name Is Nobody* (1973), directed by Tonino Valerii under 'supervision' from Sergio Leone

231-3 Jack Beauregard runs 'smack into his destiny', thanks to the irrepressible Nobody: Henry Fonda's last stand against '150 pure-bred sons-of-bitches on horseback'

234-6 Henry Fonda as an ageing 'national monument', 'Terence Hill' as his scriptwriter, his audience, and the stage-manager of his final appearance 'in the history books'

1974-SERGIO LEONE/TERENCE HILL : Mon nom est personne

1976-TERENCE HILL explose dans

Un Génie
Deux Associés
Une Cloche

RAFRAN CINEMATOGRAFICA
présente
TERENCE HILL
Un Génie Deux Associés Une Cloche
Mise en scène DAMIANO DAMIANI

MIOU-MIOU • ROBERT CHARLEBOIS avec PATRICK McGOOHAN • RAIMUND HARMSDORF
et avec JEAN MARTIN • KLAUS KINSKI "DOC FOSTER"
Musique ENNIO MORRICONE dirigée par l'auteur • Produit par FULVIO MORSELLA et CLAUDIO MANCINI
Une coproduction Italo-Franco-Allemande • RAFRAN CINEMATOGRAFICA s/f.a Rome • A.M.L.F. Paris • RIALTO FILM PREBEN PHILIPSEN GMBH Berlin
Distribué par Sojof

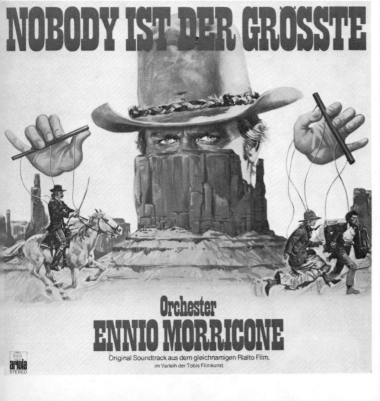

NOBODY IST DER GRÖSSTE

Orchester
ENNIO MORRICONE

Original Soundtrack aus dem gleichnamigen Rialto Film,
im Verleih der Tobis Filmkunst

237-8 French and German publicity for *A Genius* (1975), also known as *Nobody Is the Greatest*, directed by Damiano Damiani and 'presented' by Sergio Leone
239 (*Below*) 'Ford country' revisited. Sergio Leone stands in Monument Valley during the shooting of *A Genius*

size — he shoots the stilts from the dwarf, frees the unfortunate negroes ('Fun, isn't it?' he says, as he throws an extra-heavy custard pie at the manager), coolly wins the machismo games (much to everyone's surprise), uses the 'effects' in the ghost train to spook the opposition, and treats Sullivan's men as human fairground punch-bags (to the accompaniment of a children's nursery rhyme on the soundtrack). Only when he has shown the Street of Pleasure to be an empty facade, it appears, can he really begin to stage-manage Beauregard's destiny. Before he reaches the Street (at his first real meeting with Beauregard), he recounts the gunfighter's previous exploits, while the camera picks out a poster for a spectacular entertainment ('Western tableaux', 'The Ill-Fated Ship') on the wall behind. It is the era of the dime-novel, the Wild West circus, the origins of the popular Western genre: but there are still men around (ageing and bespectacled — far from the cool, flashily dressed gunmen in Sullivan's employ — but still with undeniable charisma) who can transcend the empty circus tricks which are the Easterners' only experience of the Wild West. It is partly *because* he has no reputation that Nobody can make fools of the Street of Pleasure people.

But 'to confront a myth with the negation of that myth' implies more than simply seeing through the cheap clichés which others accept as mythology. It also implies (within the frame of reference of the film) redefining the myth, in terms of 'its negation', prior to achieving (and acting out) some kind of synthesis — the final stage in the process of getting a living legend to come to terms with his own status, and also of preparing the ground for the destruction (thus 'enshrining') of that legend. And this is where the third major theme of *My Name Is Nobody* becomes important. For the film can be read as an exploration (in retrospect) of the relationship between the Italian Western (especially Leone's films) and the cherished myths of the Hollywood genre. The man with no name is more than simply the trickster of Sicilian puppet plays: in this film, he also resembles little Ivan, the wise young fool. He hero-worships the 'monuments' of the American West. He is proud of himself (especially of his drinking prowess and his 'expertise'). He succeeds in charming us with his free and easy behaviour: when he pinches an apple from a baby, or catches a fish, or messily eats a plate of beans, or torments an engine-driver in a stand-up lavatory, he somehow disarms us. Nobody is Trinity, the incredibly popular comedy hero of the post-Leone Italian Westerns.

Ever since Giuseppe Colizzi's *Revenge in El Paso* had appeared only a few grades below *Once Upon a Time in the West* in the box-office takings for 1968-9, the partnership of 'Terence Hill' with 'Bud Spencer' — derived from that of Clint Eastwood with Eli Wallach in *The Good, the Bad and the Ugly* — had dominated the production of successful Italian Westerns at Cinecittà. They had first worked together the previous year in *God Forgives, I Don't*. By 1971, their films were making more money at home than even Leone's 'Dollars' films had made five years before. Despite various attempts to fuse Spaghetti Westerns with popular fashions of the moment (for example, Lucio Fulci's *Four Horsemen of the Apocalypse*, which tried to look like *Easy Rider*, and Enzo Castellari's *Keoma*, which had the sheriff behaving like a Civil Rights marcher), the 'Trinity' films, starring the same partnership and directed by Enzo Barboni, continued to outsell them all. Apparently, the combination of an 'engaging' superstar who enjoys childish pranks, scenes of slapstick comedy, and a lot of stunts, was an unbeatable one — representing, perhaps, a reaction against the more political Spaghettis on the part of Italian producers (and audiences). So it was inevitable that Nobody should be Trinity himself. He is also, of course, the anonymous Italian audience, the moviegoer who made it all possible. (This was not the first time Leone had showed an affection for his audience, at the same time as revealing what he calls an urge to 'get even with the spectator'.) Beauregard, the icon worshipped by Nobody, is more than simply the venerable hero of John Ford's West — he is also an ageing legend (still with influence over the minds of the impressionable), who should be more conscious of the fact. He is reluctant to face up to this — preferring instead to talk about complications, or questions of survival: all he really wants to do is to retire (to Europe!), his last view of the West being from the deck of the *Sundowner*. His complexity as a character belies his charisma as a legend. *If* he 'runs smack into his destiny', then he can be relied on to stand his ground. But he has long since stopped looking for trouble. After his confrontation with the Wild Bunch, he actually hands his destiny over to Nobody — 'How do I quit?' Beauregard is Henry Fonda, or any other great hero of the traditional Western. From the point of view of the film, in a sense he *is* the Hollywood Western. Nobody — like the Cinecittà production system, always responsive to popular taste — pushes the traditional Western hero further and further in the direction of a 'Superman' comic. His prowess with a gun is speeded up — comic-strip style — as are the elaborate punch-ups he so evidently enjoys. (In *A Genius*, directed by Damiano Damiani in 1975 as a kind of sequel to *My Name Is Nobody*, this gag is extended further when Nobody's pistol comes out of its holster *before* Terence Hill has drawn it, and fires without anyone even touching it.) Not content with stories of Beauregard's past triumphs — involving the deaths of one man, two men, perhaps three — Nobody wants to see his hero face it out with 150 pure-bred sons-of-bitches, in a final, truly bizarre *extension* of the myth and of the genre. The Italian (and American) Western had been going in that direction anyway (witness the climax to a film like Buch's *Vengeance Is Mine*, 1969, where a gang of four outlaws shoot it out with the entire Mexican army in a bullring, or the climaxes of American Westerns of the post-Spaghetti era, such as *Butch Cassidy* — two against the Bolivian army — and, of course, *The Wild Bunch* — four against Mapache's army). This extension becomes in *My Name Is Nobody* mythic in a much more abstract way (baddies/riders in the sky/valkyries against Western hero/grand old movie star — with musical accompaniment provided by Morricone and Wagner). We know that Beauregard will not die (that we are present at some sort of living apotheosis) just as we know that Butch and the Kid, Bishop and the Gorches *will* die ('Hell . . . why not?'). Nobody is also, crucially, a liberalising influence: on two occasions in the film, much play is made of the fact that he goes out of his way (a rare commitment) to free Negroes who are being abused, and he clearly gets on well with the Navajo Indians — or rather, with the tatty remnants of that tribe who move on, *Cheyenne Autumn* style, from their graveyard. (In *A Genius*, Nobody stands in opposition to religious fanatics — even in a whorehouse — and to Indian-haters who are *posing* as anti-racialists.) During the scenes where Nobody is the focus of attention, there is an extraordinary emphasis on vulgar comedy (*Canterbury Tales* variety) — farting, pissing, belching, messy eating and so on: this, in direct contrast with the lyrical, twilight quality of the scenes involving Beauregard. (The film was shot in both American and Spain — the final shootout actually being filmed in New Orleans.) After ensuring that Beauregard will 'go down in history' (saving the

legend from himself), Nobody, in convincing him that he must 'die' (in fact saving the legend *and* the person), convinces us that we are *really* going to watch Beauregard's death. Like the crowd which gathers to watch this confrontation (a linear one, as in traditional Westerns), and like the photographer who is capturing the 'moment' for posterity, we accept the illusion. And the illusion is a scene from *Once Upon a Time in the West* — complete with a musical pastiche from the same film. This is where the central antagonism is leading — and it is, in the last analysis, an empty illusion (of a higher order, perhaps, than the Street of Pleasure clichés, but still . . .): it is also an illusion (and a ritual) which is essential for sustaining the legend. The schoolchildren, the schoolmarm, the blacks in the 'ghetto' area of town, the photographer, the myth-makers, and, in the cinemas, the audience who expect it — all believe that the duel is meant to be taking place. Only if they do can Beauregard retire with honour. The settling of accounts, like many of the *reflections* (or 'images') of Beauregard's legend throughout the film, takes the form of a replay of a scene from Leone's previous Westerns.

At first, Beauregard fights against the 'influence' of Nobody — he is too exuberant, too coarse, and his motivations are far from clear: 'I've always tried to steer away from trouble — but you seem to be looking for it all the time.' Eventually, however, Beauregard comes to accept that Nobody's qualities can in fact enhance his legend, for his exuberance is born of love for it: 'You can still do one thing — you can preserve a little of what made my generation tick. Maybe you'll do it in your own funny way, but we'll be grateful just the same.' By the end (when Beauregard gives his advice to Nobody, who is finally 'somebody after all'), the two men have both come to understand 'the moral of these new times' — which is contained in the parable of the little bird, the cow and the coyote. The 'moral' could not, by any stretch of the imagination, have come from a classic Hollywood Western: 'Folks that throw dirt on you, aren't always trying to hurt you. And folks that pull you out of a jam aren't always trying to help you. But the main point is: when you're up to your nose in shit — keep your mouth shut!' Within a philosophy like that, society's moral labels (as commonly recognised in classic Westerns) — Good, Bad or Ugly — cease to have much meaning. The Hollywood Western has come up against what looks like its negation, but has learned from the experience. So, the living legend can now retire to Europe with a good conscience. In Monte Hellman's *China 9, Liberty 37*, known in Italy as *Amore, Piombo e Furore* (1978) — another commentary of sorts on the rise and fall of the Spaghetti Western — a similar point is made, from another point of view: the two lovers on the run, a gunfighter (Fabio Testi) and a farmer's wife (Jenny Agutter), encounter a travelling myth-maker named Wilbur Olsen (played by Sam Peckinpah); he wants to turn their exploits into a dime novel ('I just want to buy a little legend — the lies we all need . . . Wild Bill Hickok left a rich widow. She made a fortune'). But the two lovers walk away from him, to continue their strange journey having learned about the 'legend' — but this time without feeling any compulsion to become a part of it. Perhaps the European Western can survive that way: its rhetoric needs to be stripped away. The point is similar, because both Peckinpah and Leone, by extending the Western genre in all sorts of outlandish directions, may well have succeeded in killing it off altogether. Monte Hellman's film (made six years after Valerii's) reflects on the failure of the Spaghetti Western genre — and the traditional one from which it was derived — to keep in touch with its audience, once the rhetoric could be taken no further.

As Beauregard writes, just as the ship is setting sail at the end of *My Name Is Nobody*:

> Looking back, it seems to me we were all a bunch of romantic fools; we still believed that a good pistol and a quick showdown could solve everything. Then, the West used to be a lot of wide open spaces, with lots of elbow room — so you never ran into the same person twice. By the time you came along, it was changed — it got small and crowded, and we kept bumping into the same people all the time. . . . If you are able to run around the West peacefully catching flies, its only because fellows like me were there first — the same fellows you want to see written up in history books. . . . Violence has changed too — its grown, better organised, and a good pistol don't mean a damn thing any more . . . its your kind of time not mine. That's why people like me have got to go: and this is why you fixed that gunfight with me — to get me out of the West clean. Guess I'm talking like a damn preacher — but its your fault. What can you expect of a national monument! I kinda miss you — even if you have been a stinkin', nasty trouble-maker all the time. Thanks for everything just the same.

Leone has made the transformation from Nobody to Somebody: for *A Fistful of Dollars*, he was billed as 'Bob Robertson'; for the next two films his real name revealed itself letter by letter, first from the barrel of a revolver, then from the barrel of a cannon; for *Once Upon a Time in the West*, the wide-screen credit read 'A Sergio Leone film.' His reflections on this transformation constitute a very appropriate *arrivederci* to the Italian Western.

Appendix 1
Critical Filmography

Well over 300 Spaghetti Westerns were released in Italy between 1963 and 1969 alone: the peak year for production was 1966-7 (when 66 were made) lying midway between the two least productive years, 1963 (when 10 Westerns were made) and 1969 (when only 7 Westerns were made). Fewer than 20 per cent of these Spaghettis have been distributed internationally. I have seen approximately 55 Italian Westerns (most of them distributed internationally). A thorough (if not always accurate) list of *all* Italian Westerns made between 1963 and 1969 has been published in Germany (Goetz and Banz, *Der Italo Western*, Society of German Film Clubs, 1969), and an equally thorough (if not always accurate) list of those Italian Westerns distributed in the UK is also available (in Staig and Williams, *Italian Western*, London, 1975). David Austen (*Films and Filming*, July 1971) has compiled a list of 172 Italian and German Westerns made between 1962 and 1969, with credits. The 'Cinéma Bis' section of the French magazine *Vampirella* (1970 onwards, bi-monthly) has included useful filmographies of the 'Django' formula, the 'Sartana' formula, and Sollima's work. Plot summaries (with stills) from most Westerns made for domestic Italian consumption are available in the annual pressbooks prepared by Unitalia Film; despite quaint translations ('the hill of boots', 'Drop them or I'll shoot') these are key sources of information. The *Monthly Film Bulletin* (January, 1967, February 1969) has published two checklists of pseudonyms. The directors of Spaghettis are usually Italian, the locations crews Spanish, the casts international. Nearly all Spaghettis are co-productions (often with Italian companies having the major commitment). The following Filmography deals only with those European Westerns which I have selected for thorough analysis in this book. The films are listed under individual directors. Asterisks refer to separate entries elsewhere in the Filmography.

DIRECTORS AND KEY FILMS

Sergio Corbucci (alias 'Stanley Corbett', 'Gordon Wilson, Jr')
Born 6 December 1927, in Rome. Film critic on the journals *Schermi del Mondo* and *Stars and Stripes*. Film training began in 1948. Was assistant director to Roberto Rosselini. As well as working in the Italian film industry, made documentaries for Canadian television, in the mid-1950s. His brother Bruno (with whom he is often confused in filmographies, such as Goetz and Banz) is a prolific Cinecittà screenwriter and occasional director. Corbucci has tried his hand at most popular Cinecittà genres (he has been associated with well over 50 films), and his speciality seems to be parodying visual clichés — often in rather a manic way. Has called his specific contribution to the Italian Western 'Zapata-Spaghetti', the films in question characteristically being 'proletarian fables — where the baddies are on the Right, the goodies on the Left'. At his best, he reckons, when working with Franco Nero ('John Ford had John Wayne — me, I have Franco Nero'). Enjoys black humour (especially, he says, when associated with bizarre forms of violence) and detests happy endings (his *Great Silence*, 1968, closes on the brutal death of the hero). The success of *Django*, especially in West Germany, assured Corbucci large budgets ($1 million to $1½ million) for the later Franco Nero Westerns. According to his costume designer on *Companeros*, Jürgen Henze, 'like most Italian Western directors, Corbucci pays an enormous amount of attention to detail'. This shows, in his big-budget Spaghettis.

Films analysed in the text:

Django (1966)
Italian-Spanish co-production. Wide screen. Eastmancolor.
Director: Sergio Corbucci; Producer: Manolo Bolognini; Screenplay: Sergio and Bruno Corbucci, with Franco Rossetti, José G. Naesso, Piero

Vivarelli; Photography: Enzo Barboni;* Music: Luis Enrique Bacalov.*
Cast: Franco Nero (Django), Loredana Nuscick (Maria), with José Bodalo, Angel Alvarez, Gino Pernice, Simone Arrag, Ivan Scratuglia, Erik Schippers, Raphael Albaicin, José Canalejas and Eduardo Fajardo.

A Professional Gun (Il Mercenario) (1968)
Italian-Spanish co-production. Techniscope. Technicolor.
Director: Sergio Corbucci; Producer: Alberto Grimaldi;* Story: Franco Solinas, Giorgio Arlorio; Screenplay: Sergio Corbucci, Luciano Vincenzoni, Sergio Spina; Photography: Alejandro Ulloa;* Music: Ennio Morricone, Bruno Nicolai.*
Cast: Franco Nero (Sergei Kowalski, the 'Polak'), Tony Musante (Eufemio), Jack Palance (Curly), Giovanni Ralli (Columba), Eduardo Fajardo (Alfonso Garcia), Bruno Corazzari (Studs), Remo De Angeles (Hudo), Joe Camel (Larkin), with Franco Giacobini, Vicente Roca, José Riesgo, Angel Ortiz, Fernando Villena, Tito Garcia, Angel Alvarez, Alvaro De Luna, Raf Baldassare.

Compañeros (Vamos a Matar, Compañeros!) (1970)
Italian-Spanish-West German co-production. Techniscope. Technicolor.
Director: Sergio Corbucci; Producer: Antonio Morelli; Story: Sergio Corbucci; Screenplay: Dino Maiuri, Massimo de Rita, Fritz Ebert and Sergio Corbucci; Photography: Alejandro Ulloa;* Music: Ennio Morricone, Bruno Nicolai.*
Cast: Franco Nero (Yod Peterson, the 'Penguin'), Tomas Milian* (Basco), Jack Palance (Wooden-handed John), Fernando Rey (Professor Xantos), Iris Berben (Lola), Francisco Bodalo (General Mongo), Karin Schubert (Zaira), Eduardo Fajardo (Colonel), Gerard Tichy (Lieutenant), with Lorenzo Robledo and Jesus Fernandez.

The following films, dating from various stages in Corbucci's career, are also of interest: *The Last Days of Pompeii* (1959, co-writer and assistant); *Totò Against Maciste* (1962, co-writer, the first of several films featuring the comedian Totò, including parodies of *Lawrence of Arabia* and *La Dolce Vita*, the latter directed by Corbucci); *Son of the Leopard* (director, with the comedy double-act Franchi and Ingrassia); *Maciste Against the Vampire* (1961, director, with Gordon Scott as the muscleman); *Romulus and Remus* (1961, director, with Gordon Scott and Steve Reeves); *Son of Spartacus* (1962, director, with Steve Reeves); and a series of over 10 Westerns, with Corbucci as director (and usually co-writer), including *Minnesota Clay* (1964, the first

Spaghetti to be distributed with the director's real name on the credits), *Ringo and his Golden Pistol* (1966), *The Hellbenders* (1966, with Joseph Cotten), *Navajo Joe* (1966, with Burt Reynolds in a part he was to re-create for *Deliverance*), *The Great Silence* (1968, with Jean-Louis Trintignant and Klaus Kinski*), *The Specialist* (1969, also known as *Drop Them or I'll Shoot*, with Johnny Halliday — an anti-hippie polemic), and the three Franco Nero films listed above.

Damiano Damiani

Born 23 July 1922, in Pasiano, near Udine. Student at the Academy of Fine Arts, Milan. Between 1946 and 1956 directed short documentaries. After that worked as a scriptwriter (usually on neo-realist projects, with Cesare Zavattini among others). Directed two of Zavattini's scripts in the early 1960s (*Red Lips*, 1960; *Arturo's Island*, 1962), then made *Empty Canvas* (1963, an adaptation of a Moravia novel), and *Day of the Owl* (about the Mafia). Like Lizzani,* has only made two Spaghetti Westerns, both with overtly political themes: in 1975, under the 'supervision' of Sergio Leone, made *Un Genio, Due Compari, Un Pollo* (roughly *A Genius, Two Companions, an Idiot*), known in Germany as *Nobody Ist der Grösste* (*Nobody Is the Greatest*) and marketed as a sequel to *My Name Is Nobody*. This post-Leone Western, largely set in Monument Valley, contains much satire on the military (Indian-haters posing as liberal officers, pig-headed sergeants) and the church (fanatics caught with their pants down): but the fast-moving gags, parodies of other films, and *coups de théâtre* predominate.

Films analysed in the text:

A Bullet for the General (Quien Sabe?) (1966)
Italian. Techniscope. Technicolor.
Director: Damiano Damiani; Producer: Bianco Manini; Story: Salvatore Laurani; Adaptation/Dialogue: Franco Solinas; Photography: Tony Secchi; Music: Luis Enrique Bacalav* (supervision: Ennio Morricone*).
Cast: Gian Maria Volonté* (El Chuncho), Lou Castel (Bill Tate, the Gringo), Klaus Kinski* (Santo, the priest), Martine Beswick (Adelita), Jaime Fernandez (General Elias), Andrea Checci (Don Felipe), Spartaco Conversi (Cirillo), Joaquin Parra (Picaro), José Manuel Martin (Raimundo), Santiago Santos (Guapo), Valentino Macchi (Pedrito).

A Genius (Un Genio, Due Compari, Un Pollo) (1975)

Italian-French-West German co-production.
Panavision. Technicolor.
Director: Damiano Damiani ('supervised by Sergio
Leone'); Producers: Fulvio Morsella, Claudio
Mancini (Rafran); Screenplay: Ernesto Gastaldi,
Fulvio Morsella; Music: Ennio Morricone* (Singer:
Catherine Howe).
Cast: 'Terence Hill'/Mario Girotti (in the 'Nobody'
role), Miou Miou, Robert Charlebois, Patrick
McGoohan, Klaus Kinski,* Jean Martin.

Sergio Leone (alias 'Bob Robertson')

Born 3 January 1929 in Naples, into a family which
was deeply involved in the Italian cinema.
Originally, he intended to be a lawyer, and went to
law school in Rome. Characteristically, Leone's
early film training was during the neo-realist period
(working as 'voluntary assistant' to de Sica, among
others), his first important film work during the
'American invasion' of the 1950s (as assistant on
over 50 films, side by side with Hollywood directors
such as Aldrich, Marton, Walsh, Wise, Wyler and
Zinneman, and stunt directors such as Canutt).
Took over the direction of *The Last Days of
Pompeii* (Bonnard, 1959), supervising the two
assistants, Duccio Tessari and Sergio Corbucci. In
1960, directed Lea Massari (Dalia), Rory Calhoun
(Dario), George Marshall (Periocles) and Angel
Aranda (Periocles' friend) in *The Colossus of
Rhodes*, an Italian-Spanish co-production written
by Duccio Tessari, de Martino, Giavoli and others.
In 1961-2, directed the Italian version of *Sodom
and Gomorrah* (under Robert Aldrich's
'supervision'), a French-Italian co-production, with
dialogue by Michael Audley, starring Stewart
Granger (Lot), Pier Angeli (Ildith), Stanley Baker
(Astaroth), Anouk Aimée (Berah), Rosanna
Podesta (Shuah), Giacomo Rosi Stuart (Ishmael),
Scilla Gabel and Gary Raymond. To my mind, this
is the first recognisably 'Leone' picture. Although
in interviews Leone has suggested that his
Westerns can be 'read' as commentaries on the
classic Westerns of John Ford, he seems to owe a
lot to the aesthetic of less mainstream Westerns by
Fuller, Ray, Boetticher, Aldrich and Wise (*Two
Flags West*, perhaps, for the prison camp sequences
of *The Good, the Bad and the Ugly*). Leone's major
contribution, however, has been to redefine the
language of the Western within an authentically
Italian cultural context. After *Fistful*, which was
derived from the story of Kurosawa's *Yojimbo*,
Leone preferred to work from his own story
outlines (in the case of *Once Upon a Time*,
originally written in collaboration with Bernardo
Bertolucci), with two favourite Cinecittà scenarists

to fill out the dialogue: Luciano Vincenzoni (*For a
Few*, *The Good . . .*, and especially, *Duck, You
Sucker*) and Sergio Donati (who, in addition to
co-writing the dialogue for *Once Upon a Time*,
helped to write the screenplays of Sollima's
political Spaghettis, *The Big Gundown* and *Face to
Face*). Age and Scarpelli, well known for their
work on picaresque costume adventures (such as
L'Armata Brancaleone) were also brought in for the
script of *The Good . . .* Ennio Morricone's most
inventive (and appropriate) scores were written
for Leone, and *Once Upon a Time*, the high point
of their creative partnership, was shot *after*
Morricone's score had been recorded.

Films analysed in the text:

A Fistful of Dollars (Per un Pugno di Dollari)
(1964)
Italian-Spanish-West German co-production.
Techniscope. Technicolor.
Exteriors: Almeria. Interiors: Cinecittà.
Director: Sergio Leone; Producers: Arrigo Colombo,
Giorgio Papi; Screenplay: Sergio Leone, Duccio
Tessari, Victor A. Catena, G. Schock, based on the
film *Yojimbo* by Akira Kurosawa; Photography:
'Jack Dalmas'/Massimo Dallamano; Music: 'Dan
Savio'/Ennio Morricone.*
Cast: Clint Eastwood (The Man With No Name),
'John Wells'/Gian Maria Volonté* (Ramon Rojo),
Marianne Koch (Marisol), Pepe Calvo (Silvanito),
Wolfgang Lukschy (John Baxter), Sieghardt Rupp
(Esteban Rojo), Antonio Prieto (Benito Rojo),
Margherita Lozano (Consuela Baxter), Daniel
Martin (Julian), 'Carol Brown'/Bruno Carotenuto
(Antonio Baxter), Benito Stefanelli (Rubio),
'Richard Stuyvesant'/Mario Brega (Chico), Josef
Egger (Piripero), with Antonio Vica, Raf
Baldassare.

*For a Few Dollars More (Per Qualche Dollaro
in Più)* (1965)
Italian-Spanish-West German co-production.
Techniscope. Technicolor. Exteriors: Almeria.
Interiors: Cinecittà.
Director: Sergio Leone; Assistant Director: Tonino
Valerii;* Producer: Alberto Grimaldi;* Story:
Fulvio Morsella, Sergio Leone: Screenplay: Sergio
Leone, Luciano Vincenzoni; Photography: Massimo
Dallamano; Music: Ennio Morricone, with Bruno
Nicolai.*
Cast: Clint Eastwood (The Man With No Name/'Il
Monco'), Lee Van Cleef (Colonel Mortimer), Gian
Maria Volonté* (Indio), Klaus Kinski* (Hunchback),
Mara Krup (Hotelier's wife), Josef Egger (Old
Prophet), Marianne Koch (Colonel's sister), Mario
Brega (Nino), with Aldo Sambrell, Luigi Pistilli,

Benito Stefanelli, Panos Papadopoulos, Roberto
Camardiel, Luis Rodriguez, Diana Rabito,
Giovanni Tarallo, Mario Meniconi, Lorenzo
Robledo.

*The Good, the Bad and the Ugly (Il Buono, il
Brutto, il Cattivo)* (1966)
Italian. Techniscope. Technicolor. Exteriors:
Almeria, Burgos. Interiors: Cinecittà.
Director: Sergio Leone; Assistant Director:
Giancarlo Santi;* Producer: Alberto Grimaldi;*
Screenplay: Sergio Leone, Luciano Vincenzoni,
Age-Scarpelli; Photography: Tonino Delli Colli;
Music: Ennio Morricone, with Bruno Nicolai.*
Cast: Clint Eastwood (the Good), Lee Van Cleef
(the Bad), Eli Wallach (Tuco, the Ugly), Aldo
Giuffré (Northern Officer), Mario Brega
(Sergeant Wallace), Luigi Pistilli (Padré Ramirez),
Marianne Koch (Maria), Al Mulock (one-armed
Gunslinger), with Rada Rassimov, Enzo Petito,
Claudio and Sando Scarchelli, Livio Lorenzon,
Antonio Castale, Benito Stefanelli, Chelo Alonso,
Silvana Bacci, Antonio Basas, Aldo Sambrell,
Molino Rojo.

*Once Upon a Time in the West (C'era una Volta
il West)* (1968)
Italian-American co-production. Techniscope.
Technicolor. Exteriors: Utah, Arizona; Almeria,
Guadix (where 'Flagstone' was constructed).
Interiors: Cinecittà.
Director: Sergio Leone; Assistant Director:
Giancarlo Santi;* Producer: Fulvio Morsella
(Rafran); Story: Bernardo Bertolucci, Sergio Leone,
Dario Argento; Screenplay: Sergio Leone, Sergio
Donati; Photography: Tonino Delli Colli; Music:
Ennio Morricone.*
Cast: Henry Fonda (Frank), Claudia Cardinale
(Jill McBain), Jason Robards (Cheyenne), Charles
Bronson (Harmonica), Frank Wolff (Brett McBain),
Gabriele Ferzetti (Mr Morton), Keenan Wynn
(Sheriff), Paolo Stoppa (Sam), Marco Zuanelli
(Wobbles), Lionel Stander (Barman), Jack Elam
(Frank's man), Woody Strode (Stony), Al Mulock
(Knuckles), John Frederick (Member of Frank's
gang), Enzo Santianello (Timmy McBain), Dino
Mele (Harmonica as a young man).

In 1970, together with Visconti, Petri, Monicelli,
Zavattini and others, Leone directed part of the
Document on Giuseppe Pinelli, 12th December —
an 'alternative newsreel'.

*Duck, You Sucker/A Fistful of Dynamite
(Giù la Testa/Il était une fois la Révolution)* (1971)
Italian-American co-production. Techniscope.

Technicolor. Exteriors: Dublin, Almeria, Granada,
Madrid. Interiors: Cinecittà.
Director: Sergio Leone; 2nd Unit Director:
Giancarlo Santi;* Producer: Fulvio Morsella
(Rafran); Story: Sergio Leone; Screenplay: Luciano
Vincenzoni, adapted by Sergio Leone; Photography:
Giuseppe Ruzzolini; 2nd Unit Photography: Franco
Delli Colli; Music: Ennio Morricone.*
Cast: Rod Steiger (Juan Miranda), James Coburn
(Sean Mallory), Romolo Valli (Dr Villega), Maria
Monti (Adolita), Rick Battaglia (Santerna), Franco
Graziosi (Dom Jaime), Antonio Domingo
(Guttierez), Goffredo Pistoni (Nino), Roy Bosier
(the Landowner), John Frederick (the American),
Nino Casale (the Solicitor), Jean Rougeul (the
Priest), Vincenzo Norvese (Pancho), Corrada
Solari (Sebastian), Biaco La Rocca (Benito), Renato
Pontecchi (Pepe), Franco Collace (Napoleon),
Michael Harvoy (a Yankee).

My Name Is Nobody (Il Mio Nome è Nessuno)
(1973)
Italian-French-West German co-production.
Panavision. Technicolor. Exteriors: New Orleans,
Almeria. Interiors: Cinecittà.
Director: Tonino Valerii* ('supervised by Sergio
Leone'); Producer: Fulvio Morsella (Rafran); Story:
Sergio Leone, adapted by Fulvio Morsella, Ernesto
Gastaldi; Screenplay: Ernesto Gastaldi;
Photography: Giuseppe Ruzzolini (America),
Armando Nannuzzi (Italy/Spain); Music: Ennio
Morricone.*
Cast: Henry Fonda (Jack Beauregard), 'Terence
Hill'/Mario Girotti (Nobody), Jean Martin
(Sullivan), Piero Lulli (Sheriff), Leo Gordon (Red),
R.G. Armstrong (Honest John), Remus Peets (Big
Gun), Mario Brega (Pedro), Antoine Saint Jean
(Scape), Benito Stefanelli (Porteley — also, the
stunt arranger), Mark Mazza (Don John), Franco
Angrisano (Treno), Alexander Allerson (Rex),
Angelo Novi (Barman), Tommy Polgar (Juan),
Carla Mancini (Mother), Antonio Luigi Guerra
(Official), with Emile Feist, Geoffrey Lewis,
Antonio Palombi, Neill Summers, Steve Kanaly,
Humbert Mittendorf, Ulrich Muller, Claus
Schmidt.

See also *A Genius* (1975, Damiano Damiani).

Carlo Lizzani (alias 'Lee Beaver')
Born 30 April 1922, in Rome. Film critic on the
journals *Cinema* and *Bianco e Nero* — his
contribution being a series of manifestos in favour
of 'neo-realism'. Film training began in 1946. Wrote
scripts for Rosselini. Author of a study of *The*

Italian Cinema (1953), again with an emphasis on
the contribution of the neo-realists. Since 1951
(when he directed *Achtung! Banditti!* with Gina
Lollobrigida — 'a co-operative experiment') has been
a specialist in films about bandits of all descriptions
(including Mafiosi, contract killers, street gangs,
and Mexican bandits/revolutionaries). *The Hills Run
Red*, his most impressive Western and a great
box-office hit in Italy, represents a fusion of motifs
from *Fistful*, with revenge themes and political
themes (represented by the tyranny of Mendez and
his henchmen) which were later to become staple
formulae in Cinecittà Westerns. *Requiescant*, with
Lou Castel (from *A Bullet for the General*) and
Pasolini (who had acted in a Lizzani film once
before — *Il Gobbo*, 1960), owes much to Damiani's
film, with the main emphasis on a theme which
had provided the subplot to *A Bullet* — the role
of the church in the Mexican Revolution. In 1974,
Lizzani directed *The Last Days of Mussolini* (with
Rod Steiger) — a project that had originally been
announced as a possible Leone film.

Films mentioned in the text:

The Hills Run Red (Un Fiume di Dollari) (1966)
Italian. Techniscope. Technicolor.
Director: Carlo Lizzani; Producers: Dino de
Laurentiis, Ermanno Donati; Screenplay: Dean
Craig; Photography: Antonio Secchi; Music: Ennio
Morricone.*
Cast: Thomas Hunter (Jerry Brewster), Henry Silva
(Mendez), Dan Duryea (Getz, the Lawman), Nando
Gazzalo (Ken Seagall), Nicoletta Machiavelli (Mary
Ann), Gianna Serra (Hattie), Loris Loddi (Tim),
Geoffrey Copleston (Horner), with Paolo Magalotti,
Tiberio Mitri, Vittorio Bonos, Mirko Valentin,
and Guido Celano.

Requiescant (1967)
Italian-German co-production. Techniscope.
Eastmancolor.
Director and Producer: Carlo Lizzani; Screenplay:
Adriano Bolzoni, Armando Crispino, Lucio
Battistrada, based on an idea by Renato Izzo and
Franco Bucceri; Photography: Sandro Mancori;
Music: Riz Ortolani.*
Cast: Lou Castel (Requiescant), Mark Damon
(Ferguson), Pier Paolo Pasolini (Don Juan), Barbara
Frey (Princy), Franco Citti (Burt), Nineto Davoli
(Trumpeter), with Rossano Martini, Mirella
Maravidi, Carlo Palmucci, Nino Musco, Anna Carres,
Lorenzo Guerrieri, Pier Annibale Danovi, and
Vittorio Duse.

Domenico Paolella (alias 'Paul Fleming')
Born 15 October 1918 in Foggia. His family was
originally from the province of Apulia (Puglia). Film
training began in 1935 when, still at law college in
Florence, he directed two experimental shorts with
Remigio Del Grosso (later to be the scriptwriter of
Moulin des Supplices). After graduating, he wrote
film criticisms for *Milano* and *Mondo Latino*, and
was one of the assistants on Gallone's *Scipio
Africanus* (with Giorgio Ferroni and Romolo
Marcellini — both of whom were to become prolific
directors after the war). Paolella was responsible for
much of the battle footage. In 1938, he began work
on a series of short documentaries (nearly 100 in
all), with *Castel Sant'Angelo*, and in the following
year wrote a critical study of *Experimental Cinema*,
published in Naples. One of his documentaries,
Fantasmi a Cinecittà (1940), is about the making of
films at that studio (still a relatively recent
institution), and features Totò, Alessandro Blasetti,
Valli, plus other stars of the day. Two of his films
about the Russian campaign were banned outright
by the censor. Immediately after the fall of
Mussolini, he made *L'Italia S'è Desta*, one of the
first films about Italian resistance to Fascism. In
1946, he founded the film journal *La Settimana
Incom*, which he edited for the first 600 issues,
then went to the States to make *America*
(commentary by Orson Welles) and two gangster
films for television (1952). On returning to Italy,
Paolella directed two very successful musicals
(*Canzoni di Mezzo*; *Canzoni, Canzoni, Canzoni*),
several Totò films, and *Blue Jeans* (starring Pascale
Petit). Then, in 1958, he published an 'exposé'
novel, *Le Italiane Furiose*, and worked with Pasolini
on a screenplay derived from it. After directing
I Teddy Boys della Canzone (1960), he began to
specialise in swashbuckling adventures such as
Il Terrore dei Mari; *Il Giustiziere dei Mari*;
Prigioniere dell'Isola del Diavolo; and *Il Segreto
dello Sparviero Nero* (all 1961 — a sudden increase
in productivity). In the following year, he made
one 'Maciste' film, one 'Ursus', and one 'Scotland
Yard' thriller in West Germany. Then, in 1964, he
made four 'peplums' — featuring Maciste, Goliath,
Hercules and 'the Gladiator'. Several directors of
Spaghettis (among them Sergio Sollima) gained
valuable experience either assisting or co-directing
with Paolella, who abandoned 'mini-epics' after
1964 to concentrate on thrillers, horror films —
and Westerns.

Paolella directed two Spaghettis: *Hate for Hate
(Odio per Odio)*, 1967, an Italian-Spanish co-
production, screenplay by Bruno Corbucci,*
photographed by Alejandro Ulloa,* starring
Antonio Sabato, John Ireland, Gloria Milland,

Fernando Sancho; and *Execution*, 1968, an Italian production, screenplay by Paolella, photographed by Aldo Scavarda, starring John Richardson and Mimmo Palmara.

In his article 'La Psicoanalisi dei Poveri' (1965), Paolella showed himself to be one of the few Italian directors to have thought seriously about the social implications of the shift in popularity from muscleman epics to Westerns among Italian cinemagoing audiences.

Giulio Questi

Born 18 March 1924 in Bergamo. A journalist in Rome. Film training began in 1954. Assistant director on (among many other films) *La Dolce Vita* (Fellini, 1960). Only one Italian Western, which operates as a bizarre commentary on the first phase of the Spaghetti boom, and especially on derivatives from *Fistful*.

Django, Kill (Se sei Vivo Spara/Gringo Uccidi) (1967)
Italian-Spanish co-production. Techniscope. Technicolor.
Director: Giulio Questi; Screenplay: Giulio Questi, Franco Arcalli; based on an idea by M. del Carmen and M. Roman; Photography: Franco Delli Colli; Music: Ivan Vandor.
Cast: Tomas Milian* (Django), Piero Lulli (Oaks), Milo Queseda (Tembler), Paco Sanz (Hagerman), Roberto Camardiel (Zorro), Marilu Tolo (Flory), Patrizia Valturri (Elizabeth), Raymond Lovelock (Evans).

Harald Reinl

Born 9 July 1908, in Bad Ischl, Austria. Film training began in the late 1920s, as assistant director to Arnold Fanck, on a series of 'mountain films', some with Leni Riefenstahl and Luis Trenker. In the war years, assisted Leni Riefenstahl (another of Fanck's 'discoveries'), and took over some of her (uncompleted) projects just after the war. Between 1949, when he made his first solo film as a director, and 1970, Reinl directed 46 films — usually winter sports adventures, swashbucklers, and Edgar Wallace thrillers: characteristic products of his pre-'Winnetou' career include *Weisse Hölle Mont-Blanc* (1952), *Die grünen Teufel von Monte Cassino* (1958), *Die Prinzessen von St. Wolfgang* (1957). In 1962 Dr Reinl directed the first of the 'Winnetou' films, loosely based on the works of Karl May, *The Treasure of Silver Lake* (*Der Schatz im Silbersee*, West Germany): this Western, which used locations in Yugoslavia, set the tone for future adaptations of the 'Winnetou' stories, and the same production team (writer Harald G. Petersson, director of photography Ernst Kalinke, musical director Martin Böttcher) was to collaborate on three more Karl May projects, as well as one (less successful) Fenimore Cooper adaptation (*The Last Tomahawk/Die Letzte Mohikaner*, 1965, with Italian Western hero Antonio de Teffé in the lead role). In 1966, director Alfred Vohrer took over the series, with *Thunder at the Border/Winnetou und sein Freund Old Firehand* (West Germany), while Reinl completed his spectacular two-part version of *Die Nibelungen*: Reinl's *Nibelungen* used the same locations as his 'Winnetou' films, the same scriptwriter (Petersson), and the same director of photography (Kalinke, who, presumably because he was too busy, did not photograph *Thunder at the Border*); Brunhild was played by Karin Dor (who had recently worked with Reinl on *Winnetou II*, as the Big Chief's daughter), and the *Monthly Film Bulletin* called Reinl's saga 'a de luxe edition of one of his Karl May Westerns'. Lex Barker (ex-Tarzan) and Pierre Brice (ex-Zorro) appeared as 'Old Shatterhand' and Winnetou in the four Reinl Westerns, but after that, a series of new sidekicks were introduced to act opposite Brice, including 'Old Surehand' (Stewart Granger) and 'Old Firehand' (Rod Cameron) — not all of whom had featured in the original Karl May stories. Marie Versini (who, as Ntscho-tschi, was killed at the end of *Winnetou the Warrior*) was resurrected for *Thunder at the Border*. Later films in the series (from *Winnetou II* onwards) often featured a foppish English gentleman (again, a new invention) for comic relief. Reinl's *Winnetou II* (the first of the series to be co-produced in Italy) introduced Mario Girotti in the role of a young American hero, Lieutenant Merril: as 'Terence Hill', the same Mario Girotti was later to become a major star of the Italian popular cinema. Harald Reinl's Karl May Westerns were *The Treasure of the Silver Lake* (1962), *Winnetou the Warrior* (1963), *Last of the Renegades* (*Winnetou II*, 1964), and *The Desperado Trail* (*Winnetou III*, 1965). As a veteran of the German cinema ('mountain' sagas, Riefenstahl's projects) who had worked through the period of the Third Reich, Dr Reinl must have seemed the ideal choice to direct popular films based on the works of Karl May: Petersson sensibly decided to send up the wilder excesses of May's strange morality, and Reinl had, since the war, made a name for himself as an action director of bland adventure stories. Kalinke's images occasionally recall the 'mountain films', but, on the whole, the emphasis is less on May's *Übermensch*, the noble savage, than on special effects, elaborate stunts, and action (with more violence than Karl May would have accepted).

Film analysed in the text:

Winnetou the Warrior (*Winnetou I*) (1963)
West German-Yugoslavian-French co-production.
Cinemascope. Eastmancolor.
Director: Harald Reinl; Producer: Horst Wendlandt;
Screenplay: Harald G. Petersson; Photography:
Ernst W. Kalinke; Music: Martin Böttcher.
Cast: Lex Barker (Old Shatterhand), Pierre Brice
(Winnetou), Mario Adorf (Santer), Marie Versini
(Nscho-tschi), Ralf Wolter (Sam Hawkens), Walter
Barnes (Bancroft), Mavid Popovic (Intschu-tschuna),
Dunja Rajter (Belle), Chris Howland (the Agent).

Sergio Sollima (alias 'Simon Sterling')
Film training began in 1959. Between 1959 and
1964, co-directed or co-wrote a series of 'peplums'
for Domenico Paolella and Gianfranco Parolini,
including *Maciste Against the Pirate King* (1962),
Battle of the Giants (1962), *Revolt of the
Gladiators* (1963), as well as other films for Paolella
(such as *I Teddy Boys della Canzone*, 1960).
Directed three spy adventures in 1965-6 (two
featuring Agent 353, acted by George Ardisson, and
Requiem for a Secret Agent, 1966, with Stewart
Granger and Peter van Eyck) before turning to
Italian Westerns. Little evidence of interest in
popular political cinema (except, perhaps, in
Requiem) before he made *The Big Gundown*, based
on Solinas' original idea. Since the Spaghetti boom,
has made *Violent City* (1970), a contemporary
film noir about a contract killer (Charles Bronson),
which he co-scripted, and which attempts to relate
the concerns of his Westerns (at least, of the two
which were released internationally) to the world
of American business life — with strange, often
effective results. Also *Revolver* (1973), a thriller
with Oliver Reed, Fabio Testi and Johnny Halliday,
and a six-part Franco-Italian TV series, *Sandokan*,
based on the novels of Emilio Salgari, with Kafir
Bedi in the title role, and Adolfo Celi as the nasty
English colonial administrator, Brooke. The third of
Sollima's political Westerns — *Run, Man, Run*
(1968, again featuring Tomas Milian as Cuchillo,
this time playing 'cat and mouse' with a Gringo
named Cassidy (John Ireland), and 'persuading'
him to donate some hidden treasure to the
revolutionary cause) — has not been released
internationally. Sollima lists Glauber Rocha among
the influences on his work, and considers that his
Westerns are particularly noteworthy for 'their
total disregard of the folklore of the West'. Alain
Petit has written that Sollima's films 'have little

connection with the surrealist madness of the
early films of Corbucci, or with the megalomania
of the later Leone films . . . they have an
atmosphere of *anger*, tinged with much bitterness'.
Sollima's political comments may be crude (in
Run, Man, Run, the gold is hidden in an antique
printing press), and his strange sense of humour may
sometimes belie what commitment he has, but he is
certainly less hampered by considerations of
formula than most other Spaghetti directors.

Films analysed in the text:

The Big Gundown (*La Resa dei Conti*) (1966)
Italian-Spanish co-production. Techniscope.
Technicolor.
Director: Sergio Sollima; Producer: Alberto
Grimaldi;* Story: Franco Solinas, with Fernando
Morandi; Screenplay: Sergio Sollima, Sergio
Donati; Photography: Carlo Carlini; Music: Ennio
Morricone, with Bruno Nicolai.*
Cast: Lee Van Cleef (Jonathan Corbett), Tomas
Milian* (Cuchillo), Walter Barnes (Brokston),
Luisa Rivelli (Lizzie), Fernando Sancha (Captain
Segura), Nieves Navarro (the Widow), Benito
Stefanelli (Jess), Lanfranco Ceccarelli (Jack),
Roberto Camardiel (Jellicol), with Nello
Pazzafini, Spartaco Conversi, Romano Puppo,
Tom Felleghi, Calisto Calisti, Antonio Casas
and José Torres.

Face to Face (*Faccia a Faccia*) (1967)
Italian-Spanish co-production. Techniscope.
Technicolor.
Director: Sergio Sollima; Producer: Alberto
Grimaldi;* Story: Sergio Donati, Sergio Sollima;
Screenplay: Sergio Sollima; Photography: Rafael
Pacheco; Music: Ennio Morricone.*
Cast: Gian Maria Volonté* (Brad Fletcher), Tomas
Milian* (Solomon 'Beauregard' Bennett), William
Berger (Charly Siringo), Jolanda Modio (Marie),
Carole André (Cattle Annie), Gianni Rizzo
(Williams), Lidia Alfonsi (Belle de Winton), Angel
de Pozo (Maximilian), Aldo Sambrell (Zachary
Shot), with Nello Pazzafini, José Torres, Frank
Brana, Antonio Casas, Linda Veras, and Rosella
D'Aquino.

Duccio Tessari
Born 11 October 1926, in Genoa. Film training
began in the early 1950s, as cameraman and director
of documentary films in Genoa. After moving to
Rome, Tessari worked as assistant director with
Carmine Gallone and Vittorio Cottafavi, and co-
scripted (among many other films) *The Last Days of
Pompeii* (1959, Bonnard/Leone, Tessari also

assistant director), *The Colossus of Rhodes* (1960, Leone), *Hercules Conquers Atlantis* (1961, Cottafavi), *Romulus and Remus* (1961, Corbucci), *A Fistful of Dollars* (1964, Leone — Tessari uncredited), and *Seven Guns for the MacGregors* (1965, Franco Giraldi — one of the few comedy Spaghettis which succeed in sustaining the joke). Directed four films on his own (including two spy adventures, and the very lively 'peplum' *Sons of Thunder*, 1962, with Giuliano Gemma) before turning to Italian Westerns. Like Corbucci, Tessari is a specialist in parodies of Cinecittà genre films — but his humour (both in *Sons of Thunder* and in the Westerns) is more subtle, and his 'comments' on an assortment of favourite Hollywood directors (in the 'Ringo' films, Ford, Walsh, Hawks among them) more sophisticated. In interviews, Tessari has stated that his specific contribution to the Western has been to challenge the worst forms of Hollywood cliché (the 'sheriff's girl' as a star vehicle; the 'dialogue on the verandah' interrupted by gunshots, for example), whilst retaining the most telling stylistic effects of the Hollywood 'masters'. Tessari's Westerns are well constructed (he always has a hand in the screenplay) — less episodic (or perhaps the word is manic) than Corbucci's comic-strip anthologies of visual clichés. After the 'Ringo' films (which were made with the same production crews and leading players, almost simultaneously) Tessari turned his attention to the political Spaghettis (in *Et Viva la Révolution/Viva La Muerte . . . Tua/Long Live Death . . . Preferably Yours*, 1971, with Franco Nero, Eli Wallach and Lynn Redgrave) — and, predictably, parodied the formula, with a few side-swipes at Don Siegel's *Two Mules for Sister Sara* on the way. The kind of director nameless critics on the *Monthly Film Bulletin* did not feel too ashamed to admire.

Films mentioned in the text:

A Pistol for Ringo (*Una Pistola per Ringo*) (1965)
Italian-Spanish co-production. Techniscope. Technicolor.
Director: Duccio Tessari; Producers: Luciano Ercoli, Alberto Pugliesi; Screenplay: Duccio Tessari; Photography: Francisco Marin; Music: Ennio Morricone.*
Cast: Giuliano Gemma (Ringo), Lorella de Luca (Ruby), Fernando Sancha (Sancho), Antonio Cases (Major Clyde), Nieves Navarro (Dolores), Jorge Martin (Sheriff), with Paco Sanz, José Holupi, Narrareno Zamperla, José Manuel Martin.

The Return of Ringo (*Il Ritorno di Ringo*) (1965)
Italian-Spanish co-production. Techniscope. Eastmancolor.
Director: Duccio Tessari; Producers: Luciano Ercoli, Alberto Pugliesi; Screenplay: Duccio Tessari, Fernando Di Leo; Photography: Francisco Marin; Music: Ennio Morricone.*
Cast: Giuliano Gemma (Ringo), Fernando Sancha (Esteban), Antonio Cases (Sheriff), Lorella de Luca (Hally), Nieves Navarro (Rosita), Jorge Martin (Paco Fuentes), with Pajarito, José Torres, Victor Bayo, Tuet Vila.

OTHER DIRECTORS, PHOTOGRAPHERS, MUSICAL DIRECTORS, OR ACTORS MENTIONED IN THE TEXT, WITH KEY WORKS

Alfredo Antonini (alias 'Albert Band')
Directed *The Tramplers* (1966, with Joseph Cotten, James Mitchum and Franco Nero — about the fate of Southern 'chivalry' after the American Civil War), before producing a sequel (Corbucci's *Hellbenders*, 1966, also with Joseph Cotten) and Giraldi's *Dead or Alive* (1967).

Luis Enrique Bacalov
Composer (and pianist), who collaborated with Morricone on the score of *A Bullet for the General*, and also scored Corbucci's *Django* and Valerii's *The Price of Power*. Although he trained with Morricone, Bacalov, a Spaniard, works from outside the Cinecittà 'repertory' system of composition.

Enzo Barboni (alias 'E.B. Clucher')
Photographed *Red Pastures* (1963, a pre-*Fistful* Western, with James Mitchum), Corbucci's *Django*, Corbucci's *Hellbenders* (1966), Baldi's *Rita of the West* (1967, with Rita Pavone), Bazzoni's *I Live for Your Death* (1968, scripted by, and starring, Steve Reeves) and many others, before directing (pseudonymously) the double-act of Mario Girotti ('Terence Hill') and Carlo Pedersoli ('Bud Spencer') in the 'Trinity' series of slapstick Westerns (which included *They Call Me Trinity*, 1970; *Trinity Is Still My Name*, 1971; and, with 'Terence Hill' alone, *Man of the East*, 1972). The double-act had first been a real success in Giuseppe Collizi's *Revenge at El Paso*, 1968. Post-Barboni 'Trinity' films have been directed by formula merchants such as Parolini — with even more emphasis on the stunts.

Giuliano Carmineo (alias 'Anthony Ascott')
Just as Corbucci* launched the 'Django' series
(see Chapter 2), Parolini* the 'Sabata' series,
and Barboni* the 'Trinity' series, Carmineo was
associated with the most interesting 'Sartana' films.
Gianni (or John) Garko — a graduate of the
Academy of Dramatic Art in Rome, who had acted
in several of Visconti's stage productions — first
appeared as the mysterious (almost supernatural)
avenger Sartana in Alberto Cardone's *Guns of
Violence* (1967) and Parolini's *Sartana* (1968). In
1969, Garko made his first film for Carmineo,
Sartana the Grave-Digger, a critique of his previous
Sartana films. A year later, he appeared in *Sartana
Kills Them All* for Rafael Romero Marchent (a
Western which was released in Italy at the same
time as two 'Django Meets Sartana' films, produced
by Tarquinia, a rival company). In 1971, he
appeared as Sartana in another Carmineo film,
Have a Good Funeral, Sartana Will Pay . . ., which
attempted to fuse the spy thriller genre (gadgets,
throwaway lines, 'infiltrating the organisation')
with the elements of a low-key parody Western.
This inventive variation on the formula was
followed in the same year by Carmineo's *Light
the Fuse, Sartana's Coming*, again with Garko, a
more spectacular version of the previous film, and
probably the high point of the series. For
Carmineo's next film in the cycle, *Sartana's Coming
— Get Your Coffins Ready* (1972), the avenger
was played by George Hilton: unable to defeat
the crooked banker (a standard ingredient in the
series), who is in league with a gang of Mexican
heavies, Sartana finds himself accepting help from
Sabata (Charles Southwood). In the same year,
Carmineo made *They Call Him Holy Spirit* (with
Garko as a mysterious, white-clad pistolero, who
always has a white dove perched on his shoulder,
and who bears more than a passing resemblance to
Feuillade's *Judex*), which again manages to resist
the self-parody of the later formula Spaghettis —
the slapstick humour of 'Trinity', the wild
acrobatics of 'Sabata' — by sustaining an
atmosphere of what Francois Joyeux styles
'*controlled* irony', akin to the best of the spy
films. Together with the 'Django' series (analysed
in the text), the 'Sartana' films represent useful
examples of what happens to Cinecittà formulas
as they develop, before dying the usual death.

Tonino Cervi
Director of *Today Its Me, Tomorrow You* (1968),
with Brett Halsey, William Berger, Carlo
Pedersoli ('Bud Spencer') and Tatsuya Nakadai —
a stylish, and fairly straightforward variation on
the *Magnificent Seven* formula.

Bruno Corbucci
Director of *Ringo Against Everyone* (1966, a
parody) and co-writer of *For a Few Dollars Less*
(1966, with his brother), *Hate for Hate* (1967,
Paolella), *The Great Silence* (1968, with his
brother), and *The Dirty Story of the West* (1968,
an adaptation of *Hamlet* in a Spaghetti Western
setting, with Gilbert Roland in the Claudius part).

Gianni Garko — actor: see under Giuliano Carmineo

Franco Giraldi (alias 'Frank Garfield')
Director of *Seven Guns for the MacGregors* (1965)
and the sequel *Seven Brides* (1966) as well as *Dead
or Alive* (1967, with Alex Cord, Robert Ryan and
Arthur Kennedy).

Alberto Grimaldi
After the commercial success of *Fistful*, Leone
instituted a lawsuit against Jolly Films, the Italian
co-production partners, who had attempted to force
him (by withholding payment) to make his next
Western with them. Alberto Grimaldi, a lawyer
in Rome, was put in charge of Leone's dossier.
Grimaldi had already produced one or two minor
Italian Westerns, and agreed to take over as
producer of Leone's next two projects. Largely as
a result of his association with Leone's money-
spinners, Grimaldi is now a top-line Cinecittà
producer (in recent years, Bertolucci's *1900*,
Fellini's *Casanova*, and many others).

Klaus Kinski
West German actor, specialising in bizarre
characterisations (with a unique talent for nervous
tics). Appeared in a Cinecittà spy film (*Operation
Istanbul*, 1965), and a Karl May Western (Reinl's
Winnetou II, 1964) before upstaging everyone in
numerous Spaghettis, including *For a Few Dollars
More* (1965), *A Bullet for the General* (1966),
Parolini's *Sartana* (1968), Carmineo's *Sartana the
Grave-Digger* (1969), 'Anthony Dawson's' *A Man,
a Horse, a Gun* (1969), 'Miles Deem's' *Nevada Kid*
(1971) and Damiani's *A Genius* (1975). One of his
most memorable performances was in Corbucci's
Great Silence (1968), the story of a deaf-mute
bounty-hunter (Jean-Louis Trintignant) who keeps
his victims' thumbs as souvenirs. In his
autobiography (*Dying to Live*, Paris, 1976), Kinski
describes the perils of working on low-budget
Spaghetti Westerns (such as falling off crazy horses),
and the difficulties of making the transfer from a

career in Spaghettis to more serious acting parts: 'It's not really your thing: you'd do much better to work on the next Corbucci Western instead.'

Tomas Milian
Cuban actor, who became, in his own words, a 'symbol of poverty' to Italian Western audiences — especially in the Third World. Arrived in Italy in 1959, and made *Boccaccio '70* and *The Leopard* (both for Visconti), before appearing in Sollima's Westerns, 'always as the same character' (Sollima remains his favourite Western director). Has subsequently appeared in send-ups of the political Spaghettis, and Liliana Cavani's *Cannibals*, among many others. Unlike Gian Maria Volonté,* he argues (in interviews) that actors should not confuse their screen image with their political activities off the set.

Ennio Morricone
Bruno Nicolai
A Conservatory-trained musician, Morricone (born in Rome, 1928) had scored two Italian Westerns (*Gunfight at Red Sands*, *Pistols Don't Argue*) before his creative partnership with Leone began (*Fistful*). Since then, he has scored over 35 Westerns, several of them with musical themes rejected by Leone as inappropriate for his films. Often, Morricone's scores are 'directed' or conducted by Bruno Nicolai, and this has caused some confusion as to who writes what: apart from anything else, Nicolai is quite capable of writing pastiche Morricone scores (*The Bounty Hunters*, 1970). But Nicolai can also compose in a distinctive style (*Run, Man, Run*, the third of Sollima's political Spaghettis, where there must have been a great temptation to repeat the success of *The Big Gundown* score). Nicolai trained with Morricone, and it is possible that he sometimes 'adapts' scores rejected by Leone. It is equally possible that he does much of the work on scores that finally go out under Morricone's name. In addition to his Western work, Morricone has been extraordinarily prolific in other genres (some of his best music was written for Pontecorvo's *Battle of Algiers* and *Quiemada*, and his recent score for Bertolucci's *1900* is one of his finest). But his non-Western scores are not always so successful — or interesting: the year after *Fistful*, for example, his music for *The Bible* was rejected out of hand by director John Huston. With *My Name Is Nobody* and *A Genius*, he has taken to parodying his own music (which, of course, was parodic in the first place), in a jokey, up-tempo fashion. According to both Leone and Pontecorvo,

Morricone works very fast (and, if requested, in close consultation with the director, during shooting). His music reached its widest English market through the rock music of Mike Oldfield — which seems to be strongly influenced by the Leone scores. A character based on Morricone was played by Belmondo in Claude Lelouch's *Un homme qui me plaît* (1969).

Riz Ortolani
Composer; one of the few artists to contribute to both German and Italian Westerns (Mario Girotti/ 'Terence Hill' is another). Scored *Apache's Last Battle* (1964, West Germany, Hugo Fregonese — with Stewart Granger as 'Old Surehand'), before composing for several Spaghettis, including Lizzani's *Requiescant* (1967), Stegani's *Beyond the Law* (1967) and two of Valerii's* films, *Day of Anger* (1967), *The Price of Power* (1969).

Gianfranco Parolini (alias 'Frank Kramer')
Director of *Left-Handed Johnny West* (1965), *Sartana* (1968, with William Berger and Klaus Kinski*), the incredibly successful *Sabata* (1969, with Lee Van Cleef and William Berger), *The Bounty Hunters* (1970, with Yul Brynner in the *Sabata* role), and *The Return of Sabata* (1971, with Lee Van Cleef) — all with an acrobat or two featured in the story. Before directing Westerns, Parolini was a prolific director of 'peplums', and since, he has turned to war adventures: the consistent feature seems to be the acrobats.

Giulio Petroni
Director of *Death Rides a Horse* (1967, with Lee Van Cleef and John Philip Law) — a stylish revenge Western, with very dramatic flashbacks to herald the deaths of the killers; the film also makes good use of the 'old man' and 'boy' relationship from *For a Few Dollars More*.

Giancarlo Santi
Assisted on *The Good, the Bad and the Ugly* (1966) and *Once Upon a Time in the West* (1968), before directing part of *Duck, You Sucker* (1971) (and directing the second unit, after Leone had been persuaded to take over the direction of the film).

Alejandro Ulloa
Director of photography, responsible for the two 'MacGregors' comedy Westerns for Giraldi,

Paolella's *Hate for Hate* (1967) as well as Corbucci's *Professional Gun* and *Compañeros* (and many others).

Tonino Valerii

Assisted on *For a Few Dollars More* (1965), before directing *Per il Gusto di Uccidere* (1966), *Day of Anger* (1967), *The Price of Power* (1969), *A Reason to Live, A Reason to Die* (1972, with James Coburn, Telly Savalas and 'Bud Spencer', scored by **Ortolani** and photographed by **Ulloa** — a fast-moving derivative of *Duck, You Sucker*, and the later political Spaghettis) and, under Leone's 'supervision', *My Name Is Nobody* (1973). Normally a rather nondescript director, Valerii came into his own parodying Leone.

Gian Maria Volonté

Before appearing as the heavy in *A Fistful of Dollars*, Volonté had played Romeo at the Arena di Verona (1960), and had featured in two significant films: *The Man Who Burned* (1962) and *The Terrorist* (1963, a film which Lino Miccichè categorises as 'antifascist', and which first brought Volonté to the attention of left-wing critics in Italy). So, by the time he appeared as Ramon Rojo and El Indio, Volonté had already established a minor reputation as an actor specialising in political films (as well as a major reputation for his work on the Italian stage). But he lacked box-office appeal. Since appearing in the first two Leone Westerns (which he now despises, but which, embarrassing though it is for him to admit, succeeded in making his name), and in two 'populist' Spaghettis, *A Bullet for the General* and *Face to Face* (which he considers more ideologically sound), Volonté has become what Noel Simsolo calls 'a one-man political myth' (to French and Italian audiences, at least). His work for the Tavianis (*Under the Sign of the Scorpion*), Petri (*Investigation of a Citizen above Suspicion, The Working Class Goes to Paradise*), Montaldo (*Sacco and Vanzetti*) and Rosi (*Lucky Luciano; The Mattei Affair; Christ Stopped at Eboli*), as well as his activism off the set, have kept him in the Italian public eye for over ten years.

Appendix 2
The Cut Sequences in Leone's Westerns

Most Italian Westerns were severely cut for international distribution. Sometimes (as in the case of *Fistful*), this appears to have been for censorship reasons; sometimes (as in the case of Questi's *Django, Kill*), the cuts were made in order to squeeze the movie into a 'B' feature slot *and* in order to tone down the violence; sometimes (as in the case of *Once Upon a Time*), to make ample room for three showings a day. To take a few examples: Sollima's *Big Gundown* was cut from 105 to 84 minutes, *Face to Face* from 110 to 102 minutes; Questi's *Django, Kill* was cut from 120 to 101 minutes, Damiani's *Bullet for the General* from 135 to 77 minutes(!) No wonder critics found the story-lines difficult to follow, and spotted 'surreal' qualities where none existed. Corbucci's *Django* was banned outright (in England). Of these cut versions, Leone's *The Good, the Bad and the Ugly* and *Once Upon a Time in the West* probably suffered as much as any: both seem to have been cut because distributors quite simply thought them too long ('The cuts really started when my debate grew longer,' recalls Leone). In the following description of the cut sequences, I have included (1) scenes which appeared in the Italian versions, but which disappeared in the international prints, and (2) scenes which were shot, but which did not appear even in the fullest (Italian) prints.

A Fistful of Dollars
Italian print: 100 minutes. International print: 95 minutes. Most of the cuts occur in the sequence outside the Baxters' house, where the Rojo gang have 'smoked them out'. Baxter offers to leave town. Ramon replies 'Are you sure? Better ask you wife. Maybe she won't be too happy about it.' After much laughter, Ramon shoots Baxter. The death of Consuela Baxter was also trimmed. Clint Eastwood recalls that the original cut of *Fistful* (for the Italian market) was nearly two hours, and absolute 'mayhem'.

For a Few Dollars More
Italian print: 130 minutes. International print:

128 minutes. Two very short sequences cut. In the first, Indio baptises his gun in holy water, and makes a sign of the cross; in the second (the final, explanatory flashback — essential for understanding the story), Mortimer's sister takes Indio's gun and shoots herself, after she has been raped.

The Good, the Bad and the Ugly
Italian print: 180 minutes. International print: 148 minutes. Four sequences cut:

1 Just before the Bad (Lee Van Cleef) interrogates Maria about Carson's whereabouts. A wagon-full of drunken Confederate soldiers careers round a corner and pushes Maria into the gutter. She screams abuse at them. She then gets up, and walks along a corridor into her room. The ensuing sequence, where the Bad beats her up to get his information, was also cut (presumably for censorship reasons) — creating the false impression that she is prepared to betray Carson at the mere threat of violence.

2 After Tuco (Eli Wallach) has crossed the desert, and recovered at a water-trough, he looks up, and sees that he is outside a gunsmith's shop. He goes in, and is greeted by the sales patter of an elderly gunsmith — 'Remingtons, Colts, French models . . .' Tuco looks at the many guns on show, sniffs some of them, including a pepperbox, and selects a Navy model: he revolves the chamber, listening to the 'clicks', and substitutes another chamber, and another barrel, from the pistols laid out for his inspection. He obviously knows what he is doing. 'Cartridges' — the gunsmith hands him a box, and asks if Tuco would like to test his weapon on the range outside. They walk out, and Tuco aims at four brightly-coloured wooden Indians, for target practice. He knocks over three of them, and thinks he has hit the fourth, but it remains standing: he then jumps up and down on the duck-boards, until the fourth Indian falls over. Tuco smiles: 'Another cartridge.' He stands with his back to the gunsmith: 'How much?' he asks. 'Twenty dollars,' is the reply. (*Pause*) 'Forty dollars' (*pause*), and eventually,

'Two hundred dollars — its all I've got!' Tuco takes the money, and, after having some difficulty reading the 'Closed' sign on the door, leaves.

(Like the 'Old Prophet' scene in *For a Few Dollars More*, this is a good example of Leone's bizarre sense of humour: we think that Tuco is asking the price of his gun, until it suddenly becomes clear to us (and the gunsmith) that we are watching a robbery. The sequence comes straight out of James Cagney's *Public Enemy*.)

3   As Tuco and Blondy arrive at Betterville prison camp, we see the camp commandant, an elderly man with a gangrenous leg, hobbling towards his office window: he picks up a telescope and surveys the new arrivals, stopping when he sees the back of the Bad's head. (Then comes the roll-call sequence, included in the international print.) An adjutant rushes over to the Bad, and tells him the commandant would like to see him. We return to the office, where the commandant has struggled over to his bed. The Bad is criticised for not treating the 'prisoners as prisoners': apparently, he has been running a protection racket in the camp, with help from his gang of heavies. The Bad replies that the same sort of thing goes on in the Southern camp at Andersonville. 'Not while I'm commandant.' 'That won't be for ever.' 'While I am alive, I will do everything in my power to look for men who will do honour to the Union uniform.' 'I wish you luck . . .' As the Bad leaves, sneering, he whispers to his men who are waiting outside, 'lie low for a while.' Later, when Tuco is called in to see the Bad, the sequence of his beating up (inter-cut with shots of the camp orchestra playing outside), was also considerably longer in the Italian print. More violence, and more of the Union sergeant telling the orchestra to play with 'feeling'. By the perimeter fence, Blondy is standing next to an old man: 'While the music plays, your friend "Carson" will get the treatment. We've all had the treatment from Wallace.' They both stare at the few Union sentries guarding the fence. Cut back to the orchestra, where a young man has dropped his violin: 'Play that fiddle, son . . .' snaps the sergeant.

(Like the crippled Mr Morton in *Once Upon a Time*, the camp commandant is a good example of Leone's 'portraits of power', and his relationship with the Bad resembles that between Frank and his boss in the later film. In both cases, the man in charge is ultimately responsible for all the violence, but sits safely behind a desk while the dirty work is done.)

4   As Tuco is frogmarched to Betterville station,

handcuffed to Wallace, he passes a formal group of Union officers, posing for Matthew Brady's camera. The group is standing by a mortar-cannon. The photograph is taken, and the group disbands. Later, when Tuco pulls Wallace off the train, he kills him viciously with a pointed piece of stone (like the Maria sequence, and the previous Wallace sequence, this was presumably censored).

(The Brady sequence epitomises Leone's 'peep-show' presentation of history — at the same time as showing how the famous portraits by Mr Lincoln's cameraman succeed in glamorising the realities of war. Just outside Brady's field of vision, wounded soldiers line the platform.)

In addition to these, eight extra sequences were shot, but were cut by Leone before the *Italian* print was put together:

1   Tuco recruits three Mexican gunfighters, to kill Blondy (just after the gunsmith sequence).

2   After Blondy has fled from the hotel, Tuco follows him into 'the countryside near New Mexico'. He tracks him down. In the background, there are Confederate soldiers trying to press-gang the peasants ('taking them off to be massacred in a pointless war'). Tuco takes pity on them, and starts a collection to bribe the Confederate soldiers: he goes into a saloon to ask for money. Upstairs, Blondy is with a woman. The woman flees ('in a farcical manner'), taking all Tuco's collection money with her. 'Again, Tuco has been completely foiled.'

3   The Bad arrives at a ruined fort. Several Confederate soldiers are scavenging among the ruins, many of them badly wounded during the Union advance. The Bad asks one of them where he can find Bill Carson. 'If he did not fall in the battle, he's probably ended up in the prison camp at Betterville.'

4   Close-up of Blondy's scarred face, as he is crossing the desert. Blondy is trying to drink from a water-can — but the camera pulls back to show that it is not water he is trying to drink: Tuco is, in fact, pissing into the can, and, when he gets fed up with this joke, he pushes the can away, laughing heartily.

5   Tuco, now disguised as 'Bill Carson', arrives at a Southern encampment (with Blondy in the wagon). He asks where he can find a nurse. He is told that if he goes on to the Mission of San Antonio, he may be able to find help for Blondy there.

6 Tuco consults a map. All around are 'bodies, and evidence of desolation'.

7 Blondy, now teamed up with the Bad and his gang, wakes up in the middle of the night, at their encampment. The raucous cawing of crows, and the sound of cicadas, can be heard in the background. The Bad's six henchmen are sleeping nearby. 'Six is the perfect number,' says Blondy. 'I always thought three was the perfect number,' replies the Bad. 'Yes,' says Blondy, 'but I have six shots in my pistol.'

8 As the commander of the Union outpost at Langstone Bridge (Aldo Giuffré) is demonstrating the advantages of alcohol ('the most potent weapon in war') to Blondy and Tuco, he adds, 'What the Yankees and the slave-owners have in common, is a taste for liqour.'

Once Upon a Time in the West
Italian print: 168 minutes. International print: 144 minutes. Four important sequences cut, of 14 minutes, 2 minutes, 75 seconds and 4 minutes respectively; also, various sequences trimmed by seconds:

1 Just after the sequence where Jill McBain (Claudia Cardinale) and Sam (Paolo Stoppa) travel in a buggy through Monument Valley, we see them arrive at a ramshackle trading post in the desert. Sam pulls up his horse, Lafayette. 'Why are we stopping?' asks Jill, 'I told you I was in a hurry.' 'Don't the trains stop?' replies Sam. They both go into the trading post (blacksmith, general stores, stables, a bar) and there is a lull in the conversation as Jill arrives. The bartender (Lionel Stander) leers at her as he asks, 'What can I do for *you*, ma'am?' 'I would like some water, if it's no trouble!' 'Water?' says the bartender; 'well, you see that word is poison around these parts, ever since the days of the great flood.' 'You mean you never wash . . .?' 'We sure do.' 'Well, I'd like to use the same facilities you people do.' 'You sure can. Just happen to have a full tub in the back. And you're *lucky* — only three people have used it this morning!' 'Used it one at a time or all together?' asks Jill provocatively. The bartender sighs: 'I can tell you're accustomed to fine living. Bet you come from one of those big Eastern cities.' 'New Orleans.' '*New Orleans*!' 'You've been there?' 'No . . . but I've got a cousin down there. She runs a bar. You know she . . .' The conversation is interrupted by sounds of a scuffle outside — gunshots, horses whinnying, three or four men

biting the dust: we see close-ups of various faces reacting to these sounds — travellers eating near the bar, Sam, and the bartender. There is sinister music, turning into a few bars of 'Cheyenne's theme', as Cheyenne (Jason Robards) walks in, framed by the door, with his back to the bar. Reaction shots of people staring at him, as he slowly turns round. 'Jug,' he snaps. As he pulls the cork with his teeth, he holds up his hands — they are chained together. The sound of a harmonica, from the far corner of the room, breaks the silence. Cheyenne, Jill and Sam turn to see who is making this strange music. Cheyenne gets hold of an oil lamp, and swings it along a wire towards the sound: as the 'Harmonica theme' swells on the soundtrack, we see the Man's (Charles Bronson's) face, lit by the swinging lamp, unshaven, and grimacing with pain. Cheyenne walks over to the Man and lifts his coat, to reveal a deep bullet wound in his left shoulder. Close-ups of their two faces. Harmonica has, as usual, got a gun lying flat, placed just by his right hand (as the scripts puts it, 'it looks as though he does not quite know what to do with it'). Cheyenne gently moves the gun out of Harmonica's reach: 'D'you only know how to play, or do you know how to shoot? D'you know how to blow music from that?' The Man calmly continues to play his harmonica. Cheyenne slides the gun towards him — 'Pick it up!' Harmonica takes the gun (holding it by the barrel to show he does not intend to use it). At that moment, one of the travellers standing near the bar goes for his gun: Cheyenne whips round, his own gun at the ready. '*You* — you don't know how to play!' The 'Cheyenne theme' swells on the soundtrack. Cheyenne takes Harmonica's gun, revolves the chamber, cocks it and offers it to the scared traveller: 'Try this one — go on, take it!' The traveller cautiously takes the weapon. Cheyenne holds up his manacled wrists, and, while pointing his gun at the traveller, waits for the traveller to shoot through the chains. 'Here.' There is a shot (and the sound of a horse whinnying outside). Cheyenne and Harmonica both smile: 'Bravo!' The traveller (much shaken by the experience) has succeeded in shooting through the manacles. We can hear the sound of some riders arriving, from outside the door: as Cheyenne turns towards the door, his gun at the ready, four of his men enter (in a cloud of dust) and tell him breathlessly, 'Cheyenne, we thought we'd never make it.' 'It's all right. You're right on time — to bury my escort. If I'd waited for you, I'd be in jail by now.' Cheyenne takes a good long look at Jill and sighs. Harmonica 'enters' the picture ('in his usual way'): 'Hey — the gun,' he says. As Cheyenne returns the weapon, Harmonica looks closely at one of the leather 'dusters' belonging to a member of the gang. 'You interested in fashions, Harmonica?' asks Cheyenne. 'I saw three of these dusters a short time ago,' Harmonica explains; 'they were waiting for a train. Inside the dusters there were three men.' 'So?' 'Inside the men were three bullets.' (*Pause.*) 'That's a crazy story, Harmonica. For two reasons,' says Cheyenne. 'One — nobody around these parts has got the guts to wear these dusters except Cheyenne's men. Two — Cheyenne's men don't get killed. That surprise you . . .?' 'Yeah! (*Pause.*) 'Well, you know music, and you can count all the way up to two,' replies Harmonica. Cheyenne revolves the chamber of his pistol: 'All the way up to six if I have to — and maybe faster than you.' The Man simply picks up his harmonica, and plays a wailing note on it. Cheyenne laughs: 'Yeah, go on. Play, Harmonica. Play so you can't bullshit — only watch those false notes.' At that very moment, Harmonica plays a discordant sound, and Cheyenne freezes (we see a close-up of his face). 'Like so?' says Harmonica. Cheyenne smiles, and walks out followed by his men. The bartender turns to Jill, in an attempt to lighten the atmosphere: he continues talking as if nothing unusual had happened. '. . . This cousin of mine keeps writing to me to come on down to New Orleans. Come on down. Help me with the bar. Make a barrel of money. But you know — I don't think I'd get along in a big city. It's too full of fast men and loose women — begging your pardon, ma'am. Oh no, now I'm too used to a quiet, simple country life . . .'

(The next sequence shows Jill and Sam continuing their journey to Sweetwater, presumably after she has taken her bath.)

This 'trading post' scene, the longest to be cut, establishes the relationship between the three main protagonists, and makes sense of Jill's later meeting with both Cheyenne and Harmonica (also of her behaviour just after McBain's funeral). The musical *leitmotifs* associated with both Robards and Bronson are introduced in this scene, as are their characteristic ways of entering the action. Jill's 'Eastern' attitude towards those who are condemned to 'a quiet, simple country life' is highlighted as well. In other words, the scene forms an essential part of Leone's puzzle: for the rest of the film will be devoted to unravelling the strange threads which hold these three people together.

2 Just after Frank has 'appeared' at Sweetwater, and handed Jill the model of a railway station

('Looking for this . . .?'), Leone cuts from a close-up of Frank's face to a close-up of Mr Morton. Morton is standing, with the aid of crutches, outside Frank's encampment in the mountains (a few hovels, carved out of red sandstone, with some Indian squaws washing clothes, etc.). Morton complains about Frank's high-handed behaviour: 'I know the woman's here . . . I've had enough of your butchery. We're ready to make a deal for that land. To pay what's necessary. I don't want to waste any more time.' 'You made a big mistake, Morton,' replies Frank, chewing an apple. 'When you're not on that train, you look like a turtle out of its shell. It's funny. A poor cripple talking big so nobody'll know how scared you are.' Morton keeps cool: 'I'm here to make a deal, Frank. I don't have time to compete with you.' '*Compete*?' says Frank, 'why you — you can't even stand on your own feet by yourself . . .' Frank then kicks away Morton's crutches, to prove his point, and watches him fall (as he will fall during his final moments, later in the story — and a hint of the 'Pacific theme' on the soundtrack reinforces the comparison). 'Is that sufficient to make you feel stronger?' says Morton scornfully. Frank's answer is equally scornful: 'I could squash you like a rummy apply.' 'Sure,' says Morton, 'but you won't do it. Because it's not to your advantage.' Extreme close-up of Frank's face. 'Who knows how far you'd have gone with two good legs, huh?' Morton struggles to get up again. Frank turns to his men: 'Help him back to the train; keep your eye on him.' As Morton is being assisted on his way, Frank calls after him, 'Oh, Morton. Don't worry about the land. If you feel like paying for it you can pay. It doesn't make any difference to you, dealing with a new owner . . .'

The main importance of this short sequence is that it shows a key stage in the developing relationship between Frank (as gunfighter) and Morton (as businessman). Note how Frank addresses his boss as 'Morton' (when he is on home territory, when Mr Morton is far away from his railway carriage). Also how Morton knows exactly the way to exploit Frank's weaknesses: but his obsession with time makes him very vulnerable to Frank's bullying tactics. Visually, the sequence establishes many connections with other parts of the film (Morton crawling on the ground; Frank's apple — which relates to the apple in the final flashback; the desert environment). Another brief moment, cut from an earlier part of the film in some prints, gives us our first glimpse of the way in which Frank's men are being employed to spy on Morton: after chatting amiably with his boss, Frank immediately turns to his riders and says, 'Don't let that cripple out of your sight.'

(The next sequence shows Harmonica and Cheyenne 'building a station' at Sweetwater, and ends on the words, '*If* she gets back . . .' Leone then cuts, in the Italian print, to a shot of Jill and Frank facing each other: this 'vertical' shot revolves, to become a 'horizontal' shot of Frank and Jill lying on a hanging bed, inside Frank's mountain hide-out. During the ensuing scene (when Frank discusses what he is going to do about Jill), Frank starts off by lying on top of Jill, but, at the mention of marriage, Jill shifts her position, so that she ends the sequence lying on top of Frank. Clearly, Frank will have to think of a solution that is 'easier' . . .)

3 Just after the sequence where Harmonica 'protects' Frank, from a hotel balcony overlooking the main street of Flagstone, Frank rides back to the train. He discovers the corpses of members of his gang lying by the railroad track. Puzzled, he dismounts and goes into the railway carriage: inside, we can clearly see two corpses — a member of Frank's gang (the one who had been playing cards with Mr Morton) and the bearded member of Cheyenne's gang who had bought tickets for the train ('one way only'), back in Flagstone. Cheyenne's man is lying just beneath Morton's picture of the Pacific Ocean. This short sequence opens with a close-up of Frank's face, and closes with a shot of him leaving the carriage, to be greeted with the sight of Mr Morton crawling away.

It is difficult to understand why these 75 seconds of film should have been cut, for they explain so much of the story. The two members of Cheyenne's gang have obviously been shot while helping Cheyenne to escape: but, in the process, they have managed to kill all those members of Frank's gang (now working for Morton, after the card game) who stayed behind on the train. Leone never intended to show the actual gunfight: but this short sequence, together with Cheyenne's memory of what happened — see 4 below — tells us everything we need to know.

4 Just after Harmonica and Cheyenne have left Jill McBain at Sweetwater ('. . . make believe its nothing . . .'), we see them both ride over the brow of a hill opposite the farmhouse. Cheyenne lags behind Harmonica, slumped over his saddle; his horse stumbles, and Harmonica looks back to see what has happened. Cheyenne has fallen out of his saddle and is now sitting on the ground holding the reins of his horse. As the 'Cheyenne theme' swells on the soundtrack, Harmonica dismounts and walks over to him. Cheyenne is clutching at a wound in his gut. Flies are buzzing noisily. 'Sorry, Harmonica, I gotta stay here.' Harmonica lifts up the corner of Cheyenne's waistcoat, and reveals an ugly wound down his right side. 'Who . . .?' 'I ran into Mr Choo Choo,' replies Cheyenne, 'I didn't count on that half man from the train. He got scared.' 'Hey, Harmonica,' he continues, 'when they do you in, pray it's somebody who knows *where* to shoot.' Close-up of Cheyenne's face, twisted with pain. 'Go away. Go away. Go away, I don't want you to see me die.' Harmonica turns his back. As Cheyenne breathes his final death-rattle, his musical 'theme' on the soundtrack abruptly stops. Immediately after this, Harmonica hears the whistle of a train arriving at 'Sweetwater station': the camera cranes up, to show us the train steaming by, as the 'main theme' swells on the soundtrack. (Then comes the sequence of the rail gangs jumping out of the way, as the locomotive arrives.) Harmonica rides back towards the farmhouse, over the brow of the hill, with Cheyenne's body (slung over the bandit's horse) in tow; he passes a pack-mule, and a wagon, as he rides away from Sweetwater. (Then comes the sequence of Jill McBain dispensing water to the tired rail gangs.) As the locomotive gets up steam, and begins to back out of the station (to the left of the screen), the camera pans slowly to the right, showing first the group of workers gathered around Jill, then 'the end of the line' where the rails stop and only a few wooden sleepers have been laid, then Harmonica (still towing Cheyenne's body) riding towards the mountains, past various piles of wood, and empty wagons. The final title is super-imposed on the twin images of the train pulling out, and Harmonica riding off into the wilderness: ONCE UPON A TIME IN THE WEST.

Cheyenne's death scene (which lasts only 4 minutes) brings to a close the quarrel between the bandit and 'Mr Choo Choo'. The duel with Frank has completed Harmonica's revenge: (his main motivation ever since the opening sequence): but Cheyenne's quarrel, by contrast, has throughout been specifically with Morton (and with the 'slime' he leaves behind him), so this scene represents another, less happy resolution. Once the death scene had been cut, the final appearance of Harmonica (with Cheyenne's body in tow) had also to be cut. The international print ends on a frozen frame, just before the camera starts panning to the right. As I have discussed in the text, the abridged print, by cutting out all reference to Cheyenne's death, seriously distorts the point of Leone's final 'tableau' — for the arrival of the train becomes the single, grand climax. These cuts have another, rather less

240-3 Sequences cut from the American print of
Once Upon a Time in the West

244-5 Sequences filmed from the shooting-script of *Once Upon a Time in the West*, which were cut before the full-length Italian version was put together

significant, effect on the story: in the abridged print, we never once see Harmonica riding a horse.

After demanding these cuts, Paramount executives must have despaired when *Time* magazine *still* referred to the film as 'tedium in the tumbleweed'.

In addition to these four sequences, eight extra groups of scenes were shot (see stills), but were cut by Leone before the *Italian* print was put together. These extra scenes — (1) Jill McBain and Sam, in Flagstone (Sc. 7-8); (2) Harmonica, with Wobbles, at the Chinese laundry, and, with the Sheriff, at the stables in Flagstone (Sc. 14-17); (3) Jill at the Chinese laundry, Harmonica tailing Wobbles to Mr Morton's train (Sc. 30-36); (4) Mr Morton, with Frank's men, on the train (Sc. 46); (5) Jill McBain in the Flagstone Hotel foyer (Sc. 58); (6) Harmonica in the Flagstone bank (Sc. 61); (7) the building of 'Sweetwater station' (Sc. 63); (8) (intercut with the auction sequence) Frank at the barber's shop, Harmonica preparing to claim the reward on Cheyenne (Sc. 67-70, 74, 76) — provide interesting evidence about the way in which the full-length version of *Once Upon a Time* evolved, and confirm Leone's recollections about the various 'stages' of filming. As in the case of *The Good, the Bad and the Ugly*, the episodic quality of the narrative (leaving much to the audience's imagination) was in part the result of rearranging the shooting-script during the actual filming (*after* the fullest version of the script had been shot). Thus, in *Once Upon a Time*, passages of dialogue were transposed from cut sequences to scenes in the final Italian print (from Sc. 7-8, to the sequences of Jill and Sam travelling to Sweetwater; from Sc. 68, in the barber's shop, to the sequence in Sweetwater just before the final duel, etc.); brief references to cut incidents were added to later scenes, if the incidents were considered important enough in terms of a character's motivation (references to the 'documents' seen in Sc. 61, or to the reward shown in Sc. 67, and so on); and sequences were rewritten, in order to compress two or more scenes into one, with the dialogue being gradually whittled down to the minimum (Sam and Jill travelling to Sweetwater; Harmonica tailing Wobbles; the building of 'Sweetwater station', etc.). It seems clear, from Leone's own recollections, and from the important differences between the shooting-script and the (fullest) release script, that the plan for shooting was as follows:

(a) A long story outline, written by Bertolucci, with help from Leone and Dario Argento; and a score pre-recorded by Morricone;

(b) A shooting-script, compiled, with Morricone's score very much in mind, during the actual filming (sometimes on the set);

(c) A compression of this shooting-script, by a process of improvisation and negotiation about 'what works best' — a crucial factor being running time, of course.

Leone's earlier shooting-scripts (for the trilogy) were, according to Clint Eastwood, Henry Fonda and Charles Bronson, extremely wordy, far too *literary*. Eastwood and Leone 'pruned' the part of the Man With No Name as they went along, and this semi-improvisational technique seems to have set the pattern for Leone's later features. It has some obvious disadvantages: since the *elliptical* style of the final version was in part the result of cutting and rearranging during the actual shooting, there was always the danger that the final 'compressed' sequences would become *too* allusive for the audience to make the necessary connections, particularly given Leone's disregard for Hollywood conventions of linear narrative development; and since the first drafts of the shooting-scripts had been filmed *in toto*, at great expense, in the cases of *The Good, the Bad and the Ugly* and *Once Upon a Time in the West*, there was also the danger that traces of the 'optimum' script would remain in the compressed version (thus, Charles Bronson appears at Sweetwater with unexplained scars on his face — the result of his fist-fight in Scenes 14-17, cut from the final print; and in *The Good . . .*, there is no explanation at all as to why the Bad should be working in Betterville internment camp, or why Tuco should decide to visit the San Antonio mission). On the whole, however, since Leone's mature works constitute a type of commentary on the usual narrative conventions (with a preference for the picaresque), this method of shooting may be interpreted as playing an integral part in the construction of the 'riddles' or 'games' with which Leone deliberately challenges his audience.

Sequences cut *before* the Italian print was assembled (transcribed from the shooting-script):

1 Interior. Stables. Day. Sam is sitting, struggling to read a book, inside the stables at Flagstone (originally Abilene). As the owner of the stables enters, with Jill, Sam hastily puts his book aside ('as if he has been caught stealing'). Sam is hostile and suspicious, preferring to talk to his horse, Lafayette, than to the 'intruders'. Owner: 'This signora wants you to take her to Sweetwater.' Sam (to Lafayette); 'Hey . . . do you hear him, stinker of coal! . . . What do you say, Lafayette?' Jill sends

the owner away: Sam pretends not to hear her, as he cleans the mud off his horse's muzzle. A hand, clutching two banknotes, appears in the frame: 'I can pay you well.' Lafayette the horse nods his head. 'The horse is hungry,' says Sam. 'What did you say the name of the place was?' (At this point, the dialogue is almost identical to that in the final print, as Jill and Sam leave Flagstone). 'Are you a relative?' 'In one sense.' Jill waits to be helped up on to the carriage: Sam eventually helps her, still in a surly manner. In the next scene (8), the carriage is crossing a desert: Jill is looking more and more troubled, as the topography changes 'for the worse'. 'Pull yourself together,' says Sam. 'We're almost there.' As the carriage continues round a bend in the track, Sam says, 'There you are — over there.' In the distance we can see a few people, who seem to be busy 'with construction'. Jill is surprised: 'This is the McBain ranch?' 'If you want to call it a ranch. I call this heap of bones a horse.' 'But, I thought it would be bigger. More beautiful . . .' As the carriage draws into Sweetwater, we can see a line of figures, all very neatly dressed, in black. Sam: 'It's full of people. They're all dressed up . . . What the hell can they be celebrating at the McBains?' Jill: 'A marriage, Sam . . .'

(These scenes in the shooting-script (7-8) were eventually to be augmented by three major sequences in the final version: the ride through Monument Valley; the disruption of the rail gang; the arrival at Lionel Stander's trading post.)

2 Interior. Chinese Laundry. Night. Wobbles, the proprietor, is busily walking around the mangles, steam-pressers, baskets of washing, and groups of Chinese workers who are sleeping on the floor. The Chinese workers watch, 'with half-opened eyes, timid and frightened'. Harmonica glances at Wobbles. Wobbles: 'You must be tired. Certainly, after a long journey like that. My home is yours. We can talk later, more calmly . . .' (As always, Wobbles is 'strained and nervous'.) Harmonica says nothing, but indicates that he wants to know the way to a bedroom. Wobbles shows him. As Harmonica passes an oil-lamp, he picks it up, lifts it above his head, and 'spinning round with it, watches the startled faces of the Chinese disappear, like magic, behind laundry baskets'. (This effect was later to be transposed into the 'trading post' sequence.) The next scene (15) shows Harmonica settling down for the night, in an upstairs bedroom; he is lying on a bed which is too short for him, fully-clothed, his gun ('that pistol which he never seems to know what to do with') by his side. The door opens, but Harmonica remains motionless. We

can dimly see the shape of a 'voluptuous, still young, Mexican woman': 'My husband sent me up, to see if you needed something . . .' Harmonica smiles: 'He could have sent one of the Chinese women.' The woman shakes her head slowly: 'He was afraid you wouldn't like one . . . he could have offended you . . . the worm! Now he's mad with jealousy. He's at the bottom of the stairs, suffering like a dog.' (It is clear that she is talking about Wobbles.) Harmonica stares at her stubbornly, then proceeds to kick off first one boot, then the other. 'With the same indolence, she takes off first one, then the other of her shoes.' Harmonica looks at her, smiling. As she unties the strings of her bodice, and approaches the bed, Harmonica wiggles his toes: 'Massage my feet.' 'With a sigh of acceptance, the woman obeys.' (This scene may originally have been intended to relate to the (similar) 'rape' of Jill at Sweetwater.) With 'gentle and expert hands', the girl massages Harmonica's feet, and he begins to relax: 'it really seems as if he is about to go to sleep.' Suddenly, with great care, 'two big hairy hands, with short cut nails, come into view, and take over from the girl's soft and delicate hands'. The girl's hands 'seem to be pushed away with force'. The large hands, 'trying to be delicate' continue the massage: Harmonica does not stir, but his right hand gradually moves, 'as if in sleep', towards his gun. 'Another hand enters from above, and brings down the lighted tip of a cigar onto the back of Harmonica's hand': Harmonica jumps up, to be greeted with the sight of three strange men in his bedroom. The man with the cigar grabs hold of Harmonica's shoulders, a second man raises his knee and crashes it into Harmonica's face, while a third man kicks Harmonica out of the bedroom. Harmonica is rolled down the stairs (Sc. 16), and into the street: he is then forced into the stables. His face ends up near a pair of boots: a man is sitting on a 'heap of hay', and Harmonica tries to get him into focus. We see the blurred image of 'something shiny, like a luminous sun'. Harmonica blinks, unable to believe his eyes. The image is that of a sheriff's star, and the three men are in fact deputies. The Sheriff (Keenan Wynn) signals his three deputies to leave: 'No,' says Harmonica, 'let them stay. I want to remember their faces.' The Sheriff ignores him: 'Get out!' He then moves over to one of the horse-stalls, and leads a horse by the reins into a pool of light. 'Since you want to remember so much, this horse is yours?' Harmonica struggles to his feet. 'In a sense.' The Sheriff takes a 'duster' from off the saddle: 'look!' Harmonica says nothing. The Sheriff then pulls a piece of brownish material from out of his pocket: it matches the duster. Harmonica: 'I don't understand — if it's sewing you want, I can't do it!' Sheriff: 'I see my men have not destroyed your sense of humour . . . Let's try again.' He holds up the duster and the piece of material. 'This was found next to the corpses of a man and three kids who'd been shot down. I should charge you . . . I know what you'll say — you don't look like someone who'd carry around the proofs of a murder.' Harmonica says nothing, but reaches out for the duster: when he tries it on, it becomes clear that the sleeves are at least six inches too short for him. The Sheriff smiles, takes a handkerchief and passes it to Harmonica, who proceeds to bathe his wounds. 'Where did you get the duster?' asks the Sheriff. 'From someone shorter than me.' 'Where is he now?' 'At dinner with his friends.' 'Where?' 'Not where he is eating, but where he is being eaten — it's a banquet of worms.' '. . . difficult to digest,' says the Sheriff. 'Have you ever heard of a bandit called Cheyenne?' 'Have you ever heard of an animal called a chameleon? He stands on a stone and seems to be a stone. He stands on a leaf and seems to be a leaf. This allows him to live for a long time.' Harmonica continues, smiling: 'Think how amusing it would be, if you were a chameleon, with two legs and a pistol, and in your mind the idea of making a heap of money. In one place there's a Jesse James. You take on the colour of Jesse James, commit two murders and disappear. Who was it? Well — Jesse James naturally. In another place, there's a Cheyenne. You take on the colour of Cheyenne . . .' The Sheriff nods: 'And what name would you give this particular kind of chameleon . . . What would you say if we called him Frank?' Harmonica remains cool: 'I can see you know a lot about chameleons. Why don't you try and catch one?' The Sheriff laughs. Harmonica continues: 'How much do they pay Sheriffs in this town?' 'Twenty-eight dollars and sixty-five cents a week.' 'Well, until there's a pay rise, this city will be infested with chameleons.' The Sheriff shrugs: '. . . sooner or later they turn the wrong colour, and they meet someone who can see them.' Harmonica moves towards the door: 'Can I go, while you're waiting?' As he walks outside, there are sounds of a scuffle: the three deputies stagger into the stables, one by one. Harmonica appears in the doorway, holding out the Sheriff's handkerchief to one of the deputies, who has developed a black eye: 'Like this, we don't hold anything against each other.'

(These sequences were substituted, in the final print, by a scene in Wobbles' laundry, where Harmonica gets his revenge on Wobbles for setting up the meeting at Cattle Corner station. Traces of the dialogue with the Sheriff remain ('That was always one of Frank's tricks . . . faking evidence!'). But Harmonica's part has become far less vocal (the Hamlet reference would seem very out of place in the release print!). Throughout the middle section of the final version, Harmonica bears the scars of his fight with the Sheriff's deputies.)

3   Chinese laundry. Day. The place is a hive of activity. Wobbles is supervising the Chinese workers. He rummages in a laundry basket. 'Eight sheets. There should be eight, you yellow faces!' He holds up eight fingers: 'Can't you count, for Christ's sake?' The Chinese women silently go back to work. As the bell rings, Wobbles instantly changes his manner: he is now 'all respectful solicitude'. Jill McBain enters. In the next scene (31), Jill leaves the laundry, and walks towards the Flagstone hotel. She passes a saddler's shop: Harmonica is examining the merchandise (we see his face, as he puts down a saddle). Jill walks by without stopping, but it is clear that 'all is going according to plan'. As Jill enters the hotel, Harmonica continues to inspect the saddle ('making sure it is made by hand, not one of those mass-produced mock-ups arriving in the West by train'). But he also keeps an eye on the back door of the laundry, where Wobbles is trying to leave inconspicuously. As Wobbles walks away, Harmonica follows him (his face 'appears, round the corners of houses, carriages, and from behind horses'), until Wobbles goes into the main station building. The next sequence (33) shows the railway track, with a locomotive (plus passenger carriages) pointing in the opposite direction to the one which brought Jill to Flagstone (it has been turned around, on a wooden platform constructed on the branch line just outside Flagstone). As the train leaves, Wobbles jumps into one of the carriages: Harmonica jumps on to the running board of the following carriage. In the next scene (34), Harmonica looks for Wobbles in his carriage (it is a guard's van). There is no sign of him. Scene 35 shows Harmonica looking for Wobbles in a crowded compartment (see Chapter 4 for a full description of the scene). Still no sign of Wobbles. Harmonica jumps from the moving train (36), which by now is several hundred yards from the station. There is a stretch of line which leads nowhere, parallel to the main track, with an 'improvised' wooden shack next to it. Another locomotive, with a single carriage which looks like a cattle wagon, is about to leave. (This setting remains in the final version.) Harmonica climbs a ladder at the rear of this wagon, and lies flat on the roof listening to the

conversation inside. A bell rings, and the camera zooms from a metal communication wire in the carriage, to a message bell in the cabin of the locomotive. The engine driver listens to the bell: 'Hm. The spider wants to go and make a little turn around.' The fireman shovels coal into the furnace: 'You know he likes to go fast.' The locomotive moves out.

(This cut sequence explains the apparently arbitrary decision to have *two* locomotives on display, during the final (abridged) version of Harmonica's search for Wobbles. In this final version, no attempt is made to explain how trains manage to go in opposite directions, on the same (single) line of track. The shooting-script makes clear that Morton's personal train is not intended to take passengers. In the final version, the details of train travel to and from Flagstone are extremely muddled. The reference to Morton wanting to 'go fast' relates to the scene at Frank's hide-out where the crippled railroad boss reveals his obsession with 'time' running out on him.)

4 Interior. Morton's personal carriage (a converted cattle-wagon). Harmonica has been tied up (with a length of curtain-cord), and is watching Morton's grotesque attempts to drag himself along his walking frame. Morton pours himself a large measure of liquor. Three of Frank's men are playing cards — making no attempt to help Morton. 'Now I understand,' says Harmonica to Morton. 'What?' 'Why haven't they tied *you* up?' 'Because I am not a prisoner,' replies Morton. Harmonica looks up: 'That's not the impression I'm getting.' One of Frank's men snaps at Harmonica: 'That's enough.' The expression on Morton's face shows that Harmonica has 'touched a raw nerve'. Morton turns to the prisoner: 'I am Frank's boss.' Harmonica: 'Does *he* know that?'

(This short sequence, no. 46, together with the sequence in the final Italian print set outside Frank's mountain hide-out, illustrates clearly the relationship between Morton and his employees — an important theme in the original conception, perhaps owing something to Bertolucci's contribution. In the later sequence of the final version, where Frank's men are playing cards in Morton's presence, this relationship would have been located in a clearer context, had Scene 46 not been dropped.)

5 Foyer of Flagstone hotel. Day. Jill sits down, and glances at the *Abilene Enquirer* (originally, Flagstone was to have been Abilene): the headline reads 'Railway Continues Its March Towards the West'. Jill is not concentrating, however. A shadow is cast over the newspaper. Jill is startled. Sam introduces a well-dressed man as 'Signor O'Leary, from the bank . . . He says he must talk with you.' The banker nods, and asks Sam to leave. O'Leary is clearly embarrassed: 'Useless to say . . .' 'Useless,' replies Jill. The banker gives her a sealed envelope (a legal document, given to him fifteen years before, when McBain first staked his claim to Sweetwater). Jill reads it with great interest. O'Leary recalls that McBain said to him, 'Its just a piece of earth that's worth nothing — but keep it safely — one day it could be very important.' He continues reminiscing — '. . . a strange type, that McBain. I asked him how he found the strength to work such a piece of valueless land. Do you know what he replied?' Jill has a determined look on her face: 'Yes — he answered, "In a dream, a great and splendid dream." ' O'Leary is surprised by this: Jill gets up, smiles, and returns the document. 'Will you keep it safely? It's important.' Sam pushes forward: 'If you've finished here, we've got another little problem.' He indicates something in the street behind him: '. . . what the hell are we going to do with all this wood?'

(This leads on to the sequence in the final version where Jill and Sam are inspecting McBain's consignment of wood, intended for the construction of Sweetwater station.)

6 Main Street. Flagstone. Day. A carriage passes, crammed with railway navvies ('white, black, Chinese'). In the distance, Harmonica is talking with the hotel clerk. The clerk points towards the bank opposite the hotel. Harmonica crosses the street, enters the bank, and approaches O'Leary . . .

7 Near the McBain farm, Sweetwater. Morning. Two hands are fixing up a large wooden sign, 'Sweetwater Station': the hands are Cheyenne's, and he is standing on another man's shoulders. He jumps down, and, together with his men, inspects his handiwork. 'It is not a masterpiece of carpentry, but the facade looks good . . . Cheyenne's men look at the sign in awe, as if at a Cathedral . . . It is years since they have worked with any tool apart from a pistol. Now they have built something.' Cheyenne is beside himself with excitement, and begins to imitate a stationmaster: his men join in the game. 'The exit is this way.' They open the door of the 'station', to reveal that it is simply a facade, with no interior — just miles and miles of desert. But the game continues: 'Here's the ticket office,' 'And here are the toilets . . .' The Man is leaning against this facade, cleaning his harmonica. Cheyenne turns

to him, suddenly serious: 'This little joke should draw Frank like honey draws a fly!' The Man starts to play his harmonica. Cheyenne continues: 'We can come to an agreement with the woman . . .' The Man continues to play. '. . . the station will be the first thing she sees when she gets back.' The Man stops playing: '. . . *if* she gets back.'

(In the final version, the dialogue which ends this scene (63), becomes part of a rather different sequence: the consignment of wood has just arrived at Sweetwater, and Cheyenne's men are deciding what to do with it. Harmonica mentions that he has seen a 'document' — 6 above — which has informed him that the station must be built before the rail-gangs arrive. Cheyenne immediately gets to work: 'What are you supposed to *do*? Build a station, idiots . . .!' The next time we see the station — as a locomotive pulls into Sweetwater — it has become more than a mere facade.)

8 Main Street of Flagstone. Day. Frank, dressed elegantly in a dark suit, waistcoat and white shirt, rides into town. He hitches his horse to a post outside the barber's shop. As he walks into the shop (Sc. 67), he pauses to look at a 'Wanted' poster: 'Manuel *Cheyenne* Gutierrez. Murder and Armed Robbery. $10,000.' Frank grins as he goes in to see the barber (Sc. 68). There is only one chair, and the barber — a bald, chubby man — clearly needs the work: 'Please sit down, sir.' Frank ignores him as he hangs up his hat and jacket, and adjusts his gunbelt. 'Shave and haircut?' 'Shave and silence.' Frank leans towards the basin, to wet his face; as he does so, he sees the reflection of Harmonica in the mirror. Harmonica is looking at Frank, through the window: he is impassive. *Insert. Flashback.* Out of focus, the young Frank is walking very slowly towards him. Harmonica blinks, to bring himself back to the present, and to the mirror-image of the man who jolted his memory. After a last glance at Frank, Harmonica walks away, and leans against the wall of the house: he takes out a piece of wood, and begins to sharpen it with his knife. Inside the barber's shop, Frank has arranged himself comfortably in the chair: it seems that he has forgotten about the Man. But the barber looks worried as he spreads shaving foam over Frank's chin. Eventually, the barber can hold out no longer: 'Excuse me, sir, there's someone out there, and he's whittlin' on a piece of wood.' 'And so?' 'I got a feeling that when he's stopped whittlin', something's going to happen!' Outside, in the main street (Sc. 69), the Man looks up as a carriage arrives: he stops whittling when he sees that Jill McBain is sitting in the carriage, next to one of

Frank's men. Jill shows no emotion as the carriage passes close by the Man. The carriage stops outside the Sheriff's office. Harmonica looks into the barber's shop: Frank seems to be completely relaxed. He then looks at Jill: she gets down from the carriage, and talks with the Sheriff and his deputies. The Sheriff registers surprise, seems to be making objections, then shrugs his shoulders: he gives an order to his deputies. Harmonica frowns as he continues to whittle on his piece of wood. Back inside the barber's shop (Sc. 70), a man rushes in, full of the news that 'McBain's land is for sale . . . there's an auction . . . interested? . . . it won't go for much.' The barber replies, 'Even a little is too much to pay for something that is worthless.' Frank has shown no interest in this conversation. But the barber adds '. . . unless this gentleman is interested in buying a beautiful bit of desert . . .' Frank's shoulders begin to shake as he laughs to himself . . . Scene 74 (after the first auction sequence) is located in the corridor of the Flagstone hotel. Harmonica appears 'in the usual way', and crosses the corridor. He can hear the confused murmur of voices from the auction downstairs. He knocks on one of the doors opposite him: it is clearly a prearranged signal. There are sounds of movement behind the door, and of a key turning in the lock: 'It's me,' says Harmonica. He hesitates as he glances 'with regret' at the pistol he is holding in his right hand, then decisively goes into the hotel room. Scene 76 (after the second auction sequence) takes place back in the barber's shop. Frank's face is wrapped up in a damp towel: near the chair, one of his men is telling him the news. '. . . then the Sheriff said, "OK, Cheyenne is as good as cash. He's worth $10,000" . . . The bastard's still there, Frank, in the hotel. We'd still be in time. Say the word and we'll . . .' Frank simply gestures the barber to remove the towel from his face. He is completely relaxed. As his gunman awaits further orders, Frank turns to the barber: 'Perfume!'

(These sequences are interesting for a variety of reasons. They open with a reference to the 'wedding' suggestion Frank has made in his previous scene: we are clearly supposed to think that Frank is about to get married to Jill. They continue with a tense confrontation in a barber's shop (the origin, perhaps, of the credits sequence in *My Name Is Nobody*), and with an extra flashback (which Harmonica has to make an effort to obliterate from his mind). The 'whittlin'' incident was later to be transposed to the final scenes at the McBain ranch, and Cheyenne was to be given the barber's lines. By showing *how* Harmonica discovers about the auction, and *why* he decides to turn Cheyenne in (the 'Wanted' poster), Leone cuts his character down to size. Earlier on (in the shooting-script) we have been shown *how* Harmonica discovers about Frank 'faking the evidence', what 'the document' concerning Sweetwater contains, and so on. In other words, we have shared with Harmonica the experience of piecing together the story. When Leone deleted these explanatory scenes, he also created the impression that Harmonica has an almost supernatural ability to be in the right place at the right time. The part was obviously written with Charles Bronson in mind (there are references to Bronson's facial expressions in the shooting-script): but the character of the Man With the Harmonica (like that of the Man With No Name in the trilogy) resulted from adaptations to the original script during shooting. It is also interesting that Leone reduced the price on Cheyenne's head *after* the script had been written: in the final version, the price is $5,000. And Harmonica's reluctance to turn him in is less apparent from the release print.)

In addition to these eight extra sequences, which appear in the shooting-script, but which were deleted during shooting, there is one short sequence which appeared in the shooting-script, was deleted from the Italian print, but was *put back* in the international release print: the sequence showing Harmonica at Cattle Corner station, the evening after his gunfight with three of Frank's men (Jack Elam, Woody Strode, Al Mulock). Harmonica struggles to his feet, nurses his wound, picks up his bag and walks away. This sequence was presumably deleted from the Italian print because it was clear from the subsequent scene in Lionel Stander's bar that Harmonica had survived the gunfight — with a bullet wound. It was put back in the international print because the Lionel Stander sequence had by then been deleted. It was filmed in the first place (like many of the scenes outlined above), probably because Leone had not yet decided how to strike a balance between making the story too obvious or too elliptical for his audience.

Will Wright, in his *Sixguns and Society*, interprets both the resurgence in popularity of the Hollywood Western from 1966 to 1970, and the changes in content which many of the more successful of these post-1966 Westerns represented, exclusively in terms of significant changes in the expectations of *American audiences*. John G. Cawelti, in *The Six-Gun Mystique*, interprets the same or similar issues in terms of the crucial impact of the 'international Western, in particular the Clint Eastwood films made in Italy and Spain, and directed by the Italian Sergio Leone'. Both these critics make important contributions to the analysis of 'neo-Westerns': but, at base, they are adopting two very distinct approaches to the study of film. In one sense, Wright is more concerned with *exogenous* factors (specifically the participation of audiences, changes in popular conceptions of society, the validity of consumer sovereignty theses), Cawelti with *endogenous* factors (changes in film 'style', in 'the language of the Western', variations on the formula partly analysed from aesthetic perspective). But both use 'changes in the formula' (the 'formula' being defined in terms of, on the one hand, Vladimir Propp's, and, on the other, Northrop Frye's methodology), and changes which can be readily categorised, as their primary data. So it is perhaps surprising that Wright has nothing of interest to say about the impact of the Spaghetti Westerns (at least two of which, as we have seen, come well within his 'blockbuster' category); he does not even discuss the issue.

Clearly, questions of 'impact' or 'influence' must always be problematic: 'influences' on a given film can seldom be detected with certainty. But it is worth looking briefly at (what I take to be) the more obvious Spaghetti elements in post-1966 American Westerns — if for no other reason than to fill out Will Wright's rather one-sided picture.

Several of the Italian directors discussed in this book have stressed, in interviews, the impact of their work on the Hollywood 'neo-Western', particularly on the work of Sam Peckinpah (perhaps the most obvious example). Leone: 'In retrospect, I can see that *A Fistful of Dollars* heralded the

beginnings of a new cinema: *Clockwork Orange*, for example, would never have been filmed in the way it was. And Sam Peckinpah would have hesitated before shedding so much blood. He told me himself, "Without you, I would never have thought of making the films I have made . . .".' Corbucci: 'Peckinpah made *The Wild Bunch* after thinking about the films of Leone and Corbucci.' Certainly, the success of some Italian Westerns (and especially those by Leone and Corbucci) must have helped Sam Peckinpah to interest producers in a big-budget film with a story about bandits on the run, Mexican bandit/revolutionaries, nasty children, and bounty-hunters, set on the Southwestern frontier. And the characterisation of Cable Hogue (Jason Robards) seems to have been an *extension* of Robards' previous performance as Cheyenne, the romantic bandit, in *Once Upon a Time*. However, Peckinpah's treatment of actual moments of violence in his 'twilight' Westerns (the most usual point of comparison) — which always erupt suddenly, almost casually, in his films, and are then evoked in detail *as the gun is fired* by subtle intercutting of brief slow-motion shots showing wounds spurting blood — differs fundamentally from Leone's recurring concern with the formalities which *precede* violent confrontations: the precise moment, in a duel, when guns are fired seems to be of little interest to Leone. Those critics who have noted a similarity between the two directors' attitudes towards violence are, in this sense, missing the point: the commercial success (on American release) of the films of Leone and Corbucci may have created a context within which Peckinpah was permitted not only to film the opening and closing sequences of *The Wild Bunch*, but also to include them in the final version virtually uncut (compare Jerry Bresler's less understanding view of the Apache massacre which was originally to appear in the first reel of the pre-Leone *Major Dundee*, 1964), but this is not to suggest that the 'Dollars' trilogy had any influence on Peckinpah's individual way of filming the impact of a bullet. Dr Frank Manchel in his book *Cameras West* has suggested that 'when Peckinpah told interviewers, in 1969, that in *The*

Wild Bunch he wanted to take the romance out of killing, he probably was referring to some of the conventions that the Leone films were glamorizing'. A very different view, stressing the similarities between the two directors' films — in terms of the audience's *response* to violence — has been expressed in *Violence in the Arts* by John Fraser, who writes that 'the bloodbaths in Westerns like Leone's *For a Few Dollars More*, Corbucci's *Django* . . . and Peckinpah's *The Wild Bunch*' are 'cathartic because the shocking parts provide climaxes to certain movements or phases in the films and permit certain actions to reach their logical conclusions and certain formal anticipations to be fully satisfied, just as they are satisfied in non-bloody works, such as slapstick comedies'. These assessments, by Manchel and Fraser, have more recently been challenged by Jenni Calder (in *There Must Be a Lone Ranger*, 1976): for Calder, we judge these two film-makers — Leone and Peckinpah — 'for their style. If there is a legitimate criticism of *The Wild Bunch* that is based on more than a distasteful reaction it is that the style collapses. It wobbles dangerously in Peckinpah's earlier *Major Dundee*. Realism can never be a substitute for style — in fact, it can't exist without style. If Leone has to be admired in spite of possible distaste it is because he does have a consistent and coherent style, not just, as Clint Eastwood put it, "an interesting approach to violence" . . . When Lee Van Cleef kills with such cool satisfaction in *The Good, the Bad and the Ugly*, we have a moment of particular viciousness which tells us not that killing is easy, but that the killer is evil. When in *Once Upon a Time in the West*, Fonda shoots a small boy it is an equally vicious moment but it has a ghastly logic. Leone shows little concern for the Western's traditional code. He makes Westerns without unequivocal heroes. "The Good" is only a marginal improvement on "the Bad" and "the Ugly" and has nothing like the romanticism of . . . *The Wild Bunch*. Leone's version of the West is total anarchy with scarcely any room for heroism.' We have already discussed the fundamental differences between the 'odysseys' contained in the films of Peckinpah and Leone, differences which may derive from very different cultural and economic contexts. In *The Wild Bunch*, the violence is associated with a crusading element: as Calder puts it, 'the expendable Mexican has taken the place of the expendable Indian'. In Leone's films, the violence is rather that of a grotesque puppet show. Peckinpah's emphasis on 'documentary' realism (usually based on detailed research) as in, for example, the mining camp sequences of *Guns in the Afternoon* (1962), the opening main-street scene of *The Wild Bunch*, and the whorehouse sequences of *The Ballad of Cable Hogue*, almost suggests that *description* of Western settings (the developing town, the makeshift community, life on the frontier), is, to Peckinpah, an end in itself. In Leone's films, the obsessive concern with tiny details rather provides an 'authentic' backdrop for visual experimentation, and for *extending* the rules of the genre. If Peckinpah is interested in the decline of old Western values, he does not tend to evoke this decline by manipulating the established *rituals* of the Hollywood Western (which is not to say that he hesitates before going further than other Hollywood directors had gone). Only in his first feature, *The Deadly Companions*, does he attempt to comment on these rituals, in the sequence where the Indians re-enact, in drunken mime, a stagecoach robbery. Since then, Peckinpah has used cliché dialogue not in order to satirise it, but in order to romanticise the sentiments it expresses.

Immediately after Clint Eastwood had made his name in Leone's 'Dollars' films, his most interesting work — back in the States — resulted from a collaboration with director Don Siegel. Many of the films he made with Siegel were explicitly intended to explore the 'image' he had presented in the Spaghetti Westerns. In interviews, Don Siegel has often expressed his appreciation of Leone's directorial technique, and the opening sequences of *Coogan's Bluff* (1968) and *Two Mules for Sister Sara* (1969) both contain explicit 'hommages' to the equivalent scenes in Leone's *For a Few Dollars More*. (Siegel in fact screened the three 'Dollars' films, before agreeing to direct *Coogan's Bluff*.) The interpretation of the American Civil War which runs through *The Beguiled* (1971) owes much to *The Good, the Bad and the Ugly*: the Union soldier (Clint Eastwood) is utterly cynical about his role in the war, and spends the entire movie hiding from Confederate scavengers who might drag him off to Andersonville internment camp. Ironically, since Don Siegel was later to make *Dirty Harry* (1972), his 'neo-Westerns' starring Clint Eastwood seem to effect a gradual liberalisation of the 'Man With No Name' persona — a reversal of the Leone trend. The Eastwood character comes to be concerned with justice, with righting society's wrongs — albeit in a vigilante manner: in the 'Dollars' films, he did not give a damn about society's wrongs, since he was too busy exploiting them. This is not to suggest that in Siegel's hands the character becomes more liberal in a political sense — far from it; simply that because he thinks he can do something about his environment, he becomes more recognisably human and that tends to give his violence a 'crusading element'. In addition, he actually begins to develop relationships with other people.

Most of Clint Eastwood's own films as a director also contain explorations of his cinematic 'image', and in particular of the 'lone wolf' of the trilogy. In the first of these, *Play Misty for Me*, Eastwood cast Don Siegel as a friendly neighbourhood barman. His first Western, *High Plains Drifter*, can be interpreted as an attempt (literally) to exorcise the enigmatic persona of the Man With No Name. The early sequences of *Drifter* — Eastwood's entry into Lago and 'welcome' by the inhabitants — closely resemble Leone's treatment of the Man's arrival in San Miguel (*A Fistful of Dollars*) and in Agua Caliente (*For a Few Dollars More*); the explanatory flashbacks are presented in ways which recall Indio's fantasies (also in *For a Few Dollars More*). Eastwood later said of Jim Duncan 'I had been familiar with that character for a long time . . .' But as *High Plains Drifter* progresses, Eastwood relies more on staccato visual rhythms (possibly Siegel-inspired) and becomes increasingly economical in his effects. The unsettling impact of the picture's climax, when the Stranger orders the inhabitants to paint Lago red (a Leone town, if ever there was one), and rechristens the town 'Hell', seems to owe little to devices derived from either of Eastwood's former directors: the unobtrusive use of slightly low-angle shots (to represent the dwarf's-eye view), at first apparently suggested by the conversation between the Half-Soldier and the Bad, in *The Good, the Bad and the Ugly*, and of an 'unnatural' soundtrack, for example, reveal a new assurance in Eastwood as director. *High Plains Drifter* comes over as a medieval morality play (each of the townsfolk seems to represent one of the seven deadly sins, and Duncan is the ultimate *deus ex machina*) reinterpreted through the cinematic image of Clint Eastwood — and the dwarf, standing in for little Joey in *Shane*, acts as chorus. I say 'morality play' because the film adopts a highly moral attitude *vis-à-vis* the townsfolk — even if the central character has become a superman again: in short, the simple-minded evangelism of Mickey Spillane is combined (at times) with the visual sophistication of Leone.

A press still from *High Plains Drifter* shows the Stranger (Eastwood) standing by Verna Bloom, near two gravestones: the inscriptions simply read 'Leone' and 'Siegel'. Several French critics, however, preferred to compare Eastwood's directorial technique with that of Sergio Corbucci in his Franco Nero trilogy, rather than with that of Leone (on 'Dollars' form). Leone did not enjoy *Drifter* at all. The story of *Drifter*, incidentally, closely resembles that of *Django the Bastard* (Sergio

Garrone, 1969), another Spaghetti Western, co-scripted by Garrone and the star, Antonio de Teffé, in which the avenger turns out to be a supernatural 'drifter'. But there was a fairly recent Hollywood precedent as well — Roy Rowland's *The Moonlighter* (1953, with Fred MacMurray): and the story goes back as far as 1916, when William S. Hart appeared in *Hell's Hinges*. Eastwood's more recent *The Outlaw Josey Wales* represents another 'exorcism' of the 'Man With No Name' persona. Josey Wales rides through Kansas and Missouri just after the American Civil War, bent on personal revenge ('I don't want *nobody* belonging to me'): but he is constantly being deflected from his 'quest' by various marginal people (an elderly Comanche Indian, a hippie girl, an old lady from Kansas) who refuse to take his *machismo* image seriously. Even a dog he picks up on the way seems to 'see through' his tough exterior: Josey Wales spits a wad of tobacco in the direction of the dog (hitting it right between the eyes) but the dog simply growls, then comes back for more, wagging its tail. Eventually, the 'lone avenger' is persuaded by these perceptive characters to give up his 'quest', to choose 'the word of life', and to settle down in a little log-cabin in the prairies. Like Grace Kelly persuading Gary Cooper to give up *before* the showdown. The interpretation of the Civil War in *Josey Wales* may be cynical (a ferryman sings 'Dixie' or the 'Battle Hymn of the Republic', according to whether he is ferrying Union or Confederate troops), but the conclusion to the film decidedly is not: there is hope for the post-Vietnam generation after all. It is as if *Fistful* has been challenged by *Bonanza* and lost: Henry Nash Smith was right all along. Post-Civil War society is presented as full of drifters and uprooted persons: bounty-hunters ('There's no other way to make a living'), carpet-baggers, con-men, redlegs, vigilantes, unemployed saloon folk; and the style occasionally bears the Leone stamp (low-angle shots of boots, hooves, desert landscapes). But the main themes of *Josey Wales* are far away from the world of the Spaghetti Westerns. A tree grows by the graveside. 'I guess we all died a little in that damn war.'

Ralph Nelson's *Duel at Diablo* (1965) was an underrated Western which revealed Nelson's talent for relaxing the traditionally accepted (if unobtrusive) visual conventions of the genre, and for exploring the Western's *rhetoric* — without indulging in virtuosity for its own sake — particularly in the helicopter shots which open the film, and in the scenes where a cavalry scout (James Garner) is shown crossing the desert to get help for the beleaguered settlers. *Duel* proved him to be the closest American director, in terms of technique, to Sergio Leone. Nelson's *Soldier Blue* (1970) confirmed the promise of the earlier Western: in emphasising the excessive brutality of the two massacre sequences — and ignoring the more interesting 'initiation' scenes between Candice Bergen and Peter Strauss, which provide the film with a moral centre — most critics succeeded in missing the really inventive sections of *Soldier Blue*, which involve Nelson's use of elaborate zooms, and of untraditional compositions, both of which subtly explore the relationship between the 'initiates' and the Virgin Land which surrounds them. Elliot Silverstein's *A Man Called Horse* and Arthur Penn's *Little Big Man* — released in the same year as *Soldier Blue* — were suitably liberal in their sympathetic attitudes towards the Indian counter-culture in American history, but ended up by being at least as patronising to the way of life they were so painstakingly evoking, as John Ford's cavalry trilogy had been — in a different way, of course. Almost as patronising (both to the Indians and to the audience) as Dee Brown's oversold *Bury My Heart at Wounded Knee*, published a year later. *Soldier Blue*, which dared to show the heart actually being buried, was a much more angry film — perhaps because it did not pretend to be a documentary (parallels with Vietnam were stressed throughout) and because it viewed the issue from the perspective of white liberals (rather than of Hollywood 'Indians'). It also avoided the temptation of making the Indians behave as Red WASPs. Nelson's third Western, *The Wrath of God* (1973), treated questions about an individual's attitude to the Mexican Revolution in ways which begged comparison with the political Spaghettis. Although concerned with frontier themes — such as the treatment of Indians, and the settler's way of life — which scarcely feature in Leone's films, Nelson seems to be using equally rhetorical effects to reinforce or support the polemical points he makes: alone among the liberal Westerns of the late 1960s, *Soldier Blue* challenges the language of the traditional Western at the same time as its ideological bases.

Robert Altman's *McCabe and Mrs Miller* (1971), an attempt to evoke visually the life of an expanding, primitive mining community (Presbyterian Church) in the frozen Northwest, used effects comparable to those employed by Leone in *Once Upon a Time in the West*: the long, slow panning shots of McCabe (Warren Beatty) riding into town through the snow, accompanied by a distinctive soundtrack, in this case Leonard Cohen's; Altman's fussy concern with the details of how men must have looked, dressed, walked and

behaved (details which often provide a backdrop to one of the director's characteristically 'improvised' scenarios); the ritualised confrontation between a naive cowboy and a chubby, malicious gunfighter on an improvised rope-bridge; the long sequences in which McCabe tries to outwit the three hired guns, finally winning by breaking the rules, during the climactic shootout in the snow; the expressionistic use of brown and orange colour washes for the log-cabin interiors, especially for the scenes which take place in an opium den — this in stark contrast to the freezing blue exteriors. But one of Altman's central concerns is with the relationship between McCabe and Mrs Miller (Julie Christie) — or rather, with the economic relationship this symbolises — and, perhaps because his interest in the visual conventions of the Western is peripheral to this, his photographic and editing effects are more understated, less elaborately 'set up' (within a comparably improvised framework), his attention to detail (for example in the use of language) more 'authentic' (in the sense of providing a document) than equivalent effects in *Once Upon a Time*. And Altman is, of course, less concerned with rhetoric. But the epic qualities of *McCabe* — the development of Presbyterian Church as a town, the sustained attack on Jennings Bryan's populism, the whorehouses as symbols of McCabe's 'rugged individualism', and the treatment of the business-man-gunfighter relationship (a rival mining company hires Butler and his heavies to 'persuade' McCabe) — locate the film within the same frame of reference.

Although these films by Peckinpah, Siegel, Nelson and Altman occasionally refer to, or indicate the resonance of, Leone's early Westerns, and were often financed by commercial organisations which were fully aware of the success of the 'Dollars' trilogy, they never, of course, attempt to copy Leone's work slavishly. At most, Leone (and Corbucci) provided a stimulus for individual visual effects, script ideas, characters and settings. (More emphasis was placed on the arid Southwestern frontier, even in Westerns not shot in the Spanish desert, and desolate 'Leone towns' appeared in atmospheric Westerns such as Peter Fonda's *The Hired Hand* (1971), Monte Hellman's *The Shooting* (1967), Dick Richards' *Culpepper Cattle Company* (1972) — towns which consisted solely of a saloon, a bank, and an extremely muddy main street). Other, more opportunistic directors were quick to jump on the 'Dollars' bandwagon, the resulting films simply being pale imitations. Strangely, the debate about the impact of Spaghettis has normally been concerned with films of this type, rather than with the work of more inventive directors, such as those discussed above. Andrew Sarris, for example, notes that 'the spaghetti western . . . is slithering into Hollywood westerns as well', and cites second-rate derivatives such as Hathaway's *Five Card Stud* ('killings have been replaced by murders, the vanity of villainy by an insane deviousness'), and Ted Post's *Hang 'Em High* ('catering to the lowest instincts') as evidence. 'We may be in for a long siege of stranglers with ten-gallon hats', he concludes, bemoaning the fact that post-Leone Westerns 'here and abroad' carry the message 'every man for himself'. Jeavons and Parkinson treat the most throwaway 'Paella' derivatives as characteristic of this trend. David Austen refers to the movement of American Western film crews to locations in Spain (*The Hunting Party*; *A Town Called Bastard*), and concludes from this that when Italian Westerns cease to be fashionable they will 'still be with us — for as a mass movement they have markedly influenced the American Western' (one index of this influence being the Spanish topography).

At a purely narrative level, the impact of the European Western can be traced in the 'set-pieces' written into some less enduring American Westerns, which have little else in common. We have already seen how the story-line of Garrone's *Django the Bastard* may have found its way into Eastwood's experimental *High Plains Drifter*. The gun in the bathtub gag from Leone's *The Good, the Bad and the Ugly* reappears in, of all unlikely places, the John Wayne vehicle *Big Jake* (George Sherman, 1971). An extremely unpleasant bounty-hunter named Dan Nodeen (even the baddies call him 'meaner than a gut-shot grizzly') spits his way through Andrew V. McLaglen's *Chisum* (1970), before he leaves town when there's no one left to pay him — he resembles Clint Eastwood, and John Wayne does not like him at all. The spectacular climax from Reinl's *Winnetou the Warrior*, when a locomotive is driven through the middle of a saloon, recurs in John Sturges' *Joe Kidd* (1972). The jokey, relaxed, episodic quality of Burt Kennedy's scripts and direction in such films as *The War Wagon* (1967), *Support Your Local Sheriff* (1968), *The Good Guys and the Bad Guys* (1969) and *Support Your Local Gunfighter* (1971), far removed from the concerns of those explorations of the Western hero's role which Kennedy scripted for Budd Boetticher between 1956 and 1960, owes much to the narrative structure of the 'Dollars' trilogy, and in particular to Leone's light-hearted, critical comments on the set incidents traditionally associated with the Hollywood Western myth. *Support Your Local Gunfighter* closes on a shot of Jack Elam (who plays a retired gunslinger) taking a train out of

town, and telling the audience that he can always earn a living in the Italian Westerns. Of all Burt Kennedy's films in this period, *Hannie Caulder* (1971) — financed by Tigon British — remains closest in impact to Leone's early Westerns. It is a deceptively simple revenge story, involving three itinerant gunslingers (Ernest Borgnine, Strother Martin, and Jack Elam, coming on like the Three Stooges) who seem to have walked straight off the set of a crazy version of *Once Upon a Time in the West*; and their spectacular gang-bang of Raquel Welch, a memorable enough event which is periodically recalled by the 'heroine' in a series of lurid flashbacks. *Hannie Caulder* also boasted Christopher Lee and Diana Dors in the cast.

Most of William Fraker's *Monte Walsh* (1970) looks like a movie version of Remington's paintings (which are featured behind the credits). The film opens with a reference to Jack Abernathy — a roughrider and friend of Teddy Roosevelt: Roosevelt, Remington and Owen Wister are usually cited in the history books as the East-coasters who together had the most crucial influence on the development of the Western. But, in the last part of *Monte Walsh* (from the moment when a sheriff walks into the picture, wearing a yellow oilskin in a thunderstorm), the film comes to look more and more like a Spaghetti Western: this is a pity, for if Fraker had been less fashion-conscious, his film might have sustained the effectively autumnal atmosphere of the first half. As it is, the excellent 'Slashed Y' sequences (about unemployed Remington cowboys) seem to be going in a different direction to the Leone-inspired chase which concludes the film: the clash of styles in the end breaks the back of *Monte Walsh*. The ending of Arthur Penn's *Missouri Breaks* (1976) — which departs from Thomas McGuane's script by having the crippled businessman Braxton attempt to shoot the rustler (Jack Nicholson) — contains an explicit reference to the equivalent scene in *Once Upon a Time in the West*.

More obvious derivatives (with Spaghetti elements in narrative, technique and topography), many of which conform to Sarris' model of 'the strangler in a ten-gallon hat', include Ted Post's *Hang 'Em High* (1968, the first Western made in Hollywood to cash in on Eastwood's 'Dollars' image — and cash in it did, to the tune of $17 million); Tom Gries' *100 Rifles* (1968, a depressing follow-up to the same director's *Will Penny*, an engagingly unromantic Western about the cowpuncher's way of life); William Graham and Blake Edwards' *Waterhole 3* (1967, in which the anti-hero James Coburn, in true Colonel Mortimer style, fights a 'duel' by waiting until the opponent is out of pistol range, then shooting him down with a Winchester); Lamont Johnson's *A Gunfight* (1970, the climax of which is set in a more literal version of the Leone *corrida*, where Kirk Douglas and Johnny Cash shoot it out — to no effect as it transpires, since the scriptwriter cannot decide which of the two heroes should die); John Guillemin's *El Condor* (1970, a misguided attempt to cast Lee Van Cleef in a sympathetic character part); and the dreadful *Barquero* (Gordon Douglas, 1970, which opens with a *Wild Bunch* inspired massacre, tries to get a Gian Maria Volonté performance out of Warren Oates, and was based on a script even more synthetic than rival derivatives, with the mountainman (Forrest Tucker) mouthing whole chunks of Ray Billington's frontier history). A more interesting Western, with a similar genealogy, was *Valdez Is Coming* (1970, Edwin Sherrin — a New York theatre director), which starred Burt Lancaster in the title role as the elusive Mexican Avenger, and placed the final fade-out at the *start* of a Leone-like ritual confrontation: the fact of a one-to-one confrontation was more significant than its outcome; in effect, the baddy (Frank Tanner, a capitalist 'baron') is defeated (shown to be powerless) when his henchmen desert him.

Valdez was an American film, shot on Spanish-looking locations. Of the other, 'Paella' Westerns actually shot in Spain, Robert Parrish's bizarre *A Town Called Bastard* (1971, a British-Spanish co-production, derived from Sergio Corbucci and Graham Greene!) — memorable mainly for Robert Shaw's performance as a revolutionary-turned-priest, for Stella Stevens' eye-catching funeral gowns designed by Ossie Clark, and for its extraordinarily cynical 'moral' (that in times of revolution the only genuine loyalty is to dead heroes), and Don Medford's *The Hunting Party* (1971 — a remake, in all but name, of Sergio Sollima's two chase movies *The Big Gundown* and *Face to Face*) — had the most interesting moments, but in both cases the clumsy pretensions of the directors (needless digressions, strange flashbacks, baroque violence of an unusually nasty kind) tended to swamp whatever excitement there might have been in their classically simple 'revenge' themes. A curious international Western (the crew consisted of English, Japanese, French, Swiss, Italian, Spanish, and American actors or technicians) which owed much to two earlier Spaghettis was Terence Young's *Red Sun* (1972), starring Toshiro Mifune as a samurai in the West (a samurai who, according to Stuart Kaminsky, was 'patronised' throughout); this idea was derived from Tonino Cervi's *Today Its Me, Tomorrow You* (1968), which had Mifune's sparring partner from Kurosawa days, Tatsuya Nakadai

(*Yojimbo*, 1961; *Sanjuro*, 1962), in an equivalent role as a samurai warrior stalked by 'the Magnificent Five' through the forest; and also from Don Taylor's *Five Man Army* (1969), which featured Tetsuro Tamba as one of the 'specialists', a samurai swordsman capable of splitting a man in half. The *Red Sun* team may also have had in mind an episode from the successful Ward Bond and Robert Horton TV series *Wagon Train* (1957-62), which told of a samurai ambassador's adventures among the pioneers from Eastern American, and ended on a scene in which the samurai was buried with full Indian honours. In so far as it is not a remake of *Star Trek* (Mr Spock as a resident 'alien' mystic), the recent TV series *Kung Fu* (which has as its central character a wandering Oriental sage who encounters various marginal social groups trying to settle out West) represents the fullest development of this neat idea. Clearly, attempts to keep the formula going can result in hybrid plots of a very strange kind. On the subject of which, Alexandro Jodorowsky's extraordinary attempt to make a Zen-Western, *El Topo* (1971) — which has nothing to do either with Hollywood or with Paella Westerns — contains a whole series of Leone references: it opens with a gunfighter riding through the desert under an umbrella (*The Good, the Bad and the Ugly*) and includes a 'duel of destiny' in a circular *corrida*. Jodorowsky has acknowledged this 'small homage' — 'the duel scene in the circular space — Leone'. Silvio Narizzano's *Blue* (1967) seems also to be striving (less successfully) after some kind of mystical significance: according to the director, it was concerned with youth culture of the late 1960s — 'a world allegiance that has come out of violence, the longing for peace, and the strange desire for death'. Starring Terence Stamp as a Mexican (Azul) who has been raised among Americans ('Blue'), but who has unaccountably picked up an East End accent in the process, it bears many of the hallmarks of a Spaghetti Western (the music, the landscape, the Gringo-Mexican confrontation). One scene in particular *reverses* a standard Hollywood motif: some Texans enjoy a barn-dance, to celebrate Independence Day; this is interrupted by a gang of Mexican bandits, who are attempting to reclaim the State for Mexico; the dance is presented not as a celebration of the *community*, but as a symbol of imperialism.

When Will Wright attempts to explain the resurgence in popularity of the Hollywood Western (from 1966 to 1970) in terms of a plot formula (the 'professional plot') that is more in tune with the social experience of American audiences (than the 'classical' or 'transitional' plots), he makes the assumption that Hollywood producers were in some way 'in touch' with American public demand for a variation on the Western myth which would relate directly to changed public perceptions of this social experience. Yet, even given this assumption (which has been challenged, in my view correctly), it seems more likely that producers were responding to commercial pressures from *within* the industry (rather than to the sovereignty of consumers outside — the distinction can, of course, be made), when they financed big-budget variations on the established formulae during these years. Wright also assumes that the only consumer pressure that counts (where the Western is concerned) comes from *American* audiences. Yet it seems likely that Hollywood producers of Westerns in the 1960s were becoming more and more aware of the market for their products outside the United States (*The Magnificent Seven* being the paradigm case, perhaps). After all, if the Japanese, Germans and Italians made Westerns themselves (and were prepared to saturate the home market with them), it was likely that 'authentic' Westerns (with similar themes, stories, and locales) would make as much money (if not more) than the ersatz product. And Spaghettis (in particular) had captured Third World markets more thoroughly than Hollywood Westerns had ever done. It seems to me that the commercial success of the best Spaghettis (especially those by Leone and Corbucci) — both outside the United States and in Wright's 'home market' — must in consequence be considered a

prime influence on the form and shape of the Hollywood Western from the mid-1960s onwards (as John Cawelti has suggested). Very few of the straight derivatives from Spaghettis (Paella or otherwise) did exceptionally well at the box-office: but the neo-Westerns of Peckinpah, Siegel and Eastwood — which succeeded in bringing home and absorbing the (manifestly) successful formulae of the best Spaghettis — were among the top-grossing Hollywood Westerns made since the Second World War. Will Wright's list of all-time successes includes (between 1967 and 1971) two films with Clint Eastwood, one Peckinpah, and four American 'post-Spaghettis'. Products of the Cinecittà assembly-line would seem to have given a dying American genre a much-needed shot in the arm: in 1964, there were not enough Westerns, the few that were made did not have enough shooting in them, the established stars were getting too old, they played heroes who, in Pauline Kael's words, 'nobody believed in except as movie stars', and the Western myth, like the men who epitomised it, seemed to have no vitality left; by 1971, all this had changed. At the least, Spaghetti Westerns represent *one* tradition that must be taken into account if we are to explain these changes — a tradition that has been neglected in attempts to relate the Western exclusively to the expectations of American audiences without reference to non-American — one might even say un-American — products.

Appendix 4
Box Office Receipts of
A Fistful of Dollars
in Italy

(and approximate receipts of Leone's other
Westerns in Paris, Italy, America and worldwide)

After private screenings in Naples and Rome (where distributors concluded that the film was 'not worth a lira'), *Fistful* opened at a downtown cinema in Florence ('the fixtures and fittings dated from 1908', Leone recalls) in August 1964. 'With the minimum of publicity, without a single criticism, the film took off, of its own accord, in that unknown picture house.' Of course, the context in which the film was released must be taken into account, before one accepts Leone's fairy-tale version of its initial success: although *Fistful* was treated by the industry as a marginal product, the taste for it had already been well prepared by better-publicised films in the muscleman and spy genres; as Oreste de Fornari points out, 'the Clint Eastwood character brought together both Hercules and James Bond, and in the process reconciled two classes of audience in Italy — as a Western, the film helped to recompose both the national and the international audience'. Add to this the facts that the title resembled *Un Dollaro d'Onore* (the Italian name for Hawks' *Rio Bravo* — a phenomenally successful film), and that the cast and crew were pretending to be Americans, and

Fistful becomes rather less 'marginal'. By November 1964, the film was being premièred, with much publicity, in Rome. Partly because of copyright problems involving Kurosawa's *Yojimbo*, *Fistful* did not open in the United States until 1967. The following figures, expressed in lira, cover the first fourteen months of release in Italy.

Milan	138,448,000
Turin	83,737,000
Bologna	65,407,000
Florence	52,296,000
Genoa	32,457,000
Padua	14,669,000
Trieste	13,636,000
Rome	142,108,000
Naples	50,191,000
Cagliari	13,726,000
Palermo	12,064,000

(Source: *Le Film Français*, hebdomadaire d'informations cinématographiques, 21 January 1966.)

Film	Paris (tickets sold)	Italy (dollars, gross)	America (dollars, gross)	Worldwide (lire, gross up to 1971)
A Fistful of Dollars	157,220 1966	$4,600,000 1964-8	$3,500,000	3,182,000,000 lire
For a Few Dollars More	150,724 1966-7	$5,000,000 1965-8	$5,000,000	3,492,000,000 lire
The Good, the Bad and the Ugly	137,196 1968	$4,300,000 1966-8	$6,000,000	3,210,000,000 lire
Once Upon a Time in the West	744,826 1969-70	$3,800,000 1968-70	$1,000,000	2,503,000,000 lire

(Sources: de Fornari, Miccichè, Parish, Passek and Simsolo).

Appendix 5
Umberto Eco's Model of the Superman Formula

Commercial Imperatives

Superman   *Clark Kent*

Problem One

Mythic hero, or 'fixed emblem' ('the totality of certain collective aspirations'): no enemy can possibly defeat him.

Developing hero, in a 'romance' (based on 'the unpredictable nature of *what will happen*'): he must be part of a story which is not known in advance.

Resolution

The hero always surmounts

a series of unforeseen obstacles.

Problem Two

The hero cannot be permitted to 'consume himself'.

The hero accomplishes something — thus 'consumes himself'.

God-like attributes

in a 'setting of everyday life'.

Resolution

A confused, dream-like treatment of time. The reader loses control of temporal relationships, and renounces the need to reason on their basis (for example, he sets aside questions of 'planning' and 'responsibility'). The hero always avoids 'irreversible premises', his adventures remain static, and conform to the conventions of formula fiction.

Problem Three

The hero is presented as a (predictable) 'old friend' — he is the product of 'a continuous series of connotations' (a limited repertoire of easily recognisable gestures, etc.).

The (unpredictable) story takes the form of a 'series of events repeated according to a set schema': these events must be strange enough to sustain the reader's interest, but the schema (which covers 'sentiments' and 'psychological attitudes' as well) must be reassuring.

Resolution

The 'plots' *appear* to vary significantly, and *seem* to appeal to 'a taste for the unforeseen or the sensational': but the noteworthy moments are really those when the hero repeats his usual gestures ('the reader continuously recovers, point by point, what he already knows, what he wants to know again').

Problem Four

The hero is gifted with such powers that he could 'actually take over the government, defeat the army', etc. Logically, this should lead to 'a total awareness', involving, among other things, a heightened *political* consciousness.

The hero restricts his earthly activities to the level of small-town crime, and his moral universe is equally parochial: the 'bad' is represented by offences against property, the 'good' by charity. Within this limited frame of reference, he is the perfect citizen.

Resolution

Just as the 'plots' must remain static — so as to 'forbid the release of excessive and irretrievable developments' — the hero must make 'good' consist of little activities on a small scale, a notion of 'good' which *also* represents the scriptwriters' adaptation to the particular concept of 'order' pervading the cultural model in which they live. To analyse this concept of 'order' in terms of a *premeditated* ideological position is to ignore the fundamental link between the 'hidden structure' of the formula, and Superman's activities within that formula (which function both as reflection *and* as stimulus).

Clark Kent   *Superman*

Several short stories a week — each featuring the same hero . . .

Select Bibliography

(Items marked with an asterisk proved especially useful)

Method

Althusser, Louis, 'Ideology and Ideological State Apparatuses', in *Lenin and Philosophy*, tr. B. Brewster (London, 1971).

Aristarco, Guido, 'La ville, les possibilités du cinéma, et les films', *Sociologie et Sociétés* (Montreal, April 1976).

Banfield, Edward, see under Dogan and Rose.

Barberis, Pierre, debate with Georges Duby on 'Littérature et Société', in *Écrire . . . Pour Quoi? Pour Qui?* (Grenoble, 1974).

Barthes, Roland, *Mythologies* (London, 1972).

Barthes, Roland, *S/Z* (New York, 1975).

Berger, John, 'In defence of art', *New Society* (28 September 1978).

Cahiers collective text on John Ford's *Young Mr Lincoln*, *Cahiers du Cinéma* (August 1970); translated *Screen Reader*, 1 (London, 1977).

*Cawelti, John G., *The Six-Gun Mystique* (Bowling Green, Ohio, 1971).

Cohen, Marshall, and Mast, Gerald, *Film Theory and Criticism* (New York, 1974).

*Dogan, Mattei, and Rose, Richard, *European Politics — A reader* (includes Edward Banfield on 'Amoral Familism', and a reply from Alessandro Pizzorno) (New York, 1971).

Dorfman, Ariel, and Mattelart, Armand, *How to Read Donald Duck* (New York, 1975).

*Eco, Umberto, 'The Myth of Superman', *Diacritics*, Cornell University (Ithaca, New York, Spring 1972).

Eco, Umberto, *The Bond Affair* (a more Proppian analysis of a different type of Superman) (London, 1966).

Fraser, John, *Violence in the Arts* (Cambridge, 1974).

Frye, Northrop, *Anatomy of Criticism* (Princeton, New Jersey, 1957).

Hadjinicolaou, Nicos, *Art History and Class Struggle* (London, 1978).

Hirst, Paul, 'Althusser and the theory of ideology', *Economy and Society* (November 1976).

*Jameson, Frederic, 'Ideology, Narrative Analysis and Popular Culture' (a thorough analysis of Will Wright's thesis), *Theory and Society* (Winter 1977).

King, Barry, 'Critique of Will Wright's thesis', *British Journal of Sociology* (June 1977).

Kitses, Demetrius, '*Sixguns and Society* — critique', *Quarterly Review of Film Studies* (New York, Summer 1978).

*MacBean, James Roy, *Film and Revolution* (Bloomington, Indiana, 1975).

Mepham, John, 'Theory of Ideology in "Capital"', *Cultural Studies*, 6 (Birmingham, 1974).

Orwell, George, 'Raffles and Miss Blandish', in *Mass Culture*, ed. B. Rosenberg and D.M. White (New York, 1957).

Palmer, Jerry, *Thrillers* (London, 1978).

Perkins, V.F., *Film as Film* (Harmondsworth, 1972).

Propp, Vladimir, *Morphology of the Folktale* (Austin, Texas, 1968).

Tudor, Andrew, *Theories of Film* (London, 1974).

Tudor, Andrew, 'Political Cinema', *New Society* (26 May 1977).

*Tunstall, Jeremy, *The Media Are American* (London, 1977).

Willemen, Paul (ed.), *Pier Paolo Pasolini* (especially articles by Geoffrey Nowell-Smith and Don Ranvaud), British Film Institute (London, 1977).

Williams, Raymond, 'Base and Superstructure in Marxist Cultural Theory', *New Left Review* (November-December, 1973).

Wollen, Peter, *Signs and Meaning in the Cinema* (London, 1970).

Wollen, Peter, '*North by North-West*: A Morphological Analysis', *Film Form* (Spring, 1976).

Wood, Michael, 'Critique of Will Wright's thesis', *New York Review of Books* (July 1976).

*Wright, Will, *Sixguns and Society* (Berkeley, California, 1975).

*Wright, Will, 'The Sun Sinks Slowly on the Western', *New Society* (6 May 1976).

The American Western — History, Literature and Film

Alloway, Lawrence, *Violent America — The movies, 1946-1964* (New York, 1971).

American History Hollywood Style, Velvet Light Trap special edn, 8 (Wisconsin, 1973).

Barr, Charles, 'Western', *Axle Quarterly* (Spring, 1963).

Bartlett, Richard, *The New Country* (New York, 1974).

Bazin, André, *What Is Cinema*, vol. 2 (Paris, 1961; Berkeley, California, 1971).

Billington, Ray, *Westward Expansion* (New York, 1967).

Biskind, Peter, 'Ripping off Zapata', *Cinéaste* (New York, Spring 1976).

Bogdanovich, Peter, *John Ford* (Berkeley, California, 1968).

Bogdanovich, Peter, *Fritz Lang in America* (London, 1968).

Boorstin, Daniel, *The Americans — The National Experience* (New York, 1965).

Brown, Dee, *Bury My Heart at Wounded Knee* (London, 1971).

Brown, Richard Maxwell, *Strain of Violence* (New York, 1975).

Cahiers collective text on John Ford's *Young Mr Lincoln, Cahiers du Cinéma* (August 1970); translated *Screen Reader*, 1 (London, 1977).

Calder, Jenni, *There Must Be a Lone Ranger* (London, 1976).

Cawelti, John G., *Adventure, Mystery and Romance* (Chicago, 1976).

Cawelti, John G., *The Six-Gun Mystique* (Bowling Green, Ohio, 1971).

Clapham, Walter, *Western Movies* (London, 1974).

Collins, Richard, 'The Western Genre — a reply', *Screen*, vol. 11 (September 1970); see also *Screen*, vol. 10 (September 1969).

Cunningham, Eugene, *Triggernometry* (London, 1967).

Elkin, Frederick, 'The Psychological Appeal of the "B" Western', in J. Nachbar (ed.), *Focus on the Western* (Englewood Cliffs, New Jersey, 1974).

Esselman, Kathryn, 'When the Cowboy Stopped Kissing His Horse', *Journal of Popular Culture* (Fall 1972).

Everson, William, *A Pictorial History of the Western* (New York, 1969).

Eyles, Allen, *The Western* (London, 1967; updated 1975).

Fenin, George and Everson, William, *The Western* (New York, 1962; updated 1973).

Fiedler, Leslie A., *The Return of the Vanishing American* (London, 1972).

Fiedler, Leslie A., and Zieger, Arthur, *O Brave New World* (New York, 1968).

Flinn, Tom, 'Old Ironsides', *Velvet Light Trap*, 8 (Wisconsin, 1973).

Ford, John, and Kennedy, Burt, 'On the Western', *Films in Review* (January 1969).

Foreman, Carl, 'High Noon Revisited', *Punch* (5 April 1972).

French, Philip, *Westerns* (London, 1973; updated 1977).

Geltzer, George, 'James Cruze', *Films in Review* (July 1954).

Gruber, Frank, 'The Western', in Yoakem (ed.), *TV and Screen Writing* (California, 1958).

Guzmán, Martín, *Memoirs of Pancho Villa* (Austin, Texas, 1975).

Hobsbawm, Eric, *The Age of Capital, 1848-1875* (London, 1975).

Hofstadter, Richard, *Anti-Intellectualism in American Life* (New York, 1963).

Hofstadter, Richard, *The Progressive Historians* (New York, 1968).

Hofstadter, Richard, 'American as a Gun Culture', *American Heritage* (October 1970).

Hofstadter, Richard (ed.), *Turner and the Sociology of the Frontier* (New York, 1968).

Hollen, W. Eugene, *Frontier Violence* (New York, 1974).

Homans, Peter, 'Puritanism Revisited', in J. Nachbar (ed.), *Focus on the Western* (Englewood Cliffs, New Jersey, 1974).

Jarvie, Ian, 'The Western and the Gangster Film', in *Towards a Sociology of the Cinema* (London, 1970).

Kael, Pauline, 'Saddle Sore', in *Kiss Kiss, Bang Bang* (Boston, Mass., 1968).

Kaminsky, Stuart, *American Film Genres* (New York, 1970).

Kaminsky, Stuart, 'The Samurai Film and the Western', *Journal of Popular Film* (Fall 1972).

Kitses, Jim, *Horizons West* (London, 1969).

Lavender, David, *The Penguin Book of the American West* (Harmondsworth, 1969).

Leutrat, J.-L., *Le Western* (Paris, 1973).

Lovell, Alan, 'The Western', *Screen Education* (September-October 1967).

McArthur, Colin, 'The Roots of the Western', *Cinema* (Cambridge, October 1969).

McGuane, Thomas, *The Missouri Breaks* (New York, 1976).

Manchel, Frank, *Cameras West* (Englewood Cliffs, New Jersey, 1971).

Marsden, Michael T., 'Saviour in the Saddle', in J. Nachbar (ed.), *Focus on the Western* (Englewood Cliffs, New Jersey, 1974).

*Mottram, Eric, 'The Persuasive Lips — Men and

Guns in America, the West', *American Studies*, vol. 10, no. 1.

Munden, Kenneth, 'A Contribution to the Psychological Understanding of the Cowboy', *American Imago*, vol. 15, no. 2 (Summer 1958).

Nachbar, Jack, 'Introduction to the Western', in Nachbar (ed.), *Focus on the Western* (Englewood Cliffs, New Jersey, 1974).

Nachbar, Jack, *Western Films — An Annotated Critical Bibliography* (New York, 1975).

Nash Smith, Henry, 'The American West as Symbol and Myth', in *The Virgin Land* (Cambridge, Mass., 1950).

Parish, James R., and Pitts, Michael R., *The Great Western Pictures* (Metuchen, New Jersey, 1976).

Parkinson, Michael, and Jeavons, Clyde, *A Pictorial History of Westerns* (London, 1972).

Pratt, John, 'In defence of the Western', *Films and Filming* (November 1954).

Reed, John, *Insurgent Mexico* (New York, 1914).

*Rieupeyrout, J.-L., *La Grande Aventure du Western, 1894-1964* (Paris, 1971).

Saisselin, Rémy G., 'Poetics of the Western', *British Journal of Aesthetics*, 2 (1962).

Sarris, Andrew, *The John Ford Movie Mystery* (London, 1976).

Stanbrook, Alan, '*The Covered Wagon*', *Films and Filming* (May 1960).

Stedman Jones, Gareth, 'The History of U.S. Imperialism', in Blackburn (ed.), *Ideology in Social Science* (London, 1975).

Steinbeck, John, *Viva Zapata*, ed. R.E. Morsberger (New York, 1975).

Sturges, John, 'How the West Was Lost', *Films and Filming* (December 1972).

The Popular Western, *Journal of Popular Culture* special edn. (Winter 1973).

The Western, *Velvet Light Trap* special edn, 12 (Wisconsin, 1974).

*Turner, Frederick J., *The Frontier in American History* (New York, 1976).

Turner, Frederick J., *Frontier and Section — Selected Essays* (New York, 1961).

Tuska, Jon, *The Filming of the West* (New York, 1975).

Twain, Mark, *The Mysterious Stranger and other stories*, including 'The Man That Corrupted Hadleyburg' (New York, 1962).

Twain, Mark, *Roughing it* (Berkeley, California, 1972).

Warshow, Robert, *The Immediate Experience* (New York, 1962).

Western ABC, *Kinema* special edn. (Nottingham, Autumn 1971).

Wiltsey, Norman, 'Gunfighters of the Old West', *Gun Digest* (1967).

Womack, John, *Zapata and the Mexican Revolution* (Harmondsworth, 1972).

Wright, Will, *Sixguns and Society* (Berkeley, California, 1975).

Zinnemann, Fred, 'Choreography of a Gunfight', *Sight and Sound* (July-September 1952).

The European Western

1 *Context and history*

Aimard, Gustave, *Les Trappeurs de l'Arkansas* (Paris, 1977).

Aimard, Gustave, *Les Outlaws du Missouri* (Paris, 1978).

Barr, Charles, 'Hercules Conquers Atlantis', *Movie*, 3 (1963).

*Barzini, Luigi, *The Italians* (London, 1964).

Bauer, A., *Deutscher Spielfilm Almanach, 1929-50* (Munich, 1976).

Bertolucci, Bernardo, *Novecento* (2 vols, Turin, 1976).

Carner, Mosco, *Notes on Puccini's Girl of the Golden West*, to accompany libretto and 3-record set of the La Scala production, 1959 (EMI/ HMV, 1977).

Cendrars, Blaise, *Sutter's Gold* (New York, 1926).

Chaplin, Charles, *My Autobiography* (London, 1964).

Christie, Ian (ed.), *Futurism, Formalism, FEKS* (London, 1978).

Cottafavi, Vittorio, Interview, *Positif*, 100-1 (1968).

Eisenstein, Sergei, *Que Viva Mexico!* (London, 1972).

Everson, William, 'Europe Produces Westerns Too — they resemble our own', *Films in Review* (February, 1953).

Fenin, George, and Everson, William, 'The European Western', *Film Culture*, 20 (1959).

Geduld, Harry, and Gottesman, Ronald, *The Making and Unmaking of 'Que Viva Mexico!'* (London, 1970).

Godard, Jean-Luc, *Weekend/Wind from the East* (London, 1972).

Godard, Jean-Luc, and Gorin, Jean-Pierre, Interview, in *Double Feature*, ed. Goodwin and Marcus (New York, 1972).

Grunberger, Richard, *A Social History of the Third Reich* (London, 1971).

Hammett, Dashiell, *Red Harvest* (London, 1975).

Herndon, Booton, *Mary Pickford and Douglas Fairbanks* (New York, 1977).

Honour, Hugh, *The New Golden Land* (New York, 1975).

Hull, David Stewart, *Film in the Third Reich* (Berkeley, California, 1969).

Jodorowsky, Alexandro, *El Topo* (London, 1974).

Jullian, Philippe, *D'Annunzio* (New York, 1963).

Konig, René, *The Restless Image* (London, 1973).

Kurosawa, Akira, Interview, *Cahiers du Cinéma*, 182 (September 1966).

Lane, John Francis, 'It's a Dog's Life', *Films and Filming* (June 1964).

Leiser, Erwin, *Nazi Cinema* (London, 1974).

Leyda, Jay, *Kino* (London, 1973).

*Miccichè, Lino, *Il cinema Italiano degli anni '60* (Venice, 1975).

Montagu, Ivor, *With Eisenstein in Hollywood*, including the script of *Sutter's Gold* (Berlin, 1968).

Nogueira, R., *J.-P. Melville* (London, 1971).

Nolan, William, *Dashiell Hammett* (Santa Barbara, California, 1969).

Paolella, Domenico, 'La Psicoanalisi dei Poveri', *Midi-Minuit Fantastique*, 12 (May 1965).

Passek, J.-L., 'Cinéma Italien des Années Soixante', *Cinéma 74* (September-October 1974).

Phillips, Marcus, 'The Nazi Control of the German Film Industry', *Journal of European Studies*, 1 (1971).

Richie, Donald, *Kurosawa* (Berkeley, California, 1966).

Rieupeyrout, J.-L., *La Grande Aventure du Western*, *1894-1964*, Appendix 1 (Paris, 1971).

Rocha, Glauber, Interview, *Cahiers du Cinéma*, 214 (July-August 1969).

Rosi, Francesco, Interview, *Sight and Sound* (Autumn 1978).

*Savio, Francesco, *Ma l'Amore No — realismo, formalismo, propaganda e telefoni bianchi nel cinema italiano di regime, 1930-45* (Milan, 1975).

Schmidt, Carl T., *Italy under Fascism* (New York, 1939).

Siclier, Jacques, 'The era of the peplum', *Cahiers du Cinéma*, 131 (1962).

Swallow, Norman, *Eisenstein* (London, 1976).

Torok, J.-P., 'Maciste', *Midi-Minuit Fantastique*, 6/7 (June 1963).

Whitehall, Richard, 'Days of Strife and Nights of Orgy', *Films and Filming* (May 1963).

Zimmer, Jacques, 'The Peplums', *Image et Son*, 196 (Paris, 1966).

2   The German Western

Austen, David, 'Continental Westerns', *Films and Filming* (July 1971).

Bauer, A., *Deutscher Spielfilm Almanach, 1929-50* (Munich, 1976).

Bean, Robin, 'Sex, Guns and May', *Films and Filming* (March 1965).

Bean, Robin, 'Way Out West in Yugoslavia', *Films and Filming* (September 1965).

*Cracroft, Richard, 'The American West of Karl May', *American Quarterly*, xix, 2 (Summer 1967).

*Hatzig, Hans Otto, *Karl May und Sacha Schneider* (Bamberg, 1967).

Honour, Hugh, *The New Golden Land* (New York, 1975).

*Mann, Klaus, 'Cowboy Mentor of the Fuhrer', *Living Age*, 352 (November 1940).

May, Karl, *Gesammelte Werke*, ed. Euchar Schmid (Radebeul and Bamberg, 1930 onwards). See especially vol. 7, *Winnetou I*; vol. 8, *Winnetou II*; vol. 9, *Winnetou III*; vol. 14, *Old Surehand I*; vol. 36, *The Treasure of Silver Lake*; and vol. 71, *Old Firehand*.

May, Karl, *Winnetou*, abridged and edited, with vocabulary, by Stanley Sharp and Alfred Donhauser (New Jersey, 1969).

May, Karl, *Canada Bill, and other stories*, tr. F. Gardner (London, 1971).

May, Karl, *Captain Cayman, and other stories*, tr. F. Gardner (London, 1971).

Plischke, Hans, *Von Cooper bis Karl May* (Dusseldorf, 1951).

Schmid, Euchar, (ed.), *Karl Mays Leben und Werk* (Bamberg, 1959).

Syberberg, Hans-Jürgen, *Filmbuch* (Munich, 1976).

Wechsberg, Joseph, 'Winnetou of der Wild West', *Saturday Review*, 45 (20 October 1962).

Wollschlager, Hans, *Karl May* (Hamburg, 1965).

3   The Italian Western

Abruzzese, Alberto, 'Mito della Violenza', *Cinema 60*, 54 (1965).

Badekerl, Klaus, 'Western und Italowestern', *Filmkritik* (October 1969).

Baldelli, Pio, 'Western à l'Italienne', *Image et Son*, 206 (May 1967).

*Baudry, Pierre, 'Idéologie du western italien', *Cahiers du Cinéma*, 233 (November 1971).

Bodeen, De Witt, 'Clint Eastwood', *Focus on Film*, 9 (Spring 1972).

Braucourt, Guy, 'Gian Maria Volonté', *Écran*, 6 (1972).

Bronson, Charles, Interview, *Cinema 71*, 152 (January 1971).

Chevassu, François, 'Ennio Morricone', *Image et Son*, 280-2 (Spring-Summer 1974); includes discography and filmography.

Daney, Serge, 'Il était une fois dans l'Ouest', *Cahiers du Cinéma*, 216.

*Durgnat, Raymond, 'The Good, the Bad and the Ugly', *Films and Filming* (November 1968).

*Ferrini, Franco, 'L'anti-western e il caso Leone', *Bianco e Nero* (September-October 1971).

Fofi, Goffredo, 'Lettre d'Italie: Les Westerns', *Positif*, 76 (June 1966).

Fonda, Henry, Interview, American Film Institute *Dialogue on Film* (November 1973).

*Fornari, Oreste de, *Sergio Leone* (Milan, 1977).

Fox, William Price, 'Wild Westerns, Italian Style', *Saturday Evening Post* (6 April 1968).

Frayling, Christopher, 'Sergio Leone', *Cinema*, Cambridge, 6/7 (August 1970).

Giammatteo, Fernaldo di, 'C'era una volta il West', *Bianco e Nero* (January-February 1969).

Gili, Jean, 'Sergio Leone', *Cinéma 69* (November 1969).

Goetz, Alice, and Banz, Helmut, *Der Italo Western* (Society of German Film Clubs, 1969), a filmography.

Graziani, Sandro, 'Western Italiano-Western Americano', *Bianco e Nero* (September-October 1970).

Haustrate, Gaston, 'Faut-il brûler les Westerns Italiens?', *Cinéma 71*, 154 (March 1971).

*Jameson, Richard, 'A Fistful of Sergio Leone', *Film Comment* (March-April 1973, plus note in March-April 1974 issue).

Jomy, Alain, 'West all'italiano', *Image et Son*, 218 (June-July 1968).

Joyeux, François, 'Sartana', *Vampirella*, 13 (Paris, 1970); 'Cinéma Bis', no. 5, article plus filmography.

*Joyeux, François, 'Django', *Vampirella*, 19 (Paris, 1970); 'Cinéma Bis', no. 11, article plus filmography.

Kaminsky, Stuart, 'The Grotesque West of Sergio Leone', *Take One* (May 1973).

Kaminsky, Stuart, 'The Italian Western Beyond Leone', *Velvet Light Trap*, 12 (1974)

Kezich, Tullio, 'The "Western" is alive . . .?', *Bianco e Nero* (January-February 1968).

Lane, John Francis, 'La Strada per Fort Alamo', *Films and Filming* (March 1965).

*Leone, Sergio, Interviews: *Rivista del Cinematografo* (January 1967); *Le Nouvel Observateur* (25 August 1969), *Cinéma 69* (November 1969), *Image et Son* (December 1969); *Bianco e Nero* (September-October 1971); *Cinéma 72* (May 1972); *Take One* (May 1973, translated from *Zoom*, 12, Paris); *Les Bons, les Sales, les Mechants et les Propres de Sergio Leone*, interview book presented by Gilles Lambert, Solar Press (1976); BBC TV interview (23 February 1977), as part of a documentary on Clint Eastwood.

Lodato, Nuccio, and Della Valle, Gian, 'Western all'italiana', *Civiltà dell'immagine*, 4 (1967).

Lucano, Angelo, 'Duccio Tessari', *Rivista del Cinematografo* (January 1969).

Marciano, Emanuele, and Calamandrei, C., 'Le Repliche in 35mm', *Diana Armi* (Florence, May-June 1969).

Meynell, Jennifer, 'Values and Violence — the films of Clint Eastwood', *Journal of Moral Education*, vol. 7, no. 2.

*Miccichè, Lino, *Il cinema Italiano degli anni '60* (Venice, 1975); section '. . . et circenses'.

Natta, Enzo, 'Dalla *Colt* al Mitra', *Rivista del Cinematografo* (December 1968); the connections between Italian Westerns and the cycle of 'Sexy' films.

Paolella, Domenico, 'La Psicoanalisi del Poveri', *Midi-Minuit Fantastique*, 12 (May 1965).

Pattison, Barrie, 'Sergio Corbucci', *Montage*, 24 (1973).

Petit, Alain, 'Sergio Sollima', *Vampirella*, 12 (Paris, 1970); 'Cinéma Bis', no 4, article plus filmography.

Pierre, Sylvie, 'Le Bon, la Brute et le Truand', *Cahiers du Cinéma*, 200-1 (April-May 1968).

*Pierre, Sylvie, 'Il était une fois dans l'Ouest', *Cahiers du Cinéma*, 218 (March 1970).

*Ramonet, Ignacio, 'Westerns Italiens — Cinéma Politique', *Le Monde Diplomatique* (October 1976).

Rossi, Umberto, 'È già iniziata la resa dei conti?', *Civiltà dell'immagine*, 4 (1967).

Sarris, Andrew, 'Spaghetti and Sagebrush', *Village Voice* (19/26 September 1968).

*Simsolo, Noel, 'Notes sur les Westerns de Sergio Leone', *Image et Son*, 275 (September 1973).

Solinas, Pier Nico, *The Battle of Algiers* (New York, 1973); includes interviews with Gillo Pontecorvo and Franco Solinas.

Staig, Laurence, and Williams, Tony, *Italian Western* (London, 1975); useful for the many illustrations.

Wallington, Mike, 'Spaghettis', *Time Out* (May 1970).

Wallington, Mike, 'Italian Westerns — a concordance', *Cinema*, Cambridge, 6/7 (August 1970).

Also short reviews of individual films in *Films and Filming*; the *Monthly Film Bulletin* (especially January 1967 and February 1969, both issues including checklists of pseudonyms); *Cahiers du Cinéma* and *Bianco e Nero* (especially September-October 1971, with a long article by Ferrini, an interview with Leone and full details of the cuts in his films — transcribed from the director's personal copy of the script). Reports in *Variety* (notably 15 July 1970); synopses in the Unitalia Film yearbooks (1963-1970); information in *Film Dope* (especially October 1975, on Corbucci); interviews — with actors, directors, etc. — in *Image et Son* (especially June-July 1968 and January 1971, with Corbucci, Milian and others); and bizarre details in the 'Cinéma Bis' section of *Vampirella* (the French edition of which took over from *Midi-Minuit Fantastique* in the late 1960s).

Index of Names

Index of Film Titles